Class and Politics in the United States

Class and Politics in the United States

Richard F. Hamilton
McGill University

John Wiley & Sons, Inc. New York • London • Sydney • Toronto

Library of Congress Cataloging in Publication Data:

Hamilton, Richard F
  Class and politics in the United States.

  1. Social classes—United States. 2. United States
  Politics and government—1945–   3. Political
sociology. I. Title.

HN90.S6H35   301.44   72-1951
ISBN 0-471-34710-8 (cloth)
ISBN 0 471 34709 4 (paper)

Printed in the United States of America

10 9 8 7 6 5 4 3 2

For my father and mother

Preface

The principal aim of this work is to provide an assessment of some dominant claims in the contemporary social sciences. The claims in question presume to describe the behavior of the various classes in society. In particular, this work focuses on the supposed malaise of the "lower-middle class" and the presumed intolerance and political incapacity of blue-collar workers. The main corollary of these assertions, one that came to full fruition in the 1950s and early 1960s, holds that the established elites together with the upper-middle classes are the guardians of the democratic arrangement, the defenders of civil liberties, the protectors of the poor and dispossessed, and, in general, the capable and responsible managers of the entire social enterprise. The researches reported here indicate that these claims are, to say the least, subject to considerable doubt.

A second major position that is assessed in this work is the pluralist theory, or, more specifically, that refinement of the pluralist theory that argues the incapacities or dangerous character of "the masses" and suggests, as a consequence, a need to restrict the actual processes of government to the educated, talented, and the presumably capable elites. The research directed toward the questions of class and politics, clearly, also has relevance for the assessment of these claims.

A third major position that will be given at least some attention here is the "mass society" viewpoint. In the leftist or critical variant, it is held that "the masses" are either bought off by the ruling classes or are manipulated into an acceptance of the going arrangements. This acceptance is the result of shrewd and calculating usage of the mass media on the part of the ruling elites. As will be seen, this view also proves to be inadequate, or, more accurately, it is seriously misleading.

A number of other strands of intellectual development will be discussed for purposes of criticism, or elaboration, or to provide an explanation for some of the findings.

The theoretical orientations that are considered here have been criticized in numerous other contexts. Much of this criticism, however, has been of a purely analytic character. In this respect the present work differs sharply from its predecessors; the main basis for the assessment to be presented here is empirical—it involves bringing evidence to bear on the major claims of those theories. The effort, moreover, goes beyond the task of assessment to the presentation of an alternative account of the operations of the society, one which is consonant with the evidence brought forth in the course of the analysis.

The analysis and findings presented have clear relevance for intellectual efforts in the areas of political sociology, political behavior, and social stratification. Students of American society, whether in sociology or political science, insofar as their judgments are based on the theoretical orientations discussed above, may also find this work to be of some interest. The analysis and findings would, in addition, have some relevance for the more popular distillations of these theories, those that appear in the politico-literary journals read by the formally educated upper-middle class.

It is worthwhile, perhaps, to make a few precautionary remarks. Much of contemporary intellectual effort is closely related to the supposed needs of political parties. This does not refer to anything as prosaic as Republicans and Democrats, but rather, to borrow the terminology of the nineteenth century, it refers to the party of movement and the party of order. The effort, in many cases, amounts to bringing "the world" into accord with the conceptions approved by one's chosen party. It seems much more useful to follow a neglected dictum of C. Wright Mills: "First, one tries to get it straight, to make an adequate statement—if it is gloomy, too bad; if it leads to hope, fine." This is not intended as an argument "from authority." The dictum would be just as valid if it were made by an unknown.

I have tried to follow that dictum. This means, among other things, that the discussion does not fall into simple either/or categories. A criticism or rejection of a standard claim in the repertory of the party of order does not automatically signify a victory for the party of movement. In many cases the claims put forth by both parties prove to be mistaken.

There is a third party present on the scene. While the advocates of the party of order dispute with the proponents of the party of movement, the general population goes about their routine endeavors. Various people speak for them —some claim them as an essentially conservative "silent majority," some claim them as the vital or not-so-vital center, while others claim them as the alienated masses awaiting the chance to overthrow the system. However, with rare exceptions, the members of that population are not in a position to speak for themselves. An upper-middle class intellectual may make sweeping assertions about "the Middle American" and those assertions may gain considerable currency within the intellectual's circles. But the blue-collar worker in Youngstown, Ohio (or the wife of a blue-collar worker in Akron, Ohio) is rarely in a position to answer back and say "it isn't so." I have tried, as best one can with survey evidence, to let the respondents speak, to allow their voices to be heard.

There are many people who have generously provided their assistance in this effort. I am especially grateful to Juan Linz, who first showed me how to con-

duct this kind of analysis. His work has been a continuous source of inspiration.

I also thank Chandler Davidson, William Domhoff, and Charles Perrow.
They read, commented on, and argued with early versions of the work and
saved me from many serious errors. I would like to thank the following persons
who also helped bring this book to completion: Michael Aiken, Robert Alford,
David Caplovitz, Eugen Lupri, Lawrence Felt, Peter Hall, James Jacobs, Philip
Levy, Richard Rose, Edward Silva, Donald Von Eschen, and Jonathan Wiener.

A very special debt of gratitude is owed to Dario Longhi who was my research assistant during much of this time. I would also like to thank Carla
Shagass, Marge Williams, and Janet Resnick for their help in completing this
work.

For their direct and indirect assistance I would also like to thank Irene
Hamilton, Carl Hamilton, and Tilman Hamilton.

Most of the data utilized in the writing of this book were made available by
the Inter-University Consortium for Political Research. The data were originally collected by Angus Campbell, Philip Converse, Warren Miller, and
Donald Stokes. Some of the studies were made available through the Roper
Public Opinion Research Center of Williamstown, Massachusetts. This included studies done by the Roper and Gallup organizations. A study done by
the National Opinion Research Organization was made available through the
courtesy of Peter Rossi, who was the director at that time.

I wish to thank the original researchers and the members of the Consortium
and the Roper Center for having made these materials available for my analysis.

The Social Science Research Council and the University of Wisconsin Research Committee were both generous in providing financial support for this
study. I very much appreciate their assistance.

None of these persons or agencies, of course, are responsible for the findings
or the interpretations presented here.

R.F.H.

Montreal
May 8, 1972.

Contents

1. **Introduction: Responsive and Not-So-Responsive Parties**   1
   The Responsive and Not-So-Responsive Parties
   Notes

2. **Theories of Modern Democratic Politics**   22
   Introduction: An Overview
   The Marxist View
   The Modifications of Marxism
   Pluralism
   The Theory of the Mass Society
   The Theory of Group-Based Politics
   Notes

3. **The Concerns and Issues of the Day**   83
   The Pattern of Concern
   Issue Orientations: Domestic Welfare
   Issue Orientations: Federal School Aid
   Issue Orientations: Miscellaneous Economic Questions
   Class Identification
   Party Identification
   Attitudes Toward Change
   Attitudes Toward Those in Government
   The Possible Cross-Cutting Issues: Domestic Communism
   The Possible Cross-Cutting Issues: Foreign Affairs
   The Possible Cross-Cutting Issues: Civil Rights
   Notes

4. **On the Definition, Dimensions, and Geography of Class**   152
   The Question of Definition
   The Evidence
   The Trend Question
   The "Geography" of Class and its Implications
   Notes

5. Class and Politics   188
Introduction: Some Procedures
Class Differences: A Comparative Note
Class and "Pillars": The Party Preferences
Class and "Pillars": Issue Orientations
The Southern Nonmanuals
Salaried Versus Independent Middle Class
The Manual Ranks
The Southern Workers
The Working-Class Wives
Education and the Working Class
An Overview: The Classes and the Pillars
Notes

6. Rural-Urban Differentiation   239
Introduction
Size of Community and Party Preferences
The Nonmanuals
The Manuals
Class Polarization
The Suburbs
The Evidence from other Studies: 1952 and 1956
The Suburban Development: 1952 to 1964
Issue Orientations and City Size
The Composition Hypothesis
Inter-Community Movement
The Middle-Class Returnees
Class Cleavage: Differentiation within the Nonmanual Category
Politicization and Size of Place
The Silent Democrats
The Lower-Middle-Class Activists
Peripheral Groups: The Single, Widowed, Divorced, and Others
A Note on Age
Notes

7. The Case of the South   283
The Southern Perspective: Points of Convergence and Divergence
Class, City Size, and Economic Liberalism
Class, City Size, and Party Choices
Class, City Size, and Race
Southern Nonvoters
The Concern with "Government Power"

Divisions within the South
The Party Competition in the South
Age and Politics
Notes

8. Transformations in the Working Class   **308**
The Question of Origins
Changing Origins
Background and Political Attitudes
The White Protestant Workers
Union Influence
Income and Politics
A Note on Mobility
Notes

9. Cleavages within the Middle Class   **336**
Introduction
The Question of Origins
Background and Political Attitudes
Class Identifications
The Socioreligious Cleavage
Emerging Patterns: Structural Changes
The Trend Question: Personal Influences
The Southern Exception
Summary
Notes

10. Class, Income, and Living Standards   **368**
Overlapping Income Distributions
The Well-off Workers
Income Satisfaction of Manual Workers
A Note on Recent Trends
Income and Careers
Recent Trends in Working-Class Incomes
The Question of Living Standards: Home Ownership
The Question of Living Standards: Automobile Ownership
Notes

11. Class and "Authoritarianism"   **399**
Introduction
White Attitudes and the Rights of Blacks: Manuals and Nonmanuals
White Attitudes and the Rights of Blacks: Lower-Middle and Upper-
    Middle Classes
Racism: Personal and Institutional

Age and Attitudes Toward Blacks
Black-White Contacts and Attitudes
The Housing Question
The Job Question
Some Qualitative Evidence
Some Behavioral Evidence
The Use of and Excusing of Violence
Civil Liberties
Upward and Downward Mobility
Education and Tolerance: A Note on the Dynamics of Mobility and
    Attitudes
Other Influences: Public Figures and the Mass Media
The Civil Liberties Question: A Summary
Foreign Affairs
The Previous Literature
A Postscript
Notes

12. The Future of American Politics   **507**
Introduction
Stability and Change
The Sources of Stability
The Transformation of the Party System
The Parties and Their Supporters
A New Third Party?
Change Through Revolution?
The Inadequacies of the Left
Stability and Change: A Summary
A Note on "General" Theories
Notes

Index   **577**

Class and Politics in the United States

1
Introduction: Responsive and Not-So-Responsive Parties

This work will accomplish the following objectives.

First, it will present a criticism of the dominant conception of democracy found in the contemporary social sciences, that is, the view that the existence of a "competition" between political parties guarantees accountability. This view, briefly, holds that such competition forces the parties to be responsive to public wishes since otherwise they would suffer the penalties of losing. The criticism presented below maintains that there is no necessity involved in the process; competition may be associated with "responsiveness," but it may also be associated with decade-long postponements, with minimal reactions, or with outright rejection of public demands. All of these latter options may occur without the party in power suffering any serious penalties. There are, in short, a number of ways in which political leaders can and do escape the "constraints" of the electoral process. The criticism of this dominant conception will be limited in scope since the behavior of political leaders is not the central concern of this work. Their behavior, however, does provide one of the many elements that affects public political orientations. The character of these orientations is the principal concern of this work.

The second task is to show empirically what is initially established as a mere possibility; that is, in the United States the accomplishments of the legislative and executive branches fall well short of the current desires of a majority of the population. This refers to the key area of general public concern—the sphere of domestic economic welfare and the accomplishments of the so-called welfare state. The argument of "utopianism," of technical impossibility, will not do in this case since a large number of less affluent industrial nations have surpassed the United States in their levels of achievement. It should be noted that the reference points are current accomplishments and current wants. It seems likely that with a very small effort the level of public demands could be significantly raised. For a number of reasons, however, political leaders have little interest in creating new aspirations. One of the main points made in this work is that contemporary political

1

performance falls short even of the relatively low levels of demand that are currently present.

The third task is to criticize the leading theoretical claims about the behavior of the general population—claims that appear in the contemporary social sciences and in their popular derivatives. These views may be described as theories of class. Leftist critical analyses have argued the existence of social differentiation and of serious, persisting inequalities in the distribution of power, benefits, and penalties among the various strata. The dominant "centrist" conceptions found in contemporary social science also begin with "class" but then argue that the differences are diminishing, that power is now widely dispersed, that the benefits have been or are being equalized, and that the penalties are being rapidly eliminated. They also argue that wide participation and involvement, in particular that of the poorly educated lower-middle class and of the blue-collar workers, present some threat to the quality and/or the very existence of the democratic arrangement.

Since this "centrist" framework is dominant both in the social sciences and in the popularized derivations (those that provide the intellectual substance for upper-middle-class thought), assessment of the detailed claims of this viewpoint will be the central task of this work. The question to be considered is the adequacy of this characterization of the condition and outlooks of the general population.

The centrist framework, together with a number of closely related variations, will be presented and discussed in Chapter 2. That chapter also introduces the repertory of theoretical claims that will occupy us throughout most of the subsequent chapters.

The fourth and major aim of this work consists of an empirical assessment of the principal claims of the centrist framework. The leading national surveys of the United States' adult population from the period 1952 to 1968 will be used for this purpose.

Chapter 3, on the concerns and issues of the day, contains the first systematic presentation of this evidence. It presents the distributions of attitudes on the major concerns and issues thus bringing evidence relevant to the second of the aims being considered here—the disparity between wants and accomplishment. Chapters 4 through 11 consider the detailed assertions of the centrist framework. Evidence will be presented that allows assessment of the hypotheses about the upper-middle and the lower-middle classes, about the independent businessmen, the white working class, and the black population. The intention is to provide a description of the liberal and conservative segments of the population and of the tolerant and intolerant segments, and to give some idea of their respective "locations" and of the bases of their respective power or influence. In addition to allowing an assessment of the received theories, this effort also provides the basis for an explanation of why the responses of governments on all levels have been so limited.

The fifth aim, to be considered in the final chapter, is to give some account of the changes that are taking place. Social structures and attitudes are not "constants." People are continually being subjected to new pressures, new influences, and new "educational" experiences. In the course of time, they may also develop new political capacities. The task here is to examine the processes that may lead to a greater awareness and to greater political effectiveness on the part of the general population. In short, the interest is in those processes that might lead to a more fundamental and a more effective democratization.

To summarize: the major concerns are to show the fact of "limited democracy," to provide an explanation of why things are that way, and to inquire into the trends in process to determine whether the emerging developments indicate any greater promise. In the course of this effort we shall also assess the currently dominant theories, indicating their adequacies and inadequacies.

The Responsive and Not-So-Responsive Parties

The populations of all complex societies may be divided into two categories —the rulers and the ruled, the latter forming the overwhelming majority. The rulers may consist of a small clique or of a wider class. The group may be stable, having a monopoly on all positions of leadership and passing them on to their own chosen successors, or it may be characterized by a high degree of flux, new leaders from different sections of the society frequently replacing old ones. Looking at the matter from still another perspective, the leaders may be separate from the society, independent and autonomous, paying little attention to the wishes of the general population. Or they may have close connections with that population, being sensitive to their wishes and willing to respond to them.

In complex democratic societies, the rulers, presumably at least, are chosen by a majority of the adult population and the decisions of those leaders, again presumably, in some way reflect the sentiment of that majority. This is not to say that government policy should, in any and all cases, be a mirror reflection of mass sentiment. The use of the phrase "in some way" is intentional, leaving open the complex question of the specification of details. The point here is to emphasize the irreducible minimum components of a definition of democracy; these components are: (1) leaders being chosen by the majority and (2) policy reflecting the sentiment of that majority.[1]

An adequate analysis of the politics of a complex democratic society must contain some consideration of both the rulers and the ruled and must have some accounting of the relationship between them. If one is not going to beg the question of democracy, it is necessary to show how the decisions of the leaders reflect, are responsive to, or are ratified by, majority sentiment. The a priori judgments indicated by organizational charts with "The People" at the top of a chain of command or by an arrow pointing from "Electorate" to "Leaders" and labeled "inputs" are of very limited value unless accompanied by supporting evidence.

Although the main concern in this work is with the orientations of the general population, most of the present chapter will be devoted to consideration of the behavior of political leaders. Specifically, it is necessary to consider a frequent claim made about democratic systems, that is, one arguing the presence of "constraints" which, presumably, force rulers to be responsive to the orientations of the general population.

The key defining characteristics of a democratic polity, as noted, are the public choice of the top officials and the public determination, again in some way, of the decisions of government. Rudimentary as this may seem, the latter point has been lost in much contemporary discussion, where the "competition of parties" has come to replace "representation" as the defining consideration.[2] A "competition" and public choice of top officials may occur, however, without any serious attention being paid to the wishes of the general public. The leaders of the contending parties may choose to avoid public demands. One may have a "competition" with no representation, where the parties manipulate public opinion in order to divert attention from basic felt concerns.

Those focusing on the competitive mechanism emphasize the presence of two or more parties and the possibility of the "outs" gaining popular favor. It is the presence of at least one alternative "out" party and the threat of punishment for an unresponsive "in" party that presumably *forces* the competitive effort to gain the favor of the electorate.

This viewpoint assumes, first, that winning elections is the major aim of party leaders. Second, it assumes that the party leaders are aware of the wishes of the general public. And third, it assumes that party leaders are forced to respond to those wishes, that they are "free" to make the appropriate appeals so as to enhance the party's chances and that they will, in fact, do so. This means, among other things, that the parties will not collude to avoid the "need" to respond to the concerns of the general public. These assumptions deserve more detailed consideration.

There are occasions when party leaders prefer to lose elections. Throughout the nineteenth century, but most especially in the years following the Civil War, the Democrats could have responded in some way to the widespread demand for "soft money" and could have swept many state and possibly even the national elections of the era. The Democratic leaders, however, being conservative on this and most other issues, chose to lose these elections rather than to make any concessions.[3]

In more recent times, it has been noted that urban political organizations sometimes are rather ambivalent about the possibility of statewide success of their own party. That eventuality would put a governor into power who would be beyond their control—a governor who could, to some extent at least, control the urban organization. As a result, city machines have frequently shown a noticeable lack of enthusiasm when it comes to generating a large turnout for their party, which would make a statewide win possible.[4]

Where "old ethnic" groups dominate the party in a local area, there may also be an interest in limiting turnout. This may amount to nothing more sinister than a desire on the part of long-established oligarchs to continue holding minor honorific offices. On the other hand, where the local party leaders are "old ethnics" and at the same time are the landlords of the "new ethnics," there is likely to be very little interest in "winning elections" through appeals to the majority, who happen to be the tenants.[5]

Discussions that assume that competition forces responsiveness have as a premise the assumption that politicians want to remain in office and that defeat is viewed as a serious personal loss. Rather than taking this as an article of faith, one recent study has made an effort at inquiry. The result was somewhat unexpected. One local office holder said: "I don't feel the weight of voter responsibility. I am not all fired up for a political career." Another, when asked about going against majority preferences, said: "Yes, it is easy because I don't really care if I get elected or not." Still another official said: "I am free to do as I feel. In general it is easy to vote against the majority because I don't have any political ambitions."

The key to these unexpected responses is an initial selection process that is very different from the usual or conventional image. Officeholding was an avocational enterprise for many of these men, a task performed out of a sense of "duty" rather than ambition. Many of them had been approached by political leaders and initially had been named to office through appointment to unexpired terms. They then had the considerable advantage of incumbency in the subsequent election. Very sizable percentages of those interviewed indicated that their votes while in office did not depend on their perceptions of majority opinion. This was especially so in the case of those who were initially nominated to office.[6] For this group the threat of an electoral defeat was a matter of some indifference.

There have been, in summary, some occasions on which it has been in the interest of party leaders to lose elections. This was the case where their own personal interests transcended concern for the party's success. In such cases the leaders clearly were not responsive to public demands; on the contrary, they were concerned with the containment of those demands. There have been other instances in which some party leaders have had an incentive to damage the chances of other units of their own party. Such foot-dragging efforts, needless to say, would also weaken the competition-responsiveness linkage. And in other instances the elected leaders were "free" to be indifferent to public demands by virtue of their own indifference to the rewards of officeholding.

The second assumption of the competitive position, that party leaders know what the public wants, also deserves more detailed consideration. The belief that leaders *know* the mass wants, is usually taken on faith and is rarely investigated. Writers routinely assume that party leaders are rational decision makers, that they are careful and diligent collectors of information, and that they keep close touch with the "pulse of the nation." The scattered indications from studies in the United States, however, show remarkably little direct effort by the parties to discover the concerns of the electorate. This "image" of the party as the careful follower of mass wants is, to be sure, a very convenient one for the party leaders. Without the inquiry, however, it is a claim that ought to be viewed as a hypothesis rather than as a well-supported conclusion based on extensive research.

The available evidence, limited as it is, suggests ground for considerable skepticism with respect to this established article of the democratic faith. One thinks of parties and of candidates making diligent use of polls as a key device for assessing public concerns. One commentator, however, summarized the parties' use of polls as follows: "It is remarkable that the high command of the Republican Party, which supports the finest research staff in Washington, should pay so little attention to their researches, while the Democratic National Committee, full of men who love politics, should have so primitive a research staff and resources."[7]

The use of polls has increased considerably in recent years but even now the purposes to which they have been put are rather limited. In primary campaigns the major purpose is the assessment of candidate popularity, and thus to aid in the decision of whether to stay in or bypass a given state. Another frequent use is to influence delegates at nominating conventions, the stress once again being on candidate popularity and not on public issue orientations or policy preferences.

There is, to be sure, increased use made of polls to guide campaign decisions, but even here the importance is limited. The Kennedys, major users of the campaign poll, used them to check their initial judgments, to ensure that they were not making any major errors of strategy, rather than as a basis for creation of appeals.[8]

There are a number of considerations operating that limit or restrict the use of polls. The major parties, even today, still contain large numbers of traditional politicians who prefer to operate on the basis of their "instincts" or their "feel" for public sentiment. Many of these politicians apparently recognize that they would be bypassed with the coming of a coterie of fresh, young, electoral technocrats. In some cases the objection appears to be one of political aesthetics. Anuerin Bevin, the eminent Labourite, for example, objected to polls on the ground that they would "take all the poetry out of politics."[9]

Campaign polling is a hectic operation. The studies are conducted under heavy time pressures and, as a result, suffer from faults of conception and of execution. If an adequate study is achieved, there still remains the difficulty of obtaining an adequate analysis. The time pressures force a heavy reliance on the overall distributions of attitudes and prevent detailed consideration of the results. Since political polling is such an irregular and uncertain enterprise, there is a high turnover of firms in the business and a high turnover of personnel within the firms. The problems of finding and, even more important, of retaining capable experts are formidable.

Even if an adequate study is achieved and an adequate analysis made, there still remains the problem of transmitting the findings to the relevant decision makers within the party. The results must be transmitted up one, two, or even more levels of hierarchy within the organization, before coming into the hands of the users. The finding of the studies do not always carry clear and obvious strategy implications. Some recipients may not be able to make an adequate or appropriate interpretation of the results. Some recipients may not be willing or may not be able to change strategy, even knowing the results. There is always the possibility that the results may never reach any recipient. After one particularly hectic campaign, the "archivist" in charge of sorting out his organization's accumulated papers found the report of their survey-research people; it had been sent by mail and had never been opened.

With the completion of a campaign the flurry of polling activity comes to an end. The winners turn to preparations for taking office. The losers look to means for paying off their debts. A post-mortem analysis of the reasons for a victory or a defeat is a rarity. Even at this point the studies are not analyzed. They tend rather to be abandoned.

Polling done during a term of office, either by officeholders or by the parties, appears to be a very rare experience. One commentator summarizes the matter as follows ". . . few high-level decision makers use surveys in reaching decisions on major political programs."[10]

Turning now to the third assumption, even if the party leaders did know the mass wants and were also shrewd and rational decision makers, there are still a number of reasons for anticipating less than adequate responses to public wishes. The competitive view sees the politician leading a peculiarly undetermined existence. He is viewed as free of personal psychological restraints and free also of restraining social entanglements. When put this way, it is clear that the view is rather abstract.

The normal processes of intellectual routinization serve to limit awareness of events and of solutions to problems. Party leaders, for example, who have spent a lifetime defending classical liberal economic solutions tend to be psychologically incapacitated when it comes to thinking about solutions outside that framework. Leaders with laissez-faire commitments, for example, found it difficult to plan for England's food supply during World War I. Similar commitments so incapacitated the leaders of Germany's liberal parties that they were unable to make any reasonable response to the problems facing them in the late Weimar years. Some of the "psychologically committed" recognize the hopelessness of the competition and refuse to engage in it; they refuse to play by the "rules of the game," choosing rather a personal demonstration of faith. Such "expressive" activity was indicated in the case of the representatives to the 1964 Republican Convention who nominated Goldwater even though the polls showed him to be the least attractive of their leading candidates.[11]

Party leaders will also be "constrained," as has already been indicated, by concerns with their own business interests and with the honors and advantages of office. Any party leader is going to be constrained by the sentiments of his elected associates, by the wishes of various party notables, and by the desires of the financial supporters. In the 1958 elections, for example, Senator John W. Bricker from Ohio was generally assumed to be a sure winner. He went down to a crushing defeat. The reason for this, some say, was the central issue used in his campaign, that is, the so-called right to work law. This choice of issue was made against his own personal judgment, but, as one party leader stated, "The guys who supply the money for the party in this state demanded it. It's as simple as that."[12]

Briefly, the ability of party leaders to know the public demands and their freedom to respond to them are both subject to some rather important limitations.

All this would suggest that the party leaders really want to respond and that they are hindered only by lack of adequate knowledge, by psychological and social restraints, and by their own personal interests. Some party leaders, however, do not wish to respond in any way to mass demands, their interests being fundamentally opposed to such demands. This is most striking, perhaps, in the case of classical conservative parties whose leadership played the democratic game and adopted a democratic appearance. This in no way changed their basic concern, however, which was to oppose the popular demands and to preserve the basic elements of the traditional social order. This was the point of the first two chapters of Robert Michels' *Political Parties*—"Democratic Aristocracy and Aristocratic Democracy" and "The Ethical Embellishment of Social Struggles."[13]

This third assumption of the competition of parties argument also entails that there will be no collusion between the competitors. Where, however, there is a basic refusal to cater to public wishes, or even where there is only a begrudging tactical concession to such wishes, it is likely, particularly in a two-party system, that collusion will occur. Such a development does, certainly, provide a "competition," but at the same time, there are limits set to the proliferation of issues and to the presentation or public discussion of alternative solutions. It is likely, in other words, that a cartel arrangement, or alternatively, a "political oligopoly" would develop, the polity's equivalent of the administered pricing arrangements found in the economy. For example, at one time the parties in Colombia competed in elections but had worked out an arrangement, called *alternación*, that made the outcome (who gains office) independent of the results of the elections. Another similar arrangement existed in Peru, where it was called *convivencia*, with much the same result. Such arrangements are not new to this world. The parties in nineteenth-century Spain had an agreement to trade off control over the Ministry of the Interior. This allowed falsification of election results with the aid of local notables, the *caciques*. In Italy, the system of alternation was called *trasformismo*; in Portugal, *rotativismo*.[14]

The oligopic arrangement would be most likely where there were two moderate liberal parties, one right and one left liberal, and where the electorate is basically liberal (that is, in favor of extending the welfare state), as in the United States. The left liberals initiate policies and the right liberals follow. Given the basic structure of the situation, the left liberals would never be forced very far to the left because there is no "competitor" threatening from that direction. All that is necessary for their electoral success is that they maintain a marginal differentiation in their political "product" in order to keep the differences clear. In the pure competitive model, the right liberals could "outflank" the left but in reality that does not happen. The combination of personal interests with the psychological and "social" restraints on the leaders of the right liberal parties prevents them from behaving in a purely competitive manner. For these reasons, the political development comes to be one of "imperfect competition."

The right liberals are not able to make a competitive offering. One alternative that is open to them is to follow along behind—the "me too" strategy, promising "better administration" of the achieved arrangements. Administrative improvement, however, is a theme with very limited appeal. This is especially the case for those interested in the substance of welfare-state programs as opposed to the purity of their administration. Another option is the use of irrational appeals, that is, appeals that deflect interest away from the domestic liberal concerns and toward concerns that are more difficult to assess. At the same time, these appeals are said to involve urgent, high-priority necessities. The basic aim for such parties is the discovery of suitable "cross-cutting" issues, which will divide and break up the liberal majority.

The use of diversionary or obfuscatory themes is an age-old tactic; it was tried, for example, by German conservatives who sponsored anti-Semitic parties in an attempt to break the emerging Socialist movement.[15] In the United States this task has been accomplished through more direct demogoguery: in particular, through the use of the military hero, and also through the use of "distant" issues, that is, those not easily assessed by the majority of the electorate.[16] The most prominent of these efforts have focused on foreign threats, on domestic communism, and, recently, on the "threat" of equality (that is, on the civil rights movement, on desegregation, and on the "law and order" theme with its wide range of veiled implications).

A realistic appreciation of the Republican party's need for the distracting issue has been indicated by no less a personage than Richard M. Nixon. As he stated, "If you ever let them [the Democrats] campaign only on domestic issues, they'll beat us—our only hope is to keep it on foreign policy." This statement was made during a discussion of possible vice-presidential candidates at the 1960 convention. Twenty of the party leaders who were present, we are told, agreed with the choice of Henry Cabot Lodge as "the best man to lift Americans' imagination to the problems of foreign policy."[17]

The point of this discussion is that the sheer existence of two or more parties, by itself, does not guarantee a free competition that would compel responsiveness. The presence of multiple parties provides only an obvious necessary condition for an electoral competition. Multiple parties *plus* responsiveness is the key to democracy in complex societies. Multiple parties per se, if they are engaged in a tweedledee-tweedledum competition that is purely cynical and manipulative, have little to do with democracy except, of course, to prevent its realization. The point is that "competition" does not automatically and necessarily lead to ever more adequate representation of majority interests. Stated somewhat differently, it is not the case that competition puts the parties in a position where they *must* respond to mass demand or else suffer electoral defeat. There are other forces constraining them and other options available that, in effect, allow them to "break" the competition-representation linkage.

This discussion should not be misread as implying that all parties are unresponsive and that all leaders are enmeshed in a network of special interests and, as a result, out to thwart any and all democracy. The entire discussion assumes *degrees* of responsiveness by leaders and parties. These degrees of responsiveness will vary by time, place, and circumstance. It is also reasonable to expect considerable variation in the willingness to respond depending on the kind of issue under consideration.[18] Where the theorists of the competitive mechanism have argued a set of constraining conditions that force responsiveness and require close attention to popular demands, the argument here is that the de facto conditions of party competition do not involve the insistent or compelling pressures they have claimed.

The discussion of the Democrats and of the Republicans is not intended to be a portrayal of good guys and bad guys. Neither of the parties is as responsive as they could be given the current level of technological development. The absence of a party to the left of the Democrats makes it easy for them to coast along with only a very modest level of accomplishment. As indicated above, all they have to do is maintain a marginal differentiation vis-à-vis their competition from the right liberal Republicans. The Democratic leaders are also involved with various interests, operate under a set of restraints, have their own peculiar areas of blindness, and so forth.

A persistent bias in analyses of the United States' parties involves the assumption of symmetry. There is a preference, in other words, for treating the parties as similar or parallel organizations, both doing essentially the same thing and the one easily substituting for the other. The differences in such areas as interests, restraints, and ideologies, as well as the differences in their clienteles, indicate that they are not symmetric, that one is not a "substitute" for the other. The assymetric image outlined here, the notion of limited or imperfect competition, and the assumption of a political oligopoly provides a more realistic orientation and hence a more appropriate guideline for analysis, even though it may offend traditional sensibilities.

Also, the focus on democracy as representation does not mean that government should reflect and respond to majority sentiment in all instances. There are at least three reasonable limitations: (1) technical possibility (some goals are incapable of realization given the current level of technology); (2) resource feasibility (an innovation, although technically possible, may require exorbitant costs); and (3) moral desirability (the majority might demand aggressive warfare, murder, or oppression of minorities). The leaders of a democratic society clearly should not respond to such demands since responses in these areas would endanger life, threaten the quality of the democracy, and might make impossible its continuation.[19]

The claims about competition leading to representation need not be supported by a priori judgments about the impact of "system determinants." The objections indicated here, together with the scatter of illustrations, can be no more than suggestive, the aim being to open up an area for speculation and discussion and to indicate areas where inquiry is necessary. One need not merely speculate about the linkages between governmental performance and public sentiments, however, since a direct inquiry is possible. Unfortunately, many commentators have taken the "responsiveness" claims for granted and have not bothered to undertake the needed study since, to all appearances, that would amount to testing the obvious. The use of survey research to show the alignment of majority sentiment and legislative performance (or its absence) is almost entirely lacking.[20]

For this reason the empirical study of the "responsiveness" question will be central to the present analysis. The basic substantive question to be raised is: *To what extent is legislative and executive accomplishment aligned with majority sentiment?*

As will be seen in Chapter 3, legislative and executive accomplishment, especially in the key area of domestic economic welfare, falls well below the current levels of demand. It is this disparity between wants and performance that leads to the second basic substantive question: *How does the disparity between wants and performance persist?*[21]

An answer to this second question, as suggested above, should include some consideration both of the rulers and of the general population. Although most of this book will be devoted to the latter subject, it may be helpful at this point to give a brief preliminary account of the directions to be taken.

First, a note on the method. Instead of depending on sweeping and general a priori claims about "the masses" and instead of assuming approval for "the system" or assuming the existence of something called "a sense of legitimacy," this work will attempt to make direct inquiry wherever possible. The empirical procedure allows one to check and assess the received claims and, on occasion, to open up alternative readings of the "problem of order," such as, for example, the possibility of widespread acquiescence or hopelessness in the face of the existing arrangements.

For the most part, this work is based on an analysis of national cross-sectional surveys. The principal surveys used are the 1952, the 1956, the 1964, and, to a limited extent, the 1968 election studies of the Survey Research Center of the University of Michigan.[22] The Survey Research Center's election studies are considered by specialists in the area to be the best electoral studies of the United States' population in existence. Other national surveys are drawn upon where necessary or useful, that is, where the three main ones lacked appropriate questions or where there was a need for additional supporting evidence. These studies provide the supporting evidence for the claims about the character of the American population generally and about the major subgroups within that population.

The present study is a secondary analysis. This means that the surveys are being used for a second purpose, one that is somewhat different from the original purpose. The difficulty encountered in secondary analyses is that the survey questions were not explicitly designed for the new purpose. Some questions relevant to the new aim were not asked; some questions, while adequate, are not entirely appropriate for the new purpose. While much is made of the difficulties of secondary analysis, there are also some compensating advantages that should not be overlooked. When studying past events, there exists no other alternative short of asking retrospective questions—a procedure that depends on somewhat dubious recollections. Secondary analysis also leads to useful insights in that the questions written for one purpose and derived from one theoretical orientation are being used to assess another. In the process, one may overcome the limitations set by studies that are conceived entirely within a single intellectual framework.[23]

The analysis of election studies for the period from 1952 to 1968 will be concerned only in passing with the specific features of those election campaigns. The principal task is to discover the more persistent features of the American scene, that is, the basic social structural characteristics and the relatively stable issue orientations.

The major substantive findings are summarized in brief outline in the following paragraphs. The themes to be covered, it will be noted, provide the "other side" of the picture, that is, an account of the public reactions to the appeals of political leaders.

The dominant concern in the general population is with personal and family welfare. In politics, the dominant focus, therefore, is on those issues directly affecting this family welfare, that is, on the domestic economic liberalism issues. The evidence shows that a majority of the United States' population approves of substantial government effort in this area; they approve of the welfare state and wish to see it extended.

This much of the present thesis is sometimes granted. It is argued, however, that there are other areas of at least equal concern to the general population. And it is concern with these other issues that leads to a division within the liberal pro-welfare majority. It is this conflict of personal felt interests that presumably accounts for the behavior of significant portions of the general public, that is, a sacrifice of their personal welfare in favor of these other, more distant concerns. Possibly the major "cross-cutting" issues that have dominated the media in official and intellectual discussions of recent decades have been the question of "communism" (both the domestic and foreign varieties) and, in more recent years, the questions of integration and equality. Yet, as we shall see, these issues have far less salience for the general population, despite the mass media preoccupations, than do the bread-and-butter issues linked to the welfare state. With remarkable stability, the majority of the population has remained primarily concerned with the adequacy and the quality of personal and familial circumstances throughout the entire period under study, despite the distractions of other issues offered by some political leaders.

This persistence of focus, on the whole, is not too surprising since it is the economic issues that people know firsthand and live with from day to day. Even in this era of proclaimed affluence, the "Age of the Great Society," this preoccupation still dominates, although possibly with a diminished sense of urgency. Only a small minority of the rich and of the upper-middle classes can think about and concern themselves with "other problems," with the quest for leisure, status, the arts, and so on. Even in an election in which the candidates and media centered their concern on the "communist threat" at home and abroad, only a small fraction of the electorate spontaneously mentioned this subject as a concern of theirs. Despite daily accounts of the impending "white backlash" heard throughout the 1964 presidential election campaign, no such reaction appeared, except possibly in the South. At least for the majority of the population, these "other" issues do not appear to carry sufficient weight to outbalance the salience of the domestic economic liberalism issues.

In close elections and in the short term, these "other" issues may determine the outcome by shifting a minority of the votes. This is especially likely to be the case where the economic issues are played down and not made salient. This was the case, for example, in 1952 when Stevenson refused to make use of the traditional Democratic issues, thinking they would no longer have the appeal they once had. The defection of Democrats was further stimulated by the Korean War, an event that had direct and immediate effects on many people's lives and on their domestic economic situation.

The use of distractive issues (the attempt to focus attention on distant concerns) may prove decisive in an occasional election. The argument here is that since the immediate problems of the individual household still remain and still continue to have the same high salience, the diversion would prove to be a short-run phenomenon.

Special attention has been given to the 1964 study. The presidential campaign of that year is of more than usual significance for this study because of the major use made of diversionary themes. The 1964 campaign also presents a sharper picture of the basic predispositions of the electorate with respect to the key issues of domestic policy and also, to an extent, with respect to foreign policy by virtue of what was at least the appearance of clear alternatives. As the slogan put it, one was offered "a choice, not an echo."

The 1968 campaign "remuddled" the alternatives and contained the additional complication of a third-party contender. Only very limited use has been made of the Survey Research Center's 1968 study. For the most part, the study has been used to indicate the continuity of issue orientations up to and including that date. Despite striking changes in the outcome of the voting, the basic predispositions and the basic wants remained very much the same. It appears that the 1968 campaign provided even less satisfactory alternative choices for the expression of those interests. The large shifts in the vote that year were probably due more to frustration than to changed perspectives. That frustration was indicated in one poll that showed 43 percent of the voters wanting some other candidate, that is, other than the three who had presented themselves.[24]

A problem with survey research, generally, is that the results are "outmoded" the day after the study. The skeptical commentator can always say "but that was yesterday." There is no entirely satisfactory answer to that objection. The best one can do is discover the presumed basic structural determinants of behavior (as opposed to the ephemeral campaign stimuli) and show their linkage to attitudes and to some behaviors. One can then *suggest* that as long as the structural features persist the attitudes and behaviors will also continue unchanged.

This work rejects the centrist view, which has claimed general satisfaction, approval, and feelings of "legitimacy" with respect to "the political system" and its various performances. It also rejects the sweeping claims of one prominent strand of left thinking—the assumption of hopelessly corrupt and manipulated masses. Instead, the claim here is that there are still large areas of persistent dissatisfaction, the most important of these being the economic-social welfare concern. The contemporary state of affairs is neither one of "satisfaction" nor of "narcoticized" senses. There exists, rather, a relatively clear recognition of the domestic economic needs and, correspondingly, there is a widespread willingness to extend liberal or welfare legislation to deal with these problems. There is even, as we shall see, a fair-sized interest in solutions that go beyond the conventional welfare state solutions.

The absence of significant change, the failure to achieve even relatively simple innovations designed to improve the human condition, in this view, is not due to public disinterest or lack of concern. The problem lies instead in the obstacles that prevent or make difficult the gaining of a "hearing." The character of the demand, in short, is continuously misrepresented. Where that demand, from time to time, does get expressed, there remains the additional problem of finding an adequate political vehicle, an agency that is both willing and capable of accomplishing needed and desired changes. The considerations touched on here will be discussed at greater length in the final chapter.

We turn now to a consideration of the major theoretical orientations dominant in American social science. It is these theories that will be assessed in the later chapters of this work.

Notes

1. Some of the leaders in democratic societies are "chosen" by "the people." It is well to remember that behind that "choosing" is a prior decision, the nominating decision. The eminent sociologist Max Weber described this situation as follows:

> The pure type of bureaucratic official is *appointed* by a superior authority. An official elected by the governed is not a purely bureaucratic figure. Of course, the formal existence of an election does not by itself mean that no appointment hides behind the election—in the state, especially, appointment by party chiefs. . . . Once firmly organized, the parties can turn a formally free election into the mere acclamation of a candidate designated by the party chief.

See H. H. Gerth and C. Wright Mills, translators and editors, *From Max Weber: Essays in Sociology*, (London: Routledge & Kegan Paul, 1948), p. 200.

2. The focus on competition of parties as defining may be found in the influential work of Joseph Schumpeter, *Capitalism, Socialism and Democracy* (New York: Harper & Bros., 1947), pp. 250–285, esp. p. 269. More recently the viewpoint appears in Morris Janowitz and Dwaine Marvick, *Competitive Pressure and Democratic Consent*, Michigan Governmental Studies, No. 32 (Ann Arbor: University of Michigan Press, 1956), and, possibly the most influential work containing this viewpoint, in Seymour Martin Lipset, *Political Man: The Social Bases of Politics* (Garden City: Doubleday, 1960), Ch. 1 and II. A criticism of the Janowitz-Marvick position appears in Herbert Marcuse, *One Dimensional Man: Studies in the Ideology of Advanced Industrial Society* (Boston: Beacon Press, 1964), pp. 114–120.

Three empirical studies that seriously question the assumptions about the impact of competition on policy are Richard E. Dawson and James A. Robinson, "Inter-Party Competition, Economic Variables, and Welfare Policies in the American States," *Journal of Politics*, **2** (1963), pp. 265–289; Thomas R. Dye, *Politics, Economics, and the Public: Policy Outcomes in the American States* (Chicago: Rand McNally, 1966); and Bryan R. Fry and Richard F. Winters, "The Politics of Redistribution," *American Political Science Review*, **64** (June 1970), 508–522. The latter work contains an extended review of work in this area. A useful account of the state of opposition in a wide range of countries is contained in Robert A. Dahl, ed., *Political Oppositions in Western Democracies* (New Haven: Yale University Press, 1966). Especially useful in this connection is the discussion by Otto Kirchheimer, "Germany: The Vanishing Opposition."

The viewpoint being criticized here is, to be sure, only one from among many orientations toward the subject of democracy. It is the object of attention here because of its prominence over the last two decades. For a compendious overview, see Giovanni Sartori, *Democratic Theory* (Detroit: Wayne State University Press, 1962).

3. Discussing these conservative, non-South, Bourbon Democrats, one author points out that they would rather "lose the election than make any concession to the advocates of currency reform." See Horace Samuel Merrill, *William Freeman Vilas: Doctrinaire Democrat*, (Madison: State Historical Society of Wisconsin 1954). The quotation appears on p. 38. Chapters 4–6 deal with the same problem at some length. A more extensive view of the same subject appears in the same author's *Bourbon Democracy of the Middle West: 1865–1896*. (Baton Rouge: Louisiana State University Press, 1953).

4. Some discussion of this problem may be found in Warren Moscow, *Politics in the Empire State* (New York: Alfred A. Knopf, 1948). Other accounts of this particular strain may be found in Henry F. Pringle, *Alfred E. Smith: A Critical Study* (New York: Macy-Masins, 1927), pp. 17–19, 170, and 267, and also by Pringle, *Theodore Roosevelt: A Biography* (New York: Harcourt, Brace, 1931), Book I, Chapter 15. See, also, Horace Samuel Merrill, *Bourbon leader: Grover Cleveland and The Democratic Party* (Boston, Little, Brown, 1957), Ch. III. Merrill writes that Tammany chieftains "showed no hesitancy to bring about the defeat of the Democratic party if this served [their] personal purposes. . . ." (p. 52). Party leaders, certainly, are rarely open advocates of defeat. The key to losing is inactivity, particularly with respect to registration of potential voters. See *The New York Times'* editorial entitled "The Anti-Registration Drive," August 25, 1969, p. 30. The director of a voter registration drive, not a party worker, spoke of the "apathy and indifference on the part of the Board of Elections" and of "outright subversion by political machines in various communities." *The New York Times*, August 26, 1969. Another story indicates that local party leaders hampered the registration of Negroes and Puerto Ricans. Registrars went for supper at 5:00 P.M. leaving lines of registrants waiting. Some registrars failed to show up at all (*The New York Times*, September 5, 1969, p. 39). The participation in presidential elections in New York City has steadily declined, the 1968 level being approximately 10 percent less than in 1940 (*The New York Times*, May 20, 1969, p. 39).

5. See Dan Wakefield, *Island in the City* (Boston: Houghton Mifflin, 1959), pp. 249–278. On the relatively low concern with vote getting among grass-roots party workers in Detroit, see Samuel J. Eldersveld, *Political Parties: A Behavioral Analysis* (Chicago: Rand McNally, 1964), pp. 262, 270–271, and 292–293.

In still another context, a participant and commentator, speaking of the 1920s and 1930s, pointed out that:

The Republican Party in the South has not sought to become a major party in most cases. During the years of its [national] ascendancy the leadership has been content with the spoils. The late Pope Long of Alabama, who for a time was National Committeeman of that State, was reported to have said, "We'll have to be careful or the Republican Party will get too big in Alabama." There were a few counties . . . which had strong membership in the minority party and it was all right with the State Republican leaders for them to win county offices, but they, the leaders, would reserve the luscious plums of Federal patronage for themselves.

John Wesley Kilgo, *Campaigning in Dixie: With Some Reflections on Two-Party Government* (New York: Hobson Press, 1945).

6. See Kenneth Prewitt, "Political Ambitions, Volunteerism and Electoral Accountability," *American Political Science Review*, **64** (March 1970), 5–17.

7. Theodore H. White, *The Making of the President: 1960* (New York: Atheneum, 1961), pp. 386–387.

8. See Murray B. Levin, *Kennedy Campaigning: The System and the Style as Practiced by Senator Edward Kennedy* (Boston: Beacon Press, 1966). Levin notes that "Kennedy's strategic decisions were made primarily on the basis of intuition, common sense, and the rules of thumb learned during John F. Kennedy's campaigns. Pollsters did not play a significant role in the decision-making process although public opinion data were frequently used to confirm the intuitive judgments of the candidate and his staff (p. 149). See also pp. 114–119 and p. 150. Some sense of the limited use made of polls may be gleaned from Theodore White's 1968 offering (New York: Atheneum, 1969), pp. 41, 60–61, 89, 145, 229, 238, 279n, and 340. Also of some interest, a work which expresses considerable alarm over the developing electoral technology, is James M. Perry, *The New Politics: The Expanding Technology of Political Manipulation* (New York: Clarkson N. Potter, Inc., 1968). This work contains many illustrative case studies. There is a serious problem, however, in its easy acceptance of *post hoc propter hoc* claims.

9. Quoted in Mark Abrams, "Public Opinion Polls and Political Parties," *Public Opinion Quarterly*, **27** (Spring 1963), 9–18. See also Richard Rose, *Influencing Voters: A Study of Campaign Rationality* (New York: St. Martin's Press, 1967).

10. On the use of polls in the executive branch, see Adam Yarmolinsky, "Confessions of a Non-User," *Public Opinion Quarterly*, **27** (Spring 1963), 543–548; Launer F. Carter, "Survey Results and Public Policy Decisions," same issue, pp. 549–557; and, still in the same issue, the comments of Ithiel de Sola Pool, pp. 558–561. The quotation in the text is from Pool's brief essay.

Other works of some interest in this connection are the following: Raymond A. Bauer, Ithiel de Sola Pool, and Lewis Anthony Dexter, *American Business and Public Policy* (New York: Atherton Press, 1963); Lewis Anthony Dexter, "What Do Congressmen Hear: The Mail," *Public Opinion Quarterly*, **20** (Spring 1956), 16–27, and "The Representative and His District," pp. 495–512 of Nelson W. Polsby, Robert A. Dentler, and Paul A. Smith, eds., *Politics and Social Life* (Boston: Houghton Mifflin, 1963). The first of the Dexter articles also appears in the Polsby et al. volume, pp. 485–495.

For summaries of opinion poll usage in the United States see "Congressional Use of Polls: A Symposium," *Public Opinion Quarterly*, **18** (Summer 1954), 121–142, and Leonard A. Marascuilo and Harriet Amster, "Survey of 1961–1962 Congressional Polls," *Public Opinion Quarterly*, **28** (Fall 1964), 497–506. Both reports indicate limited and erratic usage to be the rule. A later work shows more extensive usage to be the case and most users judged polls to be "helpful." See Robert King and Martin Schnitzer, "Contemporary Use of Private Political Polling," *Public Opinion Quarterly*, **32** (Fall 1968), 431–436.

11. The account of England's food supply problems appears in Mancur Olson, Jr., *The Economics of the Wartime Shortage* (Durham: Duke University Press, 1963), Ch. 4. Discussion of the situation of the German liberal parties in the last years of the Weimar republic may be found in Erich Matthias and Rudolf Morsey, "Die Deutsche Staatspartei," pp. 31–97 of Matthias and Morsey, eds., *Das Ende der Parteien: 1933* (Düsseldorf: Droste Verlag, 1960); Bruce B. Frye, "The German Democratic Party, 1918–1930," *Western Political Quarterly*, XVI (March 1963), 167–179; and Attila Chanady, "The Dissolution of the German Democratic Party in 1930," *American Historical Review*, LXXIII (June 1968), 1433–1453. Another case of "expressive" (as opposed to "goal-oriented") political activity may be found in John H. Fenton, *Midwest Politics* (New York: Holt, Rinehart & Winston, 1966), pp. 61–62.

12. See James A. Maxwell, "The Battle Bricker Didn't Want to Fight," *The Reporter*, (November 27, 1958), **19**. A description of this campaign may be found in John H. Fenton, *The Catholic Vote* (New Orleans: Hauser Press, 1960), Chapter 3.

13. Robert Michels, *Political Parties: A Sociological Study of the Oligarchical Tendencies of Modern Democracy* (Glencoe: The Free Press, 1958).

14. Collusion in these cases does involve an active conspiracy, that is, the parties must come together and work out the terms of the arrangements. In some instances, however, the same result may be obtained without any joint consultations. The latter option, which is discussed in the following paragraphs of the text, is similar to administered pricing in some sectors of the economy. Producer A publishes a new list of prices and all other producers copy his list.

The idea of collusion, or of "conspiracy," is repugnant to many contemporary social scientists. To suggest it as a possibility, however, does not at the same time imply that *all* history is a result of concerted planning and effort. There is some blundering, some incompetence, some unplanned drift. In any given instance, the task is an empirical one; the problem of whether or not a conspiracy existed is not to be settled by a priori judgments. In previous times, intellectuals were able to take a much freer and more realistic attitude toward this possibility. Without making any fuss about it, Adam Smith stated the matter rather simply: "People of the same trade," he said, "seldom meet together, even for merriment and diversion, but the conversation ends in a conspiracy against the public or in some contrivance to raise prices." From his *Inquiry into the Nature and Causes of the Wealth of Nations* (New York: Random House–Modern Library, 1937), p. 128.

15. The attempt met with no notable success. Working-class voters were not very much interested. See Paul Massing, *Rehearsal for Destruction* (New York: Harper Brothers, 1949), and also P. G. J. Pulzer, *The Rise of Political Anti-Semitism in Germany and Austria* (New York: John Wiley and Sons, 1964).

16. Taking the presidential candidates from 1832 to date who could be classified as "military heroes," we find four in the Democratic column (Jackson, Pierce,

McClelland, and Hancock) and eleven in the Whig-Republican list (Harrison, Taylor, Scott, Fremont, Grant, Hayes, Garfield, the second Harrison, McKinley, Theodore Roosevelt, and Eisenhower).

17. These quotations appear in Theodore H. White, *The Making of the President: 1960* (New York: Atheneum, 1961), pp. 206–207. Another account of the same meeting, while not mentioning the Nixon quotation, has Thomas E. Dewey giving the "sense of the meeting" as follows: ". . . he [Lodge] would put the emphasis on foreign policy, where it should be." See William J. Miller, *Henry Cabot Lodge* (New York: James H. Heineman, 1967), p. 320.

See also Bernard R. Berelson, Paul F. Lazarsfeld, and William N. McPhee, *Voting: A Study of Opinion Formation in a Presidential Campaign* (Chicago: University of Chicago Press, 1954). These authors show, through a content analysis of 1948 campaign speeches, that Truman laid the stress on domestic socioeconomic issues, on labor, agriculture, inflation, prices, housing, and social security. By comparison, the only "domestic" issue given emphasis by the Republican candidate, Thomas E. Dewey, was "conservation of natural resources." In lieu of domestic liberalism, Dewey's stress was on something entitled "unity of [the] American people," on foreign policy, and on communism, domestic and foreign. See especially pp. 235–238.

Also of some relevance is the work of Angus Campbell, Gerald Gurin, and Warren E. Miller, *The Voter Decides* (Evanston: Row, Peterson Co., 1954), pp. 46 and 50–51.

The need for conservatives to flirt with liberal themes is indicated by their near universal presence in all party platforms. If platforms were determining, for example, France should have had a sweeping welfare state in the 1920s since all the parties were so committed. See the discussion of the parties and their programs in W. L. Middleton, *The French Political System* (New York: E. P. Dutton, 1933), and Edward McC. Sait, *Government and Politics in France* (Yonkers: World Book Co., 1921). An account of the activities of the press lord and Krupp agent, Alfred Hugenberg, discusses this problem in the German context. German conservatives would buy up newspapers and transform them into direct and open agencies for the propagation of conservative viewpoints with the result that, for the readers, they became intensely dull journals, and for the owner-propagandist, they became losing ventures. Hugenberg solved this problem by yielding tactically to the "social" interests of the readers. See Ludwig Bernhard, *Der "Hugenberg-Konzern," Psychologie und Technik einer Gross-organization der Presse"* (Berlin: Verlag von Julius Springer, 1928). In the United States, Theodore Roosevelt's new-found "progressivism," after a long life of political conservatism and disinterest in social reform (as opposed to good government reforms), stemmed from a concern with growing socialism. See James Weinstein, *The Corporate Ideal in the Liberal State: 1900–1918* (Boston: Beacon Press, 1968), Ch. 6, "The Politics of Social Reform."

18. Had there been *no* responsiveness there would have been no formal democratic institutions, no elections at all, no general extension of suffrage, no welfare state, no income tax, and so on. The responses, many of them, came late, that is, long after popular demand was evident, and the achievement has been inadequate. The welfare-state accomplishment is very limited; the tax structures are pro-

gressive only in their appearance. There are, on the current scene, no inexorable pressures that have forced governments to remedy these deficiencies. The competitive mechanism, in short, proves to be a limited device.

19. As food for thought, it is worth considering some cases. In August 1951, 60 percent of the West German population "chose neutrality between Americans and Russians as the best policy for Germany." On the subject of West German postwar rearmament, a leading source says there was "no popular majority . . . pressing for it." The same source says the government was "not being driven to rearmament by any domestic popular pressure." A majority of those with opinions also opposed conscription. The government, however, proceeded independently of these sentiments and made policy. The same is true of another issue, an indemnity to Jews; disapproved by a majority of those with opinions, the measure became law. These examples come from Karl W. Deutsch and Lewis J. Edinger, *Germany Rejoins the Powers* (Stanford: Stanford University Press, 1959), pp. 23, 29, and 30. Sentiment in France was overwhelmingly neutralist with respect to a US-USSR conflict, in opposition to the underlying principle of the North Atlantic Treaty. See Richard F. Hamilton, *Affluence and the French Worker* (Princeton: Princeton University Press, 1967), p. 55. Also of some interest is Donald J. Puchala, *Western European Attitudes on International Problems: 1952–1961* (New Haven: Political Science Research Library, Research Memorandum No. 1, 1964). It is the speculation of two authorities on Norway that "substantial majorities" of the Labor party members were opposed to the party leaders' position on NATO membership and on German rearmament. With respect to defense spending, the evidence shows that the only pocket of support for Labor party policy (in favor of that spending) came from the conservatives. See Henry Valen and Daniel Katz, *Political Parties in Norway* (London: Tavistock Publications, 1964), pp. 88 and 257.

20. Two exceptions are the works of Stuart Chase, *American Credos* (New York: Harper & Bros., 1962), and Lloyd A. Free and Hadley Cantril, *The Political Beliefs of Americans: A Study of Public Opinion* (New Brunswick: Rutgers University Press, 1967). Also of some use in this connection is Hadley Cantril and Mildred Strunk, eds., *Public Opinion, 1935–1946* (Princeton: Princeton University Press, 1951).

21. This work cannot go into the question of why legislatures do not perform as one might expect. For some insights into the problem see the following: John C. Wahlke, Heinz Eulau, William Buchanan, and LeRoy C. Ferguson, *The Legislative System: Explorations in Legislative Behavior* (New York: John Wiley, 1962); John C. Wahlke and Heinz Eulau, eds., *Legislative Behavior: A Reader in Theory and Research* (Glencoe: The Free Press, 1959); Lewis A. Froman, Jr., *Congressmen and their Constituencies* (Chicago: Rand McNally, 1963); James D. Barber, *The Lawmakers: Recruitment and Adaptation to Legislative Life* (New Haven: Yale University Press, 1965); Joseph S. Clark, *Congress: The Sapless Branch* (New York: Harper & Row, 1964); Charles L. Clapp, *The Congressman: His Work As He Sees It* (Washington, D.C.: Brookings Institute, 1963); and Drew Pearson and Jack Anderson, *The Case Against Congress* (New York: Simon and Schuster, 1968), Warren E. Miller and Donald E. Stokes. "Constituency Influence

in Congress." Chapter 16 of Angus Campbell et al., *Elections and the Political Order* (New York: John Wiley, 1966).

22. Technical details about the studies and the initial presentations of findings may be found in the following: Angus Campbell, Gerald Gurin, and Warren E. Miller, *The Voter Decides* (Evanston: Row, Peterson & Co., 1954); Angus Campbell, Philip E. Converse, Warren E. Miller, and Donald E. Stokes, *The American Voter* (New York: John Wiley, 1960). Some special studies by the same authors appear in *Elections and the Political Order* (New York: John Wiley, 1966).

23. For a discussion of this point see Hamilton, *Affluence and the French Worker*, pp. 13–14.

24. Theodore H. White, *The Making of the President: 1968*, p. 352.

2
Theories of Modern Democratic Politics

Introduction: An Overview

In discussing social theories one may choose to be merely descriptive, that is, one may provide an account of the theories in question but offer no commentary or evaluation. An obvious alternative is to both describe and evaluate. All too often, however, when evaluation is provided, the effort becomes one of advocacy: Theory A is championed and some opposed Theory B is defeated. One slays the Marxist dragon and raises the colors of democratic pluralism.

It seems unlikely that theories would fall so neatly into the categories of "all right" and "all wrong." It is more likely that any position that survives over a long period contains some useful elements, that is, has some valid insights. It would make sense, therefore, to pick out the useful elements from the various current theories and ask whether it is possible to put them together in some new and better way. This is to suggest that rather than aiming toward vindication and rejection, one can criticize, sort out, retain, and synthesize the useful elements taken from a number of different theoretical orientations. It is this approach that will be adopted in the following discussion.

The major positions to be discussed here are: (1) the Marxian view, (2) a revised Marxian view that has become central to contemporary non-Marxian (or anti-Marxian) social science, (3) a pluralist view that also has great currency in contemporary social science, (4) a "mass society" view that, in a sense, is an inversion of this pluralist view, an account of pluralism "gone astray," and finally, (5) a "group-based" view of mass politics. Before undertaking a detailed consideration of these theories, a brief outline may prove useful.

These theories do different things. Because of their different aims, they are not, strictly speaking, alternatives. They are also not of equal importance for the purposes of this work, and for this reason, the attention paid them will be rather strikingly imbalanced.

The Marxian view, for a number of reasons, is of limited importance for the present purpose and will be considered only in briefest outline. For the most part, the presentation simply provides the background for the second position, the revised Marxian view, which has come to dominate the contemporary social sciences. This revised account of the "class" formations is the principal object of concern for the present work, the major task of which is to assess this dominant "charting" of the social landscape.

The pluralist view is concerned with the linkages between various segments of the society and governing agencies. The basic claim of this view is that all segments of the society have resources for influencing policy and, hence for obtaining at least some satisfaction of their wants. Put somewhat differently, this theory claims that there are a wide variety of units in the society, each with its own resources (its means for exerting influence), and that there is no clustering of resources in the hands of a single powerful elite. This theory focuses largely on instrumentalities, that is, the means for exerting influence, in particular on the role or use of voluntary associations. Such a theory may be independent of a theory of class. It focuses, in its more general formulations, on units or segments of the society, leaving open the question of the basic formations. These may be classes, religious groups, ethnic groups, regional units, and so forth.

The "mass society" view, to be considered only very briefly, sees modern societies as characterized by a widespread breakdown of the organizational units that are central to the pluralist view. This leaves the population of the society individuated, isolated, and helpless vis-à-vis the events and developments in the society. This individuation leaves the rulers of the society in an extremely powerful position in opposition to the general population. It also provides a setting in which the isolated and helpless members of the general population may be easily mobilized by manipulative "demagogues."

The fifth position, the "group-based" or socially based view of mass politics is one that has had considerably less currency. Basically this view maintains that political orientations are learned in small and personal group settings: in the family, among friends, and from co-workers. Therefore, political orientations constitute a kind of social heritage. This view amounts to a corrective to an extreme rationalist position found in some statements of the pluralist outlook. It also provides a realistic correction of the isolation and social fragmentation assumption found in the "mass society" viewpoint. The group-based view proves to be very useful in accounting for political attitudes and outlooks, particularly in the case of party identifications and party choices.

In this chapter, these theories are outlined and briefly assessed. Since the revised Marxian or "centrist" view is the main concern of Chapters 4 through 11, most of the criticism of that view will be deferred until later. The pluralist and mass society viewpoints will be assessed below; one major point to be made is that both contain valid insights but there are serious questions to be raised as to the extent of their applicability. Both, it will be argued, fit best in discussing only relatively small subgroups of the entire population.

The "group-based" view will also be discussed and assessed. We shall see that this view also errs in the extent of its claimed coverage. Intended as a corrective to rationalist pluralism and to the mass society view, it sees group bases everywhere, overlooking the fact that some isolation does exist. It also overlooks the question of the degree to which and the circumstances in which political orientations are or become rational as opposed to traditional.

Furthermore, in a number of ways the original formulation of the "group basis" position has not made maximal use of its key insights. An attempt will be made to extend the usage of the theory in order to make it more viable in discussion of changes in outlooks. In also seems useful to put this discussion and these insights together with the discussion of "class" (in the revised Marxian discussion). Sensed interests, wants, demands, and so on do not appear to stem directly as a response to the objective features of one's (or a group's) condition. Nor does it appear that the orientations are a result of mass media manipulations or of the urgings of "demagogues." The available evidence does suggest a need to specify, to break down any large category such as "class" into its more specific component communal groups. These informal groups, in turn, appear to be the bearers of political orientations that are taught to the group members. This is not to suggest that the group tradition is the only factor operating. The tradition provides a framework for the interpretation of events. When the events are no longer consonant with the framework, a new adaptation will be made. Activists, militants, or informal "opinion makers" may either supply a new framework or provide some major reworking of the old ones. Still another possibility is that people will shift from one group and join another. In the process they will be subjected to new pressures and influences and will tend to adopt the new outlooks.

An adequate account of class formations, of the orientations within the various classes, and of the changes in those orientations would have to include consideration both of the objective circumstances *and* of the informal group structures within the category. An adequate understanding of the outlooks and orientations would require a detailed knowledge of these informal group processes. The effects of distant events and of changes in one's immediate circumstances would be mediated by the received intellectual frameworks and by the influence of opinion leaders within these informal settings.

The Marxist View

Marx saw capitalist society tending more and more toward a confrontation of two classes: the owners of the means of production in a private property system (capitalists) and those who sold their labor power (the proletariat).[1] The line of cleavage expected was clear—the owners of the major means of production together with their hired agents against nonowners. While in the early stages of the capitalist epoch there would be many "classes" (remnants of earlier epochs, that is, products of early capitalism), the history of the era would be one of simplification of the entire arrangement. These remnants would disappear, being forced into the new positions determined by capitalist development. The most important development would be within the ranks of the capitalists themselves. While this group originally includes a wide range of undertakings, everything from small producers and small holders (artisans, shopkeepers, farmers) to monopoly capitalists, the processes of competition would force the small holders (*petite bourgeoisie, Kleinbür-gertum*) to give up their existence as owners and become proletarians.[2] The proletariat would, therefore, increase in size and become the overwhelming majority in the face of a small minority of big capitalists. And, as important as the quantitative transformations, the contrasts and continuous struggles between them would lead to an ever sharper awareness or consciousness of how things were structured and of the need for radical change.

A basic prediction is one of emerging separate consciousness on the part of "workers" and "bourgeoisie." Put somewhat differently, this says that the gulf *between* these classes will increase over time and that any other prior base of cleavage within the two classes will tend to diminish. This would mean that religious, ethnic, or any other traditional base of cleavage should tend to disappear.

This account focuses on the developments in the final stage of the capitalist era. Prior to the final stage, however, any given capitalist society will contain a wide variety of social formations. These will vary considerably by time and place and will reflect the differing historical developments in each country.

Another feature of capitalist societies prior to the final stage is that the consciousness of the various segments of the society does *not* fall into one or the other of the two categories, proletarian or bourgeois. In the *final* stage, events will have forced that development; they will have broken down the older formations and made necessary a change in consciousness. Prior to that time, however, the history of capitalist societies, particularly within the proletariat, is likely to be one of social fragmentation, of parcellation, of cleavages existing on the basis of religion, region, background, skill level, language, and so forth.[3] The pre-final stage history is also likely to be characterized by widespread false consciousness. One is likely to find many rural proletarians identifying with the parties of the landed aristocracy, and many urban workers supporting and identifying with liberal bourgeois parties.

The empirical tasks facing anyone investigating the operations of an ongoing capitalist society are: the identification of the existing formations, the discovery of the sources of false consciousness, and the examination of the conditions that lead to a change of that consciousness. The theory of the final stage is of limited use in this particular effort since it is not intended as a description of conditions existing prior to that time.

Most of the analysis in this work will be based, as already indicated, on cross-sectional surveys of the United States' population. Since the owners of the major units in the United States' economy constitute only a miniscule proportion of the population, they, for all practical purposes, will not appear in this analysis.[4] It would take a very different kind of inquiry to examine their orientations and outlooks. The surveys, in short, pick up the "proletariat" and also a minority of small proprietors. That "proletariat" includes a wide range of subcategories. In the language of the contemporary social sciences, it includes manual workers, white-collar workers, professionals, managers, upper- and lower-middle classes, and so forth.[5] Any useful study of the contemporary scene must recognize these differentiations within the broader category and must give some accounting of the different circumstances and outlooks of these subgroups. A major claim of the Marxian theory—the assumption of a breakdown of these subcategory particularisms —is an empirical question. Any such trend ought to be revealed in the course of one's inquiry.

It is useful to make some comment on the "deterministic" aspect of Marx's view, a focus that is especially attractive to sociologists and also to some socialists. The "inevitability" thesis assumes that the processes of capitalist development will *necessarily* lead to the transformation of the system. There would be a falling rate of profit, overproduction crises, and a struggle for colonial markets. There would be a continuous growth in the size of the working class and, as a result of the developing struggles, there would be a change in the character of their class consciousness leading to the final conflict.

That formulation leaves out any organizational role and any consideration of a place or need for militants; in short, the entire "voluntarist" component disappears from such accounts. This kind of formulation suggests that effort is not necessary; that the final conflict is an end product of normal everyday activity.

Marx does, however, make allowance for such voluntarist components. In the *Manifesto* (Part IV) he writes: "The Communists fight for the attainment of the immediate aims, for the enforcement of the momentary interests of the working class; but in the movement of the present, they also represent and take care of the future of that movement." And also, "In all these movements [the Communists] bring to the front, as the leading question in each case, the property question, no matter what its degree of development at the time." These quotations suggest the key need for organization. Without that taking "care of the future" or that bringing of the property question to the front, there is a suggestion that the development would not advance as is elsewhere predicted. In another context, Marx is much more explicit: "*History*," he says, "does *nothing*; it 'does *not* possess immense riches,' it 'does *not* fight battles.' It is *men*, real, living men, who do all this, who possess things and fight battles. It is not 'history' which uses men as a means of achieving—as if it were an individual person—*its* own ends. History is nothing but the activity of men in pursuit of their ends."[6]

These quotations indicate an important voluntarist component in the Marxian theory. Taken together with the previous discussion, they suggest the contribution of two factors—"conditions" and activity—as necessary for change. That activity consists of the behavior and efforts of militants. In part, they are essential to the "de-mythologizing" of the operations of the society, the economy, and the polity; their efforts, again in part, are also essential to the dissolution of false consciousness. To understand the processes of change, consideration must be given to these "educational" efforts, to these "small group dynamics." The militants draw the lessons of the complex, obscure, and frequently distant conditions, and pass them on to other segments of the general population.

The Marxian theory of democratic politics, briefly, is that such efforts are a sham. The governments in democratic regimes are bought by various members or factions of the bourgeoisie. The parties themselves represent nothing more than factions of the bourgeoisie plus, perhaps, some remnant parties of the previously dominant aristocracy. The participation of the socialists in electoral politics was advocated, particularly in the works of Engels. However, there was little expectation of serious reform through this effort. The basic position of socialist parties at this time was to refuse any participation in governments, awaiting instead the complete takeover. The electoral activity was seen primarily as an occasion for education, both of the population and of the Socialist activists.[7]

The Modifications of Marxism

Late in the nineteenth century, an effort was made to alter the basic Marxian outlines to take into account some significant new social and economic developments. The major innovation of the new theorizing was to recognize and focus on the emergence of a new class, the salaried "middle" class or white-collar workers.[8]

Although they were proletarians (as defined by their relations to the means of production), they, originally at least, were thought to be economically better off than manual workers. They certainly had more stable employment. The higher incomes, the greater job stability, and also, to some extent, the greater contact with the employer, contributed to the development of a different style of life, which, in turn, allowed the development of a different consciousness. Their fate did not include a "falling" into the manual ranks. Given the transformation of the occupational structure, many workers (or their children) were fated to "rise" into the salaried ranks. There was, in the original formulations of this "revised" Marxism, nothing that would lead the salaried ranks to identify with manual workers and their problems.

In this view, the anticipated disappearance of cleavages within the ranks of the proletariat was not occurring. On the contrary, an important new line of differentiation was emerging. It will be noted that the "new class" is not defined in terms of its function but rather in terms of its own sense of itself, in terms of its own consciousness of being separate. The authors of these revisions argued that the differences in income, in job stability, and in the kind of work performed, constituted "real" changes in their life circumstances and hence provided the basis for a "real" difference in their consciousness, that is, as compared with manual workers. The consciousness involved, in their view, was not false.

As this new "class" was growing in numbers and in relative size, the remaining segment of the proletariat, the manual workers, was undergoing a relative decline. The long-term development, in this view, did not entail a direct confrontation of two opposed classes. Three classes would be permanent features of the new development with this new class intervening, in a sense, between the other two preventing a polarized conflict and moderating any future struggle.

Polarization and extreme conflict, it was argued, would be limited by a number of other developments. The petty bourgeoisie, the small owners, were not being eliminated but, on the contrary, showed a rather remarkable persistence. They had not been forced into the proletariat to the extent anticipated; they continued to maintain their separate economic basis and their separate consciousness. Rather than disappearing as a factor in modern politics, they were still present and would have to be reckoned with, that is, appealed to by any serious political movement.

The lines of differentiation between categories, moreover, rather than becoming sharper, were tending to become blurred. The better-off members of the salaried middle class, for example, were buying stock in the corporations. Although their basic life chances were provided by their salaries, by becoming owners of minor fractional shares in the corporations, they gained some conflicting commitments.

Possibly the most decisive of the claims presented in this connection involved the well-off segment of the working class, that is, of the manual ranks. With increasing real incomes, more and more of the manual workers were able to afford some amenities and even to emulate some of the features of the life-style of the more affluent middle class. The pressures of sheer existence no longer had the same high salience for this segment as in the past. They, as a consequence, developed moderate political outlooks. They were willing to settle for moderate, welfare-state variety reforms. In short, it was thought that they too, like the salaried middle class, would give up on and refuse to support the traditional socialist demands for radical transformation of the economy and the society. These workers, moreover, were viewed as the forerunners of a more general well-being that would come to be shared by an ever greater proportion of the manual population.

The conclusion drawn for electoral politics was that the socialist parties would have to shift their orientation and appeals in order to draw support from the new white-collar class and to hold the support of the well-off workers. With the manual ranks undergoing a relative decline, the chances of the socialist parties gaining majorities on "pure" socialist programs would also diminish. The winning of a majority would necessitate winning the votes of this new class. To do that, it would be necessary to develop more "moderate" appeals.

There have been two major lines of development within the basic framework of revisionism: a pessimistic and an optimistic variant. The former was developed in Weimar Germany, the latter in the United States in the 1950s and early 1960s. The pessimistic variant sees the presumed differences between the "middle" and "working" classes being eroded to the detriment and consternation of the middle class. They react with anger, frustration, status panic, and fascistic politics.[9] The optimistic variant sees the erosion of differences but stresses the upgrading of the workers rather than the downgrading of the middle class. In this view, the sources of conflict or strain are gradually being eliminated.[10]

It is this second variant, the harmonist, optimistic, or American variant, that will be the focus of attention in this work. This variant has become the basic "centrist" position in contemporary social science. This theory describes the basic class formations presumed to be present, the shifts in those formations, and the attitudes presumably correlated with these "classes." Because of the general importance of this position and because it provides the main focus of attention in this work, it is necessary to elaborate the claims in some detail.

Fundamental to this view, the *beginning* point for the description of class formations and class changes, is the assumption that the major line of differentiation in modern societies was, and despite some change, still is that between manual and nonmanual work.[11] This assumption, based more on assertion than on evidence, derives largely from the "revisionist" tradition. It is assumed that the categories are differentiated in terms of income, work conditions (the onerousness, the noise, the cleanliness, etc.), differences in job stability and fringe benefits, mobility chances, and in terms of the typical social contacts on the job, the closeness to and influence of the employer being a key consideration in this connection.

Deriving from these conditions of income and work, it is assumed, are differences in consciousness, the middle class in particular having a special identification with their position and having a separate "style of life" embracing separate values, outlooks, and consumption practices that either are not shared by or are not available to the manual populations.

In discussions of the nonmanual ranks (or the "middle class") a distinction is made between the "upper-middle" and the "lower-middle" segments. However, these terms are seldom defined with any degree of precision.

For the most part, the distinction proves again to be one of income and the relative stability of job conditions. Basically, the upper-middle class has more "security" and higher income than the lower-middle class.

Frequently one also finds a parallel distinction made with respect to the manual ranks. There are the well-off workers, the skilled, who have better incomes and greater job security. And then there are the semiskilled and unskilled who have neither high incomes nor job security.

The above gives only a static picture of the "class" structure. The optimistic variant also incorporates the notion of closure, the assumption that working-class–lower-middle-class differences are being eliminated. As indicated previously, in this variant it is the upgrading of the workers that is stressed rather than a downgrading of the middle class. Counter-cyclical economic policies have more or less eliminated the crises and the resulting strains and deprivations that characterized previous times. In contrast to those previous times, sustained economic growth now pays off for all groups so that the lower-middle class, while suffering a *relative* loss of position vis-à-vis the working class, is gaining ground absolutely, that is, in terms of real changes in living standards.

Manual workers, presumably, become "integrated into the society." More and more of them come to share the living standards of the middle class. The sources of conflict, it is said, are being reduced and, with time, will be eliminated. Going along wth this affluence-moderation trend, it is argued, will be a continuous increase in educational levels and a correlated development of moderate, compromise-oriented outlooks. Accompanying the increased education and income there will be a greater development of and integration into voluntary associations. This involvement will have effects similar to those coming with increased education.[12]

Another major change assumed in this outlook involves what one might label the "class shift" hypothesis. Inherent in modern societies, it is argued, is a necessary tendency toward proliferation of administrative, technical, and clerical tasks. At the same time that these jobs are increasing in number and in proportion, the same technological development is eliminating routine manual positions. Economic development (or "modernization"), it is said, forces this shift in the occupational structure so that more and more people of necessity come to be engaged in the more desirable white-collar work.

Many commentators have mistakenly put this "fact" together with the Marxian assumption and have argued that the "proletariat" is becoming a minority, or, in the United States, has already become a minority. Rather than the dominant tendency being a "fall" into the proletariat, they say just the opposite is happening: more and more workers (or their children) are being "forced" into the middle class.[13] As a result, ever larger proportions of the populations in modern societies are coming to be rewarded with secure and stable jobs. This "inherent dynamic" also undermines radical parties and reduces the efficacy of leftist appeals.

Possibly the most important aspect of this development is that with the number of opportunities expanding there would be many "winners" and few "losers." If the occupational structure had had more or less constant proportions over the years, then upward mobility could occur only at the "cost" of an equivalent amount of downward mobility. The existence of a significant shift in the manual-nonmanual proportions means that most of the children of the middle class may continue to hold middle-class positions and that many children of workers may also achieve that status. Presumably, since the trend is likely to continue, there will be an outlet or "safety valve" available for many years to come.[14]

Improvement is also anticipated for those remaining in the manual ranks. Parallel occupational changes are occurring there with more and more workers coming into skilled positions and fewer remaining in the declining semiskilled and unskilled categories. The general upgrading of income levels and improvement of working conditions means that these skilled workers, although still doing manual work, may adopt middle-class life-styles and consumption standards when away from the job.

The discussion thus far has been focused on the occupational or "class" topography. In the 1950s, beginning in the United States, significant innovations were made with respect to the assumptions about the values and outlooks of the various classes.

The upper class, the bourgeoisie, the ruling class, for a century had been portrayed as conservative (if not reactionary), intolerant, and opposed to basic liberties. In the new formulations they came to be viewed as "moderate," well-meaning, and concerned with the welfare of the society as a whole. They also came to be regarded, because of their education and training, as capable and responsible. Perhaps even more dramatic was the new view that they were now the key defenders of individual liberties and of democratic procedures.

In some of these formulations it was claimed that the outlooks of the "elites" had changed. In times past they were rapacious and cynical, but in the present, the second- and third-generation upper classes, having the security of wealth and position and having had humanistic educations, came to have decent and responsible outlooks.[15] Much the same point is made about the upper-middle classes. They, too, as a result of their financial security, their education, and their voluntary associational involvements have devolped moderate and responsible outlooks. They, too, are claimed to be defenders of civil liberties and of democratic procedures.

The treatments of the lower-middle class vary. Some accounts view the "middle class" as an undifferentiated category. There exists something called "middle-class values" which are common throughout the rank. In other accounts one finds carryovers from the pessimistic variant.[16] The lower-middle class is presumed to be less tolerant than the upper-middle category, especially with respect to racial and ethnic minorities who are "catching up" with them in income and status. Because of their status anxieties they are thought to be susceptible to "demagogic" appeals and to those who promise "easy solutions" to their problems.

Probably the most important innovation in this new position comes in the treatment of the working class. Throughout most of the modern era, the working class, more than any other, has been considered a progressive force. Workers tended to support the parties of "movement," that is, those working for institutional changes to improve economic conditions and favoring greater equality.

In this new formulation, however, the manual workers are portrayed as opposed or indifferent to equality and civil liberties. They provide, in this view, the mass support for intolerant movements that threaten civil liberties and, ultimately, threaten the existence of democracy.[17]

Democratic societies, in this portrayal, are characterized by a very precarious balance of forces. The large mass of the manual workers are hostile or indifferent to basic democratic principles as are considerable portions of the lower-middle class. The minority upper-middle class together with the miniscule upper class constitute the key defenders of the democratic regime. In some formulations these groups at the top of the society make alliances with and protect the rights of disadvantaged minorities. The continuation of the democracy is made possible by this alliance of the minorities at the extremes of the social hierarchy against the "middle masses."

With the continued economic development of the society, another source of difficulty arises: the sudden escalation of demands above and beyond any reasonable possibility of achievement. This increase in demand, the "revolution of rising expectations," appears among previously deprived groups. If pushed beyond the capacity of "the system," there will be frustration, conflict, and strains that will threaten the "stability" of the democratic regime.

Given this new reading of the orientation of the various segments of the population, it is not surprising that the question of mass participation comes to be reevaluated. The possibility of widespread participation of the population in political affairs is viewed as a source of alarm rather than as an occasion for congratulation.[18] Low levels of involvement and participation are taken as indications of individual satisfaction and of social well-being. The twin threats of know-nothingism and high levels of demand will be minimized when such participation is low. Where a "reasonable" level of apathy exists, the direction of affairs by the responsible upper classes and the upper-middle classes may proceed with a minimum of difficulty. Their direction of the economic enterprise, according to this view, would lead to the most rapid economic growth possible and to general increases in living standards.

The social condition in this view is not static. Given the increased living standards, class transformation, expanding "educational opportunities," and the development of voluntary associations with their moderating influences, it is likely that some greater participation may occur in years to come without the same serious threat to the democratic regime. For the present, however, widespread mass participation is viewed as a hazardous development.

This social theory frequently is presented together with a definition of democracy that focuses on the competition of parties (discussed in the previous chapter). This definition, given the basic reading of the social condition as involving intolerant and appetitive masses, becomes "appropriate" or "realistic" since what is provided by the periodic elections is an occasion for either "ratification" or "replacement" but not involvement and controlling influence.

The basic substantive question raised in Chapter 1, the extent of alignment between governmental accomplishment and majority sentiment, has a fairly simple answer in this view. The "responsible" leaders will do as much as possible to satisfy public demands. They will, however, set certain strategic limitations to their responsiveness in order not to "overload" the system with unrealizable demands and they will also avoid demands that would undermine the democracy itself.

This theory, which is presented as a straightforward statement of the technical prerequisites for the maintainance of a democratic regime, does involve, it will be noted, a justification for the prevailing power relationships, for the prevailing distribution of income and other rewards, and also for the need to restrain, albeit very gently, the wishes of large segments of the general population. This is to suggest that the theory, despite its scientific-technical appearance, may well have a very considerable ideological importance. The justification for either nonperformance or for limited performance with respect to economic demands, in other words, may, either wittingly or unwittingly, provide little more than a pretense.

It is important to sort out the scientific-technical from the ideological components. One part of this sorting-out process involves an assessment of the basic descriptions of the society offered by this theory. This task will be undertaken throughout the present work. The key concerns are with the validity of the following claims: first, that the upper and upper-middle classes are moderate, responsible, and beneficent, and second, that manual workers and, to some extent, the lower-middle classes provide a source of threat or danger to the democracy.

There is a second area in which sorting out is needed, an area that can be given only passing consideration in this work. This involves assessment of the nonresponse to demands. The main concern here is whether the nonresponse is an act of statesmanship based on a realistic assessment of financial and technical possibilities or whether it is an act determined by self-interest. Leaders define programs as possible or impossible, as realistic or unrealistic (or "utopian"). In some cases it is clear that such definition is not scientific and technical, that is, that it is not "realistic" but rather is self-serving (serving the interests of well-off segments of the society). When a majority of the House of Representatives at one point voted down a measure to provide $40 million to kill rats in city slums, it is clear that "overloading" the system and technical impossibility were not the governing considerations.

Many decisions prove to be much more complicated. The claim by an interested party, by a legislator or a government official, that a decision was "realistic" may involve only pseudorealism. Whether a claim is, in fact, realistic or whether it has only the appearance of realism depends on the results of independent investigation, not repeated assertion. The theory being considered here may easily serve the convenient ideological function of justifying nonperformance decisions and discouraging the necessary investigations.

The second basic substantive question introduced in Chapter 1, the sources of any persistent discrepancy, in this "realistic" treatment drops out as not a serious question. It is the intent of responsible leaders not to respond to destabilizing or threatening demands.[19]

Pluralism

The theory just described focuses on and is concerned with class formations and the attitudes or propensities of these classes. As such, it is not a theory of democracy. It does not describe the "democratic process" or tell how democracy operates. It is basically a theory of the underlying social structure, of the component units of the society. In both pessimistic and optimistic variants, various potential threats to the operations of the ongoing democratic system are described but the specific features of that system are merely assumed.

The pluralist theory, by comparison, is concerned with describing the "political process." The pluralist theory assumes that there are a multiplicity of autonomous or semiautonomous agents or agencies in the society that represent their various followings in collective decisions and that are willing and able to check threats from either the central government or from other groups. In most accounts the agencies discussed are formally organized voluntary associations.

The theory, in effect, claims to provide a realistic and viable account of the operations of democracy in a complex society. Direct democracy does not and cannot work in "a large and complex society." Since the individual cannot participate directly (or if he does, he is going to be ineffective), there must be some intervening agencies able to take effective action; otherwise we have no democracy. The viability of a democracy, in other words, depends on the extent to which intervening organizations are present and the extent to which they are able to perform their representative and defensive functions.

The basic position may be summarized briefly as follows. A modern society, characteristically, is differentiated into a wide range of subgroups; there are occupational categories, racial and religious groups, ethnic groups, neighborhoods or larger communities, regional segments, those sharing various expressive interests, and so forth. The individuals in these categories share certain interests in common and they provide the potential for organized, planned, and coordinated action. Without organization, however, these categories would consist merely of loosely aligned collections of individuals. As such, they would be vulnerable to outside threats or incursions and they would also be unable to intervene successfully in larger political affairs to influence policies that would benefit their interests.[20]

To achieve these goals of defense and representation, the pluralist position points to the development of more or less permanent formal associations generated out of these various communal settings. The ethnic group, for example, will organize mutual aid societies and improvement associations as well as a local unit of a political party. The occupations will organize trade unions or, business or professional associations. There will be community clubs, neighborhood associations, conservation leagues, prohibition societies, and so on. Where there is a felt need, an "organizational weapon" for the defense of and pursuit of the group's interests will be developed.

The various organized groups support parties and candidates and, between elections, exert pressure to influence policies. Policy is seen as an outcome, a compromise of the various demands coming from these organizations. In the course of negotiations between the contending organizations, compromises will be worked out so that every contender gets some benefit and no contender is completely left out. A by-product of this contention is that the participants learn the processes and benefits of compromise. They learn, in short, the advantages of avoiding direct, open, and destructive conflict. A major consequence of the negotiations process is that conflict is moderated.

Multiple involvements and commitments provide another moderating influence. Most persons will not be located in a single communal grouping. They will have, for example, a neighborhood linkage, a separate occupational involvement, and still another tie with an ethnic group. This means that individuals will feel the pressures or constraints of these alternative commitments and also will be in a position to know and understand the significance of the compromise outcomes reached by their agents in the parties and the associations. The multiple involvements then serve to educate people and also lead them to check or restrain their own demands. This development, too, moderates conflict.[21]

The above account puts the case positively. It states how the system works or, more precisely, is presumed to work. Many formulations have a negative thrust to them. As Robert Dahl states: "The fundamental axiom in the theory and practice of American pluralism is, I believe, this: Instead of a single center of sovereign power there must be multiple centers of power, none of which is or can be wholly sovereign." The argument, briefly, is against those who might argue or assume undivided sovereignty. The consequences of this theory *and practice* of American pluralism are essentially those outlined above. Power "will be tamed, civilized, controlled, and limited to decent human purposes." Even minorities "are provided with opportunities to veto solutions they strongly object to. . . ." And the "constant negotiations among different centers of power" will allow citizens and leaders to "perfect the precious art of dealing peacefully with their conflicts."[22]

The key assumption is the "multiple centers of power" claim. The key implication is the opportunity for minorities to "veto" solutions. It is important to consider the "dispersion of power" assumption in more detail.

It is necessary for like-minded individuals to organize or "aggregate" in order to be heard, to get results, or to veto solutions. The adequacy of the theory depends on the actual behavior of the citizenry, or, at minimum, on their propensities when considering how to exert influence. The adequacy of the viewpoint, in other words, is dependent on the extent to which people actually see organizations as agencies for the realization of their political aims. If there were only a very restricted consideration or use of "organizational weapons," then the idea of pluralism would be useful, for empirical purposes, only in describing that limited population segment. As a description of society-wide behavior, or as an account of "how democracy works," it would have limited value.

The Almond-Verba study asks the appropriate kind of question about "what citizens would do to try to influence their national government." The most important finding in the United States is that only 1 percent said they would work through a political party and only 4 percent said they would work through a formal group such as a union or professional association. Interestingly enough, despite the theoretical focus on the formal association, a much larger proportion (29 percent) chose an informal organizational strategy (that is, they would organize friends and neighbors, get them to write letters, sign a petition, etc.). But, perhaps even more impressive is the fact that most of the Americans questioned indicated that they would act alone, that is, they would contact political figures, writing them letters directly or writing to a newspaper. This option was chosen by 57 percent of the sample.[23]

In short, only a very small part of the population thinks in the terms assumed by the pluralists. The majority is pre-pluralist in outlook, still oriented to individual petitioning. Three persons in ten opt for the weaker alternative of informal organization—weaker because typically smaller units and ones having less long-term continuity than is the case with formal organizations are involved. Only one person in twenty thought in terms of mobilizing a formal organization.

Many people are not members of voluntary associations. They have no immediate connection with such organizations such as would allow for direct representation of their interests.[24] A National Opinion Research Center study from 1953 asked about families with members in voluntary associations (including trade unions) and found 52 percent responding positively. A 1954 study by the Gallup organization found 55 percent of the adult population reporting membership in one or more such associations. A 1955 study by the National Opinion Research Center, again including union memberships, found 46 percent belonging to at least one association. A 1960 study by the NORC, which again includes trade unions, reported the membership level at 57 percent, the highest of the 4 studies.[25]

The basic finding in these studies is that a large part of the American population—close to half in three of the studies and more than half in the fourth—have no voluntary association connections. This indicates the maximum extent of applicability of the pluralist claims; at best, they apply to just over half of the adult population.

Pluralist theory, however, focuses not just on "associations" but, at least in the first line of analysis, on "instrumental" associations, that is, on those that are at least nominally concerned with exerting political influence. The theory is not concerned with expressive activities, that is, with the actions of sport clubs, bands, choruses, or adoration societies. Such organizations do not "represent" the membership in collective decisions, nor do they fend off the initiatives of the government or other organized interest groups. No simple either/or classification of organizations is possible, to be sure, but for illustrative rule-of-thumb purposes we have excluded those individuals who are members only of fraternal, religious, and recreational organizations. The portion of the population with instrumental organizational involvements, based on the 1955 NORC study, is 35 percent, as compared to the original 46 percent.

Much of this has been known for some time, that is, ever since studies of joining first appeared.[26] In response to such findings a number of variants have appeared that are designed to "save" the theory. Probably the most frequently proffered of these is the notion that nonjoining and apathy are symptoms of well-being. If the nonjoiners had real and pressing concerns they could and would either join existing organizations or form new ones. This view, however, overlooks the important disabilities suffered by some groups in the population. Organizational skills do not come into this world "full grown" but involve training and the possession of resources (money). While organization, without question, is a clear formal possibility, in practice, for those without received advantages, it proves an extremely difficult possibility to realize. The assumption that nonjoining is indicative of satisfaction does not have to be left as an a priori claim since it is easily researched.[27] Another difficulty that may be noted in this connection is the assumption that people will be activated by pressing concerns. There is a fair-sized literature available, however, which shows that in regard to one such concern, poverty, the impact is just the opposite: it depresses activity.[28]

In summary, the evidence indicates that voluntary association membership of any kind is a fact for just over half of the population. If we take only involvement in "instrumental" associations, as seems reasonable in view of the basic lines of the pluralist argument, the level falls below 50 percent. The point of this discussion is not to give any hard and fast figure on the level of involvement; that seems to be nearly impossible. The point, instead, is to indicate the limitations of the theory, the major lesson being that, at best, the theory applies to somewhere between one-third and two-fifths of the population. For the others, that is, for the majority, one needs some other kind of theoretical account.

As by-product effects of the purely instrumental concern, membership in organizations is seen both as educating and as creating conflicting commitments. By joining and participating in an organization to influence policy, one learns the attitudes and outlooks of other individuals and at the same time learns to take them into account. It is possible, however, that a single organization could "aggregate" like-minded people, cutting off potential contacts with more distant groups and thus contributing to an "immoderate" insistence on some given aims.[29] Were this to happen, it is possible that irreconcilable conflict rather than harmonious functioning would result. The assumption, however, is that individuals will have a multiplicity of organizational commitments. The interest represented by Group A will run counter to the interest being championed by Group B. The personal strain resulting from being a member of A and B is thought to be the key to the "necessary" containment of demands. The individual in such a conflict, presumably, sees that he cannot realize both demands and will, therefore, be inclined to compromise.

Given the evidence presented above concerning the overall level of membership in voluntary associations, it is clear that an even smaller percentage of the population is going to be involved in two or more such organizations. The 1953 NORC study shows 21 percent of all *families* indicating two or more memberships. The Gallup study (1954) reported 25 percent of the individuals sampled held two or more memberships. The 1955 NORC study yielded a figure of 19 percent. The Almond and Verba study, once again, has the highest figure: 32 percent. At best, then, this claim would apply to one out of three persons in the adult population.

Even this figure, however, must be discounted somewhat. In order to be "educated" in an organization one would have to show at least some minimal level of involvement. If there was none (that is, if one never went to meetings), this "education" could never occur.[30] Furthermore, the figures given here once again include all organizations. There is reason to assume that the impact of expressive organizations is different from that of instrumental ones. Where there is no bargaining, as, for example, in a choral society, there can be no development of an appreciation for aspects of the "bargaining process."[31] To give a precise figure on the de facto involvement in instrumental associations is not too fruitful. It is clear, for rule-of-thumb purposes, that this multiple involvement assumption applies to only about a quarter of the American population. Again, for the others one must have some alternative theory.

The formal associations are assumed to be internally democratic. This is obviously a major assumption of the theory of democratic pluralism. If the associations were the creations of elites and were designed to serve elite interests, the direction of influence would be the opposite of that which the pluralists anticipate.[32] To the extent that the participation "moderated" demand, in such cases, that would also serve the interests of the "sponsors" rather than of the "clients." If, alternatively, the associations were autonomous in origin but in the course of time had developed independent and self-serving leadership, the internal democracy would again be vitiated, although this time possibly with different results and implications. In short, if the voluntary associations were elite-controlled or oligarch-controlled, the assumption that they were "weapons" for those at the grass roots would be untenable. The existence of an active and flourishing organizational life in a society, by itself, says nothing about the democratic character of the society. The organization could, on the one hand, merely serve as "transmission belts" for elites, that is, as means for the easy "coordination" of the society; or, on the other hand, it could involve no more than "holding operations" for organization oligarchs.

A review of available evidence indicates a low level of democracy to be the case in most organizations. The most important work on the subject and one that has gained widespread acceptance argues the existence of an Iron Law of Oligarchy.[33] The basic condition of voluntary associations, if Michels is correct, is one of leaders who have different interests from those of their clientele-followers and who possess enormous advantages over their clientele —advantages that allow them to retain their positions even in the face of serious grass-roots disaffection.

It would be a mistake to see the matter in either/or terms, that is, to suggest that organizations either are or are not democratic. In actual cases one is likely to find degrees of responsiveness or, alternatively, to find responsiveness in some areas but not in others. The basic experience is likely to be one of organizations with only very limited responsiveness.

The term "represent" is frequently used in an equivocal manner.[34] It is said, for example, that trade unions "represent" workers, the proof being that the workers originally designated the union as their agent and have never voted for any subsequent decertification. This kind of choice, however, must be recognized as a very limited one, that is, between having a collective bargaining agent or not having one (in which case the alternative would be for each individual to negotiate in a "free labor market"). Given a choice between a "free" market and one in which one has some degree of influence, all groups (businessmen big and small, farmers, and workers) choose the latter. This kind of choice between an obvious good and an obvious bad thing will be referred to as a plebiscitarian choice. This refers to a choice that is formulated and presented by organization leaders. It takes woefully incompetent leadership to lose a plebiscite. In the ordinary course of events they will always "win" and will cite these wins as being at the same time a "ratification" of their leadership. More distant social commentators tend to draw similar conclusions.

While a union may represent workers to the extent that they prefer a bargaining agent to not having one, the key question is the adequacy of the agent's efforts in subsequent bargaining. A long-standing complaint about union leadership is the nearly exclusive concern with wages over working conditions. Union leaders prefer to work on the former issue because of the relative ease of doing so (and because management prefers this focus); the membership, while not lacking interest in the wage question, is also concerned with local work conditions. It is the situation in the local shop, after all, that occupies their attention for approximately eight hours of the day. For the union leadership, however, the local issues are "sticky" ones. Managements are more resistent in this area; it is difficult to achieve equitable arrangements, hard to enforce settlements, and so on. For these reasons there is a strong tendency in unions *not* to represent on the local issues and instead to offer a new wage settlement. The latter again turns out to be a plebiscitarian choice, and, characteristically, is approved by the membership. The problems involved in developing a more representative opposition leadership within unions have long been noted. Because these facts may well be misinterpreted, that is, the results of plebiscitarian choices and the absence of organized internal opposition, the assumption of adequate representation deserves to be questioned. Once again, it should be noted, direct inquiry is possible.[35]

In summary, there is a fair amount of evidence which suggests that even the minority that is more or less actively involved in voluntary associations faces a major difficulty—the difficulty of obtaining an adequate response from organization oligarchs.

The various organizations, it is assumed, check and balance each other; an equilibrium of forces is maintained such that no single interest is dominant over the others.

There are a number of explanations offered as to how the balance is achieved, but the major conclusion is that there is no permanent or dominant minority; nor is there a dominant majority. In Madison's view there would be a constant regrouping of forces; a different constellation, or alliance, would appear for each of the emerging issues. In de Tocqueville's view there would be some kind of rational calculation; individuals thinking of the next alliance would not act with ruthlessness or intransigence in the current venture. A "sociological invisible hand" appears in some contemporary formulations, as "veto groups," as "countervailing power," or as the "power of public opinion." Characteristically, the view is that some natural forces are operating—groups "will appear" when needed, opinion "will be mobilized," and so forth. On the whole, there is little in the way of explanation offered as to the "necessity" which is thought to be involved.

A balance of forces would depend on some rough equality in the distribution of the organizational "weaponry." Given, however, the large number of persons "left out," it is likely that their interests tend to be unrepresented in the decision-making or "bargaining" efforts. The organizationally involved are not scattered at random throughout the society; membership and involvement tend to vary directly with class level. The available evidence is in complete agreement on this point. The 1955 NORC study also shows the same pattern as may be seen in Table 2.1.[36] For this purpose we have divided the manuals and the middle classes into "upper" and "lower" subgroups using income as a crude basis for the separation (and also using a slightly lower cutting line in the South). The "upper-middle class" is most likely to be involved in organizations, to be in two or more organizations, and to be active in their organizations. There is also (not shown in table) a slight tendency for this upper-middle class to be involved with civic and service organizations, whereas the working class propensity is more toward lodges and religious associations.

Adding union membership to this picture does reduce the overall "class" differences. The significance of this for the pluralist viewpoint, however, is moot since, as previously discussed, unions tend to be strongly oligarchical and tend to restrict responsiveness to wage and fringe benefit issues. It should also be noted that approximately half of the manual workers are not represented even on these issues by trade unions.

The point of this discussion is that the organization memberships are more frequent among the higher classes than elsewhere in the society.[37] Given the original pluralist assumption, this would suggest that their interests will outweigh those of the other ranks in the society when it comes to "bargaining" efforts. A limited review of some "outputs" shows this, in fact, to be the case. In a very salient matter—taxation—the laws have been written in a way that favors the rich and the better-off and penalizes the not-so-well-off. The same is true with respect to urban renewal programs, the overall effect amounting to what Michael Harrington has called "socialism for the rich." Public schools, which are frequently viewed as involving some "progressive" redistribution of resources, have been shown to actually redistribute to the advantage of children from better-off families. Most major institutions of higher education certainly work this way; that is, they redistribute resources to the children of high-income families. Even in the case of the Medicare program, which does, in fact, aid the aged poor, there is a hidden aspect: an increase in doctors' incomes. Given the tax structure this means that modest-income families are taxed to pay a very affluent occupational group to perform services for the very poor.[38]

There are a number of other, less central, problems connected with the pluralist theory. On recognizing the inadequacy of the theory in its more

TABLE 2.1

Occupation, Income, Region, and Organizational Participation (Economically Active, Married, Nonfarm Population), NORC 1955

	Family Income							
	Non-South				South			
	Manual		Nonmanual		Manual		Nonmanual	
	To $4999	$5000 or more	To $7499	$7500 or more	To $3999	$4000 or more	To $4999	$5000 or more
Percentage of respondents in at least one organization (excludes unions)	30%	36%	53%	63%	12%	25%	33%	54%
Same including unions	51	61	59	66	21	39	38	58
Percent in two or more organizations (excludes unions)	10	17	28	38	4	11	13	29
Percent very active (excludes unions)	14	20	35	36	10	15	19	33
$N =$	(375)	(203)	(314)	(128)	(145)	(124)	(94)	(79)

sweeping formulation, one response has been to first justify the existing limitations and then argue or assume a trend toward "fulfillment." The justification takes the form of an argument (with some supporting evidence) that those not in organizations have not yet learned the "bargaining rules," that they are intolerant, intransigent, and undemocratic in their outlooks. The stability of a democracy, in this view, depends on limiting the participation of these groups in the "democratic process."[39] This limitation, however, is not viewed as permanent since the fundamental trends in the process of "modernization" include an extension of educational "advantages" to ever larger proportions of the population and an increase (because of increased wealth) in voluntary associational participation by the previously un-organized. Both of these trends are viewed as having a beneficent impact on attitudes; education and organization participation create tolerance, com-promise orientation, a willingness to abide by the "rules of the game," and so forth.

There are some questions that have to be raised about these theory-saving efforts. In most cases, a simple cross-tabulation of education and tolerance does show that higher levels of education are associated with greater tolerance. It is easy, especially for those making the defense, to take a further step and to suggest that the education causes the tolerance. If we consider, however, the other correlates of high and low education, there is at least some ground for skepticism. If, for example, we ask what kinds of people in the contemporary United States have no more than primary school education, the answer would include the following categories: the aged, small towners, Southerners, and women. The highly educated would have the opposite characteristics—younger persons, urbanites, males from outside the South. The former characteristics are all associated with low tolerance, the latter with high tolerance. Without taking all these factors into account, one cannot be sure just how much, if any, of the presumed impact may be ascribed to the influence of education. There is still another consideration that enters in here. A cross-tabulation, by itself, does not justify a causal judgment. It is conceivable that it is the tolerance that leads to higher education (and low tolerance leading to low education). The tolerant person (or his parent) may be more favorably disposed toward education and more likely to achieve it.[40]

A similar line of argument may apply to the association membership-tolerance claim. That is, the nonmembers are older, rural, Southern white women, while the enthusiastic joiners are likely to be younger, urban, non-South, and so forth. This all suggests the need for an inquiry into the actual importance of the two beneficent factors. It is possible that after all the other relevant factors are properly discounted these two would have very little importance.

An important related claim appears in the Almond and Verba study. They show a direct relationship between organization membership and "subjective competence," the suggestion again being that involvement creates this feeling of competence. Their data show that there are some very important other factors operative, since 54 percent of the nonmembers also have high subjective competence.[41] Somehow they have developed a feeling of capability without this special kind of organizational experience. Among those nonmembers with only a primary education there is still a relatively large proportion (46 percent) with high subjective competence. There is a parallel question to be raised in this connection about those who are educated and organizationally involved. Are they "subjectively competent" because of their education and organization involvements? Or, is it that their feeling of competence, their education, and their organizational involvements all stem from an upper- or upper-middle-class background? In upper-class and upper-middle-class families (and the class milieu generally) one is taught ruling and participation in ruling; the entire experience is one of "doing it," of seeing friends and relatives doing it, and thereby gaining a continuous demonstration of the possibility, and more important, of the rightness and justice of that participation. What is presented in the pluralist framework may simply be an obscuring translation of what is basically a lesson of class and the passing on of class privileges and attitudes.[42]

There is little that may be said on the subject of a trend. As indicated, the general assumption is that the level of membership will rise with increases in real incomes. The major point made in this connection is that the workers are now being "integrated into" the society. The Amond and Verba study, the most recent of the studies cited, shows the highest level of membership, thus apparently supporting the expectation. A comparison of two National Opinion Research Center studies, those of 1955 and the 1960 Almond-Verba study, shows however that most of this increase was in the nonmanual ranks. The number of nonmanuals in organizations was 59 percent in the former study and 69 percent in that of Almond and Verba. The respective figures for the manual ranks were 47 and 50 percent. That is the overall result, including the entire range of organizational types. In the case of a key instrumental organization, the trade unions, the trend was in the opposite direction, falling from 27 to 23 percent. While union memberships were falling off, there was an increase in the joining of "expressive" organizations. Seen from the perspective of control over "instrumental" organizational resources, manual workers appear to have lost ground during these years, both relatively and absolutely.

Direct evidence on union memberships (as a percentage of wage *and salary* workers in the United States) shows a steady decline from 1955 through to 1964 in the percentage of the unionized.[43] This decline, it will be noted, comes in a period of continuous increase in real income and also at a time when there was a continuous rise in the educational levels. Despite these "facilitating" conditions, the trend was toward lessened rather than enhanced affiliation in this particular kind of organization. There is little change in the *absolute* number of union members in these years but that relatively stable figure hides the fact of growing white-collar unionism and declining blue-collar affiliations.

One final comment is necessary on the presumed consequences of the "bargaining process." The processes of bargaining, so it is said, creates a sense of legitimacy. In the course of negotiating one sees, or otherwise comes to appreciate, the value of the process and the equity of the result. Although frequently repeated, there is little "hard" evidence available supporting the claim. There is, however, a large supply of contrary "soft" evidence. In everyday language there are terms for describing the same kinds of activities which do not carry the same positive connotations. Instead of "bargaining" the terms are "log rolling" and "opportunism," the suggestion being that such efforts erode legitimacy. The parties most known for their "bargaining" efforts—the parties of notables, the old-style "liberal" parties—are at the same time those that have been widely identified as the parties of questionable virtue. Such parties have also been characterized by a slowness of response in the face of objective needs where quick action has been required. In short, added to their somewhat seedy image (being parties of "politicians" in the bad sense), they are also known and identified as responsible for *immobilisme*.[44] The case for the "virtue" of the pluralist view is, in other words, made through semantic stylizing, that is, a presentation that allows or encourages avoidance of the negative evidence.

In summary, the pluralist theory proves to be quite inadequate. As an account of "how things work," it proves to have only limited applicability.[45] At best one may speak of a limited pluralism or a pluralism of the upper- and upper-middle classes. As an account of democracy in action, that is, as an account of *de facto* representation through interest groups, it is also clearly inadequate. Even the saving attempt, to recognize the limitations and to argue a trend toward this "ideal" proves to have only limited viability. Moreover, even in the upper-middle-class context there is some reason for believing that "pluralism" does not work as it is usually represented. Some orientations (the sense of "subjective competence," for example) may be the result of upper-middle-class family training; the attitudes and the organizational participation may be learned in the upper-class milieu. It may not, in other words, be a case of "membership" (which, unlike "upper-middle-class background," is open to anyone) giving rise to the attitudes.

The pluralist argument, the claim of a "widespread dispersion of power," was intended to undercut the claims about class divisions and class prerogatives. The theory, which aimed to undermine the argument of class, ironically, comes to restate and reaffirm that lesson. The resources for influencing policy are still very much in the hands of the well-off segments of the society.

In recent pluralist formulations, this state of affairs has been recognized and the effective "dispersion" of power, realistically, is claimed to extend only to the upper- and the upper-middle classes. This limited pluralism is then justified as the best possible arrangement for contemporary democratic regimes, note being made of the "unreliability" of the lower-middle class and of the "authoritarianism" of the manual workers. "Pluralism" in their latter day formulation comes to refer to a diversity of power centers within these higher ranks of the society. The party struggle amounts to a limited or restrained conflict between different segments of these ranks. The choice presented the underlying majority of the population is essentially one or the other of these high-level offerings. The range of choice presented in this "competition of parties" is, for the reasons discussed in Chapter 1, rather limited. The major concerns of the underlying population tend, on the whole, to be avoided rather than attended.

The majority of the population is not in a position to determine the issue offerings of the major parties. Voting offers them a choice only among the restricted range of alternatives. When it comes to exerting influence *between* these "ratifying" elections, the general population is even less able to exert influence given their very limited financial and organizational resources.

In the subsequent chapters, the criticism of the pluralist position will be elaborated. For the most part, however, this will be a peripheral concern and will be taken up only in passing. The major lesson to be gained from the above discussion is the relatively *limited* dispersion of power and the concentration or clustering of "resources" in the higher ranks of the society. This justifies the focus on the class stratification of the society and the attention to be paid to the claims of the stratification theories already discussed in this chapter. The major concerns will be with locating the class boundaries, indicating the values and orientations of the classes, and also, as far as is possible, indicating the presence (or absence) of resources for influencing, effecting, or vetoing policy decisions.

The pluralist account, in essence, provides a description of upper-middle-class life conditions and political behavior. There is little in this account to aid the understanding of the rest of the society. The two major alternative lines of analysis, that is, those that do offer some account of the condition of the general population, describe that population as consisting, on the one hand, of isolated individuals, and on the other hand, of *in*formal groups, of families, neighborhood groups, work groups, and so forth. The first of these viewpoints has been referred to as the theory of the mass society, the second as a theory of group-based or socially rooted politics.

The Theory of the Mass Society

This theory, in a sense, is the pathological inverse of the pluralist theory. The "mass society" is one in which the voluntary associations never developed, or have disappeared, or have come to be politically irrelevant, engaging in a round of activity with little or no serious content. There are two major readings of the "problem" of the mass society—one stemming from a conservative position and the other from liberal or left perspectives.

Both share a common diagnosis of the initial human problem; they both stress the extreme isolation of individuals and their helplessness vis-à-vis various threatening forces in the society. The personal isolation is seen, characteristically, as the result of competition, urbanization, and industrialization, all of which lead to a breakdown of primary groups, of the family, neighborhoods, communities, and so forth. The isolation and helplessness generate a considerable amount of anxiety and it is this anxiety that stimulates the desperate search for "solutions" that will alleviate their condition and that promise to eliminate the sources of their fears.[46]

In the conservative variant this condition of widespread isolation and anxiety leaves the population "vulnerable" to the simplistic appeals of "demagogues." In this view the problem is one of a "threat from below." The "demagogue," however, can offer no real solution to the complex and difficult problems of a modern society and the result can only be disruption which will further aggravate the social condition.

In the liberal and left variants the threats come from above. The shrewd and calculating elites are able to make appeals, to lead, direct, and manipulate, and in general to operate the society in any way they see fit. Because of the isolation and social fragmentation, and because of the absence of effective countering mass organizations, the general population is unable in any way to check their initiatives. In the most frequent formulations, the elites, through their use of the mass media, succeed in dominating even the consciousness of the masses. Through the use of sophisticated advertising appeals, they create artificial wants that people then adopt as their "own." The news reports are carefully manipulated so as to engineer consent to the major political directions of the elites. Moreover, to the extent that voluntary associations exist at all in the society, they are also the instruments of the elites who initially created them and who continue to use them to support their conception of the proper organization of society.

The mass society formulations have been used to explain the "susceptibility" of the German "masses" to the appeals of the National Socialist demagoguery.[47] Some use was also made of this viewpoint in post-World War II analyses of the Soviet Union and the East European nations, which were contrasted to the "pluralist democracies" of the free world. The focus on the role of the elites and their manipulative use of the mass media was also popular with left intellectuals in the 1950s. During the high tides of McCarthyism and in the later Eisenhower years, the so-called narcotizing effects of "mass culture" supposedly explained the absence of internal dissent.[48] In the 1960s, particularly in the work of Herbert Marcuse, this viewpoint was again revived in a radical critique that portrayed the general public as completely helpless, their minds totally within the grasp of cunning manipulators.[49]

This viewpoint, like the others discussed previously, is likely to contain some elements that are valid and some of dubious worth. The major initial objection to be noted involves the sweep of the claims. In essence what one has is a portrayal of an elite and of an undifferentiated "mass," the latter consisting of all the rest of the society other than the elite. There are no significant distinctions to be noted within this "mass," the key feature of the existence of its members being their dependence on and helplessness in the face of the various "offerings" of the elites.

It would seem more realistic, however, to recognize at least two sources of differentiation. In most societies, including the United States, the pattern of attention paid to the various media varies considerably by class. In general, it is the "educated" upper-middle class that follows the print media, the newspapers, the "best selling" books, and the so-called mass magazines. The manual workers and the lower-middle class tend to follow audiovisual media, that is, radio and television. There are also differences by class in the foci of attention in any given medium. This means that different media "lessons" reach different segments of the "mass" audience. The lessons of advertising also vary by medium and audience. The much-discussed emphasis on "status symbols" and "conspicuous consumption" tend to be located in the print media and those segments of the audiovisual media directed toward or, more precisely, followed by the upper-middle-class audience.

In a very general way it may be said that the most systematic attempts at the "persuasive communication" of political lessons are to be found in the media followed by the upper-middle class. This is also true of the major lessons of "consumerism." The programs followed by manual workers and low-middle-class populations tend rather to be entertainments and diversions and they generally lack explicit political content. The advertising in these programs focuses on inexpensive products used or consumed in the ordinary household, floor cleaners, soaps, deodorants, toothpastes, soft drinks, and pain-relieving patent medicines.

This means that the "lessons" purveyed in the "mass media" are differentiated by class level and that the concerns most frequently stressed by alarmed liberal and left critics apply most explicitly to the upper-middle-class audience of "the" media. The problem with the theory would appear, once again, to be one of focus or extent. The major problem is not with the mass *society* but rather, if anything, with what we might call the upper-middle-class masses.

It is also important to recognize that the success of the manipulative effort will vary according to subject matter. If the attempt is aimed at convincing the masses that they "never had it so good," there exists independent evidence that allows some assessment of the claim. This comes in the form of such hard and tangible matters as one's paycheck, the price of groceries, the rent or the mortgage payments, medical costs, and so forth. It seems unlikely that a manipulative attempt would ever succeed in this central area of human concern.

Successful manipulation would be more likely in the case of "distant" issues that cannot be immediately assessed. It would be relatively easy, for example, to misrepresent the origins of a war (as in the first and second Vietnamese wars), or to generate alarm about such matters as "communism" at home and abroad. Threats to "national honor" would also fall within the class of the not easily assessed claim.

While it is clearly the case that much alarm is and has been generated about the latter kind of issue, the effects of such efforts are not quite so obvious. It is possible that such efforts may affect the outcome of an election from time to time, but, as we shall see, even here there are some important checks on or limitations to the effectiveness of such an attempt. In great measure, the limitation is provided by the dominating, salient concern with personal or familial welfare, which tends to override the distant alarms.

These matters will be treated at greater length in Chapter 3. For the moment, by way of summary, it may be noted that it is the upper-middle class that is "most vulnerable" (or to put it another way, "most available") to the most explicitly political of the mass media. It seems likely, despite their high levels of educational achievement, that they are the most seriously "manipulated" of any group in the society. The working class and the lower-middle class are not likely to receive through the media either the explicit political lessons or the advanced lessons of "consumerism." Also, given the salience of the economic question, these classes have a kind of "anchorage" in their lives that, to some extent at least, provides a check on the attempt to distract.

The end result is the same; that is, the society is directed along lines sought by the dominant elites. To achieve that result it is not necessary to have "narcotized" masses, only inactive masses. It suffices to have the support only of the "narcotized" upper-middle class.

The fifth major position to be discussed, the theory of "group-based" politics, is essentially an empirically supported response to some of the simplified, stereotypical portrayals of "the masses" that are found in some works of the "mass society" tradition. For this reason it is expedient to defer further criticism of the latter position and proceed directly to an exposition of the "group-bases" viewpoint.

The Theory of Group-Based Politics

The basic point made in this position is that the informal group structures of "advanced" industrial societies are remarkably viable, do not undergo a rapid decline, and provide a base, or anchorage, for political attitudes and choices that is not easily overcome through the efforts of outside, distant elites. Again, the prognosis for democracy is not a highly optimistic one. The informal structures, at best, provide a defensive base against outside incursions.[50] There is little to be anticipated, in this view, in the way of new initiatives from the grass roots.

In the earlier versions of pluralist theory, the electorate was viewed as having a fairly high level of awareness and as being reasonably capable. The population generally knew what it wanted and went about looking for or creating instruments for achieving their aims. In the end, they got at least part of what they were after.

In the group-bases approach, the general population is not thought to possess this same awareness and capacity. Rejecting the implicit individualism of some formulations of the pluralist position (i.e., individuals know their wants and proceed to find means for their realization), the group-bases approach, following much of contemporary social science, stresses that, in great measure, the definition of wants and the definition of appropriate means are themselves products of "group living." The informal groups of which one is a member create the outlooks. Instead of the self-sufficient individual discussed in earlier formulations, the "individual" emerging from this analysis is very much a "group product," this "determination" extending even to aspects of his own self-conception.

Although some commentators have discussed the group-based approach as just another variant on the pluralist theory, it is important to note the decisive differences. Voluntary associations, in this formulation, do not appear as instruments for making or influencing policy. Where they are discussed it is as one more setting for the play of interpersonal influence. The analysis focuses on the impacts of the association on the individual member rather than on its impact on parties or governments. As such, the theory is not a political theory, at least not directly, but, instead, is a theory of the social psychology of mass political orientations.

The informal groups, although not active policy-making agencies, do serve some "defensive" functions. They provide a kind of insulation against outside influences. The leaders in the informal groups have some degree of expertise, more than the group members generally. Because of this, their judgments are trusted. These informal groups then provide a base or anchorage for the outlooks of their members giving the individual member some protection against outside manipulative efforts coming from upper classes, from "demagogues," or from other interested purveyors of political merchandise. It is these group bases, taken in their entirety, that provide stability to mass politics, inhibit massive swings in popular sentiment, and give mass politics what little "rationality" it has. The informal group "opinion leaders" would have some limited expertise; their evaluation and recommendations, on the whole, would be better and more adequate for the group than the appeals and judgments coming from more distant sources.

If one wishes to call this "pluralism" because of the many bases of "power" present in such an arrangement, it would be well to distinguish it from the previous version and recognize it as "defensive pluralism." It involves merely the power to defend against outside claims and appeals rather than the power to initiate and implement demands. As already indicated, the theory is social-psychological rather than *explicitly* political. It describes the real or presumed dynamics of political orientations as they are mediated within the small, informal group context.

The theory, nevertheless, does have considerable political relevance. To the extent that the majority of the electorate is removed from active involvement in political affairs (that is, to the extent that their political efforts are not carried beyond the limits of the primary groups), the traditional political elites are provided a free field for their efforts. The "containment" of the general population within the small-group contexts, provides the setting for the "free" and unhindered political practice of the elites.

The group-bases orientation also provides some explanation for the presence and persistence of false consciousness. People do not "see" most events directly. Their perceptions and understandings are mediated through the aid and guidance of friends, family, and associates. The frameworks for understanding and interpreting new and old events are, in a sense, a group heritage. Such a heritage may not be appropriate; it may involve fundamental misperceptions, untruths, and "dysfunctional" imperatives. But at the same time, supported by family potentates, by the leaders of neighborhood social activity, and by the informal leaders in the work group, that heritage appears to be solid and substantial. Moreover, to openly challenge the elements of such a world view would probably expose one to social sanctions that would make life in that context somewhat difficult.

It is through such informal group processes that confirmed working-class Democrats are created, and also, confirmed working-class Republicans (and, in other contexts, the working-class Tories and the worker Christian Democrats). The same processes, presumably, also create the dominant outlooks in upper- and upper-middle-class circles.

The basic position may be outlined as follows. In accounting for people's party preferences the key point is that most people follow their father's political lead. If one wished to predict voting and were allowed only one item of information on which to base the prediction, the preferred item would be father's vote. This means that more of the vote can be predicted on the basis of this item than would be the case with any other.[51] This does not mean that elections are thus predicted. If a two-party contest were close enough there would be sufficient shifting from the father's position to make the outcome indeterminant. One might still predict more than 80 percent of the voting without being able to forcast the outcome. Since the concern is with the entire electorate, there is as much need to understand the 80 percent as the more volatile 20 percent. Put somewhat differently, the most important determinant of voting is the parental, particularly the paternal, training. In this sense, most voting can be described as "traditional" or as a social "inheritance."

The paternal family also plays an important role in the ultimate social placement of its children. Most children are placed in the same milieu as the parents: most children of workers become workers, most children are located in the same ethnic or religious milieu as their parents, and so on.[52] This means that the family, which in the course of everyday life has trained a Democratic son, is also going to play a role in locating that son in an environment, the political complexion of which is also Democratic. This is not to suggest that there is anything sinister or conspiratorial about the process. Since there are many other values that probably outweigh the political concern, these social-political facts are probably best viewed as little more than the unintended by-products of routine social life.

The most important exceptions to these continuity generalizations occur in the case of those who are "misplaced," that is, those who for one reason or another come to be located in a milieu different from that of their father. The most important source of "misplacement" is social mobility, both upward and downward. Typically, this means the "transplantation" of Democrats into a Republican milieu (with upward mobility) and of Republicans into a Democratic milieu (with downward moves).[53]

In summary, any large collectivity consists of families that have trained their children in the "group's" political orientation. Any "new recruits" to the group are influenced and encouraged to adopt the group's standard. This explanation carries us only one generation back and thus leaves open the question as to the sources of the original group pattern (or "heritage" or "equilibrium"). The original pattern would depend on the events associated with the group's first entry into the electorate and on subsequent "realigning" events.[54] This is a reversal of the usual expectations; the suggestion is that a voting pattern is originally a "rational" one and thereafter becomes "traditional." On the whole, one would expect that the greater the extent to which campaigns are built around personalities rather than issues, the greater the extent of the traditionalizing. Some of the "group heritages" may be of very long standing. In the United States, for example, some may go back to the first entry into the electorate, say in 1832, whereas others have been shifted by some subsequent crucial events (for example, the shift in Negro voting during the New Deal). Some traditions" are being created today, as in the case of disaffected white Southerners looking for a new political direction and in the case of Southern Negroes entering the electorate for the first time since Reconstruction. The two considerations are clearly separable; one may study the origins and have no interest in the passing on of the tradition or vice versa. For the most part, the present work will focus on the contemporary dynamics and will overlook the question of the origins.

Another major determinant of an election outcome, over and above the basic "anchorage" in family training and social placement, has to do with the "new entries" and the "new exits," that is, with the new voters (either young people coming of age or the previously apathetic or disenfranchised) and the voters "retiring" from the electorate (the newly disenfranchised, the aged, the new apathetics). Some considerable part of the election outcomes from 1920 to date may be accounted for in terms of turnout, a question of entries and exits, rather than conversion. The 1920 elections were low-turnout elections (the lowest in a century) thus giving the Republicans a very pronounced edge.[55] The Democratic successes in 1932 and 1936 were associated with increases in the size of the electorate. The relative declines of 1944 and 1948 were correlated with declines in turnout.[56]

In the case of such entries and exits, however, the same basic social processes are assumed to be working. Past political training and current pressures determine their party orientations in much the same way as with the "regular" electorate. The point is that the exclusive focus on "conversion," on the "swing of the pendulum" as many have put it metaphorically, is misleading because it suggests more volatility in the electorate than is actually present.

Another long-term determinant of electoral outcomes is the demographic contribution. It is possible that two competing parties divide the vote 50–50 at time A. They each train their children in their own politics, their rates of participation are equal, and somehow, two generations later, the division is 60–40. What has happened is that the members of one party were more fertile than those of the other, trained more offspring, and thus tipped the balance. This is especially likely to be the case with left parties, having their base among the working class and poor.[57]

The group-based-politics claims do, on the whole, have a fair amount of empirical support. There has, nevertheless, been some criticism of the view, and it is worthwhile digressing a bit to consider some of these objections.[58]

The group-bases viewpoint stands in sharp contrast to classical notions of political democracy. In that view, the individual is seen as an independent collector and evaluator of data. The parties put out information on issues indicating their stance with respect to the policies to be assessed. The individual renders a judgment in the form of a vote and these are tabulated to determine who shall rule. This view assumes most people to possess a fairly high intellectual capability. Those not currently showing that capacity are thought to be developing it as a result of the extension of education. But, while the classical view sees rationality at the center of things, the group-bases viewpoint discovers rationality present only on the margins.

What does the evidence show? The available evidence indicates that a rather low level of political competence is present. There are high percentages of "don't know" responses on basic subjects including such things as the names of the candidates and the identification of important issues. On the whole, there is a low alignment of issue orientations and party choices. The classical assumption is that such discrepancies should lead to a shifting of party choice; people should choose the political instrument appropriate to the realization of the issue. One study, however, shows a distortion in the perception of issues in order to bring the "position of the candidate" into accord with the voter's party preference. In this study liberal Republicans defined Thomas Dewey (in 1948) as being for public housing, for price control, and against Taft-Hartley. This reconstruction of reality, this exceptional fantasizing, indicates that party identity, for some at least, is more important than the issues.[59]

This position, to many, is most objectionable; it is an intellectual's nightmare, this intellect-less, uncontrollable political scene. The only way, apparently, to change that scene would be through a restructuring of the group pressures and influences. To those reared in the Gladstonian school, the thought that discussion of issues must be sacrificed for mere friendly appearances, for an emphasis on tea parties and conviviality (*Gemütlichkeit* versus *Geist*), is distressing in the extreme. Or, alternatively, playing for the long term, one must try to influence birth rates; for example, birth control for one's political enemies versus continuous, enthusiastic (and uncontrolled, somewhat careless) sexual gratification for one's friends. Politics becomes, in both the short and long run, a blind, stupid process, a movement of unreasoning pawns. If the viewpoint were adequate, there would appear to be little point to campaigning on issues; one might as well have an entertainment. On the whole, like it or not, these assumptions have provided the basis for much of current political practice: for the television spot announcements and the stress on "personal interest" and "sincerity" as opposed to content. If this is "the way it is," one has to reckon with it; otherwise, scholarship would become an irrelevant fantasy.

One other implication that has been drawn from these studies is that the educated, intelligent, and concerned citizen ought to ignore the general public because their wishes are irrelevant to (or even pose dangers for) the operation of the society. It is the work in this tradition that has provided much of the justification for the elitist position with respect to the ruling of modern societies.[60]

The intellectual enterprise, however, may be pushed further by asking a causal or explanatory question; one should not take values or behavior as given, but should inquire as to their sources. Why does mass politics operate on this basis? By way of speculation, we may offer the following suggestions. American electoral history has, on the whole, been characterized by issue avoidance; it has been largely a issueless history. The experience from the first engagement in mass politics has focused on the irrelevant, on "character," personality, and sloganry ("Tippecanoe and Tyler too").[61] With this as the primary "learning experience," it is no wonder that "rationality" is absent in the electoral choice. Studies of newspaper content during campaigns have shown that the overwhelming proportion of coverage is devoted to personalities, wives, childhood simplicities, and so on. Moreover, when issues are discussed they are not explicitly linked to party position.[62] For the average man or woman it would take an unusual effort to acquire the necessary information and make the synthesis the newspapers have failed to provide. For this reason, too, it ought to come as no great surprise that people do so poorly at linking issues with parties and/or candidates.

Some political parties cannot focus on the issues. Given their conservative orientations and the liberalism of the mass electorate, to focus would be to court disaster.[63] This, for example, would be the case with the Republican party which, in essence, is an unpresentable party. They must, given their peculiarity, avoid the issues, or find some that are easier to fake, such as nationalism, patriotism, foreign policy, subversion in government, and subtle degrees of "softness" on communism. Domestically they must make do with Annie Oakley politics—"Anything you can do, I can do better. . . ."

This is to suggest that the social basis approach describes American politics "as it is" and says very little about how it could be under different prevailing conditions (for example, under the condition that parties choose to present new, interesting issues and argue them). On those occasions where issues are present, people do react and respond. As already noted, it is likely that issues are more salient at the time of first entry into the electorate, especially as many groups have to "fight their way into" the electorate, and on the occasion of realignment. The voting of Negroes in recent years has followed very closely and very sensitively the issue positions of the parties. It is obvious that the intellectual's pleasantry—that "increasing education" is the "key variable" (or, put in the vernacular, that it answereth all things) is not sufficient. In the United States, poor and uneducated farmers put forward and supported a rather complex program for monetary reform; this involved a high issue orientation on rather complex issues; they also had an impressive organizational support for this program both in the Farmers' Alliance and the Populist party. Although resisted by the elites of that age, by the educated and "respectable," the basic demand was later accepted and implemented by the very elites who had earlier opposed it.[64] The potentialities for democracy, in the classical, rational, issue-oriented sense, are obviously much greater than the generalization based on past or current practice would suggest.[65]

There is another question worth considering: Is it entirely a bad thing that people are influenced by their primary groups? And a prior question: Can it be otherwise? Put differently, is the rationalist view not based on a hopelessly unreal assumption?

In de Tocqueville's formulation, the problem is posed as follows:

> There is no philosopher in the world so great but that he believes a million things on the faith of other people and accepts a great many more truths than he demonstrates. This is not only necessary but desirable. . . .
> The question is, not to know whether any intellectual authority exists in an age of democracy, but simply where it resides and by what standard it is to be measured.[66]

De Tocqueville's point is that "faith in other people" is a simple, economical way of solving many problems. Individuals do not have time to research all problems and therefore must accept many points on faith. They will select "sources" who are believed to have some greater degree of expertise and will depend on them for political information. The group-based politics, then, is not as irrational as it at first appears. Rather, it is a necessary economy or shortcut procedure. To be sure, it is not as adequate as researching all questions; but then, that is impossible, hence unrealistic.

It is remarkable, given the ignorance of specific issues and party positions, that there is so much "objective" rational behavior. Most poor people, for example, do support the party that objectively does most for their welfare. Without knowing the answers to questions on specific issues, when asked which party is most closely aligned with their interest, most people answer correctly. This suggests that in some way the group pressures exert influence in the "right" direction. The original equilibrium of a group may have been set at a time of high rationality and awareness, and the party position and the group "interest" may not have changed. Realigning elections also serve to correct situations where a disparity has arisen—as in the case with the Negro allegiance to the Republican party.[67] Groups have, moreover, varying degrees of autonomy; to maintain their autonomy they have devices for sustaining values and for screening out and selecting from "outside" information. This is one of the tasks of a group's opinion leaders—to collect, sift, and pass on information and "lessons" to the less-informed group members.[68]

It is important to consider the "nonsocial" influences being rejected in this viewpoint; the most important of these is the role of the mass media. The "school" answer to the political influence question has been that the media have little or no impact. More specifically, it is held that information is acquired through the media but that values, particularly party preferences, are formed early in life and reinforced by contemporary influences. One's political identification leads one to select out supporting information, that is, information that is consonant with the prior party choice.[69]

The most striking evidence in support of this claim is the fact that the newspapers in the United States have been Republican in their majority for decades and yet, despite this, the Democrats have won elections.[70] Mass circulation magazines, too, with rare exceptions, have been conservative with respect to issues and Republican with respect to party, and yet Franklin Roosevelt won election four times. In this case the explanation is quite simple: those who read the magazines tended to be Republicans; the content generally did not reach those of Democratic persuasion. Among the readers there is the fact of selective attention which aids in avoiding the intent of the publishers.[71]

So, as indicated, the lesson apparently is one of either no effect, or at best, of little effect (one so small as to be undetectable with "crude measuring instruments"). This is a lesson that has been put to great use in countering the claims of mass society theorists. On the whole, these countercritics have quite justly attacked the sweeping, flamboyant claims about media manipulation, control, "narcotization," and so on. On the other hand, there is some reason to think that the rejection of the claim has been all too sweeping. To show that "the masses" are not completely manipulated does not show, of course, that no one is manipulated. If only a tiny minority were manipulated and they turned out to be the primary group opinion leaders, then there would exist what has been called a "two-step flow of communication" which, in turn, would mean support for a modified manipulation thesis.

The most important work on the subject, one that is in the "social bases" tradition and stressing the "two-step flow," is Katz and Lazarsfeld's *Personal Influence*. Ironically, despite the emphasis, many of the findings actually show just the opposite—a predominance of nonpersonal influences. The book is filled with charts showing the personal influences associated with behavioral changes. Peculiarly enough, the "bars" in these charts are broken off at a point far short of the halfway mark, let alone the 100 percent mark. In a note, for example, we find the explanation: "The difference between 37.6% [the highest incidence of personal influence] and 100% (62.4%) represents those brand shifters who were not exposed to personal contacts at all."[72] At another point we have this summary conclusion:

> Not every opinion change involved a personal contact. Fifty-eight percent (of the *changes*, not the *changers*) were apparently made without involving any remembered personal contact, and were, very often, dependent upon the mass media. But about 40 percent of the time, . . . our respondents were able and willing to recall a specific conversation with another person which they alleged played a role in bringing about their change of mind.[73]

On the basis of these findings, it would appear more appropriate if the book were entitled *Impersonal Influence* since most of the influences were of that kind. This indicates that the role of the media in decision making generally may not be so small as has been suggested.

Another major work arguing restricted media influence is the study *Voting* by Berelson, Lazarsfeld, and McPhee. Their basic finding is that: "The more exposure to the campaign in the mass media, the less voters change their positions and the more they carry through on election day."[74] Those paying much attention to the media have stable positions; those who are only casual attenders lack political commitment and are therefore more subject to change. Where most "mass society" theorizing has assumed that the "volume" of media content consumed is directly related to impact (change), the opposite appears to be the case, those moved by the media do so as a result of casual and ephemeral contact.[75] The character and location of "mass society" phenomena are, therefore, somewhat different from what has usually been suggested. The susceptibility exists among a much smaller group than has been conventionally assumed. It should also be noted that the irregular media attender who is moved by a "brief encounter" is also likely to be an irregular voter, which again reduces the political importance of such persons. This is assessing importance from the perspective of the total electorate—only a small minority operates in this way. However, that minority may be sufficient to turn the result in a close election.[76]

This discussion touches one limited kind of media influence, even though it is the influence most often discussed—change during a campaign. There is another, less dramatic kind of media influence: the reinforcement effect. The media apparently aid in "holding" people "in position." Such "holding" may be subsequent to a media induced conversion that occurred long before the campaign. Or the "holding" influence may prevent a conversion that would otherwise be likely. If so, then this kind of influence would suggest some support for the mass society theory. People may be "fed" information, which they then make "their" viewpoint. The further information received merely sustains a view that was manipulated from the beginning. This kind of influence is most likely in the case of "distant" issues, that is, issues involving factual claims that are not easily assessed by reference to immediate experience. The Detroit auto worker, for example, knows from experience that he should be suspicious of Detroit newspapers—he has compared the report with his experience—but he is much more vulnerable when it is a question of "communists in the State Department" or the behavior of insurgents in underdeveloped countries. An example of this kind of impact would involve the domestic liberal who votes for the more conservative of the two parties because of his concern with the distant "threats." To find that such a person is unmoved during the course of any given campaign does not exclude the possibility of an important media influence.[77]

There are some indications in the Berelson-Lazarsfeld work showing this kind of longer-term impact. The authors note that between campaigns there was a disaffection from the Democratic camp. As they put it: "the Democratic potential was either apathetic or concerned with other issues, mainly those dealing with international affairs. . . . the Democratic potential was 'confused' or 'led astray' by the day's topical problems." They do not indicate how the "topical problems" were communicated to the wandering Democrats but it is a fair inference that the mass media were the major contributing agency. This "dispersion of attention" in turn "had its effect upon vote intentions." The campaign itself realerted the wanderers to their political identities and, more important, the Truman campaign stressed and made salient the domestic liberal issues. This reconversion was the source of the "Fair Deal rally," the resurgence of the Democrats that, on the national scene, gave Truman his victory. It is only in a footnote that the authors report: "The saliency of class issues was brought home through the mass media." History did not repeat itself in 1952 because Stevenson did not stress the "saving issues," but, instead, avoided them, thinking they were no longer relevant. With two candidates stressing "distant" issues, the possibilities for manipulation were greatly enhanced.[78]

These comments on media impacts can, at best, only be considered as "general orientations"—as guesses as to how the events are actually structured. These guesses are not, however, pulled out of the air. They are suggested by currently available findings; there is, in short, a "thin line" of evidence supporting these speculations. A more serious difficulty is that we are unable to make any assessments as to the relative importance of the various impacts. What percentage of the electorate, for example, is "group anchored" (totally immune to the media)? What percentage, though socially rooted, are influenced over the long term? And what percentage are rootless and, to borrow Ortega's image, "moving with the wind?"

By way of guess, it seems likely that most people have a group-anchored or group-supported vote. The media-influenced votes, in any given election, are a small minority of the total. While media influence may explain only a small portion of the vote, it may, in a close election, determine the outcome.

There is one final consideration that deserves attention, namely the potential for rational, that is, issue-oriented politics. Many contemporary formulations have pointed to the available evidence and concluded that issue-oriented politics, at best, is a minority phenomenon. Going beyond the "fact," the assumption has been made that such is the nature of things, and, from there, some theorists have proceeded to construct a theory of "democracy" that accepts and justifies limited participation. Stated somewhat differently, the theory justifies the special prerogatives of the "qualified" minority.

There is some reason for believing that the rationality of the population has been unnecessarily downgraded. In one of the key formulations, that of Berelson, Lazarsfeld, and McPhee, the point is made as follows:

> . . . the amount of correct perception in the community is limited. Only 16 percent of the respondents know the correct stands of both candidates on both issues, and another 21 percent know them on three of the four. Over a third of the respondents know only one stand correctly or none at all. And these are crucial issues in the campaign, much discussed in the communication media. Thus, a good deal less than half the political perception in the community is reasonably accurate, by such definitions.

In a footnote it is pointed out that "these figures apply to the early campaign period of August," that is, before the campaign had actually begun. The authors state that similar data for October would "almost certainly" have raised these estimates.[79] The understating of issue knowledge, for this reason, is likely to be fairly sizable.

A second problem has to do with the implicit "nature of things" assumption. The study itself shows that the lack of knowledge and the inaccurate perception was closely linked to the "ambiguous" formulations of one of the candidates, Thomas E. Dewey.[80] This means, simply, that if a candidate refuses to make his position clear, respondents either will not know his position, or, if they guess, the likelihood of error will be high. The low level of accurate information, therefore, is due to the candidate's behavior rather than to the innate capabilities of the electorate. Put somewhat differently, it is evident that the "ignorance" was situational rather than characterological. This conventional reading, in short, amounts to another instance of attributing blame to a "low-status" (that is, poorer, less-educated, powerless) group when, in fact, the sources of the disability lie with rather highly placed individuals. In addition to the original misreading, ironically, in this case we also have a "theory of democracy" developed that entails further penalties for the disadvantaged groups.[81]

As already mentioned, there are occasions where groups realign, that is, where they drop a "traditional" allegiance and adopt another. It appears that these are moments in which democratic politics are "rationalized." This happened in the shift of Negro voters during the 1930s, in the case of the various farm uprisings in the course of American history, and in the sensitivity of farmers in recent decades to farm price support systems. Such events indicate the potential for rationality within the population. The contemporary surveys, for the most part, have not been focused on realigning experiences, that is, those unusual campaigns in which candidates focused on salient issues.

A linked consideration here involves the "location" of rationality. An all too easily accepted belief is the assumption of rational elites and upper-middle classes. The rest of the society, the lower-middle classes, manual workers, farmers, and, in general, those lacking formal education, are not thought to be in a position to "participate" adequately. They, so it is assumed, are subject to passions, susceptibilities, and faulty judgment such as would endanger the functioning of the "democracy." It is worth noting, in order to give a "balanced" picture, the irrationalities of elites and of the upper-middle classes.

One consequence of being located in such an elevated position is that one is very much cut off; one lacks information about the rest of the society. When one speaks of a milieu as being "exclusive" (thinking that to be a good thing), it is characteristically forgotten that such experience involves just what it says, shutting out, excluding. Those persons in the exclusive milieu are not "cross-pressured" by the excluded; they do not learn about the outsiders' values or interests. They live, in essence, within a milieu characterized by mutually reinforcing homogeneous influences. It also means that knowledge about other people must take the form of highly oversimplified stereotypes, for example, clichés about the lazy and indifferent, the relief gougers, the envious, the communists, and so on.[82] It means that their policies are going to be developed and implemented on the basis of such inadequate assumptions. The argument of "briefings" and massive media attention will not do since these alternative sources of information are under-cut by the well-known facts of yes-men and the equally well-known limitations of the media.[83]

The fixed belief in elite and upper-middle class rationality leads one to overlook much information to the contrary. One explains national disasters in terms of a "loss of leadership" (the aristocracy was wiped out by wars or plague) forgetting that, as Orwell noted, Great Britain opened up every war in the last century with a disaster, one that may be traced to the extra-ordinary inadequacies of "its" leadership. British "leadership" in World War I refused to plan agriculture and food distribution until 1917 despite objective necessity because it went against their laissez-aller predispositions. In more recent times we have the spectacle of the "president" of South Vietnam demanding misinformation from his army field commanders and punishing them for giving correct information. Even more bizarre is the fact that some United States leaders accepted these estimates and did what they could to punish those who presented correct ones. Although widely accepted at present, Keynesian economics (a plan for saving the position of those in power) is still viewed by some elites as a part of "the communist conspiracy." In the history of the world, the most tragic and frightening event of modern times, Hitlerism, was aided by an alliance with German conservatives who, with all their rationality, thought they could do business with obvious racketeers.[84]

It would be a mistake to assume that "group influence" is an all-sufficient explanation for political outlooks. Those influences can, in some circumstances, contribute to major distortions in outlook and judgment. It is not the case, however, that such influences can gain assent to any content. People, the members of such informal groups, do live in a real world; they do deal with "real" things such as wages and salaries, rents or house payments, and the price of groceries. No amount of group influence is going to convince people that "things are good" when in fact "things are bad" (or vice versa). When the received tradition gets too far out of line, it is broken and a new tradition is begun. An adequate use of the group-bases theory must recognize and make use of both the "group" and the "reality" components in one's social analysis.

It is useful, at this point, to recapitulate and expand the discussion of the main concerns of this work. The first concern is to show the inadequate, low-level performance of American democracy. This is to say that the level of accomplishment on the part of government is well below that which is both currently demanded and technically possible. The overall state of public opinion with respect to the "demand factor" will be considered in the following chapter, which will present an aggregate picture of the entire population (or, in technical language, the "marginal distributions").

The principal task of this work is to provide an empirical assessment of the revisionist Marxist claims, the claims which, in their contemporary renditions, provide the core elements of what has been referred to here as "centrist" social science. The key themes that will be assessed are the claims made about a moderate and responsible upper-middle class and the parallel assertion about the threatening or dangerous lower-middle and working classes. Another major claim to be assessed comes out of the mass society repertory—the assumption of helpless, vulnerable, and manipulated masses. The basic conclusion, to anticipate somewhat, is that the evidence does not support these claims. In fact, the evidence to be presented does not accord very precisely with any of the five theoretical "programs" outlined here.

For that reason, much of this work turns out to be largely "negative" in character. It says, basically, that many of the standard received hypotheses are not supported by the evidence. Rather than leaving the matter there, a part of the task will be to make a "positive" contribution, that is, to suggest how things are ordered. Rejecting the simplistic rationalistic assumptions of some of the theories reviewed (for example, the assumptions that individuals or groups of individuals respond directly to social and economic developments, or that the conditions of their lives would give rise to some given ineluctable, unavoidable appreciation of their interests), this work will make use of a modified and "expanded" "social-bases" approach in an attempt to account for the actual distribution of attitudes and outlooks.

It is with this view in mind that, after the initial exposition of the class–political-orientations relationship, we turn to a detailed account of the situation of the working class in different kinds of communities, in the large cities, in the suburbs, in middle-sized cities and small towns. And it is also with this view in mind that a similar inquiry is made with respect to the "location" of or likely pressures on the lower-middle classes in those communities. The likely pressures or influences within the South are also explored from this perspective. The chapters on the changes in the patterns of recruitment of the working class and the various segments of the middle class are also intended to show the shifting pattern of group influences. This task is hindered by the absence of explicit questions on social contacts and the political influences. Much of what is indicated must, for the moment at least, depend on inference. The best that may be offered in many instances is evidence that is consistent with the social-bases viewpoint.

One additional note of caution is perhaps necessary. As opposed to the "economy" of presentation that may be gained in a crude Marxian view, or in the essentially very simple framework of centrist social science or of the mass society theory, all of which are very categoric in their formulations, the basic assumption of the social-bases viewpoint is that "the masses" or, alternatively, the major class formations embrace a wide range of local, regional, familial, ethnic, or religious traditions. An adequate understanding of the "state of the masses," in this perspective, involves some knowledge of the basic traditions present in the society and the factors sustaining them or forcing them to change. This means that an adequate understanding, necessarily, is going to be considerably more complicated than are the sweeping general formulations that have provided so much of the "stuff" of the contemporary intellectual discussions. This is not to suggest that it is necessary to lose oneself in a mass of particulars. One can still try to summarize the results economically. It does mean, nevertheless, that the results are still going to be considerably more complex than in the case of the more conventional readings. There is, on the other hand, some gain to be made, in that this will be a more realistic appreciation of the state of and determinants of public or "mass" sentiment.

Notes

1. Introductions to, accounts of, and commentaries on Marx and Marxism may be found in the following: T. B. Bottomore, translator and editor, *Karl Marx: Selected Writings in Sociology and Social Philosophy* (New York: McGraw-Hill, 1956); Maurice Cornforth, *Readers' Guide to the Marxist Classics* (London: Lawrence & Wishart, 1952); Sidney Hook, *Marx and the Marxists* (Princeton: D. Van Nostrand, 1955); Karl Korsch, *Karl Marx* (New York: Russell and Russell, 1963); George Lichtheim, *Marxism: A Historical and Critical Study* (New York: Frederick A. Praeger, 1962); C. Wright Mills, *The Marxists* (New York: Dell, 1962); Stanley W. Moore, *The Critique of Capitalist Democracy: An Introduction to the Theory of the State in Marx, Engels, and Lenin* (New York: Paine-Whitman, 1957); Vernon Venable, *Human Nature: The Marxian View* (New York: Alfred A. Knopf, 1945); and Irving M. Zeitlin, *Marxism: A Reexamination* (Princeton: D. Van Nostrand, 1967). The best introductory guides to the original works of Marx are those of Bottomore and Cornforth.

2. The relative decline of self-employed workers in farm and nonfarm activity is shown in the *Manpower Report of the President* (Washington, D.C.: Government Printing Office, 1968), p. 233.

3. This point is to be seen most clearly in Marx's historical writings. See especially "The Class Struggle in France, 1848–1850" and "The Eighteenth Brumaire of Louis Bonaparte," pp. 109–220 and pp. 221–311 of Karl Marx and Frederick Engels, *Selected Works*, Vol. I (Moscow: Foreign Language Publishing House, 1951).

4. See Ferdinand Lundberg, *The Rich and the Super-Rich* (New York: Lyle Stuart, 1968), Ch. 1, for a discussion of this group.

5. A useful discussion appears in John C. Leggett, *Class, Race, and Labor* (New York: Oxford University Press, 1968), pp. 34–38.

6. Cited in T. B. Bottomore, editor and translator, *Karl Marx: Selected Writings in Sociology and Social Philosophy* (New York: McGraw-Hill, 1956), p. 63. The original source is Marx's *Die Heilige Familie*, in the *Marx-Engels Gesamtausgabe*, 1927, Vol. I/3, p. 265.

7. See Engels' introduction to Marx's "Class Struggles in France. . ." op. cit., pp. 109–127, for a detailed discussion of the electoral question.

8. The key figure in this movement was Eduard Bernstein. His leading and most influential work is *Die Voraussetzungen des Sozialismus und die Aufgaben der Sozialdemokratie* (Stuttgart: J. H. W. Dietz, 1899). A translation appeared under the title, *Evolutionary Socialism* (New York: B. W. Huebsch, 1909). It has recently been reissued by Schocken Books, 1961.

A sympathetic study of the man and his works is that of Peter Gay, *The Dilemma of Democratic Socialism: Eduard Bernstein's Challenge to Marx* (New York: Columbia University Press, 1952). An account of the Social Democratic party and its internal struggles at the time of Bernstein's effort appears in Carl E. Schorske, *German Social Democracy: 1905–1917* (Cambridge: Harvard University Press, 1955).

9. See, for example, Theodor Geiger, "Panik im Mittelstand," *Die Arbeit,* 7 (1930), 637–654. Geiger's insights were taken over and incorporated by C. Wright Mills in his *White Collar: The American Middle Classes* (New York: Oxford University Press, 1951). In particular, see his Chapter 11, "The Status Panic."

10. The optimistic versions, the 1950s revisionism, may be found in the works of such authors as Frederick Lewis Allen, Adolf A. Berle, Jr., Russell Davenport, David Lilienthal, John Kenneth Galbraith, Talcott Parsons, Peter Drucker, John W. Hill, Daniel Bell, and Seymour Martin Lipset.

11. An early work making this stress is that of Robert S. and Helen M. Lynd, *Middletown: A Study in American Culture* (New York: Harcourt, Brace, 1929), pp. 23–24. More recent works include Seymour Martin Lipset and Reinhard Bendix, *Social Mobility in Industrial Society* (Berkeley: University of California Press, 1959), pp. 14–17, 165–169; and Robert Alford, *Party and Society: The Anglo-American Democracies* (Chicago: Rand McNally, 1963), pp. 73–79. Kurt Mayer describes it as follows: ". . . there is ample evidence that the major class division in the United States, as in other Western countries, is that between the middle class as a whole and the lower or working class. This is largely a division between manual labor and white collar occupations. . ." See his *Class and Society* (New York: Random House, 1955), pp. 41–42. The same position is maintained in the third edition of this work with Walter Buckley (New York: Random House, 1970), pp. 82–85.

12. All the themes discussed in this section are central to the argument of Seymour Martin Lipset's *Political Man* (Garden City: Doubleday, 1960). See also T. H. Marshall, *Citizenship and Social Class* (London: Cambridge University Press, 1950). Also relevant are the works of Kurt Mayer; see his *Class and Society;* his "Recent Changes in the Class Structure of the United States," *Transactions of the Third World Congress of Sociology,* Vol. III (London: International Sociological Association, 1956), pp. 66–80; and his "Diminishing Class Differentials in the United States," *Kyklos,* 12 (1959), pp. 605–625. See, also, Gerhard Lenski, *Power and Privilege: A Theory of Social Stratification* (New York: McGraw-Hill, 1966), pp. 369–382. These claims will be discussed throughout this work. See especially Chapters 8 and 10.

13. It will be noted that the use of the word "class" in these formulations is not the same as that of Marx. What presumes to be a commentary of Marx (the dwindling size of the "proletariat," the forced upward mobility) is actually an account of transformations within the proletariat.

This "revisionist" or modern social science conceptualization will be used through the present work. It seems pointless to fight over word usage. The contemparary usage is so well entrenched that it appears preferable to accept the categories and to then question the· validity of the claims or hypotheses using those categories. When that assessment is accomplished, one can then consider the *usefulness* of the received conceptualization.

14. The class shift hypothesis will be discussed, with evidence, in Chapter 4.

15. Many of the points discussed here appeared in an influential and popular work, that of Frederick Lewis Allen, *The Big Change: America Transforms Itself, 1900–1950* (New York: Harper, 1962). Allen makes the contrast between the old-style and the new responsible business leaders. A very useful case study, "The Good Goldfish: A Case Study in the Corporate Conscience," by Blair Ewing appears in Charles Perrow, *Organizational Analysis: A Sociological View* (Belmont, California: Brooks/Cole Publishing, 1970) pp. 101–112.

16. See, for example, the John W. Gardner quotation in Chapter 11, note 71. C. Wright Mills' *White Collar* is the most influential work in the tradition. Lipset's *Political Man* also contains some elements of the passionistic view, although most of the book is clearly focused on the "harmonist" or "centrist" tradition.

17. The key work making this point is Lipset's *Political Man*, Ch. IV: "Working-class Authoritarianism." The chapter originally appeared as an article, "Democracy and Working-Class Authoritarianism," *American Sociological Review*, **24** (August 1959), 482–502. These claims will be considered at some length in Chapter 11 of the present work.

18. Lipset, *Political Man*, Chapter VI, especially the conclusions, pp. 216–219. See also Lester Milbrath, *Political Participation* (Chicago: Rand McNally, 1965), Ch. 6.

19. It scarcely needs saying that realistic treatments of points considered here are relatively rare. American government textbooks stress the direct, open, representative possibilities and frequently claim these to be actualities. It is infrequent that one finds a frank statement of the need for restricting responsiveness and consideration of the strategies used for accomplishing that end. Openly expressed "realism" is more frequent in discussion of underdeveloped countries. See Charles C. Moskos, Jr., and Wendell Bell, "Emerging Nations and Ideologies of American Social Scientists," *The American Sociologist*, **2** (May 1967), 67–72; and also Richard Hamilton, "A Touch of Tyranny." *The Nation*, **201:4** (August 16, 1965), 75–78. Some useful criticisms also appear in Charles A. McCoy and John Playford, eds., *Apolitical Politics: A Critique of Behavioralism* (New York: Thomas Y. Crowell, 1967).

20. Some people use the word pluralism as a synonym for diversity. Pluralism, however, involves the presence and use of "intervening" organizations. The fact of diversity by itself, (that is, that the population in any society may be divided analytically into a multiplicity of categories) has no implications for the pluralist theory. At best, that diversity could provide the basis from which organizations could grow. By itself, the fact of diverse population segments may merely provide the condition for elite domination following the principle of divide and rule.

21. Still the best work on pluralist democracy is de Tocqueville's *Democracy in*

America, Henry Reeve translation (New York: Alfred A. Knopf, 1963). An influential modern formulation is that of David B. Truman, *The Governmental Process* (New York: Alfred A. Knopf, 1951). Some of the more influential works in this tradition are Lipset's *Political Man*; Gabriel A. Almond and Sidney Verba, *The Civic Culture: Political Attitudes and Democracy in Five Nations* (Princeton: Princeton University Press, 1963); and Robert A. Dahl, *Pluralist Democracy in the United States: Conflict and Consent* (Chicago: Rand McNally, 1967).

   Useful criticisms of some of the pluralist assumptions appear in the following: Charles Perrow, "The Sociological Perspective and Politics in Pluralism," *Social Research*, **31** (Winter 1964), 423–434; C. Wright Mills, *The Power Elite* (New York: Oxford University Press, 1957), Ch. 11, "The Theory of Balance;" Henry S. Kariel, *The Decline of American Pluralism* (Stanford: Stanford University Press, 1961); Mancur Olson, Jr., *The Logic of Collective Action* (Cambridge: Harvard University Press, 1965); Grant McConnell, *Private Power and American Democracy* (New York: Alfred A. Knopf, 1966); Peter Bachrach, *The Theory of Democratic Elitism: A Critique* (Boston: Little, Brown, 1967); Robert Paul Wolff, "Beyond Tolerance," pp. 3–52 of Wolff, Barrington Moore, Jr., and Herbert Marcuse, *A Critique of Pure Tolerance* (Boston: Beacon Press, 1965); Thomas R. Dye and Harmon Zeigler, *The Irony of Democracy: An Uncommon Introduction to American Politics* (Belmont, California: Wadsworth, 1971); and G. William Domhoff, *The Higher Circles: The Governing Class in America* (New York: Random House, 1970), see especially his Ch. 9: "Where a Pluralist Goes Wrong." Also of some interest is Christopher Lasch's "The Cultural Cold War," Ch. 3 of his *The Agony of the American Left* (New York: Random House-Vintage Books, 1969).

   22. Dahl, p. 24. V. O. Key, Jr., also stresses the "wide dispersion of power" in the United States. "Actual authority," he says, "tends to be dispersed and exercised not solely by government officials but also by private individuals and groups within the society. . . . the power structure tends to be segmented. . . . All this contrasts with the model of a clear and rigid hierarchial pattern of power." See his *Politics, Parties, and Pressure Groups*, 5th edition (New York: Thomas Y. Crowell, 1964), pp. 6–7. See also David Riesman (in collaboration with Reuel Denney and Nathan Glazer) *The Lonely Crowd* (New Haven: Yale University Press, 1950), pp. 234–239, 250–255, 260, and 281.

   23. Almond and Verba, p. 203. The percentage thinking in formal organizational terms was little different in the other countries sampled: 5 percent in the United Kingdom, 4 percent in Italy, and 3 percent in Mexico. Only West Germany differed significantly. There, 13 percent chose the formal option, as opposed to only 7 percent choosing to "aggregate" with friends and neighbors. A similar picture appears with respect to attempts at influencing local government. Again only 5 percent of the American respondents chose the formal organizational tactic (p. 191). On the local scene, the effort was much more heavily oriented to informal efforts (arousing friends and neighbors, petitioning, etc.) as opposed to acting alone.

   The authors are not daunted by their findings. They comment as follows (p. 1933):

That formal organizations would be rarely invoked by individuals who were trying to influence the government does not mean, however, that these organizations are politically unimportant. They still may effect an individual's political influence, for he may have more influence over government officials merely by being a member of such a group, even if he makes no overt attempt to influence the government. And this sort of influence is of great significance—probably of greater overall significance than the overt influence attempts that ordinary citizens make from time to time.

24. Earlier formulations, by comparison, made sweeping all-embracing claims. De Tocqueville, for example, stated that: "Americans of all ages, all conditions, and all dispositions constantly form associations." Vol. II, Second Book, Chapter V, p. 106. There is also an important discussion in Volume I, Chapter XII. Charles and Mary Beard said that in the twentieth century, the "tendency of Americans to unite with their fellows for varied purposes—a tendency noted a hundred years earlier by de Tocqueville—now became a general mania. . . . It was a rare American who was not a member of four or five societies." See *The Rise of American Civilization* (New York: Macmillan, 1927), Vol. 2, pp. 730, 731.

25. The 1953 and 1955 National Opinion Research Center study results are reported in Charles R. Wright and Herbert H. Hyman, "Voluntary Association Memberships of American Adults: Evidence from National Sample Surveys," *American Sociological Review*, **23** (June 1958), 284–294. The second of these studies and a 1954 American Institute of Public Opinion (Gallup) study are analyzed in greater detail in Murray Hausknecht, *The Joiners* (New York: Bedminster Press, 1962). The figure given in the text from the 1955 NORC study comes from my own running of the study cards. This was necessary in order to add union memberships to the total. I wish to thank the Center and the then director, Peter Rossi, for making the study available for further analysis. The 1960 NORC study is the Almond-Verba study, p. 302.

It would be a mistake to put too much stress on the specific percentage figures of these studies. There are differences in question wording and differences in the antecedent questions that might have some influence here. The AIPO study reviewed the "individual's knowledge of certain kinds of organizations" that may have stimulated recall of the respondent's own affiliations. Some discussion of this problem appears in Hausknecht, p. 15, and also in his Appendix A. Hausknecht, by not including union membership, gives the NORC 1955 result as 36 percent as opposed to our 46 percent figure.

There is one study that shows a markedly different pattern from the one reported here. That is by Nicholas Babchuk and Alan Booth, "Voluntary Association Membership: A Longitudinal Analysis," *American Sociological Review*, **34** (February 1969), 31–45. Their study of a sample of adults in the state of Nebraska found that in 1961 some 80 percent were affiliated with one or more associations. There is, understandably enough, very little differentiation in the extent of affiliation by class. Their study also found a clear majority having multiple memberships.

Comparing their findings with the original Wright and Hyman (and Hausknecht) result, they note that the key question in the NORC study (No. 367, 1955) came at the end of a long interview schedule (it was question No. 135) and also that the question focused on the local community—"Do you happen to belong to any groups or organizations in the community here?" These are serious problems and do, to some extent, limit the usefulness of this particular study. One point overlooked by these authors, however, is that the previously published results did not include union memberships. That particular membership was picked up in a separate question, and, when these affiliations are added as we have done in the text, the level is higher and close to that of other national studies.

Although reviewing numerous studies in the literature, Babchuk and Booth omit any reference to Almond and Verba's study, which made detailed inquiry into associational connections. Their principal question (No. 83a of the schedule) reads as follows: "Are you a member of any organizations now (trade or labor unions, business organizations, social groups, professional or farm organizations, cooperatives, fraternal or veterans' groups, athletic clubs, political, charitable, civic, or religious organizations) or any other organized group?" (p. 535). Their study, as indicated, does not suffer from the difficulties of the NORC study, but, nevertheless, still finds a level of membership considerably below the 80 percent level reported for Nebraska. Babchuk and Booth, without giving reasons, consider it "doubtful that the high rate of membership could be accounted for by the fact that . . . Nebraska . . . is different in significant respects from a state in another region." My analysis of the Almond-Verba data, however, shows considerable variation by region, from 71 percent ($N = 31$) joining in the Mountain states and 63 percent ($N = 102$) in the west north central region, which contains Nebraska, down to 44 percent ($N = 109$) in the west south central region.

One other possible explanation for their high figure is their explicit stimulation of some connections which are not likely to be included in other studies and whose inclusion might reasonably be subject to debate such as "poker, bridge, and other card clubs."

Wright and Hyman have a follow-up study, "Trends in Voluntary Association Memberships of American Adults: Replication Based on Secondary Analysis of National Sample Surveys," *American Sociological Review*, **36** (April 1971), 191–206.

26. For example, in Mirra Komarovsky, "The Voluntary Associations of Urban Dwellers," *American Sociological Review*, **11** (December 1946), 686–698. She cites . . . studies that go back even earlier. See her "A Comparative Study of Voluntary Organizations in Two Suburban Communities," Publication of the *American Sociological Society*, Vol. XXVII (May 1933), 83–93; William L. Warner, *Social Life of a Modern Community* (New Haven: Yale University Press, 1941), p. 329; W. G. Mather, "Income and Social Participation," *American Sociological Review*, **6** (June 1941), 380–383.

27. The studies at hand are not ideal for this purpose. One suggestive result makes use of the following question: "Many people say they live only from one day to another at this time. Do you think this way too, or do you believe you can make plans for the future?" (NORC 1955). Taking married, non-South, male manual workers, the number reporting living from day to day was 26 percent among the nonmembers ($N = 215$), 22 percent among those in one organization ($N = 68$) and 10 percent among those in two or more organizations ($N = 39$).

Evidence on the intergenerational transmission of participation patterns is to be found in Robert W. Hodge and Donald J. Treiman, "Social Participation and Social Status," *American Sociological Review*, **33** (October 1968), 722–740.

28. Illustrative of the range of works making this point are the following: Marie Jahoda, Paul F. Lazarsfeld, and Hans Zeisel, *Die Arbeitslosen von Marienthal* (Leipzig: S. Hirzel Verlag, 1933); Robert S. and Helen Merrell Lynd, *Middletown in Transition* (New York: Harcourt, Brace & Co., 1937); Oscar Lewis, *The Children of Sanchez* (New York: Random House, 1961); Elliot Liebow, *Tally's Corner* (Boston: Little, Brown & Co., 1967); and Michael Harrington, *The Other America* (New York: Macmillan, 1962).

29. For a discussion of this problem and some relevant data, see Sidney Verba, "Organizational Membership and Democratic Consensus," *Journal of Politics*, **27** (August 1965), 467–497.

30. The NORC study No. 367 (1955) asked, "Do you happen to belong to any groups or organizations in the community here?" There were follow-up questions asking for a specification of which organizations they were in and the total number of memberships. Then the question was asked, "Are you very active in these groups (that group)?" While not the ideal question for the present purpose (since it left the individual respondent to define "very active") some indication of the limited commitment may be gained by the following data:

Number of Organizational Memberships

	One	Two	Three	Four	Five or More
Percent reporting they are "very active"	49%	66%	77%	86%	89%
$N =$	(463)	(215)	(97)	(43)	(26)

31. One study notes that

. . . one of the few groups in which people with low self-esteem are more likely than those with high self-esteem to be members is the Glee Club or Choir. Attention is directed to the fact that in such groups there is probably less normal time or scope for spontaneous interaction. In addition, the individual member's contribution does not tend to be unique but tends to be buried or integrated in the collective effort. Furthermore, it does not tend to be spontaneous but is controlled by the director and the implacable dictates of the music. In such a group environment, people with low self-esteem appear to be more comfortable.

From pp. 194–195 of Morris Rosenberg, *Society and the Adolescent Self-Image* (Princeton: Princeton University Press, 1965). The same point might also be made for marching societies.

32. See, for example, Justin Gray, *The Inside Story of the Legion* (New York: Boni & Gaer, 1948). Also of some interest in this connection is the discussion by G. William Domhoff of the various "transmission belt" organizations of American foreign policy elites. See "How the Power Elite Make Foreign Policy," ch. 5 of his *The Higher Circles*.

33. See Robert Michels, *Political Parties: A Sociological Study of the Oligarchical Tendencies of Modern Democracy* (Glencoe: The Free Press, 1958).

Also of relevance are the following: Seymour Martin Lipset, Martin Trow, and James Coleman, *Union Democracy* (Glencoe: The Free Press, 1956); Oliver Garceau, *The Political Life of the American Medical Association* (Cambridge: Harvard University Press, 1941); Harmon Zeigler, *The Politics of Small Business* (Washington, D.C.: Public Affairs Press, 1961); Paul Harrison, *Authority and Power in the Free Church Tradition* (Princeton: Princeton University Press, 1959). For a more general discussion and additional references, see Kariel.

Some important criticisms of Michels' position are contained in the following: Alvin Gouldner, "Metaphysical Pathos and the Theory of Bureaucracy," *American Political Science Review*, **49** (June 1955), 496–507; S. M. Lipset, "Robert Michels and the 'Iron Law of Oligarchy'," Chapter 12 of his *Revolution and Counterrevolution: Change and Persistence in Social Structures* (New York: Basic Books, 1968); and John D. May, "Democracy, Organization, Michels," *American Political Science Review*, **59** (June 1965), 417–429.

34. See Hannah Pitkin, *The Concept of Representation* (Berkeley: University of California Press, 1967).

35. See Irving Howe and B. J. Widick, *The U.A.W. and Walter Reuther* (New York: Random House, 1949); B. J. Widick, *Labor Today* (Boston: Houghton-Mifflin, 1964); Stanley Weir, "U.S.A. The Labor Revolt," *International Socialist Journal*, **4** (April 1967), 279–296, and (June 1967), 465–473. Also very useful in this connection is Alvin Gouldner, *Wildcat Strike* (Yellow Springs: Antioch Press, 1954). A similar situation is faced by farmers. A useful case study is that of Don F. Hadwiger and Ross B. Talbot, *Pressures and Protests: The Kennedy Farm Program and the Wheat Referendum of 1963* (San Francisco: Chandler Publishing, 1965). The only effective means of "communication" open to unionists and farmers is the rejection of wage or benefit settlements. This happens with fair frequency, but characteristically the significance of such communications is obscured for the larger public. The most spectacular of these rejections was in France during the May–June 1968 events. This still did not stop commentators from seeing the problem simply as one of wages and living standards. See, for example, the article by Sanche de Gramont, "A Bas—Everything," *New York Times Magazine*, June 2, 1968, pp. 23–25, 84–89.

The reactions to these signs of internal democracy are rather curious. Theodore W. Kheel described the matter as follows: "The tendency of rank-and-file members to overrule their leaders is one of the most serious problems in labor relations today," *The New York Times*, February 19, 1968, p. 42.

From the West German scene we have the following quotations: The German Trade Union Federation (DGB) chairman in Hesse said that "the democratic nonsense on the middle and lower levels of the Federation must be put to an end," and the leader of the German Employees Union (DAG) said that "the unions do not suffer from too little but rather from too much of the so-called organizational democracy." Both quotations are from the *Frankfurter Rundschau*, October 31, 1968.

36. This finding also appears in the works cited in footnotes 25 and 26. The division into manual and nonmanual occupations and by income anticipates a discussion to be developed in Chapter 4. Note that in separating a "lower" from an "upper" middle class we have taken a different cutting point in the South where the income levels are generally lower than elsewhere.

37. The discussion here, as elsewhere, makes the convenient but unrealistic assumption that $1 = 1$, that is, that one membership is like any other. One may recognize the difficulty but practically, at least for the moment, there is little else one can do. It is clear that the upper-middle classes are more likely to be involved in instrumental organizations and are more active members. It seems likely, too, given disparities in trained capacities, that their organizations would be more effective than those of other groups.

38. On the character of taxation and the absence of any significant redistribution in modern times see the following: Gabriel Kolko, *Wealth and Power in America* (New York: Frederick A. Praeger, 1962); Philip M. Stern, *The Great Treasury Raid* (New York: Random House, 1964); Louis Eisenstein, *The Ideologies of Taxation* (New York: Ronald Press, 1961); Randolph E. Paul, *Taxation in the United States* (Boston: Little, Brown, 1954). A useful overview is found in Ferdinand Lundberg, Ch. 9. An outstanding parallel study discussing the British experience is that of Richard M. Titmuss, *Income Distribution and Social Change* (Toronto: University of Toronto Press, 1962). Interestingly, Robert Dahl, in a discussion of meliorative trends, fails to mention Kolko or Titmuss. See Dahl's *Pluralist Democracy . . .* , p. 435. The distribution of educational services in one large metropolitan school system is analyzed by Patricia Cayo Sexton, *Education and Income: Inequalities in Our Public Schools* (New York: Viking Press, 1961). On the institutions of higher learning see W. Lee Hansen and Burton A. Weisbrod, *Benefits, Cost, and Finance of Public Higher Education* (Chicago: Markham, 1969); and Douglas M. Windham, *Education, Equality and Income Redistribution* (Lexington, Mass.: D. C. Heath, 1970). On the subject of medical care programs see Theodore R. Marmor, "Why Medicare Helped Raise Doctors' Fees," *Transaction*, **5** (September 1968), 14–19, and his "Congress: The Politics of Medicare," in Allen Sindler, ed., *American Political Institutions and Public Policy* (Boston: Little, Brown, 1969).

39. See the works cited previously in footnotes 17, 18, and 19. See also Lipset and Nathan Glazer, "The Polls on Communism and Conformity," pp. 141–165 of Daniel Bell, ed., *The New American Right* (New York: Criterion Books, 1955). There is no direct advocacy in these sources. The practical implication is left for the reader to draw. The evidence presented simply shows the "less tolerant" populations "to be found among the old, the poorly educated, Southerners, small-town dwellers and workers and farmers." On the other hand, it is said,

> There can be little doubt that in the United States the rights of dissidents and of Communists are protected primarily by the powerful classes who accept the traditional norms under which a democratic system operates. This seems to be true in other countries as well . . . the upper and better educated strata are more likely to be tolerant of dissent, and to recognize the need for civil liberties than the workers, the farmers, and the less educated.

(From pp. 147 and 150 of Lipset and Glazer.) This evidence will be discussed further in Chapter 11. In *Political Man* Lipset quotes other people's doubts about participation and then concludes by saying that: "To the extent that the lower strata have been brought into electoral process gradually (through increased organization, an upgrading of the educational system, and a growth in their understanding of the relevance of government action to their interests), increased participation is undoubtedly a good thing for democracy" (p. 219). An influential work making the same point is that of Bernard R. Berelson, Paul F. Lazarsfeld, and William N. McPhee, *Voting: A Study of Opinion Formation in a Presidential Campaign* (Chicago: University of Chicago Press, 1954), pp. 314–315. A very straightforward statement of the evident imperatives is made by Ithiel Pool. He says, "In the Congo, in Vietnam, in the Dominican Republic, it is clear that order depends on somehow compelling newly mobilized strata to return to a measure of passivity and defeatism from which they have recently been aroused by the process of modernization. At least temporarily, the maintenance of order requires a lowering of newly acquired aspirations and levels of political activity." From his "The Public and the Polity," in *Contemporary Political Science: Toward Empirical Theory*, Ithiel Pool, ed. (New York: McGraw-Hill, 1967), p. 26.

See the references cited in notes 19 and 21 for criticisms.

40. This matter will also be discussed at greater length, with supporting evidence, in Chapter 11.

41. Almond-Verba, p. 308. The data are preceded by a recitation of the pluralist article of faith (p. 300):

> Voluntary associations are the prime means by which the function of mediating between the individual and the state is performed. Through them the individual is able to relate himself effectively and meaningfully to the political system. These associations help him avoid the dilemma of being either a parochial, cut off from political influence, or an isolated and powerless individual, manipulated and mobilized by the mass institutions of politics and government.

The study is heavily dependent on what is called a subjective competence scale (discussed on 231 ff.). This scale depends on the respondents' beliefs about their influence in *local* politics. On this point the authors say that this procedure "allows one to locate in each nation, a group of respondents who express relatively high levels of subjective competence. If a scale based on the national government had been used, too many respondents would have fallen into the lower categories of subjective competence" (p. 232). It seems likely that responses to questions inquiring about the ability to influence local government would vary by the size of community and also, in the international comparisons, by the degree to which local affairs were controlled or centralized in the hands of the national government.

For details on the construction of the scale, see their note on p. 231.

42. Some sense of the differences in the "civic education" received in upper-middle, lower-middle, and working-class communities may be found in Edgar Litt, "Civic Education, Community Norms, and Political Indoctrination," *American Sociological Review*, **28** (February 1963), 69–75. The children in the upper-middle-class high school already showed a high level of political insight *before* they took a high school civic education course. This was, presumably, before their most important politically relevant education had occurred and before their involvement in "voluntary associations." The respective levels of awareness of politics as a process of power based on the efforts of political actors (evidenced by a special scale of question responses) were 59, 23, and 12 percent. The civic education course heightened the awareness in the upper-middle-class school and had essentially no impact in the other two contexts. The main lessons would appear to

be that, first, political awareness comes at a relatively early age in the upper-middle-class milieu and would appear to be antecedant to the formal educational effort and before any significant organizational involvement. The second lesson from this study is that education *increased* the class differences in political awareness.

It seems likely that much of this political education and much of the knowledge of organizational technique stems directly from factors in the class milieu, possibly directly from experiences in the family. This suggests that much of the observed result may be independent of the role of education. Part of growing up for the upper- or upper-middle-class child involves direct observation of the parents in politics or in politically related activity. In addition, the child sees or knows about his parent's involvements and activities in formal organizations. Even if the child were no more than a passive spectator, he or she would receive a kind of "training" in political matters that would be unavailable to either lower-middle-class or working-class children. Passive observation, moreover, seems an unlikely possibility. Most upper-middle-class parents, one would guess, are likely to be quite active in training and supporting their children's initiatives in these areas.

For an admittedly extreme case of the child raised in the political milieu, see William J. Miller, *Henry Cabot Lodge* (New York: James H. Heineman, 1967). Some useful and instructive studies of the upper-class milieu are those of E. Digby Baltzell, notably his *Philadelphia Gentlemen* (New York: Free Press, 1958), and *The Protestant Establishment* (New York: Random House, 1964).

The argument is presented schematically in Figure 2.1.

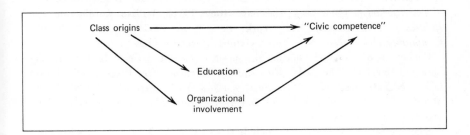

Figure 2.1.

Most studies merely abstract the relationship beginning with education and organizational involvement failing to point out that both of these are related to social origins.

Some initial support for this argument appears in the Hodge and Treiman article cited in note 27.

43. There were 33.2 percent unionized in 1955. This figure had fallen to 28.0 by 1966 From U.S. Department of Labor, Bureau of Labor Statistics, *Handbook of Labor Statistics, 1968* (Washington, D.C.: Government Printing Office, 1968), p. 300.

At the same time as the percentage of unionized persons is declining, there is a shift occurring with white-collar unionism showing a considerable upsurge and blue-collar unionism showing losses. Four white-collar unions, Retail Clerks, State and County Workers, Letter Carriers, and Retail-Wholesale Workers, jumped from a total of 676,000 members in 1956 to 1,142,000 in 1966. In addition, the government workers (AFGE) and the Teachers went over the 100,000 level in the early sixties, the former having 200,000 in 1966 and the latter 125,000. Data are from the Department of Labor, Bureau of Labor Statistics, *Directory of National and International Labor Unions in the United States*, Bulletin No. 1222, 1957 (data for 1956) and Bulletin No. 1596 (data for 1966).

The Wright-Hyman article (1971) finds greater growth in memberships among the poor, just the opposite of the trend reported here. They do not discuss the type of organizations joined.

44. A series of works appeared in the last years of France's third republic which described the "bargaining process." They all had titles that were variations on the "republic of pals" (or cronies) theme. See also Hamilton, *Affluence and the French Worker* (Princeton: Princeton University Press, 1967), p. 63.

45. But, at the same time, when presented as the end state of "de-ideologized" realism, it proves to be an extremely useful and convenient ideology. For an account of the ideological engineering done under the cover of an appearance of unplanned, spontaneous organizations, see Christopher Lasch.

46. Probably the best work in this tradition and one that explicitly links the isolation to the emergence of Nazism is that of Erich Fromm, *Escape from Freedom* (New York: Rinehart, 1941). Among the other important works with this focus are the following: Karl Mannheim, *Man and Society in an Age of Reconstruction* (New York: Harcourt, Brace, 1940); Hannah Arendt, *The Origins of Totalitarianism* (New York: Harcourt, Brace, 1951); William Kornhauser, *The Politics of Mass Society* (New York: Free Press, 1959); Robert A. Nisbet, *Community and Power* (New York: Oxford University Press, 1962).

Collections of essays elaborating this position include those of Bernard Rosenberg and David M. White, eds., *Mass Culture* (Glencoe: Free Press, 1957); Philip Olson, ed., *America as a Mass Society* (New York: Free Press, 1963); and Maurice Stein, Arthur Vidich and David M. White, eds,. *Identity and Anxiety* (Glencoe: Free Press, 1960).

Some useful recent discussions include those of: E. V. Walter, " 'Mass Society': The Late States of an Idea," *Social Research*, **31** (Winter 1964), 391–410; Joseph R. Gusfield, "Mass Society and Extremist Politics," *American Sociological Review*, **27** (February 1962), 18–30; and Raymond A. and Alice H. Bauer, "America, 'Mass Society' and Mass Media," *Journal of Social Issues*, XVI (1960), 3–66. Also of some interest is Daniel Bell's "The Theory of Mass Society: A Critique," *Commentary*, XXII (1956). This also appears as Chapter 1 of his *The End of Ideology: On the Exhaustion of Political Ideas in the Fifties* (New York: Free Press, 1960). Another critique (actually an extended *ad hominem* attack) is to be found in Edward A. Shils, "Daydreams and Nightmares," *Sewanee Review*, LXV (Autumn 1957), 587–608.

47. See particularly Fromm and Arendt.

48. A viewpoint best seen in the essays of the Rosenberg-White book. It was also a principal theme found in the "Socialist Quarterly" magazine, *Dissent*.

49. This left elitist view is frequently confused with the Marxist view. A key notion in Marx, however, is the idea of the "anarchy of production," the point being that even the most powerful men in capitalist society are *not* able to control key features of the system. Even though they have a common interest in upholding the "rights of property," they are continuously led to engage in behavior that undermines their power. Their "control" over governments amounts to little more than keeping it out of the hands of the working class, not an insignificant power obviously. Beyond the control over and agreement as to the purpose of the Ministries of the Interior (i.e., police powers), there was only very limited "control" to be seen, once again due to the "anarchy" peculiar to capitalist society. Marx's historical works are essentially extensive treaties on the use of government for private gain. Governments were "open" to any entrepreneur with a scheme and in a position to buy or otherwise manipulate legislatures and/or cabinet members. It was, in part, the resulting scandals that made the "stability" of those governments problematic.

50. A criticism of the extreme "mass society" claims together with some evidence supporting these criticisms appears in Eliot Freidson, "Communications Research and the Concept of the Mass," *American Sociological Review*, **18** (June 1953), 313–317. See also the Lazarsfeld works cited in the following footnote.

51. The single most influential work in this tradition is that of Bernard R. Berelson, Paul F. Lazarsfeld, and William N. McPhee, see particularly p. 88 ff. Also of relevance to the "group-bases" position (or "social bases," personal influence, or social pressures position) are the following: Paul F. Lazarsfeld, Bernard Berelson, and Hazel Gaudet, *The People's Choice* (New York: Duell, Sloan and Pearce, 1944); Elihu Katz and Paul F. Lazarsfeld, *Personal Influence: The Part Played by People in the Flow of Mass Communications* (Glencoe: Free Press, 1955); Angus Campbell, Gerald Gurin, and Warren E. Miller, *The Voter Decides*, Appendix C, "Primary Group Influences and Political Behavior;" and Herbert McClosky and Harold E. Dahlgren, "Primary Group Influence on Party Loyalty," *American Political Science Review*, **53** (September 1959), 757–776. A very useful discussion of this and alternative positions appears in Peter H. Rossi's account, "Four Landmarks in Voting Research," pp. 5–54 of Eugene Burdick and Arthur J. Brodbeck, eds., *American Voting Behavior* (Glencoe: Free Press, 1959).

52. See Berelson, Lazarsfeld, and McPhee, Chapters 4 and 6. For data on the intergenerational occupational continuity, see Chapter 8 of the present work.

Most discussion of this point stresses the intergenerational continuity in class levels. It is generally assumed that one group base, ethnicity, has disappeared with years and generations of assimilation. That assumption has been challenged by Michael Parenti, "Ethnic Politics and the Persistence of Ethnic Identification," *American Political Science Review*, **61** (September 1967), 717–726. See also Raymond E. Wolfinger, "The Development and Persistence of Ethnic Voting," *American Political Science Review*, **59** (December 1965), 896–908. Also of some interest is Gerhard Lenski's *The Religious Factor* (Garden City: Doubleday, 1961).

53. For more detailed discussion of this point, see Richard Hamilton and Raymond Wheeler, "Political Socialization and Political Demography," Ch. 8 of Richard Hamilton, *Restraining Myths and Liberating Realities*, forthcoming.

The usual assumption is that people convert with upward mobility, abandoning their "working-class" political orientation and taking up support for the more "appropriate" conservative party. This is the position taken in the influential work of Seymour Martin Lipset and Reinhard Bendix, *Social Mobility in Industrial Society* (Berkeley: University of California Press, 1959), especially pp. 64–71. This viewpoint has been successfully challenged by Kenneth Thompson, "Class Change and Party Choice," (Madison: University of Wisconsin, unpublished Ph.D. Dissertation, 1967). He shows that the upwardly mobile males were more likely to have been Republicans to begin with, to have come from Republican families. Republicans appear to have better chances (for some reason or other) to be upwardly mobile and Democrats have better chances to be downwardly mobile. His study focuses only on males. See also his "Upward Social Mobility and Political Orientation: A Re-Evaluation of the Evidence," *American Sociological Review*, **36** (April 1971), 223–234.

54. For discussion and data see Lee Benson, *The Concept of Jacksonian Democracy: New York as a Test Case* (Princeton: University of Princeton Press, 1961). This work is in the Lazarsfeld-Berelson tradition, sharing the basic assumptions of the "group-bases" viewpoint. It goes beyond that framework (as it is presented in the works cited in footnote 50) in adding the historical dimension and considering also realigning elections. Also of relevance is V. O. Key, Jr., and Frank Munger, "Social Determinism and Electoral Decision: The Case of Indiana," pp. 281–299 of Burdick and Brodbeck. Key's *Southern Politics* is also useful, particularly his discussion of the "deviant traditions" such as the Republicanism of east Tennessee counties. See his *Southern Politics in State and Nation* (New York: Alfred A. Knopf, 1949). Another work discussing the east Tennessee political tradition, carrying the discussion back to its "rational" (i.e., issue-oriented) origins is Thomas Perkins Abernethy, *From Frontier to Plantation in Tennessee: A Study in Frontier Democracy* (Chapel Hill: University of North Carolina Press, 1932). See especially pp. 299–304.

On realigning (or "critical") elections see V. O. Key, Jr., "A Theory of Critical Elections," *Journal of Politics*, **17** (February 1955), 3–18; also by Key, "Secular Re-alignment and the Party System," *Journal of Politics*, **21** (May 1959), 198–210; Campbell, et al., *The American Voter*, 531–538.

55. See Walter Dean Burnham, "The Changing of the American Political Universe," *American Political Science Review*, **59** (March 1965), 7–28. For data on the disproportionate turnout of Republican identifiers, see Chapter 6.

56. For the basic data, see the *Statistical Abstract of the United States: 1966* (87th edition) (Washington, D.C.: Government Printing Office), p. 368.

Another case in point involves the decline in Democratic fortunes at the turn of the century. After running a neck-and-neck race for two decades, the Democratic percentage showed a considerable decline. In most accounts this is linked to the Bryan candidacy which, presumably, drove away many Democrats. That is no doubt true. At the same time, however, it must be noted that the Bryan candidacy, understandably, also attracted considerable numbers of populists so that the Democratic percentage increased in 1896 to 46.8 percent from the 1892 level of 46.1. In the 1900 campaign the party was still doing *relatively* well with 45.5 percent of the total. The disaster came in the 1904 campaign when the Democrats abandoned any pretense of Populism and chose a conservative, Alton Parker. In that election their proportion fell to 37.6 percent, the lowest point since the Civil War. It would be a mistake to attribute this result exclusively to the "popularity of Theodore Roosevelt." As compared to McKinley in the previous election, TR did pick up some 400,000 votes and the Democrats did lose approximately the same number. The other part of the picture, however, is that the total vote was off some 400,000. It seems likely that the choice of a conservative Democrat simply drove many old Populists out of the electorate.

The Bryan elections were realigning elections. Of that there can be little doubt. The realignment, however, left the Democrats with a reasonably strong overall position. It was the Parker-Roosevelt election that appears to have been decisive in destroying the Democratic chances—in part, by generating a shift, and in part, by driving some people out of the electorate. One other fact is of some importance here. The third Bryan attempt in 1908 led to some recouping of the Parker losses. The electorate increased by about 1.3 million, the Democrats gaining approximately that number and the Republican numbers being little different from the 1904 figure.

57. See Hamilton and Wheeler. The point is discussed in Samuel Lubell, *The Future of American Politics* (2nd Ed. rev., Garden City: Doubleday, 1956), p. 28 ff, in a section entitled "A Little Matter of Birth Rates," and in Alfred de Grazia, *The Western Public, 1952 and Beyond* (Stanford: Stanford University Press, 1954), p. 22. See also Jack L. Walker, "The Republican Party and the Birth Rate," *Antioch Review*, **25** (Summer 1965), 297–306. A similar development occurred, with much higher visibility, in Belgium with the "Catholic Party" gaining a demographic edge over their competitors.

58. Some of the objections may be found in the following: Herbert J. Storing, ed., *Essays on the Scientific Study of Politics* (New York: Holt, Rinehart & Winton, 1962); W. G. Runciman, *Social Science and Political Theory* (Cambridge, England: University Press, 1963); V. O. Key, Jr., "The Politically Relevant in Surveys," *Public Opinion Quarterly*, **24** (Spring 1960), 54–62; and McCoy and Playford (note 19).

59. Berelson, Lazarsfeld, and McPhee, Chapter 10. Other behavioral studies have made a similar stress on the widespread ignorance of issues and the presumed irrational linkages between various issue positions. See, for example, Campbell, et al., *The American Voter*, Chapter 9, and Philip E. Converse, "The Nature of Belief Systems in Mass Publics," pp. 206–261 of David E. Apter, ed., *Ideology and Discontent* (New York: Free Press, 1964).

60. The argument, as noted earlier, is rarely stated directly. The evidence is presented and the implications "flow" from the findings. If, for example, the public generally does not pay attention to the issues, makes erratic linkages between them, and votes for the "party of the father," then it would appear that the general public should not be entrusted with decision making, especially in "modern, complex societies." This position is reinforced by two other claims (also presented as "findings"): (1) the widespread "authoritarianism" of the "masses" ("authoritarianism" being a cover word for intolerance, rigidity, punitiveness, and antidemocratic orientations) and (2) the presumed appetitiveness of the "masses" (a claim that most frequently, nowadays, appears as the "revolution of rising

expectations"). The lesson, for responsible democrats, then, appears to be that it is necessary to restrain those masses since their entry into the decision-making process would lead to, at best, somewhat erratic governance. These formulations, as noted earlier, are usually linked to a developmental hypothesis, one assuming that with economic improvement and with rising education levels, these untoward attitudes will change for the better and "entry" into the polity would then be permissable.

This elitism is different from that of traditional aristocratic orientations, particularly in respect to the saving developmental hypothesis. On the other hand, some of the similarities are rather striking. Where the aristocracy of the nineteenth century adhered to the "party of order," the liberal elitists of the mid-twentieth century are also concerned with the "problem of order" and seek the conditions of "stable democracy." What this means is that, in the guise of scientific and non-partisan language, they have abandoned the concerns of the "party of movement" and have committed themselves to the concerns of *Recht und Ordnung*.

61. See Freeman Cleaves, *Old Tippecanoe: William Henry Harrison and His Time* (New York: Charles Scribner's Sons, 1939), Chapters 22–24. An account of the demagoguery and issue avoidance in state campaigns may be found in Abernethy, pp. 300–308.

62. The best summary discussion of media political content appears in Robert E. Lane, *Political Life* (Glencoe: Free Press, 1959), pp. 278–281.

63. This point was discussed by Robert Michels in the opening chapters of his *Political Parties*.

64. Gabriel Kolko, *The Triumph of Conservatism* (New York: Free Press, 1963). Also, John D. Hicks, *The Populist Revolt* (Minneapolis: University of Minnesota Press, 1931).

65. One of the leading accounts showing limited public capabilities, that of Berelson, Lazarsfeld, and McPhee, may be read differently. It must be remembered that the Republican candidate, Thomas E. Dewey, did the best he could to obscure public perception of his stand on the key issues. Where there was a clear statement of position, as in Truman's presentations, there was a very clear perception of his stand—even in August (pp. 218–219). See also the later discussion in this chapter.

66. From de Tocqueville's chapter on "The Principal Sources of Belief Among Democratic Nations," Vol. II, First Book, Chapter II, p. 9.

67. See those works cited in note 54. The beginnings of one such group realignment are described in James Reichley's *The Art of Government: Reform and Organization Politics in Philadelphia* (New York: The Fund for the Republic, 1959). It is worth quoting at length from the report: ". . . the Negroes in Philadelphia . . . were overwhelmingly Republican, tracing their attachment to the GOP back to Abraham Lincoln and the Emancipation Proclamation. The Republican organization in Philadelphia treated them with about as much consideration as their 'safe' voting habits required. . . . only about fifty of the approximately 500 Negro Republican committeemen were given political jobs. Marshall Shepard, a Negro clergyman in Philadelphia in the Thirties, recalls once when he and other Negro spokesmen traveled to the Atlantic City summer home of the great

William Vare to request Negro representation on the GOP ticket for that year. The great man replied, according to Shepard: "Never! Never! The people of Philadelphia would never stand for it!" The young minister returned to Philadelphia, enlisted in the hard-to-find Democratic Party, and made his church the site for the first meeting in the city to support the candidacy of Franklin D. Roosevelt. . ." (p. 69).

In addition to group realignments, there is a fair amount of individual realigning going on in every campaign. This has been shown in Key's last and regrettably incomplete book, *The Responsible Electorate: Rationality in Presidential Voting: 1936–1960* (Cambridge: Harvard University Press, 1966).

68. For a detailed summary of the protective mechanisms (both individual and group) see Joseph T. Klapper, *The Effects of Mass Communications* (Glencoe: Free Press, 1960). A study of United Automobile Workers found high levels of distrust expressed about newspapers; see Arthur Gornhauser, Harold L. Sheppard, and Albert J. Mayer, *When Labor Votes: A Study of Auto Workers* (New York: University Books, 1956), pp. 105–110.

It is important to note that the "screening" of information, the protection of group interests may be done well or poorly. It is highly unlikely that any group would be completely autonomous or inaccessible. Most groups are "permeable" to one degree or another. It would seem likely that the "permeability" would be greatest on distant matters, that is, those not testable through immediate experience.

69. The leading compendium, which follows closely the Lazarsfeld-Berelson orientation, is that of Klapper, Chapters II and IV. The finding of a limited media impact first appeared in the Lazarsfeld, Berelson, and Gaudet work and a similar result appeared in the later Berelson, Lazarsfeld, and McPhee study (Chapter 11). Negative conclusions about the impact of television in the 1952 campaign were reached by Herbert A. Simon and Frederick Stern, "The Effect of Television upon Voting Behavior in Iowa in the 1952 Presidential Election," *American Political Science Review*, **49** (June 1955), 470–477.

Useful summary discussions appear in Robert Lane, Chapter 19, and in V. O. Key, Jr., *Public Opinion and American Democracy* (New York: Alfred A. Knopf, 1961), chapters 14 and 15. Also of interest is Kurt and Gladys Lang, *Politics and Television* (Chicago: Quadrangle Books, 1968); and by Jay G. Blumer and Denis McQuail, *Television in Politics: Its Uses and Influence* (Chicago: University of Chicago Press, 1969).

70. In one way it is very clear that the media have a limited impact. As mentioned before, for decades the bulk of newspaper recommendations and editorial approval plus news coverage, has tended to favor the Republicans. Despite this, Roosevelt won four presidential elections and even Harry Truman managed to win one. Between 1940 and 1960 the highest proportion of daily newspapers endorsing the Democrats was 22.7 percent. The highest amount in terms of newspaper circulation was 25.2 percent. Both of these results were in 1940. Truman won in 1948 with only 15.3 percent of the newspapers endorsing him, and those newspapers accounted for only 10.0 percent of the circulation. Sixty percent of the nation's newspapers endorsed Herbert Hoover in 1932 and 63 percent favored Landon in 1936. On the local level it should be noted that Tammany

candidates won New York City elections year in and year out despite the opposition of most of the city's newspapers. Mayor Hylan had the largest majority, even with nine of eleven city papers arrayed against him. For reviews of recent experience, see Frank Luther Mott, *American Journalism* (New York: Macmillan, 1950, rev. ed.), p. 719 ff., and Edwin Emery, "Press Support for Johnson and Goldwater," *Journalism Quarterly*, **41** (Autumn 1964), 485–488. Another study of some interest that does find some medium impact is James E. Gregg's "Newspaper Editorial Endorsements and California Elections, 1948–62," *Journalism Quarterly*, **42** (Autumn 1965), 532–538.

Even more striking is the late Weimar experience. The newspaper circulations and the votes in the first legislative election of 1932 were as follows:

	Newspaper Circulation (in millions)	Votes (in millions)
Liberal	3.2	0.4
Conservative	4.0	2.8
Communist	0.6	5.2
National Socialist	0.7	13.8

From Emil Dovifat, "Die Publizistik der Weimarer Zeit," pp. 119–136 of Leonhard Reinisch, ed., *Die Zeit ohne Eigenschaften* (Stuttgart: W. Kohlhammer Verlag, 1961). Both Communists and National Socialists made their electoral successes without the aid of any substantial mass media support. The radio, a public monopoly, played no significant role in this campaign.

71. One prominent exception to the rule of Republican dominance was *Collier's* magazine. For its history and demise, see Hollis Alpert, "What Killed Collier's?" *Saturday Review*, **40** (May 11, 1957), 9–11, 42–44; and Milton Moskowitz, "Who Killed Collier's?" *The Nation*, **184** (January 5, 1957), 3–5. The character of the audience of mass circulation magazines may be found in any of the frequent audience surveys. See for example, *The Audiences of 5 Magazines* by Audits and Surveys Company (1962), *The Audiences of Nine Magazines* by Alfred Politz (1955), and *The Characteristics of the Reading Audience of Newsweek, Time, and U.S. News and World Report* by Sindlinger and Company (1959).

72. Katz and Lazarsfeld, p. 176 note.

73. Ibid., p. 142.

74. Berelson, Lazarsfeld, and McPhee, p. 252.

75. See also the experimental study by Percy Tannenbaum, "The Effects of Headlines on the Interpretation of News Stories," *Journalism Quarterly*, **30** (Spring 1953), 189–197; and Jean S. Kerrick, "The Influence of Captions on Picture Interpretation," *Journalism Quarterly*, **32** (Spring 1955), 177–182.

76. Where the tendency, in the extreme formulation, is to assume a "group basis" for everyone, it should be noted that some people do not have a "group." There are some isolates and, perhaps more important, there are some people who have such limited contact that they do not know the politics of those with whom they associate. It is among the isolated and those with limited contact that we should expect to find shifting with media pressure (the only political influence in their lives).

It should also be noted that the problem is not one of either "mass society" or "social bases" approach. If this respecification is correct, both viewpoints would appear to contain valid insights. The main problem is to locate the points and extent of applicability of each.

77. Of special importance in this connection is the article by Snell Putney and Russell Middleton, "Some Factors Associated with Student Acceptance or Rejection of War," *American Sociological Review*, **27** (October 1962), 655–667. On this distant concern, one not linked to one's political identity, they report that "at least among college students, it is the most sophisticated who find nuclear war most credible and acceptable." They also link this result to media attention, reporting some experimental studies that made use of antiwar content and that resulted in a marked shift in a more pacifist direction.

78. The footnote quotation appears on p. 264. Stevenson's avoidance of the domestic liberalism issues and the implications of that avoidance are discussed by Seymour Martin Lipset in his review of Heinz Eulau's *Class and Party in the Eisenhower Years* in the *American Sociological Review*, **29** (October 1964), 760.

79. Berelson, Lazarsfeld, and McPhee, the quotation is from pp. 227–228. The note appears on the latter page.

80. Dewey's diffuse focus is discussed, together with data from a content analysis of his speeches, on pp. 235–238. A sample: "Dewey dwelt to an especially large extent on the noncontroversial desirability and need for 'unity' and 'faith' in the United States. . . . If debate is . . . defined as presenting the voters with an explicit choice between differing positions on controversial questions, Dewey generally failed to debate." The discussion of perception of the candidate positions and of accuracy of perception precedes the discussion of the stimuli on pp. 218–230.

81. It will be noted that the findings of empirical studies (associated with the social-bases" viewpoint) feed into and support the "pluralist" notions that "recognize" and justify the restriction of power to higher status groups.

82. In a study of an English working-class community, the author describes a series of weekend riots and contrasts the events with the hopeless cliché formulations that appear in the press "interpreting" the event for the distant middle classes. See Brian Jackson, *Working Class Community* (New York: Frederick A. Praeger, 1968). A similar case of opacity from another context is described in William Sheridan Allen, *The Nazi Seizure of Power* (Chicago: Quadrangle Books, 1965).

83. Kent Cooper, long-time head of the Associated Press, has indicated in his autobiography the character of the instructions given to subordinates in this important news gathering agency. "With the bureaus," he reports, "I tried to inculcate the idea that 'the member is always right.'" p. 184 of his *Kent Cooper and the Associated Press* (New York: Random House, 1959). Also of some interest is Walter Gieber's "Across the Deck: A Study of 16 Telegraph Editors," *Journalism Quarterly*, **33** (Fall 1956), 423–432.

In both cases we have instances of decision makers in news-gathering and disseminating agencies giving subordinates instructions as to how the news shall be "seen." Assuming the decision makers to be among the readers of the finished product, this amounts to a self-induced warping of consciousness on the part of rather high-status and powerful persons.

84. On the refusal to plan for wartime food supplies, see Mancur Olson, Jr., *The Economics of the Wartime Shortage* (Durham: Duke University Press, 1963), Ch. 4. The demand for misinformation from Vietnamese field commanders is discussed in David Halberstam, *The Making of a Quagmire* (New York: Random House, 1965). The American ambassador (Nolting) is also described as "pressuring his subordinates to tell him only the good news, thereby cutting off reliable lines of communication" (p. 73). Some of the best accounts of the meetings of Hitler and the German conservatives are to be found in Walter Gölitz, *Der Deutsche Generalstab: Geschichte und Gestalt, 1657–1945* (Frankfurt: A. M. Verlag der Frankfurter Hefte, n.d.) p. 358 ff. See especially p. 383.

3
The Concerns and Issues
of the Day

This chapter has several objectives. First, it attempts to show that domestic economic concerns and related "bread and butter" or welfare-state issues are the most salient, continuous, and pressing concerns of the United States' (and presumably any other) population. This is evident in the spontaneous responses to open-ended questions on people's worries and concerns. Only the periodic threat of war gains even greater salience, and this is because of the effects on the lives and welfare of the families involved. The focus on economic-liberalism concerns is present even though the United States has, apparently, the highest living standards in the world. In these areas of greatest concern, as will be seen, the government's responses have been, to say the least, rather inadequate. This is most strikingly the case with respect to the majority sentiment in favor of a job guarantee and in favor of government-supported medical care.

A second objective is to discuss the orientations of the general population with respect to various other concerns and issues of the day and to give some idea of their salience. The purpose is to give some estimate of the potential that such issues may have for diverting attention from the basic concerns of the individual household.

This chapter also contains the wordings and some discussion of the questions that will be used in the analyses in later chapters.

In conjunction with this presentation, the relevant evidence will be presented as to the levels of rationality present, in particular with respect to the degree of awareness of the political discussion and the accurate perception of party positions. This is especially important because, as noted earlier, there is a tendency to select only the negative evidence and thus to portray the potential for a rational issue-oriented democratic politics as being more or less hopeless.

Before proceeding to the evidence, it is useful to introduce a distinction between concerns and issues. By a concern we are referring to a felt or sensed problem. A concern is not necessarily a subject for widespread public discussion nor is it in any way *necessarily* of interest to political parties. An issue, characteristically defined as an object of discussion in political campaigns, nearly always has an underlying widespread concern as its basis, but there are occasions where the issues chosen by political leaders have apparently been of very little concern to the mass public.

Many discussions of American politics are heavily and gratuitously burdened with a democratic bias. It is assumed that where there is a widespread concern, there will be an issue, as if there were some automatic mechanism that brought the individual concerns to the consciousness of far-distant decision makers. If we put aside this bias, it is immediately obvious that there are a number of possible relationships between concerns and issues, or, a better formulation, between concerns and issue making (issues not being automatic emanations from a "mass will," but rather resulting from the *choices* of political leaders).[1] Basically then, we may have widespread concern that is made the subject of political discussion (actual issues) or we may have such a concern with no reaction. We will call the latter an unformulated issue.

There is still a third possibility—the undeveloped concern. For years there was no concern over the problem of air pollution. The quality of the air deteriorated gradually. Most people either did not notice the change, or if they did, they accepted and "adjusted" to it as just another fact of life. The fact that pollution control is possible, that there are ways to clean the air of a city or a region, by itself has no political significance. The connection has to be made: someone must indicate the fact of pollution, must define it as subject to human control, and must demand that control. In short, for it to become an actual issue, political leaders have to first make it an issue and by doing so generate the widespread concern. Such demand, in the ordinary course of events, will not "come from below." If individual people felt that dirty air was a problem, given the general proclivity to "small" or personal solutions, the result would ordinarily be more air conditioners or purifiers, better vacuum cleaners, and more trips to the dry cleaners. There would be no necessity that a larger solution, a regional plan, would ever be formulated as a political issue. Socialism, government ownership and direction of the means of production, is an even more striking case of a concern that is not "natural" or spontaneous. The only way such a "large" and complex solution becomes the object of majority concern is through the aegis of party leaders who must first make it an issue.

It ought, therefore, to be kept in mind that in addition to the unformulated issue and the actual issues, there is a third possible leader-follower relationship involving the undeveloped concern. For a conservative party there are obviously strong incentives to leaving many concerns undeveloped. Stated somewhat differently, there are some rather solid reasons for parties to refuse the mobilization of potential support. A party of landlords, as noted earlier, does not serve its interests by bringing tenants into the electorate. If tenants are already in the electorate, it is obviously not to the interest of such a party to stress domestic household concerns.

The Pattern of Concern

In 1954, during the Eisenhower era, in the midst of the great consensus, Samuel Stouffer's famous study asked the following question:

"What kinds of things do you worry about most?"

The answers were clear and unambiguous. "The big, overwhelming response to the question," Stouffer explained, "was in terms of personal and family problems. Eighty percent of the men and women . . . answered *solely* in these terms. And many of the remainder answered in the same terms but went on to express anxiety about other problems. . . . [but] Even world problems, including the shadow of war, did not evoke a spontaneous answer from more than 8%."[2]

In more detail, the problems are described as follows:

The largest single block of personal worries involved concern over personal business or family economic problems. A total of 43% volunteered anxieties in this general area. . . . the second largest block of answers was in terms of health, either of oneself or of members of the family. A total of 24% . . . mentioned health problems (including some who *also* mentioned family finances or other problems). As might be expected, a larger proportion of women than of men were in this category. Men were somewhat more likely than women to respond in terms of finances; women somewhat more likely than men to respond in terms of the health of the family, especially of the children.[3]

Thirty percent mentioned personal problems that were not related either to finance or health. The next highest level of concern was the 8 percent indication of anxiety about world affairs and war. The focus on the personal, for example, household problems, in other words, was overwhelming.

The striking thing about this pattern is that even at that late date in the general "move toward affluence," the dominance of such concerns for the majority of the population had not changed. This does not mean that "nothing changed" since there was and has been a general recognition that things are better than in the past, that is, either in the respondent's own life or in the life of his parents. Moreover, there was a general expectation that the improvements would continue.

The first question in the interview—the door-opening question—read: "On the whole, do you think life will be better for you or worse, in the next few years than it is now?" The author reports that only 13 percent expected life to be worse in the next few years and that a large proportion of those were in their sixties, seventies, or even older. This general optimism is found not only in the United States, but also in response to similar questions in West European countries.[4]

Some indication of the constancy of focus, to be sure with a changed saliency, is to be found in the comment of one respondent, a farm wife in Iowa, who, in describing her worries, said: "Meeting payments of interest and some principal on the mortgage. But I don't really worry compared with how my folks did."[5] The separation made between personal and distant concerns appears in the statement of a North Carolina textile worker:

> I've served my time on Guadalcanal and now I'm home minding my own business. I work graveyard shift and put in a crop besides. The plant has cut down to a four-day week. That's what bothers me. I don't worry about world problems. When trouble gets here, I can take it. I'm paying taxes for someone to do my worrying for me.[6]

Even the possibility of war is seen and assessed in highly personal terms, for example, in the comment, "With a boy 15, I'm concerned about the war."[7]

A second probing question—"Are there other problems you worry or are concerned about, especially political or world problems?"—succeeded in raising the concern with world affairs from the initial 8 percent to only 30 percent. Half of the population, 52 percent, had nothing else to add to this second question, and Stouffer reports that much of this foreign affairs concern was rather perfunctory (e.g., "Oh yes, I guess I would say I'm concerned about what's going on in world affairs."[8]).

A study undertaken by Hadley Cantril in August 1959 probes in the same area using somewhat different questions. The basic question read as follows:

> When you think about what really matters in your own life, what are your wishes and hopes for the future? In other words, if you imagine your future in the *best* possible light, what would your life look like then, if you are to be happy?

This is followed by a question probing for threats or fears:

> Now, taking the other side of the picture, what are your fears and worries about the future? In other words, if you imagine your future in the *worst* possible light, what would your life look like then?

Cantril summarizes his findings in the following words: "In the United States, as in nearly all the countries studied, the major hopes and aspirations are those involved in maintaining and improving a decent, healthy family life." Classifying the personal hopes of Americans, we find economic, health, and family concerns clustered at the top of the list with 65, 48, and 47 percent, respectively, mentioning these areas.[9] In response to the second question, the personal fears, we find the same factors listed although with a reversal of the order: health, 56 percent; economic, 46 percent; and family, 25 percent.

It is interesting to note also that, contrary to a common expectation, the concern with personal economic problems is not concentrated among the low-income groups. Cantril reports "no appreciable variation here among people in different economic brackets of the population: 63 percent of those in the upper bracket express such concerns and 66 percent of those in the lower bracket do so."[10]

In summarizing the findings for 13 countries, Cantril finds the level of economic concern in the United States to be slightly lower than the average but certainly not sharply set apart from the level discovered elsewhere. The greatest concern with economic problems was found in the Dominican Republic, Nigeria, and Panama. In the "middle range," separated from each other by no more than five percentage points, we have India, Cuba, Yugoslavia, and Egypt. The concern in all of the above countries exceeds that found in the United States; the difference, however, from Yugoslavia and Egypt is two percentage points, from Cuba, a mere four. Lower levels of economic concern were indicated in Brazil, the Philippines, and among kibbutz members.[11]

The specific economic concerns are, to be sure, markedly different in the different nations. An Egyptian agricultural worker says, "My main wishes are to have enough food to eat and enough decent water to drink." An American bus driver says, "I would like financial security and enough to be able to quit work and stay home with the children."[12]

Given this focus on the domestic welfare of the individual household, it is no wonder that the majority of the American population expresses a great interest in domestic welfare issues and that they take a liberal position on these issues.

Issue Orientations: Domestic Welfare

Contrary to common belief, majority sentiment in the United States is solidly liberal with respect to domestic economic welfare issues. The word liberal is used here in a rather restricted sense referring to a disposition to favor "welfare-state" legislation, that is, government action to aid or ensure personal or family welfare. This focus differs from the general practice in intellectual circles, where it is assumed that "liberalism" is all of one piece and that the economic liberals will also be civil rights liberals and "internationalists." While this clustering of attitudes tends to be the case among intellectuals, the relationship is not so close in the population generally.[13] Rather than impose the intellectual's concept on the general population, it seems appropriate to approach the matter somewhat more hypothetically and to ask what kind of framework, or ordering, is made by the general population. If one takes the intellectual's framework, one can only conclude that the political orientations of "the masses" are somewhat irrational. The intellectual's preconception in such a case may simply blind one to other alternatives. In any event, it proves useful to consider each of the issue areas separately.

The questions asked in the general area of "economic welfare" fall into three categories. First, there are those inquiring about pressing economic concerns, such as jobs and medical care, that offer solutions within the conventional liberal framework. Solutions in this context are those that provide aid to the helpless, minimum levels of aid for urgent necessities (as in the case of medical services), and the means for self-help for those who are otherwise able (as in the case of a job guarantee). A second kind of question asks about similar areas of concern but proposes solutions that go beyond the conventional liberal framework; these questions suggest that the government undertake tasks that are now in the private sector (such as providing electric power), or that the government go beyond the self-help principle in order to provide a direct guarantee, as in the case of a minimal standard of living. A third type of question asks about matters that are not directly and immediately tied in with domestic economic welfare, such as questions about government support for schools.

There are different response patterns associated with the three types of questions. Clear and consistent majorities are in favor of those solutions that are within the conventional liberal framework. Fair-sized minorities favor those solutions that go beyond that framework. Some shifting is indicated in the case of the more distant issues. On the question of school aid, for example, the initial majority support declines and in the later studies only a minority favor such efforts.

The liberal majority is evident in the responses to all questions of the first variety that were contained in the studies to be reviewed. In the 1952 study we have the following:

SRC 1952, Q. 21. Some people think the national government should do more in trying to deal with such problems as unemployment, education, housing, and so on. Others think that the government is already doing too much. On the whole, would you say that what the government has done has been about right, too much, or not enough?

1%	Definitely should do more
17	Should do more
47	About right, OK
14	Should do less
2	Definitely should do less
11	Should do more on some, less on others, etc.
8	DK "Don't know" and "No Answer"
100%	$N = 1799$

Just under half of the population at that time found the New Deal-Fair Deal accomplishment to be "about right."[14] Of those remaining and having some opinion on the subject, a slight majority favored doing more (this includes the 7 percent who said "should do more on some"). The conservative minority, those wishing to "put the clock back" amount to a mere 18 percent, less than one in five.

This question clearly has a number of difficulties. It refers explicitly to three items that are supported by somewhat different "constituencies" and it also allows respondents to read what they wish into the phase "and so on." For these reasons only sparing use will be made of the question. For short, this will be referred to as the "omnibus liberalism" question.

A follow-up question is also of some interest for our purposes. This reads:

Q. 21a. Now, how do you think the two parties feel about this question —Do you think there are any differences between the Democratic and Republican parties on this issue, or would you say they feel the same?

As has been noted frequently, large numbers of the population are ignorant of basic political matters; they do not know about the issues nor do they know party positions on the issues. In response to this question we find 34 percent did answer with a "don't know" or a "no answer." Another 35 percent felt there was little difference between the parties ("pro-con, same"). Twenty-nine of the remaining 31 percent saw the Democrats doing more than the Republicans in these matters. As far as this question goes, then, roughly one-third did not know, one-third reported no perceived differences between the parties, and the overwhelming majority of the remaining third had very accurate perceptions of the likely initiatives.

From the SRC 1956 study we have the following two liberalism questions. The same questions were asked in 1960 with, as may be seen, very similar overall results.

SRC 1956 Q. 12b. The government in Washington ought to see to it that everybody who wants to work can find a job.

	1956		1960	
Agree strongly	43%⎫	56	47%⎫	58
Agree but not very strongly	13 ⎭		11 ⎭	
Not sure; it depends	7		8	
Disagree but not very strongly	11 ⎫	27	7 ⎫	23
Disagree strongly	16 ⎭		16 ⎭	
DK, NA,* No opinion	10		11	
Total Percent	100%		100%	
N =	(1762)		(1954)	
Percent liberal of				
these with opinions	67%		72%	

* DK = "don't know"; NA = "no answer"

And the second question reads:

SRC 1956 Q. 12d. The government ought to help people get doctors and hospital care at low cost.

	1956		1960	
Agree strongly	39%⎫		48%⎫	
		54		59
Agree but not very strongly	15 ⎬		11 ⎬	
Not sure; it depends	8		11	
Disagree but not very strongly	8 ⎫		5 ⎫	
		26		19
Disagree strongly	18 ⎬		14 ⎬	
DK, NA, No opinion	12		11	
Total Percent	100%		100%	
$N =$	(1762)		(1954)	
Percent liberal of				
those with opinions	67%		76%	

The responses to both of these questions support the above claim. Liberal majorities are present in both cases, amounting to approximately 55 to 60 percent of the total population. We shall see below that those respondents without opinions, the "don't knows" and the "no answer" groups, fall very disproportionately in the liberal direction when they do give answers to other liberalism questions. For this reason, it seems likely that the figures underestimate the actual liberal proportion. When we take those with opinions only, presumably the somewhat better informed and more politically involved respondents, the liberal majority varies between two-thirds and three-quarters of the total. The conservative minority amounts to only one-quarter to one-third of those having opinions.

Neither of these questions was topical at the time of the study. At no time have the parties proposed legislation guaranteeing jobs and, although something that was labeled "socialized medicine" had come up for a vote during Truman's years, the idea was not under discussion in 1956. Both questions, therefore, involve unformulated issues, that is, those felt, sensed, problematic matters that had not been taken up by either party as a topic on which they chose to mobilize.

For short, we will refer to these as the "job guarantee" and the "medical care" questions.[15] These two questions will be used throughout this work for purposes of separating the economic liberals from the economic conservatives.

It could be that we are misreading the response to the job guarantee question, it being possible that supporters of the so-called right to work laws may be affirming the job guarantee question and that, in other words, agreement here actually amounts to a conservative response. Aside from the fact that "right to work" laws were and are state, not national, a cross-tabulation of the responses to this and the medical care questions makes it doubtful that for the large majority a misreading is involved. Nearly three-fourths of those who strongly agree with the job guarantee question also indicated some degree of agreement to the medical care question. There was, to be sure, a 14 percent minority who disagreed in response to the latter question.[16] (See Table 3.1.)

TABLE 3.1

Attitudes Toward Job Guarantee and Medical Care (SRC 1956)

Government Should Guarantee Medical Care	Government Should Guarantee Jobs					
	Strongly Agree	Agree	Not Sure Depends	Disagree	Strongly Disagree	DK, NA No Opinion
Strongly agree	59%[a]	30%	26%	22%	15%	22%
Agree	13	28	20	16	12	10
Not sure, depends	6	10	14	12	10	6
Disagree	4	9	7	16	14	5
Strongly disagree	10	13	21	24	44	9
DK, NA	1	1	4	1	1	2
No opinion	6	9	8	9	4	47
N =	(762)	(233)	(121)	(183)	(288)	(175)

[a] Sometimes, due to rounding off, percentages do not add to 100%.

The follow-up questions shed light both on the interpretations of the statements and on the accuracy of political perceptions. In respect to the job guarantee, the 1956 study continued with the following: (Q. 13b.) "On the question of the government seeing to it that everybody who wants to work can find a job, is the government going too far, doing less than it should, or what?" Just over one-fifth did not have an answer (DK, NA, etc.) and about one-tenth, rather appropriately, indicated they "haven't heard what the government is doing." Two-fifths thought the level of government activity "about right." Only 2.5 percent thought the government had gone "too far" as opposed to 22 percent of the respondents indicating it had done "less than it should." A third of this latter group even felt the government had done "a lot less than it should."

In 1960 respondents were asked: (Q. 18b.) "Which party do you think is more likely to see to it that everybody who wants to work can find a job, the Democrats or the Republicans, or wouldn't there be any difference between them on this?" Twenty-seven percent had no answer to this question and another 26 percent saw no difference between the parties in this respect. Four out of five of the remaining 47 percent, again quite accurately, thought the Democrats were more likely to undertake something in this connection.[17]

Without going into detail on the follow ups to the medical care question, it must suffice to note that in comparison to the job guarantee question a larger percentage had not heard "what the government is doing," the same miniscule percentage thought the government had gone too far and in this

case the percentage thinking the government performance was "about right"
is much smaller. A third of the total said the government had done less than
it should. The follow-up question in 1960 found a distribution of responses
that parallels that found on the job guarantee question; again the overwhelming majority of those seeing a likelihood of some action expected it
from the Democrats.[18]

Later studies (1962 and 1964) carry similar questions on government-
supported medical care.[19] The responses once again show a heavy majority in
favor of such a measure. The follow-up questions in these years show a
marked shift in perception of party stands on the issue. The percentage
thinking there was "no difference" falls off and the percentage expecting
the Democrats to take action shows a considerable increase. The pattern
appears clearly in the following figures:

Party likely to do more . . .?	1960	1962	1964
Democrats	34%	45%	55%
No difference	30	24	14
Republicans	8	3	5
DK, NA, etc.	28	28	25
N =	(1954)	(1297)	(1571)

What we see here is the shift accompanying the transformation of an unformulated issue into an actual issue. This allows us some rule-of-thumb
indication of the potential for rational politics present within the electorate.
Whereas up to and including 1960 we find approximately one-third of the
respondents accurately perceiving the likely party position (that is, during
a period in which the issue was unformulated), 4 years later another 20
percent have been added to those having an accurate awareness of the party
positions on this issue. This supports the observation made in Chapter 2 that
the presumed irrationality and ignorance of "the people" results more from
the parties and their failure to make or clarify the issues than from any
fundamental lack of ability on the part of the populace.

The job guarantee question drops out of the later studies. In its place there
appears the following:

SRC Q. 18. In general, some people feel that the government in Washington should see to it that every person has a job and a good standard
of living. Others think the government should just let each person get
ahead his own. Have you been interested enough in this to favor one
side over the other? (If yes) Do you think that the government [alterna-
tives repeated]. . . .

In general, the American population appears to favor provision of opportunities for achieving an adequate existence as opposed to an outright

grant. Thus, a sizable majority approves of "guaranteed work" as opposed to a "guaranteed income."[20] In contrast to the majority approving the job guarantee question, only a minority favors this option. The actual distribution of responses was: DK, NA, No interest, 15%; Depends, 11%; Should let each person get ahead on his own, 43%. Interestingly enough, although a job guarantee and a guaranteed good living standard would go against an "individualist tradition" and although such a plan had to that point, never been made an issue and advocated by either major party, nevertheless, 31 percent, or roughly one-third of the population, found the suggestion a good one. This testifies to the inadequacy of the "controls" exerted in the "mass society" and also suggests a sizable latent concern that could easily be mobilized were a party to make this an issue. For what it is worth, 45 percent see the Democrats doing more in this respect as compared with 9 percent sensing a Republican proclivity for such initiatives.

The questions on medical care and the living standard guarantee were repeated in the 1968 study. Very little change was indicated; the number of those with opinions favoring the federal medical care option was 66 percent in 1968 as compared to a 64 percent figure in 1964. The respective percentages of those with opinions in favor of the living standard guarantee in 1964 and 1968 were 42 and 40 percent.

In summary, it appears that majorities of the American population favor a federal government role in making the major means for adequate welfare (that is, jobs) available to all. They also favor a government role in providing necessary medical services at low cost.[21] Unfortunately identical questions were not asked throughout so that it is difficult to indicate any trend in the responses. Where common questions were used, no significant trend was indicated. It would appear that the differences in the results obtained from inquiries about the job guarantee and the later job-plus-living-standard guarantee stems from the different focus of the two questions. Although there is no majority favoring the living standard guarantee, it is impressive, contrary to the claims of an "individualist" heritage, that a fair-sized minority favors even this idea.

Issue Orientations: Federal School Aid

When one moves away from the direct and immediate welfare concerns, a different pattern emerges. This is the case with the issue of federal aid to education. The responses to questions in this area do not show consistent majorities favoring such measures; moreover, the responses are not as stable as those for the economic liberalism issues discussed above.

The 1956 and 1960 statement and the results follow:

SRC 1956 Q. 12i. If cities and towns around the country need help to build more schools, the government in Washington ought to give them the money they need.

	1956		1960	
Agree strongly	48%	68	37%	52
Agree but not very strongly	20		15	
Not sure; it depends	8		10	
Disagree but not very strongly	5	14	8	25
Disagree strongly	9		17	
DK, NA, No opinion	10		13	
Total percent	100%		100%	
$N =$	(1762)		(1954)	
Percent in favor of those with opinions	82%		68%	

In 1956, two-thirds of all respondents favored federal school aid. Support for such aid fell off in the succeeding years, declining to 63 percent in 1958 and to 52 percent in 1960.

This decline in support could be a reaction to the civil rights revolution. This possibility appears doubtful, however, since the civil rights attitudes were shifting in exactly the opposite direction during this period, that is, toward greater tolerance and acceptance. The expectation that the reaction would be peculiarly southern is not supported. The decline in the size of the "liberal" majority appeared in all regions of the country.

Further analysis of any trend through to 1964 is hindered by the introduction of a markedly different emphasis in the question used that year. It read as follows:

Q. 15, 15A. Some people think the government in Washington should help towns and cities provide education for grade and high school children, others think this should be handled by the states and local communities. Have you been interested enough in this to favor one side over the other? [If yes] Which are you in favor of?

Where the earlier studies asked about building schools (specifically, giving money for that purpose), this question focuses more on the role of Washington providing education, a role that is set in opposition to an exclusive state and local role. This suggests that it is impossible to say whether the 1964 responses are a result of a change in public opinion or whether they are the result of the shifted question emphases. In any event, the proportion favoring "getting help from the government in Washington" is only 31 percent. The proportion favoring state and local handling is 46 percent. The same question was asked in 1968, the results then being very similar to those of 1964. The proportion favoring the federal government role was again 31 percent and the proportion favoring state and local handling of the matter was 47 percent.

The best explanation of the 1956–1960 change to be offered at this time is that the routine, conventional conservatism of the upper-middle class had been alerted by federal government moves in this direction. The increased opposition may also have been stimulated by the conservative mass media. The evidence shows that in 1956 there were only small class differences indicated. In 1964, however, the nonmanuals were very much below the manuals in their support for federal school aid. The working class in both years, in both the South and non-South, was more favorable to this "intervention" with the Southern workers being the most favorably disposed of all. Although this preference was most pronounced among Southern Negro workers, the percentage of the Southern white workers favorable to federal school aid was also impressive.[22] Examination of this attitude by media attention did show (although the pattern was rather irregular) that non-readers were generally more "liberal" than the readers. This holds both for manuals and nonmanuals and is the case with respect to both newspaper and magazine readers.[23]

In response to the 1960 follow-up question (asking about the party positions on the issue), there were again large "don't know" and "no opinion" groups (26%), and a large group seeing no difference between the parties (33%). Of the remaining 41 percent, three out of four expected more action from the Democrats than from the Republicans.

Issue Orientations: Miscellaneous Economic Questions

One item of somewhat uncertain import in this discussion is the following (from the 1956 study):

Q. 12k. The government should leave things like electric power and housing for private business men to handle.

The meaning of the responses cannot be entirely clear because we have two items mixed here—housing and electric power—and because the implications are not detailed, that is, whether regulation or management is in order (in other words, whether a liberal or a socialist option is being considered). For what it may be worth, 23 percent of all respondents (one-third of those with opinions) disagreed with this statement. That is, they were either pro-regulation or for direct state operation. Another large number, 27 percent of the total, had no opinion and 9 percent were either unsure or said "don't know," etc. Approximately the same result appeared in 1960. It is impressive that despite considerable efforts to convince the population of the opposite position, there is still a fair-sized minority favoring government intervention and also that there is a large uncommitted minority. Despite the persuasive efforts of "independent power and light companies," only 41 percent of the total population hold to their laissez-faire conception of the proper role of government.[24]

In the 1956 follow-up question asking about the actual government role in this regard, the majority of those with opinions felt what the government was doing was "about right" and equal-sized minorities of approximately one-fifth each thought the government had done too much or too little. From the 1960 study we find, again among those having opinions, that roughly one-third saw no difference in the likely initiatives of the two parties. Three-quarters of those who did see differences between the parties expected that the Republicans would "leave things like this to private business."

The Survey Research Center's 1964 study asked a question that eliminated the above sources of ambiguity, inquiring explicitly about government ownership of power plants. The question reads:

Q. 37. Some people think it's all right for the government to own some power plants while others think the production of electricity should be left to private business. Have you been interested enough in this to favor one side over the other?" [If yes] "Which position is more like yours. . .?

19%	Government-owned power plants
4	Other, depends
39	Leaving this to private business
2	DK, NA
36	No interest
100%	
(1450)	

33 = Percent of those with opinions favoring government ownership.

A fair-sized minority, it will be seen, favors this option, which, on the whole, has not been championed in recent years by either party or by any leading political elites. For those who are convinced that "socialism" is antithetic to "American values," it is worth nothing that only two-fifths of the population oppose this suggestion. While only one-fifth currently favor such a development, roughly a third of the population are open on the subject; they are not committed one way or the other. It would appear that government ownership lies somewhere between what we have referred to as an undeveloped concern and the unformulated issue.[25]

The intellectual convention has it that "liberalism" is associated with a disdain for the activities of "big business" and some sense of enthusiasm for trade unions. Among liberal intellectuals this view once even had a special name, being referred to as the "lib-lab" outlook. As far as the majority of the population is concerned, there is little evidence of any consistent linkage of this sort. It is important to see this in the light of the statements:

(From 1956: Q. 12g and Q. 121) The government ought to see to it that big business corporations don't have much to say about how the government is run.

And,

The government ought to see to it that labor unions don't have much to say about how the government is run.

A majority of those with opinions agree with *both* statements. The results for all respondents are as follows:

	Government should limit influence of	
	Big Business	*Labor Unions*
Agree	51%	50%
Not sure	6	6
Disagree	16	19
DK, NA, no opinion	28	25
(N = 1762)	101%	100%
Percent agreeing of those with opinions	76%	72%

A cross-tabulation of the two attitudes indicated that it was not an either/or case but rather one where most people felt that both business and labor ought to have less influence. The pattern (among those with opinions) is shown in the following:

		Corporations Should Have Less Influence	
		Agree	*Disagree*
Labor unions	*Agree*	60%	13%
should have			
less influence	*Disagree*	16	11
			100%
			N = 985

In short, it would appear that the dominant view is that the government ought to be the independent arbiter of forces rather than the agent of any one. The majority of the responding population appears as classic, "Adam Smith type" liberals rather than as lib-lab (or "con-corp") types.

The 1964 study has a statement about "powerful government" that is of some relevance at this point. It reads:

Some people are afraid the government in Washington is getting too powerful for the good of the country and the individual person. Others feel that the government in Washington has not gotten too strong for the good of the country. What is your feeling. . . ?

Too powerful	30%
It depends	3
Not too strong	36
DK, NA	3
No interest	28
Total	100%
	(1571)
Percent "not too strong" of those with opinions	55%

Once again, despite the conservative agitation and the volume of "persuasive communication" in the mass media, the majority of those with opinions still remained unconvinced. Moreover, there is a large minority having no commitment on this issue.

Given the extent of the persuasion on this topic, it is worth examining the responses to this question by media attention. The pattern is very simple and very clear. The "no interest" diminishes with increased newspaper attention and the fear of government increases. This pattern appears among both the manuals and the nonmanuals. A similar development appears in connection with magazine reading. In short, it would appear that this is one of those issues that, although relevant to the bread-and-butter concerns, is not so directly linked as to be immune to the media influence.[26]

The 1968 study shows this concern with the "powerful government" increasing in the intervening four years. At the later date only 43 percent of those with opinions felt the government was "not too strong," that being down from the 55 percent level of 1964. Given the stability of the other attitudes discussed here, the willingness to have the government provide medical care and, as we shall see below, the willingness to have the government guarantee Negro rights, it would appear that this anti-big-government response stands as a peculiarly dissociated event. It would appear as if this media-stimulated reaction involves little more than an isolated semantic victory.

One final item of clear relevance to the economic liberalism area asks about the need for government tax cutting. Most intellectuals would interpret such a concern as clearly falling within the domain of conservativism. An affirmative answer to the following statement, for example, would apparently be indicative of a classical conservative low tax outlook, that is, the wish to "cut government spending" and thereby to limit the government's influence (from the 1956 Study):

Q. 12a. The government ought to cut taxes even if it means putting off some important things that need to be done.

In this case, strikingly enough, 45 percent of the total *disagreed*. The statement, it will be noted, would seem to cater to immediate self-interest, especially since the things to be cut are not specified. When we figure the disagreement as a percentage of those with opinions, a clear and fair-sized majority (64 percent) nevertheless *opposed* the tax cut.

Examination of the cross-tabulations of this response and the responses to the two basic liberalism questions shows that the initial premise—the assumption that approval of tax cuts indicates a conservative position—is not justified. When we take, for example, those strongly agreeing to the tax cut proposal, we find that 75 percent of them favor the government job guarantee and that 73 percent favor government-supported medical assistance. Only 7 percent of those who were strongly in favor of the tax cut opposed the job guarantee or the medical care proposals.

The tax cut question apparently puts some liberals in an ambiguous position. They want government services yet they do not like the price they have to pay in order to get them. The question received a higher than average "not sure, it depends" response and a very high "no opinion" appeared. Both of these groups, especially the latter came down heavily on the liberal side of things, the respective liberal and conservative percentages being 56 and 9 percent in response to the job guarantee question and 56 and 7 percent to the medical aid question. The remaining third had "no opinion" on the liberalism questions. Part of the embarrassment in response to these questions may have to do with the fact that many of these pro-welfare people who are indecisive on tax cuts happen to be Republican identifiers.

What many of these "liberal tax cutters" appear to be saying is that "the government ought to cut *my* taxes." Their behavior, in this light, is not so contradictory as at first appears. They do not see things in either/or terms. They are interested in having improved welfare services and a cut in *their* taxes. This demand for tax cutting, it would appear, indicates just the opposite of hard-nosed conservatism, that is, it appears to hide a redistributionist aim. Conservative legislators frequently point to the demand for tax cuts as justification for their negative votes on welfare legislation. Those "liberals" favoring the tax cuts, unfortunately, have not been in a position to make clear the misrepresentation involved.

To complete the picture it is necessary to note that the conservatives, that is, those rejecting the job guarantee and the medical aid options, are found among those *opposing* the tax cuts. The same is true of the strong Republicans; they, too, are disproportionately located among the *opponents* of tax cuts. We cannot discover with the materials at hand the character of their interests and concerns. One possibility, however, is that they see tax cuts as hurting "defense spending," a pressing concern of this group.

The overall picture may not be as paradoxical as it at first appears. It is paradoxical only by reference to the conventional framework, that is, the framework used by most intellectuals to order their worlds. On the other hand, the respondents themselves may have a framework that makes much better sense to them and one that may provide a nonparadoxical explanation for the observed results.[27]

Class Identification

A characteristic of the American population that deserves detailed consideration is the question of their self-conception, in particular their view of their class position. Despite claims about the "middle-class society" and about being "Americans all," and despite the repeated references to class as a "foreign" concept not at all relevant to the American scene, all surveys in which the fourfold choice of upper, middle, lower, and working class was presented, have yielded a clear majority choosing one of the two latter options, most of them saying they are working class. (See Table 3.2) Characteristically, only a third of the population have identified themselves as middle class. Given the usual sampling bias (the lowest socioeconomic groups tending to be underrepresented), this one-third figure no doubt overestimates the extent to which Americans see themselves as partaking of a "middle-class" existence.

Lest it be thought that something "Marxian" is involved, let it be said immediately that these responses, for large numbers of those interviewed, are by no means fixed and stable. Evidence on this point appeared quite early in the game. The *Fortune* magazine polls done by Elmo Roper used three response categories—upper, middle, and lower—and regularly found a majority choosing to identify as middle class. A similar result was obtained when the middle-class options were proliferated by adding an "upper-middle" and "lower-middle" choice. Richard Centers in 1945 first used the fourfold option, adding "working class" to the choices. This changed the modal case so as to yield the pattern shown in column one of Table 3.2. The volatility of these identifications was also indicated by the fact that the percentage of working class identifications in this American study increased somewhat after the Labour party victory in England, an event that occurred midway in the course of the interviewing. A later Gallup study using a split sample gave half of the respondents the "working-class" option and substituted for the other half the choice "laboring class." This substitution also had the consequence of shifting about 15 percent of the latter half of the sample—they chose "middle class" as their identification rather than "laboring."[28]

There are some simple methodological imperatives that flow from these observations. The most important of them is that any trend statement is going to have to be based on identical or, at minimum, closely parallel questions. It is also important to recognize the status of this identification. For some people, it is obviously not some kind of basic identity or anchoring point that determines the remainder of one's world outlook. Instead, the response for them appears much more epiphenomenal. The question, nevertheless, is still important to our study for the purpose of testing the claims about "middle-class society" and about the presumed tenacious identification with

TABLE 3.2
Class Identification 1945–1964

Class Iden-tification	OPOR[a] 7/17/45	AIPO #365 2/13/46	AIPO #393 3/26/47	AIPO #412 2/4/48	UNESCO[b] 9/21/48	NORC #88/166 June '49	NORC #90/168 Aug '49	AIPO #502 9/18/52	Survey Research Center 1952	1956[c]	1958	1960	1964
Upper	3%	4%	3%	6%	4%	2%	3%	3%					
Middle	43	36	38	38	42	32	32	36	37%	36%	38%	31%	40%
Working	51	51	52	53	51	61	61	56	60	61	59	64	56
Lower	1	5	3	4	...	3	3	6	4	4	4	5	4
DK	2	3	3	[d]	3	2	2	...					
	100%	99%	99%	101%	100%	100%	100%	101%	101%	101%	101%	100%	100%
N =	(1097)	(2909)	(1502)	(1583)	(1015)	(1278)	(1232)	(3052)	(1799)	(1762)	(1822)	(1954)	(1571)

[a] This is Richard Centers' study. The relatively high middle-class percentage may result from the fact that it was a wartime study and, even more important, that it was based on white respondents only. The question reads: "If you were asked to use one of these four names for your social class, which would you say you belong in: the middle class, lower class, working class, or upper class?" The same question was used in the two subsequent studies. It was the study of 3/26/47 which substituted "laboring class" for half of the sample (results appear in Buchanan-Cantril, p. 115).

[b] The Buchanan and Cantril study. The question "If you were asked to use a name for your social class, would you say you belong to the middle class, working class, or upper class?"

[c] The question (1956): "There's quite a bit of talk these days about different social classes. Most people say they belong either to the middle class or to the working class. Do you ever think of yourself as being in one of these classes? Which class?" The same question was used in 1958 and 1960. The 1952 question begins with "There's quite a bit of talk these days about four different social classes . . ." and is followed by Centers' question.

[d] Less than 0.5%.

[e] Percents do not add to 100% due to rounding.

101

the middle class held by some subgroups in the society. A fair test of such claims is a question allowing respondents to choose either that identification or an alternative of sufficient attractiveness such that the "middle-class" option is not forced.

In the 18-year span covered by these surveys, the basic fact to be observed is the remarkable stability in the distribution of the responses. This is a period during which there were considerable increases in real family incomes and, for nearly all groups, the quantity of goods per consumer unit (a measure sometimes referred to as a "standard of living") also increased considerably. And yet, these identifications remained immune to all these highly visible transformations. This suggests, therefore (contrary to the view of those who focus on "style of life" as the key determinant of outlooks), that this identification is actually dependent on something else. That "something else" must have been more or less constant over these years. One guess on the subject is that the constant determinant was occupation.[29]

The Survey Research Center studies lead into the class identification area with a prior question about whether respondents ever think of themselves as "being in one of these classes." In 1956, 63 percent said "Yes." It seems likely that the third who said "No" to this question provide the bulk of the "shifters" in those instances where the question wording is changed. It should also be noted that the SRC's question poses an explicit choice between middle and working class. For all practical purposes, it excludes the choice of upper- or lower-class identification.

At minimum, the overall distribution of the responses and the relative stability in these responses indicate that explanations of the "American experiment" that fall back on common values, common outlooks, middle-class orientations, and so forth must be treated with some skepticism. To argue, for example, that the absence of leftist parties is due to a "remarkable unity" that is different from the European experience, does not appear to be a well-founded or supported viewpoint. It seems likely that the response pattern shown here would also have been present at earlier points in our history, that is, at dates long before 1945.

Party Identification

The question on party identifications is consistent with our picture of the population as basically liberal. From 1952 to 1964, in the six studies of this series, approximately 60 percent of the population indicating at least some party leaning (this includes the independents who confessed to some preference) identified with the more liberal of the two parties. (See Table 3.3.) There was no significant change indicated in the 1968 study. Fifty-six percent of the sample identified as Democrats and 34 percent as Republicans. Among those identifying with the two major parties, 62 percent aligned with the Democrats.

TABLE 3.3

Party Identification, 1952–1964 (Survey Research Center Studies)

Party Identification	1952	1956	1958	1960	1962	1964
Strong Democrat	22%	21%	26%	20%	23%	26%
Weak Democrat	24	23	22	24	23	25
Independent Democrat	10	6	7	6	7	9
Independent	5	9	7	10	8	8
Independent Republican	7	8	5	7	6	6
Weak Republican	13	14	16	13	16	13
Strong Republican	13	15	11	15	12	11
Other	6	4	5	5	5	2
Total percent	100%	100%	99%[a]	100%	100%	100%
N =	(1799)	(1762)	(1822)	(1954)	(1297)	(1571)
Percent Democrat of two-party choice	63%	57%	63%	59%	61%	67%

(Strong Democrat + Weak Democrat braced: 1952 = 56, 1956 = 50, 1958 = 55, 1960 = 50, 1962 = 53, 1964 = 60)

(Weak Republican + Strong Republican braced: 1952 = 33, 1956 = 37, 1958 = 32, 1960 = 35, 1962 = 34, 1964 = 30)

[a] Sometimes, due to rounding off, the percentages do not add up to 100%.

If all respondents had voted and followed their identifications, there would have been solid Democratic majorities in this country. The fact that the elections of recent decades (with one exception) have not given them a series of 60–40 victories has to do with regular and persistent defections from the Democrats and to lower turnout on the part of some major groups of Democratic identifiers.

A frequent stress made in the contemporary social sciences is on the absent or low relationship between issue orientations and party choice. Such evidence is used to support the neo-elitist conception of democracy, claiming that "the people" are very confused about these matters. Actually, the correspondence of issue preference and party choice is not quite so erratic as is frequently argued. Approximately four-fifths of the Democratic identifiers, for example, have liberal preferences on the job guarantee and medical care questions. The inappropriate linkages do not occur at random in the population. They tend, instead, to be more frequent among Republicans.[30] Approximately half of the Republican identifiers approve of the job guarantee, and roughly two-fifths of them favor the medical care suggestion. Basically, as will be shown in Chapter 6, it is a matter of small towners who are liberal on the issues but who, either out of tradition and/or as a result of current pressures, favor the Republicans. It is this "unearned increment" that largely accounts for the disparity between the size of the liberal majority and that of the routine Democratic vote.

One other indication of the accuracy of majority perception of the parties appears in the answers to a question in the 1960 study, which reads: "Would you say that either one of the parties is more conservative or more liberal than the other? Which party is more conservative. . .?" (Q. 32 plus four specifying questions). The results were as follows:

3% ⎫		Democrats a lot more conservative
4 ⎬ 10%		Democrats a little more conservative
3 ⎭		Democrats more conservative
9 ⎫		Republicans more conservative
25 ⎬ 57%		Republicants a little more conservative
23 ⎭		Republicans a lot more conservative
33		No guess, DK, NA

(N = 1954)

Those giving an answer to this question have overwhelmingly described the party majorities accurately. This accuracy of perception amounts to 85 percent of those having an opinion.

Attitudes Toward Change

There are a number of other questions appearing in the Survery Research Center's election studies that are of relevance here. One series, rather than focusing on the liberal-conservative issues of the day, explores the preference for accepting the old, the traditional, or the established ways as compared to a wish for new and independent innovations. In the post-election survey of 1956, one-third of the respondents were read the following series of statements and asked whether they agreed or disagreed. ($N = 579$.)

"If something grows up over a long time, there will always be much wisdom in it."

Agree: 63%   Disagree: 31%   DK, NA: 6%

"It's better to stick by what you have than to be trying new things you don't really know about."

Agree: 50%   Disagree: 48%   DK, NA: 2%

"We must respect the work of our forefathers and not think that we know better than they did."

Agree: 47%   Disagree: 50%   DK, NA: 3%

"A man doesn't really get to have much wisdom until he's well along in years."

Agree: 45%   Disagree: 53%   DK, NA: 2%

"If you start trying to change things very much, you usually make things worse."

Agree: 46%   Disagree: 51%   DK, NA: 3%

Agreement constitutes the "conservative" response in all cases, that is, the response of faith in old or established ways.

These results do not allow any easy sweeping general summary. It is obvious that in response to these statements there is no agreement that would allow support for the claim of *Americans* being conservative nor, for that matter, is it possible to support a claim about widely shared or common values.[31] Perhaps the most striking characteristic of these results is the division in the population that in response to four out of the five statements involves a near 50–50 split.

In the 1958 study a modified version of the first of these statements was used, adding the expression "old fashioned" in describing the long-term, crescive development. The basic result is altered such that the "conservative" majority disappears and here, too, we have a 50–50 division.

Q. 74.2. If something grows up over a long time, do you think there is certain to be much wisdom in it, or do you think sometimes it may get pretty old-fashioned?

44%   Is old-fashioned
3   Pro-con; it depends
43   Much wisdom
10   DK, NA

A pragmatic, innovative majority orientation appears in response to the following questions also from the 1958 study:

Q. 74.3 Do you think it's always a good idea to look for new ways of doing things, or do you think in some cases it's better to stick by what you have than to be trying new things you don't really know about?

62%   Look for the new
3   Pro-con; it depends
32   Stick by what you have
3   DK, NA

And,

Q. 74.4. Do you think we usually should respect the work of our forefathers and not think that we know better than they did, or do you think that we must figure out our problems for ourselves?

78%   Figure out for selves
4   Pro-con; it depends
14   Respect forefathers
4   DK, NA

And finally,

Q. 74.5. Do you think that a person has many worthwhile ideas whatever his age, or do you feel that usually a man doesn't get to have much wisdom until he's well along in years?

73%   Ideas whatever age
1   Pro-con; it depends
21   Wisdom comes late
5   DK, NA

The contrasting results in questions 74.2 and 74.5 indicate the basic pragmatic orientation of the majority of the population. There is little ready respect or adulation for the purely ascribed wisdom of *persons*; there is, however, a special status accorded to institutions or procedures that have proved viable over the long term.

The reservoir of esteem for the practical is shown also in the responses to 1956 and 1958 questions, e.g., from the 1956 study:

"I prefer the practical man anytime to the man of ideas."

Agree: 68%   Disagree: 27%   DK, NA: 6%

And from the 1958 study:

Q. 74.1. Which of these types of people would you generally prefer—the practical man or the man of ideas?

27%	Man of ideas
4	Pro-con; it depends
63	Practical man
6	DK, NA

The preference for the practical man, of course, by itself says nothing about the liberalism or conservatism of the population. It is indicative of a not insignificant semantic victory that conservatives have managed to inculcate the belief that conservatism equals practicality. Given what we have indicated earlier in this chapter, it is obvious that much of the preference for the practical man must be on the part of liberals.[32]

Attitudes Toward Those in Government

There is one final series of questions that have relevance to the broad topic of liberalism and conservatism. The claims about the "conservatism" of the American population usually have as their underlying assumption the belief that the major problems of the society have been solved. This is what explains the absence of a socialist party and, insofar as liberalism is stimulated by the remaining problems, the "smallness" of these problems is what accounts for the presumed minority status of the liberals. In other formulations, it is this absence of sensed problems that provides the basis for the widespread "consent" found in the United States; there are no "outs" or no sufficient number of them, so it is said, to provide the basis for any leftist party. For the most part, it is the absence of a leftist party that is taken as the evidence for the thesis that there is no widespread disaffection. Once again, it is a case of assuming "quick and efficient" democracy: if there were dissent, either the parties would respond or a third party would appear.

At two points (1958 and 1964) the Survey Research Center asked a series that (for the sake of brevity) we may call the "disaffection questions." The focus, it will be noted, is on dissatisfaction with persons in the government, not with the institutions per se. Some preliminary exploration in this area indicated that the response pattern was to some extent party linked and to some extent determined by perception of the events of the day. The questions and results follow.

Q. 72.1. Do you think that quite a few of the people running the government are a little crooked, not very many are, or do you think hardly any of them are crooked at all?

	1958	1964
Hardly any	26%	18%
Not many	43	49
Quite a lot	23	29
DK, NA	8	5

Q. 72.2. Do you think that people in the government waste a lot of the money we pay in taxes, waste some of it, or don't waste very much of it?

	1958	1964
Not much	10%	7%
Some	41	44
A lot	42	47
DK, NA	6	3

Q. 72.3. How much of the time do you think you can trust the government in Washington to do what is right—just about always, most of the time, or only some of the time?

	1958	1964
Always	15%	14%
Most of the time	56	62
Some of the time	23	22
DK, NA	6	2

Q. 72.4. Do you think that the high-up people in government give everyone a fair break whether they are big shots or just ordinary people, or do you think some of them pay more attention to what the big interests want? (Statement not used in 1964)

Give everyone a fair break	17%
Pro-con; it depends	1
Pay attention to big shots	74
DK, NA	8

Q. 72.5 Do you feel that almost all of the people running the government are smart people who usually know what they are doing, or do you think that quite a few of them don't seem to know what they are doing?

	1958	1964
Know what they're doing	56%	69%
Pro-con; it depends	1	2
Don't know what they're doing	36	27
DK, NA	7	2

In all cases the third option is the dissenting or dissatisfied choice. The smallest disaffection in the five questions amount to 23 percent, or roughly one-fourth of the populations. One-fourth say that "quite a lot" of those running the government are crooked and the same proportion thinks that at least some of the time the government cannot be trusted to do what is right. One-third think that quite a few in government do not know what they are doing, two-fifths think the government wastes a lot of money, and finally, perhaps most surprisingly, three-fourths see the high-up people in government as giving inequalitarian treatment or favoring the big shots. The government being discussed was that of President Eisenhower who, it will be remembered, had been in office six years at that time.

In 1964, after approximately one year of Lyndon Johnson's government, we find a pattern that in most respects is not significantly different from that of 1958. There is a slight increase in the percentage sensing crookedness and waste of tax money. There is a fair-sized increase, on the other hand, in the percentage seeing the government as having "smart people" who know what they are doing. Unfortunately, the question about paying attention to the "big shots" was not repeated. In its place we have the following:

Q. 66. Would you say the government is pretty much run by a few big interests looking out for themselves or that it is run for the benefit of all the people?

64%	For benefit of all
4	Other, depends
28	Few big interests
4	DK, NA

In this case, either because of changed question wording or because of a changed perception, the dissatisfied group has dropped from three-fourths to one-fourth of the population. As already noted, there is a fair amount of party linkage involved in these responses. It may have been more difficult for Democrats to define their party as favoring big shots.

How do these "pieces" add up? It has been shown that a liberal majority exists with respect to the job security and medical assistance questions. Both of these questions, as previously noted, offer solutions that are within the classical liberal tradition. Questions about the same basic concerns that propose solutions going beyond liberalism, understandably enough, do not gain majority support. There is, nevertheless, significant minority support for such initiatives, despite all the claims about "dominant individualistic values," on the one hand, and about the "manipulated masses" on the other. There is some manipulation suggested in the case of issues that are not immediately and directly tied in with domestic economic welfare, this being the case with the federal aid to schools question and with the "government power" issue.

The "liberalism" of the general public is different from that found in the ranks of the upper-middle-class intellectuals. This may be seen in the different conception of the proper role of government vis-à-vis business and labor. Contrary to widespread belief in liberal intellectual ranks, a majority of the population is opposed to sweeping "tax cuts." Moreover, those who do favor such a move are not conservative, "antigovernment" individualists, but, instead, they tend to be economic liberals. This response, which is ordinarily viewed as indicating conservatism, is actually, if this analysis is correct, a redistributionist demand.[33]

This picture of a basic bread-and-butter liberalism is also supported by the additional data, which show persistent majorities of the United States' population identifying as working class when given the familiar two- or four-choice options. A similar pattern is found in party identification with about three-fifths of the total population choosing the more liberal of the two parties. A series of questions on attitude toward change also did not indicate any basic majority "conservatism." In one series the population split 50–50; in a later series with somewhat different wordings, the basic picture was one of an open, innovative, pragmatic majority. In fact, these results would indicate some contempt for the special claims of age and of the "old ways."[34]

A final series of questions rather directly challenges the assumptions of consensualist theorists. When asked about the perception of those running the government, we find levels of dissent that run as high as, in one case, three-fourths of the population. That this dissent does not take open or organized form means merely that it is "submerged." Since until recent years there has been little visual evidence of this dissent and since there was little published evidence from survey research showing this dissent (for the most part because this kind of question was not asked), it was easy for the consensualist theorist to read this quietude as acceptance, whereas these data suggest that a widespread sense of hopelessness or of cynicism was present.

A liberal majority might appear in support of a number of different issues. One might not, however, have the same majority in any two areas. If one assumed that the positions were in continuous flux and that they had little or no relationship to existential conditions, then it might be the case that a working-class and lower-middle-class majority would exist on one issue and a "middle mass" plus upper-middle-class majority on the next. If that were the case there would be a need for bargaining and trading, a need for reducing the level of insistance in pushing for either one of the issues, and it would mean that the party with the upper-middle-class clientele would have a reasonable chance in the "competitive struggle." If, however, the same groups constituted the majority in each case, different "imperatives" would follow. The need for "bargaining" and for "restraint" would be reduced. If the members of the adult population had relatively complete and accurate knowledge, a permanent liberal majority party considerably to the left of the present-day Democrats would be a strong likelihood. From the perspective of those concerned with "stable democracy" this should present no necessary problem; in fact, the obvious policy implication—responding to the demand —should do wonders in the short run for the enhancement of the stability and the legitimacy of the entire arrangement. In the long run, there would be some problem of stagnation and immobilism were no new parties to appear.

We have already shown the correspondence of positions on the job guarantee and medical assistance questions. A similar cross-tabulation of the job guarantee question and the school aid question shows once again a fairly high level of value coherence; those liberal on one tend to be liberal on the other. (See Table 3.4.) On these three issues, then, there does appear to be

TABLE 3.4
Job Guarantee and School Aid Questions (SRC 1956)

Gov't. School Aid	Position on Government Job Guarantee					
	Strongly Agree	Agree	Not Sure	Disagree	Strongly Disagree	DK, NA No Opinion
Strongly agree	64%	43%	37%	30%	31%	35%
Agree	16	27	24	31	20	11
Not sure	7	7	12	10	14	5
Disagree	3	5	7	11	8	5
Strongly disagree	5	8	11	16	22	5
DK, NA, etc.	6	10	8	2	6	39
	(762)	(233)	(121)	(183)	(288)	(175)

a domestic liberalism syndrome; the attitudes are not wildly scattered but instead, for the large majority of cases, they make sense in terms of the conventional views of liberalism. Again, as on the previous cross-tabulation, those who say "don't know" in response to the job guarantee tend to be strongly liberal on the school aid question.

One final point to be noted about the American population is that there is a core of knowledgeable persons, roughly one-third of the total, who appear to be aware of the issues to the extent of knowing quite accurately where the parties stand on these questions. We also saw some evidence that the level of awareness is not a constant. When the parties clarify their positions, there is a clear and fair-sized response indicated by the increased percentage who now "see" the party distinctions. This is of obvious importance to a theme touched on earlier, that is, that the low level of rational appreciation of politics in the United States is not a function of low technical ability on the part of "the masses" but rather stems from the limited differentiation of the political product made by the parties themselves.

In summary, the basic picture of the American majority is one that shows a persistent concern with and focus on domestic economic welfare and, accordingly, we find that majority taking liberal stands on the issues of domestic economic welfare. For the rest, this majority sentiment does not accord with conventional views about liberals in that they do not consider it right for the government to be the special agent of trade unions (presumably representing and supporting the interests of the liberal majority). Their view is a much more classic liberal one: that the government is the independent arbiter above the contending forces in the society. Large portions of the population are skeptical about the de facto independence of the men in government, a large majority feeling that the "big shots" received special, unequal consideration. The final point of note that comes through in these survey materials is that the majority of the population appear to be hard-headed pragmatists, persons who are willing to experiment and test for the best way of doing things rather than taking their solutions on faith. The evidence indicates that a majority is critical of old established ways and are open to new procedures.

At this point we wish to consider the question of "cross-cutting" issues, that is, issues that might break the domestic liberal majority and might fragment it so as to give the conservative party some chance of success.

The Possible Cross-Cutting Issues: Domestic Communism

The Republican success in the election of 1952 has been ascribed to, among other things, the concern with and the alarm generated by the "presence" of domestic communism. Although not strongly emphasized by Eisenhower, the theme was one of the basic elements of Nixon's standard speech, along with corruption, the cost of living, and Korea. Given both the focus in speeches and the electoral shift, it seems no problem at all to assume causality, that is, that the speeches and/or the concern was what moved some significant part of the electorate that year. We are not interested at the moment in assessing this claim or in making a contribution to the electoral history of 1952. What we wish to indicate is the extent to which this concern was present and salient in the minds of the adult population.

Fortunately, the Survey Research Center 1952 election study asked questions that allow us to assess this matter. Respondents were asked the following open-ended questions:

> I'd like to ask you what you think are the good and bad points about the two parties. Is there anything in particular that you like about the Democratic party? (What is that?)
> Is there anything in particular that you don't like about the Democratic party? (What is that?)

The same questions were also asked about the Republicans. As far as the subject of domestic communism is concerned, the authors say:

The most interesting fact . . . is that only 3 percent of the population mentioned the argument that the Democratic administration had been "soft on communism" and was "infiltrated with Communists," in spite of the fact that this argument was very prominent among the campaign stimuli to which the voters were subjected. It would appear from this that the "communism-in-government" issue was a relatively unimportant one. . . .[35]

It is clear that "domestic communism" was not a topic of widespread pressing concern; at least it did not come spontaneously to mind. It must be remembered that this result appears at a time when mobilization on this particular issue was at its peak. Not only was the vice-presidential candidate driving away at the issue, but it was also a period during which the late Senator McCarthy was close to the pinnacle of his political career.

We have an even more formidable account in the work of Samuel Stouffer in his previously discussed *Communism, Conformity, and Civil Liberties.* This large study, based on two independent samples, was undertaken in 1954, immediately after the major impact of McCarthy. It was aimed at answering the question: "How deeply concerned are the American people . . . about the Communist threat. . . .?"

The basic concern with personal and family problems has been discussed earlier. Despite the overwhelming attention given to the subject of domestic communism, the number of spontaneous references to the subject was infinitesimal. To quote the text:

The number of people who said that they were worried either about the threat of Communists in the United States or about civil liberties was, even by the most generous interpretation of occasionally ambiguous responses, *less than 1%!*[36]

After the initial opening questions, respondents were asked: "Are there other problems you worry or are concerned about, especially political or world problems?" Stouffer reports here that: "Stimulated by this second probe, the number speaking of the Communist threat rose from less than 1% to about 6%, including some of the same people who spoke about foreign affairs."[37]

Reviewing other studies, Stouffer says:

Past surveys support the finding that the internal threat of Communism has not been a matter of salient concern among the American people. Surveys have generally put the question in terms of the "biggest problem" or "biggest danger" facing the country, thus ruling out the many answers considered here in terms of personal health and financial worries. But even when the question is put in national terms, no past survey has found more than 10% of the public listing the threat from American Communists as the country's biggest problem of danger. It is of some interest, however, that the percentage who rate Communism as the Number One problem has been increasing fairly steadily—at least until 1953. Polls conducted in 1947 and 1948, for instance, reveal fewer than 1% in these groups. In 1949 it was 2%, in 1951 it reached 4% of the public, and by mid-1953 the proportion who regarded American Communists as the biggest problem facing the country had more than doubled and was at the level of 9%.[38]

These findings give some idea of the amount of ready concern about internal communism at the time of the Army-McCarthy hearings. This by no means ends the discussion, for, as we shall see, a direct question yields a much higher level of concern. For the moment, we may note that in comparison to the direct, immediate and pressing concern of household welfare, this issue occupies a distinct second- or third-rate position.

As compared to the concreteness of one's own household affairs, the matter of domestic communism is remarkably distant. Only 3 percent "said they knew a person who *admitted* he was a Communist." Another 10 percent "said they knew somebody who acted suspiciously enough to make them think he might be."[39] Some indication of the nebulous qualities of these "communists" is given by the "reasons" these people reported to Stouffer:

> He was always talking about world peace. . . . I saw a map of Russia on a wall in his home. . . . Her activities in distributing literature about the United Nations. . . . Didn't believe in the Bible and talked about war. . . . He wrote his thesis in college on Communism. . . . He brought a lot of foreign-looking people into his home. . . . Very aggressive along certain lines. Wanted to be a leader but not interested in money. . . . My husband's brother drinks and acts common-like. Sometimes I kind of think he is a Communist. . . . The way he talked. He is dead now so he can't make any trouble.[40]

The review of evidence thus far is based on open-ended questions that elicit the spontaneous, immediately sensed concerns that are in the forefront of consciousness. A direct question on communism, however, providing the subject matter and also a set of answers, yields a much greater sense of concern. When the respondents in the Stouffer study, for example, were asked how many communists there were in the government, nearly everyone had an answer and a large proportion of these would suggest at least borderline alarm. Some 8 percent of the married, economically active, college-educated males, for example, thought there were "thousands" of communists in the government and another 26 percent thought there were at least "hundreds."[41] Another indication of the underlying concern appears in a 1965 Gallup study. Asked about Vietnam demonstrations, 55 percent of the non-South whites thought there were "a lot" of communists involved and another 33 percent thought "some" were involved. Asked about civil rights demonstrations, 42 percent thought "a lot" of communists were involved. In the South, 63 percent of the whites thought "a lot" of communists were involved.[42]

This issue then is a peculiar one. The subject is not a spontaneous concern for more than a tiny minority; it is, however, one that may easily be brought to mind. It would be a mistake to assume that this reservoir of latent feeling is a "natural" characteristic of the general population. One must look to the decades of training by political leaders, mass media, and schools to account for the prevalence of the attitude.

It is necessary to give some consideration to the political impact, that is, to the potential for "deflection" associated with anticommunist demagogic appeals. In many liberal sources the image has been projected of a extraordinarily intolerant population. Underlying the widespread intolerant responses, such sources allege, is an "authoritarian" character structure. This suggests that the intolerance is not an ephemeral matter, but rather is rooted in a fixed and rigid character "structure." On the basis of such claims, it is asserted that *direct* democracy would mean the *end* of democracy. The salvation of democracy, presumably, involves holding the masses in check; the agent undertaking this "morally desirable repression" would be the established elites who are portrayed as more tolerant than the mass. It is they who come out as the supporters of the "democratic rules of the game."

This picture of the intolerant masses was not based on mere speculation; the public opinion polls of the 1950s showed relatively strong sympathy for McCarthy among low-status, low-education groups. Moreover, there were large proportions of the population who were more than willing to limit the rights of political radicals and these too were disproportionately found among the lower socioeconomic levels. It is this fact that comes through and is emphasized in one of the most widely circulated works on this period, *The Radical Right*, edited by Daniel Bell.[43]

The voting behavior of people in this period shows a quite different picture —McCarthy voting varied directly with the socioeconomic level of the district. It was not among the working class of Milwaukee that he received his strongest support. On the south side of Milwaukee, among working-class Catholics of Polish background, his performance was about the weakest in the city. Rather his voting support came from the upper-middle-class, traditional Republican areas of the city and from the north shore suburbs. This means that although some part of "the masses" were disturbed by the message he was conveying they did not vote for him.[44]

Throughout the "McCarthy Era" it was assumed that the Senator's support meant victory for his friends and defeat for his opponents. It was the combination of his "demagoguery" and the "authoritarian" propensities of "the masses" that led to this result. The best available study of the period, however, has shown that those candidates he supported tended to be damaged rather than helped. The basic conclusion was that, on the average, McCarthy "was worth about five percentage points to the Democratic Senatorial candidates whom he opposed." This result was observed in the twelve states in which he appeared in 1952 and, more specifically, in those counties in which he appeared.[45]

By way of explanation, it seems likely that many people believed McCarthy's claims about the present danger of internal subversion. The "masses" on the whole had every reason to believe the claims since, with rare exceptions, the major sources of news attested to their validity either by outright endorsement or by the equivocating view that although the man's methods left something to be desired, it was clear that he was on to something.[46] Moreover, his efforts had the support of nearly all leading Republican party figures including that of "statesman" Senator Taft who declared that "the pro-Communist policies of the State Department fully justified Joe McCarthy in his demand for an investigation." It was not that Taft was authoritarian; he was merely opportunistic. He urged McCarthy on in his work and told him that "if one case didn't work, to bring up another."[47]

This suggests that McCarthy's efforts had a considerable amount of legitimation from very high-status and authoritative personages. The average person of low education who read about the investigations and the serious "threat" posed by the communists and who saw the effort approved by leading national potentates and by his own local media of communication was easily brought to the conclusion that there was something to be worried about and, moreover, that drastic actions had to be taken. The fact that these same people did not vote either for McCarthy or for his favorites in other Senatorial races indicates that their "authoritarianism" was not characterological but was, instead, situational. Their behavior also makes clear that, although for these reasons they were sympathetic to the man and his struggle, when the choice was there, they preferred *to vote* for the liberal candidates who were more likely to guarantee them enhanced personal welfare.

In view of the concern with the "intolerant masses" it is important to examine the actual response patterns. To the one relevant statement contained in the 1956 Survey Research Center study, the majority response was a tolerant one. The statement reads:

Q. 12n. The government ought to fire any government worker who is accused of being a communist even though they don't prove it.

The responses divided as follows: Agree, 21%; Not sure, it depends, 7%; Disagree, 56%; DN, NA, 1%; and No opinion, 15%. The proportion of those with opinions who disagreed (that is, who gave the tolerant response) was 73 percent, approximately three-quarters of those responding.

Clear majorities in the Stouffer study affirmed the right of free speech for the man whose loyalty had been questioned but against whom the proof was lacking. This appeared in the two national samples and in the sample of community leaders.[48] Tolerance of an admitted communist, however, was a different matter. In such a case, approximately two-thirds of the population would deny the right of free speech and nearly half of the community leaders would make the same choice. Tolerance of athiests was also very low, coming second after the case of the admitted communist. Twenty-seven percent would allow the communist to speak in the community. In the case of the athiest, 35 percent supported his right to speak. The situation with respect to free speech for a socialist (a person who "wanted to make a speech . . . favoring government ownership of all the railroads and big industries . . ."), however, was more positive; three-fifths of the general population supported his rights and another 10 percent were unsure or had no answer.[49]

In summary, we may note the following: in two studies we find that the majority of the American public makes a sharp distinction between the accusation and (in this case) the admission of communist affiliation. The public supports the right to a job and to free speech in the former case, but not the latter. The majority position is not one of unreasoning hatred or suspicion. Instead, it is one of "fair play" and acceptance of the "rules of the game." The intolerance that was present, rather than being all-encompassing, was very much compartmentalized, being reserved for athiests and for known communists. The denial of rights for communists, curiously enough, *did* involve an acceptance of the "rules of the game," these being the new, unofficial, exceptional rules promulgated by elites and community leaders throughout the McCarthy era. This would suggest that the willingness to restrict the rights of communists was not a basic response of an authoritarian character structure, but rather was a "trained response" which, in turn, depended on journalistic persuasion and the efforts of many national and community leaders.[50]

There can be little doubt, especially when seen in the comparative perspective, that the American population had most unrealistic orientations in this matter.[51] Even here, however, the extent of the intolerance and the general nastiness of attitude was not as great as has been suggested. The majority made distinctions between types of "offenders" and were willing to penalize basically only atheists and those who had been defined by "authoritative" elites as being beyond the pale. At the worst, this behavior indicates some susceptibility to leadership initiatives; it does not, however, suggest the widespread presence of authoritarian character structures. It was only when the established elites and their prerogatives were directly and seriously attacked that the counterattack on McCarthy was undertaken. Briefly, this suggests that elites tolerated or encouraged his efforts. Given the "elasticity" of public opinion in this area, we may say that the elites were responsible for much of the hysteria from the beginning. This provides another of the many cases of not-all-too-enlightened elites giving support to radical-right demagogues in the hopes of dividing the liberal forces for the benefit of conservative interests. Although such efforts at mobilization may give rise to some mass concern, it does appear that such an interest is difficult both to generate and to sustain over a long period. Any defection in voting that is based on such efforts would probably be no more than a "flash" event; in the long run, the concern with and focus on the domestic liberalism issues would be reasserted.

The Possible Cross-Cutting Issues: Foreign Affairs

A second major diversionary concern used in modern states is the concern with foreign affairs issues. These issues are always (or very nearly so) presented as urgent or pressing ones. They demand immediate action and, more often than not, postponement of domestic liberalism programs. An early statement of this characteristic feature of "modernization" describes the situation like this:

> In a modern state based on masses, foreign affairs will be the center of every action. In this field emotions can be kept alive. An active and offensive policy can easily combat and suppress any domestic opposition, especially if the nation considers itself entitled to aggression. And this policy presupposes education for war—psychological as well as military training. The psychological education of the whole people for war again paralyzes the social groups and destroys their foundations; it canalizes mass-emotions and keeps them alive. The training for war keeps everyone busy: even the six-year-olds are made to march, to exercise, to concentrate on "war-games" to such an extent that they cease to be mere play and can be turned into grim reality.[52]

In the post-World War II period, probably the most frequent terms of analysis for foreign affairs were isolationism and internationalism, terms that all too often are taken to be synonymous with conservatism and liberalism. Foreign policy elites in the last few decades have been able to define isolationism as a "bad thing" and thus, by inference to define themselves as "liberal" and their opponents are illiberal.[53] This portrayal, this definition of the "sides," to the extent that it is accepted, could serve to fragment the liberal ranks and to aid in taking some of the pressure off the demand for domestic welfare reforms.

Such definitions, however, only very inadequately capture the "complex reality" of the situation. The unthinking acceptance of those basic terms leads to some peculiar paradoxes. The simple equation, for example, of internationalism and liberalism obscures the possibility that the actual content of a given "international involvement" may be very illiberal. It may avoid completely any concern with self-determination; it may acquiesce in the presence of and activities of dictatorial regimes; it may involve little more than the expedition of business interests, guarding against nationalization, high taxes, and so on. As for the basic economic liberalism discussed above, such involvements may have little or nothing to do with the domestic welfare of the populations—that is, the content of the "aid" program may consist largely of weaponry, permanent military emplacements, and roads to connect the various installations. Much of this contribution to the underdeveloped society is made under the noncommittal heading of "aid" or even under the (to liberals) positive heading of "economic aid."

Such use of the language allows a semantic victory of no small importance. It allows conservative elites to appear, at least in matters of foreign affairs, as "liberals." And liberals who oppose the military involvements in the foreign affairs field may easily be cast in the role of, if not conservatives, at least as the allies of the ancient, pre-war provincial isolationist conservative. Because of this problem, we shall not equate liberalism and internationalism. Rather we shall take up the subject more or less de novo with a view toward mapping the territory undisturbed by such predispositions.

The striking thing about foreign policy attitudes is that, with rare exceptions, all foreign policy initiatives of the government have majority support. This holds even with respect to the supposedly "soft," dispensable, and hard-to-defend policies, as, for example, in the case of foreign economic aid. The anxieties of supporters of these programs prove to be unfounded. Not only is the support there for these initiatives, but it also tends to be stable, or, in a number of areas where change has occurred, there has been a continuous increase in support for these policies.[54]

This pattern of increasing support is indicated in the following series. A 1952 question, to begin, is the only one in the entire series where only minority support for the policy of "involvement" appears, and even that focuses on the *degree* of involvement, not the principle itself. The question and responses follow:

Q. 24. Some people think that since the end of the last world war this country has gone too far in concerning itself with problems in other parts of the world. How do you feel about this?

Agree, 56%; Pro-con, depends, 2%; Disagree, 32%; DK, NA, 10%

A statement was given the respondents in 1956 that had an explicit focus on involvement (omitting the "too much" concern). Respondents had to disagree in order to indicate an internationalist position (usual response bias favors the agreeing choice). At that time, a clear majority of the entire sample took the internationalist position. Among those with opinions, the majority was approximately seven out of ten. By 1960, the majority had increased to nearly eight out of ten.

Q. 12c. This country would be better off if we just stayed home and did not concern ourselves with problems in other parts of the world. (Internationalist response = percent *dis*agreeing.)

	1956		1960	
Agree strongly	15%	⎫ 25	12%	⎫ 18
Agree, but not very strongly	10	⎭	6	⎭
Not sure, it depends	5		6	
Disagree, but not very strongly	14	⎫ 57	11	⎫ 64
Disagree strongly	43	⎭	53	⎭
DK, NA, No opinion	13		12	
Total percent	100%		100%	
N =	(1762)		(1954)	
Percent internationalist of those with opinions	69%		78%	

The stationing of soldiers overseas has as high a percentage approving as does the basic policy of worldwide involvement. In this respect the opposition is smaller and the "don't know" and "no opinion" groups larger so that the proportion of those with opinions who are "internationalist" in this respect proves to be enormous: 82 percent in 1956 and 87 percent in 1960. Even in the matter of giving "economic help to the poorer countries," in this "soft" and basically altruistic matter, one again finds that among those with opinions the sentiment is "pro." Here, too, the size of the majority is increasing.

Q. 12j. The United States should keep soldiers overseas where they can help countries that are against communism.

	1956		1960	
Agree strongly	39%	⎫ 58	52%	⎫ 66
Agree, but not very strongly	19	⎭	14	⎭
Not sure, it depends	9		6	
Disagree, but not very strongly	5	⎫ 13	3	⎫ 10
Disagree strongly	8	⎭	7	⎭
DK, NA, No opinion	20		18	
Total percent	100%		100%	
N =	(1762)		(1954)	
Percent internationalist of those with opinions	82%		87%	

Q. 12e. The United States should give economic help to the poorer countries of the world even if they can't pay for it.

	1956		1960	
Agree strongly	21%	43	29%	51
Agree, but not very strongly	22		22	
Not sure, it depends	15		14	
Disagree, but not very strongly	10	26	6	20
Disagree strongly	16		14	
DK, NA, No opinion	16		14	
Total percent	100%		99%	
N =	(1762)		(1954)	
Percent internationalist of those				
with opinions	62%		72%	

Lest it be inferred that this help for the poor is an instance of elite and upper-middle-class altruism (as opposed to the self-interested "isolationism" of the poor), it should be noted that the poorest groups in the American population all show majorities for this position.[55]

A somewhat different question was used in the 1964 study but the result shows the same general pattern indicated thus far. This question reads:

Q. 20, 20A. Some say that we should give aid to other countries if they need help, while others think each country should make its own way as best it can. Have you been interested enough in this to favor one side over the other? [If yes] Which opinion is most like yours?

52%	Give aid to other countries
18	Other; depends
19	Each country make its own way
2	DK, NA
9	No interest
73%	Percent internationalist of those with opinion

In part, at least, the explanation for this majority sentiment must lie in the fact that throughout the 1950s, the United States had a "bipartisan" foreign policy in support of such foreign involvements. It is worth stressing in this connection that the population, on the whole, has a very accurate appreciation of this fact. A large percentage had some perception of the party positions and those with opinions overwhelmingly felt that with respect to these matters there would be "no difference" between the parties. Unlike the domestic liberalism issues, where there was a very heavy expectation that the Democrats would make the initiatives, with respect to the three foreign affairs issues studied in 1960 there was no special tendency to be seen. Interestingly enough, again showing the relatively large size of the informed population, this pattern changed markedly in 1964 during the Johnson-Goldwater campaign.[56]

A prevalent image of "the masses" sees them as threatening, aggressive, dangerous. It is worth exploring this matter in some detail. To use the less colorful language of the age, the masses are a "destabilizing factor." The other side of the picture, of course, is that they are in need of "control." Something of this is suggested by Emil Lederer who claims that National Socialist propaganda "could always rely . . . on the predatory instincts of the masses."[57]

It is frequently assumed that an aggressive predacious response was present in the United States in the early 1950s, stimulated by the "loss of China." Given the prominence of the topic in later public discussion, one would think there was a high sense of outrage about this "loss," in particular about the United States' inability to alter the outcome of the civil war there. In October 1952, a straightforward question was asked about the subject:

Q. 25. Some people feel that it was our government's fault that China went communistic—others say there was nothing that we could do to stop it. How do you feel about this?

Seventeen percent said it was "our fault" and another seven said the same though with some qualifications ("partially our fault"). About a quarter of the population did not have an opinion. In opposition to the thesis, however, just under half (48 percent) said there was "nothing we could do to stop it." Although the impact of the 17 (or 24 percent) should not be underestimated —depending on who they were, they would make a lot of noise—the hidden part of the conventional picture is the widespread fatalistic acceptance of the event.

The subsequent question asked about the Korean War: "Do you think we did the right thing in getting into the fighting in Korea two years ago or should we have stayed out?" In this area, it is interesting to note we have a variation on the usual rule of mass support for presidential foreign policy initiatives. The results showed 39 percent saying "yes, we did the right thing," 5 percent were "pro-con," 14 percent were DK, NA responses, and 41 percent said we should have stayed out. It will be noted that if we take those with opinions only, a slight majority say we should have stayed out. Thus, interestingly enough, in a case where there was a direct attack by the "other side" (which thus aids in justifying the action, that is, in legitimating the American response), still a fair portion of the "predatory masses" showed an unusual degree of "restraint."[58]

Once committed, however, the usual picture reasserts itself. When asked "Which of the following things do you think it would be best for us to do *now* in Korea?" only 9 percent said "pull out of Korea entirely." The major other alternatives were "keep on trying to get a peaceful settlement," which was chosen by 45 percent of the total, and "take a stronger stand and bomb Manchuria and China," chosen by 38 percent.

Somewhat different questions were used twelve years later in the 1964 study in asking about the Vietnam involvement. In response to these questions, the majority of those with opinions now said that the involvement was the "right thing." This amounted to only 38 percent of the total so that the overall percentage favoring involvement was little different from that in 1952. Twenty-four percent said we should have stayed out and the remainder were "don't know" and "no interest."

A similar set of alternative policy options was presented. Again, once the commitment was made, few wished to "unmake" it; again only 9 percent chose to withdraw. The balance as far as the other two options had shifted with the larger proportion now saying "take a stonger stand even if it means invading North Viet Nam." Rather than seeing this as some kind of basic inherent pugnacity of the masses, it was found that the response stems more from the long years of cold war education and also that the stand is very sensitive to the mass media positions. Since the attention paid to the key media—newspapers and magazines—varies directly with class and educational levels, it was the "upper-middle-class masses" who were most influenced, that is, were most in favor of the "strong stand." The majority of the population at both times avoided the most bellicose of the options; they either had no position, favored pulling out, or favored ending the fighting and negotiating.[59] Even the initial acceptance of these wars, as we shall see, comes to be eroded as the "effort" continues.

The major point to be made about the "mass" outlook then is its nonpredatory character. The basis of this "moderation" will be taken up shortly. First it is useful to consider the possible explanations for the high levels of support for official foreign policy initiatives.

The following hypotheses are suggested. For many people, the president can do no wrong. One hears this in all contexts; he knows more, it is said, has more information, more expert advice, and so forth. This is to suggest that any plausible account of almost any policy will automatically pick up a considerable quantity of unreasoning support. We might refer to this as the "Oedipal support"—most people do not fight their fathers, rather they accept their dominance and the struggle is resolved in the father's favor. In addition to this unthinking support (which obviously includes authoritarians, deferentials, and so forth), we would have another large group who are brought around through the short-term and long-term influences of the mass media, the persuasive efforts of schools (again in both the long and short terms), and through the initiatives of "supportive" voluntary associations.[60]

In this issue area, we again have the problem of claims that only rarely may be tested by one's own immediate experience; hence the attitudes and outlook are more subject to distant influences. It will also be noted that in the United States, as in most countries, the parties drop their usual concerns and much effort is devoted to bipartisanship, to a formal stress on "unity," which is another reason why there comes to be a majority behind most such initiatives. In countries where party division on foreign policy exists, as, for example, where large communist parties are present, there is also a striking division in public outlook.

The relatively small support for the national leadership in the matter of actual wars (as in the Korean case discussed above) has to do with a different perception of those wars and with some very concrete impacts of those events. Far from being predatory, the "masses" show strong and persistent fear and anxiety about war. At any given time the level of anxiety among low socioeconomic status groups is considerably greater than among upper-middle-class and elite elements.[61] In great measure this is probably little more than a fear of the unknown felt by powerless groups everywhere. The same pervasive fear also appears with respect to fears of fluoridation and atomic fallout.[62] Not only does the aphorism "ignorance is bliss" fail to do justice to the actual state of mass sensibilities, but it completely inverts it; ignorance is a state of continuous fear.[63]

In addition to the general fear of war, the fear of some unknown or distant holocaust, there is good reason to believe that these people would see the war in more direct personal terms. That is, they would see that it was their sons who would be doing the fighting while, at least in the "limited" wars, the sons of the upper-middle classes would be safety sheltered in the academic enclaves—studying "vital" subjects, those necessary for the defense of the nation.

Where the widespread "fear of communism" may be used by elites in support of conventional cold war initiatives—providing support for armament budgets, for investigation of domestic subversives, and so forth—this fear of war might, if known, work in the opposite direction, to limit or restrain the use of such initiatives. Since, however, there is little knowledge of this particular distribution of attitudes on the part of elites or masses, those who were fearful and opposed to the Korean and later the Vietnam war have been largely without political influence.

It is this distinctive anxiety of the "masses" that explains another apparent paradox in the available findings. A majority of the population has regularly shown an enthusiasm for large defense expenditures. In many cases surveys have found an otherwise extraordinary willingness to spend money for an enlarged military establishment. A 1948 study, for example, showed that "even when the individual costs to the taxpayer were made explicit, 63 percent still favored a larger air force, 55 percent a larger navy, and 55 percent a larger army."[64] Such "demand" provides at least apparent support for the "pugnacious" masses claim. In this reading of the data, the national leaders are in a position where they must "restrain" this zealous, aggressive demand from below.

Another reading of the same evidence, however, suggests that there is widespread anxiety based on the conventional cold war definitions of the situation. The conventional cold war solutions for the conventional problem is armament so as to maintain a prohibitive retaliatory capacity. This is to suggest that the alarmed masses are merely responding in terms of the situation as it has been defined for them by the most authoritative figures of their nation. If their "demands" exceed those of the responsible leaders, it might indicate no more than an unrealistic appreciation of the threat and of the complexities involved.

It is not possible to offer any more than suggestive support for this view. A study in Canada found general support for all the standard cold war positions on the part of the mass of the Canadian population. Forty-two percent, for example, thought "the West should take all steps to defeat Communism, even if it means risking nuclear war."[65]

In a series of later questions on disarmament, this study discovered that there was a large group who thought such a policy would entail economic setbacks. Twenty-one percent thought a minor recession would result and another 24 percent expected a full-scale depression.

Despite the large portion of the population favoring the "deterrence" strategy and the fact that there was an awareness by many persons that their economic interest was tied to continued armament, when asked the question "In general, are you in favor of general disarmament with proper safeguards?" 92 percent said "yes" (3 percent were "don't knows" and only 5 percent were opposed). Putting it even more strongly, weighting the matter still more against disarmament, the following question read: "Would you favor disarmament even if it meant a loss of income or that you had to look for another job?" Seventy percent of the population still remained with their preference for disarmament even under the condition that financial sacrifice was thereby entailed for them. Five percent were opposed to disarmament in their response to the prior question, 13 percent favored disarmament only under the condition that no personal costs be present, and 12 percent now said "don't know."[66]

There is a widely disseminated thesis that large elements of the population, working class and middle class alike, have been bought off or corrupted through the influence of the "military-industrial complex." It is, supposedly, the fact that their well-being, that is, their jobs, are dependent on defense contracts and military spending which leads to their commitment to the "Peace Through Strength" strategy. The Canadian evidence suggests that this is a misreading. It is a misreading based on a widely accepted corollary of the "predaceous" masses assumption—one that we may call the ruthless self-interest thesis. The Canadian evidence suggests another possibility. Contrary to the view that greedy, short-run interests dominate most lives, or that most people have "an interest in armament," this discussion shows an entirely different kind of "mass man"—one who is willing to pay the costs and is willing to sacrifice his immediate personal welfare. Rather than an egoistic, self-interested man, this alternative picture shows a man who is fundamentally decent—decent but frightened. And it is this fright that leads him to support programs that alarm the "good liberal."

Even more striking as an indication of this fundamental altruism are the detailed responses to questions on foreign aid. If the American population were predaceous and self-interested, we would expect them to be strongly for military aid and very restrained in their support for economic aid. The fact is, however, that "larger proportions of the American public have favored economic than have approved of military aid." When asked which was most important, "to send . . . economic aid like machinery and supplies, or to send . . . military aid like tanks and guns?" as one source puts it, "invariably much larger percentages favored economic over military aid." The same finding occurs among respondents who might presumably have a great interest in "hard" defense spending. As reported: ". . . when a cross section of members of the United Automobile Workers around the country were asked, in late 1964 and early 1965, 'If Congress does cut down on the amount of foreign aid requested by President Johnson for the coming fiscal year, would you perfer that it cut primarily military aid (like tanks, combat aircraft, and guns) or economic aid (like machinery and supplies)?' a majority of all major educational, religious, occupational, regional, ethnic, age, and sex groups within the U.A.W. favored cuts primarily in military rather than economic aid." A series of studies undertaken by the National Opinion Research Center between 1951 and 1957 indicate that the percentage putting economic aid as more important increased from roughly 50 percent to about 70 percent during the period. Correspondingly, the support for military aid decreased as did also the no opinion and "don't know" response.[67]

Technical assistance has, in general, been even more popular than direct economic aid. There was very substantial support for the Peace Corps from the very beginning. There was equivalent high support for the suggestion of a "Great White Fleet" consisting of floating hospitals, food supply ships, training schools, and so on to help out "poorer" countries. Similarly there were majorities from the beginning favoring the use of surplus grain to alleviate food shortages. The extent of the willingness, of the altruism found in the American population is indicated by the following instances: ". . . large majorities during the first three years after the war favored continuation of . . . food and other relief to war-torn areas, even if these shipments should require shortages and rationing in the United States." Majorities, although smaller ones also "favored food and other relief shipments to defeated Germany during the initial months after surrender." Although in recent years Americans have perceived China as a greater long-term threat to the United States than any other country, just over half (52 percent) replied in the affirmative to the following question asked in February 1961: "There is now a severe food famine in Communist China. Do you think the United States should or should not send some of its surplus foods to that country?" A year later, when China "seemed even more hostile to our interests," there were still 48 percent replying in the affirmative.[68]

The above findings in no way gainsay the fact of an opposed (and possibly more influential) minority. There are also variations in the size of the minority depending on the recipient country. European countries are more favored than Asians; Greece is preferred over Turkey; Negroes favor aid to Africa, Jews oppose aid to Egypt, and so on.[69] But, the general picture is one of majority altruism. Some of the opposed minority sentiment, moreover, represents a different ordering of the altruistic priorities rather than a pinchpenny cost-cutting outlook. As one author summarized the matter: "Lower socioeconomic groups who would cut aid have typically tended to feel that these resources should be expended on disadvantaged groups, such as themselves, in this country. . . ." It is the "economically privileged opponents of aid [who] have preferred on the whole that these funds not be expended at all and that the national debt, the national budget, and taxes be reduced instead."[70]

In summary, the use of foreign affairs issues to "break" the liberal majority appears to be a procedure having only limited efficacy. The "masses," we have suggested, prove to be the least pugnacious element in the population and hence the least easily mobilized for such ventures. The ready aggressiveness is found with much greater frequency in the upper-middle classes; hence, such foreign policy initiatives would not tend to break the domestic liberal majority. The attitude cleavage that occurs on such issues tends to run along the same line that separates the economic liberals from the economic conservatives.

As we have shown or suggested, the basic attitude among "the masses" does not tend to be one of zealous pugnacity via-á-vis one's perceived enemies. If anything, the more characteristic attitude is one of shying away from distant and, as they see it, pointless confrontations. Moreover, on the other side of the coin, there is present in these circles a sizable fund of generosity as is indicated by the willingness to provide help for the poor in other nations.

We have also suggested that much of the apparent pugnacity is a trained response, a result of two decades or so of cold war education. This again, like the case of the presumed "authoritarianism" discussed earlier, suggests that the response is situational rather than rooted in character. Evidence in support of this view appears in the Canadian study, which showed a remarkable willingless to accept disarmament and to sacrifice the entire Dullesensian apparatus even when there were personal costs to be paid. This "unusual" finding, it was suggested, stems from the omnipresent fears and anxieties felt by "the masses" in the world which, as they see it, is filled with lethal potential, with "devices" that may go off at any moment.

It is worth stressing in more detail the character of the likely strains and their possible resolutions. As we have suggested, the "masses" take a dim view of involvement in actual conflicts abroad. We get a 50–50 split on the retrospective question about Korea, the pro-involvement group being the more "committed" upper-middle classes.[71] Once the involvement has occurred, there is, however, a reluctance to reconsider the decision. As suggested, there are two forces operating: first, the ability of the ruling political elites to "define the situation," and second, the widespread propensity to give assent to executive decisions. There is no possibility for an immediate check of the claims about distant events and, also, regardless of the evidence, it is felt by many as quite legitimate that the citizen-president relationship should involve an irrational component that is somewhat akin to fealty.

For these reasons the routine foreign policy initiatives in most cases have, as noted, mass support. It is more difficult for some to assent to an active military involvement, but even here, in the initial stages, at least, once the commitment is made, assent is given.

The experience of wars, however, is different from the other foreign policy initiatives because, unlike mere troop stationing or economic aid, there are some "feedbacks" that eventually provide a basis for "reality testing." The most direct and immediate "return" is in the form of casualties—sons, husbands, friends, appear among the dead, the missing, or the wounded. Because of these "direct impacts" there is a tendency for the initial high level of legitimacy given the governmental initiative to be eroded where the war continues over a number of years. Some evidence of this kind of erosion may be seen in both the Korean and the Vietnam "involvements."[72]

It is this erosion that in those two cases led to a breaking of the liberal majority which, in a sense, forced defection from the Democrats. As an explanation, or hypotheses, the following "scenario" may be offered. People who are basically economic liberals find that the war, more and more, cuts into their welfare.[73] The liberal party is no longer able to "pay off" because of their foreign commitment. Hence, the most attractive offering of the liberal party is no longer, so to speak, in play. Moreover, when direct losses are sustained in the immediate family or the immediate neighborhood, there is direct evidence that the policy is destroying life in addition to welfare. A military "commitment" of this sort makes the parties into equals since the one can no longer play its trump card. Although the conservative party may not be particularly attractive, when it can present itself as providing a solution to the war, it may be able to divert enough persons to provide a win. Those diverted are likely to be those with a lesser commitment to the welfare issues and also are likely to be the more easily moved elements, those with weaker party identifications, those with relatively low knowledge of the issues, with low sophistication and so forth.

Most accounts of the Eisenhower victory of 1952 have stressed the shrewd Republican moves—the choice of the charismatic leader, the choice of the *military* leader, the use of the "I shall go to Korea" statement. From another perspective, however, considering the performance of the other contender in the struggle, one may see that the Democratic leaders "gave" the Republicans the victory.

The original United Nations mandate was to return to the status quo ante, that is, to return to the 38th parallel. Without a decision from the UN, however (the decision came after the fact), the United States' led forces moved over the parallel thus turning the struggle into a different kind of war ("rollback" versus mere "containment") as well as prolonging it. The push to the North came to a halt, and then General MacArthur, defying orders, made the move that brought a Chinese response and thus once again prolonged the war.[74] The return to the 38th parallel had been accomplished by the fall of 1950 at which time it would have been possible to end the conflict. The commitment to cold war foreign policies led both to a continuation of the war through to the 1952 election and to a sacrifice of many domestic programs in the interim. As mentioned earlier, Stevenson soft-pedaled the welfare issue thinking it was no longer a widespread concern.[75] In short, the Democratic party leadership made the decisions that later put them on the defensive on the key issue, the war, and they also made the important tactical error of failing to stress their position on domestic welfare. If they had *not* followed the Acheson initiative of 1950, they would have taken the war issue away from the Republicans and would have been much more "competitive" as far as domestic welfare offerings were concerned. The other Republican themes (e.g., domestic communism, already discussed) proved to be ones of very limited mass concern.

The years 1965 to 1968 provide a parallel to this Korean War experience. Again the ruling Democratic party undertook "commitments" that undercut the promised welfare-state accomplishment and that brought dead and wounded in ever increasing numbers. This time the Republicans were not, as in 1952, able to offer a "saving" charismatic figure. As noted earlier, there was widespread frustration over the lack of any positive alternative.

Where most commentators choose to stress the "necessities" involved in the conflict of foreign policy and domestic concerns, this view stresses, realistically it is thought, the options involved. It is not a case of there being a "need" to repress a "warlike" demand from the masses. Nor is it the case that a government *must* make those military commitments. When such a "commitment" was made, it worked to the disadvantage of the liberal party, which "accepted" that choice.

Even in these cases, however, it is interesting to note just how overwhelmingly the advantages fall on the Democratic side of things. The shifting votes came almost exclusively to the head of the Republican ticket, not to the "party." The top-of-the-ticket defections led to no notable shift in party identification; those defecting still continued to think of themselves as Democrats. The closeness of the 1960 election was not due to any basic shift in party identification but instead proved to be largely a reaction of fundamentalist Protestants against a Catholic candidate.[76] Once again, it must be noted, what we have is a case of a Democratic "contribution" to the Republican chances rather than any basic attractiveness of the party itself.

The Possible Cross-Cutting Issues:
Civil Rights

Still another possibility for breaking the liberal majority is the use of racist themes. Although the mass of the population are domestic economic liberals, their orientation toward racial, ethnic, and religious minorities may be a different matter. In this area, the masses tend to be, at least so it is claimed, basically intolerant.

This viewpoint, another cornerstone of the liberal world outlook, rests on the previously discussed assumption that the existence of the masses consists of competition and ruthless struggle within a milieu of scarcity. The struggle over jobs leads them to easy scapegoating and targeting of the most visible competitors. Such outlooks and behaviors are overcome by well-being and education; hence, moderation and tolerance will be found in the upper-middle classes and among the elites. If true, this would mean that here we had a major cross-cutting concern—Negroes, together with white "liberals," for example, would be led to reach out across class lines to the upper-middle class in order to find allies against the ruthless and hostile white workers. The campaign of Barry Goldwater in 1964 and the so-called Southern strategy of the Nixonites are both based on the competition-reaction assumption.[77] The Goldwater campaign was a clear failure. The Goldwater appeals, moreover, found their strongest response in the upper-middle class.[78]

It should be remembered that we are dealing with the study marginals in this chapter, that is, the results presented are for the entire sample. This means the figures appearing in the following pages include responses of both black and white populations. For most purposes, these figures would not be especially useful. The appeals in question, after all, are designed to break up the white liberal population. That question or questions (how the white population breaks? who breaks?) will be considered in a later chapter. The figures as presented here indicate the overall majority sentiment and, as such, indicate what total support is "available" for equalitarian initiatives.

The basic picture of the United States adult population shows a generally tolerant position to be dominant. In 1956 and 1960, respondents were read the following statement and asked if they agreed or disagreed:

> If Negroes are not getting fair treatment in jobs and housing, the government should see to it that they do.

Approximately three-fifths of the total indicated agreement at both times, one-fifth disagreed and the other fifth consisted of DKs, NAs, and so on. If we take those with opinions only, we find that three-quarters of the American population in both studies chose the "liberal" option. Assuming that Negroes all took the "liberal" position and that the sample is an accurate representation of the population (which in respect to the Negro percentage, it is), this would still leave 50 percent of the total white population being "liberal."

Among the whites with opinions, the liberal to illiberal ratio would be 5 to 2.[79]

A statement about the government's role in school integration brought a somewhat smaller liberal response. This read:

> The government in Washington should stay out of the question of whether white and colored children go to the same school.

In this case in both years the respondents divided with about two-fifths agreeing, the same proportion disagreeing, and the last fifth not knowing or not sure. Taking those with opinions only, we find that roughly half of the population took the liberal position on this question. For what it may be worth, should one care to pay attention to the small differences indicated between the 1956 and 1960 studies, the liberal percentage showed a slight increase.

Unfortunately, in both the "jobs and housing" and the school integration questions there are two concerns mixed in the statements, attitude toward civil rights of Negroes and attitude toward the proper role of government. It is possible that one may be a liberal with respect to civil rights but at the same time have a narrow conception of the proper role of government. This linkage is fairly frequent, especially among Republican identifiers. We will consider below some direct questions that allow a "pure" or unencumbered picture of the state of tolerant attitudes. One further difficulty with respect to the first statement is that it combines "jobs and housing" in the same question. Some people may be "tolerant" with respect to one and not the other.

The 1964 study made use of somewhat different questions. The question on "jobs and housing" for example, now focuses only on jobs and also, unlike the previous formulations, now mentions explicitly the government "in Washington" which may have an impact on the responses. The question goes:

> Q. 22, 22A. Some people feel that if Negroes . . . are not getting fair treatment in jobs the government in Washington ought to see to it that they do. Others feel that this is not the federal government's business. Have you had enough interest in this question to favor one side over the other? [If yes] How do you feel? Should the government in Washington . . . .

39%	See to it that Negroes get fair treatment in jobs
7	Other; depends
40	Leave these matters to the states and local communities
14	DK, NA, No interest

If one reads this as an attitude change, that is, in comparison to the 1956 and 1960 results, it means that one-fifth of the population fell away from the pro-civil rights majority of 1960 and joined the illiberal opposition.

Alternatively, the new result may be due to the changes in the wording of the question (the omission of the prior reference to housing, the explicit inclusion of Washington and the "not the federal government's business" phrase might well make all the difference.)

The school segregation question is also slightly changed. It reads:

Q. 23, 23A. Some people say that the government in Washington should see to it that white and Negro . . . children are allowed to go to the same schools. Others claim that this is not the government's business. Have you been concerned enough about this question to favor one side over the other. [If yes] Do you think that the government in Washington should. . . .

41%   See to it that white and Negro children go to the same schools
7   Other; depends
38   Stay out of this area as it is none of its business
13   DK, NA, No interest

One reason for suspecting that question wording rather than "backlash" is operating with respect to the previous job question is the response to this school integration question. As compared with 1960, the responses in 1964 show no change. If there were any reaction it would seem likely that it should appear here since it was with respect to schools—not jobs—that the major government efforts had been made between 1960 and 1964.

In both 1964 and 1968 respondents were presented two alternatives with respect to housing. These read:

White people have a right to keep Negroes out of their neighborhoods if they want to

and

Negroes have a right to live wherever they can afford to, just like white people.[80]

These options have an advantage over the preceding ones in that they focus directly on the matter of equal rights. There is no complication posed here by the question of a federal government role in enforcement. The responses are indicated below:

	1964	1968
Keep out	26%	22%
Live anywhere	57	68
DK, NA	17	10
$N =$	(1571)	(1557)

There is, in short, a substantial equalitarian majority indicated. The previous questions, on jobs and schooling, probably understate the extent of such sentiment in the society by mixing in the question of a government role.

This picture of majority equalitarianism is contradicted by the results from one final question in this area:

Q. 41. What about you? Are you in favor of desegregation, strict segregation, or something in between?

31% Desegregation
44 In between
22 Segregation
3   DK, NA

Given the fact that most of the Negroes favor desegregation, this means that only one-fifth of the American population are white and "pure liberals." There is a counter balancing "pure segregationist" fifth and the rest choose this undefined option "in between." It is clear that the population does not fall neatly into integrationist and segregationist, liberal or illiberal camps; there is much ambiguity of feelings indicated. If we were to summarize simply, we would have to talk degrees of access, about areas of acceptance.

From the basic frequency distributions presented here, it is impossible to claim any trend. The best summary of the 1956–1960 experience, where we have the same questions, would be "no change." The same holds with respect to the nearly equivalent questions on school integration from the 1964 study. The evidence from another national study based on white respondents and using identical questions allows us to make a judgment about the longer-term trends from 1942 to 1963.[81] The following results from that study are based on white respondents only. Questions were asked in three areas as follows:

Generally speaking, do you think there should be separate sections for Negroes on streetcars and busses?

If a Negro with the same income and education as you moved into your block, would it make any difference to you?

Do you think white students and Negro students should go to the same schools or to separate schools?

The pro-integration percentages for four time periods are as follows:

	1942	1956	June 1963	December 1963
Transport	44	60	79	78
Neighborhood	35	51	61	64
Schools	30	49	63	62

The trend clearly is one of sizable increase in the percentage favoring integration (or saying they do). The trend occurred in both the South and the non-South regions of the country. The figures shown here, incidentally, are based on the entire population questioned. This means that among the 22 percent who in December 1963 did *not* favor integrated transport there were both segregationists and "don't knows."

One other question shows the same trend: "In general, do you think that Negroes are as intelligent as white people—that is, can they learn things just as well if they are given the same education and training?" The trends from 1942 to December 1963, for the South and non-South regions are as follows:

	1942	December 1963
Non-South whites	50	80
Southern whites	21	59

The percentage expecting full integration to be achieved some day has shown steady increase, amounting to three-fourths of the white population in 1963, the younger persons being even more likely to expect full equality.

The results as of 1963 showed no significant reversal of the trend such as would be consistent with a "backlash" theory. The slight (one percent) reversals between June and December of 1963 could easily have been due to sampling error. Certainly there was no "wave" of reaction indicated as of that date.

If the civil rights issue did at one time prove useful for splitting the liberal majority, its "viability" for such purposes would appear to have seriously diminished with time.

We shall see in Chapter 11 that these attitudes show very little relationship at all with class. Within the manual ranks, moreover, it is the Republican workers who prove to be the less tolerant; hence, the efficacy of this issue in cutting across or splitting the Democratic majority would appear to be very small.

In summary, our presentation thus far leads us to the following conclusions. First, the domestic liberal concerns are very high on the list of salient concerns for the overwhelming majority of the American population and the overwhelming majority takes a liberal position with respect to the political issues "built upon" these concerns. This finding is not all that is surprising; it is made noteworthy only by the persistent refusal to face up to and focus on this more or less obvious fact.

Second, two of the three areas of diversionary issues that we have considered prove to be of only very low importance for the majority of the population. In terms of their salience, that is, their presence in the "mass consciousness," the matters of domestic communism and foreign affairs do not figure very prominently at all. Spontaneous references to these as concerns are few and far between. If these issues were to provide the basis for a division of the liberal majority, it would appear that any "victory" won would be of a short-term, temporary nature—to be superseded in short by the return of the domestic liberal concerns.

Even in respect to the foreign affairs issues, there is a "liberal" position (overlooked by most commentators) that favors economic aid over military aid and, although in favor of an "armed peace" in the cold war, is extremely frightened by the implications of that solution and is very favorably disposed to the idea of mutual disarmament. The key to the apparent aggressive anti-communism among the general public is a widespread fear that is not inherent in the "mass character" but has been cultivated over the years through the efforts of influential political elites.

The concern with the Negro revolution has, in recent years, been greater than the concern over foreign affairs or domestic communism. It does not make too much sense to discuss this topic further at this point. For the moment it should suffice merely to note that the trend in attitudes is such that the potential for scapegoating efforts is reduced.

One of the great virtues of democracy, de Tocqueville said, was its self-legitimating quality. An election made clear where the majority sentiment lay. It also made clear that the opposition was in a minority and made difficult any delusions about the size of one's following. The clarity of any such mandate, however, would depend on the level of participation. Low election turnout could be (and has been) used to cast doubt on the legitimacy of the winner's mandate. In recent decades in the United States this has been a favorite argument of conservatives who, in effect, claim the nonvoters as theirs. The fact of abundant survey evidence to the contrary has not served to discourage them.

The fact that one elects a *man*, that one makes a choice between two men each of whom presumably has taken positions on a range of issues also tends to obscure the character of the "mandate." The question arises as to whether the candidate was elected because of his stand on issue A, issue B, or issue C? Was it all three? Or, was it B and C, but not A? Then, too, there is a problem that, for reasons already considered, it is advantageous for some candidates to obscure their position on some issues, particularly those in which a direct and immediate payoff is demanded.

There is still another possibility that is much more simple and direct for obscuring the liberal mandate. Because of the multiple issues in a campaign and because of the refusal to focus on the issues, it is ordinarily very difficult to give a clear "reading" of the evidence of the election. It proves a relatively simple matter to "misdefine the majority." If the test of survey evidence is lacking (or is hidden, or not believed), then it is a relatively simple matter for anyone to make claims about the "meaning" of the election. For conservatives of all varieties, this characteristically means that they define the liberal majority as a minority.

Such definition or stylizing of majorities is, on the whole, accepted by the liberals who, being anti-empirical and therefore self-disarmed, are not in a position to test those claims with the available empirical evidence. They fall back on newspaper accounts, popularizers, and highly selected spectacular cases.[82] Thus, they are never in a position to redefine that majority accurately. They are then left with their diffuse notions of a conservative majority satiated with all kinds of consumer goods, intolerant of the "lower-status" population who are now "catching up," and hostile to the interests of those outside the United States' boundaries. They see this "majority" as willing to cut aid to poor countries and more than willing to undertake aggressive efforts to definitively "put down" the Soviet Union and/or China. Given this view of a world in which the small and uninfluential minority of liberals is surrounded by conservative, authoritarian, Negro-hating and communist-hating workers, on the one hand, and by aggressive, status-striving, radical-rightist, lower-middle-class desperados, on the other, the only thing left for them to do is to make common cause with the educated, democratic, and presumably tolerant and responsible upper class. The definition of majority-as-minority, then, has the obvious consequence of sapping the willingness of the liberals to initiate their programs. Who are they, after all, to impose their will on a majority?

The stylization of a false majority is facilitated by other liberal assumptions, notably the belief that legislative behavior and accomplishment accurately represents the mass sentiments. The implicit argument is that if it were not the case, those representatives would be voted out. As discussed previously, this overlooks the extraordinary technical difficulties involved in voting out an incumbent and the fact that the poorest and least technically qualified groups in the population are supposed to undertake this task. For the conservative leadership, the stylization of a false majority and the acceptance of this claim makes their task an easy one—they initiate no new liberal legislation, oppose that which does appear, and shrugging shoulders and turning up their hands, can portray themselves as helplessly but dutifully responding to the wishes of the population.[83]

In point of fact, as has been shown here, the majority of the adult population favors significant extensions of the "welfare-state" apparatus to include a general guarantee of jobs and general medical care coverage. These interests appear to be the most salient and pressing ones felt by that majority. As noted above, it takes no diligent review of governmental performance to discover that neither demand has been adequately handled. For all practical purposes there has been no response to the first of these concerns. And with respect to medical care, the responses have been late in coming, limited in extent, and inadequate even in those areas now covered.[84]

Mass society theorists would argue, by way of explanation, that the reason for the nonresponse or the inadequate response was the manipulated or diverted masses. There can be little dispute that some diversion does occur and that in close elections that is sufficient to determine the outcome. The evidence reviewed here *suggests*, however, that there is not very much diversion occurring. Even at the peak of various diversionary campaigns only very small proportions of the population mentioned those themes as special concerns of theirs. There is some evidence, for example in the McCarthy case, that the attempt backfired, that is, it lost votes rather than gaining them.

If liberal politicians were not aware of the majority sentiment, if they thought that such sentiment had dwindled, if they thought it no longer had the same salience, or if they thought the interest had been checked by diversionary appeals, they would be led to abandon the liberal appeals. They would, in short, be led to reduce the visible differences between themselves and their conservative competition. By doing so they would reduce the incentive to vote on the part of many people within that liberal majority. By reducing the visible differences, the party leaders would also, unwittingly, make it easier for those with marginal or limited committments to shift over and vote for the competitor.

This suggests that, in part at least, the explanation for the inadequate performance—for the disparity between mass wants and political decisions —lies not with cunning manipulation on the part of the conservatives but rather with what amounts to a giveaway on the part of the liberal forces. There are, to be sure, other factors operating. As mentioned in the first chapter, some politicians intentionally choose to give away elections. Any given result is likely to involve a mixture of outlooks, some "leaders" not knowing that the liberal issues are viable and some not wishing to mobilize on those issues.

The evidence reviewed here has also indicated the presence of fair-sized minorities willing to support solutions that go beyond the conventional liberal framework. There are, in addition, other fair-sized minorities that neither favor nor oppose the suggested socialist options; they either give no answer or have no opinion. The antisocialist sentiment indicated in the responses to the few questions contained in these studies proves to be only a minority of the population. There is a suggestion here that leftist appeals might also provide the basis for electoral effort that also might have some reasonable chance for success.

This final discussion has focused again on the party leaders—on their doing or not doing certain things. The general population, for the most part, only reacts to the leaders' overtures. The options open to them, again for the most part, are very limited; people may choose one or the other of the two parties, or they may choose not to vote at all. With only very rare exceptions, the general population has not been able to intervene in the "political process" in order to make clear the direction of majority sentiment. The general population, moreover, has only on rare occasions been able to determine a party's position on the key issues, let alone compel the institution of adequate new programs.

To explain why this has been the case, it is necessary to consider the condition of the general population and of its component subgroups in some detail. Up to now we have considered only the overall distribution of attitudes. It is now necessary to raise the question of which groups hold which positions and, furthermore, to make some inquiry as to the political resources and capacities of each.

Notes

1. Poverty, for example, is an immediate concern of somewhere between a fifth and a fourth of the United States' population and yet this concern did not provide the basis for a political issue until the mid-1960s. The fact that it is possible to overlook the pressing and urgent concerns of a minority of that size makes it all too clear that there is nothing automatic about the issue-making process.

Additional insight on a necessity for consideration of the role of issue makers (indicating that the process is not natural) may be found in the following: S. M. Lipset, *Agrarian Socialism* (Berkeley: University of California Press, 1950); S. M. Lipset, Martin A. Trow, and James S. Coleman, *Union Democracy* (Garden City: Doubleday & Company—Anchor Books, 1962), especially pp. 209, 124–125, 225n, 330, and 393; and Raymond A. Bauer, Ithiel de Sola Pool, and Lewis Anthony Dexter, *American Business and Public Policy* (New York: Atherton Press, 1963), see especially pp. 299 and 316.

2. Samuel A. Stouffer, *Communism, Conformity, and Civil Liberties* (Gloucester: Peter Smith, 1963), p. 59. The original edition was by Doubleday, 1955. The study is based on two national cross-sectional probability samples. The two were undertaken by different organizations—the American Institute of Public Opinion (Gallup) and the National Opinion Research Center. The results of the two studies are nearly identical on all major questions.

3. Ibid., pp. 60–63.

4. Ibid., p. 59. A discussion of "before" and "after" in the life of English workers is contained in Michael Young and Peter Willmott, *Family and Kinship in East London* (London: Routledge & Kegan Paul, 1957), pp. 3–15. See, also, for similar findings from France, Richard Hamilton, *Affluence and the French Worker in the Fourth Republic* (Princeton: Princeton University Press, 1967), p. 73n.

5. Stouffer, op. cit., p. 60.

6. Ibid., p. 61.

7. Ibid., p. 67.

8. Ibid., p. 70. There was still another follow-up question that asked what things they had discussed with friends during the week. "Personal and familial prob-

lems" again headed the list, being mentioned by 50 percent of the respondents. This was followed by mentions of "world problems, including war," a topic discussed by 28 percent of the samples. See p. 71.

9. Hadley Cantril, *The Pattern of Human Concerns* (New Brunswick: Rutgers University Press, 1964), pp. 23 and 35–36.

10. Ibid., p. 41.

11. Ibid., p. 163.

12. Ibid., pp. 208 and 222.

13. See Seymour Martin Lipset, *Political Man* (Garden City: Doubleday, 1960), pp. 101–102; Gerhard Lenski, *The Religious Factor* (Garden City: Doubleday, 1961), pp. 189–191; and Philip E. Converse, "The Nature of Belief Systems in Mass Publics," pp. 206–261 of David Apter, ed., *Ideology and Discontent* (New York: The Free Press, 1964). A useful dissenting discussion, with supporting evidence, is that of Steven R. Brown, "Consistency and the Persistence of Ideology: Some Experimental Results," *Public Opinion Quarterly*, **34** (Spring 1970), 60–68.

14. The questions and the marginals on which the percentages are based appear in the codebooks for the 1952–1968 studies. These are available from the Inter-University Consortium for Political Research, Box 1248, Ann Arbor, Michigan.

15. The job guarantee question has relevance to the discussion in Chapter 1. A clear majority demands a job guarantee. Despite this demand, contemporary policy is guided by the notion that roughly 4 percent unemployment is an acceptable or tolerable amount. Given the fact that this is not the same 4 percent, that there is no permanent unemployed minority, and that there is a "circulation of the unemployed," this means that those who are continuously in-and-out of employment must run to about 10 percent of the population. There is no technical impediment to achieving 100 percent employment as has been shown by the experience of West European countries in recent years. The objection that there is some danger of inflation with full employment is true enough but that is not an insurmountable problem as has been shown once again by the West European experience. Moreover, any shift from defense production to the production of consumer goods would have a salutory impact as far as the inflationary pressures are concerned. The basic point, then, is that (a) the majority wants full employment, (b) it is technically possible, and (c) the decision *not* to have it was never made by the public.

16. See the previously noted article by Philip Converse, "The Nature of Belief Systems. . . ." This article stresses the extent of issue *dissociation* found in the general population. Using tau-gamma coefficients and data from the 1958 Survey Research Center study, he reports rather low levels of association between the various domestic issues. The details of the procedure are not presented, making it difficult to assess the result. If there were a large number of instances of respondents strongly agreeing on one question and only weakly agreeing on another, this would have the effect of lowering the coefficients. Such respondents, however, would be making consistent liberal responses, a fact that would not be indicated by that procedure. It is again unclear how the problem was handled, but some handlings of the "don't know" and "no answer" groups could also contribute to lowering the coefficients. The medical care question, incidentally, was not among

the domestic issues considered in this article. In another presentation, a rank-order correlation (tau-beta) between individuals' positions in 1958 and in 1960 on the same items was presented and this also indicated a relatively low degree of correspondence. Here again it is not clear from the text whether the inconsistencies involve shifts from strong to weak agreement (or from strong to weak disagreement) or actual changes in position on the issues. If the coefficient does reflect the former shifts, then the actual consistency of position is likely to be considerably greater than that account would initially suggest.

There are some points of related interest to be noted in Table 3.1. There is a persistent tendency to "break" in the liberal direction. The percentage of job guarantee "conservatives," for example, who turn out to be medical care "liberals" is greater than the equivalent percentages breaking in the opposite direction. Those who are "not sure" about the job guarantee fall disproportionately in the liberal direction in their responses to the medical care question (46 versus 28 percent). And those who answered DK and NA ("don't know" and "no answer") or "no opinion" to the job guarantee break heavily in the liberal direction in their responses to the medical care question (32 versus 14 percent). This suggests that there is a fair amount of "crypto-liberalism" to be found within the conservative ranks and even more among the DK, NA, etc. groups. It would appear that many respondents have conflicting sentiments about these matters, as if their objective needs and their value commitments did not mesh very well. These results suggest that if the parties made these concerns into issues, the result would be greater clarity in the minds of many individuals and a sharper relationship than is indicated in this table.

17. It is customary to assume that those seeing no difference between the parties are politically ignorant. While the question, technically speaking, does ask which party is "more likely" to move on this issue, a possibility exists that some respondents are hearing it as "likely" and, in turn, are saying that neither party is very likely to undertake this task. This is to suggest that they, too, are giving an accurate reading of the political map and that their answers also could be counted as "correct" or "informed." This suggests that the "no difference" response might just as well be an indication of realism as of ignorance. If one reads the response as showing ignorance, then one is giving support for an elitist and consensual image of the society. If we read it as realism, then obviously dissensus must be given more consideration. It should be remembered that in 1952 and 1956, the Democratic candidate, Adlai Stevenson, was avoiding the focus on domestic liberalism issues (having been convinced that with widespread affluence such concerns were no longer viable) and the Democratic leader in the Senate, Lyndon B. Johnson, was also not "differentiating his product."

Early in the 1950s Democrats began to abandon their New Deal–Fair Deal focus. This was stimulated by the conclusions of liberal intellectuals who argued that those concerns were passé. The welfare state and universal affluence were thought to have arrived. Except for some tidying up here and there, no major new programs were needed. As one author stated: ". . . the need . . . is not for reformers but for administrators and consolidators." See Joseph C. Harsch, "Are Liberals Obsolete?" *Reporter*, September 30, 1952, pp. 13–16; quotation from p. 16. See also Eric F. Goldman, "The American Liberal: After the Fair Deal, What?" *Reporter*, June 23, 1953, pp. 25–28; and Eugene J. McCarthy, *Frontiers in Amer-*

ican Democracy (Cleveland: World Publishing Co., 1960), p. 66. McCarthy, a Democratic Senator from Minnesota, summed the matter up at that time as follows: "As the general economic well-being of the people of the United States improved, the positive content of the liberal movement narrowed and popular support fell away." For an account of Adlai Stevenson's propensities, in the face of evidence it should be noted, see Charles Thompson and Frances Shattuck, *The 1956 Presidential Campaign* (Washington, D.C.: Brookings Institution, 1960), pp. 224–225.

18. The results: 1956 medical care question: government has gone too far, 3%; about right, 23%; less than it should, 33%; haven't heard what government is doing, 17%; DK, NA, etc., 24%. The 1960 question: which party likely to do more: Democrats, 34%; No difference, 30%; Republicans, 8%; DK, NA, etc., 28%.

19. The 1964 question wording is slightly different from that used in preceding years. Q. 17. "Some say the government in Washington ought to help people get doctors and hospital care at low cost, others say the government should not get into this. Have you been interested enough in this to favor one side over the other? [If yes] What is your position? Should the government in Washington help people get doctors and hospital care at low cost? stay out of this? depends?"

20. A Gallup study in 1968 posed both alternatives. The guaranteed income question read as follows: "As you may know, there is talk about giving every family an income of at least $3,200 a year, which would be the amount for a family of four. If the family earns less than this, the government would make up the difference. Would you favor or oppose such a plan?" The alternative question reads: "Another proposal is to guarantee enough work so that each family that has an employable wage earner would be guaranteed enough work each week to give him a wage of about $60 a week or $3200 a year. Would you favor or oppose such a plan?" The results were as follows (From the *Gallup Opinion Index*, July 1968):

	Favor	Oppose	No Opinion
Guaranteed income	36%	58%	6%
Guaranteed work	78	18	4

21. Additional evidence on the basic liberalism of the American population may be found in the following: Hadley Cantril and Mildred Strunk, eds., *Public Opinion, 1935–1946* (Princeton: Princeton University Press, 1951); Stuart Chase, *American Credos* (New York: Harper & Bros., 1962); and Lloyd A. Free and Hadley Cantril, *The Political Beliefs of Americans* (New Brunswick: Rutgers University Press, 1967).

22. The data: SRC, 1964.

	South		Non-South	
	Manual	Nonmanual	Manual	Nonmanual
Of those whites with opinion, percent favoring federal school aid	45%	27%	43%	35%
N =	(64)	(146)	(264)	(331)

A majority of Negroes in both regions and both classes favor the federal school aid. The number of cases, particularly in the middle class, is relatively small. The overall proportion in favor is 70 percent ($N = 101$).

23. The data: Percent approving federal school aid (of those with opinions) by attention to magazines and newspapers, SRC 1964.

Class and Medium	Attention Level			
	High	Medium	Low	None
Nonmanual[a]				
Newspapers	36%	27%	30%	44%
$N =$	(228)	(74)	(106)	(62)
Magazines	29	27	38	38
$N =$	(73)	(121)	(72)	(210)
Manual[a]				
Newspapers	45	39	50	59
$N =$	(126)	(52)	(107)	(87)
Magazines	36	47	51	51
$N =$	(22)	(34)	(59)	(258)

[a] Respondents classified by occupation of head of household. Retired not included.

24. This figure was somewhat larger, 48 percent, in the 1960 study. For some insight into the efforts of the companies to create opinion, see Ernest Gruening, *The Public Pays, A Study of Power Propaganda* (New York: Vanguard Press, 1931); N. R. Danielian, *A. T. & T.: The Story of Industrial Conquest* (New York: Vanguard Press, 1939); and Lee Metcalf and Vic Reinemer, *Overcharge* (New York: David McKay, 1967).

25. A tabulation of the 1956 power and housing question by age also gives some evidence of the "autonomy" or "independence" of these particular wants. One might expect that those favoring government action in these areas would be older persons, those who were around when the Socialist party was present, and who were the beneficiaries of the "old style" attacks on "the interests." The result, however, is just the opposite of this expectation. The data below indicate the percent favoring a government role (of those with opinions).

	24 or less	25–34	35–44	45–54	55–64	65 or more
Percent						
N =	46%	40%	38%	34%	26%	26%
	(67)	(286)	(280)	(218)	(155)	(122)

26. The data: Government power question (SRC 1964).

	Attention Paid Newspapers			
	High	Medium	Low	None
	Nonmanuals[a]			
Percent with no interest	17%	18%	27%	28%
N =	(275)	(89)	(137)	(82)
Government too powerful				
(of those with opinions)	57	56	43	39
N =	(216)	(68)	(96)	(54)
	Manuals[a]			
Percent with no interest	27	30	33	46
N =	(151)	(73)	(131)	(129)
Government too powerful				
(of those with opinions)	42	38	28	29
N =	(103)	(47)	(76)	(62)

[a] Respondents were classified by the occupation of the head of the household. Retirees were excluded.

A similar pattern appears with respect to magazine reading. The pattern does not appear in connection with attention paid to television. The latter, of course, as a "nonpolitical" medium is not as likely to be pushing such a theme.

27. Some discussion of the tax cutting peculiarity may be found in the original publication of the study findings. See Angus Campbell, et al., *The American Voter* (New York: John Wiley and Sons, 1960), especially p. 194 ff. where the interrelationships of the various issue positions are discussed.

28. Richard Centers, *The Psychology of Social Classes* (Princeton: Princeton University Press, 1949), pp. 138–139, and William Buchanan and Hadley Cantril, *How Nations See Each Other* (Urbana: University of Illinois Press, 1953), pp. 114–116 and 125 ff. See also, E. M. Schreiber and G. T. Nygreen, "Subjective Social Class in America: 1945–68," *Social Forces*, **48** (March 1970), 348–56. I would like to thank the Roper Center, Williamstown, Massachusetts for making available some of the study results reported in Table 3.2.

29. The 1968 study indicates a slight shift in this pattern. The proportion of working-class identifiers was only 53 percent, the lowest of all the Survey Research Center studies, and the proportion of middle-class identifiers, 43 percent, was the highest. One might easily assume this to be the beginnings of a trend. Another possibility is that it stems from methodological difficulties. The response rate in the election studies has shown some decline in recent elections. In 1956 the rate was 85.0 percent. In 1964, it was 80.6 percent and in 1968, 77.5 percent. If this increased refusal were disproportionately on the part of the poor or of manual workers, this would have the consequence of a reduction in the percentage of working-class identifiers.

30. Percentage having personal issue positions in conflict with that of their party (SRC 1956).

	Party Identification	
	Democratic % Conservative	Republican % Liberal
Issue		
Job guarantee	22	48
Medical care	19	42
$N =$	(877)	(658)

31. As, for example, where Lipset refers to "the dominant conservative values of the larger culture." *Political Man*, p. 208. Or, where Gabriel Almond refers to "fundamentalism with regard to social and political values. . . " in *The American People and Foreign Policy* (New York: Frederick A. Praeger, 1960), p. 52.

A very useful article in this connection is that of Michael Mann, "The Social Cohesion of Liberal Democracy," *American Sociological Review*, **35** (June 1970), 423–439.

32. That the demand for practicality is not indissolubly linked to conservatism is shown by the experience of the Milwaukee Socialists. They were eminently pragmatic during the years of their growth and were continuously looked to by the other parties in the city council for reasonable solutions for the day-to-day problems of the city. Apparently too, they attracted their followers by their ability to show these immediate, direct, and tangible payoffs that resulted from their "practical" orientation. The infant mortality rate, for example, was reduced by 50 percent in some areas in the year following their first assuming power. For some discussion of the work of these "practical" men, see Bayrd Still, *Milwaukee: The History of a City* (Madison: State Historical Society of Wisconsin, 1948).

33. Characteristically, given the assumptions about the "values of Americans," questions are not asked about whether or not they favor redistribution or radical equalitarianism. A notable exception is to be found in the work of John C. Leggett. See his "Economic Insecurity and Working-Class Consciousness," *American Sociological Review*, **29** (April 1964), 226–234, and by David S. Street and Leggett, "Economic Deprivation and Extremism: A Study of Unemployed Negroes," *American Journal of Sociology*, **67** (July 1961), 53–57. A more extended analysis appears in Leggett's *Class, Race and Labor: Working-Class Consciousness in Detroit* (New York: Oxford University Press, 1968). Also of interest are the following: William H. Form and Joan Rytina, "Income and Ideological Beliefs on the Distribution of Power in the United States," *American Sociological Review*, **34** (February 1969), 19–31 and, Joan Rytina, William H. Form, and John Pease, "Income and Stratification Ideology: Beliefs about the American Opportunity Structure," *American Journal of Sociology*, **75** (January 1970), 703–716.

34. It seems likely (although a test has not been made) that this antitraditionalism and openness would be more frequent among youth than among older populations. This is not to suggest a "hardening-of-the-arteries" type of conservatism, a conversion with age. Rather, it seems likely that the older populations contain more farmers, ex-farmers, and farm-reared populations, among whom a disdain for "new ways" may have been more frequent than among urban populations. Some recent studies of suburbia indicate that the "newest" child training is

designed to help the child detach himself from any undue affection for things in his past—persons, places, things (e.g., furniture styles)—because of the need for mobility, for a continuous transformation of all aspects of one's existence. See William H. Whyte, Jr., *The Organization Man* (New York: Simon and Schuster, 1956), Chs. 21 and 22; and John R. Seeley, R. Alexander Sim, and Elizabeth W. Loosley, *Crestwood Heights: A Study of the Suburban Life* (New York: Basic Books, 1956), especially Ch. 7.

35. Angus Campbell, Gerald Gurin, and Warren E. Miller, *The Voter Decides* (Evanston: Row, Peterson, 1954), p. 52.

36. Stouffer, op. cit., p. 59.

37. Ibid., 70.

38. Ibid., 86. See also Herbert H. Hyman, "England and America: Climates of Tolerance and Intolerance—1962," pp. 227–257 of D. Bell, ed., *The Radical Right* (Garden City: Doubleday, 1963).

39. Stouffer, p. 176. The answers to the question appear on pp. 176–178. See also pp. 158–159.

40. Ibid., pp. 176–178.

41. Most of the remainder indicated it was only a matter of a "few." Lest it be assumed that the sense of alarm was greater elsewhere, that is, among the less well educated, it ought to be noted that among grade-school-educated, male, manual workers, only 5 percent thought that "thousands" of communists were in the government and 19 percent thought it a matter of "hundreds." This group had the largest percentage saying "no, not any."

42. This information comes from Gallup Study No. 719K of October 1965. I wish to thank the Roper Center of Williamstown, Massachusetts for making this data available to me. Blacks, by comparison, were not particularly susceptible to this view. Only 15 percent of the non-South Negroes felt that "a lot" of communists were involved in civil rights demonstrations. In the South, the equivalent figure was only 8 percent. Blacks were more likely to believe communists were involved in Vietnam demonstrations, but the level of such belief still fell well short of the percentage among whites.

43. See particularly the Lipset article, "Three Decades of the Radical Right . . . ," especially pp. 330–332. The Hyman article, incidentally, contains data on the development of the post-war intolerance. As he puts it (p. 237): "With the cold war, public intolerance had grown and the relative tolerance of the more educated strata had been undermined."

44. Evidence on the actual voting for McCarthy and McCarthyites may be found in Louis H. Bean, *Influences in the 1954 Mid-Term Elections* (Washington: Public Affairs Press, 1954). Despite the title, this work concentrates on the 1952 experience. See also Nelson W. Polsby, "Toward an Explanation of McCarthyism," *Political Studies*, **8** (October 1960), 250–271, and Michael Paul Rogin, *The Intellectuals and McCarthy: The Radical Specter* (Cambridge: The M. I. T. Press, 1965).

45. See Bean, p. 2, 18–19. Much attention has been focused on the defeat of Senator Millard Tydings in Maryland in 1950. Tydings, who headed the first Senate committee to investigate McCarthy's communists-in-the-State Department

charge, became a prime target for his attacks. The campaign proved to be a rather ugly one. The McCarthy efforts made it seem plausible that *he* was responsible for Tyding's defeat. Bean notes, however, that the Democratic percentage in the state (as in the nation) had been declining for some years. Given the trend, which continued through to 1952, a Democrat was destined to lose with or without McCarthy's presence.

Another source points out an additional contributing factor. Tydings was a conservative Democrat. One aspect of the campaign against him involved the circulation to Negro voters of a report on Tydings' votes on FEPC, school discrimination, housing, the poll tax, and anti-lynching legislation. This account indicates considerable "apathy" in Negro wards. In addition, Tydings' share of the vote in one Negro ward fell from 51 percent in 1944 to 15 percent in 1950. "Apathy" was also noted in white working-class wards. See Stanley Kelley, Jr., *Professional Public Relations and Political Power* (Baltimore: Johns Hopkins, 1956), Ch. IV, entitled "Merchandising Doubt."

46. Robert Harry Pell, "APME Editorial Criteria vs. Comment on McCarthyism: A Study of Editorial Page Responsibility in the Daily Press of Wisconsin" (Madison: M.S. Thesis, School of Journalism, University of Wisconsin, 1963); Sharon Coady, "The Wisconsin Press and Joseph McCarthy: A Case Study" (Madison: M.A. thesis, Department of History, University of Wisconsin, 1965).

47. The first quotation is from Richard H. Rovere, *Senator Joe McCarthy* (New York: Harcourt, Brace and World, 1959), p. 179. The second is from the much more informative work by Jack Anderson and Ronald W. May, *McCarthy: The Man, the Senator, the "Ism"* (Boston: The Beacon Press, 1952), p. 352. The latter quotation first appeared in *The New York Times*, 23 March 1950.

48. Stouffer, op. cit., pp. 36–37.

49. The level of tolerance falls off when it is a question of employment in "sensitive" industries. It is impossible to make a brief summary of the complex patterns indicated in Stouffer's exposition, notably in his Chapter 2. It should be remembered that these attitudes are not spontaneous, natural, or to be viewed as "uncaused." They should be viewed in the light of our previous discussion of elite-sponsored and legitimated alarms.

Another work of some importance in this connection is Walter and Miriam Schneir, *Invitation to an Inquest* (Garden City: Doubleday, 1965).

50. A discussion of the new ground rules (and other behaviors) of neoliberals (or, if one prefers, of the illiberal liberals), may be found in Christopher Lasch, *The Agony of the American Left* (New York: Random House Vintage Books 1969), Ch. 3.

51. See Hyman, op. cit.

52. Emil Lederer, *State of the Masses: The Threat of the Classless Society* (New York: W. W. Norton & Co., 1940), p. 122.

53. This misperception was aided and abetted by the efforts of the late Senator McCarthy. His attack on the established elites of foreign affairs could easily be portrayed as an irresponsible, radical-right assault on responsible neoliberals. This led liberals of all varieties to unite in fending off this attack. The problem with this view is that McCarthy was simply very erratic (or blind) in his choice of

targets. In attacking established State Department elites he was attacking persons who were in very substantial value agreement with him over the appropriate strategies in the further conduct of the cold war. At best, the differences were ones of means, of personnel, and of aesthetics (McCarthy not liking certain features of some of the participants (e.g., mustaches, accents, attire). For a portrayal of the hard-line orientations of some of McCarthy's leading target victims, see David Horowitz, *The Free World Colossus: A Critique of American Foreign Policy in the Cold War* (New York: Hill and Wang, 1965).

54. This statement is based on the distribution of attitudes found in the Survey Research Center studies. Any such summary must necessarily oversimplify. Some of the complexity may be seen in the following review of survey findings on foreign aid, Alfred O. Hero, Jr., "Foreign Aid and the American Public," pp. 71–116 of John D. Montgomery and Arthur Smithies, *Public Policy*, Vol. XIV (Cambridge: Harvard University Press, 1965). Hero notes the paucity of public information in this area, the persistent tendency to overestimate the amount for foreign aid, and, one instance of disagreement with administration initiatives, a propensity to favor cuts in the amount of aid. It is to be noted that the AIPO (Gallup) findings show a general agreement as to the principle of foreign aid (seconding the SRC findings). It is at the point, however, where the implications of that principle touch on domestic economic concerns that we find some "countervailing" sentiment. This does not imply that the majority of Americans are indifferent to the plight of the rest of the world; in part at least, the sentiment for aid cuts would appear to stem from the fantastic conceptions of the size of current aid budgets. On the other hand, the sentiment also involves a very rational ordering of the priorities. A *New York Times* account, for example, indicated that, "as many as 100,000 to 150,000 San Antonians suffer from hunger or malnutrition. . ." (September 24, 1967). The director of the city's welfare department complained that "the Federal Government recently cut its surplus commodities meat ration per person in half when the United States announced resumption of food shipments to Egypt." As the director put it: "Let's take care of the home folks."

Also useful in this connection is Gabriel A. Almond, op. cit.

55. Sixty percent ($N = 168$) of those with opinions and in families reporting total incomes under $2000 favored giving economic help to the poorer countries of the world (SRC 1956), This probably understates the willingness of the poor somewhat since persons in these poor families tend to be older than the better-off populations. Some of the opposition is likely to be due to the contaminating age factor, to years of previous isolationist training.

56. The data:

Which party will favor...?	Demo-crats	No difference	Republicans	DK, NA, etc.
Internationalism (1960)	11%	51%	13%	23%
Giving help (1960)	14	45	14	27
Sending soldiers (1960)	10	48	13	28
Giving aid (1964)	38	35	5	21

57. Lederer, op. cit., p. 121.

58. This oversimplifies considerably. For a discussion of the complexities involved, see David Horowitz, *The Free World Colossus*, Ch. 8. See also John E. Mueller, "Trends in Popular Support for the Wars in Korea and Vietnam," *American Political Science Review*, **65** (June 1971), 358–375, and Hazel Gaudet Erskine, "The Polls: Is War a Mistake?" *Public Opinion Quarterly*, **34** (Spring 1970), 134–150.

59. This evidence appears in Richard Hamilton, "Le fondement populaire des solutions militaires 'durs,'" *Revue française de sociologie*, X (janvier–mars 1969), 39–58. An abbreviated summary appears as "A Research Note on the Mass Support for 'Tough' Military Initiatives," *American Sociological Review*, **33** (June 1968), 439–445. See also James D. Wright, "Support for Escalation in Viet Nam, 1964–1968: A Trend Study" (Madison, Wisconsin: unpublished M.S. thesis, Department of Sociology, University of Wisconsin, 1970).

60. G. William Domhoff, *The Higher Circles: The Governing Class in America* (New York: Random House, 1970), Ch. 5: "How the Power Elite Make Foreign Policy."

61. For example, we have the following questions from the National Opinion Research Center's Study No. 339 (15 November 1956) (Courtesy of the Roper Center). The questions:

Do you expect the United States to get into an all-out war with Russia during the next two years?

[If "no" or "don't know"] Do you think we can avoid a big war with Russia entirely, or will we have to fight them sooner or later?

	Occupation of Main Earner		
	Nonmanual	Manual	Farm
All-out war	18%	30%	38%
N =	(445)	(618)	(174)
Eventual war (of those saying "no" or "don't know")	39	56	54

The responses to the Survey Research Center's "war questions" show no such differentiation by occupational level. Their question, however (for example, in 1956), asks about the fear of war "at the present time." It would appear that there is a fairly realistic appreciation of current chances of war. Such responses fluctuate considerably in accordance with world events. The NORC question reported here is more of a projective question, as it asks about expectations in the distant future. It is not "bound" by current realities and gives a picture of underlying anxieties.

62. The heightened anxiety of low-education, low-status groups is indicated in Hazel Gaudet Erskine, "The Polls: Atomic Weapons and Nuclear Energy," *Public Opinion Quarterly*, **27** (Summer 1963), 155–190. This summary indicates that low-educated persons *tend* more than others to think: (a) that the A-bomb can defeat a country in "one blow," . . . that the war would be "over in a few days" and that such a war would mean the end of mankind; (b) that rains and tornadoes are caused by bomb testing in Nevada; (c) that it is a bad thing that the bomb

was developed in the first place; (d) that it will do more harm than good in the long run; (e) that continued testing of bombs constitutes a danger; (f) that fallout constitutes a serious danger; and (g) that the having of atomic bombs makes war more likely. See also, Sidney Kraus, Reuben Mehling, and Elain El-Assal, "Mass Media and the Fallout Controversy," *Public Opinion Quarterly*, **27** (Summer 1963), 191–205; Gene N. Levine and John Modell, "American Public Opinion and the Fallout-shelter Issue," *Public Opinion Quarterly*, **29** (Summer 1965), 270–279; and Eugene J. Rosi, "Mass and Attentive Opinion on Nuclear Weapons Tests and Fallout, 1954–1963," *Public Opinion Quarterly*, **29** (Summer 1965), 280–297. On the fluoridation fears, see Thomas Plant, "Analysis of Voting Behavior on a Fluoridation Referendum," *Public Opinion Quarterly* **23** (Summer 1959), 213–222.

63. A study of children showed that their fantasies were more controlled and less terrifying after they learned to read. Afterwards, they could see more order to the world and felt it to be less threatening. See Hilde L. Mosse and Clesbie R. Daniels, "Linear Diplexia: A New Form of Reading Disorder," *American Journal of Psychotherapy*, XIII (October 1959), 826–841.

64. Almond, op. cit., p. 104.

65. John Paul and Jerome Laulicht, *In Your Opinion: Leaders' and Voters' Attitudes on Defence and Disarmament* (Clarkson, Ontario: Canadian Peace Research Institute, 1963), p. 19.

66. Ibid., pp. 30–31.

67. Alfred O. Hero, Jr., op. cit., pp. 81–84.

68. Ibid., pp. 84–88.

69. Ibid., pp. 88–97.

70. Ibid., p. 100.

71. For example, the percentage thinking it was the proper thing that the United States entered into the Korean conflict varied directly with educational level going from approximately 30 percent among the grade-school educated to approximately 60 percent among the college graduates. See Chapter 11 for further discussion of this matter.

72. See, for example, Campbell, Gurin, and Miller, op. cit., p. 46, 56–57, and 175–177, and Louis Harris, *Is There a Republican Majority?* (New York: Harper & Bros., 1954), 22–31. Says Harris: "Korea grated and gnawed. . . . It worked decisively to Eisenhower's advantage. When the Elmo Roper-NBC surveys asked those people who said they were most concerned about the Korean fighting which party they thought would bring the war to a close most quickly, the answer by over a three-to-one margin was the Republicans." (p. 26) Also, Angus Campbell, et al., *The American Voter*, p. 527. See also Joel T. Campbell and Leila S. Cain, "Public Opinion and the Outbreak of War," *Journal of Conflict Resolution*, IX (September 1965), 318–329, and Mueller. On the Vietnam conflict (and also reviewing the Korean experience) see Sidney Verba, et al., "Public Opinion and the War in Vietnam," *American Political Science Review*, LXI (June 1967), 317–333. These authors, in discussing the Korean War, say that: "although its precise impact on the 1952 presidential election is difficult to assess there is little doubt that the Korean issue contributed significantly to the Eisenhower landslide."

73. Verba, et al., op. cit. They report that there was "a considerable reluctance to pay the domestic costs of the war, (among both doves and hawks) and a growing opposition as the escalation steps presented to the respondents became more severe." Asked about the alternatives, a majority in all instances put domestic welfare programs above the costs of the war; for example, "reducing the Medicare program" received a 28 percent approval and 65 percent disapproval. An interesting account of the treatment of this study in the nation's press appears in Nelson W. Polsby, "Hawks, Doves, and the Press," *Trans-action*, 4 (April, 1967), 35–41. Also of some interest is S. M. Lipset, "The President, the Polls and Vietnam," *Trans-action*, 3 (September 1966), 19–24.

74. See Horowitz, op. cit., Ch. 8; Fleming, op. cit.; and I. F. Stone, *The Hidden History of the Korean War* (New York: Monthly Review Press, 1952).

75. See note 17 of this chapter.

76. Angus Campbell, et al., *Elections and the Political Order* (New York: John Wiley and Sons, 1966), Ch. 5.

77. For discussions of the strategy see Richard Rovere, *The Goldwater Caper* (New York: Harcourt, Brace & World, 1965); Robert N. Novak, *The Agony of the G.O.P., 1964* (New York: Macmillan, 1965); and Theodore H. White, *The Making of the President: 1964* (New York: Atheneum, 1965). For a post-1964 work in the same tradition see Kevin P. Phillips, *The Emerging Republican Majority* (New Rochelle: Arlington House, 1969).

78. For the Goldwater following, see Leon D. Epstein and Austin Ranney, "Who Voted for Goldwater: The Wisconsin Case," *Political Science Quarterly*, 81 (March 1966), 82–94. See also Ch. 5 below for national data.

79. The data on the attitudes of whites will be presented in Chapter 11.

80. In 1968 this last phrase read "just like anybody else."

81. See Herbert Hyman and Paul Sheatsley, "Attitudes Toward Segregation," *Scientific American*, 211 (July 1964), 16–23. Also of some interest is their account, "Trends in Public Opinion on Civil Liberties," *Journal of Social Issues*, 9 (1953), 6–16. See also Bruno Bettelheim and Morris Janowitz, *Social Change and Prejudice* (New York: The Free Press, 1964), pp. 3–24, "Trends in Prejudice" and Mildred A. Schwartz, *Trends in White Attitudes toward Negroes* (Chicago: National Opinion Research Center, Report No. 119, 1967). Also, see Andrew M. Greeley and Paul B. Sheatsley, "Attitudes toward Racial Integration," *Scientific American*, 225 (December 1941), 13–19.

82. For example, completely misrepresenting what actually happened, we have the following from Theodore H. White's 1964 account (p. 234): "In Wisconsin, he [Wallace] scored heavily in the predominantly Italian, Polish and Serb working-class neighborhoods of Milwaukee's south side. . . ." This should be compared with the evidence as presented in Michael Paul Rogin, "Wallace and the Middle Class: The White Backlash in Wisconsin," *Public Opinion Quarterly*, 30 (Spring 1966), 98–108.

83. Compare, for example, Richard Nixon's comments during the first of the television debates with John F. Kennedy in 1960. The candidates were discussing a $1.25 an hour minimum wage proposal, federal aid to education, and medical care for the aged, all three measures having been defeated. The threat of a

presidential veto played a role the process. Nixon's explanation went as follows: "The reason why these particular bills . . . were not passed was not because the President was against them; it was because the people were against them. It was because they were too extreme." From Sidney Kraus, ed., *The Great Debates: Background-Perspective-Effects* (Bloomington: Indiana University Press, 1962), p. 362.

84. A leading study in the area reports "considerable agreement" between the opinions of 116 Representatives and those of representative samples of constituents. The correlation is described as "approximately .4." The correlation between "the constituency majority" and congressional roll call votes was reported as "nearly +.59" on social welfare policy. The correlation of district majority attitudes and those of the defeated candidates in the same area was −.44. While it is clear that from the point of view of representation, the electorate is better off with the incumbents, it is also the case that those roll call votes yielded a level of accomplishment that was well short of the majority demands of the period. See Warren E. Miller and Donald E. Stokes, "Constituency Influence in Congress," Ch. 16 of Angus Campbell, et al., *Elections and the Political Order* (New York: John Wiley and Sons, 1966).

4

On the Definition, Dimensions, and Geography of Class

The Question of Definition

Following the terminological conventions of centrist social science discussed in Chapter 2, we shall now present findings separately for manual and non-manual categories. To avoid monotony we shall also refer to these groups as "working" and "middle" classes or as "blue collar" and "white collar," respectively. There is no intention here of suggesting a collective consciousness within these groups. Whether one exists is a separate empirical question. All that is being done here is to distinguish two wide and diverse ranges of occupations. The manual jobs, in a very general way, are those involving relatively greater contributions of physical labor that is expended in the production of goods or the performance of onerous services. The manual jobs, for the most part, are paid less than the nonmanual; they involve less on-the-job autonomy, carry less prestige, and are performed in less attractive surroundings.

The use of the term "middle class" as the equivalent of nonmanual is obviously imprecise since the latter does include a small upper class or elite. The nonmanual jobs, in the majority of cases, have better pay, more prestige, and cleaner, more pleasant, and less noisy surroundings. The holders of white-collar jobs either make the major decisions in occupational life or they execute, transmit, and carry out the orders of others. Their basic function is the specification and transmission of those orders to the manual ranks together with the collection of performance records. Other functions performed by the nonmanuals include the merchandising of products or of services, as in the case of proprietors and sales personnel as well as some professionals. Still another function is the performance of services with no notable manual contribution as in the case of teachers.

The qualifying phrase—in a very general way—cannot be emphasized too much. There is a fair amount of income overlap shown in all presentations of the distributions by class. Moreover, there are some nonmanual jobs with little job control and some manual ones with a large amount. The definition here clearly can provide little more than a rule-of-thumb guide especially when it comes to classifying 20,000 or so distinct occupations. One of our aims in this book is to test some of the claims about class distinctive behavior; these claims are based on the same rule-of-thumb definition. A second aim is to examine internal differentiation within these two broad classes to see what shifts if any in attitudes and behavior have occurred such as would justify focusing on different lines of cleavage. In the next chapter we shall suggest a more precise refinement of this beginning definition. For the moment, the task is to define the classes, indicate their relative size and the character of the current trends, and also, to give some idea of the physical location of the classes. This latter task is useful in that it sheds light on some otherwise puzzling findings to be reported in later chapters.

If we were to deal with all employed persons, that is, with the entire labor force, we would run into some problems. Most men have a "permanent" full-time committment to their jobs in the sense that their life and the lives of their families depend on their performance in that job. By comparison, many employed women have only a short-term commitment to the job. They work either prior to marriage or for a short period after marriage. They may also reenter the labor force after the children have become semi-independent in an effort to supplement the earnings of the husband. An analysis that focuses on the "class" of *individuals* (by considering the entire labor force, as if all commitments had the same meaning) will lead to some paradoxical situations and will also lead to results that are markedly different from an analysis focusing on the occupational location of males or of male heads of households.

The major problem with the former analysis is that many wives and daughters in working-class families are employed in white-collar occupations. The most frequent kind of inconsistent experience is that where the husband is in a manual occupation and the wife or a daughter is in a nonmanual one. One could, to be sure, talk of them as being in different classes, however, a more reasonable procedure is to define the entire family as working class. This procedure follows another fairly well-established sociological convention that makes a good deal of sense, that is, to define the class of the family by the occupation of the head.[1] It is the family as a unit that has a life-cycle and a standard of living. If there were separate and distinct manual and nonmanual values or behaviors, one would not be likely to find them mixed within the same family, at least not with any great frequency. For these reasons, the sociological convention will be accepted throughout this work. Wives and dependent children of a manual family head will be counted as manuals even if the former are themselves engaged in white-collar occupations.

This is not to lose sight of the fact that there is a problem here. We can and will analyze the behavioral and attitudinal differences in families where husbands and wives are both in manual jobs as compared to those families in which the wife works "outside of the class." (See Chapter 5.)

For practical purposes, we are defining class in terms of the occupation of heads of families. This focus, as we shall soon see, yields a markedly different picture of American society than does one based on the entire employed population. Unfortunately, it is not always possible to get information presented by the occupation of the family head so that in many cases we shall be forced to fall back on second-best approximations. In many cases, especially when dealing with aggregate data reports, it has proven necessary to fall back on data for all males, regardless of whether they are house heads, as providing the best available approximation to our concept of class. Since four-fifths of the adult males are married, the inclusion here of a small minority of single or widower males will not make too much of a difference in the overall results. The single men are found largely within the 20–24-year age category.[2]

Our provisional operating definition is quite simple: by working class (also referred to here as manual or blue-collar workers) we mean those persons in households where the head is employed in one of the following United States Census categories: craftsmen, foremen, and kindred; operatives and kindred; laborers; private household workers; and service workers. By nonmanuals (or "middle class" or white-collar workers) we are referring to the Census categories: professional, technical, and kindred; managers, officials, and proprietors; clericals; and sales.

The Evidence

The most recent statistics for employed males, 16 years and over, show the following distribution: (1969)[3]

	Total	Nonfarm Only
Nonmanuals	40.1%	42.5%
Manuals	54.3	57.5
Farm owners	3.6	
Farm labor	2.0	
Total	100.0%	100.0%

Just under three-fifths of the nonfarm population is engaged in manual or working-class occupations. This result omits the unemployed, who would ordinarily be largely engaged in manual jobs, and for that reason probably understates the manual percentage. This result differs considerably from other accounts which suggest that the middle class forms the majority of the society.[4] Such accounts differ in two ways from the presentation here: they deal with the entire employed labor force, not just the males, and, in their examination of the nonfarm ranks, they have omitted consideration of service workers by the simple expedient of placing them in a separate category. Even placing the service workers in a separate category does not change the basic picture shown here since it would still leave a total of 23,263,000 manual workers to 19,574,000 nonmanuals. The factor that shifts the relative proportions is the inclusion of women in the accounting. The "middle class" majority results from counting the employed wives and daughters of blue-collar workers as middle class.

The question about the location of the service workers appears to have a very simple answer: they are manual workers. This judgment is based on the fact that many of the jobs contained in this category are ones that involve routine, physical labor. Among others we have attendants (for hospitals and other institutions) stewards, janitors, kitchen workers and porters. Also in this category are police and firemen, guards, watchmen, doorkeepers, and detectives. And finally, there are persons who are directly concerned with the performance of personal services: barbers, bartenders, cooks (except private ones), and waiters. This is obviously a mixed category and one could quarrel over the placement of a number of these occupations. If it helps to allay anxiety, it may be noted that a number of occupations are misplaced in the other direction; for example, in the case of the postmen who are classified by the census as clerical workers, and hence, are here treated as nonmanual.

The service workers match the manual ranks in a number of respects. The median income for males age 14 or more in 1960 was $4012, a figure which is very close to the earnings of laborers who had a reported $4018. Within the ranks of the service workers, the firemen and police are the high earners with $5544 and $5321 respectively, which means the median for the remaining service workers must put them at the bottom of the manual pay scale. The earnings of the firemen and police do not exceed those of the craftsmen.

In terms of their education, the median years of schooling of service workers 14 and over proved to be 9.7 years, slightly higher than the level among laborers, about the same as that of the operatives (semiskilled manual workers) and less than the 10.3 years of the craftsmen. The latter attainment is the high point for the manual ranks; from there we jump to 12.3 years for both the clerical and the sales groups.[5]

One other point of similarity with the manual group is that the service workers tend to be children either of manual workers or of farmers, a pattern that closely matches that of the current generation of manuals.[6] Thus, in terms of their origins as well as the kind of work, their current income, and their education, they are similar to the manual workers.

The service workers are also accorded relatively low prestige. On the revised NORC prestige ratings, this group received an average score of 46.7 as compared to the 45.6 for laborers and 53.7 for operatives. Protective service workers received a higher 57.0 but that was still below the craftsmen (69.0) or the clerical employees (67.0).[7]

Some of the complexities of the accounting question are indicated by the following considerations. The focus on employed males 16 years and over underestimates the nonmanual component since the children of nonmanuals are disproportionately located in schools, colleges, and universities between the ages of 14 and roughly 25. Counterbalancing that bias, however, is the fact that many of the children of manual workers are omitted since they are unemployed. Another consideration that works in the same direction is the fact that the children of the manuals are disproportionately located in another employment field, that is, in military activities of various kinds. Since working-class families tend to be somewhat larger, this would mean that our focus on adult or semiadult employed males would also underestimate the total size of the working class in the United States. This point would be especially important in consideration of the composition of primary schools where the working class percentage is probably greater than the rough three-fifths estimate indicated here. It is obvious that it is both difficult and not too fruitful to explore any further the question of the precise working-class percentage. For the moment we will remain with a three-fifths estimate.[8]

The Trend Question

It is commonly assumed that a rapid change in the relative size of classes is in progress. This change is shifting or, in the most frequent reading, has already shifted the relative class proportions (see the statements cited in note 4). If we take the data for all nonfarm males from 1900 to 1950 (and include the service workers among the manual ranks) we find a modest decline in the manual proportion, the proportion falling from 69.9 to 64.2 percent. Most of that change occurred between 1920 and 1950. If the trend continued at that rate, the percentage would fall to 58.5 percent in the year 2000 and from there to 52.8 percent in the year 2050. At that rate, sometime in the latter half of the twenty-first century, equality would be achieved.

In 1900, 78 percent of the employed women were in manual occupations. Although the absolute number of women in manual jobs shows (with one small exception) a continuous increase right through to the present, the increase of those in nonmanual jobs is much more rapid, so that the manual percentage had fallen to 53.2 by 1940 and fell below the 50 percent point before 1950. The basic "transformation of the classes," then, is caused by the sizable increase in the number of women working and by their increased employment in white-collar jobs. In great measure this meant a growing percentage of wives and daughters of manual workers coming into office employment. Except for the slight and slow trend noted above, the basic pattern among the males held fairly constant. (See Table 4.1.)

The employment of men in white-collar occupations showed a considerable relative increase in the years that followed between 1950 and 1960.[9] From the latter date to 1969, however, the pattern was again one of very slow change. Given that rate of change, there is little reason to expect an early transformation to a "middle-class society." It is useful to examine these results in more detail. (See Table 4.2.)[10]

Some specification of the development is possible. The claim is made that the nonmanual category in its entirety is growing. It is inherent in advanced, modern societies, given the proliferation of administrative and clerical tasks, that this development occur. The percentages in Table 4.2, however, indicate that only the first of these catgories, the professional and technical group, is expanding. It shows a growth from 7.5 percent of the employed nonfarm males in 1950 to 14.7 percent in 1969. In that same 19-year period the man-

TABLE 4.1[a]

Nonfarm Occupational Trends, 1900–1950: Males and Females (Economically Active Population)

	Year					
	1900	1910	1920	1930	1940	1950
	Males (in 1000's)					
Nonmanual	4,166	6,019	7,176	9,564	10,434	12,974
Manual (includes service	9,664	13,469	16,172	18,956	20,247	23,228
Total	13,830	19,488	23,348	28,520	30,681	36,202
Percent manual	69.9	69.1	69.3	66.5	66.0	64.2
	Females (in 1000's)					
Nonmanual	949	1,943	3,353	4,756	5,648	8,627
Manual (includes service	3,363	4,327	4,115	5,088	6,419	7,217
Total	4,312	6,270	7,468	9,844	12,067	15,844
Percent manual	78.0	69.0	55.1	51.7	53.2	45.6

[a] Table based on figures in *Historical Statistics of the United States: Colonial Times to the Present* (U.S. Bureau of the Census, Government Printing Office, Washington, D.C., 1960), p. 74.

agers, officials, and proprietors decreased slightly going from 15.1 to 14.6 percent. The clerical ranks also showed a decline, going from 8.4 percent in 1950 to 7.4 in 1969. The increase in the administrative and processing tasks have brought no increase in their relative proportion (this is for the males only). There was also a decline in the percentage of sales employees (6.6 to 5.8 percent). The change, in short, does not involve an increase in the entire nonmanual category; it is restricted to the professional and technical category.

This increase in the proportion of professionals appears to be the result of two nonrecurring developments. The first of these was the formidable growth of the "education industry."[11] This increase resulted from the combination of a commitment to "expanding educational opportunities" and a sizable increase in the numbers of those to be educated. After years of depression and war a very large cohort appeared in 1947, a cohort that first made its impact on the schools in 1952. All school facilities were expanded in response to that "generation" and its immediate successors. Each year brought new demands for academic laborers to handle the task.

In great measure this expansion is now completed, the 1947 generation being second-year graduate students in 1970 (those who were still with the educational enterprise). The smaller generations that followed may easily be "serviced" by the same staff and facilities created to handle the giant 1947 cohort. Beginning in 1961 and continuing through 1969 there was a con-

TABLE 4.2[a]

Nonfarm Occupational Trends: 1950, 1960, and 1969 (Employed Males)

	Year					
	1950		1960		1969	
	N	%	N	%	N	%
White Collar (in 1000's)						
Professional, technical, and kindred	2,696	7.5	4,766	12.0	6,751	14.7
Managers, officials, and proprietors	5,439	15.1	5,968	15.0	6,726	14.6
Clerical and kindred	3,035	8.4	3,145	7.9	3,422	7.4
Sales	2,379	6.6	2,544	6.4	2,675	5.8
Total	13,459	37.7	16,423	41.3	19,574	42.5
Blue Collar, Service						
Craftsmen, foreman, and kindred	7,482	20.8	8,332	21.0	9,854	21.4
Operatives and kindred	8,810	24.5	8,617	21.7	9,883	21.4
Laborers	3,435	9.6	3,471	8.8	3,526	7.6
Private household workers	125	0.3	30	0.1	39	0.1
Service workers	2,560	7.1	2,814	7.1	3,257	7.0
Total	22,412	62.3	23,264	58.7	26,520	57.5

[a] Table based on figures in *The Manpower Report of the President* (Government Printing Office, 1970), p. 225. The 1960 and 1969 figures are for employed males 16 years and over. The 1950 figures are from the 1967 *Manpower Report* (p. 211) and are for males 14 and over.

tinuous decline in the size of the birth cohorts. If the average size of class were to remain constant, this would entail a relative decline of the size of the "industry" in the 1970s. Increased use of "teaching technology," that is, of teaching machines and of television teaching, also would make further growth of the "industry" unlikely.

This particular source of growth in employment is not "inherent" in modern societies. It is not something that a "modern society" has to do or else suffer some severe penalty. Most of the growth took place in state-owned and controlled enterprises and most of the investment, therefore, was dependent on political decisions. These decisions were not forced; they were in no way predestined. That "amount" of education present in the society is not necessary for its adequate functioning. Much of that education, it will be noted, involves attention to literature and the arts, a focus that has only the most minor relevance to the "needs" of the economy or of the society. The provision of extended opportunities for education in the United States has had the consequence of making it the only country in the world with university-educated manual workers, the level of educational accomplishment far outstripping the *necessary* requirements (See Chapter 8 for details).

The second source of this increase in the number and proportion of professionals is the changed character of military services. With the escalation of military technology, there was a need to design and build new plants and to employ different kinds of labor. World War II depended on tanks, trucks, and jeeps—products made largely by manual workers. The new military technology—missiles, supersonic jets, electronic sighting and firing devices, and so on—requires a different kind of labor, principally that of professionals and technicians. *The New York Times*'s advertisements for engineers in the 1960s, for example, were almost all inserted by major "defense" contractors. One source, talking about the presumed shift to a white-collar majority, notes that "At the great Boeing aircraft plants, the ratio of white-collar to blue-collar workers has, in the past fifteen years, reversed itself from 3 to 1 for blue-collar worker over white-collar to 3 to 2 of white-collar over blue-collar."[12]

It will be noted that this determinant of the occupational structure is also dependent on political decisions. It is not an inherent feature of "modern" societies that such decisions be made. It is possible that here, too, the impact may not be a recurrent one. Like the universities, one builds the new plant and adds the new staff. From then on, it is a matter of maintaining the achieved through additions of relatively small numbers of replacements. That effort would not, however, work any major transformation in the character of the labor force.

The further implications of this reading of the evidence are rather important. If the working class is thought to be a minority, one destined to become even smaller and less important, one would be led to emphasize the "rapid change" and the new life conditions of the growing middle-class majority. If the reality involved a persistent working-class majority, then the need would be for a focus on the more or less stable conditions of this population segment.

The "Geography" of Class and its Implications

Since one of the major lines of analysis to be explored is the "social bases" or "group influence" viewpoint, it is useful to inquire as to the structuring of the population, the extent and character of these working-class or middle-class aggregations. Were extensive "class integration" the case, it would be no problem at all for working-class individuals to make contact with middle-class persons and to emulate their behavior. Another possibility—the middle class having contact with working-class people and knowing their wants and outlooks—would also pose no difficulty. Were there serious segregation of the classes, however, a very different development must be anticipated.

Although approximately three-fifths of the United States' nonfarm population is working class, it is obviously unlikely that a 60–40 division will obtain in all parts of the country. Some areas will be well above the 60 percent figure, some will approximate it, while others will be heavily middle class.

American cities do vary considerably in their working-class percentages with the older industrial cities typically being above the average. Taking the 25 largest cities as of 1960, the following proved to be above that average (shown in order of decreasing working-class percentages): Cleveland (73.4); Buffalo (67.7); St. Louis (66.6); Milwaukee (66.5); Detroit (65.8); Chicago (63.0); Baltimore (62.7); Pittsburgh (62.7); Philadelphia (62.5); Boston (61.2); San Antonio (59.8); Memphis 59.7); and Cincinnati (59.4). There are a number of cities below the average: New Orleans (57.7); Minneapolis (55.3); Houston (55.2); San Diego (54.9); New York (54.1); San Francisco (53.4); Washington (52.1); Denver 51.4); Dallas (50.8); and Los Angeles (50.7). Only two fall below the 50 percent level, that is, have a middle-class majority, these being Seattle (49.7) and Atlanta (46.8). A number of these "below average" cities are government or trade centers as in the cases of Washington, New York, and Atlanta. Other "below average" cities are centers of new military production (Houston, San Diego, Denver, Dallas, Los Angeles, and Seattle).

Within the cities there exists a very striking pattern of occupational segregation. The city of Buffalo, admittedly an extreme case, contained 75 census tracts in 1960.[13] Only 14 of these had a nonmanual majority. More than 80 percent of those in 17 of the city's tracts were in manual occupations. Another 10 tracts contained between 75 and 80 percent manual workers. One part of the city, the largest part, approximately 4 miles wide and 6 miles long, contains no tract with a middle-class majority and only 2 (of 38) having less than 60 percent of the population in manual occupations.

There is a convention in Europe to talk of the "working-class quarter" of a city (*quartier, Viertel*). In the case of Buffalo one must talk of the working-class "three-quarters" and the middle-class *quartier*. Even within this latter enclave some of the 14 tracts have relatively high working-class percentages. Between 1950 and 1960 some of these showed a trend toward increasing working-class dominance (one going from 36.1 to 41.4 percent, another from 42.3 to 44.4 percent, and still another from 36.2 to 48.9 percent).

Conventionally, one speaks or thinks about "the suburbs" as being "middle class."[14] This too is misleading. In the case of the city of Buffalo there are middle-class suburbs contiguous to the middle-class tracts of the central city. But, on the other hand, there are working-class suburbs contiguous to all of the working-class areas of the city.[15] Taking the tracts immediately surrounding the city one finds that only 17 of 63 have a middle-class majority.

It proved convenient to carry through the same kind of analysis with respect to the city of Milwaukee. In this case the investigation was considerably more detailed, allowing examination of claims about the differentiations within the working class and about the situation of the presumably more affluent suburban workers.

The city of Milwaukee as of 1960 was the eleventh largest city in the United States.[16] It had shown steady growth in the last 50 years. Part of this growth, however, specifically that of the 1950s, was a result of annexation rather than of birth and in-migration. One peculiarity worth mentioning is that in 1960 Milwaukee had the smallest nonwhite population of the 15 largest cities— 8.9 percent or 65,752 people. Hence, Milwaukee's ghetto was a relatively small one.

The Menomonee River separates Milwaukee into a north and a south side. The river makes a small valley, or trough, that is filled with railroad yards and manufacturing industries. Four long viaducts reach over this valley, but for all practical purposes the two sides are socially quite separate. In the common parlance of Milwaukee, the South Side is the working-class section of the city. It is also described as Polish. The North Side contains the downtown, business and shopping area, running east and west parallel to the Menomonee. Immediately to the north of the downtown is the ghetto or "core" area. The Milwaukee River divides the North Side, providing an eastern "boundary" to the core and separating it from the North Shore lakefront area, the most elegant residential location in the city. To the west and north of the core is a white working-class area. As one proceeds west from the core, there are gradual shifts in the character of the neighborhoods with some tracts having middle-class majorities.

All of the census tracts south of the Menomonee have working-class majorities ($N = 57$). One of these, a lakefront tract, had a slight middle-class majority in 1950 but that changed in the intervening decade.

There were 6 tracts with a middle-class majority in the North Side lakefront area, which contains large old houses, expensive apartments, and the University of Wisconsin's Milwaukee campus. On the western edge of the city, as mentioned, adjacent to suburban Wauwatosa, there were 15 tracts with a middle-class majority. All other tracts in the city had working-class majorities. There were, in short, only 21 middle-class tracts out of a total of 189. In this case one is not justified in referring to a middle-class *quartier*; the two enclaves together do not make up even an eighth of the tracts.

A person traveling through the city from north to south would go almost 12 miles without ever passing through a tract with a middle-class majority. This working-class cluster is approximately 3 miles wide. Within this large rectangular area, toward its center, is an even heavier working-class concentration. Here, in an area approximately 6 miles long and 2½ miles wide, are tracts in which at least three-quarters of the employed males are engaged in manual occupations.

It would be a mistake to exaggerate the "sameness" of these working-class persons and their families since there are numerous sources of differentiation. The area contains the black ghetto to the north and a white Polish-American working class to the south. There are a wide range of other nationalities present within the area. There are differences in skill levels and in the type of industry predominating. There are also, as we shall see, some important age or generational differences present.

It would also be a mistake to assume any fixity about the above picture. The above portrayal, drawn from the census materials, merely catches the development, or rather drift, as of the 1960 census date. A comparison with the 1950 census allows some sense of the trend.

There are, as indicated, two middle-class enclaves within the city—one the "best area" and the other consisting of the not-so-attractive tracts on one part of the western edge of the city. Little change appeared in the former area during the decade covered by the census. At last as indicated by the census materials, the tracts maintained approximately the same social composition in 1960 as in 1950.

The western tracts, by comparison, show signs of a major transformation. Basically, three population shifts appear to be in process. Black working-class families moved out from the 1950 core area into the immediately adjacent tracts. White working-class families appear to have moved out of these adjacent tracts into the middle-class tracts further to the west. And the middle-class families from these tracts appear to have been moving out of the city, possibly to suburban Wauwatosa. Taking one cluster of 11 tracts that were middle class in 1950, one finds only 7 still with nonmanual majorities in 1960 and some of these were at the point of transition. Three of the remaining 7, for example, were less than one percentage point away from a manual majority in 1960. One of the middle-class enclaves in short, is in process of disappearing, giving way to working-class occupants.

One may dismiss with relative ease the experience of the central cities. It is well known that they are losing their middle-class populations. It is in the "middle-class suburb" that the great modern drama is occurring, where "the blue-collar worker learns to behave more like his white-collar colleague . . ."[17]

The Milwaukee pattern, however, is a direct parallel to the Buffalo experience. The areas of the urban ring match the central city areas in social composition. For Milwaukee that means that the North Shore is elegant and upper-middle class, matching the North Shore tracts of the city. This area contains the "best" suburbs: Shorewood, Whitefish Bay, Fox Point, Bayside, and River Hills. In these communities one finds the highest nonmanual concentrations of the entire county; the lakefront tract of Fox Point, for example, is 97.1 percent nonmanual.

Adjacent to the city's west side middle-class enclave is middle-class suburban Wauwatosa. Although middle class in its majority, this city does have a significant manual minority. Approximately one-third of the employed men are in blue-collar occupations. For all practical purposes, this community provides *the* center of significant class mixing.

These communities, with four other tracts, form *the* middle-class suburban areas. All other areas in the surrounding urban ring have working-class majorities. Here too, in short, working-class suburbs or industrial satellite cities dominate in the surrounding territory.

Most of the city's blue-collar workers obviously live in neighborhoods with other blue-collar workers. Typically, between three and four of every five neighbors would be blue-collar families. Children who are born and raised in these areas will attend school with working-class children. Their friends and later co-workers will, overwhelmingly, be from other blue-collar families. As far as *personal* contacts and influences are concerned, the structure of the city is such as to almost guarantee exclusive patterns of association.

The chances of persons from such a working-class milieu entering into either of the two middle-class enclaves are rather small. The occasions for contact with persons in those settings, occasions where workers could "see" middle-class people and learn their ways are going to be few and far between. The person born and raised in the central city's working-class "rectangle" is in a context where "*the* middle class" can provide only a very far-distant model. One of the consequences of "urbanization" is that the distance between the working class and "the middle class" becomes ever greater. The opportunities for gaining detailed and accurate information about the other's outlook become ever smaller.

The image of the "middle-class suburb" as the "great new 'melting pot' " is clearly inadequate. There are not enough "middle-class suburbs" to allow the assimilation of any significant portion of the blue-collar ranks. If large numbers of blue-collar families were to enter the middle-class suburbs, they would no longer be middle class in their majority. As it happens, most of the working-class suburbanites are located in working-class suburbs. The dominant orientations there, as indicated by one leading study on the subject, are quite different from those in the middle-class suburbs.[18] In fact, as we shall see later, the orientations found there bear a striking resemblance to those found in the working-class neighborhoods of the central city.

Although there have been attempts to refocus attention and show the widespread presence of such communities, the tendency has been to consider "working-class suburbs" as somewhat bizarre, a new and peculiar exception to the rule of middle-class communities. The older, conventional, and inaccurate image persists because intellectuals, teachers, and university students come from the upper-middle-class enclaves and make the assumption that their experience "is" the suburban world. The major routes they take into the city rarely show them any other part of the city.

It is necessary to guard against some frequent misconceptions. When one uses the term "working class" it is easy to conjure up a picture of densely populated slums, of tenement houses, of people sitting on the front steps on hot summer nights. In addition to the visual images it is also easy to assume that a corresponding consciousness will also be present.

The data presented in this chapter show nothing at all about consciousness.

Such concerns will be discussed in a later context and with different research materials. As for the visual image, the following corrective observations ought to be considered. Beginning at the Menomonee and proceeding southward we have the following developments. In the tracts bordering immediately on the valley, the most frequent types of housing unit are single and double detached dwellings. These types of housing are the most frequent everywhere on the South Side; the only significant differentiation being in the frequency of the single family unit. Roughly a third (35.1 percent) of these units are owner-occupied. The median estimated values of the owner-occupied dwellings in this row of tracts is well below the citywide median. In two of these, the figure falls below $10,000 whereas the citywide figure is $15,100. The rentals in the area are all below the city median.

Somewhat farther to the south the proportion of single-family units increases but double units are still the most frequent. About half of the homes here are owner occupied (49.2). The value of those homes is not especially high. Rents are again all below the citywide median.

A few miles further to the south we have another "row" of tracts that again show the gradual transformations that occur as one moves out from the center of the city. These tracts, overwhelmingly, contain single-family dwelling units. The rate of owner occupancy runs to 76.1 percent of all occupied units. The average home values here are equal to or slightly exceed the citywide median figure. The rentals all exceed the citywide medians. Unlike the former two "rows" of tracts, which had relatively high vacancy rates (5.2 and 4.0 percent), these homes are nearly all occupied, only 1.1 percent being vacant.

Still further to the south we find tracts that have a "suburban" appearance and that are heavily working class. One such tract is over 70 percent working class and consists largely of single-family dwelling units (88.8 percent). Approximately two-thirds of these were owner-occupied. Another similar tract, this one over 75 percent working class in 1960, was situated just outside the city limits. About 89.4 percent of the housing there consisted of single-family dwelling units and 77.7 percent of the units were owner-occupied.

One other point to be noted about this working-class suburban tract is the high percentage of automobile ownership; 71.4 percent of the homes had one auto in 1960, 15.2 percent had two or more, and only 13.4 percent had no car. The majority of the employed population report that they go to work either with their own car or travel in a car pool.

Rather than thinking of tenements, at least for this part of the working class, one must think of detached frame houses, of flats or duplexes, and of single units. The flats and duplexes are in the older part of the area, the single units in the newly developed areas. Where flats or duplexes predominate, the highest effective ownership rate ordinarily would be 50 percent; hence, the 35 percent rate in the first row of tracts ought to be viewed as a relatively high figure.

Since so much is said about the "new" suburban workers, it is useful to discuss the contrast with the "old" central-city worker in more detail. For this purpose we took one tract at the edge of the Menomonee and the briefly mentioned working-class suburban tract. Both are predominantly (i.e. 75 percent or more) working class. Less than one-fourth of the homes in the former tract are owner-occupied while the latter has more than three-quarters. In the former area about 11 percent of the units are deteriorating or dilapidated while in the suburban tract only a fraction of a percent are so described. In the former area, 36 percent of the families have no automobile as compared to only 13 percent of the families in the suburb.

The size of the houses are approximately the same in both areas, the median being 5.1 rooms in the center-city tract and 5.0 in the suburb. This means, in effect, that they have a kitchen, dining and living room, and two bedrooms plus bath as the basic housing unit.

The median family income in the city tract was $6797 in 1959 whereas in the suburban tract it was $7169. There is, effectively, very little difference in the income of the central-city and suburban working classes. Here it would amount to $372 per year or about $7 per week. If we were comparing renters, that seven dollars would go for the higher rent. The higher income must also be taken up in transportation costs; the absence of public transportation means that they have to pay the higher charges involved in automobile ownership.

In summary, comparing the suburban and central-city workers as best we can with aggregate census data, it would appear that they have much the same size houses; the one owns, the other rents. One house is new, the other is more than 30 years old and in a neighborhood having a fair amount of run down property. The suburban worker is not especially affluent. What advantage he has (by being skilled as opposed to semiskilled) is taken up in the extra added charges of suburban "living." In addition to the higher mortgage (or rental) charges and the increased costs of transportation, one should also consider the enhanced costs of lawn care.

It is difficult to give any definitive answer to the claim about working class and middle class "looking alike" when away from the job.[19] The middle-class suburban tracts characteristically contain higher income families and homes with higher median values than do the suburban working-class areas. There are a number of other details that make clear that the "looking alike" thesis is rather exaggerated. In the suburban working-class tract where, as noted, nearly 90 percent of the homes are owner-occupied, we find the following elements: Interstate Highway 94 cuts through the district; the Chicago, Milwaukee, St. Paul, and Pacific Railroad also cuts it; the Howard Avenue Water Purification Plant is located on one corner of the tract; touching another corner is Mitchell Field, the city's airport. A major runway points directly at this area of working-class suburbia. Although the individual houses may look like houses elsewhere, the overall "tone" of the area is obviously very different from that of middle-class suburbia.

That is the South Side working class. On the North Side, particularly in the case of the Negro working class, the housing fits with the more classical images of the proletariat. Even here, however, this is the case only within the tracts of the old 1940 ghetto. There one finds the multiple dwelling units. The breakout from that area brought Negroes into the more typical single- and double-unit housing of the city and made fairly high levels of ownership possible on the margins of the ghetto area. The median value of owner-occupied units are all far below the citywide median. The median rentals at the center of the ghetto are below the city median (as is also the median size of the units); on the edges of the ghetto the rentals are equal to the city median. A little more than one-third of the units in the area are described as dilapidated or deteriorating, the highest level for any area of the city. Here, again, the most deteriorated sections are the old ghetto areas with the condition improving somewhat toward the periphery. In the center of the ghetto the decaying proportion in one tract was 70 percent, the general experience being at least half. In the peripheral areas, the percentage falls to approximately 15 percent. Although the housing units are of approximately the same size as those of workers on the South Side, it is clear that one pays more for the average rental property and one receives lower-quality housing for this greater payment. It is obvious that in basic life conditions the situation of Negro and white working-class families are worlds apart.

One other point deserves consideration, given the widespread fantasies about Negro automobile ownership. Just under half, or 45 percent, of the occupied units reported that the family did not own an autombile. Ownership was lowest in the poorest tracts in the center ghetto. The percentage of families owning cars on the periphery of the ghetto was also low relative to other working-class areas. In the *relatively* high-income (all ghetto tracts are more than $1000 below the city median family income) tracts on the periphery of the ghetto we still find about a third of the homes lacking an automobile. There was some complaint in these areas about the inadequacy of public transportation.

From one perspective it might be claimed that the boundaries of the ghetto are breaking down. The Negro population did "break out" of the seven-tract area in which most lived in 1940. In another respect, however, it is more realistic to note that it is merely a question of the boundaries having expanded without any serious integration having occurred. One very striking characteristic of the ghetto tracts is the very low median age of the population. Separate consideration of Negroes and whites shows the median age of the latter to be well above the citywide median. The whites in the "integrated" districts are elderly persons who may merely lack the money needed for a move. In other words, even this minimal degree of integration bodes ill for the future. When these older whites die it seems unlikely that they will be replaced by other whites.[20]

It is worthwhile reconsidering some of the basic claims made about class structure in the United States in the light of this picture of working-class predominance. In a previous chapter we considered the discussions of the "lower-middle class," of the economically depressed clerical and sales workers. The basic image, it was noted, involves a group having middle-class origins, who sense a loss of status and feel they have "come down" in the world. A frequent correlated argument is that the skilled workers have "come up" in the world, are living in middle-class neighborhoods, are associating as equals and so forth.

We have examined the residential locations of some of the occupational categories so as to ascertain the proportion living in areas of different working-class concentration. Looking first at these craftsmen living in the central city, one finds little support for this "mixing in neighborhoods" claim. Less than one skilled worker in ten lives in a tract with a middle-class majority. By comparison, nearly three-tenths of them live in tracts that are 75 percent or more working class. By a rough rule-of-thumb estimate we may suggest that three-fifths of the city's skilled workers live in tracts where two out of three neighbors are engaged in working-class occupations. (See Table 4.3.) Seen

TABLE 4.3
Distribution of Selected Occupations in Milwaukee and Suburbs (1960, Males)

	Working-Class Percentage in Tract[a]					
	75% or More	70–74.9%	65–69.9%	50–64.9%	Less Than 50%	N
Central City						
Professionals	13.0%	6.9%	20.9%	35.9%	23.2%	(18.457)
Managers, etc.	15.0	6.2	19.1	34.0	25.7	(14,765)
Sales	16.4	7.2	18.2	33.5	24.7	(12,080)
Clericals	25.4	10.3	20.5	30.3	13.4	(16,718)
Craftsmen	28.6	10.4	23.2	28.1	9.6	(43,510)
Urban Ring						
Professionals	3.1	7.2	13.4	13.3	63.0	(12,668)
Managers, etc.	3.2	4.8	9.4	12.2	70.3	(10,867)
Sales	2.8	6.3	10.2	12.8	68.0	(7,659)
Clericals	6.0	13.3	21.5	16.9	42.3	(5,903)
Craftsmen	10.2	16.7	25.4	19.5	28.1	(17,531)

[a] Percentages add across to 100.

from the perspective of the "group-bases" theory of mass politics, this would suggest that the skilled workers are still very much "embedded" in the working-class milieu and subject to its influences.

In the surrounding urban ring there is a greater degree of integration.

About three-tenths of the skilled in this context are found in areas having middle-class majorities. At the same time it ought to be noted that less than one skilled worker in three lives in the "ring" and also that half of those in this area live in tracts that are 65 percent or more working class.

One further point about the skilled: the census category is "Craftsmen, foremen, and kindred." Roughly 15 percent of the category consists of foremen and they, in turn, earn roughly $1000 more than do skilled workers. They are, moreover, increasingly drawn from among those of middle-class background. It is frequently used as a step in the executive career line rather than a terminal reward for the manual workers. It seems likely that it would be the foremen who are living in the middle-class areas and the skilled who are in the working-class areas.[21] Thus, the possibilities for contact and for direct knowledge of upper-middle-class life are not frequent for this latter group of the economically best-off workers.

It will be noted that there is a "middle-class" minority present in all of the working-class districts of the central city. Obviously if one added each of these minorities together we would find a fair proportion of the clerical workers living in working-class areas. Within the central city, as it turns out, only about one clerical worker in eight lived in a middle-class tract. The overall distribution of the clerical workers was not much different from that of the craftsmen. Over half of them live in districts in which two-thirds of their neighbors are in manual occupations. Even in the case of the "higher-status" nonmanual categories we still find only a small minority, approximately one in four, living in middle-class districts. Again, we find fairly large proportions of these categories living in districts with fair-sized working-class majorities.

It will be remembered that the "manager" category is a mixed one. It seems likely that most of those in this category who live in working-class tracts are proprietors, that is, the owners of small retail establishments. The presence of professionals in these districts appears at first to be somewhat more difficult to account for. Most people hearing the word professional think "doctor, lawyer." The census category, however, is much broader. It seems likely that the professionals in working-class districts are low status professionals—draftsmen, marginal lawyers, some teachers, medical and dental technicians, and probably also some clergy. It seems likely that their situation would be very similar to that of clerical employees living in working-class districts.

The picture in the urban ring is more familiar. Here one finds majorities of the professionals, managers, and the sales categories living in middle-class areas. The segregation of the classes is indicated by the fact that about 70 percent of the managers live in such areas in contrast to only 28 percent of the skilled workers. Once again the clericals occupy an equivocal position. A majority of those in the ring live in working-class areas. To be sure, the minority living in the middle-class tracts is considerably larger than in the central city. It seems likely that these segments of the white-collar category differ in terms of their backgrounds. Those who live in the middle-class areas are likely to come from middle-class families originally. Those who live in areas with working-class majorities are likely to come from working-class, or possibly farm, backgrounds. It also seems likely that they are in different kinds of white-collar jobs.

In 1960 the city contained roughly twice as many women clerical workers as men. Looking at their residential locations, one finds a pattern that is very similar to that of the men clericals. In this case just over half (52.1 percent) live in districts that are at least 65 percent manual. Only 16.3 percent of the women clerical workers live in middle-class tracts. The women sales workers also have a similar pattern; 56.1 percent live in districts that are 65 percent or more manual and only 16 percent live in middle-class tracts. In the suburban ring, the pattern for the women clerical workers is very similar to that of the men (shown in Table 4.3). The pattern for the women sales workers is somewhat different in that a majority of them live in working-class districts. Only 47.3 percent, as compared to 68.0 for the men, live in middle-class districts.

Obviously, in many of these cases, the husband is likely to be in a working-class occupation. One might hypothesize that such families will exhibit "status strains" or that they will suffer from the tribulations imposed upon them by being "status inconsistents." The matter can not be solved by speculation, however, and will, therefore, be considered in our analysis in the next chapter.

One can only speculate about the future developments. In the 1950s and 1960s the upper-middle-class made its exodus from the central city. For all practical purposes, this exodus is now complete. In the course of the move out, given the haste involved, much of the settlement proved to be rather chaotic. In the initial exodus, a fair amount of mixing of populations occurred in various border tracts. Populations moved into fringe areas that had no planning and no zoning with the result that trailer parks and suburban bungalows came to be located alongside the drive-in theaters and the hot dog stands.

It seems likely that future decades will involve a "sorting out" of populations and consolidations of the emerging patterns. There will probably be more struggles to "establish the character of" areas as well as resistance to such attempts. Where upper-middle-class groups "win out," that is, where they establish strict zoning, take over the school boards, and upgrade the schools, the areas will no longer be "livable" for many blue-collar workers. As the school taxes increase and as the free-and-easy and relatively low-cost conditions disappear, the life there will become less and less congenial for them. Where the upgrading effort loses, the incentives will be for the white-collar families, particularly those of the upper-middle class, to move out. This suggests that there will be a fair amount of exchange of populations among the suburban communities, an exchange that will result in a "sorting out," or a more systematic segregation of the occupations than existed even in 1960. The future development will consist less of a "filling up" of previously vacant areas and will involve more of a mutual displacement of populations.

At this point we may introduce for consideration an alternative reading of the psychology of the "lower-middle class," that segment of the nonmanuals who live in working-class districts. It seems likely that many of them issue from working-class families, and that they went to school with working-class children. It seems likely that they continue to see and associate with them informally in these working-class neighborhoods. These blue-collar workers are, after all, their lifetime friends and/or kinsmen. These white-collar workers do not, one may guess, aspire to "middle-class status" (by which is meant actually *upper*-middle class) but rather work out a life that is little different from that of the others in the neighborhood. It would probably be extremely difficult, not to say unpleasant, were they to begin behaving differently; the penalty would be a severance of informal relationships and sanctions for any such attempts to "put on airs."[22] It seems unlikely that there would be much incentive or much personal interest in changing behavior and emulating the upper-middle class. These lower white-collar workers have learned the values of the immediate milieu during their entire lifetimes. The values of the upper-middle class are husbanded and cared for in enclaves that are far distant from their home base.

Still another consideration enters in here: these white-collar groups are not too well-off economically. They earn less than skilled workers, hence, would not be in a position to maintain upper-middle-class standards. In fact, they are not likely to be dominant in the social hierarchies of their own working-class neighborhoods. This is to suggest that they are not models for the manual workers in the neighborhood and also that they do not consider themselves to be such. Some evidence of relevance has appeared in survey materials. Americans, when asked what they would prefer for their sons—a skilled-workers job at $100 a week or a white-collar desk job at $75 a week—showed an overwhelming preference for the former.[23] The lower the educational level, the more likely were they to prefer the skilled job. The white-collar job may well be seen as a soft touch, as not deserving equivalent pay. There appears to be some tendency to define such jobs as "woman's work." There is some reason to believe that many of the occupants of such jobs are older persons, those who have retired from the rigors of semiskilled jobs on the production line. This would again make it unlikely that they have any high prestige accorded them by others or that they themselves have any high pretensions.

The aggregate census materials do not allow us to explore this matter further. In a later context we will consider some of these questions with the use of survey data.

Are we misrepresenting the picture of working-class domination by focusing on Milwaukee County? That is, are we leaving out some middle-class areas by omitting consideration of outlying counties?

To the north of Milwaukee County lies Ozaukee County, to the west is Waukesha, and to the south is Racine. The respective working-class percentages are 58.1, 65.9, and 65.9. Further south, beyond industrial Racine lies industrial Kenosha with manual workers accounting for 72.2 percent of the population.

Looking at this from a still larger perspective, we have to go beyond the Milwaukee area. There are two other cities with more than 50,000 population in Wisconsin that have not yet been mentioned. The first is Green Bay, a manufacturing center, with a manual population of 61.2 (the county 60.0). The second is Madison, the state capital. There is some manufacturing in this city, but even more important are the administrative offices of the state, the head offices of insurance companies and of numerous voluntary organizations, and the presence of the state university. This means that the working-class percentage in this case is relatively low, in fact, it is well below the 50 percent mark with 44.8 percent. The city's manual percentage is even below that of the county which is 47.7 percent. The city of Madison, it should be noted, is essentially two cities with manufacturing operations and populations living on the East Side, their children going to East High and the professionals on the West Side, their children going to West High.[24]

This "exception" in the case of Madison points to another kind of segregation on the American scene. Not only are the classes segregated within cities but also, to some extent, there is a segregation between cities with high-status occupations clustering in select administrative centers and workers clustering in manufacturing communities.[25] Increasing use of computerized administration makes it possible for more and more of the upper-middle class to remove from center cities and to establish in outlying high-status, administrative, and professional communities. This again has the consequence of removing high-status, upper-middle-class models from working-class and lower-middle-class life. Again, in this second way, we see a gradual "building in" and institutionalization of class segregation in modern society.

Thus far, we have focused mainly on "big city" workers, that is, on class in the metropolis. This makes a standard, although unwarranted, assumption about class that deserves further consideration. Looking at the pattern by city size, we find that the percentage of manual workers *increases* in the smaller communities. (See Table 4.4.) A correlated tendency (not shown in the table) involves the percentage of proprietors which also increases in the smaller communities. It is the managers and officials who are present in the larger cities.

In the large cities, then, we have working-class populations concentrated in the central cities and, for the most part, one finds "new middle-class" salaried employees in the upper-middle-class suburbs. The small towns and villages have larger working-class components, disproportionately operatives and laborers. To the extent that classes mix in these communities, the workers there come together with old middle-class populations, with independent

TABLE 4.4
Occupations of Nonfarm Males by Size of City[a]

| | Urbanized Areas of | | | | | Places Outside Urbanized Areas | | | |
	3,000,000 or More	1,000,000– 3,000,000	250,000– 1,000,000	Less Than 250,000	25,000 or More	10,000– 25,000	2,500– 10,000	Rural Nonfarm
Professional	13.3	14.0	12.8	11.9	12.3	11.6	10.6	8.1
Managers, officials, and proprietors	12.1	11.4	12.7	12.7	12.9	13.3	13.4	10.0
Sales	8.3	8.3	9.0	8.6	8.4	7.9	7.4	5.2
Clericals	10.1	9.9	8.8	7.8	7.2	6.6	6.0	4.7
Craftsmen	20.7	21.5	21.8	21.4	20.8	20.9	21.6	23.1
Operatives	20.9	19.4	19.5	21.3	21.4	21.9	22.7	25.4
Service	8.1	7.4	7.1	7.5	7.8	7.3	9.3	4.6
Laborers	5.7	7.2	7.1	7.3	7.3	7.8	8.0	9.5
Percent manual	55.4	55.5	55.5	57.5	57.3	57.9	67.6	62.6

[a] Source. 1960 Census, Size of Place, p. 1; V. III, selected area reports, PC(3)-1B.

proprietors. The central city workers are in trade unions and to some extent have their own indigenous class leadership. In the small towns, they tend to be non-union and dependent on the local provincial middle-class leadership.

One other point must be added to this picture. In general, the *average* socioeconomic status of large city suburbs is higher than that of the central cities. Most people talking of suburbs have a picture in mind of the elegant New York, Chicago, Cleveland, or Philadelphia suburbs, which stand in sharp contrast to the blighted city. In the case of the smaller cities, however, the reverse tends to be the case. This is particularly the case in urbanized areas of 250,000 or less. Specifically, this means that the percentage of those engaged in white-collar occupations is higher in these central cities than in the surrounding suburban areas.[26] This finding, in turn, proves to be linked to the age of the central city. Basically, in the United States, it would appear that the upper-middle classes make and destroy a city. In the course of time, they abandon it for the suburbs and, in effect, turn the city over to manual populations. In the beginning of cities, the working class tends to live outside, in fringe areas or to commute from farms. In the course of what is mistakenly called "development," they trade places. Once the city becomes unlivable, the upper-middle class moves to the fringe areas, displacing the workers there, and leaves the city to the new recruits from the farm.

In terms of the social influences and social pressures—in terms of the social determinants of political attitudes—it is important to note that a sizable portion of the working class does not live in large cities but lives on the edges of middle-sized cities or in small towns. This means that in great measure they are located in a setting that shields them from the influences resulting from continuous contact with other workers. It is this that, as we shall see, makes a major contribution to the "moderation" of working-class outlooks.

Some of these workers live in thinly populated fringe areas and some live on back roads in rural communities. For all practical purposes these are isolated families having no contact with their "community." They work outside it; their trip to work does not take them into "their" community. They shop at "centers" somewhere outside the community and they are not integrated into voluntary associations there. Their contacts with the outside world prove to be essentially with people in the factory and with those persons they see on television. Hence, although many of these workers are "small town" or village workers, they show traits that reflect the influences of somewhat larger communities. In a sense, they "skip over" their community of residence, avoiding contact there (or perhaps more precisely, being avoided), and rather loosely integrating into a part, at least, of the middle-size city milieu.[27]

What is the significance of this dissociation of classes? One consequence is immediately clear. Children of workers in the huge working-class enclaves associate with children of workers; their peer influences overwhelmingly reflect that background and there is little or nothing immediately and directly present in the way of alternative values that would be able to make an impact in this setting. This statement clearly assumes that there are differences in value orientations; the evidence already "in the record" supports this view.

It is known that the classes differ in their levels of educational aspiration. Recent studies have shown that these differences are reinforced by influences within the neighborhood and the schools. A study by Alan Wilson, for example, of high school boys in thirteen high schools in the San Francisco-Oakland Bay area found support for the proposition "that the aspirations of the bulk of the students in a high school district provide a significant normative reference influencing the educational aspirations of boys from varying strata . . . ." The author summarizes his findings as follows: "The *de facto* segregation brought about by concentrations of social classes in cities results in schools with unequal moral climates which . . . affect the motivation of the child, not necessarily by inculcating a sense of inferiority, but rather by providing a different ethos in which to perceive values."[28]

This article also provides support for some of the claims we have made with respect to Milwaukee. Wilson divided the schools into three groups in terms of the socioeconomic status of the families "served." In the lowest-level schools, there are some children of professionals, some white-collar employees (including "executives"), and some self-employed. He shows that the non-manual parents in the low-status neighborhood are obviously quite different from their occupational peers in the high-status neighborhoods. The percentage of "white-collar" parents, for example, having at least some college falls off from 65 to 47 and finally to 20 in the lowest-level schools.

It is also obvious that the working-class "deviant cases" are quite different from the others in their class. We find, for example, that 50 percent of the manual children in the "best" schools consider themselves to be Republicans as opposed to only 24 percent in what was called the "C" group. Only 36 percent of the white-collar children in the "C" schools, by contrast, consider themselves Republicans as opposed to 72 percent in the "A" group.

Wilson does an excellent job in controlling for detailed occupation and for parents' education, a procedure that still suggests that residential segregation has an impressive impact. One consideration not pointed out is that there appear to be subcultures operating within the schools. The children of non-manuals in the working-class high schools, although their level of college aspiration is lower than nonmanual children elsewhere, still show aspirations that are higher than those shown by the children of manual parents. The children of semiskilled and unskilled manual worker families who attend the elite high schools (only 15 cases out of a total of 373), by comparison, show a level of aspiration that is just as low as that of equivalent children in the "C" schools. At least some of the middle-class children who attend the working-class schools would appear to "keep their distance" so as to protect their special value orientations.[29] The children of poorer manual families who happen to be located in the "best" schools appear to be outcasts, so far out, in fact, that they assimilate nothing of the dominant aspirations of the milieu.

The article, unfortunately, does not indicate what colleges are considered in their plans. Attendance at "good colleges" obviously would provide the means for gaining or maintaining a middle-class position. A milieu-induced trip to poorer colleges (to junior colleges, and so on) might provide the base for, at best, a lower-middle class position (and housing within a working-class majority area) or, should one drop out in the process, for a job in the working class.[30]

Another study points in the same direction. This one is based on questions addressed to Milwaukee County seniors, both males and females.[31] The high schools were divided into low, middle, and high on the basis of the "proportion of males fourteen years and older living in the area who are employed in white-collar occupations." The "high" neighborhods are the "four high status suburbs located on the northern and western borders of the city and two high status neighborhoods adjacent to them but within the city limits of Milwaukee." Both the latter proved to be West Side schools. The Lake Shore high schools serve mixed populations including children of the North Side working class.

Whether one came from a "low" or "middle" neighborhood made little difference in the aspirations; the key difference was associated with residence in the "high"-status neighborhoods. Children from low and middle socio-economic status families appear to have had their interest in college increased by being located within this high-status context. This comes through clearly and consistently in 18 detailed comparisons (which included a control for intelligence). Being in a "middle"-status school appears to have little impact as compared to being in "low" schools. There are, in fact, 6 clear reversals among the 18 comparisons of low- and middle-level schools, and in 4 other cases there is essentially no difference.[32]

Both of the central-city schools classed as "high status" are serving an area which, as we have seen, is undergoing transformation—the West Side. Hence, the salubrious impact of the higher-status children in those schools is, at the time of this writing, largely a thing of the past.

On the whole, among the males, just over three-fifths in the high-status schools intend to go to college. In the other contexts, only one-third intend to go. It is clear that there was a large dropout before achieving senior class status (and thereby being represented in this sample), hence these results if anything understate the impact of the varying contexts. Among the girls, the pattern is even more striking with just over half of those in the high-status context intending to go to college and only a fifth of those elsewhere intending to do so. This report also, unfortunately, makes no mention of the kinds of universities or colleges in which they intend to enroll.

Once again, there is evidence that the context is not all-determining. The high-status families in the low-status neighborhoods can, with some degree of success overcome the impact of that milieu. It is the children of high-status parents in this context who have the highest percentage indicating college aspirations. More of them indicate college aspirations, for example, than do the children of low-status parents in high-status neighborhoods. This suggests that the former voluntarily segregate themselves from their low-status milieu. The children of low-status parents in the high-status schools are probably segregated by the others in the milieu. . . . The experience of the high-status child in the low-status school must be gratifying for the ego; the opposite case, that of the low-status individual in the high-status school, must be a shattering, ego-destroying experience.

It is clear from these findings that most of the schools within the city of Milwaukee do little to outfit their "clientele" for anything except a continuation of the family's current class position. A comparison of the sex ratios in the three contexts, for example, makes clear that many of the males are already out of those middle- and low-status schools and, therefore, on their way to semiskilled jobs. As noted, only a third have been motivated to go on to college and they are primarily the children of the higher-status families. The net long-term impact then would appear to be that the school aids in the "sorting out" process—it gives (or in the conventional formulation, it "provides opportunity") to the children of the remaining middle-class families a means for escape from that milieu. Such a school context must give them an enormous benefit in the form of a very high class ranking, a benefit that must help in gaining admission to desirable colleges.

To be sure, one-fifth of the low socioeconomic status males in the low- and middle-status schools intend to go on to college. What colleges they attend, how far they get, and what happens to them subsequently are as yet unstudied topics. Some of this "interest" must be pure fantasy. For example, 13 percent of the males from low-status families and in low-status schools and who have the additional disadvantage of low intelligence say they intend going on to college. A real difference in aspirations and in likely chances for carrying through does occur in the case of children from families of skilled workers who happen to be located in the high-status schools. Their experience, however, gives little ground for optimism (should one accept the implicit liberal values) given the small number of such schools and the small number of such children in them. Only a very small number of working-class children can be fitted into such a context without changing its character and thus losing the presumed benefit.

Still another study offers confirmation of the above findings. This is based on questionnaire results from students in 500 public high schools in 1955. The study finds a persistent impact made by the "high school climate" in the same directions as those noted previously. The children of low-status families show "some benefit" from the high-status milieu. Interestingly enough, the enhanced educational aspirations are found primarily within the highest socioeconomic status settings, a develpment that again parallels the experience of the Milwaukee area. This study also found that the children of high-status families are relatively well able to resist the impact of a "low-status" milieu.[33]

The implications of class segregation in city and suburb come through in more detail in James Coleman's study of school climates. He notes that the "leading crowds" in most schools are of higher status families than average. This is particularly the case in schools having a white-collar clientele. On the other hand, discussing the experience of a working-class suburb located outside Chicago, he reports:

> The boys and girls from lower-class backgrounds tend to "take over". . . . [In Newlawn] they . . . reverse the tendency toward middle-class control, leaving those few middle-class students outside the leading crowd.
>
> The implications of this result are important. The leading crowd of a school, and thus the norms which that crowd sets, is more than merely a reflection of the student body. . . . The leading crowd tends to accentuate those very background characteristics already dominant, whether they be upper- or lower-class.[34]

The impact of this alternative leadership, of these working-class models, is markedly different from the experience in middle-class high schools. Car ownership is linked to membership in high school "elites" in all ten schools studied. Elites in high-status schools use their cars for transportation, to go on dates, and so on. Generally speaking, in all the schools it was the outsiders who were "interested in cars" per se. But in Newlawn, it was dominant lower-status "elites" for whom "being up on cars [was] important." As Coleman puts it, "some adolescent cultures are *themselves* focused around cars."

In contrast to the concern with cars and the stress on athletics, the social rewards for the scholar in Newtown were "very meager." "In absolute quantity," Coleman reports, the scholar's "prestige is lower than in any other school." Even the scholars in this setting, moreover, are different from those elsewhere: the percentage of frequent users of the mass media among them is second highest of the ten schools studied. The media attention of Newlawn scholars is also higher than the rate among the nonscholars (a reversal that appears only in Newlawn and in working-class Elmtown). The average grades of the boys in this school are lowest of the ten studied and, using another measure of performance, it turns out that the best grades tend not to be made by the most qualified students. That is to say, the milieu is not such as to stimulate high performance on the part of those with high ability. Regardless of the educational level of the father, the boys in Newlawn put in less time studying than do boys in four other equivalent city schools and, again regardless of father's education, the Newlawn boys have the lowest educational aspirations. As in the previously discussed studies, it is the boys whose fathers had higher educational accomplishment who intend to go to college, which again shows that the school is a means for further segregation and for sorting out the population.

Controlling for the level of the father's education, Coleman also shows that, with one exception, the boys in elite Executive Heights High School have higher percentages of college aspirants than in four equivalent schools. The one exception occurs in the case of children whose fathers had only a grade school education. Again it appears that the low-status students in the high-status schools are crushed by the experience.

Summarizing his findings, Coleman says that in general

> . . . the [high school] elites contained more sons and daughters from the higher-status segments of the community. Beyond this, however, there was a tendency for the elites to be like the student body in their characteristics. In the elites of the more working-class schools, the middle-class bias was either reduced or vanished altogether. Consequently, the backgrounds *and* the interests come to be closer to the rest of the school, more infused with out-of-school concerns.

In much of the sociological literature the factors involved in this low level of academic achievement are somewhat obscure. Most frequently mentioned are parental stimulation and, increasingly, the role of peer group pressures. In great measure these concerns omit the most obvious consideration, that is, the differing impact of the schools themselves. Without going into the matter in any detail, the relationship appears to be a very simple one. Schools, particularly those in working-class areas, do a very poor job in the teaching of reading. The reasons are that the schools serving the working class and the poor have larger classes, have less qualified and less experienced teachers, and, relative to the upper-middle-class schools, are lacking facilities.[35]

The result is that these children get further and further behind their grade level, although, to protect the schools from embarrassing evidence of *their* failure, the children are promoted nonetheless. The students must, in great part, sit there not knowing what is happening and not understanding it. School for them becomes a continuous insoluble mystery and a constant humiliation, especially since it is obvious that there are some who can and do pierce through the mystery. To the extent that the school is merely holding on or retaining those who do not understand the materials, it is obvious that the task of the school has shifted from educational aims to custodial ones. It is not too surprising that the "inmates" react by engaging in diversionary entertainments, many of them directed at their tormenters.

Part of this educational procedure is justified and supported by the teachers and administrators under the cover of a so-called readiness ideology. This holds that people have natural maturation processes and natural top levels of development. The teacher is there to work with the children when (and if) they mature. For the rest, the matter is simply one of waiting and hoping that they will mature at some later date. A study by Charles Walcutt analyzes this damaging ideology at some length with special focus on the early reading problems.[36] He cites evidence showing that the overwhelming majority of unselected classes can be taught to read in the first grade, a fact that effectively disposes of the readiness mythology. The "waiting for readiness" period is time in which the child is learning far below his "natural capacity," that is, for him it is wasted time. That time must also be both frustrating and humiliating.

From the teacher's and from the school's vantage point, the readiness ideology serves the important function of shifting the blame for poor (or no) performance from the school and teacher onto the student. It eases their moral and professional burden. Insofar as the claim is backed up by "scientific studies" they might even succeed in convincing the parents of these children.

Most harmonist social theorists, especially those in the United States, see the school system as a key device for teaching common democratic and achievement values. Not only do schools "teach values" but they also "provide opportunity" for the talented. This review of the evidence indicates that *the* schools do not do this. Working-class schools, given their malperformance, serve to humiliate persons and do damage to their abilities. By doing so they succeed in driving many of them out of the schools at the earliest possible date (at which point they are labeled "drop outs" thus again shifting the fault from school to student). As for the common values, in particular, the "all-embracing" middle-class value of going to college, it is obvious that only a minority of the surviving seniors in these schools share that value. For the rest, they have been led to adopt some other life career. To the extent that such schools do provide "opportunity" it is for the children of those members of the middle class who still remain in the working-class milieu. To the extent then that these schools do "provide opportunity," they are aiding the development of the more highly segregated community of the future.

The segregation of the classes carries with it many more implications than those mentioned thus far. There are implications for occupational aspirations. Only certain kinds of jobs will be "visible" from one's position in the heart of the urban working class or in an upper-middle-class enclave. Those visible jobs will develop a kind of naturalness to them; there is a certain "rightness" about them.

Given the social structuring of the city, there is also a correlated structuring of the marriage chances of the city's populations. Males living in the working-class center would have to travel quite a distance to find a wife who is other than working- or lower-middle class. Upper-middle-class males in the days of yore, in the smaller, more integrated community with one common high school could and did make contact with daughters of workers and did marry them. The growing distance separating them makes this less and less possible. Hence, as will be seen in a later chapter, there is a growing tendency for the classes to become endagomous subcommunities. The removal of increasing numbers of these daughters to colleges and universities (that is, to even more strictly segregated middle-class enclaves) at the age of potential marriage also contributes to this developing class endogamy.

It seems likely that the combination of separate neighborhood locations, separate schools, separate jobs, and separate lines of descent will, in the long run, lead to progressively differentiated consciousnesses. If it ever did make sense to talk about common values, these developments should have the consequence of undoing that condition. The emergent development of separate consciousness, moreover, would occur without any special efforts on the part of political activists, that is, merely by virtue of the fact that subpopulations have such sharply differentiated life circumstances. Were intelligent and capable political activists present, the rate at which attitudes were differentiated would be markedly increased.

In addition to the more or less central differences in life circumstances already considered, it is to be noted that there are emerging differences in the more peripheral aspects of human existence, differences that are also, in a sense, built into the very architecture of the city. In the working-class area we have the baseball stadium; in the middle-class area, we have tennis courts and, in more outlying areas, we have the golf courses. The cultural institutions, those that are not hopelessly built into the decaying central city, are located in or near the middle-class enclave. This is the case with the legitimate theater (the repertory theater and the summer theaters), the philharmonic hall (and the summer outdoor concert shell), the music school, and the bookstores of the community. Thus, once again, insofar as propinquity has an effect, the location of urban facilities will have the consequence of reinforcing already existent differences.[37]

Notes

1. Justifications for treating all family members as members of the same class appear in the following: Bernard Barber, *Social Stratification* (New York: Harcourt, Brace, 1957), pp. 73–74; Kingsley Davis, *Human Society* (New York: Macmillan, 1948), p. 364; A criticism of this approach appears in Walter B. Watson and Ernest A. T. Barth, "Questionable Assumptions in the Theory of Social Stratification," *Pacific Sociological Review,* 7:1 (Spring 1964), 10–16. Using the 1/10,000 U.S. Census sample they found 62 percent of the husbands and wives employed in the same class. In 8 percent of two-earner families the husband was in a white-collar job and the wife in the manual ranks. The more frequent disparate case, however, involved a husband in a blue-collar and a wife in a white-collar job. Thirty percent of the two-earner families were of this variety.

2. See *Current Population Reports,* Population Characteristics, Series P-20, No. 114, January 21, 1962, "Marital Status and Family Status."

3. The figures are recalculated from United States Department of Labor, *Manpower Report of the President* (Washington: Government Printing Office, 1970), p. 225

4. Everett Kassalow has put the matter as follows: "The United States is the first country in the world in which manual or blue-collar workers have ceased to be the largest single occupational group of the labor force. They have been displaced in recent years by white-collar workers." "White Collar Unionism in the United States," p. 305 of Adolf Sturmthal, ed., *White-Collar Trade Unions*

(Urbana: University of Illinois Press, 1966). Sturmthal also points up this change, beginning his preface with the following: "The great manpower revolution of the post-World War II period has focused attention upon a change in the structure of the American labor force that has been underway a long time: the shift from blue-collar to white-collar. For the first time in history, the Census shows that this heterogeneous group is larger than manual labor."

5. The discussion of the service workers is based on the following source: 1960 Census of Population, PC (2) Subject Reports, Table 16, pp. 232–233.

6. This may be seen in *Current Sociology*, IX, 1 (1960), "Comparative Social Mobility," S. M. Miller, ed., p. 78. The 1964 SRC study shows 17 of 37 male service workers to be children of manual workers and another 13 to be of farm parentage.

7. Albert J. Reiss, Jr., *Occupations and Social Status* (New York: The Free Press, 1961), pp. 68–69.

8. Some indication of the selectivity of the "national service" may be found in James W. Davis, Jr., and Kenneth M. Dolbeare, *Little Groups of Neighbors* (Chicago: Markham, 1968), Ch. 6. See also, Albert J. Mayer and Thomas Ford Hoult, "Social Stratification and Combat Survival," *Social Forces*, **34** (1955–1956), 155–159. This study concludes that "The variation [in Detroit] was such that the data reported herein substantiate the charges made by a number of observers that Korea was a 'poor man's war.' "

9. The percentage of women in manual occupations continued to decline in the years after 1950, dropping to 43 in 1960 and to 39.4 by 1969. See *Manpower Report of the President*, p. 225 (recalculated).

Typical of the discussions of the occupation trends, emphasizing the presumed sweeping changes involved, is the following: "With every decade, more of the jobs available in our society require a high level of training. As our industrial economy comes of age, it has less and less room for laborers and skilled workers, more and more room for engineers and managers. Thus, not only do we relegate education to an institution outside the family, we must keep a child there longer before he is 'processed' and fit to take his place as an adult in society." From p. 3 of James S. Coleman, *The Adolescent Society* (New York: The Free Press, 1963). It is true that there are fewer jobs for laborers. The number of skilled workers employed in the American economy, however, has shown continuous increase (except in the depression decade) from 1900 to date. The same holds even more strikingly for the operatives, the semi-skilled workers. For these (numbering 9.9 million in 1969) there are no formidable educational requirements that would require long formal educational processing. The "tightness" of the linkage between education and the economy has obviously been very much overstressed. The fact of continuously increasing levels of educational attainment in the United States and elsewhere is in great measure due to considerations that are quite independent of the "demands of the economy." To a much greater extent, it reflects a widespread mobility drive and a concern with "equal opportunity." For a more extended discussion of this topic, see Richard F. Hamilton, "Work and Education: The Problem Facing Us," pp. 25–33 of John L. O'Brien, ed., *The Advanced Degree and Vocational-Technical Education in Leadership* (New Brunswick: Rutgers Graduate School of Education, 1966).

10. The discrepancy in the 1950 figures of Tables 4.1 and 4.2 stems from the fact

that the former is based on the "economically active population" (which includes the unemployed) and the latter is based on the employed only. The former table shows the manual percentage in 1950 to be 64.2 percent. Exclusion of the unemployed, as in Table 4.2, results in the manual percentage of 62.3 percent.

For those who assume a continuous inherent process of development toward the "middle-class society," it should be a matter of some interest to know that between 1960 and 1966 there was no change in the occupational distribution. The manual percentage was 58.6 percent in the first of those years and 58.8 percent in the latter. It is clear that the entire question of occupational trends and the determinants of those trends needs much more detailed attention; the sweeping, global claims will no longer suffice.

11. The number of male professionals in education jumped from 475,470 in 1950 to 802,069 in 1960, an increase of 68.7 percent. See U.S. Bureau of the Census, *United States Census of Population: 1950*, Vol. IV. Special Reports, Part 1, Chapter C., "Occupation by Industry" (Washington, D.C.: Government Printing Office, 1954), and *United States Census of Population: 1960*, Subject Reports, "Occupation By Industry," Final Report PC (2)-7C (Washington, D.C.: Government Printing Office, 1963). About one-fifth of the growth of the male professional rank occurred in this industry.

12. Theodore White, *The Making of the President: 1960* (New York: Atheneum, 1961), p. 221. A useful technical summary is that of Joseph F. Fulton, "Employment Impact of Changing Defense Programs," *Monthly Labor Review*, **87** (May 1964), 508–516.

13. The information presented here has been derived from the following: U.S. Bureau of the Census; U.S. Census of Population and Housing, 1960; *Census Tracts*, Final Report, PHC (1)-21 (Washington, D.C.: U.S. Government Printing Office, 1962). Information for the discussion of Milwaukee (which appears later in the book) was gained from the Final Report PHC (1)-92.

14. For example: "Suburbia is . . . preponderantly, native-born and white. . . . the suburbs become overwhelmingly white, higher in social class, tending toward Republican affiliation" pp. 4 and 9 of Scott Greer, *The Emerging City: Myth and Reality* (New York: The Free Press, 1962). This assumption is in great measure based on the more famous suburbia studies of the 1950s. Among the most noted are: William H. Whyte, Jr., *The Organization Man* (New York: Simon and Shuster, 1956); John R. Seeley, R. A. Sims, and E. W. Loosley, *Crestwood Heights: The Culture of Suburban Life* (New York: Basic Books, 1956); and A. C. Spectorsky, *The Exurbanites* (Philadelphia: Lippincott, 1955). Additional citations plus discussion of the early postwar suburban scene may be found in Maurice R. Stein, *The Eclipse of Community* (Princeton: Princeton University Press, 1960), and Robert C. Wood, *Suburbia: Its People and Their Politics* (Boston: Houghton Mifflin, 1959). A late appearance is the recent work of Herbert J. Gans, *The Levittowners* (New York: Pantheon Books, 1967).

15. For analysis of this other kind of suburbia, see Bennett Berger, *Working-Class Suburb* (Berkeley: University of California Press, 1960) and Leo F. Schnore, "Satellites and Suburbs," *Social Forces*, **36** (December 1957), 121–129. The latter essay also appears in William Dobriner, ed., *The Suburban Community* (New York: G. P. Putnam, 1958, pp. 109–121, and as Ch. 7 of Schnore, *The Urban Scene* (New York: The Free Press, 1965).

16. The city had a population of 741,324 according to the 1960 census. It came after New York, Chicago, Los Angeles, Philadelphia, Detroit, Baltimore, Houston, Cleveland, Washington, and St. Louis. U.S. Bureau of the Census, *Statistical Abstract of the United States: 1966* (Washington, D.C.: Government Printing Office, 1966), p. 21.

17. The quotations are from Harold L. Wilensky and Charles N. Lebeaux, *Industrial Society and Social Welfare* (New York: The Free Press, 1958), p. 129.

18. The reference is to Bennett Berger's work. Another good, brief description of a working-class suburb appears in James Coleman's *The Adolescent Society* (New York: The Free Press, 1963), pp. 63–64. Some salient characteristics of the town are described as follows:

The fact that there is no program for youth has been attributed by some to the lack of interest on the part of Newlawn parents. In many instances, both parents are working in the factories in or near the community and don't take time with their children. . . . Although most parents are extremely proud of the education their children receive at Newlawn High School, little evidence was available in the questionnaires to show that many graduates attend college or that there is much inspiration to go. The teen-age boys seem to spend much of their time working on cars, and the school has a place and facilities for them to do this type of work conveniently.

19. One sociologist, Francis E. Merrill, observes that: "Away from the job, many manual workers cannot be separated from white-collar workers by any obvious criteria." See his *Society and Culture* (Englewood Cliffs, N.J.: Prentice-Hall, 1961), p. 302.

20. In one ghetto tract (No. 29), the median age of the 96 white males was 57.2 (1960) as compared with a median of 19.4 for the 1006 nonwhite males. There were 18 white males under age 20 in the tract and 511 nonwhites. The overall white-black ratio is 1:10. Among those under 20, it is 1:28.

A more detailed account of the Milwaukee ghetto may be found in the following: Charles T. O'Reilly, Willard E. Downing, and Steven I. Pflanczer, *The People of the Inner Core-North: A Study of Milwaukee's Negro Community* (New York: LePlay Research, Inc., 1965). Also of interest is Charles O'Reilly and Willard E. Downing, *Property and Race: A Case Study of Property Change in a Racially Changing Milwaukee Neighborhood* (mimeographed paper: in State Historical Society, Madison, Wisconsin).

21. This question is discussed in Richard F. Hamilton, "The Income Difference Between Skilled and White Collar Workers," *British Journal of Sociology*, **14** (December 1963), 368. In Milwaukee (1950) the foremen constituted 11.3 percent of the craftsmen, foremen, and kindred rank. In the surrounding ring within the Standard Metropolitan Area, they made up 14.5 percent of the total. United States Census, 1950. Vol. II., Characteristics of the Population, Part 49, Table 73.

22. The informal social controls of middle-class communities have been frequently described. William H. Whyte, Jr. (in *The Organization Man*) devotes an entire chapter to "inconspicuous consumption" and to keeping *down* with the Joneses. The "next step up" for these middle-class families necessitated a change of location; then they could leave both old neighbors and the old furniture behind them, picking up both a new, higher-level community and consumption standard.

184   Class and Politics in the United States

Some suggestion of the equivalent social controls in working-class communities are found scattered throughout the following works: William Foote Whyte, *Street Corner Society* (Chicago: University of Chicago Press, 1955), and Herbert Gans, *The Urban Villagers* (New York: The Free Press, 1962). Another source describes the "common man" outlook as follows: "They believed that people like themselves who were not overly bright or ambitious had, as a matter of course, a certain style of life which might be questioned in detail but not in substance. Some said this way of life was not only to be accepted, but to be preferred, that the competitive game to rise higher was not worth the candle. These . . . families . . . espouse the core value of 'getting by.'" From Joseph A. Kahl, "Educational and Occupational Aspirations of 'Common Man' Boys," pp. 348–366 of A. H. Halsey, Jean Floud, and C. Arnold Anderson, eds., *Education, Economy, and Society: A Reader in the Sociology of Education* (New York: The Free Press, 1961), quotation from p. 354.

23. S. M. Lipset, *The First New Nation* (New York: Basic Books, 1963), p. 184.

24. For a more extended discussion of the Madison case see Robert Alford, *Bureaucracy and Participation: Political Cultures in Four Wisconsin Cities* (Chicago: Rand McNally & Co., 1969), Ch. VI.

The dominant pattern of working-class majorities does not change even in the smaller cities of the state. Janesville, with a 1960 population of some 35,000 people, was 67.6 percent working class. The city of Eau Claire (38,000 in 1960) was 57.0 percent working class. Eau Claire County, without that city, was 70.8 percent working class (taking the nonfarm male populations only). Eau Claire County, again without the city, contained 2294 manual workers in 1960 and 1727 persons in farm occupations, 521 of whom were farm laborers.

25. Professor Michael Aiken has made an analysis of United States cities with a population of 10,000 or more ($N = 1654$). In a special analysis of the top decile (in terms of professionals in the labor force) he reports that 122 of the 165 communities are suburbs, that is, political units located in a Standard Metropolitan Statistical Area. Of the remaining 43 cities, 37 have less than 20 percent of the labor force in manufacturing. Most of these 37 cities contain large universities— those of Oklahoma, Illinois, Florida, Kansas, Missouri, Georgia, Indiana, Iowa, Oregon, and others. One contained a major medical complex (Rochester, Minnesota) and one was a state capital (Pierre, S.D.).

Only six of the 165 top professional cities are manufacturing cities with their own independent economic bases. Three of them are based on chemical processing industries and three are based on military manufacturing. One of these communities—Midland, Michigan, the home of the Dow Chemical Company—is the subject of an article that suggests that this very exceptional case is a forerunner of the coming middle-class society. See William A. Faunce and Donald A. Clelland, "Professionalization and Stratification Patterns in an Industrial Community," *American Journal of Sociology*, **72** (January 1967), 341–350. I am very much indebted to Professor Aiken for making his data available to me.

26. Leo F. Schnore, *The Urban Scene* (New York: The Free Press, 1965), Ch. 11. "The Socioeconomic Status of Cities and Suburbs," originally published in The *American Sociological Review*, **28** (February 1963), 76–85.

27. See, for example, the discussion of the industrial workers in Arthur Vidich

and Joseph Bensman, *Small Town in a Mass Society* (Princeton: Princeton University Press, 1959).

28. Alan B. Wilson, "Residential Segregation of Social Classes and Aspirations of High School Boys," *American Sociological Review*, **26**:6 (December 1959), 836–845. The quotations are from p. 837 and 845. One of the unapplauded advantages of such class segregation is that it does spare the egos of the disadvantaged children. One study of the "adolescent self-image" found no relationship between the self-esteem of children and the occupation of the parents. This is not because they do not see or are not aware of differences between their families and others. It is rather that the class-homogeneous school environment makes much more favorable comparisons possible. The student of low-status parents who is in a mixed school, by comparison, appears to be crushed by the contrast.

On the class–self-esteem relationship, see Morris Rosenberg, *Society and the Adolescent Self-Image* (Princeton: Princeton University Press, 1965), p. 47. For the awareness of the family disadvantage sensed by students, see Patricia Cayo Sexton, *Education and Income: Inequalities of Opportunity in Our Public Schools* (New York: Viking Press, 1961). In her study, fifth and seventh graders were asked the question: "Do you wish your father (or mother) had a better job?" Eight percent of the fifth graders in schools located in predominantly high-status districts answered "yes" as did 15 percent of the seventh graders. By comparison, 42 and 61 percent, respectively, of the children from the schools in low-status areas felt the need for some improvement in the family's position (pp. 90–91). The impact of mixed schools will be considered in the text. For a discussion of the different "ethos" of the working class school see Edgar Litt, "Civic Education, Community Norms, and Political Indoctrination," *American Sociological Review*, **28** (February 1963), 69–75.

29. It seems likely, following what was said earlier, that we have two types of nonmanual families located in these working-class districts, those of middle-class background and those coming from working-class families. It seems likely that it is the children of the former group who have the higher aspirations.

30. Discussions of the desirability of "more and more" higher education and of the "need" to extend "opportunity" to more and more persons stress that education is the key to better jobs and higher income. What is left unsaid is that without transformation of the job opportunities, increasing levels of educational attainment can *only* mean increasing numbers of college-educated manual workers. The United States, as already noted, is unique in being the only country in the world with college-educated workers. In Samuel Stouffer's study (discussed in Chapter 3) from 1954, we find 1.2 percent of the manuals to be college graduates and another 5.7 reporting having had some college. (Recalculated from Lipset, *Political Man*, p. 109.) A study of children in four San Francisco area high schools in 1959 (selected in order to overrepresent children of manual workers) showed 15 percent of the manual fathers as having "some college." See Irving Krauss, "Sources of Educational Aspirations Among Working-Class Youth," *American Sociological Review*, **29** (December 1964), 867–879 (Percentage recalculated from Table 4, p. 871). Contemporary studies of workers in West Germany and France show no college-educated workers. The Krauss study, incidentally, also shows us that "other" middle class within the working-class milieu. Eighteen

percent of the middle-class fathers in this study had not completed high school. Their children's post-high school aspirations were little different from those of equivalent working-class children. Thirty percent intended to go to technical school and another 30 percent reported no further educational aspirations.

31. William H. Sewell and J. Michael Armer, "Neighborhood Context and College Plans," *American Sociological Review*, **31**:2 (April 1966), 159–168.

32. There has been some dispute over the significance of the neighborhood or school context. Sewell and Armer downgrade its import, laying their stress on family status and intelligence. A major difficulty here stems from their assumption that the relationship between the school contexts and the aspirations will be linear. Since it is not and since, in fact, there are these reversals between the low and the middle schools, the correlation of context and aspirations is a relatively low one. This had led the authors to overlook the fact that the difference between a working-class context and an essentially upper-middle-class one is rather sizable. See the discussion in the *American Sociological Review*, **31**:5 (October 1966), 698 ff.

33. John Michael, "High School Climates and Plans for Entering College," *Public Opinion Quarterly*, **24** (Winter 1961), 585–595. Another study reports: ". . . at given levels of occupational background, the higher the status of the community, the more likely it is that a boy will go to college. However, when IQ is held constant, the independent effect of community status evaporates at all occupational levels but the highest." Stuart Cleveland, "A Tardy Look at Stouffer's Findings in the Harvard Mobility Project," *Public Opinion Quarterly*, **26** (Fall 1962), 453–454. This study questioned 4000 boys in nine suburbs of Boston. See also Richard P. Boyle, "The Effect of the High School on Student's Aspirations," *American Journal of Sociology*, **71** (May 1966), 628–639. The studies reviewed here ought to be assessed in light of the questions raised by Robert M. Hauser, "Context and Consex: A Cautionary Tale," *American Journal of Sociology*, **75** (January 1970), 645–664.

34. Op. cit., p. 109. Quotations in the following pages are from the same source, pp. 129–130, 158–159, 270–271, and 280. Additional references on school contexts and aspirations are to be found in the Sewell-Armer article (footnote 31) and in the comments on their article (footnote 32).

35. Patricia Cayo Sexton, *Education and Income: Inequalities of Opportunity in Our Public Schools* (New York: Viking Press, 1961); James S. Coleman, et al., *Equality of Educational Opportunity* (Washington, D.C.: Government Printing Office, 1966). An on the spot portrayal of the scene is to be found in the work of Jonathan Kozol, *Death at an Early Age* (Boston: Houghton Mifflin, 1967).

36. Charles C. Walcutt, *Tomorrow's Illiterates* (Boston: Little, Brown, 1961). See also Frank Riessman, *The Culturally Deprived Child* (New York: Harper & Row, 1962).

37. Still another kind of experience that may have some significant effect on future class outlooks involves direct participation in United States military efforts abroad. A list of Vietnam deaths was obtained from the State of Wisconsin Department of Veterans' Affairs, and (a) Milwaukee County decedants were

located by census tracts, and (b) information was obtained on their parents' occupations from the City Directory. Up to and including Supplement No. 8 (25 January 1968), we found 78 listings, 69 of whom had locatable addresses. Of these 69, some 86 percent lived in districts that had at least a working-class majority. Sixty-five percent of these persons came from districts that were 65 percent or more working class. Finding information on occupations of individuals proved rather difficult but, for what it is worth, the scattered listings indicated that many of those living in middle-class areas or in low-percentage working-class areas had also been in manual jobs or their parents did manual work. For example, of the ten who came from middle-class districts, four had parents in manual work —a janitor, a saw operator, a warehouseman, and a carpenter. A fifth was himself a painter. Taking them chronologically and dividing them into early wartime deaths, middle, and late, we find that the percentage coming from heavy (65 percent or more) working-class districts increases—from 57, to 61, to 78.

See also the Mayer and Hoult article cited in note 8.

5
Class and Politics

Introduction: Some Procedures

In this chapter, after a few introductory considerations, we shall examine the relationship between class and party alignment in the United States and then compare that result with those from Great Britain and West Germany. Relatively little "class polarization" is indicated in the United States. This result does not stem from the presence of a large contingent of Republican workers, as is argued in a well-established tradition, but depends rather on the large proportion of middle-class Democrats. This peculiarity of the middle class in the United States is shown to be linked to the religious/ethnic factor, a consequence of structures, organizations, and allegiances that have long historical roots in the United States. The political differences associated with lower-middle- and upper-middle-class position are then explored along with the differences linked to this "vertical" division, that is, to the socioreligious cleavages. A similar analysis is made of the manual ranks. Finally, the question is raised as to whether the emphasis that has been placed on the manual-nonmanual division is justified. The evidence indicates that this emphasis has been misplaced. A more important division is that between the upper-middle class and the combined lower-middle and working-class categories. An adequate understanding of the social structural cleavages must also take into consideration the vertical divisions or "pillars."

We turn in this chapter to the results of opinion and attitude surveys. For the first time in this work we are able to draw the manual-nonmanual lines in a way that suits the present purposes rather than having to follow the conventions forced on one by the census categories. The categories to be used from this point accord with those of the theories discussed in Chapter 2. We are, therefore, in a position to make a more adequate assessment of those theories than would be the case had we followed the usual conventions.

Basically, we are still focusing on families as the basic units of analysis and are once again classifying the families by the occupation of the head of the household. We are now able to shift the foremen out of the category "craftsmen, foremen, and kindred" and have located them with the middle class. In the detailed comparisons they have been combined with the managers and officials. Since they are salaried and, as it is frequently stated, since they constitute the "first line of management," this placement is more reasonable than the usual one. While it is obvious that there is an enormous distance between top management and the foremen, this is a problem that we may consider when we explore the internal differentiation of the nonmanual ranks. A second change we have made is to remove all self-employed persons from the manual ranks. We have located them too among the nonmanuals. In the detailed comparisons they appear with the proprietors. Again, there is the problem of the immense gap between the *petit* and the *grand* bourgeois ranks, between the newspaper vendor, the independent welder, and the candy store owner, on the one hand, and the proprietor of the firm having 1000 employees, on the other. This problem will also be considered later in this chapter when we discuss the internal differentiation within the nonmanual ranks.

In most of what follows, both in this chapter and in the subsequent ones, we will be dealing with married respondents only and with those in which the head of the house is either employed or else unemployed but seeking employment. Essentially we have omitted the retired, the economically active single persons, the widows and widowers as well as the divorcees. What we have then are husbands and wives in intact families.[1] We are also going to be working only with nonfarm populations.

To explain why we have proceeded this way, it is perhaps best to consider first the alternatives. The reasons for working with families rather than individual employed persons have been discussed already in Chapter 4. If we were to take all persons, married and unmarried, and classify them by the occupation of the head of the house and were then to proceed with our analysis, we would be faced with a number of problems. In any given presentation of findings, the question would arise as to whether the results were not due to the different age composition of the categories or to a disproportionate number of broken homes in one case, or to the surplus of widows in the other. Thus, if we followed the most obvious procedure, we would frequently find it necessary to present first the basic findings and then either to present further tables, or otherwise assure the reader that with all these other factors controlled the same result would be obtained.

By excluding these "groups on the periphery" from the outset, we can save ourselves the necessity for making all these controls. We are, in other words, going to present the evidence for the basic cases and thus, hopefully, give the main outline of the class-politics relationship. The excluded cases can best be treated in separate inquiry, which can then be contrasted with or set in the context to be outlined here. That is to say, subsequently one could undertake study of the young unmarried worker (preferably with a special sample), or of the retired workers, or of the working-class widows, and so forth. It is difficult to have a "definitive" position as to which procedure is the best one.

In some discussions we shall follow a somewhat different procedure. At other times, we shall indicate in either the text or in the notes at the end of the chapter the implications of making the exclusions.

Class Differences: A Comparative Note

There is a persistent problem which appears in the discussion of class: how to assess the differences that do appear. Most studies do show some percentage difference in the political choices and in the attitudes on issues. It then becomes a question of whether to express astonishment over the enormity of the differences or satisfaction that they are so small. Those who are convinced that the past consisted of a thoroughly radicalized working class pitted against an equally monolithic and conservative bourgeoisie find anything short of that extreme polarization as a cause of self-congratulation. It is, so one says, an indication of just how effectively the "developing industrial society" has moderated the once radical demands.

An alternative view of the political history of the last century makes just the opposite assumption. The classes were never internally unified and were never sharply opposed to each other. In Europe, the "radical element" in the early working class development was no more than a tiny minority amidst a *potential* clientele which at that time consisted of very religious and deferential small-town workers and ex-peasants. As the socialist parties grew, the radical intellectuals counted for less and less in party affairs as their influence was overwhelmed by that of party bureaucrats devoted to established routines. Although the parties of the left showed a steady growth in the number of party members and steadily increased their share of the vote, the development, no matter how threatening it was seen to be by the established elites of the day, in point of fact did not represent any serious radical threat. This fact became most clear in July and August of 1914 and once again in November of 1918 in the case of the most developed of the Social Democratic parties.[2]

The declining influence of the intellectuals combined with the growing domination of the party *Apparat* served to contain any radical potential. Thus, one part of the "classical" imagery proves to be a myth—the myth of the radical past. A second point that needs correction is the notion of a sharp division between the classes. Early in this century a report appeared that indicated that a third of the German Social Democratic voters were nonmanual. This was a pattern that persisted through to the last elections in the Weimar period. It was the Social Democratic success within the nonmanual ranks (or alternatively, the defection of the nonmanuals from "middle-class" politics) that reduced the "class polarization." It is important to note that the *way* in which the polarization was reduced is just the opposite of that which so completely dominates social science discussions. Rather than "workers becoming bourgeois," the actual case was one of nonmanuals (particularly the urban "lower-middle class") turning to Social Democracy.[3]

American political history differs quite markedly from this European pattern. In the American context Socialism has played only a very restricted role and even that development was broken during and shortly after World War I.[4] Although it is currently common practice to equate the Democrats with the European Socialist and Labour parties as the "liberal-left" direction, the procedure leads one to overlook some important differences.[5] Even though the latter parties have of late adopted left-liberal programs that are very similar to those of the Democrats, such late transformations do not change the underlying patterns of support for the parties, patterns that were created and institutionalized in the course of more than a century.

The Democrats, unlike the European Socialists, had majority (or near majority) status from the beginning of mass politics in this country. Unlike the European Socialists, the Democrats were never a threat to the prerogatives of the *entire* ruling class. The Democratic party did not constitute a case of late developing insurgency with a strong class base. Rather, the situation in the United States was much more one of competing elite parties, each challenging the other's interests and claims to preference; neither of them, however, avowing the "abolition" of the other. Neither Jackson nor the party were interested in improving the condition of the masses. The struggle against the National Bank was not a struggle of elites and masses, but, as far as the party leaders were concerned, it was a struggle between one privileged element and another. The defeat of the National Bank did not signify a victory for the masses but rather was a victory for state and private banking interests.[6]

Concretely what this means is that the composition of the Democratic clientele is different from that of the European Socialist and Labour parties. Because of this different composition, the character and the significance of the "class polarization" in the United States is also different.

From the beginnings, the main lines of cleavage in the United States tended to be vertical rather than horizontal. The division was along ethnic and religious lines rather than being primarily along class lines. This means that the parties in the United States, from the beginning, had a structure that was more akin to the "pillars," or vertical divisions, of Netherlands' society than to the image of parties with near-exclusive class clientele. The basic situation involved two competing parties, each with its own elite and mass support. The English-Yankee elements, to be sure, were somewhat better off and therefore, to a limited extent, there was some original class differentiation in the party clientele. On the whole, however, it seems unlikely, were we in a position to examine mass attitudes in 1840, 1860, or 1890, that we would find any great difference indicated in the party choices made by the manual and nonmanual ranks.[7]

In the American case then, the relative absence of polarization is due to the fact that the parties have never been divided along elite-mass lines. The Democrats had their "own" elites from the very beginning. Given this differing history, the contemporary result is that the Democrats have a much larger following in the upper- and upper-middle classes than do the Socialist parties of Europe. (See Table 5.1.) Especially in the continental countries such as

Party Preference by Socioeconomic Status in Three Countries[a] (Marrieds Only)

Socio-Economic Status (Interview Rating)	Manual				Nonmanual				
United Kingdom									
	Group D	Below Average	Average		Below Average	Average	Above Average		
Percent Labour[b]	76%	67%	53%		43%	20%	11%		
N =	(45)	(578)	(45)		(256)	(297)	(71)		
West Germany									
Family income (DM monthly)	599 or less	600–799	800–999	1000 or more	599 or less	600–799	800–999	1000–1499	1500 or more
Percent SPD[b]	55	54	66	51	34	29	24	15	13
N =	(266)	(143)	(47)	(37)	(108)	(83)	(84)	(95)	(47)
U.S.A.									
Family income (yearly in 1000's)	Less than 6	6–7.5	7.5–10	$10+	Less than 6	6–7.5	7.5–10	10–15	$15+
Percent with Democratic identification[b]	81	78	68	72	74	67	57	50	46
N =	(135)	(160)	(85)	(54)	(77)	(124)	(106)	(123)	(70)

[a] The British data are combined results from British Gallup studies CQ 332 and CQ 333, both of August 1963. The IBM cards were made available through the Roper Center, Williamstown. The questions read: "If there were a General Election tomorrow, which party would you support?"

The West German data are from DIVO Study 326, November 1961. The IBM cards from this study were made available to me by Eugen Lupri of DIVO. The question asked which party they voted for in the 1961 Bundestag election.

The United States' results are from the SRC 1964 election study. Because the 1964 election was not at all a "normal" vote, the party identification has been used for this comparison.

West Germany where the opposition has long been Socialist, it comes as no surprise that the upper classes are still overwhelmingly nonsocialist in their voting behavior and that the appeal in the middle classes is rather restricted. Accordingly, in such contexts (as opposed to the American scene) it is not too surprising that the "class polarization" is fairly sizable.[8]

Most studies of class polarization focus on the "defection" of *working-class* populations from a pure class vote, the most widespread hypothesis being that workers "convert" as the prevailing income levels rise. To the extent that such conversion does occur, it would, to be sure, contribute to a reduction of "polarization." The focus on the working-class deviation from "class politics" has led analysts to forget or overlook the fact being stressed here—that *non-manual* "defections" are the more important factor in the United States. This peculiarity has nonclass sources (in the ethnic politics of more than a century) and persists as a result of segregated institutions in middle-class ranks (such as "exclusive" clubs) that inhibit assimilation of the outlooks of the white Protestant majority. One of the ironies of American history is that the "Whiggish elements," those who were obsessed with "assimilation" of the newcomers, developed institutions that made achievement of this aim impossible.[9]

One further point to be noted about "class polarization" in the United States is that, as previously noted, the parties only rarely mobilize on the basis of class themes. More specifically, this means that the Democrats do not do so. It is obvious, from a rational viewpoint, that this is not the kind of strategy that can be used by the Republicans. Interestingly enough, when class issues were made salient by the Democratic candidate—the most striking case being the Truman campaign in 1948—the class cleavage increased very sharply. Robert Alford's trend data show that from 1936 to early 1948, the "Index of Class Voting" averaged somewhere between 15 and 20. (This means that the manual ranks were between 15 and 20 percent more Democratic than the non-manuals.) In the course of the 1948 election, that figure went from 20 percent in August to 29 percent in September and then to 41 percent in November. In the following election years, 1952 to 1960, the index fell to its "normal" 15 to 20 percent range.[10] Interestingly enough, what happened in 1948 was a conversion of the manual ranks. They were brought around to a Democratic position, reaching the highest Democratic percentage in the entire 24-year period. The presence of the bland above-the-parties candidate in the 1952 and 1956 campaign together with a general avoidance of class issues by the Democratic candidate led to a falloff in the Democratic percentage among the manuals to the lowest point in the 24-year period.

Class and "Pillars": The Party Preferences

In the 1964 Survey Research Center election study, following Alford's procedure, we find that 79 percent and 60 percent of the active manuals and nonmanuals, respectively, reported a vote for the Democrats. Thus, the "class polarization" was again of a relatively low order (+19), that is, of much the same magnitude as was found in the Eisenhower period. In this election, to be sure, there was a very marked shift in voting toward the Democrats on the part of both ranks. Even, however, when we work with party identification, the polarization is of a very low level (+16). In both cases, the lowness of the cleavage is a result of the high level of Democratic sentiment on the part of the nonmanuals. What has to be explained, in other words, is just the opposite of what is called for by the conventional assumption.[11]

Following the previous discussion of the "uniqueness" of the American party followings, it is important that we examine the evidence. Since the key to the relatively limited class cleavage lies in the nonmanual ranks, our effort will be concentrated there. Since, as has also been noted, the original party divisions in the United States followed ethnic and religious lines, we have divided the nonmanuals in such a way as to approximate this division, separating them into (1) white Protestants and (2) a category that we have labeled "all others."[12] An examination of the party identifications found in the two "pillars" or "columns" confirms our expectation in that the former divide nearly 50–50 (actually 53 percent Democratic, $N = 295$) and the latter divide 75–25 (actually 73 percent Democratic, $N = 182$). Once again it is clear that to think of the nonmanuals as Republican, as if that were the basic, most frequent position, is not at all adequate.

We have suggested in Chapter 4 the existence of a very important cleavage within the nonmanual ranks, that is, a division between those living in the working-class districts (essentially constituting a lower-middle class) and those living in the segregated middle-class enclaves (who are, for the most part, upper-middle class). The study does not allow us to divide the populations by the character of their home neighborhoods; however, we may approach this aim in a very crude way by arbitrarily separating the "pillars" by income at the $10,000 line (this is an estimate of 1964 total family income).[13] This is not to suggest that the income determines either one's class, one's party choice, or one's political attitudes. The procedure is intended rather to provide a crude indication of one's social location.

Three of the middle-class groups (shown in Table 5.2) had majorities identifying with the Democrats. Only the upper-middle-class white Protestants showed a Republican majority. Despite frequently voiced claims about lower-middle-class "reaction," this is not indicated in this result, both such groups having higher levels of Democratic identification and voting than the equivalent upper middles. The question of whether or not these party identifications actually represent liberal issue orientations will be considered later in this chapter.

This presentation still tends to obscure the picture by failing to consider the regional pattern. Since we have many Whig-Democrats in the South, that is, upper-middle-class Democratic conservatives, it is important to make a sep-

TABLE 5.2
Party Identification in the Nonmanual Ranks (Married; Head in Labor Force)
SRC 1964

	Nonmanuals			
	White Protestants		All Others	
Family Income:	To $9999	$10,000 or More	To $9999	$10,000 or More
Percent identifying as Democrats (of those with party identification) [a]	59%	42%	83%	62%
N =	(182)	(103)	(93)	(82)
Percent reporting Democratic vote in 1964 (of 2-party choices) [a]	52	37	84	74
N =	(146)	(92)	(81)	(77)
Same for non-South respondents[b]				
Percent identifying as Democrats	51	31	80	59
N =	(107)	(70)	(80)	(65)
1964 Vote	55	30	82	75
N =	(89)	(64)	(72)	(60)

[a] The percentages are based on those choosing one or the other of the two major parties. To obtain the Republican percentages, therefore, it is necessary to subtract these figures from 100%.
[b] Data for the South are to be found in Table 5.6.

arate consideration by region. When we consider the non-South middle-class populations separately, we find much the same picture as that shown for the nation as a whole (also in Table 5.2). Here it is even more pronounced that the white Protestant upper-middle-class constitutes *the* Republican stronghold. The lower-middle-class white Protestants are less conservative dividing 50–50 in their party identifications. Both upper and lower groups in the "other" column are considerably less Republican than their class peers among the white Protestants. Again the upper-middle-class "others" are more Republican than the lower middles but that still leaves somewhat more than half of them in the Democratic camp. Perhaps the most striking fact about this "column" is that the lower-middle class here is overwhelmingly Democratic, only one in five identifying as Republican.

It would not seem worth the effort to stress these lessons except for the fact that opposite and misleading claims have so frequently been asserted. It has been argued that the lower-middle class is somehow a "reactionary" class in opposition to moderation and reasonableness to be found among the educated upper middles. This first view of the subject does not support the claim of "reaction." A second difficulty with the conventional claim is the propensity to speak of "the" lower- or "the" upper-middle class. In the light of these findings, on such occasions one must ask the questions: Which lower-middle class? And, which upper-middle class?

We may carry the analysis a step further in order to specify in greater detail the location of the white Protestant Republicanism. As we noted in the analysis of Milwaukee, the upper- and lower-middle classes live in very different neighborhoods. It is reasonable to assume that the *urban* lower-middle class (including those living in the surrounding ring) would either have or would take on the political complexion of the working-class majority districts in which they live. The white Protestant lower-middle class in the smaller towns, however, would be more closely tied to the upper-middle classes there and hence would tend to fall in the Republican direction. We have taken only the non-South respondents for this analysis.

These expectations are generally supported. In the city we find three-fifths of the upper-middle class white Protestants identifying as Republicans. In the urban lower-middle class, however, we find a Democratic majority. (See Table 5.3). Small town and rural white Protestants, those in both the upper- and lower-middle classes, both show Republican majorities.

A similar picture appears with respect to the 1964 voting. The urban lower-middle-class white Protestants were again the most Democratic. In the 1964 election, the equivalent small town and rural group divided nearly 50–50. It is instructive to note that it was the upper-middle class in both locations (the

TABLE 5.3
Differentiation of the Non-South Nonmanual White Protestants (Married; Head in Labor Force) SRC 1964

| | Nonmanual, Non-South White Protestants | | | |
| | In Cities of 50,000 or More Plus Environs | | Other Communities | |
Total Family Income	To $9999	$10,000 or More	To $9999	$10,000 or More
Democratic identification				
(of 2-party choice)[a]	60%	41%	46%	25%
N =	(35)	(34)	(72)	(36)
Democratic vote, 1964				
(of 2-party choice)[a]	60	38	53	22
N =	(27)	(32)	(62)	(32)

[a] To obtain the Republican percentages, subtract these figures from 100%.

educated, pragmatic, responsible, and presumably tolerant upper-middle class) that, with sizable majorities. remained with the Republican party so as to support the Goldwater candidacy.[14]

The pattern among white Protestants indicated in Table 5.3 also appears with respect to the liberalism questions. The lower-middle-class urban white Protestants were the most liberal with respect to the medical care and the living standard questions. The small-town upper-middle classes were the most conservative.

On the whole, the lessons appear to be that the locus of Republicanism within the middle class is within the white Protestant ranks. As for the differentiation within this context, we find that Republicanism is predominant in the upper-middle class, both urban and small town, and also, to a lesser extent, within the small-town lower-middle class. The latter group, incidentally, happens to be the largest of the four categories under consideration. The political coherence of the white Protestant middle class is broken by the lower-middle-class populations in the cities, a group that shows a fair-sized Democratic majority. It seems likely that this latter group has lost contact with the "Whig heritage" and responds more directly to the problems posed in the work and neighborhood milieux.

Class and "Pillars": Issue Orientations

The examination of middle-class differentiation and party identification may, certainly, hide some important confounding findings. Party identification may be a simple matter of family tradition and as such may be in conflict with issue orientations that more closely reflect present realities. Specifically, it is possible that the Republican clustering in the upper-middle classes may hide a "flexible" or "pragmatic" position on the issues and the Democratic presence in the lower-middle classes might actually be associated with some proportionately greater degree of conservatism.

A first exploration of this question indicates that the conservatism of the upper-middle-class white Protestants, which was indicated by their party identifications, is also indicated in their positions on the issues. (See Table 5.4.) Both upper-middle classes tend to be less liberal than the lower-middle classes. And once again the "other" lower-middle class tends to be the most liberal segment of the entire class.[15] (We have chosen to show the percent "liberal" in this and the following tables to facilitate comparison with the manual workers discussed later in the chapter. The percent "conservative," obviously, is indicated by subtracting the figures in the table from 100%. It should be kept in mind that there are small numbers of persons saying "don't know" and "no answer." They have been omitted from these tables.)

The cutoff at $10,000 hides some characteristics of the white Protestant upper-middle class. This is revealed by making a further subdivision into those receiving between $10,000 and $15,000 and those with $15,000 or more.

TABLE 5.4

Issue Orientations in Non-South Nonmanual Ranks (Married; Head in Labor Force) SRC 1964

	Nonmanuals, Non-South			
	White Protestants		All Others	
Family Income:	To $9999	$10,000 or More	To $9999	$10,000 or More
Economic Liberalism Questions	*Percent "liberal" of those with opinion*			
Medical care	41%	28%	71%	65%
N=	(87)	(57)	(69)	(54)
Living standard guarantee	26	18	43	35
N=	(86)	(62)	(63)	(54)
School aid	26	27	49	49
N=	(85)	(66)	(67)	(57)
Government too powerful (% saying "no")	50	33	65	56
N=	(78)	(64)	(60)	(55)

Among these very high income white Protestants, the identifications are four-to-one Republican. They also tend to be strongly identified with that party. Another point: this group has a high level of decision; there are few independents or "don't knows." A similar picture appears with respect to the 1964 vote with 84 percent ($N = 19$) voting for Goldwater. There were no nonvoters in this rank. This heavy vote for Goldwater ought to be taken in conjunction with the fact that this is a highly educated group and also with the fact that, at least as social scientists have stated it, education is associated with tolerance, compromise-orientation, flexibility, pragmatism, and so forth.

On the issues we find the same lopsided distribution: 89 percent opposed the medical care suggestion, 90 percent opposed the guaranteed living standard, and 89 percent thought the government too powerful. On these questions there is also a very high level of "decision." Only on the school aid question does the pattern vary. In this case, a one-third minority felt that government support of schools was acceptable. The peculiarities of the white Protestant upper class will be explored in more detail in Chapter 9.

Thus far we have focused on the economic liberalism questions, those concerned with domestic economic welfare. In the 1960s, the basic line of centrist theorizing shifted somewhat, the claim now being that the lower-middle class "reaction" would be associated with the arrival of (or the threatened arrival of) Negroes in their neighborhoods. The results do not support this particular claim. (The findings appear in Chapter 11, Table 11.3.) In response to the job rights question, it was the white Protestant upper-middle class that, by a small margin, provided the *least* approval for a government guarantee. In the matter of equal schooling there was basically no difference between upper- and lower-middle-class Protestants. If the claim were valid, one should find very little lower-middle-class support for a government role to guarantee equal rights and there should be a large difference between them and the upper-middle class. Neither expectation is supported.

Both the upper- and lower-middle-class Catholics are more approving than the equivalent white Protestants. In this context, too, "class" makes very little difference in the outlooks (also in Table 11.3). It should be noted, especially with regard to the lower-middle class in this context, that they are overwhelmingly "new" immigrant groups who have only just recently "made it" and who, presumably, have the weakest grasp on their newly acquired middle-class "status." Despite this presumed source of "strain" and "reaction," they still respond with greater support for a government effort than the equivalent Protestant group.

The evidence presented here fits much more closely, on the whole, with the older line of theorizing, which stressed the Whiggery of the white Protestants. It also should be noted, however, that the question is a mixed one, touching on equalitarianism and consideration of the proper role of government. It might be that little more is indicated by this result than the presence of a laissez-faire orientation on the part of the middle-class Protestants. It is also possible that the ambiguity here provides merely a convenient and "legitimate" cover for a basically intolerant, inequalitarian outlook. It might, in other words, be merely a more acceptable alternative to open and straightforward Know Nothingism.[16]

Possibly the most important point to be made about the analysis thus far in this chapter is the extent to which the original socioreligious contextual determinants are still present on the scene. Despite a persistent focus on "class," the remarkable fact is the extent to which classes are divided along this "other" line. The relatively limited import of the class factor is a result (at least the 1948 election campaign would suggest this) of the absence of a focus on class issues, or alternatively, of the refusal by party leaders to make use of these issues. This being the case, there should be little cause for astonishment in the fact that mass politics show so little rationality and that the traditional basis of United States' politics still tends to prevail. It is, however, important to note that the urban white Protestants who are lower-middle class do tend to deviate from the political orientations of their socioreligious "pillar." It seems likely that this context is one in which political orientations are shifting from a pillar-based to a class-based outlook.

It is now necessary to turn to the Southern case to see how political orientations are distributed within the nonmanual ranks in that region.

The Southern Nonmanuals

The same "pillar" phenomenon is to be observed within the Southern middle class. In this case, however, there is a difference in the relative size of the two pillars, with approximately four out of five nonmanuals being white Protestants. Roughly seven out of ten of these white Protestants identify as Democrats. In the "other" column, the Democratic percentage is even more striking, with 87 percent identifying as such.

Although a little more than two-thirds of the white Protestants identified as Democrats, just under half of those reporting on their 1964 vote indicated that they voted Democratic. Unlike the rest of the country, the South showed a fair-sized movement to the Republicans. Moreover, what we have is a defection in the *non*manual ranks—not in the working class as has been so frequently claimed. Among the voters in the "other" column, the Democratic percentage is approximately the same as it was in the case of the party identifications; hence, the defections were specifically from the white Protestant middle class.

It is also worth noting the tendency of the relatively large numbers of middle-class nonvoters in 1964, most of them being in the white Protestant column. Unlike the voters, this group showed a pronounced Democratic preference. Since nonvoters tend to be poorer, more marginal, and so on, this is one further instance of the fact that the so-called backlash response—the attraction to racist themes—was not a peculiarity of poor whites but instead was more a characteristic of the better-off whites.[17]

Since in the South there are so few cases in the "other" pillar, we shall not explore the internal differentiations there, but instead shall concentrate on the white Protestant group. The cutting point used to divide the lower- and upper-middle classes has been set somewhat lower, at the $7500 level, in order to accord with the lower prevailing incomes in the region. There is a natural break at this point in the sense that the groups below that point tend to be substantially more Democratic than those above it. The lower-middle-class white Protestants in the South prove to be 79 percent Democratic in party identification (as compared to 50 percent outside the South). The Southern upper-middle-class white Protestants are 61 percent Democratic (as opposed to 31 percent elsewhere). The differences between the religions are fair-sized, amounting to about 30 percentage points at both class levels. It remains to be seen whether this preference for democracy hides a convergence on the issues —that is, whether this heavy preference for the "liberal" party does or does not mask a common position on the issues of the day.

Comparing the white Protestants in the South with those in the rest of the country, we find both similarities and differences in the issue orientations. (See Tables 5.4 and 5.5.) The upper-middle classes in the two regions prove to be very similar in outlook on the issues; that is, both are strongly conservative. The Southern group has 35 percent taking a liberal position on the

TABLE 5.5
Issue Orientations in Southern Nonmanual White Protestant Ranks (Married; Head in Labor Force) SRC 1964

	Southern Nonmanual White Protestant	
Family Income:	To $7499	$7500 or More
Economic Liberalism Questions	*Percent "liberal" of those with opinion*	
Medical Care	60%	35%
N =	(45)	(48)
Living standard	50	9
N =	(38)	(47)
School aid	26	26
N =	(43)	(57)
Government too powerful (% saying "no")	41	31
N =	(34)	(55)

medical care question as compared to 28 percent elsewhere; the respective percentages on the guaranteed living standard question are 9 and 18 percent. Approximately the same percentages favor government-supported schools and approximately the same low percentages feel the government is not too powerful. On all of these questions there is a substantial agreement on the rightness of the conservative position. It comes as little surprise that for this upper-middle class, the preponderant Democratic identification does in fact hide a marked conservative issue orientation.

The propensity of the Southern white Protestant lower-middle class is somewhat different from that of their peers elsewhere in the nation in that there is a considerably higher level of support for two key liberalism questions, the medical care one and the one on a guaranteed living standard. The proportions in favor of these programs are 60 and 50 percent, respectively (versus 41 and 26 percent elsewhere), a level of concern that finds little reflection in the actual conduct of Southern legislators. This part of the Southern lower-middle class is no different from the equivalent group elsewhere in the nation in their outlook on school aid. With respect to the "too powerful" government, they are slightly more conservative.

Comparing upper- and lower-middle-class white Protestants in the South, we find the lower middles to be more liberal on three of the four questions. There is no difference on the school aid question. On the others, however, the disparity ranges from 10 percentage points in respect to the "powerful" government to a rather large 41 percentage points in response to the living standard question. In the Southern context also, there is no basis for the claim of an especially reactionary lower-middle class.

The percentages of white Protestants approving government action to guarantee job equality and equal schooling for Negroes was considerably lower in the South, a fact that also comes as no surprise. For what it may be worth, there was no difference between the lower- and upper-middle classes in regard to government action on job rights but there was a 9 percent less favorable attitude on the part of the lower-middle class in the school desegregation question. This 9 percent difference was one of the few fragments of support found for the received claim in this entire study.[18]

A parallel analysis examining the party choices and issue orientations of the major segments of the nonmanual ranks was made using the 1956 Survey Research Center study. Space limitations do not allow a presentation of this evidence. In all significant respects, the 1956 results showed complete correspondence with those from the 1964 study.

Salaried Versus Independent Middle Class

It is worthwhile exploring another source of differentiation within the middle-class populations: the independence-dependence question. The independents, according to a long and well-established line of social theory, are closely tied to the market and suffer all the strains and uncertainties associated with economic fluctuations. Presumably, too, in recent times independent businessmen are the victims of "big government," "big business," and "big labor unions." As such, they are thought to be hostile to these "new" developments, preferring instead a return to some prior condition in which the independents were the dominant factor in social affairs.[19]

An examination of the pattern of party identification and of voting outside of the South showed some support for the basic notion of greater conservatism among the independents. It would be a mistake, however, to make much of a point about this since the overall differences were not very large, the independents being only seven percentage points less Democratic than the salaried in their identifications. In their 1964 voting, the difference was only six percentage points.

Since outside of the South the independents are somewhat more likely to be upper-middle class, we have made class-specific comparisons. (See Table 5.6.) When this was done, the differences are reduced still further. Whether one is salaried or independent, therefore, makes very little difference in party identification or in the 1964 voting choice. The same general pattern of small differences appears with respect to the economic liberalism issues. It will be remembered that in the 1964 election, people were "given a choice," one that presumably would appeal to the independents; for them, it was not just another run-of-the-mill issueless election.

This finding indicates that the "relationship to the means of production" and the "dependence on the market" make very little difference in the United States' electoral affairs. That does not, to be sure, say anything about other times and other places; in this study, however, this presumably key factor

TABLE 5.6

Politics and Issue Orientations of Independent and Salaried Nonsouth Nonmanuals
(Married: Head in Labor Force) SRC 1964

	Nonsouth Nonmanuals			
	To $10,000		$10,000 or More	
Family Income	Independent	Salaried	Independent	Salaried
Democratic identification				
(of 2-party choices)	60%	65%	42%	46%
N =	(55)	(129)	(50)	(82)
Percent Democratic, 1964				
(of 2-party choices)	65	68	47	53
N =	(46)	(113)	(47)	(73)
	Percent "liberal" of those with opinions			
Medical care	52	57	40	49
N =	(46)	(108)	(40)	(68)
Living standard	26	36	26	24
N =	(42)	(105)	(38)	(75)
School aid	35	36	36	40
N =	(43)	(106)	(45)	(75)
Government too powerful				
(percent "no")	53	58	41	45
N =	(38)	(98)	(44)	(71)

proved to be of very little significance. The relevance of this finding for
standard Marxist or neo-Marxist orientations is too obvious to require further
discussion. Since, however, the finding may prove difficult to accept, it is
important to make further exploration and to note that this finding could
conceivably depend on the cross-cutting socioreligious factor discussed earlier
in this chapter. Even if this proved to be the case (which it does not), the
above finding is still relevant to the Marxist position, since the economic factor
should make itself apparent; it should outweigh that purely traditional heritage and make itself shown in the overall result.

It is imperative that we look at the impact of independence within the two
socioreligious columns discussed earlier. If independence is associated with
special strains that, in turn, gave rise to a special kind of politics we ought
to see it clearly reflected in both subgroups. The special conservatism of the
independents ought to come through in each of the four possible comparisons.

The findings, however, do not accord with this expectation. In the white
Protestant ranks the lower-middle-class independents are slightly *more* Democratic in both identification and in their 1964 voting than are the equivalent

TABLE 5.7
Politics and Issue Orientations of Independent and Salaried Nonsouth White Protestants (Married; Head in Labor Force) SRC 1964

	Non-South, Nonmanual White Protestants			
	To $10,000		$10,000 or More	
Family Income:	Independent	Salaried	Independent	Salaried
Democratic identification				
(of 2-party choice)	54%	48%	14%	40%
$N =$	(37)	(69)	(21)	(48)
Percent Democratic, 1964				
(of 2-party choice)	59	53	14	39
$N =$	(29)	(59)	(22)	(41)
	Percent "liberal" of those with opinions			
Medical care	40	42	11	37
$N =$	(30)	(57)	(18)	(38)
Living standard	18	30	11	19
$N =$	(28)	(57)	(18)	(43)
School aid	18	29	24	30
$N =$	(28)	(56)	(21)	(44)
Government too powerful				
(percent "no")	56	46	20	40
$N =$	(25)	(52)	(20)	(43)

salarieds. (See Table 5.7.) In response to two of the liberalism questions the lower-middle-class white Protestant independents are more conservative, by 12 percent in the case of the living standard question and by 11 percent in response to the school aid question. There is, on the other hand, virtually no difference with respect to the medical care question; two-fifths of both independents and salaried favor such a program. And in response to the question on government power, 56 percent of the independents, 10 percent more than among the salaried, say that the government is *not* too powerful. The evidence, in summary, is somewhat contradictory. At minimum, however, we may say that the thesis of lower-middle-class independent business conservatism receives no significant support; three of the comparisons in Table 5.7 go against the hypothesis, and one shows no difference. The two supporting cases involve differences of 11 and 12 percentage points.

We do find that the *upper*-middle-class white Protestant independents are much more conservative, by all measures, than are the equivalent salaried. These findings for the white Protestants, however, mean that the opposite pattern obtains among the "others." The "other" upper-middle-class independents are somewhat less Republican than are the equivalent salaried. The impact of the socioreligious factor is made clear by the fact that only 14 percent of the upper-middle-class white Protestant independents identify as Democrats as opposed to 62 percent among those in the "other" column (not shown in the Table).

The hypothesis about the role of the economic determinants cannot be excluded, however, without showing first that the groups do in fact have similar interests. It is possible that, due to differing times of immigration and different urban-rural location, they are engaged in different kinds of business with different "objective interests." A more detailed questioning would be necessary in order to assess this possibility.[20]

As the picture stands, the initial small support for the view of a special conservativism among the independents stems from an averaging together of the diverse patterns of the two socioreligious columns. It is impossible to explore the matter in more detail at this point, but one lesson is clear—the upper-middle-class white Protestant independents prove to be a very special enclave of conservatism. The significance of this fact is rather striking. Given the special historical advantages of white Protestants generally and given the freedom of independents (especially those from the upper-middle class) to express "authoritative" positions, their voices are ordinarily going to count for much more than those of the "dependent" salaried—the managers, the teachers, the engineers, and so on.

Again, for reasons of space, we shall not make a detailed presentation of the Southern experience. There, too, the evidence provides no clear support for the conventional thesis. The lower-middle-class independents in the South are more Democratic in party identification, slightly more favorable to government-supporetd medical care and the living standard guarantees than are the equivalent salaried. They are, on the other hand, less favorable toward school aid and are more worried about government power.

Since the point is such an important one, equivalent runs were made using the 1956 SRC study. Taking the non-South lower-middle classes, it was found that in five comparisons (three liberalism questions, party identification, and 1956 vote) that the independents were consistently *more* liberal than the salaried. There is only an insignificant difference in the case of the school aid question but the other differences range from 14 to 21 percentage points. In the non-South upper-middle class there is some evidence of greater conservatism on the part of the independents but once again the evidence is contradictory. The upper-middle-class independents are less Democratic than the salaried (by 10 percent), but then they are very slightly more favorable to the job guarantee and the school aid options. The 1956 evidence from the South also offers no clear cut support for the received claim.

All of this suggests that the heavy emphasis that has been given to economic determinants and to special "structural strains," at least in the case of the United States, has not been justified. Once again, in terms of the social pressures and the personal influence hypotheses the finding comes as no great surprise. "Lower-middle-class" independents live in working-class communities, come out of working-class families, have associated with working-class children in school, and have clients who are largely working class. It would be very difficult for them, openly, to take a political line that was opposed by most persons in the neighborhood area. That assumes that they would want to take a different line. As small proprietors, in great measure their personal well-being depends on the efforts of "strong unions." Where unions get good wage settlements, the position of the independents would also improve. Most small proprietors, having no employees (other than family members) are not competing with giant firms in labor markets and are specifically excluded from participation in government-sponsored aid and welfare programs. This latter exclusion means that they are not forced to make contributory payments into any welfare fund and also they are not involved with government "red tape." In short, the familiar lines of analysis about the small independent businessmen simply do not apply to them.[21]

The Manual Ranks

We shall follow a procedure here that is similar to the one used in our analysis of the nonmanuals. That is, we shall consider the South and the non-South separately and, within each region, the ranks will be divided by "pillar" and income. The purpose of the income division is somewhat different in this case. Rather than providing an indicator of a different territorial base or membership in different community areas, the purpose here is rather to assess the classical "economism" hypothesis, that is, that better-off workers are more conservative.

The same differentiation in party choices by pillar appears with the white Protestants once again more Republican (or less Democratic) in identification than the "others." In the manual context, however, the pillar differences are somewhat smaller than among the nonmanuals. Within the manual ranks also the "upper" and "lower" income distinction is not as systematically associated with differences in party identifications and choices as among the nonmanuals. Among the white Protestants, for example, there is a 4 percentage point difference in identification associated with income. (See Table 5.8.) Among the "other" workers we find the lower-income category to be 14 percentage points more Democratic than the better-off one.[22] The overall 4 and 14 percent differences must be contrasted with differences among the equivalent nonmanuals of 19 and 22 percentage points.

Although we cannot find room for the presentation here, equivalent runs from the 1956 study showed the *lower*-income workers in both pillars to be slightly less Democratic than the high-income groups. In summary, the evidence suggests that both sources of differentiation count for less in the manual ranks. The manuals, in other words, tend to be more homogeneous in

TABLE 5.8

Politics and Issue Orientations of Nonsouth Manuals (Married; Head in Labor Force) SRC 1964

	Non-South Manuals			
	White Protestants		All Others	
Family Income:	To $7500	$7500 or More	To $7500	$7500 or More
Democratic identification				
(of 2-party choices)	67%	63%	88%	74%
N =	(95)	(71)	(68)	(54)
Percent Democratic, 1964				
(of 2-party choices)	82	64	96	75
N =	(71)	(61)	(51)	(48)
	Percent "liberal" of those with opinions			
Medical care	70	51	86	70
N =	(83)	(63)	(58)	(44)
Living standard	38	45	61	36
N =	(64)	(58)	(62)	(42)
School aid	39	34	51	44
N =	(79)	(56)	(65)	(45)
Government too powerful				
(percent "no")	68	56	75	70
N =	(60)	(50)	(48)	(30)

party preference than do the nonmanuals. Of the two sources of differentiation considered here, the socioreligious proves to be generally the more important.

Turning to the issue questions, we find here a tendency toward greater liberalism among the lower-income groups. Exploration of the equivalent questions in the 1956 study (where we found lower-income groups to be slightly more Republican) also showed the low-income groups to be slightly more liberal. This points to a degree of independence between the two factors. Party identification tends to run "within the family," to be traditional, handed down, and relatively independent of events. Position on the issues is not given as part of the family heritage and is much more directly dependent on events; stated simply, poor people want medical care, job guarantees, and guarantees of minimal standards of living.[23]

Working-class conservatism is slightly more prevalent in the white Protestant ranks. More specifically, the 1964 study shows slightly more Republican identification and a greater percentage of Republican voting among the better-off white Protestant workers. With respect to the issue orientations, both the 1956 and 1964 studies agree about the relative conservatism of the better-off white Protestant workers. One additional bit of evidence that shows this "Toryism" appears in examination of the 1964 defections. In the 1964 election campaign, the upper-income white Protestant working-class populations tended to vote in accordance with their party identifications. Elsewhere, however, the Republicans suffered considerable losses; this was especially the case among the low-income white Protestant workers. The Goldwater candidacy did indirectly what the Truman campaign did directly—it contributed to a "rationalization" of the behavior of a significant proportion of the electorate. A major consequence of the Goldwater candidacy was the conversion of "Tory workers."[24]

Given the widespread conservative fantasy that there are many people sitting out elections awaiting a suitable candidate, it is worth noting that the largest quantity of nonvoters discovered thus far is found among the low-income manual groups and that their dispositions—in both socioreligious columns—are overwhelmingly Democratic. The obvious lesson is that if the entire or near-entire electorate were mobilized, a sizable liberal "input" would be contributed to "the political system."[25]

Many social scientists have focused on the "destabilizing" impact of heightened participation, this presumably meaning the mobilization of "authoritarians," of intolerance, and of antidemocratic sentiment. Insofar as the heightened participation meant the mobilization of economic liberal sentiment, and to the extent that legislators were moved by that sentiment, it would mean a more adequately functioning democracy, one with more equity, and possibly also one with more "legitimacy" and hence more "stability."

The Southern Workers

The Southern working class presents a more complex picture. The white Protestants, putting the matter as simply as possible, tend to be the upper-income workers and the "others"—overwhelmingly Negro—tend to be the low-income workers. Since the South as a whole is heavily Protestant, there is no significant Catholic population present as among the Northern manuals.

In party identifications the "others" are more heavily Democratic than the white Protestants but that means the former group are more than 90 percent Democratic while the latter are "only" somewhat more than 80 percent. (See Table 5.9.) In 1964 voting behavior, the four groups were all about 80 percent Democratic. Better-off white Protestant workers had the largest Republican percentage (23 percent) and, allowing for the small numbers involved, had a high percentage of nonvoters indicating a Republican preference (7 of 16 cases).

Summarizing the issue orientations as simply as possible, we may note the following: the "others" in the South are uniformly more liberal than the white Protestant workers, and, among the latter, the poorer white Protestants

TABLE 5.9
Politics and Issue Orientations of Southern Manuals (Married; Head in Labor Force) SRC 1964

Family Income:	Southern Manual Workers			
	White Protestants		All Others	
	To $5000	$5000 or More	To $5000	$5000 or More
Democratic identification				
(of 2-party choices)	81%	85%	93%	93%
N =	(21)	(39)	(28)	(15)
Percent Democratic, 1964	80	77	85	80
N =	(15)	(26)	(13)	(10)
	Percent "liberal" of those with opinions			
Medical care	69	60	96	80
N =	(16)	(30)	(27)	(15)
Living standard	73	39	89	89
N =	(15)	(31)	(28)	(18)
School aid	44	39	76	71
N =	(16)	(33)	(25)	(17)
Government too powerful				
(percent "no")	57	27	79	71
N =	(14)	(26)	(19)	(14)

are uniformly more liberal than the better-off workers. Relative to other workers, the better-off Southern white Protestant segment is somewhat more of conservative. This is not so marked in response to the medical care question but it is very sharp in regard to the guaranteed living standard and the government power questions. Interestingly enough, although these Southern white Protestant workers proved to be relatively conservative, the role of tradition appears once again in that this issue orientation has no significant payoff in terms of voting for the more conservative of the parties. The level of Democratic voting in 1964, when people were "given a choice," was little different from that of the other three more liberal groups of Southern workers.

It is important to emphasize that this discussion is of the *relative* conservatism of the better-off white Protestant workers both in the South and elsewhere. On the whole, white Protestant workers are also a liberal group. Fifty-one percent of the better-off non-South group favor the medical care option, a level that is still above that of the equivalent white Protestant middle-class groups. Forty-five percent of them favor the guaranteed living standard, a figure that is to be contrasted with the 26 percent figure among the lower-middle-class non-South white Protestants. The question to be explained is the presence of a fair-sized conservative working class minority within this context.

The evidence as presented thus far would appear to support the conventional "economism" hypothesis. Before one fits this new evidence into the conventional framework, however, it is necessary to consider an obvious alternative that might also account for this finding. It is possible, for example, that rather than a "conversion" taking place with "new found" affluence, what is operating is merely a traditional or handed-down party identification. Exploration of this possibility does support this latter alternative since 21 of the 22 well-off Republicans in the sample who knew their father's politics reported that he too was a Republican. This suggests, in turn, that somehow or other these workers have come to be located in a milieu that protects or insulates their received orientation from the dominant influences within the working class. The SRC study does not have many questions that allow us to chart out in any detail the character of their segregation within the working-class milieu. Some clues, however, are available. Taking the better-off white Protestants, we find the Republican identifiers are less likely to be unionized than are the Democrats (54%, $N = 26$ versus 73%, $N = 45$) and they are somewhat more likely to be located in smaller communities than are the Democrats (in places of 2500 or less, 31% versus 16%).

The pattern of party shifting among the well-off is deserving of more detailed attention. In this context, among the "affluent" workers, only one respondent has shifted away from his father's Democratic position as opposed to five Republicans shifting to the Democrats. Among the workers who possibly had less firm political anchorage, that is, those whose fathers were independents or apolitical, we find that 75 percent ($N = 16$) fell to the Democrats. From the perspective of the "economism" hypothesis it is rather ironic that the Republicans do slightly better among the less-well-off workers, that is, a larger percentage shift away from a Democratic heritage to Republicanism. These poorer workers who shifted from the father's Democratic or apolitical position into the Republican camp tend to be very disproportionately small-town dwellers and non-union (10 of the 14 were non-union and 8 lived in places of 2500 or fewer persons).[26]

What we have said thus far focuses on the presence or retention of a Republican heritage among the better-off workers. There is a parallel process operating among the less-well-off. Southern-reared workers migrate to the North and bring their Democratic party orientations with them. Since most of the Southern-reared end up in low-paid positions, this has the result of providing spurious support for the economism thesis. As an illustration of the impact of this migration and transfer of allegiances, we may note that the Democratic identifications of the low- and better-paid non-South white Protestant workers were 67 and 63 percent (from Table 5.8). Eliminating the Southern-reared yields a slight reversal, the new figures being 63 and 65 percent, respectively.

In conclusion, we may note that there does tend to be more Republicanism among better-off workers but this orientation appears to be a result of a special, well-retained heritage rather than due to the "affluence" itself.

The Working-Class Wives

As noted in Chapter 4, the working-class family may be subject to varying influences depending on the position of the wife; she may live solely within a working-class neighborhood or home milieu (as a housewife) or she may be employed in either a manual or nonmanual occupation.[27] If the latter, it is possible that she could come in contact with middle-class populations and pick up "middle-class" values. It could be a setting in which some significant change might occur.

Three SRC studies indicate that somewhat less than one-third of the non-South working-class wives were employed. Of these, just over half were in manual and somewhat less than half were in nonmanual occupations. We have taken the attitudes of housewives as the reference point for this analysis, as providing a "normal" level of Democratic sentiment for working-class wives.

Taking both party identification and voting, we may make six comparisons. (See Table 5.10.) Those working-class wives in middle-class employment were less Democratic than working-class housewives in two comparisons (thus

TABLE 5.10
Party Identification and Vote of Working-Class Wives by Employment Status

	Working-Class Wives who are:		
	In Nonmanual Occupations	In Manual Occupations	Housewives
Party identification	*Percent Democratic of Two-Party Choices*		
SRC 1964	81%	70%	67%
N =	(21)	(27)	(100)
SRC 1956	45	80	57
N =	(29)	(35)	(138)
SRC 1952	57	72	58
N =	(23)	(32)	(133)
Voting			
SRC 1964	88%	91%	77%
N =	(17)	(21)	(81)
SRC 1956	41	57	41
N =	(27)	(28)	(112)
SRC 1952	39	64	48
N =	(18)	(22)	(110)

offering support for the hypothesis), equally Democratic in two comparisons, and more Democratic in the two comparisons from the 1964 study (thus challenging the received hypothesis). There is, in short, no clear and consistent evidence in support of this hypothesis to be found in these studies.

When we look at the working-class wives engaged in manual occupations we find in all six comparisons that they are more Democratic than the working-class housewives.

From the perspective of the present study, these findings—the absence of clear and consistent support for the received hypothesis—is not much of a surprise. These wives come out of urban working-class families and neighborhoods. It is likely that their jobs are very much "lower-middle class" and that many of their co-workers are also from working-class backgrounds. We have noted also that some segments of the lower-middle class are heavily Democratic in their orientations. Hence, a venture into the lower-middle class, which is made five times a week by these working-class wives, is not likely to be a move that takes them into a markedly different social or political milieu. The jobs themselves are probably not in the downtown or front offices of the firms but rather are likely to be in fringe areas, in working-class neighborhoods, next to the factory, and so on. The strongest evidence in support of the received hypothesis is the twelve percentage point difference in party identification shown in the 1956 study. If we were to take this as a genuine finding and if we were to attribute this difference to the influence of the milieu (and not to family background or to small-town location), we would still have to take that finding in connection with the greater difference in the opposite direction indicated in the 1964 study.

To have any significant influence on elections, one would have to assume that the "new" political orientation that the wife has supposedly acquired in her middle-class milieu is going to be passed on to her husband. It should, however, be noted that this is a direction of influence that is very unlikely. Husbands give political direction to wives but it is rare that political influence flows from the wife to the husband.[28]

Education and the Working Class

Much has been said about the "rising levels" of education in the United States.[29] It is this development that "provides more and more opportunity," aids in the creation of "consensus," and creates, if not middle-class jobs, then at least middle-class outlooks. About the fact of "rising levels" there can be little question. The significance of the development, however, is open to considerable question. One point that is frequently made is that the "increased education" constitutes a "necessity" for a modern society; because of the complexity of modern technology there is more and more need for high skill development.

This point, however, would seem a somewhat dubious one since increasing numbers of those with this "necessary training" end up in working-class occupations. The rising educational level, for example, has been associated with a continuous increase in the percentage of the working class who report having at least "some college." The actual percentages (taking all economically active male manuals) were 4 in 1952, 9 in 1956, and 11 in 1964.[30] There are a few college graduates among them but most of the college-educated workers report only "some college."

This finding strongly suggests that the "necessity" argument is a false one. It also suggests that the education these workers have received was not of very high quality; it obviously provided very little basis for their mobility. What seems more than likely is that we are dealing with "debased" units of education; the 13 or 14 years of education that they report are very likely to, in fact, be equal to 8 or 9. It is likely that the last "years" of this education were spent in the process of "dropping out" or of being "cooled out." As such, this "education" would constitute little more than a digression or detour in the course of a normal working-class career.[31]

It has sometimes been suggested that education plays a role in the presumed processes of "bourgeoisification." In the course of all those years of education, one would acquire middle-class values and outlooks, one would acquire strong mobility values, and one would be led, through some process of "anticipatory socialization" to imitate the values of the rank one wished to enter. It is worth inquiring as to whether this is in fact the case.

Non-South white males were studied for this purpose. This procedure allows us to control for a number of extraneous factors and leaves us with the largest core group of the American working class, a group with sufficient homogeneity to allow a reasonable test of the political impact of education. One runs again into the small numbers problem and for this reason we have used three different studies. The overall picture is one that provides no clear support for this modern variant of the "bourgeoisification" hypothesis. The evidence is contained in Table 5.11.

It is worth bearing in mind that this lack of difference is present even though "educated" workers are of higher social background than others, that is, a greater percentage of them come from either skilled or middle-class families. Higher education, in other words, touches those who are somewhat better off to begin with; the majority of workers are, as yet, still scarcely influenced by it.[32]

These findings—that there are college-educated workers and that they are no different politically from other workers—come as a surprise only in the light of conventional assumptions about education in America. If one makes the mistaken assumption that one equals one (that one year of education at Prairie State is equal to one year at Princeton), the findings come as a surprise. At the lesser-prestige institutions, not only is it obvious that the quality of the education leaves much to be desired, but also the content of the education—that which comes through both the formal and the informal

TABLE 5.11
Party Identification and Education (Married, Manual Non-South White Males in the Labor Force)

	8 or Less Years	9–11, Same Plus Non-college	High School Grad-uate	H.S. Grad Plus Non-college	Some College
			Education		
	Percent Democratic of 2-party identifiers				
SRC 1952	78%	74%	52%	71%	67%
N =	(83)	(62)	(27)	(17)	(9)
SRC 1956	45	80	61	53	56
N =	(64)	(44)	(41)	(15)	(18)
SRC 1964	86	75	74	59	77
N =	(28)	(32)	(35)	(17)	(17)

channels—is not likely to lead to much change in political orientation. One has to raise the question of just how much "bourgeoisification" is likely to occur in the course of study at the two-year community college in the industrial city, especially when the student lives at home.

An Overview: The Classes and the Pillars

The use of income to subdivide the manual and nonmanual ranks has served two purposes. The first (the major one intended here) has been to provide an indication of membership in separate communities such as those typified by the middle-class suburbs of Milwaukee and, on the other hand, the majority working-class districts of the center city. The second purpose, more of a by-product, has been to allow exploration of the "economism" thesis, that is, to inquire as to the relationship between income differences and political attitudes. In this discussion we would like to look at the overall picture in more detail, both with more detailed income breaks and, for the first time, with the "other" pillar broken down into its components.

Taking the non-South white Protestant working class, we find that in this context, income makes no systematic difference in party identification. (See Table 5.12.) The "affluent" workers are as Democratic as the poorest. The only difference of note here is that the better-off workers tend, more than others, to be weak Democrats or independent Democrats. There is no associated shift to "strong" Republicanism among the better-off Republican workers. In short, the economism thesis would appear to be completely useless in describing this segment of the population.

TABLE 5.12
Party Identification by Class, Column, and Income for Non-South (Married; Head in Labor Force) SRC 1964

	Manual				Nonmanual				
Family Income:	Less Than $6000	$6000– $7499	$7500– $9999	$10,000 or More	Less Than $6000	$6000– $7499	$7500– $9999	$10,000– $14,999	$15,000 or More
	Percent identifying as Democrats (of 2-party choice)								
White Protestants	72%	61%	60%	70%	61%	48%	42%	36%	20%
N =	(54)	(41)	(48)	(23)	(43)	(21)	(43)	(50)	(20)
Catholics	84	86	71	67	77	82	89	61	43
N =	(19)	(28)	(21)	(18)	(17)	(17)	(26)	(28)	(14)
Jews		100%			100%			78%	
N =		(4)			(8)			(9)	
Negroes	91%				71%			50%	
N =	(22)				(7)			(4)	
Others	91%				20%			60%	
N =	(11)				(5)			(10)	
All	79	73	67	70	67	66	58	47	39
N =	(86)	(77)	(79)	(46)	(67)	(44)	(76)	(91)	(44)

Among the white Protestant nonmanual population, the evidence is *consonant with* the economism thesis; there are sharp and consistent changes in party identification associated with five levels of income. Whether the income is causal or merely indicative of background differences is another question demanding separate consideration. At minimum, however, the political correlates of high income in this context are very clear. As will be shown in a later chapter, a very high percentage of those in the higher income categories indicated that their fathers were Republican. The "upward mobiles" into these categories also showed a high rate of conversion to Republicanism.

It is important to dwell briefly on the political character of the white Protestant "lower-middle class" and to note the likely significance of mobility into that class from the manual ranks. It is unlikely that the best-off manual workers would care to move into lower-middle-class jobs. The bases of their incomes are very specific manual skills that are not transferable and usable in middle-class occupations. For these workers, the price to be paid for mobility would be a lower income. Given what we know about manual worker motivations, it is unlikely that they would care to make this sacrifice for the sake of any prestige associated with "white-collar" work.[33] This means that the most likely candidates for mobility would be the middle-income manual workers, those for whom there would be either no great financial sacrifice involved or for whom the security of white-collar positions (versus the uncertain employment in physically demanding semiskilled jobs) would be an important consideration.[34] A move by workers into the lower-income middle-class categories of Table 5.12 would involve little change for them as far as the political character of their new environment is concerned. If they came into the lowest-paid group of nonmanual white Protestants there would be no change at all, both the new and the former contexts being approximately three-fifths Democratic. If they arrived in the next highest "middle-class" income group, they would still be in a context that is only marginally differentiated from their former milieu, the members of this context dividing 50–50 in their party preferences. In short, a move into the lower-middle-class would have very little meaning for such upward mobiles since that context, contrary to popular theorizing, is so heavily Democratic.[35]

Within the Catholic working class there is some evidence that is consonant with the economism thesis; the better-off categories do show some tendency toward increased Republicanism. Given, however, the overwhelming Democratic percentages among the poorer working-class Catholics, this still means a two-to-one Democratic edge even among these working-class "aristocrats." The Republicans here also tend to be non-union and small town.

The Catholic nonmanual ranks show a pattern that stands in very marked contrast to the white Protestant pattern. The three income categories up to $10,000 are all at least three-fourths Democratic and the tendency is for the percentage to increase in the higher of these categories. It is only in the highest-income categories (over $10,000) that we find a break in the conservative direction. Even here, the levels of Democratic sentiment are nearly double those of the equivalent white Protestants. These findings provide eloquent testimony to the fact that, at best, level of income could have only a very restricted impact in the determination of outlooks. There is much more impressive support for the alternative explanation—the notion of "social determinism"—the findings indicating a much greater differentiation associated with the socioreligious factor.

The same point can be made about manual to nonmanual mobility as we made with respect to the white Protestants. For those workers in the $6 to $7.5 thousand working-class range, for example, a move into any middle-class rank below the upper-middle class would mean a move into a very similar political milieu. The better-off manuals, should they make the same move, would be moving into a rank that is even more Democratic than their former "location."

The two remaining groups from the "other" pillar differ somewhat from the Catholic column in that they are rather "imbalanced." The Jews are almost all located in the nonmanual ranks and two thirds of the Negroes are found among the manuals. Both groups are very heavily Democratic.

There are only very limited income-related political differences in any of the component groups of our "other" column. This is the case with the white Catholics and also, allowing for the problem of small numbers, for the Jews and Negroes. The income-related differences or, more generally, the class differences in politics appear primarily in the white Protestant column and even there it is more specifically among the nonmanual white Protestant that the significant differences appear.

The white Protestant numbers, fortunately for the democracy of the society, are too large to allow for the formation of a cohesive body or to allow a common outlook. This group, therefore, fragments into more or less distinctive subgroups. Most importantly, it proves impossible for the leaders or elites in that "pillar" to influence, engineer, or otherwise guarantee consent to their "establishment" position.

The Protestant upper- and upper-middle classes have been exclusivist, Whiggish, and "know nothing" in their outlook over the years. Their construction of separate formal and informal institutions has meant that they have unwittingly limited their influence by cutting themselves off from the rising (or "emergent") upper-middle classes in the "other" column. By so doing they forced the various leaders outside their ranks to organize, in a sense, *down* across class lines, to maintain subgroup solidarity, and to proceed somewhat more defensively than they would have done had things proceeded otherwise in the course of American history. The fact that the elites and upper-middle classes were thus divided has meant that "class polarization" (as initially discussed in this chapter) has never been very great since many nonmanuals were led to maintain their Democratic identifications and loyalties.[36]

There is one final point to be made in this summary. There is a sweeping consensus in the sociological literature on the importance of the manual-nonmanual line. So important is this cutting point that many researchers have incorporated it into their studies and have used those or some equivalents as the key focal terms of the analysis. There is a general assumption that the "biggest differences" in attitudes and life styles occur at this breaking point and that the most significant mobility involves the crossing of that line.

We cannot speak generally and can only discuss the political questions studied here, but as far as party identifications go, that position is not supported. If we take the poorest of the nonmanuals (that is, those who earn considerably less than the best-off manual category), we find that their Democratic percentage is not substantially different from any of the four income categories of manuals presented here (bottom line of percents, Table 5.12). One should also keep in mind that the poorer nonmanuals are disproportionately white Protestants, older, and from small towns. Even if we proceed one step higher and take those nonmanuals earning between $6 and $7.5 thousand, we find that they too are not especially different from three of the four working-class groups. None of the percentage figures in the six lower left-hand columns of Table 5.12 are more than eight percentage points away from the overall figure for these working-class and lower-middle class categories, which is 71 percent.[37] The more sizable defections from that "consensus" appear first in the higher income nonmanual categories. The higher we go in the nonmanual ranks, the greater the percentage difference from the working-class–lower-middle-class "consensus." All this adds up to saying that the biggest "break" in the class structure is not between manuals and nonmanuals but rather is between the lower-middle and upper-middle classes. This finding is possibly the most significant one in the entire book.

The pattern in the South is essentially the same as the one described above. A move by a white Protestant from the high-income manual rank to the lower-middle class shifts one from a context that in the 1964 study was 80 percent Democrat to one that was 81 percent. A move upward by the low-income manuals would involve a shift to a more Democratic milieu.[38]

It is important to consider two additional questions. The chapter has been focused on married manuals and nonmanuals, hence the question arises: what about other groups? And a second question arises: what about possible shifts in political orientation? To answer these questions as economically as possible, we have taken the party identification questions from the 1952 and 1964 studies. Looking first at the 1964 non-South populations, we find that the nonmarried middle class (that is, those who are single, divorced, separated, or widowed) are very similar to the married in their identifications. (See Table 5.13.) The nonmarried manuals, by comparison, prove to be more heavily Democratic than the marrieds. Retired nonmanuals have a strong Republican tendency in opposition to the Democratic majority among those who are economically active. This peculiarity of the retired middle class

TABLE 5.13
Party Identification: 1952 and 1954 (All Respondents with Party Choice)

	Nonmanual			Manual			Farm		
	Married Employed	Not Married Employed	Retired	Married Employed	Not Married Employed	Retired	Employed	Retired	Other
	Percentage identifying as Democrats of 2-party choice								
Non-South									
1952	45%	50%	39%	67%	75%	49%	58%	44%	50%
$N=$	(341)	(62)	(33)	(400)	(64)	(37)	(101)	(18)	(101)
1964	55	58	31	73	85	63	61	44	61
$N=$	(336)	(71)	(55)	(294)	(58)	(51)	(41)	(16)	(61)
Difference	+10	+8	−8	+6	+10	+14	+3	0	+11
South									
1952	86	80	100	78	71	67	68	93	82
$N=$	(104)	(25)	(8)	(144)	(28)	(9)	(69)	(14)	(45)
1964	74	76	52	88	93	96	75	80	69
$N=$	(141)	(29)	(23)	(105)	(15)	(26)	(40)	(15)	(39)
Difference	−12	−4	−48[a]	+10	+22[a]	+29[a]	+7	−13[a]	−13

[a] Based on small numbers.

219

is not due to a "conversion of the aged," but rather to the socioreligious character of the group, it being much more heavily white Protestant than is the case with those currently is nonmanual positions.[39] The retired manuals show a Democratic majority although it is not as strong as among those still active.

It may come as a bit of a surprise that the farmers show a Democratic majority; this, it will be remembered, is among the non-South farm population. The figure includes both farm owners and farm labor, but even if we take the former group alone we still find a Democratic majority.[40] Once again, we see the inadequacy of a "time-honored" or "classical" hypothesis. The number of cases is rather small, but, for what it is worth, the retired farmers show a Republican majority. Finally, the others (mostly housewives together with some students) show a fair-sized Democratic majority.

Allowing for the generally higher level of Democracy, we find a similar picture in the South. The only finding of special note here is the strength of Republican sentiment among the retired nonmanuals. In this case there is a near 50–50 split. The explanation for this deviation from Southern politics generally is relatively simple. A large portion of the retirees spend their careers outside of the South (9 of the 23). Eight of the 9 reported a Republican identification. Among the retirees of Southern origins the Democrats constituted 73 percent.

A similar picture appears with respect to voting in 1964 (not shown in the table). The pattern of Democratic voting has the same emphases or clustering as the identifications. Of special note is the fact that the retired nonmanuals, both those in the South and the non-South, turned out Republican majorities. The Goldwater themes apparently appealed to a previous generation, to the middle class of an earlier age.

The groups considered in this extended discussion would not reduce the differences observed earlier with respect to the active manuals and non-manuals alone. The heavy Democratic sentiment among the nonmarried manuals and the strong Republicanism among the retired nonmanuals could only accentuate the differences noted earlier.

It is not possible to go into the issue orientations in any detail. The medical care issue was taken as possibly most salient to the largest number of individuals. The picture here mirrors the picture of the party identifications. The significant new observation in this connection is that the retired nonmanuals outside the South show a pro-medical care majority. Retired manuals are overwhelming in their support for such a program. If these groups were included in our basic presentation, that too would accentuate the differences already shown. Farmers, moreover, favor the suggestion by a two-to-one majority. This holds, too, for all farm subgroups, South and non-South, active and retired.

With respect to the question of the trend, we may begin by referring back to the data contained in Table 3.3. There we noted small fluctuations in the pattern of party identification. The Democratic two-party percentage, for example, declined six percentage points between 1952 and 1956, recovered completely in 1958, and with minor fluctuation ended at 67 percent in 1964. Study of the 1952 to 1956 pattern showed most subgroups within the population making some shift to the Republicans, the pattern appearing to be one of across the board "drift." There was no specific class location in the shifting.

The presentation here will focus on the 1952 to 1964 trend. The overall pattern is one of very little change between the two dates, the net result being a four percentage point increase for the Democrats. This evident stability, however, overlooks a considerable amount of two-directional shifting that is balanced out in this "net" result.

In Table 5.13 a "plus difference" indicates a shift of a subgroup toward the Democrats, a "minus" means a shift toward the Republicans. It may be seen that aside from the stability in the farm sector, the Democrats made general across-the-board gains in most of the major non-South population segments. The only area of Republican gain is in the relatively restricted and politically not-all-too-promising context of the retired nonmanual population. The Republicans are faced with the problem that not only are retireds (the non-manual ones) a poor base for a future party revival, but also there is every reason, as suggested earlier, to assume that this pattern will shift to their disadvantage in the course of time.

A different pattern appears in the South. The Democrats made gains among the Southern manual workers, but among the nonmanuals, the reverse is the case. Here we find some Republican advance. There are also advances indicated among the South's retired farmers and the residual subgroup (mostly housewives). Another center of Southern Republicanism happens to be the nonmanual retired, notably the *immigrés* discussed earlier. The Republicanism in the South tends to be upper-middle class with no important resonance, as of 1964, to be found in either the lower-middle or the working class (see Chapter 7).

The minor flow of mobility associated with the retirement of upper-middle-class populations has an ironic consequence. Elderly, influential conservatives from Northern and Midwestern states remove themselves and regroup in a few select watering spots, notably in Florida, Arizona, and southern California. This reduces the electoral chances for the Republicans in northern areas and at the same time provides them with enhanced chances in these centers for the retired. The concentration of the retired upper-middle classes no doubt goes a long way to account for the unique brand of Republicanism associated with those states (as evidenced in the presence of such successful politicos as Governors Kirk and Reagan and Senator Goldwater).

The chances for more adequately representative politics are somewhat enhanced in other regions as a result of this self-selected removal of conservatives. Whether or not something will come of this new condition will depend on the character of the (by default) somewhat stronger Democrats or of new party developments that might arise. Nothing, of course, is "in the cards" in this respect; it all depends on the character of the political efforts to be undertaken.

It is important, finally, to consider once again the question of the class divisions. The Alford method for summarizing class "polarization" errs in the assumption that the manual-nonmanual cleavage is the most significant one. In this respect, to be sure, he is merely following a long tradition that grew out of revisionist Marxism and that has become incorporated in the contemporary social sciences. The basic difficulty is that the nonmanual average combines two diverse patterns of political orientation, that of a relatively liberal and Democratic lower-middle class and a relatively conservative and Republican upper-middle category. Also, there is the additional complication of the pillars and their diverse political outlooks.

It proves useful to undertake a modification of the Alford procedure. When we took the married, non-South populations who give a party identification, the difference in Democratic party identification between manuals and nonmanuals was +18, a "normal" low level for the United States. But that nonmanual figure is an average of two diverse experiences, the Democratic percentages being 63 and 44 percent for the lower- and upper-middle class, respectively (using $10,000 as the cutting point as we have done throughout this chapter). This means that we actually have the following picture:[41]

Between lower and upper manuals	Between upper manuals and lower middle	Between lower and upper middle	Between all manuals and upper middle
+8	+5	+19	+29

This presentation still leaves much to be desired. The Catholic and Jewish upper-middle classes are different from the equivalent white Protestant category. It seems likely that the latter group is more directly linked to the national and metropolitan ruling or upper classes since they are, in many cases, high-level employees who are close to the top of the chains of command in major industrial bureaucracies. It seems likely that there would also be systematic informal connections along religious lines in city and country clubs and in other voluntary associations.

The Catholic and Jewish upper- and upper-middle classes tend to be located in different business and industrial bureaucracies and in different communities and associations. In governmental affairs, other than the relatively restricted sphere of local government, they are likely to be engaged in the performance of what we may call the "minor" governmental tasks. Many of the tasks of the society have been left in private hands in the United States. Much of welfare activity, for example, is still performed by private voluntary associations, mutual improvement associations, and "immigrant's" banks. These tasks, in great measure, are directed by the boards of trustees of these institutions and the boards are staffed from among the upper-middle classes in the respective "other" pillars. The direction of these institutions and the decisions made by them, will depend in great measure on the character of the upper-middle-class leadership within the pillars. Such, in rough outline, is the locus of the "minor tasks" of government, or, of what we may also refer to as private or informal government. These private governments have their own taxing powers (called "charity drives" or "fund raising campaigns") and make their own "allocative" decisions.

To call the tasks of private or informal government "minor" is not to suggest that these private welfare functions are unimportant. To the recipients of that welfare, clearly, they are of the utmost importance. These tasks are only "minor" by comparison to the major tasks of government which are those performed by the (more or less) public government in Washington. The major tasks are those of foreign affairs management, of policing (both internal and external, the latter usually referred to as "defense"), and of stabilizing the economy. The decisions made in these areas have implications of major importance to both public and private welfare. The tasks of these private governments are obviously minor in comparison to these decisions. The decision makers in this "public" government determine how much is left over for private incomes and welfare; they determine (through progressive or not-so-progressive taxation) how personal income shall be allocated; they determine, in part, the choice and scale of wars that will divert resources from private welfare; and they determine what shall be "acceptable" levels of unemployment and thus also determine the size of what is then called the welfare problem.

According to a number of commentators, perhaps the most notable of whom are Mills and Baltzell, the managers of the de jure public government in Washington are overwhelmingly white and Protestant. Stated somewhat differently, the government in Washington is the basic field of operation of the dominant political group in the United States, a group that happens to be very disproportionately white and Protestant. This group has a number of front organizations that serve as "transmission belts" to local elites and upper-middle-class populations.[42]

It makes sense to contrast the politics of the upper-middle-class white Protestants with those of all "subordinate" populations, not just with those in the white Protestant ranks. Since the upper-middle-class "others" occupy what Mills would call an "interstitial" position with respect to the rulers of major government affairs and the ruled, we shall leave them aside for the moment. The results for the non-South populations are as follows:

	All Lower-Middle and Working Class	Upper-Middle-Class White Protestants	Percent Difference
Party identification (percent Democratic)	69%	31%	+38
1964 vote—percent Democratic	74%	31%	+43

We can refine these results somewhat more. In the above figures we have followed the arbitrary usage of this chapter and taken $10,000 as the cutting line. If we were to take the $15,000 cutting line as providing a closer approximation to the Protestant ruling class (and thus eliminating many members of the upper-middle class who are not close to the "transmission belt") we obtain even more striking findings:

	All Lower-Middle and Working Class	Upper-Class White Protestants	Percent Difference
Identification	69%	20%	+49
1964 vote	74%	16%	+58

The disparity which is indicated here in party identification and in 1964 voting is also indicated in attitudes toward some of the key welfare issues. Taking the same groups as in the last figures, we have the following:

Issue	Percent Liberal		Percent Difference
Medical care	64%	11%	+53
Living standard	40	10	+30
Government power	63	11	+52

On a national basis, the percentage differences in voting and identification are not quite so great, largely because of traditional Democratic sentiment in Southern upper classes and because the latter are slightly more liberal than their peers elsewhere. In this case we have again taken white Protestants who report $15,000 or more in income.

	Percent Democratic		Percent Difference
Party identification	73%	40%	+33
1964 vote	73	41	+32

	Percent Liberal		Percent Difference
Medical care	64	19	+45
Living standard	46	13	+33
Government power	60	26	+34

These figures summarize the character of the political contest in the United States. The majority (of those with opinions) want, for example, a comprehensive government-supported medical care program. Among the tiny ruling elite with its circle of upper-middle-class support, however, there proves to be strong opposition to this idea. Judging by legislative performance through to the present, it is clear who wins out in this contest.

This picture probably understates the degree of polarization on this issue because, as noted in an earlier chapter, many of the "don't knows" are hidden "do knows," being cross-pressured between their own wants and interests, on the one hand, and their lingering commitments to a handed-down self-help tradition, on the other. Many of the "mass" opponents of medical care are located in small towns and rural areas and again are moved by the dominant pressures in that milieu. This is to suggest that if "equal time" were granted to both pro and con positions, the polarization on this question would be much greater than the +45 indicated here. It is interesting to note, moreover, that although there had been (through to 1964) no official support for a guaranteed living standard, close to half of those in the working and lower-middle classes had come to accept this as a good idea. This high degree of acceptance occurred with no special advocacy and in the face of the long-term and well-engrained tradition of self-help. It is worth adding that the 1956 question, which focused on a mere job guarantee (which would be much more acceptable from the vantage point of the received tradition), had the support of 70 percent of the working- and lower-middle-class populations.

It is clear that the conservative white Protestant upper- and upper-middle classes "get their way" and that the liberal majority does not. This finding in itself does not indicate *why* it is that the established ruling group gets its way; that is necessarily the task of a different kind of study, a decision-making (or perhaps more precisely, a decision-deferring) inquiry. For the moment, we can simply indicate the lay of public sentiment and thereby dispel a range of false explanations—such as the idea that we have "liberal elites" who, despite their good intentions, are thwarted by a combination of conservative workers together with a reactionary lower-middle class; or, an alternative favorite, the belief that there is a widespread "consensus" on the value of individualist, self-help approaches to the problems of welfare, that "people" are satisfied, and that they like things the way they are.

We turn now (in the next two chapters) to a more detailed specification of the locations of conservatism and liberalism in the American population. This will involve the more detailed examination of class characteristics associated with communities of different sizes outside the South and also of the peculiar features of the Southern development.

Notes

1. The presentation in this chapter and in the remaining chapters of this book will be based largely on the 1964 Survey Research Center election study. Addi-

tional supporting evidence is drawn from the 1956 and 1952 studies and, where appropriate, from some Gallup studies (all dated 1965).

Following the procedure outlined in the text, the 1964 sample (of 1751 persons) breaks down as follows: active nonmanuals, 634; active manuals, 553; active farm, 91; retired nonmanuals, 82; retired manuals, 88; retired farm, 32; and "others," 111. The latter divides into 74 housewives, 9 students, and 28 who gave no answer to the occupation question.

We have, as indicated, taken only the married active manuals and nonmanuals, hence, the basic groups considered decrease to, respectively, 448 and 524 cases. The distributions, for the sake of the record, are indicated as follows:

	Nonmanual	Manual
Married	524	448
Single	38	20
Divorced	30	17
Separated	11	14
Widowed	31	34

The manual rank in this study is smaller than the nonmanual because we have transferred the foremen and the self-employed manuals into the nonmanual category for the reasons already discussed. The numbers transferred were: foremen, 34; self-employed skilled workers, 27; and other self-employed manuals, 18. The exact same procedure has been used in the 1956 SRC study. Unfortunately, it was not possible to do the same with the 1952 study, the basic problem being that the foremen could not be separated out and transferred. Another difficulty with the 1952 study which could not be surmounted is that farm laborers were classified together with nonfarm unskilled and service workers and it was impossible to remove them. Judging from the experience with the other studies, these would constitute only a very small number of cases.

2. Some preliminary discussion, a somewhat more extensive sketch of the matter, appears in Richard Hamilton, *Affluence and the French Worker* (Princeton: Princeton University Press, 1967), Ch. 12. Also of relevance are; Carl E. Schorske, *German Social Democracy: 1905–1917* (Cambridge: Harvard University Press, 1955); Guenther Roth, *The Social Democrats in Imperial Germany* (Totowa, New Jersey: The Bedminister Press, 1963); and Robert Michels, *Political Parties* (Glencoe: The Free Press, 1949). Some suggestions of the deference to be found among the populations born near the turn of the century are to be found in Gabriel A. Almond and Sidney Verba, *The Civic Culture* (Princeton: Princeton University Press, 1963), p. 338 ff. See also Ralph Miliband, "Socialism and the Myth of the Golden Past," pp. 92–103 of Miliband and John Saville, *The Socialist Register: 1964* (New York: Monthly Review Press, 1964).

3. The early report is that of R. Blank, "Die soziale Zusammensetzung der sozialdemokratischen Wählerschaft Deutschlands," *Archiv für Sozialwissenschaft und Sozialpolitik* (Tübingen: J. C. B. Mohr—Paul Siebeck) **20** (1905), 507–550. Another early report of some interest in this connection is Robert Michels' "Die deutsche Sozialdemokratie. I. Parteimitgliedschaft und soziale Zusammensetzung," *Archiv für Sozialwissenschaft und Sozialpolitik*, **23** (1906), 471–556. A study of

the 1930 election showed the same picture; see Hans Neisser, "Sozialstatistischen Analyse des Wahlergebnisses," *Die Arbeit,* **7** (1930), 654–659.

4. The best work on American socialism of this period is James Weinstein's *The Decline of Socialism in America, 1912–1925* (New York: Monthly Review Press, 1967).

5. See the articles in Seymour M. Lipset and Stein Rokkan, eds., *Party Systems and Voter Alignments: Cross-National Perspectives* (New York: The Free Press, 1967); Juan J. Linz, *The Social Bases of West German Politics,* (New York: unpublished Ph.D. dissertation, Columbia University, 1959), Ch. II: "The German Party System in Comparative Perspective," and Robert Alford, *Party and Society: The Anglo-American Democracies* (Chicago: Rand McNally, 1963).

6. The best discussion of this matter appears in Lee Benson's *The Concept of Jacksonian Democracy: New York as a Test Case* (Princeton: Princeton University Press, 1961), Chs. III and IV. Also of some interest in undermining mythology about Adams aristocrats versus Jacksonian masses is Benson's earlier article, "Research Problems in American Political Historiography," in Mirra Komarovsky, ed., *Common Frontiers of the Social Sciences* (Glencoe: The Free Press, 1957), especially pp. 146–155. On Jackson and the poor debtors, see the essay "Andrew Jackson and the Rise of Liberal Capitalism" by Richard Hofstadter, which appears as Ch. III of his *The American Political Tradition* (New York: Alfred A. Knopf, 1948). Recent studies have very much undercut the notions of Democrats as "mass" party and Whigs as agency of "elites." See Richard P. McCormick, "New Perspectives on Jacksonian Politics," *American Historical Review,* **65** (January 1960), 288–301 and his "Suffrage Classes and Party Alignments: A Study in Voter Behavior," *Mississippi Valley Historical Review,* **46** (December 1959), 397–410; see also J. R. Pole, "Suffrage and Representation in Massachusetts: A Statistical Note," *William and Mary Quarterly,* **14** (October 1957), 560–592, and his "Election Statistics in North Carolina, to 1861," *Journal of Southern History,* **24** (May 1958), 225–228; and Grady McWhiney, "Were the Whigs a Class Party in Alabama?" *Journal of Southern History,* **23** (November 1957), 510–522.

Cutting through the mythology of Jackson as spoilsman we have Erik M. Erikson, "The Federal Civil Service Under President Jackson," *Mississippi Valley Historical Review,* **13** (1927), 517–540 and Sidney Aronson, *Status and Kinship in the Higher Civil Service: Standards of Selection in the Administrations of John Adams, Thomas Jefferson, and Andrew Jackson* (Cambridge: Harvard University Press, 1964). A short but useful overview of the social conditions of the period may be found in Douglas T. Miller, *Jacksonian Aristocracy: Class and Democracy in New York* (New York: Oxford University Press, 1967). On the bank question see Bray Hammond, *Banks and Politics in America* (Princeton: Princeton University Press, 1957).

7. For an overview of the class and religious patterns in New York state in the 1840s see Benson, op. cit., Chs. VIII and IX. An analysis of politics at the end of the eighteenth century does put the religious factor in a very definite second place to the class factor, at that time; see Manning Dauer's, *The Adams Federalists* (Baltimore: Johns Hopkins Press, 1953), pp. 25–32. Lipset has summarized the role of religion in mass politics throughout the course of American history in his

article "Religion and Politics in the American Past and Present," pp. 69–126 of Robert Lee and Martin Marty, eds., *Religion and Social Conflict* (New York: Oxford University Press, 1964). This article also appears as Ch. 8 of Lipset's *Revolution and Counterrevolution: Change and Persistence in Social Structure* (New York: Basic Books, 1968).

There is a fairly sizable literature on the "did labor support Jackson" question, a literature that largely rejects the pure class analysis. Two examples must suffice: Walter Hugins, *Jacksonian Democracy and the Working Class* (Stanford: Stanford University Press, 1960) and William A. Sullivan, *The Industrial Worker in Pennsylvania, 1800–1840* (Harrisburg, Pennsylvania: Historical and Museum Commission, 1955).

The best work on the political correlates of the religious "pillars" in the United States is that of Gerhard Lenski, *The Religious Factor* (Garden City: Doubleday, 1961), especially Ch. 4. A very careful and detailed community study that also shows the pillar structure of one city is the work of Kenneth Underwood, *Protestant and Catholic: Religious and Social Interaction in an Industrial Community* (Boston: Beacon Press, 1957).

A portrayal of the division in the elite ranks appears in E. Digby Baltzell's *The Protestant Establishment: Aristocracy & Caste in America* (New York: Random House, 1964). His book *Philadelphia Gentlemen* (Glencoe: The Free Press, 1958) is also very useful on this subject.

8. The discussion of class polarization rests largely on the work of Robert Alford, op. cit.; see especially the summary presentation in his Appendix B. He also presents the findings in his article in the Lipset and Rokkan volume, op. cit. Basically what he has done is calculate the difference in the percentage vote for the liberal/left party on the part of the manual and nonmanual populations in order to yield an "Index of Class Voting." If all manuals vote "left" and no nonmanuals do so we would have total polarization and an index of +100. If 60 percent of the manuals voted left and 40 percent of the nonmanuals did so, we would have a relatively low +20. It is important to note that we might have the same index figure for quite different situations; the following manual-nonmanual percentage combinations—60 and 40, 100 and 80, 20 and zero—all would have an index of +20 although the situations are rather markedly different.

9. See both Baltzell books on this subject. Also useful in this connection is Gustavus Myers, *History of Bigotry in the United States* (New York: Random House, 1943).

There are a number of other factors, aside from those considered in the text, that have aided in the reduction of class polarization in the United States. Agrarian radicalism of the nineteenth century, favoring as it did "cheap money," was not particularly attractive to the urban working class. The promise to, in effect, cut working-class purchasing power was used effectively by the opponents of Populism and Bryan Democracy to shift urban working-class populations away from any traditional Democratic sympathies. The Bryan campaign of 1896 proved rather disastrous for the Democrats because it created so many "Tory workers."

One other contribution to the reduction of "class polarization" (at least as indicated by the Alford procedure) occurred in the South following the Civil War.

Many of the elites of the area had been Whigs prior to the war. Their initial political effort in the postwar period consisted of a try at Republicanism. This, however, for more or less obvious reasons, proved to be unsuccessful. With great reluctance, not to say revulsion, they "converted" and became the leaders of the Democratic party in the South. These "Bourbon Democrats," supply, on the national scene, a large part of the upper-middle-class Democrats of white Protestant background. To give some indication of this, we took the active (not retired) nonmanuals, both the married and not married, from the 1952 SRC study. Democrats who were white and Protestant made up only 28 percent of this group. Fifty-two percent of these white Protestant middle-class Democrats were located in the South (this includes the border states). Since then, there has been a fair-sized reconversion within the Southern nonmanual population back to their first love—Whiggery. This is indicated in the SRC studies, which showed the number of Republican identifiers in the nonmanual ranks to have been 18 percent in 1952 and 34 percent in 1964. This has meant that class cleavage in Alford's sense has shown some increase in the South since the manual trend is in the opposite direction. The history of Southern Whiggery is to be found in C. Vann Woodward, *Reunion & Reaction* (Garden City: Doubleday—Anchor Books, 1956).

10. Alford, op. cit., p. 352. The best picture of the dynamics of the 1948 campaign and of the role played by the domestic liberalism issues in the "Democratic rally" is to be found in Bernard Berelson, Paul F. Lazarsfeld, and William N. McPhee, *Voting: A Study of Opinion Formation in a Presidential Campaign* (Chicago: University of Chicago Press, 1954), Ch. 12. Another useful account that discusses the decisions to focus on those issues is Irwin Ross, *The Loneliest Campaign: The Truman Victory of 1948* (New York: New American Library, 1968). Stevenson, as we have noted previously (see Chapter 3) chose to abandon the stress on the same issues.

11. With retired house heads excluded, we have the following result (SRC 1964):

	Manual	N	Nonmanual	N	Difference
Percent Democratic of 2-party vote	79%	(301)	60%	(407)	+19
Percent Democratic of 2-party identifications	77	(399)	61	(477)	+16

Throughout this work we have focused on those respondents with opinions and those with party positions. In most cases this yields dichotomous choices (liberal or conservative, tolerant or intolerant, Democratic or Republican). To simplify the presentation, in most cases only one percentage has been presented since the opposite percentage may easily be obtained by subtracting any given result from 100%. Where it is indicated that 70 percent of a group is liberal, it means that 30 percent are illiberal. Implicit in this procedure is the assumption that the "don't knows" and the nonresponse groups will divide in the same way as those who "do know." For reasons indicated previously this procedure probably understates the liberalism of the entire population. In presenting data on party identifiications, we have counted the independents with Republican or Democratic leanings with those respective parties. The pure independents and the other responses have been omitted (see Table 3.3).

12. This "all other" procedure is obviously no more than a crudity forced on us by methodological necessity. Within this category we have Catholics, Jews, and Negroes; each group, to some degree, has its own separate "pillar" or "column"— its own neighborhoods, voluntary associations, places of employment, and so forth. Since there are so few cases of Jews and Negroes in a national sample (especially when divided by class), it is pointless to give separate consideration in all tables. Since, however, these groups all share a strong Democratic party identification and liberal positions on the issues, it proves convenient to combine them for the purposes of the presentation at hand. Detailed breakdowns appear in notes 16 and 22.

The image of a series of vertical cleavages in the society, of pillars or columns as opposed to the more frequently discussed horizontal cleavages or strata, derives from the Netherlands experience where this pattern is most pronounced. In that country the religious groups have separate trade unions, schools, radio and television stations, and periodicals. For an overview of the Netherlands pattern (called *Verzuiling*) see Hans Daalder, "Parties and Politics in the Netherlands," *Political Studies*, **3** (February 1955), 1–16, and his chapter "The Netherlands: Opposition in a Segmented Society," contained in Robert A. Dahl, ed., *Political Oppositions in Western Democracies* (New Haven: Yale University Press, 1966). See also David O. Moberg, "Religion and Society in the Netherlands and in America," *American Quarterly*, **13** (Summer 1961), 172–178.

13. This arbitrary division into upper and lower middles obviously leaves much to be desired. What we would like to do, following the implications of the analysis of Milwaukee, is to sort them into those living in the predominantly middle-class community areas and those living in other settings. The use of income can be no more than a crude clue to the community type. Many lower-middle-class persons have a high family income in mid-career—through the efforts of a wife or of employed children. By the use of the arbitrary procedure, we pay the cost of counting such persons as "upper-middle class." For many people who are "upper" it must be noted that they begin "low" when just out of college; also some people with high incomes throughout their careers "lose out" just prior to retirement. For these reasons there is some "mixing" of the classes. It should be remembered, therefore, that the findings given here probably understate the actual differences between the lower- and upper-middle classes. A discussion of the problems involved in the procedure used here can be found in Richard Hamilton, "Einkommen und Klassenstruktur," *Kölner Zeitschrift für Soziologie und Soziolpsychologie* **20:2** (1968), 250–287.

14. On the differentiation within the Protestant column see Lenski and Berelson, Lazarsfeld, and McPhee. See also N. J. Demerath III, *Social Class in American Protestantism* (Chicago: Rand McNally, 1965). The various articles by Benton Johnson are also of interest in this connection: see, for example, his "Theology and the Position of Pastors on Public Issues," *American Sociological Review* **32** (June 1967), 433–442; "Ascetic Protestantism and Political Preference," *Public Opinion Quarterly*, **26** (Spring 1962), 35–46; and "Ascetic Protestantism and

Political Preference in the Deep South" *American Journal of Sociology*, **69** (January 1964), 359–366; and "Theology and Party Preference among Protestant Clergymen," *American Sociological Review*, **31** (April 1966), 200–208. See also Oscar Glantz, "Protestant and Catholic Voting Behavior in a Metropolitan Area," *Public Opinion Quarterly*, **23** (Spring 1959), 73–82; and also, Charles H. Anderson, "Religious Communality among White Protestants, Catholics, and Mormons," *Social Forces*, **46** (June 1968), 501–508.

Very few of the Democratic identifiers among the white, middle-class Protestants defected to the Republicans in 1964. Those who did tended to be from the smaller communities, the proportions being 8 and 16 percent, respectively. There was a considerable defection from the Republicans. This shifting does not vary significantly by size of place; it does, however, vary with class level, the defection amounting to 25 percent among the lower middles as against only 14 percent for the upper middles.

Runs similar to those of Table 5.3 were made with the SRC's 1956 and 1952 voting studies. The same pattern (that is, of the relative liberalism of the urban, lower-middle-class, white Protestants) appeared in 1956, although somewhat weaker than in 1964. In 1952, however, the pattern did not appear, both urban and small-town lower-middle classes being roughly the same in voting and identification. This result could be due to methodological difficulties (the class categories and the income cutting line not being entirely equivalent in 1952) or it could indicate a breakaway from traditional voting patterns.

15. The information presented in Table 5.4 to be sure, is not entirely appropriate for the purpose of showing the overlap of party identifications and issue positions. A more detailed cross-tabulation, however, does bear out the point: Democratic identifiers tend to be liberal; Republican identifiers tend to be conservative. For example, (SRC 1964):

	Non-South, Nonmanuals (Married; in Labor Force)			
	White Protestant		*All Others*	
Family Income:	To $9999	$10,000 or More	To $9999	$10,000 or More
Party identification	*Percent favoring medical care (those with opinion)*			
Democrats	60%	71%	84%	74%
N =	(38)	(14)	(50)	(31)
Republicans	23	12.5	17	55
N =	(44)	(40)	(12)	(20)

While this limited presentation can only be suggestive, it does show very sizable differences. It is also interesting to note that the upper-middle-class white Protestant Republicans have the greatest consensus on this issue. There is a slight tendency for Democratic upper-middle-class "others" to lean toward conservatism (as compared with the equivalent lower middles), but the difference is small and the majority there still is solidly liberal. That tendency toward conservatism is offset by a striking liberal tendency on the part of the small number of Republicans in that context. A similar pattern among "other" Republicans also appeared in the 1956 study.

16. See Chapter 11, note 9, for further discussion.

The use of the category "other" is clearly little more than a practical convenience forced by the small number of cases in some of the "pillars." The composition of the nonmanual "other" categories in the 1964 SRC study is as follows:

	Non-South		South	
Income:	To $9999	$10,000 or More	To $7499	$7500 or More
Nonwhites	8%	9%	45%	19%
Whites:				
Catholic	73	63	45	71
Jewish	10	16	—	10
Other	9	13	9	—
N =	(90)	(70)	(11)	(21)

The comparable figures for the manuals are in note 22.

17. The data for married Southern white nonmanuals:

	White Protestants	All Others
Percent Democratic		
(of those with opinions)	69%	87%
N =	(111)	(30)
1964 Vote: Percent Democratic		
(of 2-party choices)	49	81
N =	(86)	(26)

Sixty-nine percent of all the nonvoters ($N = 32$) indicated they would have voted Democratic had they actually voted. For comparable data on Southern white workers, see note 25 of this chapter.

18. See Chapter 11, note 9, for details.

19. One such discussion is that of C. Wright Mills, *White Collar: The American Middle Classes* (New York: Oxford University Press, 1951).

Respondents in the following analysis were differentiated in terms of their response to the question (asked of heads of households): "Do you work for yourself or someone else?"

20. A study of some interest in this connection (since the businessmen are all gas-station operators and presumably share the same interests) is that of Ivar Berg and David Rogers, "Former Blue-Collarites in Small Business," pp. 550–566 of Arthur B. Shostak and William Gomberg, *Blue-Collar World: Studies of the American Worker* (Englewood Cliffs, N.J.: Prentice-Hall, 1964).

Paul Eberts and I have reviewed a large number of surveys, both national and local, in an attempt to assess the "business conservatism" hypothesis. The findings, which are similar to those reported here, appear as "The Politics of Independent

Business," Ch. 2 of Richard Hamilton, *Restraining Myths and Liberating Realities* (forthcoming).

The best-known work which supports the thesis of business "extremism" is that of Martin Trow, "Small Businessmen, Political Tolerance, and Support for McCarthy," *American Journal of Sociology*, **64** (November 1958), 270–281. This article shows that the small businessmen in Bennington, Vermont, were more pro-McCarthy (Joseph R.) than the salaried middle class. At the same time, note 10 indicates that they were not notably conservative in regard to the issues. The study also found that the small businessmen who were nineteenth-century liberals (that is, opposed to big business and big labor) were especially likely to be pro-McCarthy. An attempt to replicate these findings (through the use of a large sample from 11 non-Southern states) failed. See Seymour Martin Lipset, "Three Decades of the Radical Right—1962," in Daniel Bell, ed., *The Radical Right* (Garden City: Doubleday, 1963), pp. 340–341. It is worth quoting the finding: "Efforts at partial replication of Trow's analysis with the I.N.R.A. data did not yield comparable results. . . . The hypothesis must be placed in the category of the not proven."

It is instructive to make a more detailed examination of the original Trow dissertation, that is, *Right-Wing Radicalism and Political Intolerance* (New York: Columbia University, unpublished Ph.D. dissertation, 1957). Most of that pro-McCarthy sentiment appears among the Protestant businessmen. Among the better-educated Catholics (that is, high school or more) there is a one percent difference between the salaried and independent middle class (see p. 115). This means that the pattern does not hold across the board and that what has to be explained is the peculiar propensity of the *Protestant* businessmen, rather than the reactions of businessmen generally.

21. It is impossible in this brief discussion to do justice to the complexities of the subject. The number of cases of independents, moreover, is too small to allow all the controls and exploration that are needed. For what it is worth, the reader must consider the facts that independents are older and also tend to be, as compared to salaried populations, located in small towns. This would suggest that if the needed controls were present, we would find the evidence going even more against the "business conservatism" hypothesis than it does in our tables.

22. The composition of the Southern and non-South manual "others" is as follows (SRC 1964):

| | Non-South | | South | |
	Lower Income	Higher Income	Lower Income	Higher Income
Nonwhites	20%	19%	84%	78%
Whites:				
Catholic	66	75	13	17
Jewish	3	3	...	...
Other	11	3	3	6
N =	(80)	(59)	(32)	(18)

See note 16 for the equivalent nonmanual figures.

The greater conservatism among the better-off "others" is not due to compositional factors (such as Negroes being disproportionately in the lower-income, Catholics in the higher-income group). Separate consideration of the Catholics showed greater conservatism among those with higher incomes. There is a question to be raised, however, about the source of this greater conservatism. These high-income Republican Catholics tend to be small towners and to be non-union. They might, in other words, merely happen to be located in conservatizing contexts.

23. Even here, it will be noted, there is a rather striking exception to this rule of the relative conservatism of the better-off workers with respect to the guaranteed living standard question. Forty-five percent of the better-off white Protestant workers (non-South) favored that policy, a higher level of approval in this case than was found among the equivalent "others." From the 1956 study, which asked about a job guarantee (rather than a guaranteed living standard), we find a considerably higher overall level of approval and only very small differences between the better-off and poorer workers. Among the non-South white Protestants, for example, 69 percent of the poor and 64 percent of the better-off workers approved the suggested policy. Among the equivalent "others" the numbers were 80 and 71 percent. See also the discussion of income and politics in Chapter 8.

The strain between party identification and issue orientation is indicated by the following data. Two-fifths of the low-income Republicans show a strong interest in government-supported medical care.

	Non-South White Protestant Manuals (1964)			
	Income to $7500		Income $7500 or more	
Party identification:	Democratic	Republican	Democratic	Republican
Percent favoring government-supported medical care	80%	38%	63%	26%
N =	(54)	(21)	(38)	(23)

24. The pattern of "rationalization" is indicated in the data below. Very few Democrats went over to the Republicans, a sizable minority of better-off white Protestant workers shifted to the Democrats, and a majority of the low-income Protestants went over (SRC 1964).

	Non-South White Protestant Manual Workers			
	Lower Income		Higher Income	
Party identification:	Democratic	Republican	Democratic	Republican
Percent 1964 Democratic voters	95%	58%	89%	26%
N =	(39)	(26)	(37)	(23)

25. Data on the nonvoting workers and their preferences follows: non-South white Protestants, 94% Democratic ($N = 34$); non-South "others" 82% Democratic ($N = 28$); Southern white Protestants, 60% Democratic ($N = 20$); and Southern "others," 100% Democratic ($N = 19$). For comparable data on the nonmanual population, see note 17.

A more detailed discussion of the underlying realities can be found in Philip E. Converse, Aage R. Clausen, and Warren E. Miller, "Myth and Reality: The 1964 Election," *American Political Science Review*, **59** (June 1965), 321–336.

26. The data on fathers' and childrens' party identifications follow (SRC 1964).

	Non-South White Protestant Manuals					
	Income $7499 or less			*Income $7500 or more*		
Father's politics:	*Dem*	*Rep*	*Indep. Other*	*Dem*	*Rep*	*Indep. Other*
	Percent Democratic (of 2-party choice)					
Respondent's party identification	83%	32%	72%	97%	19%	75%
$N =$	(52)	(25)	(18)	(29)	(26)	(16)

The pattern of intergenerational changes will be considered in more detail in Chapter 8. For another parallel discussion of the "economism" thesis, which focuses instead on skill levels, see Richard Hamilton "Skill Level and Politics," *Public Opinion Quarterly*, **19** (Fall 1965), 390–399 and *Affluence and the French Worker*, Ch. 7.

27. The following works are useful in this connection: Mirra Komarovsky, *Blue-Collar Marriage* (New York: Random House, 1964); F. Ivan Nye and Lois Wladis Hoffman, eds., *The Employed Mother in America* (Chicago: Rand McNally & Co., 1963); and Lee Rainwater, Richard P. Coleman, and Gerald Handel, *Workingman's Wife* (New York: MacFadden Books, 1962).

28. See Elihu Katz and Paul F. Lazarsfeld, *Personal Influence* (Glencoe: The Free Press, 1955), pp. 140–142, 276, 282–283; and Berelson, Lazarsfeld, and McPhee, op. cit., p. 102.

29. For example, by Harold Wilensky in his "Class, Class Consciousness, and American Workers," Ch. 2 of William Haber, ed., *Labor in a Changing America* (New York: Basic Books, 1966).

30. The claim of increasing skill levels has been effectively challenged by James R. Bright in his *Automation and Management* (Boston: Harvard Business School, 1958) and in his article "Does Automation Raise Skill Requirements," *Harvard Business Review*, **36** (July–August 1958), 85–98.

Other evidence on the presence of college educated workers has already been cited. See Chapter 4, note 30.

31. Burton R. Clark, "The 'Cooling-out' Function in Higher Education," *American Journal of Sociology*, **65** (May 1960), 569–576.

32. The college-educated workers are disproportionately in the younger age groups. The pattern, however, is not one of continuous increase among the younger cohorts. The very youngest groups, those who were in their twenties in the 1960s, tended to have less education than the generation that immediately preceded them. The most frequent explanation of this is that the younger cohorts are still working on their degrees and that they will finish them at a later age. An alternative explanation, however, would seem equally if not more likely. The somewhat older generation received their education with the aid of the G. I. Bill.

A more comprehensive study that shows this same slight reversal among the young and that also shows that the education gap is increasing over time is that of William G. Spady, "Educational Mobility and Access: Growth and Paradoxes," *American Journal of Sociology,* **73** (November 1967), 273–286. His major point is that the "educational explosion" of recent decades has meant a very sizable increase in the education of the children of the educated and relatively little change for other groups in the population. This ties in with one of the central points of this work, that is, the likelihood of increasing class differences.

33. See, for example, the data in Seymour Martin Lipset, *The First New Nation* (New York: Basic Books, 1963), p. 184. The basic finding was reported in the previous chapter of the present work. My own investigation of that study showed that the preference for the skilled worker's job increased among the low education groups. A general disdain for white-collar work was also indicated by the workers interviewed by Herbert Gans as reported in his *The Urban Villagers: Group and Class in the Life of Italian-Americans* (New York: The Free Press, 1962).

34. The Blau and Duncan study shows a greater percentage of operatives moving to clerical and retail sales jobs than is the case with the craftsmen. The numbers and 6.8 and 5.6 percent, respectively. Recalculated from Peter M. Blau and Otis Dudley Duncan, *The American Occupational Structure* (New York: John Wiley and Sons, 1967), p. 498.

35. For a more extended discussion, see Kenneth Thompson, Jr., "Class Change and Politics: Social Mobility and Voting" (Madison, Wisconsin: University of Wisconsin. Unpublished Ph.D. dissertation, 1967).

The results from the 1956 SRC study show strong similarities to the findings reported here for 1964. Taking first the non-South white Protestant manual workers, we found little systematic variation among five income categories; the point of the working-class homogeniety was again supported. The slight variation that did appear involved the Democratic percentage *increasing* slightly in the higher-income categories, again casting doubt on the economism thesis. Secondly, there was little systematic variation in party identification among four income categories of the lower-middle class (to $7500). For the white Protestant worker "going up in the world" meant changing from a milieu that was 47% Democratic to one that was only 34%, a difference of 13 percentage points.

The same points about the homogeniety of manual and lower-middle classes may be made with respect to the equivalent white Catholic groups surveyed in 1956. Since there is once again less differentiation by income in the Catholic column, the upward mobile person would be shifting from a 71% Democratic milieu to one that was 69% Democratic.

Roughly the same picture appears in the 1952 study. The working-class homogeniety appears in the overall pattern for four broad income groups. The lower-middle-class pattern is somewhat more fluctuating than in the other studies, but even here the picture is erratic rather than systematic. The overall consequence of mobility is a shift from a milieu that was 67% to one that is 53% Democratic. The difference here is 14 percentage points, the largest of the three studies.

36 Another possibility, of course, rather than "organizing down" is "organizing up." That is, by taking advantage of the ethnic "improvement association," by

performing services for the subgroup, some of the leaders are able to "go up in the world." Their existence, however, is still dependent on the contribution of the group members; hence it is incumbent on the "successful man" that he maintain solidarity with the group in question. For this kind of success, complete assimilation is impossible. Even many of those who end up as Republicans retain much of their subgroup liberalism.

37. The lowest paid manual workers, it will be noted, are the most Democratic. Since that category in Table 5.12 includes families earning up to $6000, it is important to undertake a more detailed examination of these cases. There is little internal differentiation within the category. Those earning between $5000 and $6000 were 78% Democratic ($N = 37$), those earning $4000 to $5000 had the same percentage ($N = 23$), and those with less than $4000 were 81% Democratic ($N = 26$). Again the question may be raised as to whether it is low income or some background characteristic that is at work here. Taking the 49 respondents reporting incomes of less than $5000, we find that five were Negro and five were Southern-reared whites. All of these respondents were Democrats. The level of Democratic identification among the remaining low-income workers was 74%. Removal of the Catholics, who were highly Democratic, would again lower the level among the remaining workers.

38. The data (SRC 1964) below are for Southern, married, head in labor force.

Family Income:	Manual		Nonmanual	
	Low	High	Low	High
	Percent Democratic (of 2-party choice)			
White Protestant	68%	80%	81%	61%
$N =$	(41)	(59)	(52)	(56)

39. The non-South retired nonmanual population was 72 percent white and Protestant ($N = 58$) compared to a figure of 55 percent ($N = 444$) among the equivalent economically active population. These figures include married and nonmarried alike.

40. Thirty-four of the 41 persons in farm employment were owners, tenants, or farm managers. This means, among other things, that the survey simply did not pick up the proper proportion of farm laborers. This is the case with all surveys. These "hidden" or "overlooked" people are also part of the immense liberal majority; they are obviously even less likely to be heeded by virtue of their nearly complete "invisibility."

Fifty-nine percent of the non-South farm owners ($N = 34$) reported a Democratic identification in 1964 and 66 percent voted for Johnson in that year.

41. Just as a reminder and as a precaution against reading in either an "economist" interpretation or a "middle mass" theory, it should be noted that the low paid workers are disproportionately from the South and bring Democratic identifications with them. Without the Southern-reared, the equivalent figures are:

$$-3 \quad +9 \quad +20 \quad +27$$

42. See the two previously cited Baltzell works and, C. Wright Mills, *The Power Elite* (New York: Oxford University Press, 1957), Ch. 5. Also, G. William Domhoff, *Who Rules America?* (Englewood Cliffs, N.J.: Prentice-Hall, 1967); and Chapter 5 of "Who Made American Foreign Policy, 1945–1963," of his *The Higher Circles: The Governing Class in America* (New York: Random House, 1970).

The relationship between the outsider, John F. Kennedy, and the dominant political group is described by Arthur Schlesinger, Jr., in his *A Thousand Days* (Boston: Houghton Mifflin, 1965), p. 128 ff. Schlesinger does not use the Mills's term but rather refers to the circle as "the American Establishment." Otherwise, the lines of analysis are very similar.

6
Rural-Urban Differentiation

Introduction

In this and the following chapter we shall further specify, or locate, the centers of conservatism in the population and shall point out the significance of our findings for the future development of class relations in the United States.

These two chapters are almost necessarily interrelated. If we were to show political differentiations along the rural-urban dimension for the entire population, we would find, first of all, very little relationship. That result, however, would be misleading since the small communities happen to be disproportionately Southern and heavily Democratic. Because the South has its special peculiarities, it makes sense to treat that region separately. That is the reason for the two chapters. In the present one we shall be examining the political correlates of city size in the non-South regions.

In previous work, the basic hypothesis has been that liberal or left political orientations would increase with the size of the city. This is nothing new in the literature, the main point having been touched on some centuries ago by the Italian legal reformer, Cesare Beccaria, who feared the *immense moltitudini* of the cities. De Tocqueville noted the significance of the Paris agglomeration and the clustering of laboring populations there, a development that was perceived by some as a threat, but about which no one seemed able to do anything. Frederick Engels said that the great cities would be the "birthplace of the working class movement."[1]

The major previous line of explanation for this finding has been that in the larger cities the working class constitutes an "isolated mass." In isolation the workers develop their own leadership and, simultaneously, lose contact with the presumedly more conservative middle-class populations.[2] The major received hypotheses, then, are the following: first, a mistaken one, that the middle class is uniformly conservative in all sizes of community, and second, that it is changes within the urban working class that make or account for the overall differences associated with city size. The initial discussion here

239

will remain with the manual-nonmanual formulation in order to address these claims. We shall also consider some alternative hypotheses to explain the city size–politics relationship; first, we shall discuss a compositional hypothesis —that differing proportions of white Protestants and "others" explain the result, and second, we shall discuss the hypothesis that patterns of inter-city movement may contribute to the result. We shall then examine the internal differentiation within the white-collar rank, in particular the differences between the lower middles and upper middles noted in the previous chapter. An attempt will be made to explain the preponderant Republican influence in the smaller communities despite the presence of majorities with Democratic identifications. And finally, some consideration will be given to the changes that have occurred or that are in process within the various community contexts.

One of the most difficult tasks in discussing the role of community size is the development of an adequate set of categories. The major problem stems from the presence of small communities adjacent to metropolitan areas and whether to classify them as "small towns" or as "metropolitan." It is easy to envision small towns as pristine, unspoiled, nineteenth-century trade centers for a surrounding rural population. Often, however, despite the appearances, such communities contain commuting workers (and a few nonmanuals). The workers have taken over the old farm houses so that effectively there is no "rural" population.[3] One can "solve" this problem by having a large number of categories but then one runs into the problem of small numbers and unreliable percentage figures.

A second major problem is closely related to this first one, that is, what to do with, or how to handle, the suburbs. One view, discussed in Chapter 4, sees "suburbs" as middle-class housing areas. If so, they ought to receive special or separate treatment, especially if we are attempting to show the pattern of differentiation associated with increased size in "normal" (that is, mixed, heterogeneous) communities. This view, however, misrepresents the actual frequency distributions and, as we have shown in connection with the city of Milwaukee, the surrounding areas have the same general character as the parts of the city on which they border. This means that the suburbs, on the whole, will have very much the same composition as the cities although with some overrepresentation of upper-middle classes. This would mean that we can include them together with the large cities in any combined presentation. It would be necessary, however, to remember that the overall results for the category "suburbs" involves an average of highly Republican upper-middle-class neighborhoods and of Democratic working-class suburbs.

The basic city code in the 1964 study contains 10 categories. Use of all 10 would give us a small numbers problem. For this reason, the "detailed" breakdown in this chapter will use 7. This results from combining 2 classes of suburbs and by combining various nonmetropolitan categories. For most purposes, it proves necessary to make further combinations. In this case we have used three categories: large cities of 50,000 or more (plus suburbs);

middle-sized cities (those between 2500 and 49,999) ; and places of less than 2500 (here called small towns or rural areas). In both the middle-sized city and small-town categories, there are some communities that are located within Standard Metropolitan Statistical Areas (SMSAs). In both cases, it will be noted, the populations outside the SMSAs tend to be more Republican than those within.

Size of Community and Party Preferences

The overall picture shows some support for the basic hypothesis, that is, the larger the city the more liberal the populations (see Table 6.1). As indicated by the party identifications, for example, we find nearly three-fourths of those persons from the central cities of the twelve largest SMSAs to be Democratic identifiers. Other large cities have a level of Democratic identification that is only slightly lower and in the suburbs the level is just below two-thirds. It is clear that there is a falling off in the Democratic percentage in the middle-sized cities and even more falloff in the small towns and rural areas. That said, it should also be noted that the overall variation is not very great. It is not a case of "radical" cities and archconservative villages. Taking the extremes, we find that the largest central cities are 74 percent Democratic as opposed to a 53 percent level in those small towns and rural areas not included in the SMSAs. The smallest and most provincial of the community categories, surprisingly, turns out not to be overwhelmingly Republican, but rather divides more or less evenly between the two major parties. Since this finding goes against "common sense," we will have more to say on this matter later in this chapter. The basic point to be noted at the moment, however, is that the Democrats have a majority in all community size categories with the possible exception of this smallest category where they have "only" a 50–50 chance.

When we condense the presentation, going from 7 to 3 categories, we find the Democratic percentage falls off from 69, to 60, to 56 percent as we go from metropolitan cities to small towns and rural areas. The basic conclusion is that the original hypothesis is supported although the community context makes relatively little difference. The point, in other words, is supported but its importance has been somewhat exaggerated.

When we turn to the indicated 1964 vote we do not find the hypothesis supported. The metropolitan cities are still the most Democratic, but the middle-sized cities now prove to be the least Democratic, and the towns and villages are now in-between. All of the differences, moreover, are very small. The big cities were only 3 percentage points more Democratic than the villages in this election. This result is not dependent on nonvoters. The percentage of nonvoters was nearly the same across the board. The nonvoter predispositions, moreover, were overwhelmingly Democratic (to a greater extent in the middle-sized cities and the small towns than in cities), so that if they

TABLE 6.1

Party Identification and Size of Place (Married, Economically Active Manuals and Nonmanuals, Non-South Only) SRC 1964

	Large Cities			Middle-Sized Cities		Small Towns—Rural	
	Twelve Largest Central Cities	Suburbs of Twelve Largest	Other Cities 50,000 or More	In SMSAs	Not SMSAs	In SMSAs	Not SMSAs
Strong Democrat	36%	22%	29%	23%	11%	16%	21%
Weak Democrat	23	21	19	22	27	27	20
Independent Democrat	9	14	18	16	14	13	7
Independent	10	11	6	5	7	6	8
Independent Republican	4	6	6	8	12	13	6
Weak Republican	9	13	12	14	17	17	28
Strong Republican	11	13	10	13	12	8	9
$N =$	(104)	(143)	(89)	(101)	(84)	(77)	(85)
Percent Democrats (of 2-party choice)	74%	64%	70%	64%	56%	60%	53%
$N =$	(94)	(128)	(84)	(96)	(78)	(72)	(78)
Percent Democrat	69%			60%		56%	
$N =$	(306)			(174)		(150)	
1964 vote	71%			64%		69%	
$N =$	(257)			(143)		(132)	

had voted, the community size differences would have been reduced still further.

One point of some importance is hidden in this presentation. Of the seven categories, the middle-sized communities outside the SMSAs were the most strongly Republican in their 1964 voting; even then, however, it amounted to only 42 percent. Interestingly enough, the provincial communities, or county seats, appear still to be the centers of conservatism, more even than the rural populations that surround them.[4]

If we look at the relative proportions of strong versus weak party identifications in Table 6.1, there are some important discoveries to be made. In the largest cities, not only is there a heavy preponderance of Democrats, but we find also that they tend (except in the suburbs) to be disproportionately strong Democrats. Something of the same is true in the other large cities. Elsewhere, the strong-to-weak ratio is either equal or reversed. In the middle-sized cities outside SMSAs, for example, the typical Democratic attachment tends to be a weak one. In the small towns and rural areas there is some tendency in both party camps for the identifications to be weak.[5] The rural areas, in short, tend to show low levels of political commitment, or, put differently, the rural areas tend to be lacking firm political roots.

Although one tends to think of the smallest communities as the most "organized" and the largest communities as being characterized by "anomie" and "disorganization," the evidence here *suggests* that the conventional expectation is not justified. In depopulated (or depopulating) rural areas, in areas with high population turnover, and in areas with large numbers of commuting ruralites, it seems likely that there will be very limited "organization"—the bare minimum necessary to conduct business. It seems likely that small-town politics would be very low key. There would be little explicit political organization and political discussion would be relatively rare. The latter is a feature of "small units" everywhere (small factories, small colleges, small offices); potentially disruptive conversations are avoided.[6]

All this suggests that the middle-sized communities are the more important for the Republicans by virtue of the fact that the party there is better organized and the members more committed. Some suggestion of the relative stability there is contained in Table 6.1. In the middle-sized communities there was—comparing the identifications with the vote—only a very small difference of 4 percent between the 2 figures. In the small towns, by comparison, there was a difference of 13 percent.

The Nonmanuals

The second basic hypothesis, as noted, holds that the nonmanual populations are conservative across the board, presumably equally so in all sizes of community. That the middle class is not monolithic has been shown in the previous chapter so that our revised hypothesis, for the present purpose, must hold merely that one would expect at least the same Republican percentage in all community size groups.

The evidence does not support this assumption. Among the nonmanuals the Democratic percentage varies directly with city size, the difference between the smallest and largest communities being even greater than among the combined manuals and nonmanuals. Basically, the middle-sized and smaller communities are not at all different in party identification. In both, slightly under one half of the middle-class populations indicate Democratic allegiance. In the larger cities, on the other hand, close to two-thirds identify themselves with the Democratic party (see Table 6.2).

TABLE 6.2
Party Identification and 1964 Vote by Size of Place for Manuals and Nonmanuals (Married, Economically Active, Non-South Only) SRC 1964

	Size of Place		
	Large Cities	Middle-Sized Cities	Small Towns, Rural
Party Identification: Percent Democratic (of 2-party choice)			
Nonmanuals	64%	48%	47%
N =	(163)	(98)	(75)
Manuals	75%	76%	65%
N =	(143)	(76)	(75)
1964 Vote: Percent Democratic (of 2-party choice)			
Nonmanual	69%	48%	58%
N =	(145)	(83)	(67)
Manual	74%	87%	80%
N =	(111)	(60)	(65)

The voting pattern also provides little support for the received hypothesis. Approximately seven-tenths of those in the large cities report a Democratic vote in 1964. The next highest Democratic percentage, (58 percent) was reported in the smaller communities. Once again we find the middle-sized cities as both most Republican and as containing the most loyal Republican forces. The percentage of middle-class Republican voters is identical with the percentage of Republican identifiers.

The basic lessons, as far as the middle classes are concerned, involve first, the "Democraticness" of those in the big cities; second, the stable, inflexible Republicanism of those in the middle-sized cities; and third, the relative openness or flexibility of those in the small towns. Since the words "open" and "flexible" tend to be weighted or loaded terms, we might also express the point somewhat differently by noting that they are easily swayed, that is, they bend with the winds.

The Manuals

Corresponding to the assumption of uniform conservatism among the non-manuals, is the assumption of a "break to the left" among the manuals living in the larger cities. The evidence does show the manual workers in the small towns and open country to be somewhat less Democratic than those living elsewhere.[7] Otherwise, there is no difference of note; the workers in big cities and those in the middle-sized ones are both equally Democratic in identification, to the extent of three out of four.

In voting behavior we have a complete *boulversement* of the expectations; those in the middle-sized communities are the most Democratic, those in small towns are next, and those in the large cities are only 74 percent Democratic. The relatively low figure here is caused by the suburban workers, only 62 percent of whom supported the Democratic candidate. Without their influence, the big-city workers would have had a one-in-five Republican minority, a minority that would still have been larger than that found among their working-class peers in the middle-sized cities.

Class Polarization

Following the Alford procedure for assessing the degree of "class polarization," we find that the differences between manuals and nonmanuals in Democratic party identification in the large and middle-sized cities and small towns, respectively, to be as follows:

$$+11 \qquad +28 \qquad +18$$

When we look at the differences in voting in 1964, the pattern is even more pronounced:

$$+5 \qquad +39 \qquad +22$$

In short, class polarization as defined by Alford is almost nonexistent in the large metropolitan areas—not because the workers have "come around," but because such a large percentage of the middle classes stand for the same party. The great class division is in the middle-sized communities, those of from 2500 to 50,000 persons, or what we might call the Muncie (or Middletown) size, or alternatively, the Elmira size.

One might think that in these *relatively* small communities, a collective conscience, a shared set of values, a common outlook, and so forth ought to be present. Presumably the working-class persons would have so much contact with middle-class persons, that their influence would most certainly "rub off."

It is worth noting, just to illustrate the difficulties in this view, the case of Janesville, Wisconsin. In 1960 the population was 35,164, about 10,000 being under age 14. Taking adult males, we find that there were about 9100 who were employed and that 68 percent of these were manual workers. As far as the "close contact" and the "rubbing off" theses are concerned, that would involve 6181 manual workers coming in contact with 2957 nonmanuals in some more or less continuous way. On the average, each middle-class male would have to serve for two manual workers. The manuals, most of them, are employed in the giant Chevrolet and Fisher Body assembly plants to the south of the community or in the Parker Pen factory to the north. Residential neighborhoods, too, are very neatly segregated. On the whole, therefore, it would seem highly unlikely that any continuous contact could take place. In a sense, the workers in the middle-sized cities live with the same kind of segregation as do those of the larger cities. To be sure, the upper-middle class is only a mile away as compared to being five miles distant in Milwaukee. But as far as contact is concerned, here one mile is as good as five.

There are, however, some differences. A major one is that the elites in middle-sized communities are more likely to be known; one can personalize more clearly and more accurately than in a larger city. Also, compared to the situation of the workers in the larger city, the condition is much more hopeless. The unions have less importance; there are fewer committed activists; the Democratic party means little or nothing. At-large elections (where the council members are elected from the entire city rather than from wards) are more frequent than in larger cities and the local governments tend to be almost completely in the hands of the dominant political cliques whose members come from the "other side" of town. In short, the conditions that generate a separate consciousness for workers are very much the same as those in the larger cities but the conditions that make for an even minimally viable, organized opposition are absent. It is this absence of organized opposition that accounts for the fact that the day-to-day politics of these communities are more thoroughly dominated by Republicans than would be suggested by an examination of the underlying loyalties. It is also clear that if there were an alternative political movement present in those contexts, with adequate cadres, that the entire political scene could be radically changed. "Insurgency" in these contexts, one should note, would run up against very intransigent and very well-organized conservative Republican forces.[8]

Before leaving the discussion of Table 6.2, it is worthwhile to take a look at the marginal distributions. When one talks of "workers" or of "industrial workers," the near automatic response is to think "big city." Interestingly enough, however, roughly half of the manual workers live in communities of 50,000 or less. A quarter of the workers live in communities of 2500 or less. This is speaking of the legal entity in which they are housed; to be sure, some of these small towns are within Standard Metropolitan Statistical Areas and, once again, it is at least an open question as to whether they are to be viewed as "urban" or "rural." The important lesson is that when talking of "workers," rather than thinking exclusively in terms of Detroit, Pittsburgh, St. Louis, Cleveland, and so on, one must also include Mechanicville, McKeesport, Muncie, Muskeegan, and Fond du Lac as well as still smaller communities of the "Springdale" variety.

The Suburbs

Taking the suburbs of the twelve largest metropolitan areas and examining the political orientations of manuals and nonmanuals there, we find what initially are some puzzling findings. Contrary to popular expectation, we find 58 percent of the middle class (N = 76) identifying as Democrats and 71 percent (N = 70) reporting a Democratic vote in 1964.

The explanation for this finding follows from the previous discussion of class and "pillars." Upper-middle-class white Protestant suburbanites are quite heavily Republican. That statement, however, may not be said of the upper-middle-class suburbanites of the other religious faiths. Also in the suburban nonmanual category are a fair-sized group of lower-middle-class persons, many of whom are Catholic and also heavily Democratic in political orientation. The next largest group are the white Protestant lower-middle-class suburbanites who divide about 50–50 between the parties.[9]

The suburban manual workers had approximately the same level of Democratic identification as the workers in the central cities. In the 1964 election, however, the level of Democratic voting fell approximately 20 percentage points behind that of other metropolitan workers. The explanation for this difference appears to be largely a matter of disproportionate Republican turnout rather than any serious defection. Eighty-three percent of the Goldwater supporters among the suburban workers indicated they had actually voted as compared to only 71 percent of the equivalent Johnson supporters.

Thirty-one of the suburban workers in this study were white Protestants, 22 were white Catholics, and there were 2 Negroes and three "others." Twelve of the 14 Republican identifiers among the working-class suburbanites were white Protestants. The suburban milieu clearly had very little political impact on the other workers.

Looking at the matter from another perspective we can compare the respondents' identifications with those of their parents. If the familiar conversion hypothesis is operating, we ought to see a marked shift toward Republicanism by those who had Democratic fathers; also there should be a disproportionate falling to the Republicans on the part of those with uncommitted fathers. The results do not support these expectations. Ninety-one percent of the working-class suburbanites with Democratic fathers (N = 22) reported Democratic identifications. Eighty-nine percent (N = 19) of those with a politically uncommitted father are currently Democratic identifiers. The working-class suburban Republicans are, quite simply, the children of Republicans.[10]

The Evidence from other Studies: 1952 and 1956

Since the major points made so far in this discussion are so important and since they are so at variance with previous work in the area, it is important to review the evidence from the other major studies being used in this work. We have, therefore, divided the respondents in two other Survey Research Center studies by city size categories, approximating as closely as possible the 1964 division, and we have, once again, examined the variation with city size among manuals and nonmanuals and have also looked at the class polarization in each of the categories.

The 1952 study showed a remarkable correspondence with the results of the 1964 survey. The nonmanual level of "Democraticness" in that year was generally lower than in 1964; but aside from that, the variations by city size were quite similar to the 1964 results and support the points already made. These are, in summary, that there is greater differentiation in party identifications by city size in the nonmanual than in the manual ranks and that the greatest degree of class polarization is to be found in the middle-sized cities.[11] Although the data cannot be presented here, the same approximate results (allowing for different overall levels of party division) appear in the 1948 and 1952 voting patterns.

It would be nice to have the three studies come up with identical results. Unfortunately, however, that does not happen to be entirely the case. The 1956 study is in agreement with the other two in showing that there is greater differentiation by city size in the nonmanual ranks, the big-city middle classes being again more Democratic than those in the other two contexts. Once again, there is little consistent variation in the manual ranks, the small towns being 60 percent Democratic compared to the 61 percent in the big cities. The difference between this study and the other two lies in the fact that the working classes in the middle-sized cities turn out to be the least Democratic of the three contexts, whereas in the other two studies they were very heavily in favor of that party. It is because of this difference that the pattern of greater class polarization in the middle-sized cities does not appear in the 1956 study.[12]

The easiest solution would be to write off the "deviation" either as a fluke in the 1956 sample, or, alternatively, as resulting from somewhat different city size categories. While it is impossible to reject these hypotheses, it is worth considering other possibilities. While we have, thus far in this work, accepted the near-dogma of the stability of party identifications, it is a possibility that, under heavy pressure, there was a shift on the part of many workers in this milieu. We can offer some evidence suggestive of the apparent pressure in the setting. Workers in all contexts swung in a Republican direction in 1956, but the extent of the shift in the middle-sized cities, as shown by the swing of Democrats away from their identifications, was considerable. The likelihood of special pressures there also is shown in the preferences of the nonvoters. The working-class nonvoters indicated Republican preferences everywhere in that year, but again, in this middle-sized city, the sentiment was greater than elsewhere. (All of the middle-class nonvoters there, incidentally, reported a Republican preference.) Republican workers in middle-sized cities in 1956 were slightly more likely than their peers elsewhere to report a shift from earlier Democratic allegiance. It is possible, given the suggested pressures, that some shifting of identification did occur in this context—more than is indicated by the actual reports by respondents. It is possible that the combination of local and national media influence together with the availability of an attractive candidate image was sufficient to move workers in ways that were not possible either in big cities (where there would be stronger countervailing informal influences) or in the small towns. This accomplishment depended on a rare set of circumstances. In 1964, however, the Republican candidate was not "above the parties" and thus could not escape the constraining influence of party identifications. Both candidates probably helped to realert workers to their traditional identifications and both helped make clear the threat to worker interests. Against these conditions the local media and political efforts in the middle-sized communities would be more or less helpless.[13]

The Suburban Development: 1952 to 1964

Looking back at the political orientations in metropolitan suburbs in 1952 and 1956, we find in those years that the nonmanual suburbanites were Republican in the majority, the number of Democratic identifiers in those years being only 39 percent (N = 46) and 29 percent (N = 66), respectively. The tendency, moreover, was for those Republicans to be strong identifiers, unlike the 1964 results. The working-class suburbanites in both years showed Democratic majorities.

Something happened between the earlier two studies and 1964 that affected the party identifications of the middle-class suburbanites. The explanation appears to lie in the composition of this group and the political outlook associated with the various socioreligious categories. Basically, in 1952, the middle-class suburbanites were white Protestant in their majority. This majority fell from 61 percent ($N = 54$) in 1952 to 55 percent in 1956 ($N = 73$). In 1964 they were a minority with only 41 percent ($N = 85$) of the total.

Issue Orientations and City Size

It is important, once again, to examine issue positions to see whether the patterns of party loyalties actually reflect liberal-conservative positions or whether they are merely traditional, hand-me-down allegiances with little or no relationship to the issues. The overall picture shows rather erratic results. The liberal percentages for the three size categories in response to the medical care question, for example, were 63, 55, and 57 percent, going from large to small. For the guaranteed living standard, the figures were 42, 32, and 32 percent. On the whole, one might say there is slight support for the received hypothesis, but again, as in the case of the party identifications, the differences between the extreme categories are relatively small and the pattern not one of consistent increases in liberalism with size of place.

When we look at the breakdown for the manual and nonmanual groups separately, it becomes even more difficult to maintain the thesis of liberalism (or leftism) increasing with city size on the basis of these findings (see Table

TABLE 6.3
Liberalism Questions and Size of Place (Married, Economically Active, Non-South) SRC 1964

| | Size of Place | | |
Issue	Large City	Middle-Sized City	Small Town, Rural
	Percent liberal (of those with opinions)		
Medical care			
Nonmanual	59%	42%	47%
N =	(141)	(79)	(62)
Manual	68%	73%	67%
N =	(126)	(64)	(63)
Difference	+9	+31	+20
Living standard			
Nonmanual	33%	27%	28%
N =	(133)	(84)	(57)
Manual	52%	38%	36%
N =	(125)	(60)	(44)
Difference	+19	+11	+8
School aid			
Nonmanual	43%	34%	30%
N =	(141)	(80)	(66)
Manual	41%	48%	40%
N =	(129)	(58)	(63)
Difference	−2	+14	+10
Gov't. power			
Nonmanual	55%	40%	51%
N =	(131)	(75)	(61)
Manual	66%	80%	57%
N =	(95)	(49)	(49)
Difference	+11	+40	+6

6.3). Looking at the pattern of class differences, we do find, in response to three of the four issue questions, a pattern of cleavage similar to that noted with respect to party identification and voting—that is, one of greater cleavage in the middle-sized cities. This is clearly indicated in the response to the medical care question. Again, the greatest differentiation appears within the nonmanual rank, with the big-city nonmanuals being more liberal and those in middle-sized cities being more conservative. There are no significant differences among the manuals. The greatest class polarization is also found in the middle-sized cities in the responses to the school aid and the government power questions, although here there are some differencs in detail as compared to the patterns noted previously.

A quite different pattern appears with respect to the guaranteed living standard. In this case the manuals in the middle-sized cities and small towns are considerably more conservative than are their peers in the big cities. One possible explanation is that in response to this kind of program the small-town individualistic heritage still has some hold on a fair-sized proportion of the manual workers there.

Some of the responses to the liberalism questions, however, suggest the instability of the individualist heritage. Workers in the middle-sized cities (who showed a conservative majority on the living standard question) were very liberal in their responses to the medical care and the government power questions. It would appear that the tradition holds with respect to what for them may seem a very "far out" option—the living standard guarantee. On the other hand, the spector of "government power," which figures so prominently in conservative rhetoric, does not appear to move them to any significant extent.

It is possible to show this conflict of ideological versus existential commitments in another way. Small-town workers showed a relatively low level of approval for the living standard guarantee. It would be easy, given this evidence and given that they are "small town," to assume a consistent, ideological conservatism, rooted perhaps in a long tradition of individualism. A crosstabulation with the medical care question, however, indicates very serious countervailing concerns. A near-majority of the opponents of the living standard guarantee favor government-supported medical care (see Table 6.4). Those with "no interest" in the living standard guarantee prove to be very much interested in the medical care possibility and, on the whole, positively disposed toward it. A similar division of the presumed conservative ranks appears in response to the government power question. Those saying no to the living standard guarantee and having an opinion on the government power question split nearly 50–50. To the extent, therefore, that there is conservatism in these locations, one ought to recognize that it is a very "flimsy" conservatism, a variety that might very well disappear on the first contact with serious advocates of either a liberal or left program. Similar findings also appeared in an exploration of attitudes in the nonmanual ranks.

The conflict of existential concerns and ideology may be shown in another way. The manuals and nonmanuals were divided by party identification and the positions on government-supported medical care examined. For the purpose at hand, we calculated the percentages (of those with opinions) who were in a position of conflict with their party, that is, who were anti-medical care Democrats or pro-medical care Republicans. The highest percentage of such conflict is among the *nonmanual* small-town populations, one-third of whom hold an issue position at variance with the most likely position of their

TABLE 6.4
Liberalism Issues and the Small-Town Workers (Married, Economically Active, Non-South) SRC 1964

	Attitude Toward Living Standard Guarantee			
	For	Depends	Against	No Interest, DK, NA
Attitude Toward Medical Care				
For	69%	36%	46%	52%
Depends	...	...	...	4
Against	19	43	32	12
No interest, DK, NA	12	21	22	32
Attitude Toward Government				
Too strong	6%	43%	36%	20%
Depends	6	7	7	...
Not too powerful	31	43	39	24
No interest, DK, NA	56	7	18	56
N =	(16)	(14)	(28)	(25)

party. The social and political processes within the small-town middle-class milieu clearly do not result in any very high level of rationality. There is, in short, something about this setting that either generates or allows such conflict to persist. The parallel finding here is that the manual workers in the small-town milieu, despite their lower level of formal education, are less likely to be conflicted than the middle classes. Among the manual workers, moreover, such conflict is more frequent among the Republicans than among the Democrats.[14]

The Composition Hypothesis

A recurrent problem in the social sciences is the failure to test the obvious. When a time-honored hypothesis is once again supported, the task is considered to be finished. For this reason, it is with respect to just these kinds of hypotheses that one is actually very poorly informed. One could, for example, have stopped with our presentation in Table 6.1 showing the increase in the percentage of Democratic identification associated with the larger communities, assumed it was due to "isolated masses" of city workers, and gone on to other considerations. Had we done so, however, we would have overlooked much of what actually underlies this pattern.

To this point, we have accepted the basic explanatory hypothesis—the influence of occupational segregation in the larger cities (although with some significant respecification). It proves rewarding, however, to consider a completely different line of explanation: the socioreligious composition of the various sized communities. A moment's thought would suggest that the heavy Democratic sentiment in non-Southern cities could very well be a result of the disproportionate presence there of Negroes, Jews, and Catholics; whereas, the disproportionate Republicanism of the small towns might result from the white Protestant predominance there. The 1964 survey shows the white Protestant proportion increasing from 43 to 71 percent as one moves from the metropolitan to the small-town context. A separate consideration of the party identification among the white Protestants shows that city size makes practically no difference at all; the metropolitan Democratic figure was 56 percent, in the middle-sized cities it was 55 percent, and in the small towns it was 51 percent. This indicates that the overall pattern shown in Table 6.1 is, in fact, largely a result of the socioreligious composition of the various community size categories.[15]

There is some variation by city size among the "other" socioreligious groups. In the metropolitan communities, 80 percent identified as Democrats as against 68 percent in the middle-sized communities and 69 percent in the small towns. In this case, the difference was not to be accounted for by the conventional explanation (isolated working-class masses in cities), but just the opposite experience, isolated or uprooted middle-class *individuals* in small towns.[16] This kind of experience is not very frequent and, therefore, is not likely to be of great importance in the future development of party loyalties. Few of those in the "other" category are found in the smaller communities and very few of them become isolated from their socioreligious communities, so that even there the majority still retain their traditional party loyalties.

The absence of widespread conversion on the part of the socioreligious "others" in the middle-sized and smaller communities suggests the existence of a socioreligious segregation. Rather than the relative or absolute "smallness" of community being associated with complete "integration," with absence of barriers, and with monocultural orientations, it is apparent that both class and religious barriers can persist even in the smallest communities.[17]

Inter-Community Movement

It is important to make some examination of the political correlates of movement between communities. Those who are either traditional or diffuse small-town conservatives may well shift position after migration to the cities and exposure to the different pressures or influences present there. And, if the "backflow" movement, from city to smaller community, were of sufficient strength and had a distinctive political character, it might have some considerable impact on the small towns.

For this discussion it was necessary, in order to allow a sufficient number of cases, to combine the small and the middle-sized communities and contrast them with the large cities. For the purpose of examining stability or change in party identifications, the political orientations of the fathers have been

contrasted with the current identifications of the respondents. We are again
focusing on the manuals and the nonmanuals.

The middle class currently resident in the smaller communities was divided
into those born and raised there and those who came there from the large
cities. Looking first at the former group, the indigenous population, one
finds that the most important political development is a considerable (i.e., 31
percent) shift away from the father's position on the part of those coming
from Democratic families (see Table 6.5). The children from Republican

TABLE 6.5
Inter-Community Movement and Political Change (Married, Economically Active,
Non-South) SRC 1964

Father's Politics:	Size of Place					
	Large City			Middle-Sized City, Small Town		
	Democrat	Republican	Other	Democrat	Republican	Other
	Percent Democratic (of those with opinion)					
Nonmanuals						
Indigenous	80%	50%	65%	69%	20%	53%
N =	(49)	(22)	(23)	(62)	(49)	(17)
New arrivals	79	25	77	58	10	56
N =	(28)	(28)	(13)	(26)	(10)	(9)
Manuals						
Indigenous	81	38	90	89	38	67
N =	(31)	(8)	(19)	(70)	(32)	(30)
New arrivals	95	21	79	73	a	a
N =	(37)	(19)	(28)	(15)	(3)	(1)

a Too few cases. Combined results are: 50% Democratic, $N = 4$.

families hold fairly well to the family position and those few from politically
indeterminate families (father shifted, had no politics, etc.) divide 50–50.
The evidence suggests that these middle-class settings do involve pressures
leading to some conversion in a Republican direction. It is important to note,
however, the limited impact even of this milieu. The current generation of
the indigenous population is still 48 percent Democratic. After a lifetime in
the smaller community middle class, there is a *net* shift toward Republicanism
of only 9 persons out of 128.

The remainder of the middle-class population in the smaller communities
comes from the larger cities. While most attention has come to be focused on
the larger country-to-city movement, it is important to note that there exists
a fair-sized "backflow." Thirty percent of the nonmanual population in these
smaller communities had their origins in larger cities.

Originally, as judged by the father's politics, this backflow population was heavily Democratic. Here again, the influences of the milieu would appear to make themselves felt. The small number of those from Republican families remain heavily Republican. There is a considerable shift among those from Democratic families, more even than among the indigenous Democrats. Once again, it is important to note that despite the obvious drift within this setting, there must also be some important limiting or constraining factors since 47 percent of the new arrivals in the smaller communities have a Democratic allegiance. One other point of some interest: the "converts" to Republicanism, both among the indigenous and among the new arrivals tend to be weak identifiers. The strong identifiers are found among the indigenous populations, especially among those who themselves come from Republican families.[18]

It is clear that the nonmanual setting in the smaller communities is, as has long been asserted, a conservatising one, although the extent of the influence has perhaps been exaggerated. As we shall see below, much of what has been called "conservatising" is merely a "quieting" of the Democratic voices in that milieu rather than a changing of the orientation.

Turning now to the middle classes in the large cities, we find a somewhat opposed picture. Here, taking first the indigenous population, we find that the children of Democrats retain their political direction fairly well and, by comparison, there is serious defection from the Republican families. Indicative of the general tenor of the milieu, the children whose parents were of indeterminate political orientation fall heavily to the Democrats.

As is to be expected, a large proportion of the contemporary middle-class urbanites have their roots in smaller communities. Judging once again by the orientations of the parents, a relatively strong Republican sentiment was to be found in this group. They were even more Republican in their origins than their class peers, left behind in the smaller communities. But here again, reflecting the new milieu, there is a slight overall drift to the Democrats. One other point of note is that more than half of the strong Republicans in the urban middle class have their origins in the smaller communities.[19]

Turning to the working class in the smaller communities, we find that here, too, contrary to widespread expectations, the net drift among the indigenous population is very much in the Democratic direction. The experience of the relatively small number of working-class "new arrivals" also suggests some "insulation" or protection against the "dominant" climate of opinion in this setting.

It is a work of supererogation to comment on the trend within the big-city working-class context, but, for what it may be worth, the retention of Democratic orientations and the drift to that party is somewhat more pronounced there than in the small towns. A majority of the big-city working class consists of new arrivals from smaller communities and their pattern of shifting very closely mirrors that found within the indigenous population. Not all of the new arrivals, of course, make the shift. There is a fair-sized "Tory worker" contingent still remaining. It is also worth noting that 64 percent ($N = 23$) of the urban Republican workers came from these smaller communities.

In summary, we have one conservatising milieu—the middle class in the smaller communities—the other three contexts discussed here being, in essence, "liberalizing."

The focus on party identification and the absence of major differences between the manual groups in the various sized cities could easily lead one to overlook some less obvious attitudinal changes associated with residence in, and migration to, the different communities. Taking the manual workers who were raised and are living in small towns and inquiring as to their views on the guaranteed living standard, one does find a conservative tendency indicated (see Table 6.6). But perhaps even more striking, is the fact that one-third report no interest in the matter and one-eighth say that "it depends."

TABLE 6.6
Working-Class Rural-Urban Migration and Attitude Toward Guaranteed Living Standard (Married, Economically Active, Non-South Manuals)

	Manuals Reared In			
	Large City	Small Town		
		Now Living In		
	Large City	Large City	Middle-Sized	Small Town
Attitude toward living standard guarantee				
Approve	49%	39%	29%	21%
Depends	1	11	10	13
Disapprove	35	39	41	32
No interest, DK, NA	15	11	20	34
$N =$	(68)	(62)	(49)	(62)
Percent approving of those with opinions	58	50	41	40

In short, the most important fact about this group is not their conservatism, but their indecisiveness or indifference toward the matter.

When we take the manuals who were reared in small towns but who are now located in middle-sized and large cities, we find much higher levels of decision with much of the shift being "to the left." The level of opposition remains nearly constant but the percentage in favor of the program nearly doubles among those now living in the big cities. This still does not equal the level among the indigenous big-city workers, but they appear to have shifted significantly from the position of the small-town working-class peers they have "left behind." One cannot say with certainty that this represents a change, an adoption of big-city working-class values (since it might be that leftist workers leave the small towns and conservative workers prefer to remain there). If it does prove to be change, it would mean that "small-town conservatism" undergoes a considerable transformation in the cities. The point to be emphasized, if change is the case, would not be the entrenched, rigid conservatism of the group, but rather the lack of commitment, the indecision, or openness of the group. This would mean that on migration to the city they are easily moved to a more appropriate position.

The Middle-Class Returnees

The backflow, the returnees, those going against the mainstream flow from country to city are deserving of more detailed attention. As compared to the city-reared group who remained in the large cities, they tend to be very highly educated, and they tend to have a very high sense of political efficacy. One other characteristic of some possible importance is that they tend to be rather young.[20]

We cannot, of course, give any very definitive answer as to the motivations of these returnees. Some of them might, conceivably, be looking for a milieu that is more favorably disposed toward their political preference than tends to be the case in big cities. Although possible, it seems unlikely that the need for a friendly, congenial political environment would be sufficient to motivate a move of this importance. Another possibility involves an identity that is likely to be of greater significance—the socioreligious identity. Those remaining in the cities are Catholic or Jewish in their majority whereas those returning to the smaller communities have a Protestant majority.[21]

These migrants, in essence, provide a "staff" for the small towns, doing much legwork for the indigenous elites and providing specialized services (teaching, ministering, etc.). With their education and skill, they can easily gain more power, influence, and prestige than the indigenous lower-middle and working class. At the same time, they are likely to be very much "out-classed" by the indigenous upper class who would be "independent" businessmen and who would, in essence, "own" the local political party. By virtue of the fact that these migrants are not likely to be permanent residents, this would mean that they never become integrated in such a way as to seriously challenge the entrenched powers in the community even though, with their numbers and abilities, they could do so with relative ease. It is this "free flowing" character of the "migratory elite" which. in part at least, limits their power and also leaves the control of the smaller communities unchallenged.[22]

Class Cleavage: Differentiation within the Nonmanual Category

In the last chapter we showed that the middle class is rather sharply divided into lower and upper subgroups. It is worthwhile specifying the picture by city size categories.

Taking the white Protestants and the "others" separately, we have six comparisons. In four of these, the differences between the Democratic percentages in the working and lower-middle classes are very small, one being 12 percentage points, another being 3 percentage points (in the case of the big-city white Protestants) and in two cases there were even small reversals, the lower-middle class being slightly more Democratic than the manuals (see Table 6.7). The much discussed manual-nonmanual differences appear only

TABLE 6.7
Overview: Class, Socioreligious Category and Party Identification (Married, Economically Active, Non-South) SRC 1964

	Class			Percent Difference between	
Size of Place	Manual	Lower Middle	Upper Middle	Manual and Lower Middle	Lower and Upper Middle
Percent Democratic (of 2-party identification)					
Large city					
White Protestant	63%	60%	38%	+ 3	+22
N =	(62)	(35)	(34)		
Others	84%	85%	66%	− 1	+19
N =	(81)	(46)	(41)		
Middle-sized city					
White Protestant	75%	50%	22%	+25	+28
N =	(48)	(36)	(23)		
Others	79%	67%	53%	+12	+14
N =	(28)	(21)	(15)		
Small town					
White Protestant	62%	42%	31%	+20	+11
N =	(61)	(36)	(13)		
Others	79%	85%	33%	− 6	+52[a]
N =	(14)	(13)	(9)		

[a] Small number of cases.

among the white Protestants in the middle-sized and the small communities. In these cases the manual-lower-middle-class differences are 25 and 20 percent, respectively.

It is only in the middle-sized cities and in the small towns that serious cleavage exists between the manuals and the lower-middle class, and even there it appears only in the white Protestant ranks. It seems likely that some of the lower-middle-class white Protestants in those communities do have contact with and are influenced by the local upper-middle classes. Such influence would be possible for a larger proportion of that segment of the lower-middle class in those communities than in the larger cities. It might also be the case that those lower middles who have such contact in the smaller communities would suffer "status strains" by virtue of their peculiar connections and aspirations.

The lower-middle–upper-middle cleavage is, with one exception, either the same as or considerably larger than the equivalent manual-nonmanual divisions. Even among the white Protestants in the middle-sized cities where there was some division between blue collars and white collars (a division of 25 percentage points), there exists another sharp break within the latter rank, amounting to some 28 percentage points.

This evidence indicates once again, that manual-nonmanual focus is misleading since some very diverse outlooks get combined in the latter category. The further significance of this lower-middle–upper-middle cleavage will be made clear in the next section.

Politicization and Size of Place

Throughout this chapter we have stressed the relative depoliticization of the smaller communities. Support for this claim may be found in Table 6.8, which shows the small-town populations to be less interested in politics and less likely to talk politics, to attend meetings, to work for the party, or to belong to a political organization. With respect to low-effort activities, such as wearing a button or having an auto sticker, there are no significant differences between the communities. There are also no significant differences in letter writing to officials, although this indicator is of another character than the foregoing since here we are asking for activity over one's entire lifetime and since this result will therefore depend on the age structure of the various populations.[23]

Another exception to the pattern of lower small-town involvement appears with respect to voting turnout in which case there are essentially no differences associated with size of city. This means that in the small towns we have a somewhat larger percentage of the population whose effort may be characterized as "participation without interest."[24] It seems likely that these low-interest participators supply a fair proportion of the "irrational" vote which is, as already noted, more prevalent in that setting. It is also likely that these persons are more subject to distant or casual stimuli and do much to account for the greater "swing vote" found in this milieu.

One other point of note in this connection is the fact that the pattern is not one of continuous increased activity in the larger communities. The middle-sized cities in some comparisons show more political effort than the metropolitan areas. We shall explore this matter in more detail below.

In all three community size categories the level of political activity and concern generally varies directly with class level.[25] (Table 6.9) There are

TABLE 6.8
Size of Place, Political Interest, and Activity (Married, Economically Active, Non-South) SRC 1964

	Large City	Middle-Sized City	Small Town
Interest in campaign[a]			
Very much	40%	37%	29%
Somewhat	36	42	49
Not much	24	21	22
$N =$	(339)	(186)	(164)
Talked Politics[a]	35%	42%	28%
$N =$	(315)	(170)	(161)
Attended meetings[b]	12%	12%	6%
Worked for a party	9	7	3
Belongs to political organization	6	7	3
Wore button, had car sticker	17	15	15
Ever written officials	19	23	18
Participation in past elections; voted in:			
All	59	56	57
Most	13	20	21
Some	9	8	10
None	7	4	5
Other[c]	12	12	7
1964 election participation[b]	81	84	82

[a] See note 23 for question wordings.
[b] The participation questions were post-election, hence the smaller number of cases. For the sake of economy, the remaining Ns have been omitted. In no case are they more than two cases away from those in the "talked politics" row.
[c] "None of them because not old enough to vote before or not a citizen before. Resident of Washington, D.C." The question is pre-election and the Ns very close to those for the above "interest in campaign" question.

some important specifications of this pattern, however, that deserve more detailed consideration. Taking "interest in the campaign," for example, we find very low interest indicated on the part of the small-town workers and also by the small-town lower-middle class. For both working and lower-middle classes, the pattern of diminished concern in the smaller communities comes through very clearly. In the case of the small-town upper-middle class, however, the opposite is the case; they have a very high interest. In this respect, the class differences are greatest in the small towns, the workers and lower-middle classes being very much "out of it" and the upper middles very much "in."

It is this fact, the depressed interest on the part of the "subordinate" ranks

TABLE 6.9

Size of Place, Class, Political Interest and Activity (Married, Economically Active, Non-South) SRC 1964

	Size of Place								
	Large City			Middle-Sized City			Small Town		
Class:	WCᵃ	LMCᵇ	UMCᶜ	WC	LMC	UMC	WC	LMC	UMC
Very much interested in campaign	31%	48%	51%	28%	46%	41%	19%	30%	61%
N =	(160)	(88)	(83)	(81)	(61)	(39)	(83)	(54)	(23)
Talked politics	28%	38%	44%	33%	41%	61%	25%	29%	35%
N =	(150)	(81)	(79)	(72)	(58)	(36)	(81)	(52)	(23)
Attended meetingsᵈ	5%	11%	25%	4%	9%	36%	4%	49%	9%
Worked	5	9	15	1	5	22	3	4	⋯
Member of political organization	3	7	12	4	5	17	4	⋯	⋯
Wore butten; had car sticker	16	17	18	11	14	22	17	14	13
Has written letters	9	21	34	11	26	44	18	19	17
Voted in all past elections	49	61	73	45	55	77	53	54	78
Voted in 1964	75	85	94	83	81	91	82	81	91

ᵃ Working class.
ᵇ Lower-middle class.
ᶜ Upper-middle class.
ᵈ The Ns are very close to those of the "talked politics" question. See the note to Table 6.8 for further explanation.

in these communities which, in great measure, is responsible for the dominant Republicanism in the smaller communities—despite the fact that the Democratic identifiers are in the majority. Generally such facts are interpreted "individualistically"—it is presumably a matter of *their* apathy, or *their* disinterest; they could participate if they wanted to, and so on. It is, however, important to consider the social organizational and institutional factors such as the absence of Democratic party organization and the link between "nonpartisan" arrangements and low participation. Such nonpartisan arrangements are de facto partisan devices which, in fact, lead to the dissolution of the Democrats and the replacement of a local Republican organization by a less accessible clique or private voluntary association. Manual workers, in short, are *made* apathetic by the destruction of a key political agency.[26]

When it is a matter of political activities (as opposed to mere interest), we find a somewhat different pattern, one of peculiarly high effort on the part of the upper-middle classes in the middle-sized cities. This means that the middle-sized cities, the location with greatest class polarization as far as political orientations are concerned, are not especially given to organized political confrontation. The actual development appears to be one of very active upper-middle classes and more or less routinely inactive working classes. For this reason, once again, a development that might be suggested by the distribution of attitudes does not become the case either in organizational fact or in the facts of electoral results.[27]

It is worth noting that the high level of interest shown by the small-town upper-middle classes is not correlated with a high level of political activity. They are low both in talking politics and attending meetings (that is, in comparison to their class peers elsewhere). They are only moderately differentiated from the "lower ranks" in the small towns. One possibility is that in the small towns, politics, so to speak, "takes care of itself." Things proceed in their traditional way with little or no special efforts being necessary to "mobilize the masses." Since there is virtually no challenge from below, there is little need for the community leaders to undertake any special organizational efforts. Moreover, with the removal of campaigning to the national level there is less and less for these leaders to do. None of them were members of a political organization and none reported working for a party.

The Silent Democrats

The introduction of a formally nonpartisan arrangement cripples the Democrats but, on the whole, probably has very little impact on the strength of the Republicans. In both the small towns and the middle-sized cities the Republicans can conduct political affairs in the course of their ordinary routine life activities. Their situation has been well described by Alfred De Grazia who points out that:

Since the parties do not have generally effective party organizations,

Republicans gain a strong initial advantage from the "natural" organization. By natural organization, it is meant that the Republicans number among their supporters by far the greater proportion of the business and professional groups who, without changing their way of life, engage in politics as a matter of course. . . . the Republicans have a great many individual supporters who belong to real estate organizations, publishers' associations, insurance groups, Rotary, Kiwanis, and other fraternal organizations that function continually, and that, without breaking step with their routine operation, can convert themselves into political organizations. The transformation is often not a conscious one. Indeed it may not even be a transformation at all. But society is like a giant spider web of communication and contacts, and Republicans tend to be stationed at the centers of contacts and communications with the society at large. As spare-time politicians, such contact-controllers and opinion leaders can easily bring to bear upon the political process their strong influences and political leadership. In brief, the normal social structure provides an informal Republican party organization.[28]

As was seen in Table 6.1, the Democrats have a majority of the party identifiers in all community sizes. Clearly, if people voted their identifications the political history in the non-South regions of the United States would be one long unbroken history of Democratic rule. Since non-South states have gone Republican in presidential elections and since they do elect Republican governors and Republican legislatures, it is more than clear that somehow or other the threat of "perpetual Democracy" has been avoided.

Most analysis has focused on defection from the Democrats, that is, on the "swing voters." This view has the advantage, from the viewpoint of more conventional perspectives, of according with the images of rational voters, of the "give-and-take" of electoral competition, and so forth. One can argue that the opposition has put up "attractive candidates" and developed "appealing programs" and thereby the momentarily less responsive party has been punished. Their defeat serves as a lesson to them to respond accordingly in the next election. This viewpoint has the advantage, therefore, of providing a highly acceptable view of the electoral arrangements and their operations.

While not completely without merit (there are, after all, some "swing voters" and some of them are more or less rational in their decision making), the view does overlook the impact of differential turnout and differences in political effort.

It is useful to begin this discussion once again with a consideration of campaign interest. We have divided the respondents by city size, class, and then by party (see Table 6.10). Significantly, we find relatively little difference by party in the amount of interest shown in the campaign. In the big cities the maximum difference is 10 percentage points. In the small towns there is equality in one comparison and a fair-sized reversal in another. The one

TABLE 6.10

Size of Place, Class, Party Identification, Political Interest and Activity (Non-South, Economically Active, Married) SRC 1964

	Size of Place								
	Large City			Middle-Sized City			Small Town		
Class:	Manual	Lower Middle	Upper Middle	Manual	Lower Middle	Upper Middle	Manual	Lower Middle	Upper Middle
Party Identification[a]									
Percent very much interested in campaign									
Republican	39%	57%	47%	39%	61%	48%	19%	22%	67%
N =	(36)	(21)	(34)	(18)	(23)	(27)	(26)	(23)	(15)
Democratic	31%	47%	50%	28%	33%	43%	20%	39%	43%
N =	(106)	(60)	(40)	(57)	(30)	(14)	(49)	(26)	(7)
Percent talking politics									
Republican	40%	57%	58%	31%	74%	83%	40%	41%	47%
N =	(35)	(21)	(33)	(13)	(23)	(24)	(25)	(22)	(15)
Democratic	25%	33%	32%	32%	19%	18%	17%	23%	14%
N =	(100)	(55)	(38)	(54)	(31)	(11)	(48)	(26)	(7)
Percent attending meetings									
Republican[b]	11%	14%	33%	...	17%	50%	8%	9%	7%
Democratic	4	11	21	4	...	18	2	...	14
Percent working for party									
Republican[b]	11	19	21	8	13	21	...	5	...
Democratic	4	6	11	...	...	18	4	4	...

	Size of Place								
	Large City			Middle-Sized City			Small Town		
Class:	Manual	Lower Middle	Upper Middle	Manual	Lower Middle	Upper Middle	Manual	Lower Middle	Upper Middle
Percent members of political club									
Republican[a]	11%	14%	16%	8%	13%	21%	8%	...	...
Democratic	1	6	11	4	...	9	2	...	...
Percent with buttons, stickers									
Republican[b]	23	24	22	15	22	29	8	14	13
Democratic	16	18	13	9	13	9	25	15	...
Percent ever writing a letter									
Republican[b]	23	29	43	15	48	58	28	9	20
Democratic	3	20	26	11	10	18	15	31	...
Percent "always" voting									
Republican[c]	58	71	83	67	56	84	69	44	87
Democratic	51	62	60	40	50	62	49	65	57
Percent voting in 1964									
Republican[b]	74	95	91	100	96	96	96	82	93
Democratic	80	86	87	80	74	82	75	85	86

[a] This question is pre-election. *N*s are similar to those of the "talked politics" question.
[b] Post-election. *N*s are similar to those of the "campaign interest" question.
[c] Pre-election. The *N*s are similar to those of the "campaign interest" question.

instance that supports the major previous finding of a consistent Republican edge is based on a very small number of upper-middle-class Democrats in that location $(N = 7)$. The major support for the basic finding appears in the middle-sized cities; there the Republicans are consistently ahead of the equivalent Democrats, the differences ranging from modest to fair-sized (28 percentage points). We may take these figures as a reference point for the subsequent discussion. It will provide an indication of "level of carry-through."

The first and, in a sense, the easiest carry-through effort would involve "talking politics." Here we find a markedly different picture that, with a single exception, shows consistent and sizable differences between the Republican and Democratic party identifiers. The most notable finding is the extremely high participation in political talk on the part of middle-class Republicans in the middle-sized cities and the extremely low level on the part of the equivalent Democrats. It would appear that among Democrats the working-class milieu in these communities is more congenial to political conversation than is the middle-class setting. It is apparent that the middle-class Democrats in this setting sense some strain in the open expression of or advocacy of their views.[29]

Another point of some interest appears when we compare the level of interest in the campaign with the level of those talking politics. Taking Republicans first, we may note that in the big cities 47 percent are very much interested but that even more, 58 percent, have tried to convince others. In the middle-sized cities, particularly in the upper-middle class, we find that the proportion engaging in political talk far exceeds the level showing "very much" interest, the figures here being 48 and 83 percent. The same tendency is found in two of the small-town categories, that is, among manual workers and lower-middle classes. In the case of the Democrats, on the other hand, with only one exception (workers in middle-sized cities) the proportion "talking politics" is consistently below the proportion of those showing much interest.

The lesson would appear to be that Democratic "interest" does not get translated into the most rudimentary form of political effort. The Republican situation tends to be just the opposite; not only do those with "very much" interest transfer their concern but even those with limited interest also do so.[30]

The levels of participation in the other, more demanding, activities are consistently below those involved in talking about politics. In general, the same patterns appear as are found with respect to the talking of politics, that is, the same class and party relationships and the same high involvement of the upper-middle-class Republicans in middle-sized cities.

Talking politics, wearing buttons, going to meetings, and so forth is one part of the electoral scene. This is not an unimportant part, to be sure, but the decisive factor is obviously the winning of the vote. This may be accomplished either through convincing the waverers or through differential turnout of the already convinced. Some indications as to the impact of the latter process may be gained by examining the results of the voting turnout question and of the 1964 vote question. Taking the percentage who report they have "always voted," we see, with one exception, Republicans consistently leading the Democrats, the differences for the most part running between 10 and 20 percentage points. Examining the reports on whether or not they voted in 1964, we find much the same pattern. In this case we have the same reversal among the lower-middle-class partisans in the small towns, and we also have a reversal in the metropolitan working classes.

The major point to be noted, however, is the nearly 100 percent turnout among Republicans in middle-sized cities. With the exception of the lower middles, the same holds in the small towns. This must be set against a roughly 80 percent turnout among the Democrats in these settings. Many of these Republicans, it must be noted, defected to the Democrats in their 1964 voting. What is being attempted here, however, is to give some sense of the *usual* basic dynamics of turnout in the different settings. Some sense of the usual Republican advantage may be seen in the responses to the question about the regularity of voting in previous elections.

The importance of the differences in turnout may be seen by consideration of the small-town experience. There, in 1964, we had 64 Republican and 82 Democratic identifiers. If 100 percent of the Republicans turned out and voted for their party and only 80 percent of the Democrats did so, the number of voters, respectively, would be 64 and 66. If even two Democrats shifted to the Republicans, there would be a Republican majority. This direction of shift is more than likely given the political orientation of newspapers and the dominant personal influences in most non-South small towns.[31]

The Goldwater candidacy made the 1964 campaign a very exceptional one. It was different enough to "convert" Republicans, to lead some Republican newspapers not to make their usual endorsements, and to generate a very high working-class turnout. In more "normal" elections, it seems likely that the assymetrical process outlined above would be the more typical development.

The Lower-Middle-Class Activists

We have argued to this point that the division between blue collar and lower white collar is not a significant one; the two groups share the same backgrounds and formative experiences and, hence, are very much alike in their outlooks. With respect to "interest in campaign," and talking politics, this expectation was not consistently supported. In the six class comparisons made in Table 6.10, we found, for example, in the case of talking politics, two sharp exceptions to our expectations in the case of lower-middle-class Republicans in large and middle-sized cities. Elsewhere the pattern is one of very little consistent class difference and, among the Democrats in the middle-sized cities, there exists an inversion (previously discussed) of the usual expectation with the manual workers being more active. Since these instances of "middle-classness" on the part of lower-level nonmanuals challenge the position taken in this work, it is important to inquire into the source of this deviation from our expectations.

It is worthwhile to go back to our original, arbitrary definition of these upper- and lower-middle classes. By using an income level for our cutting point we have introduced some ambiguity (as noted earlier) and thereby have, in a sense, misplaced some individuals. One of the characteristics of a bureaucratic society is that people tend to begin low in the hierarchy and "work their way up." Persons born and raised in upper-middle-class families, outfitted with a "proper" education, and so forth, will, at the beginnings of their careers, frequently be found with an income that is relatively low. Their presence in the "lower-middle class" is misleading since they are on a career line that will carry them (barring extreme difficulties) once again to their original station in life. This is to suggest that among the younger lower-middle-class populations, particularly among the Republicans, there are some who are not going to be "lower-middle class" over their entire lifetimes; they come with different expectations and training and they have a high probability of leaving the class ranks. Their "consciousness," for these reasons, is not likely to be either determined by or reflective of their current "lower-middle-class" income level. There are a range of determinants in their lives that are of much greater salience than their current salary level and the "life chances" determined solely by income.[32]

It was possible to check out this possibility in a crude way. Taking younger (age 39 or less), married, non-South lower-middle-class respondents, we found the Republican identifiers among them to be more optimistic about their future incomes than were Democrats. We were not able to discover whether or not they came from upper-middle-class backgrounds but this was suggested by their higher level of education. A majority of this group indicated that they came from middle-class families (unlike the Democrats, a majority of whom said their families were working class). It was the Republican identifiers who were confident of their futures who showed the high interest in the campaign.[33]

The lower-middle-class Democrats, on the whole, have less education than lower-middle-class Republicans. The same holds in the comparison of upper-middle-class partisans. It is obviously possible that these differences in political activity reflect these educational differences rather than community pressures. This did not, however, prove to be the case. Taking the married, non-South, middle-class respondents we found, as above, essentially no difference in the political interest of the party identifiers when we controlled for education. Fifty-two percent of both Republican and Democratic identifiers with at least "some college," for example, indicated a high interest in the campaign. Again, however, when we turned to political *activity*, sizable and consistent differences appeared. Forty-seven percent ($N = 32$) of the lower-middle-class Democrats with at least "some college" talked politics as opposed to 67 percent $(N = 30)$ of the equivalent Republicans. The figures for the upper-middle-class are 25 percent $(N = 24)$ and 67 percent $(N = 45)$, respectively. Differences in the same direction and of approximately the same size appeared in the four other education comparisons made. This evidence is consistent with the assumption that the middle-class Democrats feel a need for prudent restraint in their political effort.

Peripheral Groups: The Single, Widowed, Divorced, and Others

The analysis in this chapter, like the previous one, has been based on married respondents in families with an employed house head (or one who is unemployed but seeking work). In this section, we shall examine briefly the political orientations of the excluded groups. These include the economically active nonmarrieds (single, divorced, widowed), the farm populations, and retired populations (see Table 6.11).

The patterns of party identification for the nonmarried, economically active manuals and nonmanuals are very similar to those of their married peers. The distributions of attitudes in these groups would do little to change the

TABLE 6.11
Party Identification of Other Categories by City Size (Non-South) SRC 1964

Category	Large City	Middle-Sized City	Small Town
		Size of Place	
	Percent Democratic (of two-party identification)		
Nonmarried, economically active			
Nonmanuals	66%	48%	55%
N =	(38)	(21)	(11)
Manuals	86%	82%	80%
N =	(42)	(11)	(5)
Retired			
Nonmanuals	30%	29%	33%
N =	(23)	(14)	(18)
Manuals	71%	56%	57%
N =	(21)	(16)	(14)
Active farm	40%		64%
N =	(5)		(36)
Retired farm	50%		42%
N =	(4)		(12)
Others	60%	86%	30%
N =	(37)	(14)	(10)

patterns indicated in Table 6.2. One point to be noted in this connection is the marginal distribution for these groups; both manuals and nonmanuals are disproportionately located in the large cities. It seems that there are very few nonmarried adults in middle-sized or small towns. If the "free-floating" talents of the single population were to be geared in with any political movements, it would be a major factor only in the cities.

The retired nonmanuals in all three city size categories, proved to be heavily Republican, the ratio running at approximately two-to-one. Among the retired manuals there is a Democratic edge in all communities—a very strong one in the big cities and a slight one elsewhere. On the whole, the number of cases are so small that the results in Table 6.2 would, once again, not be seriously affected.

There is no surprise about the location of the active farm population (including here both married and nonmarried). The only observation of note in this connection has been made before, that is, the heavy Democratic preference of these rural (non-South, it will be remembered) populations. Even among the retired, the balance is only slightly Republican, a far cry from the image of a Republican and conservative monolithic "bloc."[34]

The final group is a residual category consisting largely of housewives. This is a very heterogeneous collection and the results as far as political sympathies are concerned are equally diverse. There is little intelligent comment that may be offered at this point.

A Note on Age

There is a suggestion contained in the preceding review that Republican identifications are directly related to age. This was shown in the Republican predominance among the nonmanual retired, the slight edge among retired farmers, and in the relative strength among retired workers in middle-sized cities and small towns.

Taking all non-South populations (regardless of marital status, economic activity, farm or nonfarm sector), we do find a strong age relationship with 68 percent of those under 30 indicating a Democratic choice, the level falling off to only 40 percent among those of 70 or more years. We have a similar pattern with respect to the 1964 vote (see Table 6.12). It should be remembered that many older Republicans have already moved off to St. Petersburg, Ft. Lauderdale, Palm Beach, and other Southern watering places, so that this picture actually somewhat understates what must have been the original situation. That particular flow, however, is countered by a movement of Southern Democrats to the North. Without the two migration flows, the Democratic figure among those non-South persons of age 60 or more would have been 44 percent instead of the 48 percent actually present in 1964. The flows, in other words, work to enhance Democratic chances outside the South. The movement of upper-middle-class retirees out of northern and midwestern cities,

TABLE 6.12

Politics and Age (All Non-South) SRC 1964

	Age					
	To 29	30–39	40–49	50–59	60–69	70 or More
Percent Democratic						
identification	68%	68%	61%	66%	53%	40%
N =	(190)	(202)	(197)	(187)	(118)	(86)
	68%		63%		48%	
Percent 1964						
Democratic voters	75%	73%	67%	71%	63%	53%
N =	(135)	(171)	(179)	(163)	(104)	(61)
	74%		69%		58%	

as previously noted, leads to a peculiar concentration of their political sentiments (McKinley-vintage Republicanism) in a few locations, especially in
Florida, Arizona, and southern California.[35]

The significance of the age relationship depends, of course, on how it comes
about. If it were due to conversion with "age and maturity" (the geriatric
thesis), it might not have any all-too-serious implications either for the Republican party or for the "two-party system." The prime concerns would be
merely that such shifting continued and that it did so in sufficient quantity
so as to allow some "reasonable" balance. Such a development would involve
the problem of parties divided on age lines and that might give rise to some
difficulties but, on the whole, it might still yield a passably functioning arrangement.

Unfortunately this view, salutary as it may appear to some, does not accord
with the available evidence. We took the non-South Republican identifiers and
divided them into three broad age groups (to 39, 40–59, and 60 or more).
If there were anything to be said for the geriatric thesis, we should find an
increase in the percentage reporting former Democratic allegiance among the
older age groups. This is not the case, the older group having the smallest
percentage of self-reported converts. Among the Democrats, on the other hand,
we find a slight increase in the percentage of those who report a conversion
from Republicanism, just the opposite direction from that which would be
expected. Looking at the matter in terms of the absolute numbers, the basic
point to be noted is that approximately equal numbers shift in both directions
within each broad age group. In the older group, 21 Republicans became
Democrats and 22 Democrats became Republicans for a net Republican gain
(thus supporting the thesis) of 1 individual. In the middle-age category 51
Republicans became Democrats while 46 Democrats became Republicans for
a net loss to the Republicans of 5 individuals. In the youngest category, 45

Republicans became Democrats and 38 Democrats became Republicans for a net Republican loss of 7. As far as this evidence is concerned, the picture would appear to be very dim for the Republicans.[36]

Another way of assessing the Republican chances is to examine the shift from the parental political orientation within the three broad age categories. This investigation does initially suggest some net gain for the Republicans. Taking those with either a Republican or Democratic father, we find a net Republican gain of 8 persons in the youngest group, 3 in the middle-age group, and 7 in the older group.

This analysis, however, does not account for those who did not know the father's position or whose fathers were vacillating in their loyalties. In the younger and middle-age groups these respondents fall heavily to the Democrats. In the older category, they fall to the Democrats, but this time by no large majority. The important point is that the original Republican net gain of 7 individuals for this age group is completely wiped out by the distribution of the latter respondents. The older generation is, to be sure, more Republican than the younger cohorts but, on balance, the assumption of conversion as the explanation for this finding is a very dubious one.

The actual mechanism appears to be a quite different one. A larger percentage in the oldest cohort came from Republican families than in any subsequent cohort. This older cohort was born at the turn of the century or even earlier and it contains a larger proportion of white Protestants than the later generations.[37]

One other fact that is frequently overlooked is that Democrats have larger families than do Republicans. Since most children follow the parental direction and since there is no net shift to the Republicans, this means that it is a simple matter of political demography that the Democratic identifiers should grow both in numbers and proportions.[38]

As might be expected, it is the older populations in the middle-sized and smaller communities that are most heavily Republican (see Table 6.13). It seems likely that the passage of time will, barring as yet unforeseen develop-

TABLE 6.13
Age, Size of Place and Party Identification (All Non-South Respondents) SRC 1964

Size of Place	Age		
	To 39	40–59	60 or More
Large city	73%	66%	58%
$N =$	(199)	(183)	(87)
Middle-sized	67%	64%	36%
$N =$	(105)	(96)	(53)
Small town	57%	59%	44%
$N =$	(88)	(104)	(64)

ments, bring a major transformation in those contexts. Given, however, the relative disorganization of the Democrats there, the pickup in electoral chances will probably take longer than would be anticipated on the basis of numbers alone.

Because they are the centers of Republican voting strength, the transformation in the middle-sized cities and the small towns deserves more detailed examination. Combining the two and looking at the picture by class and age, we find the following. In the oldest cohort, both upper- and lower-middle classes were heavily Republican and the working class divided almost 50–50[39] It is in this cohort that we have a heavy representation of Tory workers. In the younger cohorts we find a shift toward the Democrats within all class levels. The lower-middle class divides 50–50 in the middle-aged cohort, and among the young the same group is heavily Democratic. The working class of the younger two cohorts is heavily Democratic in both cases. Something appears to be happening in the course of the years which is loosening the hold of the conservative elites in these smaller communities. Not only are they losing their Tory worker allies, but the lower-middle class also is becoming Democratic.

Another aspect of the transformation deserves mention. The 1964 study contains a series of "political efficacy" questions that tap the sensed ability to influence events. Respondents fell into a 5-point scale ranging from 0 (no sense of efficacy) to $+4$. We have taken those with a $+3$ and $+4$ rating as having "high" efficacy. It is interesting to note that the older workers are very low on this scale, only 2 of 40 (5 percent) being classed in the "high efficacy" category. It would appear that the older working-class populations in the smaller communities were, as we have suggested earlier, extremely passive and deferential. The younger cohorts are somewhat different in this respect, 28 percent of the middle-age group ($N = 86$) showing high efficacy and 36 percent of the younger group ($N = 94$). Although these figures fall far short of the equivalents for the upper-middle classes, there is some suggestion of, if not a "revolution in participation," at least a small stirring of participation.

It may seem superfluous to note, in conclusion, that a part of the answer to one of our original questions is contained in the analysis of this chapter. The question of why the liberal majority is not heard has to do with the fact that in the smaller communities they are very quiet people. In fact, it is easy for the opposition to deny their very existence and argue nearly universal consent. In contrast, the conservative upper-middle classes are highly active and well organized; their frequent political conversations and the high level of voting participation serve to create the illusion in these communities of *their* majority status. It would be easy, as noted, to pass off this disparity in terms of individual attributes (such as laziness or apathy). There appear, however, to be some important institutional considerations that, in effect, break the strength of organized opposition; the most important we have suggested is the typical local communications monopolies and the presence of "nonpartisan" electoral arrangements that make it difficult for manual and lower-middle-class groups to maintain any effective political organization at the local level.

Notes

1. See Juan Linz, *The Social Bases of West German Politics* (New York: unpublished Ph.D dissertation, Columbia University, 1959), Ch. X: "Size of City and Working Class Politics"; and also Ch. XI of Richard Hamilton, *Affluence and the French Worker* (Princeton: Princeton University Press, 1967). The Engels quotation is from *The Condition of the Working Class in England*, W. O. Henderson and W. H. Chaloner, eds. (New York: Macmillan, 1958).

In the same vein, although from a different political perspective, we have the following:

> The true relationship between the Prussian people and the old regime was perhaps never better demonstrated than during a debate in the Prussian Diet in 1852. In answer to complaints that the government distrusted its people, Bismarck said that this was true especially in regard to the populace of the big cities "where one cannot find the true Prussian people." "Should these big population centers again rise against their government as they had done in 1848, the Prussian people (viz. the army and the police) would know how to deal with them and would wipe them off the map."

Quoted from pp. 116–117 of Albert C. Grzesinski, *Inside Germany* (New York: E. P. Dutton, 1939).

The most important studies in the United States are those of Leon D. Epstein, "Size of Place and the Division of the Two-Party Vote in Wisconsin," *Western Political Quarterly*, **9** (1956), 138–150 [also found as Chapter 4 of his *Politics in Wisconsin* (Madison: University of Wisconsin Press, 1958)]; and Nicholas Masters and D. S. Wright, "Trends and Variations in the Two Party Vote: The Case of Michigan," *American Political Science Review*, **52** (1958), 1078–1090. There is also a general discussion and data to be found in Seymour Martin Lipset, *Political Man* (Garden City: Doubleday, 1960), p. 248 ff. Another very useful discussion and data presentation is that of V. O. Key, Jr., *Public Opinion and American Democracy* (New York: Alfred A. Knopf, 1961), pp. 110–118. Key uses the 1956 Survey Research Center study and presents data on city size and issue orientations for the entire country. An overview based on 1950 census data and also making no regional breakdown is that of Otis D. Duncan and Albert J. Reiss, Jr., *Social Characteristics of Urban and Rural Communities: 1950* (New York: John Wiley and Sons, 1956).

2. The notion of the isolated mass, as applied to manual workers, appears in Clark Kerr and Abraham Siegel, "The Inter-industry Propensity to Strike—An International Comparison," Chapter 14 of Arthur Kornhauser, Robert Dubin, and Arthur M. Ross, eds., *Industrial Conflict* (New York: McGraw-Hill, 1954).

3. As an illustrative case in point, the community described by Granville Hicks in his book *Small Town* (New York: Macmillan, 1946) lost its last working farmer in the early 1960s. Some additional insight can be gleaned through examination of census materials. The city of Eau Claire, Wisconsin (1960 population, 37,987) would appear to be a commercial center serving an agricultural *Hinterland*. It is isolated in that it is not close to any large city. One would, following outdated and inappropriate bucolic imagery, expect a large group of businessmen and shopkeepers in the city and farm population outside. Fifty-seven percent, however, of the employed males in the city are in manual occupations (as defined in Chapter 4). In the surrounding county, we do find, to be sure, some farm populations. Taking once again the males only, there were, in 1960, 1206 farmers and 521 farm laborers. Among their neighbors, however, again contrary to the outdated imagery, we find 2294 manual workers. There are, in other words, more manual workers in the countryside than there are farm populations.

The best study of the transformations in a one-time agricultural community is the work of Arthur J. Vidich and Joseph Bensman, *Small Town in Mass Society* (Princeton: Princeton University Press, 1958).

4. The reported Republican vote in the middle-sized communities outside the SMSAs was, as indicated, 42 percent ($N = 65$). In the equivalent small towns and rural areas, the Republican figure was only 17 percent ($N = 23$). The classical statement on provincial small town conditions is that of Thorstein Veblen, "The Country Town," pp. 142–165 of *Absentee Ownership and Business Enterprise in Recent Times* (New York: Viking Press, 1938).

5. The "weakness" of Democratic party identifications in the small towns also appears in the 1952 and 1956 studies.

6. The point about the relative absence of political discussion will be considered later on in this chapter. The lack of political "roots" in small towns has been indicated in previous work. The greatest shifting between 1948 and 1952, for example, came from "rural areas." See Angus Campbell, Gerald Gurin, and Warren E. Miller, *The Voter Decides* (Evanston; Row, Peterson, 1954), p. 71. An analysis of gubernatorial voting in Wisconsin shows the smaller communities as being especially volatile, this is in Leon Epstein, *Politics in Wisconsin,* op. cit., p. 60. From an entirely different context, Weimar Germany, we find again sweeping transformations occurring in the rural areas. See Rudolf Heberle, *Landbevölkerung und Nationalsozialismus: Eine soziologische Untersuchung der politischen Willensbildung in Schleswig-Holstein 1918–1932* (Stuttgart: Deutsche Verlags-Anstalt, 1963).

7. The 65 percent figure in Table 6.2 breaks down into 76 percent ($N = 34$) for those small-town workers in SMSAs and 56 percent ($N = 41$) for those outside the metropolitan areas.

8. A case in point is Sheboygan, Wisconsin, scene of the Kohler strike, the longest strike in American history. For a description of the event see Walter Uphoff, *Kohler on Strike* (Boston: Beacon Press, 1960). A very good discussion of the politics of such a community, indicating the virtual absence of organized opposition under a so-called nonpartisan regime may be found in Alden D. Hays, "City Manager Government in Janesville, Wisconsin, 1939–1951: Its Recent

Political Experience" (Madison, Wisconsin: unpublished M.A. thesis, 1953). A discussion of the larger implications of such "reform" arrangements appears in James Weinstein, "Organized Business and the City Commission and Manager Movements," *Journal of Southern History*, XXVIII (May 1962), 166–182, and in his *The Corporate Ideal in the Liberal State, 1900–1918* (Boston: Beacon Press, 1968), Ch. 4.

9. Space allows only an abbreviated presentation. The Democratic percentages are as follows: Upper-middle-class white Protestants, 39 percent $(N = 23)$; lower-middle-class white Protestants, 46 percent $(N = 13)$; upper-middle-class "others," 68 percent $(N = 19)$; and lower-middle-class "others," 79 percent $(N = 19)$.

10. These findings are in line with those of Bennett Berger; see his *Working Class Suburb* (Berkeley: University of California Press, 1960). Divergent findings, based on a small sample from the Minneapolis area are reported in Irving Tallman and Ramona Morgner, "Life-Style Differences among Urban and Suburban Blue-Collar Families," *Social Forces*, **48** (March 1970), 334–348.

11. The data: SRC 1952 (married, non-South):

	Size of Place		
	Big City	Middle-Sized	Small Town
	Percent Democratic of 2-Party Identification		
Nonmanual	53%	33%	34%
$N =$	(198)	(60)	(83)
Manual	73%	68%	58%
$N =$	(219)	(82)	(89)
Percent difference	+20	+35	+24

12. The data: SRC 1956 (married, non-South):

	Size of Place		
	Big City	Middle-Sized	Small Town
	Percent Democratic of 2-Party Identification		
Nonmanual	47%	38%	34%
$N =$	(173)	(78)	(96)
Manual	61%	53%	60%
$N =$	(237)	(77)	(88)
Percent difference	+14	+15	+26

13. In the small towns and rural areas where political activity is practically nonexistent, workers would not be subject to the impact of local Republican pressures. This entire line of analysis, clearly, is highly speculative. It is based on inferences from data (such as that in Table 6.11 below) and accounts such as that of Vidich and Bensman.

14. The figures of those showing this conflict among the nonmanuals are 23 percent (132), 23 percent (73), and 33 percent (58). This is going from large

communities to small. The picture for the manuals is as follows: 24 percent (115), 22 percent (58), and 26 percent (58). Another study showing this conflict between conservative ideology and "liberalizing" realities is that of Gertrude J. Selznick and Stephen Steinberg, "Social Class, Ideology, and Voting Preference: An Analysis of the 1964 Presidential Election," pp. 216–226 of Celia S. Heller, ed., *Structured Social Inequality* (New York: Macmillan, 1969).

15. When we consider still another compositional factor, migration from the South, and take it into account, the differences are still further reduced. The results for non-South manual and nonmanual white Protestants omitting those reared in the South are as follows: percent Democratic, 52 percent (116), 53 percent (95), and 50 percent (100). This is again going from largest to smallest community categories.

16. Because the "others" in middle-sized cities and small towns were so similar in political outlook, we have combined them and made the contrast with their socioreligious peers in the large cities. Big-city workers were 84 percent Democratic in identification ($N = 81$) as against 79 percent ($N = 42$) elsewhere, a falling off of only 5 percentage points. The equivalent figures for the nonmanuals, however, were 76 percent ($N = 92$) and 62 percent ($N = 60$), a falloff of 14 percentage points.

The falling off in the Democratic percentage of the middle-class "others" may be located even more specifically among those with either limited or no church attendance. Those who disaffiliate, it seems, assimilate the politics of the dominant small-town Protestants. The data: (married non-South, nonmanual "others" living in middle-sized cities or small towns)

	Church Attendance		
	Regular	*Often*	*Never*
Percent Democratic	69%	64%	38%
$N =$	(36)	(11)	(13)

17. This same point is indicated in the Berelson, Lazarsfeld, and McPhee study of Elmira. See Bernard Berelson, et al., *Voting* (Chicago: University of Chicago Press, 1954). The authors stress the impact of something called a "dominant community ideology" that presumably influences all who live there. About workers, for example, it was said that they are "in an ambivalent position in which their political values are derived from the dominant culture . . ." (p. 59). It is clear, however, that the Catholic population somehow escapes from this pervasive influence because, as the authors put it, "The longer Catholics lived in Elmira . . . the more Democratic do they vote." (p. 67)

The following works are also useful and insightful: John P. Dean, "Patterns of Socialization and Association between Jews and Non-Jews," *Jewish Social Studies*, **17** (1955), 247–68; Joseph Greenblum and Marshall Sklare, "The Attitudes of the Small-Town Jew Toward His Community," pp. 288–303 of Marshall Sklare, ed., *The Jews: Social Patterns of an American Group* (Glencoe: The Free Press, 1958); and Peter I. Rose, "Small Town Jews and Their Neighbors in the U.S." *The Jewish Journal of Sociology* (England) **3** (1961), 174–191.

18. Twenty of 31 strong Republicans in the middle classes of the small towns and middle-sized cities stem from indigenous Republican families.

19. Fourteen of the 25 strong Republicans in the urban middle class stem from Republican families in the smaller communities.

20. As might be expected for a group with these characteristics, the "new arrivals" in the smaller communities tend to fall disproportionately into the "upper-middle class."

21. Thirty-six percent of the middle classes reared and remaining in the large cities were Protestant. This compares with 53 percent among those moving to smaller communities. Following previous lines of analysis, we would predict that these returning Protestants would integrate into their new milieu with relative ease and it is they who would convert from Democratic parentage. Taking those of Democratic fathers, we find 6 of 10 Protestants converting to Republicanism as against only 5 of 16 (31 percent) among the others.

22. Vidich and Bensman have a detailed portrayal of the small-town "new middle classes" and their position vis-à-vis the local elites. They mention the fact that the "new arrivals" carry on the voluntary associational life, a point that is also made by Basil G. Zimmer in his article, "The Participation of Migrants in Urban Structures," *American Sociological Review*, **20** (April 1955), 218–224. From the English context, another community study shows much the same picture; see A. H. Birch, *Small-Town Politics* (London: Oxford University Press, 1959). A summary discussion may be found in Frank Musgrove's *The Migratory Elite* (London: Heinemann, 1963).

23. The interest in campaign question reads as follows:

Q. 59 (pre-election) Some people don't pay much attention to the political campaigns. How about you? Would you say that you have been very much interested, somewhat interested, or not much interested in following the political campaigns so far this year?

The talked politics question asks for more than a casual conversation or for mere passive reception of someone else's message. The wording is as follows:

Q. 24A (post-election) Did you talk to any people and try to show them why they should vote for one of the parties or candidates?

The remaining questions were straightforward (e.g., "Did you belong to any political club or organization?") and had yes or no answers.

With respect to the "ever writing a letter" question, the differences were small ones, but in all three community size categories, the 40–59-year-old cohorts had a larger percentage responding positively than those of ages 39 or less. Again, the differences are small but within the two age groups, the small towners were least likely to have written.

24. The small-town "participation without interest" has been noted also in France (Hamilton, 258–268) and in West Germany (Linz, 368–371).

We have abbreviated the presentation that follows in the text, showing only the percentage indicating "much interest." Those responding that they were "somewhat interested" turned out to be very similar to those with no interest in respect to talking politics, attending meetings, working for a party, and so on. In the small towns, for example, 53 percent of those very interested in the campaign ($N = 43$) had talked politics with someone. This compares with only 21 percent among both those with only "some" interest ($N = 63$) and those with no interest ($N = 24$).

The small towns were not always politically inactive. If memories are correct, just the opposite was the case in the previous generation. When asked about their fathers' political interest, it is those living in small towns, manuals and non-manuals alike, who are most likely to report that the fathers were "very much" interested. Many of those who said their fathers were very interested in politics were raised elsewhere, that is, in larger communities. It is to be noted, however, that whether native or new arrival, the *contemporary* small-town context appears to markedly depress political concern. Fifty-two percent of nonmanuals ($N = 79$) and 40 percent of the manuals ($N = 78$) in the small towns indicated that their fathers were "very much interested" in politics. They themselves reported only 38 and 19 percent, respectively, as being very interested in the 1964 campaign. In the large and middle-sized cities, by comparison, the level of current interest exceeded that reported for the fathers.

25. While these data do not indicate precisely "who has power" within the party organizations, the findings are certainly of relevance to the notion of *stratarchy*, the belief in the "proliferation of the ruling group and the diffusion of power prerogatives and power exercise." See Samuel J. Eldersveld, *Political Parties: A Behavioral Analysis* (Chicago: Rand McNally, 1964), p. 9 and also Harold Lasswell and Abraham Kaplan, *Power and Society* (New Haven: Yale University Press, 1950), pp. 219–220.

The main exception to the rule of increased activity among the upper-class levels is in the case of buttons and stickers. There would appear to be some aversion to this kind of politicking on the part of middle-class groups and, on the other hand, that it is somehow a more acceptable thing for manual workers. The question on letter writing, as already noted, is not entirely in keeping with the rest of the series since it asks whether one has *ever* written officials rather than focusing directly on the 1964 campaign activities. This result would therefore be affected by age differences unlike the other findings.

26. See Weinstein, op. cit. The relationship between "reform government" and voting turnout is shown in Robert Alford and Eugene C. Lee, "Voting Turnout in American Cities," *American Political Science Review*, **62** (September 1968), 796–813. The impact of "reform government" on the parties is treated in Hays, op. cit. Another account is that of Charlotte Frank, "Politics in the Non-partisan City," (Chicago: University of Chicago, unpublished M.A. thesis, 1957–1958). Also useful is Phillips Cutright's "Nonpartisan Electoral Systems in American Cities," *Comparative Studies in Society and History*, **5** (January 1963), 212–226.

Another device that works to the same end is the use of restrictive registration procedures. For the influence of such mechanisms on voting turnout see Stanley Kelley, Jr., Richard E. Ayres, and William G. Bowen, "Registration and Voting: Putting First Things First," *American Political Science Review*, **61** (June 1967), pp. 359–377.

A look at occupation and participation in France shows no systematic class differentiation. It is also clear that the key agency in eliminating the class differences is a party, see Hamilton, pp. 45–50. No difference in the voting turnout of the different classes has also been reported in Norway, see Henry Valen and Daniel Katz, *Political Parties in Norway* (London: Tavistock Publications, 1964), pp. 158–162, and also Stein Rokkan and Angus Campbell, "Norway and the United States of America," *International Social Science Journal*, XII:1 (1960), pp. 69–99. Pages 88–94 of the latter are especially appropriate.

27. This suggests the difficulty entailed in the focus on "values" and the attempt to project social structural developments from the distribution of mass outlooks as in the case of Lipset's *The First New Nation* (New York: Basic Books, 1963).

28. From his *The Western Public: 1952 and Beyond* (Stanford University Press, 1954), p. 185. This "natural" advantage is recognized by the main victim groups, that is, those who are penalized by "reform" government arrangements. The opposition, those who have opposed the "reform" plans, have been working-class organizations. See Edwin O. Stone and George K. Floro, *Abandonments of the Manager Plan* (Lawrence, Kansas: University of Kansas Publications, 1953), and also Hays, op. cit. A study of some interest in this connection is that of J. Leiper Freeman, "Local Party Systems: Theoretical Considerations and a Case Analysis," *American Journal of Sociology*, **64** (November 1958), 282–289. His study of a Massachusetts industrial city of 50,000 inhabitants shows that a two-party structure managed to persist despite the nonpartisan innovation. The prohibition of national party labels in local elections meant simply that Republicans and Democrats reappeared as Non-Partisans and Progressives, respectively. The successful maintenance of a functioning party in this case seems to have been the result of a parallel set of informal organizational structures, for the most part, located in ethnic subcommunities. Freeman also notes that "A united Progressive party could usually produce a comfortable majority. It is known that certain Non-partisans have not been above helping finance a discontented Progressive in his campaign as a third candidate" (p. 286).

29. See note 23 for the question wording. There is a serious problem of "small numbers" here. The same finding does not appear in the 1956 study. The upper-middle-class Democrats in middle-sized cities and small towns were, again allowing for the small number, very restrained in their political conversation. The equivalent Republicans, although more talkative than the Democrats, were very restrained in comparison to the 1964 activity. The working-class Democrats in middle-sized cities were, as in 1964, more likely to report political conversations than were the equivalent nonmanuals.

30. Taking the nonmanuals in the middle-sized cities we find that only a third of the "very interested" Democrats talked politics (i.e., ". . . tried to show [someone] why they should vote for one of the parties . . .") as against 88 percent of the equivalent Republicans. Very few of the low interest or disinterested Democrats talked politics (12 percent, $N = 26$). By comparison, only one middle-class Republican in this context had no interest at all in politics. For those Republicans who were only "somewhat interested" the limited interest provided no deterrent to their conversation since 71 percent of them ($N = 21$) talked politics.

A very insightful and useful study in this connection is that of Robert E. Agger and Daniel Goldrich, "Community Power Structures and Partisanship," *American Sociological Review*, **23** (August 1958), pp. 383–392. They studied two far western communities, Valley City with 2000 adults and Boomtown with 16,000, both of which would fall into our middle-sized city category. About Valley City they say that the "field workers [felt] that there was not a single Democrat on . . . Main Street." Survey evidence, however, showed this feeling to be incorrect. It was largely a matter of the Republicans being well organized and the Democrats having "almost no formal organization in Valley City." They report further that "In Valley City, the Republican atmosphere did not seem to weaken or transform Democratic party identification (50 percent Democrats, 39 percent Republicans and 11 percent independents). In spite of the pervasive Republican climate on Main Street, 47 percent of the businessmen and white-collar workers were self-identified Democrats. . . . The Republican atmosphere, while not undermining Democratic party identifications, functioned to inhibit more overt partisan activity." In summary, it was felt that "Even though registered Democrats outnumbered Republicans in the community, there was a general feeling that continued Republican domination was inevitable."

31. An examination of the situation in Wisconsin in cities of 25,000 to 50,000 showed 8 of 12 to be below the statewide Democratic percentage in the 1956 presidential election, that is, 38 percent. One city was at the average and another was one percent above that average. Two cities, however, far exceeded that average: Superior (55 percent Democractic) in which the local paper made no endorsement, and Sheboygan (50 percent Democratic) in which the paper endorsed Stevenson. In all elections from 1948 to 1964 the Democratic percentages were consistently well above the state average in these two cities where there was consistent non-endorsement in the one case and consistent Democratic endorsement in the other.

32. For a preliminary discussion of this point, see my "Marginal Middle Class: A Reconsideration," *American Sociological Review*, **31** (April 1966), 192–199. Further evidence appears in Richard Hamilton, *Restraining Myths and Liberating Realities* (forthcoming).

33. Eighty-five percent ($N = 27$) of the Republican identifiers and 75 percent of the Democratic identifiers ($N = 69$) were optimistic about their future earnings. The percentages indicating that their fathers were "middle class" were 52 and 39 percent, respectively. Among the Republicans who were optimistic about their future, 59 percent ($N = 22$) indicated a high interest in the campaign. The equivalent figure among the younger lower-middle-class Democratic respondents was 34 percent ($N = 70$).

34. The farmers, like the small-town populations previously discussed, tend to be weak party identifiers. This again suggests the lack of "rigidity" in their outlooks and the ease with which they might shift given an attractive political stimulus. Only 5 of the 23 economically active small-town Democrats were strong identifiers and only 4 of 13 equivalent Republicans showed the same intensity. Taking all farm respondents (active or inactive, regardless of residence) we find 8 of 32 Democrats having strong identifications and 6 of 25 Republicans.

35. The political correlates of the flows are summarized in the following table:

	To 39	40–59	60 or More
	Percent Democratic identification		
Southern reared, now non-South	89%	67%	65%
N =	(36)	(49)	(23)
Non-South Reared, Now South	75%	46%	26%
N =	(24)	(28)	(19)

36. Taking those with a Republican identification, the question was raised as to whether they had ever changed identification or whether they had always been of this persuasion. The proportions reporting that they were always Republican were 68 percent for the youngest cohort ($N = 126$), 67 percent for the middle group ($N = 140$), and 79 percent for the oldest ($N = 107$). The equivalent Democratic figures were 83 percent ($N = 265$), 78 percent ($N = 243$), and 77 percent $N = 97$).

The work of John Crittendon does report a very modest Republican drift with age. See his "The Relationship of Age to Political Party Identification" (Chapel Hill: University of North Carolina, unpublished Ph.D. dissertation, 1960); "Aging and Party Affiliation," *Public Opinion Quarterly*, **26** (Winter 1962), 648–657; and, "Aging and Political Participation," *Western Political Quarterly*, **16** (June 1963), 323–331.

Crittendon's work has been criticized in a dissertation by Karen Oppenheim. Using SRC data and multiple regression methods she found no evidence of a Republican drift. See her "Voting in Recent Presidential Elections" (Chicago: Department of Sociology, 1970).

37. The white Protestant percentages (all non-South respondents) were: age to 39, 49 percent (214); age 40–59, 57 percent (240); and age 60 or more, 61 percent (137).

38. The point is considered at greater length in Richard Hamilton and Raymond Wheeler, "A Note on Political Socialization and Political Demography," Chapter 7 of Hamilton, *Restraining Myths* . . . .

39. Taking the nonfarm populations in middle-sized and small communities, including this time, the retireds and the nonmarried (this is to maximize the number of cases available for the breakdown), we have the following picture for manuals, lower-middle, and upper-middle classes, respectively: the Democratic figures among those 60 or more were: 53 percent (34), 33 percent (36), and 10 percent (10). Among those who were 40 to 59, the equivalent figures were: 80 percent (80), 48 percent (48), and 33 percent (30). And finally, among those 39 or younger; 67 percent (84), 63 percent (62), and 43 percent (30).

7

The Case of the South

In this short chapter we wish to consider the thesis that the South is an especially conservative region. This is the impression one would get from the behavior of legislators from the region and, were one to make the usual "democratizing" assumption, it would be suggested that their behavior reflects underlying mass sentiment. As we shall see, this is not the case.

The Southern Perspective: Points of Convergence and Divergence

How does the Southern adult population stand on the election issues of recent years? Are they more conservative on domestic liberalism issues as is suggested by the voting records of Southern legislators? In what days do the Southern attitudes converge, and in what ways are they different from those of persons in other regions?

Fortunately, the basic outlines of the answer are already in, having been researched by V. O. Key, Jr. Using the SRC 1956 election study, he has shown, contrasting all Southern (including border states) with all non-Southern respondents, that the former are somewhat more liberal in their responses to the two most relevant questions (i.e., those on medical care and the job guarantee), while on three other questions there were no differences to be noted.[1]

Our data from the 1964 study show a similar picture. The Southern population (again, for the moment, including the border states) is somewhat more liberal in their response to the medical care question than are those in the Midwest and West but somewhat less liberal than were those persons from the East.[2] In response to the living standard guarantee question, the South proves to be the most liberal region, half of the respondents there favoring this option, which, as noted, goes so sharply against the standard image of a conservative self-help America. In respect to government aid to education the South, as a whole, surprisingly, shows very little distinctiveness. It will be remembered that the wording of this question (as given in Chapter 3) was

such as should discourage the ordinary states' rights advocate. In response to
these three questions, the midwestern respondents prove to be slightly more
conservative than those from the other regions, although the differences are
shall and their importance should not be overemphasized. In response to
the final question presented in Table 7.1, on "government power," the finding

TABLE 7.1
Region and Economic Liberalism (All Respondents) SRC 1964

Liberalism Question	New England, Middle Atlantic	Mid-West	South, Border	Mountain, Pacific
	Percent liberal (of those with opinions)			
Medical care	74%	57%	66%	61%
N =	(280)	(382)	(364)	(190)
Living standard guarantee	42	37	50	37
N =	(255)	(359)	(370)	(180)
Aid to education	41	37	42	43
N =	(259)	(374)	(392)	(191)
Government not too powerful	60	57	48	54
N =	(213)	(321)	(323)	(178)

does accord with popular understandings; the Southern population is more
likely to feel that there is a problem here. Even in this case the differences
are not great—12 percentage points vis-à-vis the Northeast, only 6 in comparison to Western states.

In a summary way, we may say that the South (including the border states
as in Key's procedure) is either as liberal as the rest of the nation's population or is slightly more liberal, this latter being the case in the very concrete
concerns of jobs and medical care. Only in response to the "government
power" question is there an exception to this general finding. The claim of a
special conservatism characteristic of the region is, with the one exception,
unsupported. This would suggest that the basic fact about the politics of the
region is the *mis*representation by Southern legislators.[3]

It goes without saying that this overall result for the South hides very
diverse distributions of attitudes on the part of whites and blacks. On the
medical care question, for example, 56 percent of the whites with opinions
($N = 227$) favored the suggestion. Among the blacks the equivalent figure
was 97 percent ($N = 87$). Some of the respondents, to be sure, had no

interest in the subject or were undecided on the matter, saying "it depends." Interestingly enough, it was the whites who, disproportionately, chose one of these alternatives, 27 percent of them ($N = 382$) falling here as against only 11 percent of the Negroes ($N = 98$).[4]

Similar patterns appear with respect to the three other liberalism questions considered in Table 7.1. On these, the whites show a conservative majority and the blacks a sizable liberal majority. Thirty-six percent of the whites with opinions ($N = 277$), for example, favored the government-supported living standard question. Among the blacks, 90 percent favored the suggestion ($N = 93$). Forty-six white respondents said "it depends" and another 46 said they had no interest in that question. Among the blacks only 1 said "it depends" and only 4 had no interest in the matter. Indifference, equivocation, or conservatism on this question appears to be a luxury available only to the white majority. In contrast to the standard portrayal of low-income, low-education groups as lacking interest and concern, in this instance we see a very high level of concern and commitment. The question, it will be noted, differs from most questions on political awareness in that this one focuses directly on a matter of prime concern to the respondents, unlike questions on foreign affairs, administrative reforms, or knowledge of specific legislation.

One other observation to be made in this connection is that the "individualistic" or "self-help" tradition, at least in this part of the United States, is found only among the whites. To equate that tradition with "America" or to take that orientation as "the American value system" is to ignore the black population and, moreover, in regard to the medical care question, it is to ignore 56 percent of the whites. In regard to the living standard guarantee, it means ignoring 36 percent of the Southern whites with opinions on the subject.

It is not necessary to go into the federal aid to education question in any detail; the results closely parallel the above presentations. Thirty-two percent of the whites ($N = 308$) favor Washington's aid to the schools; 79 percent of the blacks ($N = 84$) also do so. Again there were few blacks who were indifferent or had no interest in the matter.

On the subject of "government power," 62 percent of whites ($N = 260$) thought there was too much concentration in Washington as opposed to only 8 percent among the blacks ($N = 63$). This particular theme differs from the three previous ones in that it does not probe for a matter either of direct or immediate concern to every household (as with the medical care and living standard questions) or even of clear indirect concern, as in the case of the school aid question. In comparison to these concerns, there were nearly twice the number of both blacks and whites who indicated no interest in this more distant "government power" theme put forward by modern conservatives. About 3 out of 10 among both whites and blacks indicated a lack of position on this issue, that is, they had "no interest" in this matter. It is worth noting that among the blacks who did "get the point" and were interested there was not one who said "it depends."[5]

Class, City Size, and Economic Liberalism

As this point we wish to show the distribution of issue orientations in more detail, by class and city size. This discussion will parallel the account in the previous chapter. We will, therefore, be considering married persons in family units where the head is economically active. Since we are interested in popular sentiment in its entirely and are essentially raising "what if" questions, namely, what if they all voted, or, what if their sentiments actually determined policy, we will postpone consideration of the differences in black and white outlooks.

The pattern, on the whole, is a relatively simple and familiar one (see Table 7.2). (For a limited comparison with the non-South population see Table 6.3). With respect to medical care and the guaranteed living standard we find heavy working-class support and a tendency toward upper-middle-class disapproval, the lower-middle class having an intermediary position. The middle classes are more approving of the medical care option than of the guaranteed living standard, hence the class differences with respect to the former are not very great. In respect to the guaranteed living standard, however, we find a very solid conservatism in the upper-middle classes in opposition to majority leftism among the working classes in all three settings. Again, the lower-middle class has the intermediary position. It is important to note, once again, that the lower middles do not uniformly share the upper-middle-class outlook; there is no consistent avoidance of liberal or left or "working-class" outlooks.

Looking at the city size pattern, we find that the middle-sized cities show a marked conservative tendency. The upper-middle classes in these communities are extremely conservative and here, unlike the experience outside the South, we find this tendency also in the working class. A comparison with Table 6.3, however, shows that the Southern working class in all three community settings is much more approving of the guaranteed living standard than are workers elsewhere.

The working-class liberalism in all three contexts extends also to the federal school aid question. The preference is strongest in the large cities where three-quarters of the workers approve this suggestion; elsewhere the level is somewhat under half. The upper-middle class tend to be least approving of federal aid to education, and once again this disapproval is especially pronounced in the middle-sized cities. In middle-sized cities and in the small towns the lower-middle classes also have a very low level of approval of such aid.

A similar picture appears with respect to the government power question, although here we get some erratic developments especially in the working

TABLE 7.2
Class, City Size and Economic Liberalism (Married, Economically Active Southern and Border State Respondents) SRC 1964

| | Size of Place | | | | | | | | |
| | Large City | | | Middle-Sized City | | | Small Town | | |
Class:	Manual	Lower[a] Middle	Upper Middle	Manual	Lower[a] Middle	Upper Middle	Manual	Lower[a] Middle	Upper Middle
Medical care	83%	73%	61%	64%	63%	23%	81%	53%	b
$N =$	(35)	(11)	(36)	(28)	(24)	(26)	(26)	(19)	(5)
Living standard	72	b	31	55	42	7	82	63	b
$N =$	(36)	(7)	(32)	(29)	(26)	(27)	(28)	(16)	(4)
Aid to education	75	55	39	42	28	21	48	12	b
$N =$	(36)	(11)	(39)	(31)	(25)	(29)	(25)	(16)	(7)
Gov't. power	67	b	50	33	52	33	57	36	b
$N =$	(30)	(6)	(36)	(21)	(21)	(30)	(23)	(14)	(6)

[a] The cutting line used in the South is $7500 to take into account the lower-income levels in this region.
[b] Too few cases.

287

class of the middle-sized cities. Another point, as noted earlier, is that there are fewer respondents having an interest in this more distant issue than is the case with the other three questions. The distinterest in this matter is greatest in the working and lower-middle classes.

In summary, it is to be noted that we do get considerable class cleavage on these issues. There is a fair-sized minority (or in some cases a majority) of the lower-middle class who take a liberal position on some of these, contrary to widespread assumption. And, there is, to be sure, a fair-sized group of workers who take conservative positions with respect to some of these issues, this development being most likely in the middle-sized communities.

The middle-sized communities, like their equivalents elsewhere, prove to be peculiar centers of conservatism. A significant difference between the Southern and non-South middle-sized communities is that in the former the workers are more susceptible to conservative influence on the government aid to education and government power questions than is the case elsewhere.

One final point deserves reiteration. The claims about "American" individualism and about "American" self-help values appear once again to be mistaken. Rather than these orientations being cultural "universals" they appear to be more "class specific" and that means specific to the upper-middle class. Even this would appear to be much too generous since it is most appropriate for the upper-middle classes in the smaller communities. As such, the claim would appear, at best, to be a generalization based on very limited and perhaps dated experience.

Class, City Size, and Party Choices

The basic pattern of party identification may be summarized simply; the Democratic percentage declines in the higher class levels and, in all classes, the percentage tends to be somewhat lower in the middle-sized cities. The inverse of this picture finds the upper-middle class to be disproportionately Republican and the same holding for all classes in the middle-sized cities (see Table 7.3).

Looking at the pattern of 1964 voting, one finds that in nearly all contexts a shift toward the Republicans is evident. The Southern experience, in short, is just the opposite of that seen elsewhere. The amount of shifting ought not be exaggerated since some of the result is due to disproportionate turnout. The nonvoters in all contexts were more heavily Democratic in their expressed preferences than were the voters; most of these nonvoters were working class.

Southern Republicans, it may be noted in passing, are more likely to describe themselves initially as "independents" than are Republicans elsewhere. This would suggest a much greater willingness (or ability) to shift to another party when the opportunity presents itself than would be the case with the more typical "strong" Republican found in the Midwest.

TABLE 7.3

Class, City Size, and Party Preference (Married, Economically Active Southern and Border State Respondents), SRC 1964

City Size	Class		
	Manual	Lower Middle	Upper Middle
Percent Democratic Identification (of two-party choices)[a]			
Large city	92%	92%	75%
$N =$	(40)	(12)	(40)
Middle-sized city	81	77	48
$N =$	(31)	(31)	(29)
Small town	88	84	[b]
$N =$	(34)	(19)	(7)
Percent Democratic: 1964 voting (of two-party choices)[b]			
Large city	82	[b]	65
$N =$	(22)	(6)	(37)
Middle-sized city	65	59	44
$N =$	(20)	(22)	(25)
Small town	91	62	[b]
$N =$	(23)	(13)	(7)

[a] The Republican percentages are obtained by subtracting these figures from 100%.
[b] Too few cases.

If votes and/or opinion counted, Tables 7.2 and 7.3 would show the various components of the overall picture of demand. Since, under the going arrangements, such an assumption is less than realistic, it is important to examine the pattern among the dominant white populations in order to see whether or not the basic lessons there are any different. For this purpose it is necessary to turn first to some geographical matters.

City Size, Class, and Race

The overwhelming majority of Negroes in the South (here again including the border states) are in manual positions, and, according to the 1964 study, just over half, of these manual workers are in the large cities. In contrast, approximately two-thirds of the white workers are living in the middle-sized or smaller communities.[6] Looked at from an alternative perspective, we find that approximately half of the large city manual workers are Negro. The working classes in the middle-sized and smaller communities are very disproportionately white. The middle classes there, both upper and lower, are overwhelmingly white. The only context in which there is any significant Negro non-manual representation is in the large cities (see Table 7.4).

The basic picture in the middle-sized and smaller communities is one of a white upper-middle and lower-middle class and a working class that is also

TABLE 7.4

Race, Class, and City Size (Married, Economically Active, Southern and Border State Respondents) SRC 1964

		Class	
Size of Place	Manual	Lower Middle	Upper[a] Middle
Large cities			
White	47%	77%	91%
Negro	53[b]	23	9
N =	(45)	(13)	(46)
Middle-sized cities			
White	79%	97%	100%
Negro	21	3	...
N =	(39)	(33)	(32)
Small towns			
White	74%	95%	100%
Negro	26	5	...
N =	(38)	(22)	(8)

[a] The cutting line used in the South was a family income of $7500 or more.
[b] There is one "other" included here.

very predominantly white. As far as the trends are concerned, it appears that there is a very disproportionate outmigration of Negroes from these communities.[7] In the large cities it would appear that there are two rather assymetrical "pillars" developing; this time the lines are primarily racial rather than socio-religious.[8] The whites are very disproportionately found in the middle class whereas the blacks have only a very limited middle-class representation. Since they both work in the same economy it must be noted that black and white workers are likely to have somewhat more frequent contact than black and white nonmanuals.

The location of blacks here is similar to the non-South pattern. The smaller communities in both areas tend to be the most racially homogeneous and are likely to provide a context supportive of racist outlooks. In these settings there would be little or no contact with the other groups and no learning of the other's outlook or concerns; also knowledge of the Black Revolution would be only very inadequately portrayed through the mass media.[9]

The pattern of party choices shown in Table 7.3 might be affected by the composition of the working class, especially in the case of the large-city working-class. A separate examination of the pattern among the whites, however, shows only small changes in the percentages of working-class Republican identification. Among the big-city white manuals, the overwhelming majority were still Democratic (83 percent, $N = 18$). The largest Republican minority among the white workers was in the middle-sized cities, but even here the majority was still heavily Democratic (76 percent, $N = 25$). In the small towns the Democratic percentage was highest of all (88 percent, $N = 34$). There is no point in reviewing the middle-class percentages since they are only marginally different from those already shown.

With respect to 1964 voting, there is an initial problem of a small number of cases, the level of working-class participation being relatively low. The Republican percentages among the Southern white workers in big cities, middle-sized cities, and small towns, respectively, were: 33 percent (12), 44 percent (16), and 11 percent (19).[10] While the Republican voting percentage is consistently above the level of Republican identification, in no context did Goldwater receive a majority of the Southern white workers. This picture would not be altered if we included the preferences of the nonvoters since there, too, the majority sentiment in each context was Democratic. Given a clear choice (". . . instead of an echo!") Southern white workers proved rather remarkably immune to the suggestive "law and order" themes. The heaviest white working-class support for the Goldwater candidacy, it will be noted, came in the middle-sized cities, that is, in that context where a majority of the upper-middle class supported Goldwater.[11]

The basic lessons thus far would appear to be the following. First, that there is heavy support for economic liberalism in the working class and in the lower-middle class in the South. And, second, on being given "a choice" as in the 1964 election, the majority of the white Southern working class remains with the "liberal" candidate. This is a point of obvious relevance to the so-called working-class authoritarianism thesis. There is, in short, a failure to "react" as predicted (or to lash back) on the part of most of the working class there. The 1968 experience and the reaction to George Wallace's appeals will be considered in Chapter 11.

Southern Nonvoters

It is worthwhile pursuing the question of the nonvoters. For this purpose, because of the limited number of cases available, we shall revert for the moment to using *all* Southern and border state respondents, black and white, employed and retired, married, single, widowed, and so on.

There has been a widespread concern, a sense of anxiety, on the part of contemporary social commentators about nonvoters. Unlike de Tocqueville, who saw elections (and implicitly high participation) as legitimizing the outcome and thus providing support for the regime, contemporary commentators have stressed the dangers of high participation. High participation, it is argued, means bringing "know nothings" into the "political process" and they, in essence, can destabilize. Neglecting or overlooking the fact that contemporary conservatives have used the fact of low turnout to challenge the legitimacy of election results (there are, it is said, millions of conservatives sitting out the election waiting for the proper candidate), these advocates make their point dependent on selected aspects of contemporary survey data and on the correlation of increased turnout in late Weimar with the increase in Nazi voting.[12] The contemporary survey evidence has shown that non-voters are less likely to know things (candidates' names—particularly lesser candidates—details of legislation, information on foreign policy, etc.); therefore, the "know nothing" claim is supported, at least as far as facts of campaigns and legislation are concerned. We have suggested that the procedure is selective in that it overlooks what else would be "brought to the polls," namely, a strong demand for performance in the area of domestic economic liberalism. It is worth reviewing the relevant evidence in some detail, both to fill in this gap in contemporary analysis and, as we shall see, to point up some contrary findings.

In addition to their ignorance of affairs, the nonvoters also, presumably, pose a threat to the stability of a democratic regime by virtue of their intolerance and antidemocratic propensities. They are, so it is said, highly susceptible to the appeals of demagogues willing to make use of such themes. The 1964 election campaign should provide a useful setting in which to test this particular claim. The South, moreover, should be an especially appropriate location for such testing since it is here that there exists a considerable reservoir of intolerance and of ready anxieties.

Fifty-eight percent of the Southern white voters $(N = 250)$ in 1964 reported a choice for the "responsible" candidate. If there were anything to the argument outlined here, the nonvoters should have indicated markedly *lower* sentiment for the Democratic candidate; but as it turns out, the opposite was the case, 62 percent of them indicating a Democratic preference $(N = 89)$. The difference of four percentage points is not the important fact here. Rather, if the line of theorizing were adequate, there should have been a sizable difference in the opposite direction.

For the sake of the record, the study shows that 100 percent of the Negro voters $(N = 47)$ supported the Democratic candidate in 1964 and 100 percent of the Negro nonvoters $(N = 41)$ indicated the same preference. The finding is of some interest in the light of the widespread assumption of public incapacity for handling the "complex issues of modern politics." These findings suggest that when positions are clarified and when there is a choice everyone gets the message.[13]

On the issues, we find that the white nonvoters show somewhat greater economic liberalism than the equivalent voters. The differences are small with respect to the medical care and the living standard questions, but in the expected direction. Negroes, voters and nonvoters alike, are heavily liberal in response to both questions (see Table 7.5). One of the implications of the high levels of nonvoting then is that much liberal "demand" is not being "expressed."

TABLE 7.5

Race, Participation, and Liberalism Issues (All Southern and Border State Respondents) SRC 1964

1964 Election Issue	Whites		Blacks	
	Voted	Did Not Vote	Voted	Did Not Vote
	Percent liberal (of those with opinions)			
Medical care	54%	62%	93%	100%
N =	(190)	(68)	(45)	(38)
Living standard	36	41	89	90
N =	(188)	(70)	(46)	(40)
Gov't. Power	37	40	91	92
N =	(182)	(62)	(32)	(26)
Aid to education	27	43	78	81
N =	(213)	(73)	(45)	(32)

There are no differences between voters and nonvoters with respect to the government power question. The differences here are between whites and blacks, the former having a majority believing in a "too strong" government and the latter being overwhelmingly skeptical of the claim.

The final question in the series deserves some special emphasis since here, with respect to federal aid to education, we find the nonvoter whites to be much more in favor of that aid than voting whites. The pattern, in other words, is the reverse of the usual expectation. These nonvoters may be "know nothings" but there is a greater interest indicated among them in obtaining aid in "knowing something" than is expressed among the presumably more responsible voters. It should be noted that among the nonvoting white population one is likely to find many of the so-called red-necks.[14]

The simultaneous existence of a liberal electorate and a conservative elect would ordinarily pose something of a problem. It was this discrepancy that was originally discussed in Chapter 1 and elaborated on with data in Chapter 3.

The explanation for the disparity is relatively simple. The liberal segments of the population tend to have very low levels of participation. Taking the large cities, for example, only about one in three workers report having voted in "all or most" of the past presidential elections as against some seven out of ten of those in the urban upper-middle class (see Table 7.6). The overall pattern (in general and specifically in the 1964 campaign) is one of participation varying directly with class level. The outcomes of elections in the South are heavily dependent on the upper-middle-class propensities. Given all the discussion of the role of "poor whites" in Southern politics, the re-

TABLE 7.6

Class, City Size, and Participation (Married, Economically Active Southern and Border State Respondents) SRC 1964

	Large City			Middle-Sized City			Small Town		
	Manual	Lower Middle	Upper Middle	Manual	Lower Middle	Upper Middle	Manual	Lower Middle	Upper Middle
Voted in "all or most" elections	36%	42%	71%	50%	70%	84%	53%	48%	a
N =	(36)	(12)	(45)	(34)	(30)	(32)	(36)	(21)	(6)
Voted in 1964	58	50	86	56	69	83	69	71	a
N =	(38)	(12)	(43)	(36)	(32)	(30)	(35)	(21)	(7)
Very much interested in campaign	44	15	63	46	39	69	29	23	a
N =	(45)	(13)	(46)	(39)	(33)	(32)	(38)	(22)	(8)
Talked politics	26	33	42	25	44	47	23	33	a
N =	(38)	(12)	(43)	(36)	(32)	(30)	(35)	(21)	(7)

Size of Place

a Too few cases.

markable fact is their relative unimportance in the electorate. Until very recently they could not have played any important role in Southern politics.[15]

In addition to the low level of working-class voting, there is also a relatively limited expression of interest in the campaign itself and also a low percentage of workers who say they have talked politics, that is, who have attempted to convince someone of their point of view.[16]

In general, the upper-middle class showed very disproportionate participation in elections, evidenced a high level of interest in the campaign, and were likely to be vocal about that interest. If one were to judge by the "voices heard" in a typical community, there would be a very disproportionate expression of upper-middle class and conservative opinion such that one could easily mistake the actual distribution of opinion. Given such a distortion, it would also appear that elected officials actually do "represent" mass sentiment and hence for some liberal observers, although there might be some regret about the lay of opinion, there would at least be no problem about the "functioning" of the democratic system.[17]

The Concern with "Government Power"

It would be easy to assume that the emergent concern with "government power" might break up a domestic liberal majority. This would especially be the case in the South where the issue, linked to black-white relations through the government desegregation guidelines, could conceivably lead to widespread defections. The 1964 election, once again, is a good testing ground because voters there had to make the choice, in effect, between welfare programs sponsored by a pro-civil rights party (on the national scene) and a party that favored "law and order" and limited government, and that was not known for its efforts in aid or domestic welfare.

Following the lines of argument developed earlier, it is suggested that the "government power" issue is a rather distant one. For many of those moved by the issue there would still be the more salient, day-to-day, bread-and-butter concerns that would serve to counter any impetus to change party loyalties. For this reason, it seems likely that many of those who thought the government in Washington was "too powerful" would remain with the Democrats when faced with a choice affecting these very concrete interests.

For this analysis we have taken only the whites since it is about the whites that the claim is made. Most of the Southern whites did not, as of 1964, consider the government too powerful; they either rejected the claim outright or else reported no interest in the matter. As one would expect, those who felt that the government was too strong tended to be more conservative on the liberalism issues (see Table 7.7). On the government-supported medical care idea, however, approximately a third "defect" from their ideological position in favor of a liberal stance vis-à-vis this immediate and concrete concern. On the generally less approved suggestion, the guaranteed living standard, there

is still a one-quarter "defection." It is interesting to note that the highest
level of issue consistency is to be found on the somewhat more distant school
aid question.

The concern with the "powerful government" was correlated with a heavy
Republican vote in the 1964 election. The Republican figures for the three
groups shown in Table 7.7 are, respectively, 66 percent ($N = 113$), 17 percent ($N = 66$), and 25 percent ($N = 71$). Not all of this 66 percent, however, was defection from the Democratic camp since many of these were
Republican identifiers and presumably were disposed to make this electoral
choice even before this specific campaign. Thirty-seven percent of the white
Southerners who thought the government too powerful were Republican identifiers and the overwhelming majority of these voted Republican in the 1964
campaign. Forty-five percent of the white Democratic identifiers who felt
the government to be too powerful defected to the Republicans in the 1964
election.

The peculiar strains generated by this concern with "big government" is
illustrated in the following. Among the conservative Democrats (those oppos-

TABLE 7.7
Government Power and Economic Liberalism Questions: Southern White Respondents (All Southern Whites) SRC 1964

	Government in Washington		
	Too Powerful	Not Too Powerful	No Interest Depends, etc.
	Percent liberal (of those with options)		
Medical care	34%	75%	77%
$N =$	(131)	(69)	(77)
Living standard	26	45	45
$N =$	(133)	(71)	(73)
School aid	19	48	38
$N =$	(145)	(79)	(84)

ing the "powerful" government and government medical aid), there was a
Republican majority in 1964 (57 percent, $N = 30$). Among those opposed
to "powerful goverment" but who favored the medical care (or who were
uncommitted on the issue) only 36 percent ($N = 25$) went Republican. The
hostility to "big government" is, in a sense, a "luxury" attitude in that only
those who are well-off can "afford" that kind of position and, more particularly, can afford to hold it consistently. The attitude is, as noted, especially
prevalent among the upper-middle-class Republican identifiers. Interestingly
enough, among the Democratic identifiers who are opposed to "big government," consistency occurs most frequently in the better-off income categories.

For example, 64 percent of those having a family income of $6000 or more ($N = 28$) consistently opposed government-supported medical care. Among the less-well-off, the level of consistency fell to 54 percent ($N = 24$).

It would appear that in the short run the "big government" issue has some viability for a conservative party, that is, it does lead some people to defect from the liberal majority. On the other hand, it must be recognized that this concern does not exist in a vacuum. Respondents still have to face the day-to-day existential problems (such as the price of medical care) and for that reason, as we have shown, many of them appear to be somewhat ambivalent on the issue. It would seem, however, in view of the constancy of day-to-day concerns, that the liberal interest would, in the long run, "win out" over the distant "government power" issue.

Divisions within the South

Clearly the South is not all of one piece. Following Mathews and Prothro, we have divided the respondents by subregion into three groups: the Deep South, consisting of South Carolina, Georgia, Alabama, Mississippi, and Louisiana (the Goldwater states); the Peripheral South, which includes the six remaining states of the Confederacy; and the Border States, including Kentucky, Maryland, Oklahoma, West Virginia, and Washington, D.C. The Democratic figures in 1964 in these three subregions were 42 percent ($N = 26$), 68 percent ($N = 186$), and 65 percent ($N = 85$).

For many years prior to 1964 conservatives claimed that many people sharing their outlook did not vote because there were no candidates representing their position. It is ironic that if there had been full participation in the Deep South, the one area of their success, they would have lost there, too. That is, if the nonvoters had participated and voted their reported preferences, the result in the "Goldwater States" would have been 55 percent for the Democrats ($N = 64$). That contrary-to-fact "result" would have depended on the mobilization of nonvoting blacks. Among Deep South whites, the preferences of both voters and nonvoters were heavily for Goldwater. In both the Peripheral South and the Border States, the Democratic majorities were heavy among both voting and nonvoting whites. Here, too, the "susceptible" populations had somehow or other failed to take advantage of their "opportunity."

Heavy majorities of the populations of each of these subregions favored the government-supported medical care possibility. The level of support for the living standard guarantee was high, relative to the regions outside the South, in both the Deep and Peripheral South. In the Border States there was a majority in favor of that option.[18]

This similarity hides some important underlying differences. Liberalism, particularly in the Deep South, is found mostly among the black populations. Among the whites there is a very clear and consistent pattern with heavy conservatism in the case of the Deep South, a moderate degree of it in the

Peripheral South, and relative liberalism in the Border States. Moving from the Deep South to the Border States, the number favoring the living standard guarantee among the whites increased from 16 to 36 to 47 percent.

The Deep South white popuation shows a conservative majority on all four domestic economic liberalism issues. The black population in that region has a liberal majority on the same four issues. Given the difference in voting of the two groups, the conservatives among the white population dominate the electoral process, that is, they select the conservative candidates to represent what is basically a liberal region. It would be a mistake to see the matter as simply another instance of white against black since there are liberal minorities within the white population, 43 percent of them favoring the medical care suggestion, and a quarter of them favoring federal school aid and not worried about government power.[19]

The Deep South was *the* area of Democratic defection in 1964. A majority of white Democrats from that subregion favored Goldwater in that campaign. The size of the defection dwindled in the Peripheral States and even more in the Border States. There was some tendency for the Republicans to defect to the Democrats in the Peripheral States and even more in the Border States.[20]

It is clearly a mistake to speak of *the* South as if the same processes dominated the entire region. The Border States appear to be similar in their characteristics to the non-South states, particularly in their lack of susceptibility to the Goldwater candidacy. There are differences of degree, to be sure, but the Peripheral South states also would appear to share the "non-South" pattern more than that of the Deep South. Most of the white Democrats, three-fourths of them, remained with the Democratic party in this key election; and most of the Republicans were Republicans presumably even before the appearance of the special appeals of the 1964 campaign.

The Party Competition in the South

There has been some question as to whether the Republicans and Democrats will take on the same conservative and liberal pattern that is found in the North or whether, as for example in Virginia, there might be an attempt to reverse these roles.

To address this question we have taken the nonmanual whites, this on the assumption that it is they who would determine the formation and character of the parties. We have divided them again into a lower- and upper-middle class on the further assumptions that key decision makers would be from among the upper-middle-class populations and that the lower-middle class would be important largely for supplying votes.

The picture that emerges is one of relatively strong liberal tendencies in the Democratic party and very strong conservatism in the Republican (see Table 7.8). This is indicated, by way of illustration, in the responses of the upper-middle-class Democrats to the medical care question. We find a fair-

TABLE 7.8

Issues Orientations of Southern Nonmanual Whites by Party Identification (Married; Head in Labor Force) SRC 1964

| | Southern Nonmanual Whites | | | |
| | Democrat | | Republican | |
	Lower Middle	Upper Middle	Lower Middle	Upper Middle
Economic Liberalism Questions	*Percent "liberal" of those with opinions*			
Medical care	63%	62%	a	10%
$N =$	(38)	(37)	(8)	(20)
Living standard	41	24	a	...
$N =$	(32)	(33)	(8)	(18)
School aid	24	38	a	17
$N =$	(33)	(39)	(9)	(23)
Government too powerful (percent "no")	48	54	a	12.5
$N =$	(29)	(37)	(8)	(24)
Civil Rights Questions	*Percent "liberal" of those with opinion*			
Equal job rights	34	43	a	13
$N =$	(35)	(37)	(9)	(23)
Equal schooling	34	48	a	27
$N =$	(38)	(44)	(9)	(22)
Open housing	43	48	a	48
$N =$	(35)	(42)	(9)	(23)

[a] Too few cases.

sized majority in favor of such action and they are backed up by a two-to-one liberal sentiment among the lower-middle-class Democrats. By comparison the small number of upper-middle-class Republicans are overwhelmingly opposed to the plan. The Republican have only a very small lower-middle-class following and they, too, shared the conservative outlook. The inclusion of the middle-class Negroes would only serve to accentuate this division. There were only eight in the subsample—all were Democrats and all took the liberal position on both the medical care and the living standard guarantee questions.

When conservative Democrats defect to the more "appropriate" party, they appear to be leaving behind the beginnings of a much more liberal Democratic party. It also appears that the opportunities for the acquisition of new recruits from the Democratic ranks are relatively small for the "new" Southern Republicans. The advantage for the Democrats and the problems for the Republicans are even more striking when we consider the economic liberalism of Southern working-class ranks and reckon with the likelihood of increased voter registration in years to come.

While neither of the party followings in the middle class has a majority favoring a federal government role with respect to civil rights, the Democrats have the relatively larger percentage favoring a government role to ensure equal opportunity (as in the jobs and school questions) as opposed to fairly solid opposition in the Republican ranks. Here, too, were any party initiatives to be made, they would be *more* likely to come from the Democrats.[21]

In short, it appears that the Southern party arrangements are coming to approximate the Northern pattern. Given the initial advantages and given the possibility of drawing on a large working class with basically Democratic predispositions, the Southern party competition is likely, ultimately, to be even more asymmetrical than that found elsewhere.

Age and Politics

In the previous chapter we saw that younger age groups tended to be heavily Democratic. In all the younger categories three-fifths or more identified with the Democrats. Among those in the 60–69 category there was an approximate 50–50 division. Only among the very old (70 or more years) was there a Republican majority among the identifiers.

Examination of the age-politics relationship within the South shows no significant pattern; all age groups have more or less the same Democratic percentage. If one wished to pay attention to the small differences indicated in the first line of Table 7.9, there is a somewhat lower Democratic percentage in the very old category, which was the contribution of retirees coming from outside the South.[22]

The Southern pattern, then, is not the same as that found elsewhere. While the evidence here does not suggest a dwindling of Republican chances,

TABLE 7.9
Politics and Age (All South) SRC 1964

	\multicolumn{6}{c}{Age}					
	To 29	30–39	40–49	50–59	60–69	70 or More
Percent Democratic identification	80%	75%	76%	86%	82%	69%
N =	(64)	(81)	(98)	(77)	(60)	(52)
		77%		80%		76%
Percent 1964 Democratic voters	61	63	64	75	58	63
N =	(31)	(62)	(73)	(63)	(33)	(35)
		62%		69%		60%

neither does it suggest any special inroads among younger groups that would allow the party a favorable prognosis.

Tieing in with points made earlier, it would appear that the party is restricted to the white-upper-class ranks and has limited potential in any other context in the society. The impact of one of the leading "appeals"— the "powerful government" threat—is limited and, as we have seen, even those moved by it are subject to some important "countervailing forces" that prevent enthusiastic defection.

The impact of changing black-white relations on the Southern population will be discussed in Chapter 11.

Notes

1. V. O. Key, Jr., *Public Opinion and American Democracy* (New York: Alfred A. Knopf, 1961), pp. 100–110. To summarize his findings briefly, ". . . More southerners than midwesterners . . . agree that the government 'ought to help people get doctors and hospital care at low cost' (68 percent against 54 percent) . . ." (p. 103). Sixty-nine percent of the South agreed to a government job guarantee as compared to 60 percent elsewhere. With respect to big business influence, union influence, and a government role in power and housing, there was essentially no difference between regions.

Key's *Southern Politics* (New York: Knopf, 1949) is also an invaluable source. Also of interest are the following: Alexander Heard, *A Two-Party South?* (Chapel Hill: University of North Carolina Press, 1952); Donald S. Strong, *The 1952 Presidential Election in the South* (University, Alabama: Bureau of Public Administration, 1955); and, also by Strong, *Urban Republicanism in the South* (University, Alabama: Bureau of Public Administration, 1960).

2. A hidden point here is that the white Protestants in the South show a slight tendency to be more liberal than white Protestants elsewhere. Thirty-seven percent ($N = 236$) of those in southern and border states favored the guaranteed living standard as against 30 percent elsewhere ($N = 318$). It ought to be kept in mind that these Southern white Protestants are poorer and more rural than their socioreligious peers elsewhere. This would suggest that when they move out—to larger cities, to the north or the west—their initial political predisposition will be somewhat different from those of white Protestants from similar settings in the nation.

3. See, for example, the voting records of the 89th Congress tabulated in the October 22, 1966 issue of *The New Republic*. Also showing the same tendency among the region's Senators and Congressmen is the *Index of Americans for Constitutional Action* (1967 and 1968 editions). Still another tabulation with a different set of votes shows the same conservative pattern: the *ADA* (Americans for Democratic Action) *World Magazine*, November 1968. They have a "Liberal Quotient" calculated for each Representative, the scores running from zero to 100. The average for the eight Alabama Representatives was 7.2; for the eleven from North Carolina, 5.2; for the five from Mississippi, 5.0; and for the ten from

Virginia, 1.6. The white South is more conservative on race, of course, as Key points out.

Among the recent discussions of things Southern are the following: Allan P. Sindler, ed., *Change in the Contemporary South* (Durham: Duke University Press, 1963); Charles O. Lerche, Jr., *The Uncertain South* (Chicago: Quadrangle Books, 1964); *The Virginia Quarterly Review*, entire issue, 41 (Spring 1965); John C. McKinney and Edgar T. Thompson, eds., *The South in Continuity and Change* (Durham: Duke University Press, 1965); Donald R. Mathews and James W. Prothro, *Negroes and the New Southern Politics* (New York: Harcourt, Brace, 1966); Robert Sherrill, *Gothic Politics in the Deep South* (New York: Grossman Publishers, 1968); and Marshall Frady, *Wallace* (New York: World Publishing, 1968). On Republicanism in the South see Bernard Cosman, "Deep South Republicans: Profiles and Positions," pp. 76–112 of Cosman and Robert J. Huckshorn, eds., *Republican Politics: The 1964 Campaign and Its Aftermath for the Party* (New York: Frederick A. Praeger, 1968).

4. Although the terms Negro, black, and nonwhite have been used interchangeably throughout this chapter (for the sake of style), there is one "other" (of a total of 98 cases) in the category, that is, a respondent who is both nonwhite and nonblack.

5. These findings are difficult to reconcile with Philip E. Converse's statement about the "great majority" of southern Negroes. He reports that "Most of these respondents are extremely ignorant, disoriented, and in the most utter confusion about politics." See his "On the Possibility of Major Political Realignment in the South," pp. 212–242 of Angus Campbell, et al., *Elections and the Political Order* (New York: John Wiley and Sons, 1966). The quotation is from p. 234.

6. The 1964 study showed 41 of 50 economically active nonfarm Southern Negro family house heads were in manual occupations. Twenty-three of the 41 were located in large cities. Seven of the 9 middle-class Negroes were in big cities. By comparison, only 21 of 80 white manual families were in big cities.

7. Taking those Southern (plus border) respondents who were reared in middle-sized or small towns we find the following picture. Twenty-seven percent of the whites ($N = 226$) had moved to large cities as against 37 percent of the nonwhites ($N = 75$). Among the younger populations, those 39 or less, the differences were more pronounced, with 30 percent ($N = 84$) and 55 percent ($N = 29$) now living in the large cities. This does not include Southern-reared populations now living outside the South.

8. The data (SRC 1964) for married active population in large cities:

Class	White Protestants	Negroes	Catholics, Jews, Others
Upper middle	51%	13%	76%
Lower middle	16	10	6
Working	33	77	18
$N =$	(57)	(30)	(17)

The political correlates of membership in one or another of the pillars are the same as outside the South. Taking the large-city upper-middle class, we saw that some 35 percent of them voted for Goldwater in 1964. If we consider separately the white Protestants in that category, we find the Republican figure to be 48 percent ($N = 21$). Among Catholics and Jews (combined), the figure was 25 percent ($N = 12$). Most Catholics and Jews are in the large cities. In the middle-sized and small communities almost all populations are either white or black and Protestant.

9. For further discussion, see Chapter 11.

10. Not all of this white working-class Republicanism is caused by conversion or "backlash" since some were Republican identifiers. The actual distribution of the cases, showing votes and preferences of the nonvoters is as follows (Southern white working class):

Party Identification

	Democratic	Republican	Independent, Other
		(*distribution of cases*)	
1964 vote			
Democratic	32	1	1
Republican	5	8	...
Preferences of nonvoters			
Democratic	10	...	3
Republican	3	2	3

Because of the importance of the claim being tested and because the number of cases in the SRC 1964 study is so small, similar runs were made using five 1965 Gallup studies containing retrospective questions asking about voting in the previous November. With the community size division, we have essentially fifteen additional independent samples of the Southern white working-class population (five in each size category). Of that total, only three show majorities for Gold-water and one showing a 50–50 split. Including the 1964 SRC study this would mean that Goldwater majorities appeared in only three of eighteen contexts. If there were anything to the working-class "authoritarianism" hypothesis and if the Southern white workers were prone to react to the "law and order" theme with all its overtones, one should see it indicated with much greater consistency than is the case in these studies.

The combined results for five 1965 Gallup studies show a similar pattern. It will also be noted that Goldwater support is greatest in the upper-middle classes in all three contexts. The data are as follows:

	Southern Whites		
	Manuals	Lower Middle	Upper Middle
	Percent for Goldwater (of 2-party vote)		
Large cities	34	40	53
$N =$	(218)	(139)	(261)
Middle-sized cities	38	32	58
$N =$	(119)	(68)	(62)
Small town	35	45	47
$N =$	(241)	(93)	(76)

11. The SRC 1964 study shows that Republican sentiment among the white workers *tends* to be greatest in the middle-sized communities. The combined result for the five Gallup studies also shows the same tendency. Workers in the middle-sized cities also showed relatively high turnout. If we assume that this tendency is neither spontaneous nor a result of media influences but rather caused by organizational efforts centered in the middle class, the question arises as to why Southern workers are vulnerable to middle-class influences whereas that is not the case elsewhere (see Table 6.2).

One can only offer speculations at this point as to why the situation in the South is different. Conceivably, because the region is more settled and has less immigration from outside, there is greater kinship linkage across class lines making for greater access. Then, too, since most of the adult population went to segregated high schools, this too should make possible greater contact between the white upper-middle class and working-class populations than would be the case elsewhere. This is based on the assumption that in the North where two high schools exist in a middle-sized community, the clientele would be divided along class lines. In the South the clientele would be divided along racial lines, the high school for whites containing the entire class range. One other consideration, perhaps worth mentioning, is the role (or lack thereof) of unions. The level of organization outside of the large cities is minimal so that there would be no countervailing effort opposing the upper-middle-class initiative in those contexts.

The focus here is on the middle-sized cities since they tend to be strongest for Goldwater. The upper-middle class in those cities have the highest percentage for Goldwater. The small towns and rural areas appear to have been *relatively* immune to the Goldwater stimulus. This point is also generally supported with the data from the five Gallup studies. Since the Goldwater enthusiasm did not get implanted in the upper ranks of the small towns, political practice there continued along in its customary channels.

This peculiarity of the middle-sized communities appears even when we excluded the Deep South (Goldwater) states. That is, the result does not depend on any special contribution of the most exceptional subregion.

12. See Seymour Martin Lipset, *Political Man* (Garden City: Doubleday, 1960). His Chapter VI "Elections: Who Votes and Who Doesn't?" ends by citing a number of works skeptical of the virtue of high participation. While not himself explicit on the subject, Lipset clearly leans to the same conclusion. See also his discussion of the increased turnout in the last Weimar elections in his Chapter V.

13. The SRC studies ask respondents who they voted for and if they did not vote, there is a follow-up question asking who they preferred. In 1964 this read: "Who would you have voted for for president if you had voted?" It is on this basis that we have been able to present figures both on the choices of the electorate and the preferences of those who did not so participate.

The findings in the text once again do not accord with Converse's conclusion given in note 5. The 1964 election, it will be remembered, was one in which the positions were (or at least appeared to be) very clear so that choosing the appropriate candidate was not much of a problem. In other contexts, where the stimuli were much more diffuse and the candidates attempted to hide positions, it is remarkable just how high the level of rationality (appropriate choice) became. A dissertation by Chandler Davidson reviews a series of 17 elections in Houston,

Texas (state, local, school board, and referenda included) and has calculated "pro-Negro" voting in each of these elections, the percentage in Negro precincts averaging 90.6 percent. Considering the efforts to obscure issues and positions in some of these elections, this is a very remarkable accomplishment. See Davidson, "Negro Politics and the Rise of the Civil Rights Movement in Houston, Texas" (Princeton: unpublished Ph.D. dissertation, Princeton University, 1968). For the data summarized here, see his p. 171.

14. Consideration of the civil rights questions will be found in Chapter 11.

15. Davidson presents data on the registration of whites in Harris County, Texas. This contains Houston, which in 1960 was the sixth largest city in the country. Registration of whites was at its peak in presidential years running at 57 percent of white adults in 1956 and 59 percent in both 1960 and 1964. The respective figures on Negro registration were 35, 35, and 44 percent. At least two-fifths of the white adult population played no role at all in the determination of the presidential outcomes. In off-year elections between 1956 and 1966 there was no occasion on which the majority of the white adults were registered. Considering the low rates of Negro registration (in the same period the percentage of blacks registered never exceeded 40 percent and considering also the fact that actual voting falls short of registration, this means that all candidates elected in this county were elected by minorities of the population.

Average turnout for whites (as a percent of the voting age population) was 29.2 percent in the elections from 1960 to 1966 inclusive, and for Negroes it was 20.4 percent. That includes two presidential elections, the peak participation there being 49 percent among whites in 1964. If one excludes these two "high participation" elections, the averages are 24 and 17 percent, respectively, for whites and blacks. In these elections, somewhat less than one-eighth of the adult, voting-age population is clearly all that is necessary to determine the outcome. See Davidson, pp. 74–78. Registration rates in major American cities in 1960 may be found in Stanley Kelley, Jr., Richard E. Ayres, and William G. Bowen, "Registration and Voting: Putting First Things First," *American Political Science Review*, **61** (June 1967), p. 373. Houston is relatively high for southern cities. Also of obvious importance is the work of Matthews and Prothro.

16. There is one exception to this generalization about participation varying directly with class level. The Southern lower-middle class, in all three city size contexts, proved to be less interested in the campaign than were the workers. It is difficult to account for this development. One possibility has to do with age; in all three community contexts the lower-middle class tends to be older than either the manuals or the upper-middle category. The Southern workers expressed a higher degree of interest in the campaign than workers elsewhere. This was the case with blacks, with white Johnson supporters, and, most enthusiastic of all, with the working-class Goldwater supporters.

17. Of considerable interest in this connection is the article by Warren Breed and Thomas Ktsanes, "Pluralistic Ignorance in the Process of Opinion Formation," *Public Opinion Quarterly*, **25** (Fall 1961), 382–392. By asking people their own opinion on integration and their estimate of opinion on the subject generally, it was possible to contrast actual distributions of attitudes with general estimates of the distributions. As they put it, ". . . there is clear and systematic error in

guessing 'public opinion,' and the error is in the traditional direction." That means that there was a tendency to overestimate the size of the segregationist sentiment. Pro-integration people were more accurate in their assessments than segregationists. "The Segregators," report the authors, "were . . . unable to envision even the existence of an antisegregationist public."

Another work of some relevance here is George R. Boynton, "Southern Conservatism: Constituency Opinion and Congressional Voting," *Public Opinion Quarterly*, **29** (Summer 1965), 259–269. He presents data (from the Matthews and Prothro survey) showing that politically active Southerners are highly conservative and that members of politically relevant organizations have the same tendency. It is difficult to agree with Boynton's conclusion (based on the 1956 Survey Research Center study) that "Southern Democratic Congressmen do represent the views of their constituents in their conservatism on social welfare policies." (p. 265) My calculations indicate that the overwhelming majority of Democratic identifiers in the South took a liberal position on the 1956 job guarantee and medical support questions. The least conservative of the Democratic identifiers were the nonmanuals but even here 62 percent ($N = 97$) favored the job guarantee and 65 percent ($N = 102$) favored the medical support idea.

18. The overall percentages in favor of the medical aid, going from Deep South to Border States are: 64 percent (58), 67 percent (217), and 63 percent (89). The equivalent figures for the living standard guarantee are: 47 percent (60), 48 percent (223), and 55 percent (87).

19. Approximately two-thirds of the whites in each of the subregions are in nonmanual occupations, which ordinarily would account for some of this conservatism.

The distribution of domestic liberalism attitudes by class, however, is the same in the Deep South as elsewhere; hence, one might suspect the same kinds of strains would exist for white working-class and lower-middle class persons as noted above. The number of cases is very small: eight of thirteen workers and lower-middle-class Deep South whites favored the medical aid option as against only one of eight in the upper-middle class. Even on the school aid question, there is a similar distribution although not quite so pronounced. Five of eleven of the former categories (of those with opinions) favored government aid to the schools. Only one of eight in the upper-middle class took that position.

20. Taking those with Democratic indentifications, the percentage of defections in the Deep South, Peripheral South, and Border States, respectively were: 62 (26), 22 (153), and 19 percent (54). These percentages include those reporting a Republican vote and the nonvoters reporting Republican preferences. The equivalent percentages for Republican identifiers shifting to the Democrats were: 8 percent (12), 12.5 percent (40), and 25 percent (32).

Useful for its portrayal of Goldwater voting in the different areas of the South is Bernard Cosman's *Five States for Goldwater* (University, Alabama: University of Alabama Press, 1966). In Deep South cities, there was very little variation in the vote by income level in the white precincts. In Birmingham, for example, it ran at approximately 80 percent in all areas. Elsewhere in the South, the Goldwater tendency was strongest in the affluent precincts. See pp. 87 and 106.

21. The exclusion of workers from this analysis implicitly makes the assumption

that they would count for little or nothing. On the whole, this does make sense in Southern party affairs. In essence, it is not at all necessary for the parties to take their interests into account, at least, not at the moment. See Stanley Kelley, Jr., et al.

By way of illustration, only Dallas, Corpus Christi, and Houston among the larger Texas cities had 60 or more percent of the eligible population *registered* for the 1960 election. Austin, Fort Worth, and San Antonio ranged between 40 and 50 percent registered. Columbus, Georgia, had only 32.1 percent of its adult population registered. It seems likely that most of these nonvoters are manual workers. For discussion of the attitudes of Southern white workers toward civil rights, see Chapter 11.

An examination of the Gallup studies showed much the same pattern as is shown in Table 7.8. Neither Democrats nor Republicans in the white Southern middle class were overflowing with tolerant sentiment but the comparison between them shows that the Democrats have the decisive edge on what small quantities are available. Asked if a Negro moved next door whether or not they would move, 50 percent of the middle-class Democrats said they would *not* as opposed to 23 percent of the Republicans. Asked if clubs and fraternities should have the right to exclude "otherwise qualified Negroes," 23 percent of the white middle-class Democrats ($N = 93$) said no. All of the equivalent Republicans ($N = 32$) were in favor of the right to exclude.

22. If one examines the age-politics relationship for the nation as a whole, the differences prove to be relatively small as a result of this lack of difference in the South. The consistent Democratic allegiance of all age groups in the South also helps to cancel out the difference on the national scene since the older cohorts are disproportionately Southern. Twenty-five percent of the adults of age 29 or less are Southern. The Southern percentage increases to 40 among those who are 70 or older.

8
Transformations in the Working Class

In this chapter we shall consider the working class in terms of its origins and its likely future development. Curiously enough, for a subject matter originally having a very explicit historical focus, the discussions of class, on the whole, have been peculiarly ahistorical. The question of where a class came from is rarely raised, the processes of its formation seldom considered. And the possibility of contemporary transformations in patterns both of recruitment to and exits from the class are also topics given very little attention. For these reasons, we wish to explore the matter of the social origins of the working class, to give some idea of the political outlooks and capabilities associated with different origins, and finally, to give some assessment of the future trends in the development of the class.[1]

The Question of Origins

In discussions of "working-class culture" and "working-class consciousness," the question of the possibility of any such culture is continually overlooked. For a world of shared understandings to arise there must be a common background from which such a heritage is derived, a background involving a wide range of common life experience. A key consideration here would be the experiences associated with "growing up" particularly those linked to or dependent in one way or another on the father's occupation. This would include the experiences in the home, in the neighborhood, in the school, among peers, and so forth. Although one may, for some purposes, talk about coming of age *in America*, it also makes sense to consider more specific contexts: coming of age in white working-class America, in Negro working-class America, in white farming regions, in Negro farm settings, in the white upper-middle class, and so forth. The prerequisite to any significant development of a *class* consciousness would be the sharing of life experiences in that class milieu. It is useful to consider the extent to which such sharing occurs.

The contemporary working class is made up of people who grew up in

TABLE 8.1

Occupational Origins of the Working Class by Region (Married Respondents in Working-Class Families Excluding those Families with a Retired House Head)

	Region				
Father's Occupation	North-east	Mid-west	South	West	All
1952 SRC					
Working class	63%	43%	35%	40%	46%
Farm	14	36	48	34	33
Middle class	19	15	10	17	15
Other, N.A.	4	6	7	10	6
$N =$	(155)	(194)	(163)	(83)	(595)
1964 SRC					
Working class	58	50	37	49	48
Farm	11	31	52	24	31
Middle class	20	10	7	20	13
Other, N.A.	11	9	4	7	8
$N =$	(105)	(146)	(122)	(75)	(448)

one of the following settings: within manual families, nonmanual families, or farm families. The 1952 and 1964 Survey Research Center election studies show about half of those adults currently in manual families to be descended from working-class families; they are (at least) second-generation manual workers (see Table 8.1). The largest group of newcomers to the manual ranks consists of the children of farmers; they make up about one-third of the total. A small minority in the contemporary working class have nonfarm middle-class parents and thus are "downwardly mobile" or, in other words, having "fallen" into the working class. Only about half of the entire working class, therefore, could have been born and raised in working-class families and thus have shared at least that much in the way of common experience. The "other half" had either "middle class" or farm experience when growing up, experience which they might then have "imported" into the working class.[2]

The pattern varies considerably by region. The non-South working class is most likely to be of working-class background, especially in the northeastern states, the region of earliest industrialization. The South, on the other hand, has a "new" working class with roughly half of the manual workers there being "new entrants" from the farms.

Changing Origins

For any kind of assessment of the future of the working class it is important to consider the trends, that is, the changing pattern of recruitment over time. One way of doing this is to examine the origins of those in the different working-class age cohorts. The basic finding is a pattern of sharply reduced recruitment from farm ranks and a corresponding increase in the proportion of second-generation working-class individuals (see Table 8.2).

TABLE 8.2
Working-Class Composition by Age (Married Respondents in Working-Class Families, Excluding those Families with a Retired House Head)

Age of Respondent	Father's Occupation				
	Worker	Farm	Middle Class	Other	N
SRC 1952					
to 24	52%	24%	20%	4%	(46)
25–34	51	30	14	6	(189)
35–44	46	31	15	8	(178)
45–54	45	31	18	6	(94)
55 & over	30	52	13	5	(84)
SRC 1964					
to 24	63%	17%	8%	12%	(59)
25–34	52	20	19	9	(138)
35–44	51	31	12	6	(111)
45–54	38	49	7	5	(95)
55 & over	31	42	18	9	(45)

In the oldest cohorts of both studies the farm recruits outnumbered the second-generation workers. In the youngest cohorts there were at least twice the number of working-class children as farm children. In the 1964 study the proportion was three to one. The basic findings, then, indicates that in the early years of this century a majority of the persons in the working class were raised on farms. At present the farm-reared group is a minority and destined to dwindle still further. In its place the working class will more and more come to be made up of people born and raised in a working-class milieu.

It is obvious that in the early stages of industrialization the working class is going to be drawn from other elements or sectors of the society. In terms of social origins then, the class is going to be most divided by background when it is first formed. In other words, the working class, during its beginnings, is going to be more heavily populated with ex-farmers than at any other time in its history. The entire subsequent history of the class involves ever increasing recruitment from within its own ranks, that is, from the children of workers.[3] In the long run, too, it would appear that the principal source of "outside" recruitment is destined to shift from children of farmers to children of urban nonmanuals, that is, to downwardly mobile persons.

Working-class males in the past also had fair opportunities for meeting and marrying outside of the manual ranks, with the daughters of middle-class or farm families. Looking at the pattern of the various age cohorts we find a tendency toward class endogamy. Table 8.3 shows the family background

TABLE 8.3
Cross-Class Marriage by Age

Occupation of the Wife's Father	Working-Class Wives: Age		
	18–29	30–44	45 or More
SRC 1952			
Worker	55%	49%	37%
Farmer	25	29	36
Middle class	15	15	18
DK, NA	5	7	10
N =	(79)	(128)	(73)
SRC 1964			
Worker	56%	47%	31%
Farmer	21	28	49
Middle class	10	15	13
DK, NA	13	10	7
N =	(78)	(93)	(70)

of working-class wives by age groups. Reconstructing the courtship patterns indicated there, the data suggest that the opportunities of working-class men are increasingly restricted to the daughters of workers. The reason for this is more or less obvious. There are fewer farm daughters available and a relative increase in the number of working-class daughters. This development too, for the children of these unions, reduces the chances of cross-pressures; it would mean less chance for the mixing of experience or for conflict over values stemming from different backgrounds. The correlate of the trend in class recruitment clearly is a parallel trend in intra-class marriage and this, in turn, means that an ever larger number of working-class children will come out of families in which both parents knew only working-class experience.[4]

Background and Political Attitudes

The available evidence from other countries (to be discussed below) indicates rather large differences in the political orientations of manual workers drawn from these different backgrounds. In the United States too, given the belief that middle-class or farm background "means something," one would anticipate a similar development. The initial findings, however, do not accord with this expectation. The first exploration of workers' political orientations by family background showed only very small differences. Some initial exploration showed this finding of essentially little or no difference to be linked to the regional factor since those of farm background happen to be disproportionately Southern. Both Negroes and whites in this category were overwhelmingly liberal with respect to welfare-state-type activities and were overwhelmingly Democratic in their party preferences.

Since the heavy economic liberalism and Democratic sentiment in the Southern group leaves little room for variation by background, and given the even higher liberal-Democratic consensus in the black working class, the arena in which background might make a difference would be among the non-South white workers. This category, which contains a majority of American workers, would be central to any collective class action (were such to occur) and for this reason it is useful to focus here.

Even with this restriction, however, the differences associated with backgrounds among the non-South whites prove to be very restricted. In the 1952 study the percentages identifying as Democrats among those of manual, farm, and middle-class backgrounds, respectively, were 68 percent (182), 65 percent (96), and 62 percent (68). The differences in reported voting prove to be somewhat greater but even here they are not sizable. The retrospective question asking about 1948 voting found 74 percent ($N = 130$) of those with working-class backgrounds reporting a Democratic vote as against 58 percent ($N = 66$) of those from farms; the middle class group fell in-between at 63 percent ($N = 48$). The equivalent figures for 1952 voting were 56 percent (145), 45 percent (77), and 53 percent (57). The largest difference then proved to be between those of manual and farm background in 1948, that being a matter of 16 percentage points. In the 1964 study, taking the same two groups, there was no difference between them in party identification and a very small edge among the former in Democratic voting, amounting to 4 percentage points.

With the exception of the 1952 voting (that is, in the first Eisenhower election), the tendency is for all three groups to be strongly Democratic. The Democratic identifications in 1952 were all in excess of 60 percent. In 1964 Democratic identifications, all three groups were at the 70 percent level. Democratic voting in 1964 was at the 75 percent level or higher for all three.

A similar pattern appears in the responses to the domestic liberalism questions. With respect to government-supported medical care, for example, there are once again rather small differences; again the children of manual workers have the highest liberal percentage (70 percent versus 66 percent for those of farm backgrounds and 62 percent from those from middle-class origins). On the question about a government guarantee of a job and a good living standard the equivalent figures are 45, 33, and 37 percent.[5]

Given that original expectation that background "should mean something," there is an obvious question posed by these findings. Why is it so unimportant?

One initial possibility is that we still have not completely excluded the regional factor. The non-South white working class still includes many people reared in the South and they are disproportionately found among those of farm background. An examination of the pattern without these southern-reared populations, however, does very little to alter the picture described above. The largest difference is made with respect to the question on a government guarantee of jobs and living standards. Removal of the southern-reared leaves a more individualistic ex-farm group than that originally indicated, but the increase is one of a mere 4 percentage points, this being the largest impact to be discovered.

There are two other lines of explanation that prove to be more rewarding. The first has to do with the original assumption, central to the revisionist or centrist theoretical repertory, that class as here defined "means something," that is, membership in or origin in the nonmanual ranks should be associated with a markedly different, more individualist, more conservative outlook. We have seen in Chapter 5 that the "lower-middle class" (the point of origin of most of the downwardly mobile individuals) is actually quite similar to the working class in political outlook, hence that original assumption of difference was unwarranted.[6]

Something of the same holds with respect to the farm ranks. The non-South farm ranks are not as heavily Democratic as the lower-middle-class ranks but, again contrary to widespread expectation, these ranks are far from being monolithic Republican. It simply is not so that farmers "are" Republican in party politics and conservative on the issues. Since the point is so crucial, it is worth digressing for a paragraph to present the evidence on the political orientations of contemporary farmers.

The category that is of most importance for this discussion is the non-South, white farm population. We will restrict ourselves to farm proprietors since the number of non-South white farm laborers in the available studies is miniscule. The proportion of Democratic identifiers among the white non-South farmers was 56 percent ($N = 85$) in 1952, 41 percent ($N = 73$) in 1956, and 59 percent ($N = 27$) in 1964. The farm *vote* for the Democrats fell off sharply during the Eisenhower years, to 35 percent ($N = 77$) in 1952 and 34 percent ($N = 70$) in 1956. In the Goldwater-Johnson campaign, the Democratic proportion among these farmers was 69 percent ($N = 26$). Three-fifths of the non-South white farmers favored the government supported medical care program in 1956 and an equal proportion in the same year favored the government job guarantee. In 1964, two-thirds of them favored the medical care option. In response to the living standard guarantee question, mirroring other groups, the liberal proportion was considerably smaller, but even here about 29 percent of them ($N = 24$) favored this kind of intervention.

In response to these questions then, we find that the white, non-South farmers are not, as is frequently imagined, solidly conservative, individualist and opposed to government interventions and assistance. There are liberal and/or Democratic majorities in many of these cases and even with respect to the "demanding" living standard guarantee question there is still a fair-sized "interventionist" minority. The better-off farmers are the most conservative and their children are largely destined to occupy urban middle-class positions. The poorer farmers tend to be the liberal ones and they or their children appear destined for working-class positions.

Given this considerable liberalism among the farm ranks, it is no surprise then that children of farmers who are now located in the manual ranks should be so similar to the second generation manual workers in their outlooks. Southern white farmers, Negro farmers, and farm laborers are all considerably more Democratic and more liberal than the non-South whites considered here.[7]

The second major explanation for the finding of no or very limited difference has to do with "conversions." Again we are dealing with a standard item of the centrist social science viewpoint, one that assumes a rather formidable attachment to one's middle-class or "independent" position and that assumes a steadfast refusal to "give up" one's position, or, failing in that and having "fallen" into the working class, assumes a refusal to give up the marks or signs of "middle-class" status. This latter group is not "threatened" with a loss of status; they have already lost it and, again following the conventions, they ought to be steadfastly resisting contact with the manual workers, protecting their middle-class "heritage," and attempting to recoup their former position. Something of the same ought to be true of large numbers of farmers, at least of that segment that has lost its "independent" status.

We may explore this question by comparing the respondent's politics with those of the father in order to see the extent of shifting or of steadfastness. In both the 1952 and 1964 studies we find that the overwhelming majority of the non-South working-class whites reporting Democratic fathers remain identified with that party. This is true of all three background subgroups (see Table 8.4). In all three subgroups we find that the children of Republican fathers also tend to remain with the party of the parent. In five of the six comparisons, however, the percentage of those defecting to the Democrats is greater than of those shifting to the Republicans. More specifically this means that among the "new entrants" from the farm and middle class who had a "Republican upbringing" there is a fair-sized conversion to or adoption of the modal working-class political position. Perhaps even more striking is an observation that is frequently omitted from these accounts: those who did not know the father's politics tend to divide in favor of the Democrats. The lack of a familial direction, the absence of positive "political socialization," apparently leaves these individuals open to the dominant influence within the working-class milieu.

TABLE 8.4

Father-Respondent Politics by Background (Married, Non-South Whites—Working Class)

Father's Politics:	Father's Occupation								
	Worker			Farm			Middle Class		
	Dem	Rep	Other	Dem	Rep	Other	Dem	Rep	Other
Respondent's party identification (SRC 1952)									
Democrat	84%	40%	56%	79%	22%	76%	71%	55%	52%
Independent	2	2	9	6	9	5	4	0	0
Republican	14	58	35	15	69	18	25	45	48
*N*s									
	79	21	30	26	7	29	20	11	11
	2	1	5	2	3	2	1	0	0
	13	30	19	5	22	7	7	9	10
Respondent's party identification (SRC 1964)									
Democrat	83%	19%	61%	89%	32%	80%	64%	13%	56%
Independent	4	5	14	4	8	20	20	0	25
Republican	13	76	25	7	60	0	16	87	19
*N*s									
	80	4	27	24	8	12	16	1	9
	4	1	6	1	2	3	5	0	4
	12	16	11	2	15	0	4	7	3

Since the number of cases on which these percentages are based happens to be very small, it is worthwhile noting the absolute numbers. In all six contexts (the three from 1952 and the three from 1964) the pattern is one of net absolute gain for the Democrats, this conclusion depending largely on the division among the children of the uncommitted fathers. This result suggests a considerable long-term advantage for the Democrats as a result of shifts occurring among second-generation workers and also among the two segments of new additions to the working-class ranks.

It will also be noted that in both 1952 and 1964, the basic assumptions about the downward mobiles proved to be erroneous. The modal downward mobile individual comes from a Democratic family. In short, it is not the case that the process of downward mobility brings "alien" political orientations into the working-class milieu. And, it is also not the case that assimilation is strongly resisted; at least the data from these studies do not support that position.[8]

Returning to the beginning point of this discussion, the second major reason for a lack of difference by background has to do with the fact that a fair amount of conversion does occur, thus reducing the original disparities.[9]

In an effort to show further support for this point—the assimilation by downward mobiles of typical working-class outlooks over the lifetime—we examined the political choices of the downward mobile group by age. The findings, however, were directly the opposite of the initial expectation. This led us to explore, in addition to the conversion hypothesis, a "selective recruitment" hypothesis, that is, the guess that different kinds of people were downwardly mobile in times past as compared with those suffering the same fate in the present. A brief examination of this possibility showed, first, that older downward mobile persons were likely to report that they had Republican fathers while the younger ones reported Democratic parentage. A second step in the exploration showed that seven out of ten of the older "skidders" were Protestants while less than half of the younger ones were of the same religious persuasion.[10]

Our explanation for this shift in the social and political backgrounds of the downward mobile populations over time, put epigramatically, is that people have to "get up" in the world before they can "fall down." Less cryptically this means that it took some generations for a sufficient number of Catholics to achieve middle-class standing before they could provide the basis for any considerable quantity of downward mobility.[11]

This finding perhaps accounts for the apparent ease of adjustment to an event that many theorists have thought to be the source of very extreme rightist reactions. For many, particularly for the Catholics in the younger age cohorts, it would appear to be a relatively easy adjustment because their families issued from the working-class only recently and because they probably have friends, neighbors, and relatives who, in a sense, are there to make things easy for them.

These "new" downward mobiles do not add "conservative" or dissonant political values to the working-class milieu. In essence, they are adding values that are close to identical to those already found in the setting. This means that this "new" downward mobility, far from "mixing up" or cross-pressuring, in fact, contributes to the increasing homogeniety of the class.

Shifting away from the basic centrist or revisionist framework, that is, from the view that it is the manual-nonmanual line that makes the difference, we may put these findings together with our conclusions in Chapter 5. The pattern evidenced here suggests first, mobility by a grandparent or father from the manual to the lower-middle-class rank and, second, downward mobility by the respondent. Given the character of the "lower-middle class" shown in Chapter 5, this would mean that the "upward mobile" individual arrived in a rank that politically was little different from the milieu of his origin. This formulation still is encumbered with the original basic image—

the notion of mobility as involving a move one *place* to another. For many the "move" from manual to lower-middle class may involve very little in the way of a place change. If a man employed in a small establishment moves from the shop into the office, he may still live in the same neighborhood, associate with the same people, retain the same contacts with kinsmen and friends, and so forth. For the child of this same man, a child who is raised in this context, a return to the shop (possibly with higher pay than the father) is not likely to be experienced as an important "move" or as a grievous threat to his status. At no time, moreover, has he been in a position to associate with the upper-middle class and to learn their values and take them as his own.

Another standard position in need of reconsideration is the assumption that those raised in the middle class will "identify with" the middle class. While it is true that the downward mobile group has the highest percentage of the three subgroups indicating that their families were "middle class" when they were growing up, the remarkable finding is that only a minority (37 percent, $N = 46$) do so. Roughly three-fifths of this group, in other words, identified their family's position when they were growing up as "working class." This strongly suggests that although they were middle class by the centrist or revisionist definition (and the one accepted in this work for heuristic purposes) most of these downward mobiles must have lived precariously close to the margins of that "class." It seems unlikely that they were ever integrated into the tone-setting upper-middle class. On the contrary, they probably have had continuous contact with working-class people since, as suggested in Chapter 4, they live so close to them. Many of the "middle-class" parents were independent businessmen, shopkeepers, and so on, and were probably in business in working-class neighborhoods or in industrial satellite cities. In such cases they would, again, never have had any extensive contact with the upper-middle class located in the affluent suburbs.

It seems likely that downward mobility would have different meaning, on the one hand, for a lower-middle-class Catholic raised in close contact with manual workers in a large city, and on the other hand, for a white Protestant coming from a smaller community. Conceivably for those Protestants identifying with the nativist heritage, for those who feel, as the then Secretary of State Dean Rusk put it, that "After all, we are an Anglo-Saxon country," downward mobility would be a threat.[12] And it is conceivable that it is the Protestant subgroup that tends to resist this loss of position and strives to recoup, and so on. It is impossible, given the small number of cases at our disposal, to pursue this alternative line of analysis.[13] If subsequent work, however, were to substantiate the suggestions put forward here, then it would mean that the received line of theorizing was adequate within a limited context; it would be appropriate for the analysis of the white Protestant segment of the American population. If the present analysis is correct, the theorizing based on the white Protestant experience would appear to be historically dated, having failed to recognize the developments that have emerged since white Protestants dominated the society. Again, if the present analysis is correct, there is an obvious need for a parallel line of theorizing to account for the other groups in the society.

The unexpectedly high Democratic sentiment in the farm and lower-middle-class ranks in the United States may result from the specific historical development of the country, in particular from the absence of a left party.[14] The Lipset-Zetterberg data on background and politics of West German workers show 65 percent of the children of manual parents supporting the Social Democrats compared to only 38 percent of those having farm parents, and only 24 percent of those who were downwardly mobile from the middle class. A study from Finland reported by the same authors shows still another pattern. There, 80 percent of the (at least) second-generation workers supported either the Socialists or Communists. Among the children of farmers the percentage was relatively high at 67 percent and among the downward mobiles the figure was 42 percent.[15]

These varying results stem from historical factors, that is, from different historical "inputs." West Germany has, on the whole, a relatively conservative middle-class and farm population. In part this result was "made" by the nineteenth-century socialist performance. They taught the lessons of class. They alarmed the bourgeoisie in city and countryside and in great measure they created the differences that to this day are still associated with backgrounds in that country. The conservatives too made their contribution. They erected the tariffs to keep out American grain and manufactures, and therefore they were responsible for creating the bases for a persisting common outlook shared by big business and farmers as against industrial workers, the matter coming to a sharp focus in one very simple ordinary everyday reality —the price of bread. The contempt of the socialists for the small farmers and for the petty bourgeois "elements" generally, together with their failure to put forward an adequate farm program, must have further contributed to and solidified the antipathies felt on both sides.[16]

The situation in Finland involved very serious agrarian unrest early in the century. The established conservative government repressed the movement and, in the long run, gave rise to the distinctive alignment of forces evidenced in the Lipset and Zetterberg data. No more than a brief historical sketch is intended here. The aim is to show the range of different historical developments that have occurred and to suggest that these histories, once "implanted," have been carried foward to the present. Social scientists bent on developing generalizations that are intended to characterize either all societies or all advanced ones, will have difficulty achieving their aim, at least with respect to mass political choices, considering these original and persisting divergencies in the social histories of nations.

In recent decades, a line of theorizing that was originally developed in the German context and that was, apparently at least, adequate for describing the developments in that context, has been carried over and applied to the American scene. The evidence presented here suggests, however, that the theory does not fit, at least, not without considerable delimitation and specification. It is necessary to supplement that theory with another one to describe and account for the behavior of those not covered by its assumptions.[17]

The political differences associated with the various backgrounds are, as indicated, rather small. There are, however, some ways in which the background does have a greater impact, for example, in regard to turnout. The basic pattern is one of relatively low turnout on the part of those from farm backgrounds.[18] If their children were to adopt the regular voting habits of the current second-generation working class, that would suggest a higher and more stable level of Democratic voting in most constituencies throughout the nation, thus further reducing the normal Republican chances. In addition to being a group that influences elections by their erratic participation, they also, at least as is indicated by the 1952 election experience, proved to be a group with less firmly rooted party loyalties. They were the only working-class segment of the three considered here that gave a majority to Eisenhower.[19] This would suggest that they are still subject to either the influences present in the smaller communities or, alternatively, in that particular wartime election, they were influenced by the Eisenhower image as it was communicated in the media. Again, if the contemporary experience involves the integration of their children into urban working-class settings, this source of "volatility," which in exceptional circumstances could pay off for the Republicans, would be diminished.

The White Protestant Workers

One conservatising link that is peculiar to the white Protestant workers and particularly to those who are children of farmers is the link to the church. When we take the non-South white Protestant workers, we find that among the regular church attenders about 35 percent ($N = 37$) voted for Goldwater. Among those who "often" attend, the figure was 27 percent ($N = 30$), and among those seldom or never attending the figure was 17 percent ($N = 66$). The pattern is regular and persistent as is indicated by the party identifications in three studies[20] (see Table 8.5).

Regular or frequent churchgoing on the part of the white Protestant workers appears to be most likely among those who have never migrated. Among the migrants who have moved from smaller to larger cities attendance tends to be infrequent. Among the nonmigrants, the highest level of attendance is to be found, not unexpectedly, among those in the small towns, that is, in communities of less than 2500 persons. If one takes those white Protestant workers who were raised in small towns, for example, one finds that among the minority still residing there, over half are regular or frequent attenders and one-third of this group identified themselves as Republicans. If we look

TABLE 8.5
Church Attendance and Party Identification: Non-south, White Protestant Workers
(Married, Economically Active)

	Attend Church			
	Regularly	Often	Seldom	Never
	Percent Democratic Identifiers			
SRC 1952	36%	43%	62%	66%
N =	(42)	(37)	(108)	(29)
SRC 1956	31%	40%	53%	61%
N =	(42)	(42)	(103)	(18)
SRC 1964	57%	58%	71%	82%
N =	(44)	(31)	(80)	(11)

at those who had moved to larger communities, we find that among the sub-group still maintaining links to a church there was a similar high level of Republican identification. Among those who were infrequent attenders, however, Republicanism was a comparative rarity. It must also be noted that among those who have left the small towns, regular or frequent attendance is a minority phenomenon.[21]

In short, it would appear that these processes of uprooting and transplanting associated with "economic development" are such as to break one of the few remaining supports for "Toryism" in the working class. The situation is not hopeless for the Republicans. Where the workers from the small towns do manage to reestablish church connections in the cities, some of them also appear to find support for or aid in maintaining a Republican identity. The problem, however, would seem to lie in the well-known difficulties of the urban Protestant churches and their inability to create that linkage.

Protestant churches tend to be heterogeneous with respect to their class composition. It seems likely that one of the unintended consequences of religious activity for manual workers is more cross-class contact than would occur otherwise and this, in turn, leads to the "unearned increment" for the Republicans. One other consequence of the heterogeneous congregation, however, is a sense of strain felt by "low-status" participants. This leads to the dropping away that has already been noted and to the breaking off of more class-specific sectarian subgroups. The emphasis in these fundamentalist sects on other worldly solutions may also play some part in creating the observed result.[22]

Union Influence

Some commentators, mostly professional pluralists and alarmed conservatives, have asserted the existence of some strong, imbalancing union influence. It is possible to make some assessment of this claim that the union is an agency capable of "moving" a sizable clientele.

An initial inquiry among the non-South white workers does provide some support for this view. The level of Democratic party identification in 1964 among large-city union families runs to 84 percent as against 57 percent in the non-union families, a difference of 27 percentage points (see Table 8.6).

TABLE 8.6
Union Membership, City Size, and Politics (Married, Economically Active, White, Non-South Manuals) SRC 1964

	Size of Place					
	Large City		Middle-Sized City		Small Town	
	Union	Non-Union	Union	Non-Union	Union	Non-Union
Party identification						
Percent Democratic	84%	57%	83%	67%	67%	64%
N =	(67)	(51)	(46)	(30)	(39)	(36)
1964 vote						
Percent Democratic	75	63	92	77	84	75
N =	(52)	(41)	(38)	(22)	(37)	(28)
Percent favoring						
Gov't.-supported medical care	59	67	79	62	56	75
N =	(56)	(46)	(43)	(21)	(27)	(36)
Gov't. guaranteed living standard	50	43	39	37	36	36
N =	(62)	(42)	(36)	(24)	(22)	(22)

In the middle-sized communities there is a similar pattern, although this time the difference between the two groups is only 17 percentage points (and that reduction stems from the higher Democratic sentiment among the non-union group). In the small towns it would be difficult to argue the union influence thesis; there, the difference between union and non-union families is miniscule.[23]

Looking at 1964 voting, we once again find the union people to be consistently more Democratic than the non-union groups. The maximum difference with respect to voting is 15 percentage points.

If we take the mobilizing of support for candidates as a prime political concern of a union, we find some evidence that does not support an extreme claim about union influence and power. When we contrast the levels of Democratic identification with the levels of 1964 Democratic voting we find that where generally the latter exceeds the former, in the case of the large-city unionists, the opposite is the case. That result, certainly, depends on a very small number of cases and one would not be justified in paying it much attention. Somewhat more striking, however, is the fact that some 25 percent of the large-city unionists favored the Republican candidate in 1964 and another relatively large percentage did not get out to vote—this presumably where the organized resources of unions would be greatest.

When we examined attitudes on some key bread-and-butter issues, the medical care question and the support for a reasonable living standard, we found little consistency between union affiliation and the attitudes. The unions appear to have only a very restricted influence on the *attitudes* of their membership. If the differences in voting are attributable to the union influence, the 1964 data suggest that the influence is a relatively modest one.

This 1964 picture, however, is somewhat misleading. It was, after all, a campaign in which the sides and the issues were made clear, or at least, so it appeared at the time. The campaign, then, was one in which the activity of the Republican candidate did much to drive people from all walks of life into the Democratic camp, without any special organizational effort on the part of pro-Democratic agencies being necessary. The relatively small voting differences between union and non-union families, it will be noted, resulted from a relatively high level of Democratic voting on the part of *non*-union families.

A better test of union influence would be in a campaign where the "tide" was against the Democrats. In such a case one could assess their ability to withstand the tide. The Eisenhower elections were clearly of this variety and the results from the studies of these two elections are strikingly different from those of 1964.

We find a similar picture of initial predispositions, the union groups tending to have somewhat higher levels of Democratic identification than the non-union groups. The big difference vis-à-vis the 1964 pattern appears in the defections of the non-union families and in the ability of the union to "hold" its members for the Democratic candidate against the Republican tide. Taking the 1952 large-city workers, for example, we find the initial levels of Democratic identification were 77 percent ($N = 137$) and 57 percent ($N = 56$) for union and non-union groups, respectively. In the voting, the Democratic percentage within the union group fell to 62 percent ($N = 118$) whereas among the non-union group it fell to 35 percent ($N = 37$). The falloff amounted to some 15 percentage points among the unionists as opposed to 27 among the non-union group. In the middle-sized communities we find a similar pattern; a falloff of 4 percentage points among the unionists as compared to one of 35 percentage points in the non-union group. These results do suggest a greater union "impact" than was suggested by the 1964 data. It must be noted, however, that this impact amounts to an ability to "hold" most of its members, to resist a contrary drift. The "power" of the unions appears to be more defensive than offensive; they are better able to hold "achieved positions" than to initiate developments. One should also note that their "defenses" leave much to be desired. A fair-sized minority of the union group identified with the Republican party. There were sizable "defections" in 1952 and more serious ones in 1956.[24]

In passing, it is of interest to note that the Eisenhower victories, in great measure, appear to have been dependent on the party shifts of non-union manual workers. This would appear to provide some support for the "mass society" theory. Those workers who were not "integrated" into the key voluntary association representing, in one way or another, their occupational interests proved most subject to the enchantments of the distant political figure whose "image" came largely through the mass media.

There is some reason to believe that the union influence is greatest in the large and in the middle-sized cities. This is consistent with the point made in the preceding section. For many Protestants, the conservatising link to the church becomes broken in the larger cities. In its place, there appears an influence that works in the opposite political direction.[25]

Income and Politics

Increased affluence might be a "saving" possibility for the Republicans. If better-off workers were to become more conservative, if they "converted" upon achievement of high and sustained income, there would be some ground for a positive assessment of Republican futures. It is difficult to judge this possibility in all the detail that might be desired. Some exploration of the matter, however, does allow limited conclusions. For our present purposes, following the explanation given earlier, we are still restricting ourselves to the married, economically active, white, non-South, working class.

Looking at income and party identification we find no support at all for the standard expectation in the 1952 and 1956 studies and only slight support (previously discussed) in the 1964 study, the two higher categories there being less Democratic by approximately 10 percentage points (see Table 8.7). If one were to count this latter finding as evidence of the impact of "affluence," it must be noted that the impact is very restricted, with two-thirds of those in the better-off categories still retaining a Democratic identification. The evidence in support of this conventional hypothesis then, at best, amounts to an impact on one worker in ten in the two highest categories and even this experience is countered by the evidence of the two earlier studies.[26]

The evidence with regard to the 1964 *voting* would appear to give somewhat stronger support to the income-conservatism thesis. The pattern here is clear and linear, the Democratic percentages falling from 88 percent ($N = 58$) in the lowest category, to 85 percent ($N = 55$), to 70 percent ($N = 63$), to 63 percent ($N = 38$) in the highest. This clear support for the claim was not found in the 1952 and 1956 studies.[27]

TABLE 8.7

Income and Politics (Married, Economically Active, White, Non-South, Manuals)

	Low	Medium Low	Medium High	High
		Family Income[a]		
		Percent identifying as Democrats		
SRC 1952	63%	67%	68%	65%
N =	(59)	(124)	(88)	(98)
SRC 1956	58	54	54	64
N =	(88)	(86)	(81)	(110)
SRC 1964	77	73	66	68
N =	(77)	(73)	(73)	(41)

[a] The categories differ. In 1952 they were: less than $3000, $3000–$3999, $4000–$4999, and $5000 or more. In 1956, the categories were: less than $4000, $4000–$4999, $5000–$5999, and $6000 or more. In 1964, the categories were: less than $6000, $6000–$7499, $7500–$9999, and $10,000 or more. The aim was to get four nearly equal-sized categories in each study.

While it would be easy to assume that this difference in 1964 is due to the income factor, that initial impression is cast into question by the fact that the higher-income workers are more likely to report having Republican fathers. This would suggest, in line with the Lazarsfeld-Berelson orientation, that the somewhat greater propensity toward Republicanism found among the better-off workers in the 1964 study is a result of a family political heritage rather than a direct result of the immediate, contemporary well-being.

It is worthwhile exploring this matter in greater detail. An examination of the party identifications of high- and low-income groups by father's party preference showed that the children of Democratic fathers in the higher-income categories were just as likely to identify with the Democrats as were the equivalent low-income group. The same was the case with those high-income workers whose fathers had no definite political direction. For these two groups, in short, the income factor played no role.

The overall difference between the high- and low-income groups in 1964 depends exclusively on those groups having Republican fathers. In the low-income category a relatively high proportion of this group (37 percent, N = 27) converted to the Democrats. In the equivalent high-income group the amount of conversion is relatively limited (19 percent, N = 31).[28] The "income effect" in this study then does not involve a conversion *to* Republicanism but rather appears to be somehow tied to conditions that limit conversion *from* Republicanism. That high-income group of Republican parentage must have rather unique circumstances within the working class.

They are the only group of non-South workers giving a majority to Goldwater in 1964, 68 percent of them ($N = 28$) favoring his candidacy.[29]

While the relationship of income to party identification and voting is at best a tenuous one, there is a clearer relationship in the case of some issue orientations. In both the 1956 and the 1964 studies the largest differences appear with respect to the medical care question, the percentage in favor of the government aid option showing a tendency to fall off in the higher-income categories. The differences between the extremes amount to 22 and 25 percentage points in the respective studies.[30] There is a similar pattern, although one that is less consistent and of less importance, in the case of the 1956 job guarantee question. And there is a similar but still less consistant result in the case of the 1964 living standard guarantee.[31] In these instances the differences between the extremes amounted to twelve percentage points in the 1956 study and fourteen in 1964.

There is one other correlate of income that is hidden in the figures as presented thus far. The 1956 study asked respondents whether their position on the issues involved strong or weak agreement and disagreement. With respect to both the job guarantee and the medical care question the lower-income groups, if they agreed, tended to agree "strongly." If they disagreed, they tended toward weak disagreement. Among the higher-income groups the opposite was the case. Relative to the lower-income groups, the agreement tended to be weaker and the disagreement, that is, the conservatism, tended to be stronger, more committed.[32]

This does suggest then at least some limited support for the conventional "economism" hypothesis. The situation, however, is somewhat more complex than the ordinary readings of the situation. High income by itself appears to have, at best, only a limited impact on party identification and voting. As already indicated, the studies yield inconsistent results in this matter but even if one accepted the "confirming" 1964 study, the "impact" would still involve only one worker in ten, which still leaves a fair-sized Democratic majority even in the highest income category. And also, as indicated, the dynamics involve fewer defections from Republicanism rather than an attraction to it. A second possible impact is to be seen in the attitudes on the domestic welfare issues. Among the better-off workers, that is, among those for whom the economic pressures are somewhat lessened, there is less approval of and commitment to welfare measures.

Despite the sweeping claims made about the better-off working class, about the "aristocrats of labor" or the "bourgeoisified" workers, it is to be noted that in 1956, majorities of those with opinions took a liberal position on both the medical care and job options. The highest income group in 1964 showed a 50–50 split on the medical care issue. It should also be kept in mind that we are dealing here with the non-South whites and that in the 1964 study a relatively large proportion of the better-off subgroup reported having had

Republican fathers. The basic lesson is that a large portion of the "affluent workers" remain committed to the Democrats and maintain liberal economic outlooks even with their well-being. A second major lesson is that some of the conservatism of the better-off is a result of a family heritage rather than a direct effect of affluence.

A Note on Mobility

Another much discussed "saving" option for a conservative party involves the possibility of a sizable movement of workers out of a "liberal" context into one that is more moderate or, possibly, into one that is even conservative. This is the point of the discussions of the transformation of the occupational structure discussed in Chapter 4. As was pointed out there, the optimism of those commentators is not justified. The amount of change is nowhere near as formidable as their figures would suggest. And, the mobility of workers, it was suggested, is largely into the lower-middle class, a context that is little different from their place of origin.

For a number of reasons it is worthwhile taking a more detailed look at the mobility processes. There is a strong ideological interest in the process of *upward* mobility; this focus has been so dominant that it has over-shadowed all other considerations. One consequence is a widespread misconception as to the actual frequencies involved. Another source of mis-representation is the focus on non-farm populations. By excluding those of farm origins one also excludes from consideration the largest single stream of movement.

For the present purpose we have taken all married, active males. We have also considered the mobility processes separately in the South and the non-South regions. For this purpose too, we have made use of the National Opinion Research Center Study No. 367, which gives us a relatively large number of cases. The SRC 1952 and 1964 studies showed very similar results.

As Lipset and Zetterberg have shown, there is a considerable amount of "upward mobility" from the manual ranks, the proportion of sons from manual families "making it" running somewhat higher than one out of three (see Table 8.8). This movement, however, is very disproportionately into the lower-middle-class ranks (as defined here), only 7 percent of the non-South manual children arriving in the "upper-middle class." There is also a con-siderable amount of downward mobility. The proportion of downward mobiles, as has been previously reported, is smaller than the proportion of upward mobiles. In absolute numbers, the exchange is such that approxi-mately two manual children move upward for each nonmanual child moving down.[33] If the presentation were restricted to these two groups, as has been done, for example in the Lipset-Zetterberg discussion, the picture would suggest a considerable movement into and expansion of the middle-class ranks.

TABLE 8.8

Intergenerational Mobility by Region (Married Active Males) NORC Study No. 367—1955

	Region					
	Non-South			South		
Father's Occupation:	Manual	Non-manual	Farm	Manual	Non-manual	Farm
Respondent's occupation						
Upper-middle class[a]	7%	22%	7%	17%	41%	6%
Lower-middle class[a]	30	46	13	24	27	16
Manual	61	31	48	51	21	55
Farm	3	1	32	8	11	22
$N =$	(243)	(139)	(188)	(71)	(44)	(141)

[a] The cutting for the non-South was a family income of $7500. In the South the line was $5000.

The third major observation, however, involves the children of farmers. We find that only a minority of them remain in farm occupations and that the principal terminus for those entering urban occupations is the manual ranks. Approximately seven out of ten of those leaving the farms end up as workers. Most of the others acquire lower-middle-class occupations. This means that the working-class children who leave the manual ranks are more than replaced by the combined numbers of the new entrants from the farm and nonmanual ranks.[34]

In summary, the data presented in this chapter point to the following conclusions.

In the course of the twentieth century the working class has been transformed from a rank made up largely of ex-farmers and children of farmers to one that is increasingly drawn from the children of manual workers. This development is most advanced in the areas of earliest industrialization and is least advanced in the less developed regions. It is among the younger workers in the larger cities of the industrially advanced regions that this development is especially evident, thus providing some sense of the likely future for the entire country.

As indicated, there is a striking lack of political difference associated with background. Part of this is due to peculiar compositional factors: those of farm background are disproportionately from the South and are also heavily Democratic in their party preference and liberal in their orientation to the issues. Somewhat larger differences appear when we examine the white, non-South workers, but even then the differences are not very great.

The relative lack of difference, in comparison with some European countries apparently result from the fact that much conversion occurs on the part of the new elements in the working class. It was seen that, contrary to wide-spread expectation, the outlooks of American farmers and of the lower-middle class originally were not very different from those of workers. This relative liberalism of the farm ranks and of the lower-middle class was explained as the result of different historical developments in the creation of and the political education of those two groups. In particular, American farmers came to be pitted against "the interests" unlike German farmers who were brought into coalition with the interests, this coalition being very concretely *against* the manual workers. As for the lower-middle class, we showed some changes occurring there, the older downward mobiles from that class being Protestant and tending toward Republicanism, but, given the changed composition of that rank, the new "recruits" (the more recent down-ward mobiles) now are very similar in social background and political out-look to the second-generation workers.

The small differences that do appear with respect to background among the non-South white workers involve a small edge of preference for the Demo-crats among the second-generation workers and a small but consistent edge in favor of the liberal position on the issues. The segment from farm back-grounds tend to be the most conservative of the three groups. Given the long-term development, this should mean that the largest and most con-servative source of recruitment from "outside" the class is dwindling and is destined to all but disappear with the continued reduction in the farm sector. If the next generation follows the pattern evidenced here and the children of the contemporary ex-farmers come to behave like the second-generation workers, there ought to be some enhancement of the liberal and Democratic potential.

That potential is likely to be enhanced in still another way. The workers coming from the farm sector tend to be less decided on issues and less regular in their election turnout. If their children were to adopt the behavior patterns of the current second-generation workers, this, too, would have the result of increasing both the liberal sentiment and the Democratic party potential. Another consequence would be a reduction of the "volatility" of American politics were these persons from the farm sector to become more "integrated" and committed to the political values presently dominant in the milieu.

Religious involvement appears to have an important political impact among the non-South white Protestants; those who are regular or frequent church attenders tend to be more Republican. Regular or frequent church attendance appeared most often in the small towns. Among migrants to the larger cities there was a tendency to drop the church connection and those dropping the connection tended to become Democrats, once again adapting to the dominant influences in the milieu.

Those who were union members (or in union families) were consistently more Democratic than was the case with the nonmembers. There was, however, little evidence to suggest that union membership shaped issue orientations in any significant way. The union influence appeared to be largely confined to "stabilizing" the voting commitment of members. It was largely the nonmembers who were swept into the Eisenhower camp in the 1950s and who swung back to the Democrats in 1964. Again, if the future were to involve an increase in unionization of the manual labor ranks, this rather sizable shifting population would become committed, the shifts from election to election would be considerably reduced, and the chances for charismatic Republicans of the Eisenhower variety would also be diminished.

Many accounts treat "mobility" (meaning "upward" mobility) as playing some important meliorative role in the politics of advanced nations. We have shown that most of the upward mobility on the part of working-class children consists of a move into the lower-middle class. By now it should be clear that such a move does not involve night and day contrasts in life conditions but rather can perhaps be best summarized by suggesting that the typical lower-middle-class milieu contains "more of the same," that is, it provides continuity with working class experience rather than the contrary. For all those "leaving" the class, there are approximately twice the number of "new recruits" coming in, these coming principally from the farms but many also coming from the lower-middle class.

The kind of mobility most theorist-speculators have in mind—a movement from the working class into the upper-middle class—is a relative rarity. It must also be noted that no matter what importance such movement may have for upper-middle-class publicists (such as providing useful symbolism and aids in touting the virtues of "the system"), that mini-minority experience has little impact whatsoever on the life circumstances of those who are left behind. For them, the job demands continue uninfluenced by someone else's "success"; the housing situation, the neighborhoods, the schools, and so forth are also uninfluenced, and the weekly struggle to balance the pay check against the grocery costs also continues unchanged by the facts of some one else's "mobility." The point is that the symbolism of "some people making it" is largely of benefit to the established upper-middle class. It soothes their anxieties and justifies their ways. That symbolism, however, is likely to be a minor and passing concern for most working-class people as compared to the day-to-day realities of the job, wages, and prices.

Notes

1. It should be noted that we are still working within the revisionist conceptualization, that is, assuming the manual-nonmanual division to be meaningful. This is a point that, by now, is clearly contrary to fact. It is, however, useful to

continue with the assumption for heuristic purposes in order to elaborate and detail the critique we are making. A respecification is not precluded by this procedure. This will be undertaken in the next chapter.

2. It is necessary to make drastic oversimplifications in some of these formulations. Possibly the statement that *at maximum* half would be the bearers of a class culture would be more appropriate. This still makes an unwarranted assumption (to be explored below) that there are sharp differences in outlook associated with different kinds of background. It assumes, too, that all second- (or more) generation workers share a "working-class" culture, and this would seem doubtful. Some 26 percent of the second-generation workers live in communities of fewer than 2500 persons, and another 29 percent live in communities of 2500 to under 50,000. It seems likely that many of these people are not living in a "pure" working class context. In discussing these large categories (e.g., non-South white working class), it is easy to assume a homogeneity that does not in fact exist.

By way of precaution it is worth a reminder that this category includes workers in New York and Chicago, in Youngstown, Akron, and Columbus, in Eau Claire, Janesville, and Fond du Lac, in Compton, and in the innumerable "Springdales" of the nation.

3. This point is shown in the contemporary data. For example, taking the northeastern states, the region of earliest industrialization, we find about 72 percent of the workers under age 45 to be second-generation working class ($N = 131$, NORC Study No. 367).

4. Those working-class wives who came from nonmanual families appear to have come from lower-middle-class families. In the 1964 study, for example, 81 percent of them ($N = 74$) reported that when growing up their family had been "working class," usually an indication of marginality.

It is to be expected, given the massive shift away from farm occupations, that the basic pattern indicated in Table 8.3 would occur. One additional fact that is not as obvious is that the relative "availability" of wives from middle-class families also declines. It is difficult to separate the developments in the farm and the non-farm sectors; however, a crude approximation may be reached by examining those marriages in which the wife's father was engaged in a nonfarm occupation. In the older cohorts, approximately one out of three working-class males who married into a nonfarm family found a wife whose father was middle class. In the younger cohort, the ratio was only one in five.

5. Those of farm background also tend to be less decided on the issues. For example, in response to the government living standard guarantee question, 32 percent ($N = 163$) of the second-generation worker group had no opinion (no answer, undecided, etc.) as against 40 percent ($N = 67$) of those with farm background and only 16 percent ($N = 49$) among those who are downwardly mobile.

6. See the data presented in Chapter 5, particularly that contained in Table 5.12.

7. There is one exception here. In 1964 voting, Southern white farmers divided 50–50 ($N = 20$). These findings have some importance for the pluralist assumptions since they show that the American Farm Bureau Federation, the so-called voice of the farmer, clearly does not represent *the* farmer but rather the conservative minority among them. For a useful account of the organizational dynamics

in the farm sector see Wesley McCune, *Who's Behind Our Farm Policy* (New York: Frederick A. Praeger, 1956). A useful recent account of American Farm Bureau Federation operations appears in Robert G. Sherrill's "Harvest of Scandal," *The Nation*, **205**:16 (13 November 1967), 496–500. The best work on the political behavior of farmers is in Angus Campbell, et al., *The American Voter* (New York: John Wiley & Co., 1960), Ch. 15: "Agrarian Political Behavior."

8. It is necessary, once again, to stress the fact that the assertions in the text are based on a very small number of cases. On the other hand, the points made here may be enhanced by considering the alternatives. If the conventional formulations were correct (for example, the claims about the down mobiles), then the large majority of such cases should be found both coming from Republican families and themselves remaining Republican. That is, they should be very disproportionately concentrated, in the 1952 data, in that cell (bottom line, second column from the right) containing nine cases. It is possible that a single study might misrepresent the realities, especially where we are dependent on a very small number of cases. The fact that a second study with an equally small number of cases yields a similar picture attests to the very strong likelihood that the conventional formulation is not adequate. In any event, one should not definitely accept or reject the claim on the basis of the data presented here. These findings would serve, hopefully, as a stimulus to the designing of an appropriate study for testing these claims.

9. Some suggestive evidence on the point is contained in Harold L. Wilensky and Hugh Edwards, "The Skidder: Ideological Adjustments of Downward Mobile Workers," *American Sociological Review*, **24** (April 1959), 215–230. See also Joseph Lopreato and Janet Saltzman Chapetz, "The Political Orientation of Skidders: A Middle-Range Theory," *American Sociological Review*, **35** (June 1970), 440–451.

10. It seems likely that both processes—conversion with time spent in the working class and differential recruitment at different times—are operating. If this is the case and if some conversion has occurred among the older downwardly mobile white Protestants, the fact of their still relatively heavy Republicanism is due to the high "beginning" level.

The data supporting the points made in the text follow: Taking the 1952 study, which had the larger number of cases, we divided the downward mobiles into those of ages 44 or less and 45 or more. The percentages of Democratic fathers were, respectively, 66 percent ($N = 29$) and 42 percent ($N = 19$). The respective Protestant figures were 44 percent ($N = 43$) and 70 percent ($N = 27$). Similar patterns were found in the 1964 study.

11. This pattern of families who rise in the father's generation tending to fall in the son's and vice versa is shown in Ramkrishna Mukherjee, "A Study of Social Mobility Between Three Generations," Chapter IX of D. V. Glass, ed., *Social Mobility in Britain* (London: Routledge & Kegan Paul, 1954); in Kaare Svalastoga, *Prestige, Class and Mobility* (Copenhagen: Gyldendal, 1959), p. 342, 409; and in John D. Allingham, "Class Regression: An Aspect of the Social Stratification Process," *American Sociological Review*, **32** (June 1967), 442–449. The Kenneth Thompson work, while not considering the three generational pattern, does show the "political" implication of the "class regression" pattern; workers

from Republican families are more likely to be upwardly mobile and persons from Democratic middle-class families are more likely to be downwardly mobile. The previous tendency, based on data showing only mobility and politics without information on political "origins," had been to treat these as instances of "conversion" subsequent to the "move." See Thompson's studies cited in Chapter 2, note 53.

12. The quotation appears in Abba P. Schwartz, *The Open Society* (New York: William Morrow, 1968), p. 119.

13. Again taking the 1952 study because of the larger number of cases, we do find the downward mobile Protestants tending more to identify themselves as "middle class" (47 percent, $N = 38$) than is the case with the Catholic down mobiles (29 percent, $N = 24$).

14. See the initial discussion in Chapter 5.

15. These figures are recalculated from Seymour Martin Lipset and Reinhard Bendix, *Social Mobility in Industrial Society* (Berkeley: University of California Press, 1959), p. 70.

16. The comments in this paragraph are based largely on Alexander Gerschenkron, *Bread and Democracy in Germany* (Berkeley: University of California Press, 1943), and on Sten S. Nilson's "Wahlsoziologische Probleme des Nationalsozialismus," *Zeitschrift für die Gesamte Staatswissenschaft*, **110** (1954), particularly pp. 295–311.

17. The leading importer of Weimar Germany social theorizing was C. Wright Mills, particularly in his *White Collar* (New York: Oxford University Press, 1951). An earlier attempt, Lewis Corey's *The Crisis of the Middle Class* (New York: Covici-Friede, 1935) had little impact in academic circles.

18. Taking the 1952 study, the percentages reporting having voted in all elections (excluding the new voters, new citizens, etc.) were as follows: those of working-class background, 56 percent (185); farm background, 39 percent (99); and middle-class background, 50 percent (62). The equivalent figures from the 1964 study were 59 percent (130), 45 percent (64), and 66 percent (44).

19. The data are presented in the first pages of this chapter.

20. The most illuminating discussion of the political-religious linkage is to be found in the work of Benton Johnson. See his articles cited in Chapter 5, note 14.

21. Among those workers who have moved on to larger communities and who are regular or frequent church attenders, the proportion of Republican identifiers in 1964 was 38 percent ($N = 29$). The figure among the equivalent group who were irregular attenders was 21 percent ($N = 33$). Examination of the 1952 and 1956 results showed that churchgoing workers of small-town origins, no matter what the present community context, were consistently more Republican than the nonattending workers.

22. For an outstanding discussion of the Protestant churches and the workers in one industrial community see Kenneth Underwood, *Protestant and Catholic: Religious and Social Interaction in an Industrial Community* (Boston: Beacon Press, 1957). Also very useful is Liston Pope's *Millhands and Preachers* (New Haven: Yale University Press, 1942).

23. There is, of course, an obvious possibility that the basic assumption about

the direction of influence is mistaken. It is conceivable that some Republican workers in the cities go out of their way to choose work that does not require them to join unions. Such, for example, might be the case in the instance of very committed ideological conservatives. We cannot assess this alternative possibility with the data at hand. It seems unlikely, however, that there would be many committed ideological conservatives in the working class, especially ones in a position to put ideology ahead of high earnings. We can, by presenting the evidence as we have (that is, by *assuming* the influence to run as originally claimed), give some sense of the maximum union "impact."

24. A suggestive discussion of "union influence," (one that challenges the sweeping claims), appears in E. E. Schattschneider, *The Semisovereign People* (New York: Holt, Rinehart and Winston, 1960), p. 49–52. Some evidence from the 1956 study appears in Angus Campbell, et al., *The American Voter* (New York: John Wiley & Sons, 1960), pp. 302, 305, and 314–316. See also Arthur Kornhauser, Harold L. Sheppard, and Albert J. Mayer, *When Labor Votes: A Study of Auto Workers* (New York: University Books, 1957) and Harold L. Sheppard and Nicholas A. Masters, "The Political Attitudes and Preferences of Union Members: The Case of the Detroit Auto Workers," *American Political Science Review*, **53** (June 1959), 437–447. A useful compendium containing a large number of relevant articles on the subject is that of Charles M. Rehmus and Doris B. McLaughlin, eds., *Labor and American Politics: A Book of Readings* (Ann Arbor: University of Michigan Press, 1967). A very useful account that makes clear the research gaps in the area is that of Harry M. Scoble, "Organized Labor in Electoral Politics: Some Questions for the Discipline," *Western Political Quarterly*, **16** (September 1963), 666–685. Some paradoxical results are reported by Samuel J. Eldersveld, *Political Parties: A Behavioral Analysis* (Chicago: Rand McNally, 1964). Based on a study in Detroit, he reports that "union members did not respond well to the precinct leadership of union officers." There was, he found, "high enthusiasm for party activity in precincts not led by union people: 67 percent of Democrats and independents were enthusiastic in such precincts, compared to about 25 percent in union officer precincts" (p. 448).

25. This expectation assumes at least some constancy in the level of and location of union memberships. Contrary to the customary pluralistic expectation of increasing membership with advancing "modernization," the evidence available for the United States suggests the opposite. The data from three SRC studies, 1952, 1956, 1964, respectively, show the following proportions of economically active, working-class males to be members of unions: 58 percent ($N = 358$), 48 percent ($N = 326$), and 47 percent ($N = 243$). If the trend were, in fact, toward more "integration" of the manual workers, it seems likely, considering the implication of the 1952 and 1956 results, that such sizable "swings" in the aggregate vote would be eliminated. The division of the vote between the parties, in other words, would approximate much more closely the pattern indicated by aggregated party identifications.

26. The earliest of the 1965 Gallup studies at our disposal (the one least subject to faulty recall) gives the following result: The percentages of Democratic party identifications, going from low- to high-income categories, were 63 percent ($N = 121$), 73 percent ($N = 109$), 64 percent ($N = 100$), and 62 percent ($N = 39$). The Democratic vote percentages for the same categories were 76 percent

$(N = 92)$, 76 percent $(N = 107)$, 61 percent $(N = 101)$, and 71 percent $(N = 45)$. These results are for economically active, non-South, white, working-class persons.

This finding of essentially no difference in party choice is in line with previous evidence on the subject. Kornhauser, et al., for example, reported the following in 1956:

> Our study of auto workers contributes rather striking evidence that it is possible for wage earners to experience vast social and economic gains and yet remain steadfastly union oriented in their political views. This may well be the most significant of our findings. . . . Detroit area auto workers are not going "middle class" in political outlook. They are predominantly oriented in agreement with the union; they approve of union political activities; they trust labor's voting recommendations and the great majority cast their ballots accordingly; they are inclined to distrust the recommendations of business groups and newspapers; they want organized labor to have a larger voice in government and they want business to have less influence; they are overwhelmingly Democratic and they look upon the Democratic Party as the party that protects and advances the interests of working people; they identify themselves as members of the "working class" rather than the middle class . . . (pp. 281–282).

27. The pattern with respect to voting in these years is somewhat erratic. The Democratic percentages for the four income categories in 1952 were, reading from low to high, 49 percent $(N = 43)$, 51 percent $(N = 101)$, 65 percent $(N = 71)$, and 46 percent $(N = 76)$. The equivalent figures for 1956 were 40 percent $(N = 72)$, 48 percent $(N = 75)$, 41 percent $(N = 75)$, and 45 percent $(N = 102)$.

28. The analysis is based on the married, active, non-South, white working class. The group was divided into those with family incomes up to $7499 and those of $7500 or more. Taking those who reported having Democratic fathers, the proportions of Democratic identifiers among low- and high-income categories were 85 percent $(N = 87)$ and 89 percent $(N = 54)$, respectively. Among those reporting that the fathers had no clear political position, the equivalent figures are 78 percent Democratic $(N = 36)$ for the low-income group and 76 percent $(N = 29)$ for the high category. The figures for those with Republican fathers are given in the text.

29. The assumption throughout this discussion is that it is not the money per se that affects the political orientation but rather a set of social conditions that isolates these individuals from the dominant outlooks found in the milieu and that either engenders or allows the persistence of conservatism. For a more detailed discussion of the effects of income as opposed to social influences see my *Affluence and the French Worker* (Princeton: Princeton University Press, 1967), Ch. VII: "Income and Politics." For a study using data from the United States, paralleling the account in text but based instead on skill level, see Richard Hamilton, "Note on Skill Level and Politics," *Public Opinion Quarterly*, **29** (Fall 1965), 390–399. Also of some interest in this connection is my "Affluence and the Worker: The West German Case," *American Journal of Sociology*, **72** (September 1965), 144–152.

30. In the 1956 study, the percentage of those with opinions favoring the government-supported medical care fell from 78 percent $(N = 79)$ in the lowest-

income category, to 69 percent ($N = 74$), to 66 percent ($N = 70$), to 56 percent ($N = 98$). The pattern is very similar in 1964.

31. The 1956 study showed the percentages favoring the government job guarantee to be 72 percent ($N = 83$) in the lowest-income category, 71 percent in the next ($N = 84$), then 72 percent ($N = 86$), and 60 percent in the highest ($N = 108$).

32. Taking those with opinions on the medical care question, for example, the 1956 results are as follows. In the low-income group we find 65 percent to be strongly in favor and 14 percent indicating weaker support. Eleven percent were moderately opposed and some 10 percent strongly opposed ($N = 79$). In the highest income category the equivalent figures were 40 percent strongly in favor, 16 percent favoring but not strongly, 10 percent somewhat opposed, and 34 percent strongly opposed. Most of those who were opposed to the medical care option were Republican identifiers.

33. The Lipset-Zetterberg account appears in Lipset and Bendix, op. cit. Most of this downward mobility occurs outside of the South. In the South, only a small proportion of the children in nonmanual families lose that position. This peculiarity appears also in both the 1952 and the 1964 studies.

34. Stating the point somewhat differently, we have the following picture. Outside the South, the working class "lost" 90 members of this sample to the middle class. At the same time, 90 members were "gained" from the farm ranks. And, in addition, 43 members were gained from the middle class, that is, the downward mobiles. In the South, the working class lost 29 members to the middle class and gained 78 from the farms. There were only minor gains from the middle-class ranks ($N = 9$).

9

Cleavages within the Middle Class

Introduction

This chapter is intended as a parallel to the preceding one. It is, in other words, concerned with the transformations within the middle-class ranks. For reasons already indicated, it has been necessary to consider the upper-middle and lower-middle segments separately. The origins of these categories have been explored in a manner similar to that of the working class in the previous chapter. An analysis was also made of the pattern of recruitment by age in an attempt to assess changes but, because of the complications encountered, it was impossible to establish any clear-cut trends. There follows a discussion of the structural changes occurring in the white-collar ranks, that is, changes affecting their current situation apart from the question of their origins. The likely result of these changes, it is suggested, would be an increasing differentiation in the political outlooks of the upper- and lower-middle-class groups. An examination of the class segments by age does confirm this prediction. The chapter ends with a discussion of the locations of Republicanism within the population and an analysis of that party's "core" and "peripheral" supporters.

The Question of Origins

There are a number of possibilities that one might reasonably anticipate with respect to the trend in recruitment of the nonmanual ranks. One might expect that these ranks would show a development similar to the manuals; this time, however, the tendency is toward increased middle-class recruitment. Another possibility is that the development in the lower-middle class parallels the working-class pattern and that in the upper-middle class one finds the trend toward exclusive middle-class recruitment. There are a number of other more complex possibilities. These will be developed at a later point.

Looking first at the pattern of recruitment of the lower-middle class (that is, examining the family backgrounds of those in the rank, as in the previous chapter), we find that outside the South the major source of its "members" is the working class. Four out of ten lower-middle-class persons come from

336

TABLE 9.1

Occupational Origins of the Middle-Class Ranks (Married Respondents in Middle-Class Families; Excludes Families with Retired House Head)

Region	Father's Occupation					
	Manual Worker	Farm	Middle Class	Other; No Answer	%	N
Non-South						
Upper-middle class						
SRC 1952	26%	9%	57%	8%	= 100%	(76)
SRC 1964	32	12	52	3	= 99	(145)
Lower-middle class						
SRC 1952	40	25	32	3	= 100	(291)
SRC 1964	41	23	33	3	= 100	(204)
South						
Upper-middle class						
SRC 1952	8	22	62	8	= 100	(50)
SRC 1964	26	17	49	8	= 100	(86)
Lower-middle class						
SRC 1952	19	50	21	10	= 100	(58)
SRC 1964	25	56	18	1	= 100	(68)

manual families (see Table 9.1). Approximately one-quarter of the lower-middle-class individuals are from farm backgrounds and, perhaps somewhat surprisingly, only one in three of its members comes from a middle-class family. In the South, those from the farms far outnumber those from the manual ranks and there only one in five are second-generation middle class. A majority of the "lower-middle class," therefore, is drawn from outside the rank. Only a smallish minority are in a position to contrast two different generations of middle-class experience in order to assess whether one has "come up" or "come down" in the world, a judgment that is central to the revisionist social theory. Most people in that rank are "new" to the rank; their intergenerational comparisons would have to be with a different kind of experience.

Second-generation middle-class persons constitute just over half of those in the upper-middle class. That is the case in the non-South regions. In the South, we find a similar picture although here the proportions differ somewhat, being 62 percent in 1952 and only 49 percent in 1964. Outside the South, the principal source of "outside" recruitment is from the manual ranks. In the South in 1952, the main source of newcomers was from the farm sector. This pattern had shifted, if we accept the percentages based on the small number of cases, so that by 1964 those from the manual ranks outnumbered the farm recruits.

In summary, the lower-middle class appears to be more like the manual rank in social origins, and in the upper-middle class we find a relative predominance of the second-generation middle-class populations.

An analysis of the pattern by age, similar to that undertaken for the manual workers in Chapter 8, poses a number of difficulties. Because the nonmanual rank is smaller than the manual, the number of cases is somewhat reduced. This smaller category is then divided into upper and lower subcategories. When considering the manuals, both the South and non-South were combined. Here, however, because of the different cutting lines used to divide the upper- and lower-middle classes, it is necessary to consider the developments separately by region. When these delimited categories are then divided into four or five age cohorts, it is clear that there are going to be some problems. The basic lessons (and problems) may be illustrated by consideration of the pattern among the non-South middle classes. We will use the 1955 NORC study here, once again, because this study contains the largest number of cases.

There is very little evidence of any trend, that is, of any shift in the recruitment pattern within the upper-middle class. The percentage of those drawn from middle-class families does show some fluctuations from cohort to cohort but, aside from the farm predominance in the oldest category, there is no clear pattern evident (see Table 9.2). The farm dominance and the corresponding low percentage from middle-class families indicated in the oldest cohort of this table should not be overstressed since both SRC studies show an opposite pattern; the middle-class percentages in the oldest categories of the 1952 and 1964 studies are 67 percent ($N = 21$) and 62 percent ($N = 26$), respectively. These studies also show no clear trend.

TABLE 9.2
Occupational Origins of the Middle-Class Ranks by Age; Non-South Only (Married Respondents in Middle-Class Families, Excludes Families with Retired House Head) NORC 367, 1955

Class and Age of Respondent	Father's Occupation				
	Manual Worker	Farm	Middle Class	Other	N
Upper-middle class					
To 34	18%	18%	59%	4%	(27)
35–44	29	17	51	2	(41)
45–54	25	14	61	...	(28)
55 and over	21	38	34	7	(29)
Lower-middle class					
To 34	50	13	37	1	(127)
35–44	39	18	42	1	(85)
45–54	39	26	33	2	(46)
55 and over	25	31	40	4	(48)

We may speak with some greater confidence about the lower-middle-class developments. There is no change indicated in the percentage recruited from middle-class families.[1] There is, as in the manual ranks, a tendency for the younger cohorts to be drawn disproportionately from manual families and less frequently from farm families. This tendency toward increased dependence on manual ranks and the corresponding decrease in the recruitment of farm children also comes through in both SRC studies.

The discussion to this point, it will be noted, has treated the "new arrivals" in a class as having come there in their youth, that is, at the beginnings of their careers, and stayed all their lives. This simplification is clearly not entirely adequate. It has much less justification in the case of nonmanuals than in the previous discussion of the manuals.[2]

The upper- and lower-middle classes have been defined arbitrarily in terms of income, specifically, it will be noted, on the basis of the estimated total *family* income. There are a number of problems involved in this procedure. To illustrate, one may consider first a typical upper-middle-class career. The person born and raised in the upper-middle-class setting characteristically goes to a university and proceeds from there to a job in a large bureaucratic enterprise. The careers in these firms usually involve some kind of a "beginning at the bottom" and a "working one's way up." In many cases this amounts to little more than a highly stylized imitation of an Horatio Alger career line. It is clear, however, that for some brief and consciously delimited period, the Yale graduate with the telephone company, for example, does work as a lineman or set poles. At one time, beginners in the Wall Street law firms started with rather marginal earnings. From that humble beginning, however, they proceeded with $1000 yearly increments. Their real beginnings, moreover, were in very well-off families and their backgrounds included education at the best universities and law schools.[3]

This means that the normal upper-middle-class career begins with a temporary period of relatively low income. Given the definition used here, this would mean that the youngest age cohort of the lower-middle class probably contains some persons of upper-middle-class backgrounds, persons who possess the characteristic educational training of that class, and who are involved in planned (by the firms) career lines that, barring grievous mishaps, will soon bring them back to an upper-middle-class earning level. It is to be noted that these "temporary" lower-middle-class persons will be well aware of the "plan" involved in their careers and will be able to develop their lives, particularly their consumption patterns, accordingly. In addition to being differentiated from the more-or-less permanent lower-middle class in terms of their "great expectations," they would also be differentiated in terms of the help they could expect from their families during this period of temporary privation. It seems unlikely that they would abandon their "inherited" political outlooks during this "transitional" period. For this reason one may expect this group to provide some otherwise unexpected conservatism in the youngest cohort of the lower-middle class.

One indication of this "temporary decline" may be seen in the Ns in the right margin of Table 9.2. The youngest cohort of the upper-middle class, it will be noted, is relatively "underpopulated" (containing 22 percent of the class total) in comparison to the equivalent cohort of the lower-middle class, which contains some 41 percent of that total.[4]

Another indication of this temporary "downward mobility" is to be seen in the educational accomplishments of the various groups. The formal educational level of most segments of the lower-middle class tends to be rather low. Only smallish minorities of those from manual or farm families have gone beyond high school to achieve at least some college. In the older categories of those from middle-class families, the percentage of those with at least some college, although somewhat higher, still is less than half of the total. But among those of 34 or fewer years who are from middle-class families we find 69 percent ($N = 29$) have some college experience and most of these have completed college. Another 17 percent have had some other kind of training beyond high school such as a trade, business, or technical education. The equivalent figures for those younger persons of manual and farm backgrounds (combined) are 35 percent ($N = 46$) having at least some college and 11 percent having some business or technical training beyond high school. There is, in short, a strong suggestion here that many of these young people of middle-class families are "lower-middle class" for the time being only.

There is some additional supporting evidence in the responses to the survey questions. It must be remembered that we are dealing with very small numbers of cases. For the present purpose we are comparing the younger second-generation lower-middle-class cohort with equivalent older ones. There is a tendency for the younger cohort in the lower-middle class to show behaviors that would indicate the presence of such "temporary" lower-middle-class persons. For example, from the 1964 study, we find a higher percentage of the younger cohort of the lower-middle class reported having Republican fathers. Moreover, a higher percentage of the fathers of this group were reported to be politically interested. The respondents themselves were more likely to favor Goldwater in the 1964 election. The younger cohort also indicated considerably higher expectations with respect to their future income than the older cohorts. Perhaps more relevant here is the comparison of the younger cohort stemming from middle-class parents with those coming from fam and working-class backgrounds. The former have the higher expectations for the future. This same finding appears in the National Opinion Research Center Study (No. 367, 1955). In addition to the young second-generation middle-class group having the higher future expectation, they also indicated less current satisfaction with their incomes despite the fact that they had on average higher incomes than the other groups.[5]

A second difficulty with the arbitrary definition used thus far in this work stems from the fact that we have been working with family income. If the wife of a lower-middle-class man works, it would be relatively easy, given the low cutting line used, for her effort to bring the family into the upper-middle class (as here defined). Since women in the younger cohorts tend to be at home, not in the labor force, the working wives first appear in significant numbers in the middle-age categories. The income pattern over the career of many lower-middle (and working-class) persons for this reason involves an inverted-U pattern. When the husband and wife are both young, the unit has one earner, the wife typically being engaged in child-rearing activities. The wife reenters the labor force once the children are older and semiautonomous, and her efforts (and to some extent also the efforts of the children as they come of age) contribute to provide the years of peak earnings for the family during the "middle years." Later, as the children leave home and as the wife once again retires from the labor force, the family returns to its original single-earner status.

This would mean that there are some lower-middle-class people who, as a result of the arbitrariness of the definitions used here, have been classed as upper middles. Like the previously discussed career pattern, these too happen to be "temporaries," that is, temporarily "mislocated." It seems likely that they too will retain the political outlooks that they originally learned despite their new and temporary condition of relative affluence. Unlike the previously discussed career line, this group is unlikely to have any "great expectations," their source of income, promotion chances, and futures being all too clear.

The data at hand indicate support for this line of speculation. Once again it is necessary to keep in mind that all this support is based on a very small number of cases. The likely presence of "temporaries" appears to be greatest in the 35–44 age cohort.[6] Here we find that 87.5 percent ($N = 32$) of those of middle-class background have achieved the $10,000 family income level through the efforts of the house head alone. Among those of working-class and farm background, the equivalent figure is 63 percent ($N = 35$). A sizable minority, therefore, of those present in this category are there only through the efforts of multiple earners. Those of farm and working-class background who are "upper-middle class" and in this 35–44 age cohort also have dimmer expectations as far as their future earnings are concerned, this is in comparison to the equivalent group of middle-class background. This pessimism is most pronounced among those families of working-class and farm background having two or more earners. Most optimistic about the future are those of middle-class background, particularly those families with a single earner.[7]

When treating the age groups in the middle class as cohorts in order to undertake a crude assessment of the trends (such as was done for the manual workers in Chapter 8), it is necessary to keep in mind or make some correction for these temporarily misplaced persons.

Background and Political Attitudes

It is worthwhile addressing the questions raised previously about the newcomers to the rank and about any possible conversion in that rank. As noted earlier, there is an assumption in revisionist or centrist thinking that the middle-class rank is "different" (specifically, conservative and Republican) and that mobility from the manual level into this new milieu would be associated with a shift in the direction of more conservative politics. This view would also, presumably, apply to mobility from the ranks of the poorer farmers into the "middle class."

The pattern of intergenerational party shifts, however, does not accord with those assumptions. Instead, the results prove to be consistent with the expectations outlined in this work. Those persons of working-class and farm background who "arrive" in lower-middle-class positions show a considerable drift toward the Democratic party (see Table 9.3). There is, to be more specific, only a very limited "defection" on the part of those having Democratic fathers. There is a relatively sizable shift to the Democrats among those reporting Republican fathers. Those persons whose fathers had no fixed political party commitments fall heavily to the Democrats.

The major conclusion, then, is that contrary to the widespread expectations that "upward" mobility would involve movement into a different political milieu (and consequent adaptation of the politics of that milieu), what we have shown is a very similar political context. These two groups form a majority of the "lower-middle-class" ranks. A sizable proportion of the fathers in both categories were Democrats. And finally, the point indicated here, within both groups of "newcomers" there is a net shift toward the Democrats.[8]

The lower-middle-class persons of middle-class parentage show a somewhat different pattern, this difference, however, being largely one of degree. There is a greater defection from the Democrats, less shifting to the Democrats, and the children of the politically indeterminate fathers divide evenly between the two parties. There is, as a result of this shifting, no net advantage gained by either party within this segment.

The overall pattern for the lower-middle class, then, is similar to that in the working class. The class is very disproportionately drawn from Democratic families and the pattern of shifting in the current generation is one that favors the Democratic party.[9] It seems likely that among the minority (those who are second-generation middle class and who are Republicans), one would find many who are in career lines that will either take them or return them to an upper-middle-class income level. It seems unlikely that they have any significant political influence within the lower-middle-class ranks. It would seem more likely that they both live and work in locations different from those in which the majority of the rank find themselves.

A similar analysis of the pattern of intergenerational shifting within the upper-middle class is hampered by the small number of cases available for analysis. When we consider the patterns indicated by these few cases we find that the result is a net gain for the Republicans in all three subgroups. Among the upward mobiles, specifically among the children of Democratic manual workers, one finds a majority shifting to the Republicans.

The major conclusion to be noted about these findings is that the kind of

TABLE 9.3

Father-Respondent Politics by Background (Married, Non-South Upper- and Lower-Middle Class; SRC 1964)

	Father's Occupation								
	Worker			Farm			Middle Class		
Father's Politics:	Dem	Rep	Other	Dem	Rep	Other	Dem	Rep	Other
Respondent's party identification									
Lower-middle class									
Democrat	88%	37.5%	69%	79%	39%	57%[a]	72%	18%	36%
Independent	7	...	6	...	...	43	7	11	27
Republican	5	62.5	25	21	61	...	21	71	36
*N*s	38	9	11	15	7	4	21	5	4
	3	...	1	...	...	3	2	3	3
	2	15	4	4	11	...	6	20	4
Upper-middle class									
Democrat	36%	33%	50%	67%	...	33%[a]	63%	15%	56%
Independent	8	...	20	...	...	...	6	7	...
Republican	56	67	30	33	100[a]	67[a]	31	78	44
*N*s	9	4	5	8	...	1	20	4	9
	2	...	2	...	...	...	2	2	...
	14	8	3	4	3	2	10	21	7

[a] Note small number of cases.

conversion that is thought to occur generally throughout the nonmanual ranks in fact occurs only in the upper-middle class.

Within the lower-middle class, there are fair-sized differences in party identifications associated with the different background (see Table 9.4). This

TABLE 9.4
Party Identification and 1964 Vote of Middle-Class Respondents by Rank and Background (Married, Active, Non-South Respondents) SRC 1964

	Lower Middles			Upper Middles		
Father's Occupation	Manual Worker	Farm	Middle Class	Manual Worker	Farm	Middle Class
Party Identification						
Percent						
Democratic	73%	63%	50%	42%	50%	46%
N =	(79)	(41)	(60)	(43)	(18)	(71)
1964 Vote						
Percent						
Democratic	73	66	61	64	33	48
N =	(63)	(35)	(57)	(39)	(15)	(67)

is the one context in which there is recruitment from genuinely different settings, this being particularly the case with those who in all likelihood come out of upper-middle-class ranks. In addition to the background differences, it seems likely that there are differences in the places where these people live and work. Those of working-class background are likely to be more closely linked to manual workers in terms of physical proximity and personal connections. It also seems likely that many of those of middle-class background would tend to have close contacts with the upper-middle class. Again it should be noted that one cannot talk about *the* lower-middle class. One must ask about the specific subgroups within the broader category.

In the upper-middle class, by comparison, there are only very small differences in party identification associated with background. This lack of difference results from the sizable conversion, particularly among those of working-class backgrounds, noted in the previous discussion.

The pattern of 1964 voting yields unexpected results. When we contrast the percentages of Democratic identifiers with those of Democratic voters we find in the lower-middle class some drift away from the Republicans. In essence, this pattern is similar to that found in the working class. In the upper-middle class we find that the upward mobiles, those of working-class background, show a striking shift *back* to Democratic voting when faced with that season's choice.[10] It would appear that many of the "new converts" still retain some feeling for their original roots and, given a clarification of the political issues and the party positions, return to their original loyalties. This would suggest that the significance of the "conversion," the interest in assimilating and identifying with their new milieu, is not as strong as has been frequently suggested.

Some of this "lingering liberalism" among those people coming out of the working class and having "made it" into the upper-middle class is indicated by the responses to the economic liberalism questions. When we contrast the upward mobile group with the farm and middle-class children combined, we find a fairly consistent pattern. Roughly half (51 percent, $N = 35$) of the upward mobiles favored government-supported medical care as against 42 percent ($N = 78$) of the other group. Forty-nine percent ($N = 37$) of the upward mobiles favored government aid to education as against 33 percent ($N = 85$) of the others. And forty-six percent ($N = 37$) of the upward mobiles thought the government in Washington had too much power as opposed to 60 percent ($N = 78$) of those from farm and middle-class backgrounds. The only question in which this liberal tendency does not come through is in the one on a government guarantee of a job and a decent living standard. It would appear that there is some ambiguity in the outlooks of many upward mobiles, some being devoted to "self-help" and at the same time being willing to have the government help in the case of medical needs or to provide "enabling" education.[11]

Class Identifications

Many commentators have claimed that the lower-middle class "identifies" as middle class. Implicit in this viewpoint is the assumption that such people avoid any suggestion of working-class behaviors or connections. The portrayal is one of a rather desperate effort involving fierce and tenacious attachment to all the signs and symbols of middle-class status.

As indicated elsewhere, this view runs into the immediate difficulty that a sizable proportion of lower-middle-class persons respond to the class identification question by identifying with the working class.[12] When the pattern is examined by family background the result that emerges is a very simple one. Only 46 percent ($N = 81$) of those from working-class families currently identify themselves as "middle class." The equivalent figure for those of farm background is 41 percent ($N = 41$), whereas among those who are second-generation middle class, the figure is 73 percent ($N = 66$). As far as this minimal verbal "commitment" goes then, the pattern is rather strikingly at variance with the received notions. Those lower-middle-class persons who had their origins in the middle class tend to identify as middle class. Those who had their origins elsewhere, either in the farm sector or in the working class, show only a very limited propensity to make the expected identification, clear majorities of both groups still choosing to call themselves working class. That presumed fear and anxiety is rather strikingly absent.[13]

The Socioreligious Cleavage

As indicated in Chapter 5, there are very sizable differences in the political outlooks of white Protestants and the other groups in the population, this difference being greatest in the nonmanual ranks. The findings presented thus far in this chapter clearly involve an averaging of two very diverse kinds of experience. It is worthwhile at this point, therefore, to make some inquiry into the role of the socioreligious factor.

An examination of the non-South middle-class ranks looking at background and religion shows the following results (see Table 9.5). Although a majority

TABLE 9.5
The Middle Class by Rank, Background, and Religion (Married, Active, Non-manuals) SRC 1964

	Lower Middles			Upper Middles		
Father's Occupation:	Manual Worker	Farm	Middle Class	Manual Worker	Farm	Middle Class
Religion	Non-South					
Protestant	53%	76%	56%	51%	83%	50%
Catholic	39	17	32	43	11	28
Jewish	2	...	10	4	...	11
Other	6	7	2	2	6	12
N =	(83)	(46)	(68)	(47)	(18)	(76)
	South					
Protestant	94%	95%	75%	70%	79%	81%
Catholic	6	5	17	26	21	17
Jewish	...	...	...	4	...	2
Other	...	...	8	...	...	...
N =	(17)	(38)	(12)	(23)	(14)	(42)

of the upward mobiles in both upper- and lower-middle class are Protestants, there is a very sizable Catholic minority. Those of farm background are, as one might expect, overwhelmingly Protestant. And those of middle-class background are also heavily Protestant, the Protestant-Catholic ratio here being approximately two-to-one.[14] This second-generation middle-class category also contains most of the Jews in the non-South middle class.

In the South all categories are heavily Protestant. In all three categories of the upper-middle class, however, there is a fair-sized Catholic minority. Middle-class Catholics in the South, interestingly enough, tend to be located in the upper-middle class.

There is some possibility that the results that we have presented thus far in this chapter in "class" terms might well be caused by the socioreligious composition of the various categories being considered. A separate examination of the party identifications of the white Protestants and the others indicates once again the substantial division between the two groups (see Table 9.6).

TABLE 9.6
Party Identification and Class Identification in the Middle Class by Rank, Background and Socioreligious Category (Married, Active, Non-South Non-manuals) SRC 1964

Father's Occupation:	Lower Middles			Upper Middles		
	Working Class	Farm	Middle Class	Working Class	Farm	Middle Class
Socioreligious category	*Percent identifying as Democrats*					
	(of two-party choices)					
White Protestant	62%	53%	36%	29%	47%	28%
N =	(42)	(30)	(33)	(21)	(15)	(32)
All others	87	91	67	55	a	62
N =	(37)	(11)	(27)	(22)	(3)	(39)
	Percent identifying as middle class					
	(of those with responses)					
White Protestant	54	50	76	70	67	80
N =	(41)	(28)	(37)	(20)	(15)	(35)
All others	37.5	23	69	60	a	86
N =	(40)	(13)	(29)	(25)	(3)	(35)

a Small number of cases.

In addition, we see the same fair-sized political party differences by background within both the lower-middle-class segments, both the second-generation middle-class subgroups being the most Republican. We also find a relative absence of differentiation by background within both upper-middle-class subgroups.

For a number of reasons it seems unlikely that the pattern shown in Table 9.6 will continue unchanged in the years ahead. It is likely that with developing bureaucratization of firms and increased size and differentiation in the cities, the lower-middle-class white Protestants of working-class background will be more and more "detached" from the traditional Protestant linkages and consequently will be free to adopt the more liberal political values present in their milieu. If the barriers in the upper-middle class were broken down there would be some possibility for the "others," the previously excluded Catholics and Jews, to associate with the upper-middle-class white Protestants. It is possible that there might be some assimilation of white Protestant political outlooks were these formal and informal barriers to fall.

In the short run, an opposite development appears to have been stimulated among the upper-middle-class "others" by the Goldwater candidacy. If we take the Republican identifiers as constituting the basic potential of that party and chart additions or losses of voters with respect to that level, we find, as has been noted many times by now, that there were near across-the-board losses suffered in this election. We saw, however, that the upper-middle class, particularly those of farm and middle-class background, held strong at this "basic" level in the 1964 campaign. Separate consideration by socioreligious category shows a hidden divergence here. There was actually a slight gain for the Republicans in this white Protestant subgroup. There was, moreover, only a very limited loss among the white Protestants of working-class origins. Among Catholics and Jews in the upper-middle class, there were, in percentage terms, considerable Republican losses.[15] Within both the second-generation and upward mobile subgroups the Democrats registered very large gains. Almost all of the shifting among the upward mobile group noted earlier is to be found among this "other" group, that is, from among those Catholics and Jews coming from working-class origins. The Republicans had, over the years, attracted votes of upper-middle-class Catholics and Jews. The choice of candidate and themes in 1964, however, drove many of these more recent adherents back into their traditional party.

The pattern of class identification also differs by "pillar." With one exception, the white Protestants are more likely to identify as "middle class" than are the others (also shown in Table 9.6). Within each pillar and class segment, it is the second-generation group that is most strongly identified with the middle class. This indicates that a "pure" class analysis is inadequate. It also suggests that the claims about the special anxieties of new arrivals, particularly of the newer ethnics just "up" from the working class, do not appear supported. Once again it appears to be a case of a claim being appropriate for the white Protestants but not for others.

The formulation used thus far in this discussion has focused on the "outsiders" or newcomers and neglected the "insiders." This latter group, the white Protestant upper-middle class, is unusual in many ways. They are the main *committed* bearers of the minority political orientation.[16] Theirs is the only context in which the newcomers, the upward mobiles, both adopt and for the most part retain the political outlook of the more permanent occupants of the rank. And also, they are a group characterized by a peculiar political immobility. All other groups outside the South show a distinctive reaction to the 1964 campaign. Only this one remains unmoved. This would suggest either the very special isolation of this group from the events and influences touching others in the society or, alternatively, that they possess some very special "internal" controls, that is, a different character structure. It is, of course, also possible that both conditions obtain. One other unusual characteristic of the group has already been mentioned—their extreme conservatism on domestic liberalism issues.[17] This orientation (for example, the heavy opposition to federal aid to education) is difficult to reconcile with the widespread assumption that these educated, upper-middle-class populations are characterized by a sense of "responsibility."

Emerging Patterns: Structural Changes

What may one expect in the future? If the future were to involve a continuous expansion of the upper-middle-class ranks, there probably would also be continued addition of "new" elements and some conversion of those upward mobiles just as in the past. If there were to be a continuous "upgrading" of skill levels, an increase in the demand for managerial and technical talent, something of that sort might occur. Even that kind of change, however, in all likelihood would involve little more than a change in the *relative* size of the upper-middle class rather than some wholesale transformation of the entire society. That is, it seems unlikely that the proportion of managers, professionals, and technicians will, in the foreseeable future, ever be more than a small minority of the population.

It is useful to review some of the relevant evidence. Most of the discussions of the "big changes" in modern societies have stressed the role of automation; in this connection they have focused on the impact of automation in the factory, arguing a reduction in the number of blue-collar jobs. This emphasis, however, overlooks a parallel and perhaps even more significant development of automation in the office.

One study of office automation investigated the effects in a wide range of firms in the San Francisco area and came to the following conclusions. On the whole, a firm using electronic data processing (EDP) equipment created one new job for every five that were terminated. The lesson obviously, is one of drastic reductions in the need for white-collar personnel. For the most part, since the equipment was brought in over a period of some years and was operated simultaneously with the old-style data processing until the system was debugged, there were few firings necessary. One simply did not hire and, in the course of time, the usual attrition solved the problem of redundant labor.

For the most part, the jobs eliminated were those involving routine clerical work, such as payroll, billing, filing, inventory and so forth. Large numbers of typists, calculating machine operators, and file clerks disappeared from the office. It will be noted that most of these positions are filled by women and that ordinarily there is a high turnover in such jobs—hence the relative ease with which the attrition process "solved" the problem.[18]

A more difficult problem involves supervising management and the personnel departments. With the numbers of routine office operatives drastically reduced, the need for supervisors and office managers is also diminished. In turn, there is less need for a large personnel staff as the demand for high-turnover labor is reduced.

The character of the work is significantly changed. In place of the former masses of routine clerical workers there are now a relatively small number of key punch operators. This work has very low skill requirements with speed and accuracy being the main essentials. These jobs, too, are mostly held by women. The need for supervision, as noted, is reduced and the task for the remaining managers consists largely of maintaining the data flow and checking for error.

The only other major change in personnel is the addition of a programming staff. This group is described, even for a relatively large enterprise, as constituting only a very small "committee." Both the numbers involved and the skill requirements of programmers are frequently exaggerated. It should be remembered that the tasks involved are routine and that for such operations one works out basic programs. Once worked out, the subsequent demands with respect to billing or payroll are not going to be all that great. Some suggestion as to the actual skill requirements of programmers is given by consideration of their previous careers. One such staff contained an ex-farmer, a cellist, a former tabulating machine operator, an ex-key punch operator, a girl from the secretarial ranks, and a math major with a M.A. degree. The latter was considered to be the least competent in the group.

The use of EDP equipment leads to some centralization of operations. Rather than having a number of regional offices, it becomes possible and advantageous to bring all operations into one center. Within the new center, there are some important further transformations affecting the character of office work and the position of those employed there. Frequently, because of the size and requirements of the new data processing equipment, a new location is needed for this part of the office. Unless a completely new building is involved, especially designed for this operation, the alternative is to remove the data processing operations from the front office into somewhat drab fringe areas just outside the central business district. The rents there are low (or the buildings less expensive) and remodeling can easily be done to suit the user. In short, the front or downtown office is split up with the executive offices remaining in the central business district and the clerical work being removed elsewhere. Paralleling the experience with capital intensive production in the blue-collar sphere, here, too, there is a considerable incentive for the firm to operate the new machinery around the clock. In short, shift work comes to the office.[19]

There would seem to be every likelihood that the development described here would accentuate the cleavage already existing between the lower- and upper-middle classes.[20] The pre-automation office allowed opportunities for mobility to men of working-class origins. They could, in some contexts, begin as office managers, supervising eight or ten women employees, and from there work up to positions of greater responsibility and higher earnings. Such jobs, obviously, do not lead to top management positions, but they do provide a large range of "opportunity" in middle- and low-level management ranks. When the large numbers of women are removed from the office, however, that "opportunity" is removed simultaneously. Those who remain at the lower levels of the hierarchy will, in all likelihood, be involved in the work of the new, physically removed, data processing division and they will also be involved in shift work. The possibility of moving from one office to the other, in terms of career possibilities, would clearly be diminished. As for "personal influence," that is, contact with and emulation of the top executives in the front office, that possibility too is sharply reduced when the locations are so widely separated. The "old" office, conceivably, provided a setting that encouraged deference and emulation, including in particular the acquisition of the employer's political perspectives. This new office, it would appear, provides the basis for a separate consciousness.

Basically the new arrangements reduce the number of paths by which one can travel "upwards" in the social structure.

In addition to knowing the "terrain," however, a complete account must also consider the pattern or, more specifically, the changing pattern of "population settlement." In times past, fertility has varied inversely with class level. Stated simply, this means that, formerly, poorer people had larger families than richer ones.

Given that roughly half of the upper-middle-class offspring are girls, and that among the boys there would be some who do not "enter the firm" (either through lack of interest or because lacking in capability), the result has been the creation of openings that had to be "filled from below."

That inverse relationship between class and fertility, however, is in the process of changing. The conclusion of one leading work on the subject described the situation as follows: "In the United States as a whole there tended to be a direct relation of children ever born to husband's income among white married women under 25 years old and an inverse relation among those 30 years of age and over. There was virtual equality of average number of children by income of husband among women 25–29 years of age."[21]

The reversal of the historic pattern would have different implications for mobility depending on its specific character. If the fertility of all groups were drastically reduced with that of the poorest families being most affected and that of the high-income groups least, there would be a still greater shortage of eligible upper-middle-class sons available to take over the top and middle management positions than is now the case. If, however, the change resulted from a decrease in the average family size among lower-income groups and an increase in family size among the more affluent, that change would obviously increase the number of upper-middle-class sons available and simultaneously reduce the chances for those further down in the social structure. The actual development is closer to the latter picture than to the former. With respect to the key consideration, the size of the typical upper-middle-class family, the pattern is clear, namely, one of absolute increase in size. This conclusion is based on a comparison of the size of families of professionals and of managers, officials, and proprietors in 1910 with those in 1960. The size of these families is not so great as to allow their filling of all upper-middle-class positions; the point concerns their *relative* ability. The size of both the professional and the managerial categories is greater in 1960 and with larger average sized families, the possibilities for internal recruitment are clearly going to be at least somewhat enhanced.[22]

"The middle class," to summarize, turns out to be comprised of many different kinds of persons. There is, first, the division, shown throughout these chapters, between an upper- and a lower-middle class. It is clear that there is no hard-and-fast "line" separating the two. It seems likely, however, that they tend to be separated by geography, by background, and by contemporary jobs and job expectations. Rather than thinking of these ranks as providing a more or less permanent condition for its members, it is important to recognize the movements undergone in the course of a typical career. People of upper-middle-class backgrounds receive the best educations and then commence on the most well-paying careers.[23] Such a career involves some kind of a "humble" beginning, a "lower-middle class" clerical job probably being the most frequent starting point. This kind of start, however, unlike the case of other lower middles, is planned to lead quickly to other jobs, these having considerably greater incomes and standing.

Another group of lower-middle-class jobs do not and are not intended to lead to promotion. Some of these more or less permanent lower-middle-class families, through the efforts of second and third earners, do make out relatively well financially in mid-career. The additional efforts put them, temporarily, into a higher income bracket. Such "episodes" in lower-middle-class careers might easily give rise to misleading conclusions with respect to the study of political party preferences and issue orientations since the definition of middle-class subcategories purely in terms of income artificially "blurs" the division within the middle class.

Because of the problems of delineation, it is difficult to show the stability or change in the recruitment of subgroups within the middle class. We have, however, presented some argument suggesting that because of demographic and technological changes there is likely to be more "internal" recruitment in the future.

In addition to the pure "class" analysis, it was found, repeating what was shown before, that both the upper- and lower-middle classes may be divided along the socioreligious dimension, the white Protestant groups being consistently more Republican and also more prone to identify themselves as middle class. There would appear to be separate middle-class structures for Catholics, Protestants, and Jews, a point that merely extends along the occupational dimension the notion of the "triple melting pot."[24] It seems likely on the whole, that one hundred and fifty years of nativist episodes together with the recurrent efforts of conservative Republican campaigns have done much to maintain the distinctiveness of the "out" groups.

The Trend Question: Personal Influences

It has been argued above that because of the growing separation of the classes within the cities, because of the differences in careers and the different locations of those careers, it is likely that the outlooks of lower-middle and upper-middle classes will, over time, show even greater divergence. In the smaller communities and smaller workplaces of former times there was frequent occasion for contact between owners and managers, on the one hand, and the dependent employees, on the other. With the growth of city size and development of the firm, the physical distances increase and the number of intervening layers of hierarchy also increase, which reduces the chances for effective influence "downward" in the social structure or "down" across the organizational ranks. At the same time this development means that the previously dependent and the previously influenced groups now come to have a degree of autonomy that was rare in times past. Given also a heavy influx of members from contexts still more distant from the upper and upper-middle classes, that is, from the working class and farm ranks, it would not be too surprising to find the "lower-middle class" developing a substantially new and different political orientation.

The trend question has also been discussed (with very different conclusions) in the revisionist Marxist framework, that is, in the intellectual development that eventually formed the core of contemporary "centrist" social science theorizing. In that view, it will be remembered, the line separating the manuals from the nonmanuals is believed to be of central importance. It is assumed that the modal political orientations are sharply differentiated along that line with conservatism dominant in the middle classes and liberalism and/or leftism dominant among the workers. The position of groups or individuals relative to that "line" is fundamental for all such analyses.

A leading contemporary variation on this theme has argued that the attitudes found on the nonmanual side of the line have permeated into the skilled working-class ranks. This extension of the middle-class orientations has resulted in the formation of a broad "middle mass." The persons within the "middle mass" are thought to share in common not only the majority value orientations, but also basically similar life chances. Only the upper class and the lower, or "under class," are left out of this broad consensus.

The analysis presented thus far in this work has indicated the inadequacy of both the theme and the variation. As far as the class dimension is concerned, it has been shown here that the major line of division is not between manuals and nonmanuals, nor between the semiskilled and the skilled. Instead, the most significant division appears between and lower- and the upper-middle classes. Rather than the orientations of the middle class permeating the upper ranks of the working class, something of the opposite appears to be the case. The political orientations of the working class are increasingly present within the lower-middle class.

This change may be seen by examination of the class cleavages within the pillars when divided into younger and older age categories. Among the older, non-South, white Protestants, the conventional viewpoint is supported; there, the greatest difference is between the manuals and the nonmanuals and also one finds little difference between the upper- and the lower-middle classes (see Table 9.7.) In the younger group of white Protestants the picture is strikingly

TABLE 9.7
Party Identification and 1964 Vote by Class, Socioreligious Status and Age: Non-South (Married, Active) SRC 1964

Age:	White Protestants		All Others	
	To 44	45 or More	To 44	45 or More
	Percent identifying as Democrats			
Upper middles	28%	35%	60%	54%
N =	(39)	(31)	(40)	(24)
Lower middles	56	41	81	77
N =	(70)	(37)	(58)	(22)
Working	64	69	81	84
N =	(109)	(62)	(91)	(32)
	Percent voting Democratic in 1964			
Upper middles	24%	37%	77%	71%
N =	(34)	(30)	(36)	(24)
Lower middles	61	42	81	83
N =	(57)	(31)	(48)	(24)
Working	73	74	86	86
N =	(86)	(50)	(71)	(29)

different. Most important, the level of Democratic identification is fifteen percentage points higher in the younger lower-middle-class group. This means that the significant cleavage is now between the upper- and lower-middle classes and that the difference between the lower middles and the working class is now minimal. This change is also to be observed with respect to 1964 voting.

This transformation may be summarized easily by looking at the percentage differences between the classes (based on Table 9.7). Taking first the party identifications of the white Protestants, we have the following picture:

Difference Between	*Younger*	*Older*
Upper and lower middle	+28	+ 6
Lower middle and working	+ 8	+28

The equivalent figures showing the differences with respect to 1964 voting are as follows:

Differences Between

Upper and lower middle	+37	+ 5
Lower middle and working	+12	+32

This increase in Democratic sentiment among the younger lower-middle-class white Protestants is due to a change in party preferences within the group. That is, the possibility of changed recruitment may be immediately rejected. The political "inheritances" of both older and younger groups are very similar. The younger group actually report a slightly higher proportion of Republican fathers. But approximately three-tenths of these children of Republican fathers shift to become Democrats (see Table 9.8). The few chil-

TABLE 9.8
Father's and Respondent's Politics by Age: Upper and Lower-Middle Class Non-South White Protestants (Married, Active) SRC 1964

	Age					
	To 44			45 or More		
Father:	Demo-cratic	Repub-lican	DK, NA, Other	Demo-cratic	Repub-lican	DK, NA, Other
Upper-middle respondents						
Democrat	43%[a]	. . .	33%	44%	11%	71%
Independent	5	. . .	. . .	11	11	. . .
Republican	52	100%	67	44	78	29
N =	(21)	(13)	(6)	(9)	(18)	(7)
Lower-middle respondents						
Democrat	78	29	50	63	13	43
Independent	3	3	25	. . .	7	. . .
Republican	19	68	25	37	80	57
N =	(32)	(34)	(8)	(16)	(15)	(7)

[a] Many of these percentages can only be suggestive due to the small number of cases on which they are based.

dren of politically uncommitted fathers fall disproportionately to the Democrats, and there is only a relatively restricted "defection" on the part of the children of Democratic fathers. This net gain for the Democrats is even more striking when we exclude those who are likely to be lower-middle class "temporaries," that is, those who have completed college. Within this small group of temporaries, the net shift is toward the Republicans.

Within the older category of non-South lower-middle-class white Protestants, by contrast, the opposite trend was present; there, the net shift was to the Republicans.

It seems likely that the different developments stem from different social-political influences on the two groups. The older group tends to be located in smaller communities, the younger one in larger cities. Within the larger cities it seems likely that the younger white Protestants tend to be located in "mixed" settings and to lose contact with the more self-enclosed white Protestant communities of their previous experience. As opposed to living in smaller communities, life in the large cities also involves a loss of contact with the upper-middle class so that the political choices and reactions come to depend more on individual judgment or on the cues offered by a different kind of "informal opinion leader" in the new urban milieu.[25]

Within the younger segment of the white Protestant upper-middle class, sizable gains are achieved by the Republicans (also shown in Table 9.8). Approximately half of the children of Democrats in this location convert to the Republicans. There is no conversion in the opposite direction. This pattern of "retained" Republicanism and conversion of the other groups very strongly suggests the isolation of those in this particular milieu. If the pattern of shifting indicated in this study were to continue, the gulf between the white Protestant upper-middle class and the entire remainder of the society would widen. There is good reason for assuming that this is the case and that the class differences within the white Protestant pillar are increasing rather than, as conventionally assumed, decreasing.[26] The implications of this emerging class cleavage will be discussed at greater length in the final chapter.

There is little to be said at present about the other non-South groups. The combined result for Catholics, Jews, and others (also shown in Table 9.7) indicates that in both the older and younger groups the major division has been between the upper- and lower-middle classes. In both age groups the lower-middle-class–working-class division is negligible. There are some indications of a decline in the differences between upper- and lower-middle classes here. This is the result not of a more conservative (or "assimilated") lower-middle class but of a more liberal upper-middle category. The key claim of the revisionist line of theorizing, it will be noted, up to this point has been supported only in the experience among the older white Protestants.[27]

The Southern Exception

Among the dominant white Protestants of the South there appears to be an opposite development under way (see Table 9.9). All three younger segments show a reduction in the level of Democratic identification. The differences among the segments, however, are approximately the same in both age categories. The opposite development appears in the pattern of 1964 voting. The working-class voters for the most part remained with their traditional identifications. There was a significant defection, however, in the lower-

TABLE 9.9
Party Identification and 1964 Vote by Class and Age: Southern White Protestants
(Married, Active) SRC 1964

	Age	
	To 44	45 or More
	Percent identifying as Democrats	
Upper middles	53%	70%
N =	(32)	(23)
Lower middles	71	86
N =	(24)	(28)
Working	81	89
N =	(42)	(19)
	Percent voting Democratic in 1964	
Upper middles	47%	53%
N =	(30)	(19)
Lower middles	44	56
N =	(18)	(18)
Working	76	81
N =	(25)	(16)

middle categories, both old and young, with the result that there was essentially no difference between the lower and upper middles in their voting patterns. There was, on the other hand, a sizable gap between the lower-middle groups and the manuals. There would appear to have been a decided lower-middle-class white "reaction" in the Southern setting resulting in a relatively sharp manual-nonmanual division.[28] This is one of the few instances to be found in this work where a received claim has gained some support.

Because of its potential significance, it is worth undertaking a more detailed examination of this development. While the Goldwater upsurge in the South has some of the characteristics of a "classical" rightist movement, other available evidence does not accord with that picture. Such rightist movements have presumably involved an immense politicization of the electorate. In this case, however, except for the Southern upper-middle class [where the level of those very much interested in the campaign was 66 percent $(N = 86)$] and the Southern black population (where the equivalent high interest ran to 55 percent, $N = 62$), there was remarkably little interest in the campaign. Among the Southern white Protestant lower-middle and working classes, the level of interest was a relatively low 30 percent in both instances $(Ns = 57, 71)$.

The lower-middle-class shift involved the defection of a number of Democrats. Interestingly enough, these shifters also showed a general low level of interest in the campaign. Most of them had made no efforts to convince others; most had not attended meetings. In short, it would appear that this shift was not associated with a high level of interest, mobilization, or involvement. This is indicated also by the fact that many of those who favored Goldwater did not even bother to get out and vote for him. It would appear, instead, that the shift involved apathetic and uncommitted voters rather than devotees of a high-powered movement. This does not mean that the development is unimportant. The votes count and have their effect regardless of the character of the underlying drive. The shifting provides some indication of a potential for rightist mobilization. Conceivably, if this base were organized and mobilized, the political direction would be much more significant than was indicated in the South in 1964. It should also be remembered, however, that in terms of numbers there is a larger group of unmobilized Southern Democrats available for a mobilization in an opposite direction, there being approximately twice as many of these.[29]

The response to the somewhat different appeal of George Wallace in the 1968 campaign will be considered in Chapter 11.

Summary

To put the previous discussion in perspective, it is useful to present a synoptic overview. In discussion of the various class components, some of the "parts" loom rather large. One tends to think, for example, of a sizable "upper-middle class" and of a impressive white Protestant component within the larger category. In fact, however, taking the non-South populations, the white Protestant upper-middle class amounts to only 5.2 percent of the total (see Table 9.10). In part, that small percentage is a function of the arbitrary income line used in that study, but even if a lower level had been available it still would have made a difference of only a few percentage points.

Earlier in this chapter it was indicated that the only segments having Republican majorities were the three upper-middle-class white Protestant subgroups (shown in Table 9.10) and the second-generation lower-middle-class white Protestants. These four categories combined form only about one-tenth of the non-South population and only about three-tenths of the non-South middle class. These rough estimates ought to be considered in conjunction with the belief that the entire middle class is Republican or, at least, that the entire upper-middle class may be so characterized.

These four categories provide a kind of "center" from which Republican influence emanates. The Republicanism of those contained within these categories is of a somewhat different character from that located elsewhere in the society. The resources of those located in the categories (together with those in the white Protestant upper-class ranks) are considerably greater than the overwhelming majority of those elsewhere in the society. The remarkable thing about the Republican "operation" is the ability of this small minority

TABLE 9.10

Distribution of the Non-South Respondents by Class and Socioreligious Categories (Married, Active, Non-South Respondents) NORC 367

	Socioreligious Group							
	White Protestants							
Class	Father Middle Class	Father Farm	Father Working Class	Catholics	Jews	Negroes	Others	
Upper middle	2.6%	1.6%	1.0%	2.9%	1.2%	0.1%	0.5%	9.9%
Lower middle	4.9	3.5	4.6	7.4	1.7	1.0	1.3	24.4
Working	40.3			15.5	0.8	7.1	2.2	65.9
								100.2%
								(N = 1291)

of the population to hold onto and maintain majority and near-majority electoral status in many states and sometimes in the nation.

To give some idea of the character of the Republican "coalition" of forces it is useful to begin with those who are located in these four "center" or "core" categories. Among the married, active, non-South and nonfarm respondents in the 1964 SRC study, there was a total of 224 Republican identifiers. Thirty-one percent of these were white Protestants located in these four "core" categories. Another 13 percent of the Republican identifiers were lower-middle-class white Protestants of working-class and farm background. And a third major source of their identifiers was the additional 26 percent who were white Protestant manual workers. The other three-tenths of the party's basic supply of identifiers are to be found scattered, very thinly, in the other categories of Table 9.10, that is, outside the white Protestant column. Except where Republicans happen to congregated, electoral victories for that party depend on holding "their own" and gaining some Democratic or independent defectors, or, alternatively, hoping to have the differences in turnout be such as to allow a "victory through apathy"—that is, as a result of nonvoting Democrats.

It is important to consider the relationship of the "center" or "core" Re-

TABLE 9.11

Orientations and Characteristics of Two Groups of Republicans (Married, Active, Non-South, Republican Identifiers) SRC 1964

	Republican Identifiers	
	"Core" Group[a]	All Others
Government too powerful (of those with opinions)	81%	65%
$N=$	(58)	(117)
Percent without opinion on government power	16	27
$N=$	(69)	(161)
Oppose medical care	89	65
$N=$	(56)	(126)
Oppose living standard guarantee	88	77
$N=$	(57)	(118)
Voted in all elections	82	75
$N=$	(66)	(138)
Very much interested in the campaign	55	38
$N=$	(69)	(161)
High or medium-high political efficacy	68	44
$N=$	(69)	(161)
Percent for Goldwater	84	62
$N=$	(63)	(133)

[a] Upper-middle-class white Protestants plus those white Protestants who are second generation and lower-middle class.

publicans with those identifiers who may be appropriately described as on the margins or periphery of its "territory." The "core" group might be said to form an "isolated mass." Isolated from the rest of the society, they mutually reinforce each other in their views and thus come to sustain a peculiar and distinctive world outlook. Their separation from the larger society puts them at a distance from the problems found in that society; that distance allows them to know the problems of the society only inexactly, at second hand, and with a minimum of detail (if they are known at all). The isolation of the context also allows them to carry over, perpetuate, and maintain viewpoints that were current and perhaps appropriate in previous generations.[30]

This small minority of the non-South population cannot compete in electoral politics without a large number of allies who are not found in their immediate context. Most of them, as indicated, are to be found further "down" in the white Protestant pillar. There are, in addition, some allies to be found scattered outside that pillar.

The "center" or "core" Republicans appear to be more conscious, convinced, and ideologically oriented. The Republicans-of-the-periphery appear to be more "traditional" in their commitments. Their commitments seem less strong and they are more frequently in conflict with typical Republican issue orientations (see Table 9.11).

The key to the future of the party, were it to gain no new sources of support, would be its ability to maintain the loyalties of this less committed periphery. For a number of reasons touched on throughout this work and particularly in this chapter, the links to the periphery would appear to have been weakened, to have become more tenuous.

Notes

1. The percentages for the four age categories from the 1964 study, going from youngest to oldest are: 38 percent (76), 26 percent (62), 35 percent (40), and 32 percent (25). The equivalent figures from the 1952 study does show increased middle-class recruitment, the figures here being 41 percent (80), 33 percent (84), 30 percent (66), and 20 percent (59).

2. What is needed, obviously, is a detailed study of jobs held over the course of lifetimes. The best work at present that has information on first and present jobs is that of Peter M. Blau and Otis Dudley Duncan, *The American Occupational Structure* (New York: John Wiley & Sons, 1967). Also of some interest is S. M. Lipset and Reinhard Bendix, "Social Mobility and Occupational Career Patterns," *American Journal of Sociology,* **57** (January 1952), 366–374, and (March 1952), 494–504. See, also, S. M. Lipset and F. Theodore Malm, "First Jobs and Career Patterns," *American Journal of Economics and Sociology,* **14** (April 1955), 247–261 and also S. M. Lipset and Reinhard Bendix, *Social Mobility in Industrial Society* (Berkeley: University of California Press, 1959), Chs. 5–7.

3. On the lineman to vice-president pattern see Sidney J. Kaplan, "Up From

the Ranks on a Fast Escalator," *American Sociological Review*, **24** (February 1959), 79–81. Robert Lovett "began" as a "clerk" in the National Bank of Commerce and then worked as a "runner" in his father-in-law's banking and investment firm. Approximately five years later, however, he was a partner in the firm (Brown Brothers) and in the same year (at age 31) he was made a director and member of the executive committee of the Union Pacific Railroad.

His father was an attorney for E. H. Harriman and also, at one time, was president of the Union Pacific. The son was graduated from Yale and spent a year in Harvard Law and another in the Graduate Business School before "beginning as a 'clerk'."

The claiming of humble origins is an age-old game. Charles Dickens portrays one Thomas Gradgrind of Coketown as endlessly parading his self-made being only to be exposed later in the book by his own mother. See his *Hard Times* (Chicago: W. B. Conkey, Co., n.d.). A parallel to the Gradgrind case appears in the case of Lyndon Johnson. Johnson was showing the reporters around the ranch and he stopped in front of "a ruined shanty about the size of a chicken coop." Johnson, it is reported, "stretching forth his hand and speaking in hushed and reverent tones, identified it as the place in which he was reared to manhood. His mother . . . piped up, 'Why Lyndon, you know we had a nice house over on the other side of the farm.'" This is reported in Robert Sherrill, *The Accidental President* (New York: Grossman Publishers, 1967), p. 24. Still another such case is to be found in Erik Erikson, *Young Man Luther* (New York: W. W. Norton, 1958), pp. 51–54.

On the Horatio Alger stories see Richard Wohl, "The 'Rags to Riches Story': An Episode of Secular Idealism," pp. 501–506 of Reinhard Bendix and S. M. Lipset, *Clan, Status, and Party* (New York: The Free Press, 2nd ed., 1966).

On the Wall Street lawyers, see Erwin O. Smigel, *The Wall Street Lawyer* (New York: The Free Press of Glencoe, 1964). The tendency to begin high-level careers in "lower-middle class" positions is indicated in Blau and Duncan, pp. 30–31, 37, 58. Much work in sociology has failed to recognize this use of the lower-middle-class jobs, such as clerical and sales occupations, as the first steps in executive career lines. One recognizes the importance of bureaucracy in modern life and yet fails to consider the basic characteristics of bureaucracies. As Max Weber stated: "The official is set for a 'career' within the hierarchical order of the public service. He moves from the lower, less important, and lower paid to the higher positions." From p. 203 of H. H. Gerth and C. Wright Mills, translators and editors, *From Max Weber: Essays in Sociology* (London: Routledge & Kegan Paul, 1948).

4. The same picture obtains when we considered only the males. About 29 percent ($N = 161$) of the lower-middle-class males are in the youngest cohort as against only 19 percent ($N = 107$) in the upper-middle class. Something similar appears when one examines the census categories. Taking employed males from the 1960 U.S. census we find that 19 percent of both the clerical and sales categories were 24 years of age or younger. This is to be compared with a 3 percent figure for the manager, official, and proprietor category and a 9 percent figure for the professionals. From U.S. Bureau of the Census, *U.S. Census of Population: 1960*. Subject Reports, Occupational Characteristics. Final Report PC (2)–7A. (Washington, D.C.: U.S. Government Printing Office, 1963). Table 6, pp. 71–80.

5. Taking lower-middle-class persons of middle-class background and dividing them into two groups, those 34 or younger and those 35 or older, we find the following (SRC 1964) : 58 percent of the former group ($N = 26$) report having Republican fathers as opposed to 43 percent ($N = 30$) among the latter. About 61 percent ($N = 28$) of the fathers of the former group are reported to have been very much interested in politics as opposed to 45 percent ($N = 33$) among the latter. Considering the respondents' candidate preferences in 1964 (this combines the reported votes with the indicated preferences of the nonvoters), we find 63 percent ($N = 19$) of the younger subgroup favoring Goldwater as opposed to 40 percent among the older groups. Asked about their expected future earnings, the respective percentages indicating things will get better are 86 ($N = 29$) and 57 ($N = 37$). Among the young lower-middle-class persons of farm and working-class background, the proportion expecting things to improve is 80 percent ($N = 44$). There is a similar question in the NORC study No. 367, asking about the expectations in five years. About 92 percent ($N = 52$) of the younger second-generation middle-class respondents expected improvement as opposed to 68 percent ($N = 82$) of those from farm and working-class backgrounds. Forty-two percent of the younger second-generation group report dissatisfaction with the main earner's present income. The equivalent figure for those of farm and working-class background was 32 percent ($N = 84$). A majority of the second-generation group falls in the highest of the lower middle income categories, that is $5000 to $7500, and even in this category the dissatisfaction runs high, being 46 percent ($N = 24$). Those of working-class and farm background tend to be more satisfied at that income level, only 32 percent ($N = 28$) indicating dissatisfaction. At the same level of income there are differences in the expectations with respect to future earnings. Twenty-nine ($N = 24$) and 11 percent ($N = 27$), respectively, expect their earnings to be very much higher in five years. On the other hand, eight and 33 percent, respectively, expect to be earning the same.

6. The percentage reporting working-class backgrounds is greatest in the 35–44 upper-middle-class age category in the NORC 367 study and the 1964 SRC study. A more detailed and extensive consideration of this point appears in my "Einkommen und Klassenstruktur: Der Fall der Bundesrepublik," *Kölner Zeitschrift für Soziologie und Sozialpsychologie*, **20**:2 (1968), 250–287.

7. We have taken upper-middle-class respondents in the 35–44 age category and divided them into those from middle-class families and those from either working-class or farm families. The respective percentages expecting future economic improvement are 71 percent ($N = 21$) and 58 percent ($N = 24$). From the NORC study No. 367 we have the following: nine of thirteen second-generation middle-class families in this age group expect financial improvement in the future. Five of the ten families coming from farm or working-class backgrounds and having two or more earners expect future improvement. The families of middle-class background tend to be disproportionately single-earner families, the figures being 64 percent ($N = 22$) and 55 percent ($N = 22$).

8. The pattern in Table 9.3 may be compared with that shown in Table 8.4. These tables are not entirely comparable since the latter includes only the non-South *white* working class. Four percent of the non-South middle-class respondents are nonwhite.

9. The number of cases is very much reduced in the South. For this reason it does not make much sense to consider the result separately by background. In the lower-middle class, taking first those reporting Democratic fathers, we find only 11 percent ($N = 46$) defecting to the Republicans. Fifty-seven percent ($N = 14$) of the children of Republicans become Democrats. All six of those having fathers with no clear political direction became Democrats.

That is speaking of (Southern) Democratic party identifications. Although there were only 10 Republican identifiers in the Southern lower-middle class, there were 18 Goldwater voters and another 7 who were nonvoters favoring the Goldwater candidacy. However, there still was a Democratic majority within the Southern lower-middle class, 59 percent ($N = 61$) favoring Johnson's candidacy. The same percentage for Johnson appeared in the Southern upper-middle class ($N = 74$). Most of that Democratic edge is contributed by those of working-class and farm background. Among the second-generation Southern upper-middle class the proportion favoring Johnson was only 51 percent ($N = 41$) and among the voters in the same category only 47 percent ($N = 34$).

10. A total of 43 non-South respondents "made good," that is, moved from the working class into the upper-middle class. Exactly 23 of these were children of Democratic fathers and 14 of these changed party identification to become Republicans. Six of the 14 "came back" and voted for Johnson in 1964.

11. The combination of this "conversion" of the upward mobiles together with this "lingering liberalism" means that upper-middle-class *liberal* Republicanism is found disproportionately among those of working-class background. For example, 39 percent ($N = 18$) of the upper-middle-class Republicans of working-class background favor government-supported medical care as opposed to only 18 percent ($N = 39$) among those of middle-class or farm backgrounds. The respective percentages of those favoring the living standard guarantee are 24 percent ($N = 21$) and 9 percent ($N = 35$).

One other point of some interest in this connection involves the attempts at exerting political influence. The upper-middle-class Republicans of working-class backgrounds are less likely to make such efforts (46 percent, $N = 24$). It is the second-generation group, the established upper-middle-class Republicans, who show a high level of political effort (73 percent, $N = 37$).

12. See Richard Hamilton, "The Marginal Middle Class: A Reconsideration," *American Sociological Review*, **31** (April 1966), 192–199. For more recent evidence see Hamilton, *Restraining Myths* . . . , op. cit., Ch. 3.

13. A similar pattern appears in the upper-middle class. Sixty-four percent of those from working-class backgrounds ($N = 45$), identify as middle class. Among the children of farmers the equivalent is 61 percent ($N = 18$). And among the second-generation middle-class group, the figure is 83 percent ($N = 70$). Some of these from working-class backgrounds are probably in lower-middle-class career lines and only temporarily fall here as "upper middle" because of second and third earners.

14. Most of these Protestants are white. As indicated earlier, the number of nonwhites in the middle class is miniscule. For the non-South, the numbers present in the six columns of Table 9.5 are, reading from left to right, 2, 3, 2, 3, 0, and 3.

In the South, only the second and fourth columns contain nonwhites, both of these having four.

15. Taking the non-South upper-middle-class white Protestants of middle-class or farm background, we find only 2 Republican identifiers (out of 28) voting for Johnson. Three of 13 Democrats in this circle came over to vote for Goldwater, and all 3 independents voted for Goldwater. Among the equivalent upward mobile Republicans, we find 4 of 15 voting Democratic. All 3 upward mobile Democrats remained with their party. Taking the equivalent results for the other (that is, other than white Protestant) groups we find that among the second generation plus the farm group, nearly a third of the Republicans shifted their vote (5 of 18) and there was only one (out of 21) Democrat who voted Republican. Among the upward mobiles, 5 of 8 Republicans came to the Democrats as did both independents. No Democrat defected $(N = 11)$.

16. The upper-middle-class subgroup of middle-class background contains a very high proportion of strong Republicans. Among the Republican identifiers 61 percent $(N = 23)$ report a strong commitment. Among the remaining upper-middle-class white Protestants, those from farms or working-class backgrounds, the proportion of strong identifiers is 33 percent $(N = 75)$.

17. See Chapter 5, Table 5.4.

18. That solved the problem for the firm. There would be a problem for the people not hired, mostly young women, wishing to enter the labor force for the first time.

Most of the claims made in this and the following paragraphs are based on the work of Ida R. Hoos, *Automation in the Office* (Washington, D.C.: Public Affairs Press, 1961).

19. Some other accounts pointing generally in the same direction are the following: C. Edward Weber, "The Impact of Electronic Data Processing on Clerical Skills," *Personnel Administration,* **22** (January–February 1959), 20–27; Edgar Weinberg, "Experiences with the Introduction of Office Automation," *Monthly Labor Review,* **83** (April 1960), 376–380; Richard W. Riche and William E. Alli, "Office Automation in the Federal Government," *Monthly Labor Review,* **83** (September 1960), 933–938; Einar Hardin, "The Reactions of Employees to Office Automation," *Monthly Labor Review,* **83** (September 1960), 925–932; Rose Wiener, "Changing Manpower Requirements in Banking," *Monthly Labor Review,* **85** (September 1962), 989–995; and Richard W. Riche and James R. Alliston, "Impact of Office Automation in the Internal Revenue Service," *Monthly Labor Review,* **86** (April 1963), 388–393; see also Ben B. Seligman, *Most Notorious Victory: Man in an Age of Automation* (New York: The Free Press, 1966), Ch. 5.

20. See Harold J. Leavitt and Thomas L. Whisler, "Management in the 1980's," *Harvard Business Review,* **36** (November–December 1958), 41–48. Some consideration of this point also appears in Thomas O'Toole, "White-Collar Automation," *The Reporter,* **29** (December 5, 1963), 21–27; and in C. Edward Weber, "Change in Managerial Manpower with Mechanization of Data-Processing," *Journal of Business,* **32** (April 1959), 151–163.

21. Clyde V. Kisser, Wilson H. Grabill, and Arthur A. Campbell, *Trends and*

Variations in Fertility in the United States (Cambridge: Harvard University Press, 1968), pp. 208.

22. A fragment of the data (from Kiser, et al., p. 186) follows:

Number of children ever born per 1000 women,
white, married, and husband present

Age of wife and occupation of husband	1910	1940	1960
30–34			
Professional	1820	1321	2377
Manager, official, proprietor	2206	1526	2465

The same pattern appears in the still younger cohorts. An opposite pattern appears in the older ones.

23. Another conception deserving correction is the notion that the middle class generally is *the* educated class. It is true that most of those with higher education are in the middle class. The opposite, however, is not the case, namely, the assumption that most of the middle class are college educated. The data follow:

Married, Active, Non-South Middle-Class Respondents (SRC 1964)

	Father's Occupation		
	Manual	Farm	Nonmanual
	Percent who have completed college		
Upper-middle class	36%	28%	45%
$N =$	(47)	(18)	(76)
Lower-middle class	11	2	31
$N =$	(83)	(46)	(64)

24. The idea of the "triple melting pot" stems from some research on inter-religious marriage by Ruby Jo Reeves Kennedy, see her "Single or Triple Melting Pot? Intermarriage Trends in New Haven, 1870–1940," *American Journal of Sociology*, **49** (January 1944), 331–339, and "Single or Triple Melting Pot? Intermarriage in New Haven, 1870–1950," *American Journal of Sociology*, **58** (July 1952), 56–59. The idea has been popularized in Will Herberg, *Protestant-Catholic-Jew* (Garden City: Doubleday, 1955).

25. Taking the younger white Protestants, we find that those who remain Republican (like their fathers) tend to be small towners (48 percent; $N = 23$) and tend to be regular or frequent churchgoers (61 percent; $N = 23$). Those who shift to the Democrats tend to be located either in big or middle-sized cities (seven of ten) and tend to be irregular in church attendance (only five of the ten being regular or frequent in attendance).

26. Examination of the non-South white Protestant upper-middle class in the 1964 SRC study showed the younger members less approving of government aid to education, less approving of a government medical care program, and more sus-

picious of the power of big government than the older equivalent group. There was, surprisingly enough, a small increase in the percentage favoring the government living standard guarantee. By comparison, looking at the equivalent lower-middle class, there was no difference between old and young on three of the issues and a fair-sized increase in the percentage favoring the living standard guarantee. The younger white Protestant workers showed increased liberalism in response to three of the questions, but were somewhat more conservative on the distant "government power" question. On the whole, then, the upper-middle class appears to be getting more conservative and the lower middles and working class are either standing still or becoming more liberal.

27. The class differences in party identification among the other groups (that is, other than white Protestants) are as follows:

	Age	
Differences	*To 44*	*45 or more*
Upper and lower middle	+21	+23
Lower middle and working	0	+7

The differences in 1964 voting are

Upper and lower middle	+4	+12
Lower middle and working	+5	+3

28. The voting indicated in Table 9.9 underestimates the size of the "defection" since among the nonvoters in both the lower-middle class and the working class there were some significant additions of "unrealized" Goldwater strength. This strength is almost exclusively among the younger white Protestants there. The Goldwater movement in the South was something of a youth movement.

29. Of the 70 nonvoters located in the South, 52 favored Johnson and 18 were for Goldwater. Even among the white Protestants, the majority was for Johnson.

30. This notion of the "isolated mass" has, for the most part, been applied only to working-class populations. It seems equally if not more useful in the analysis of upper-middle-class subgroups, elites, and large academic enclaves. For the classic discussion of this topic, see Clark Kerr and Abraham Siegel, "The Interindustry Propensity to Strike—An International Comparison," 189–212 of Arthur Kornhauser, Robert Dubin, and Arthur M. Ross, eds., *Industrial Conflict* (New York: McGraw-Hill, 1954).

10

Class, Income, and Living Standards

There is little else that can be offered from the available studies with respect to the political transformations of the manual, lower-middle, and upper-middle categories. An alternative line of analysis that concerns the same questions involves claims about incomes and living standards. This view assumes the existence of a trend toward the equalization of incomes. That development, presumably, provides the basis for the acquisition of equivalent life-styles. It is this improvement in the condition of manual workers, this creation of "middle-class" workers, that has reduced the objective class differences and provided the basis for a broad "moderate" or "middle ground" consensus. This viewpoint, sometimes referred to as "economism," assumes that political outlooks are more or less direct responses to economic conditions, that is, apart from the influence of received political traditions, party positions, political activists, and mass media efforts.

The basic general orientation of the present work, by comparison, has not put the primary stress on income. Instead, it has been argued that the most important factor will be social pressures or influences. Implicit in this notion is the assumption that the political orientations may be relatively independent of income fluctuations.[1] This is, perhaps, best indicated by the fact that in a period characterized by general improvement in income levels the proportion of Democratic party identifiers has been more or less constant.

It is worthwhile undertaking a rather detailed exploration of the question of class and income. In the conventional centrist formulations it is assumed that at some time in the past there was a wide separation of middle-class and working-class income levels. In recent decades, however, the tendency has been toward convergence and overlap.

With the materials at hand, it is difficult to make any assessment of the convergence claim. Most such accounts merely assume the disparity in the past rather than presenting evidence on the subject. Because of that difficulty, most of the attention in this chapter will be given to the indisputable fact of the contemporary picture—that there is considerable overlap of the manual and nonmanual income distributions. There may, however, be some grounds for reconsideration of the significance of that overlap, a question to be considered below.

Overlapping Income Distributions

If we take the $5000 cutting line in the 1952 study (a line close to the nonmanual median), we find 24 percent of the working-class families were above that level (see Table 10.1). Approximately one-quarter of the working-class families were better off than the "average" middle-class family or, more precisely, were better off than half of the middle-class families. To that extent there was "overlap" or, to cite the cliché of the day, a "blurring of class lines."

On the other extreme, the poor side of the middle class, we find a very large portion of that group falling into the lowest income categories. It is clear that any suggestion of a uniformly affluent middle class is far from adequate. On the basis of the arbitrary dividing line used in this work, only 20 percent of the nonmanuals were "upper-middle class" as of 1952, that is, having a family income of $7500 or more. Roughly half of the nonmanuals might be labeled at best "middle-middles," falling between $5000 and $6000. At that time nearly one-third of the nonmanual ranks outside the South made less than $4000. At that same time, just over half of the non-South manual families earned less than $4000. In the following years there is an upward movement but the relationship between manuals and nonmanuals remains constant.[2]

The Well-Off Workers

While there is some similarity in the distributions, that appearance hides some important differences in details. To illustrate, one may consider a key group—the well-off workers. Who are they and what kind of circumstances put them into the high-income brackets? The answer to these questions are quite simple. They are in families having more than one earner. Taking the National Opinion Research Center study and looking at those with an "upper-middle-class" earning level ($7500 or more), we find 72 percent ($N = 58$) reporting two or more earners. As may be seen in Table 10.2, there is a very sharp direct relationship between working-class income and the porportion of second earners.

The equivalent picture for the nonmanuals is very irregular. The most important finding is that in the highest income category we find two-thirds of the middle class families "making it" on the basis of the main earner's efforts alone. The second or third earners appear in only a minority of the high-income middle-class families. Apart from the head, the other members of these middle-class families are free of gainful employment. Roughly nine out of ten of the equivalent working-class families, by comparison, have second and third earners.[3]

The lessons appear to be very simple. Affluent working-class families are

TABLE 10.1
Class and Family Income, Non-South (Married, Active, Families)

	Family Income									
	$2999 or Less	$3000–3999	$4000–4999	$5000–5999	$6000–7499	$7500–9999	$10,000–14,999	$15,000 or More	=100%	*N*
SRC 1952										
Nonmanual	13%	19%	18%	30%		12%	8%		= 100%	(367)
Manual	19	34	23	20		3	1		= 100	(427)
NORC 1955										
Nonmanual	7	10	21	34		14	15		= 101	(441)
Manual	21	22	26	24		5	2		= 100	(847)
SRC 1964										
Nonmanual	4		6	11	14	23	27	14	= 99	(349)
Manual	10		8	13	27	27	13	2	= 100	(320)

TABLE 10.2
Number of Earners by Class and Family Income (Married, Active, Non-South)
NORC 367—1955

	Family Income					
	To $2999	$3000– 3999	$4000– 4999	$5000– 7499	$7500– 9999	$10,000 or More
	Percent of families having two or more earners					
Nonmanual	31%	26%	27%	35%	51%	31%
N =	(29)	(43)	(92)	(150)	(63)	(64)
Manual	34	39	39	56	66	93
N =	(179)	(184)	(222)	(205)	(44)	(14)

not like equivalent middle-class families. The majority of well-off working-class families achieve "affluence" through a greater expenditure of effort. Where the wives and children of the well-off middle-class families are free for leisure activities, their working-class "peers" are at work. The determinants of income, moreover, in the typical middle-class case are linked to the head's job and career. In the typical working-class case the family's "affluence" is dependent also on the wife's job and her "career." The stability of such incomes and the expectations for the future are likely to be quite different. It is clear that if a "trend toward equality" were based on these diverse experiences, the end result would still not be equality.[4]

Income Satisfaction of Manual Workers

All too frequently discussions of income make unrealistic assumptions about the "objectivity" of the subject. One assumes simply that those who are poorly paid will be dissatisfied and will react accordingly. The evidence at hand provides an immediate challenge to such an assumption. The Survey Research Center's question provided respondents with three options, asking whether they were "pretty well" satisfied with their financial situation, more or less satisfied, or not satisfied.[5] Taking for this purpose the non-South manual workers in 1964, we find that in the lowest paid category, those under $4000, roughly one-quarter say they are pretty well satisfied and another two-fifths say they are more or less satisfied (see Table 10.3). Only one in three report dissatisfaction with their financial circumstances. This is not to gainsay the expected direct relationship between income and satisfaction. The point to be noted here is that even at the lowest income level there is a majority indicating some degree of satisfaction.[6]

For all the talk about rising expectations and the assumption of envious, appetitive masses, it is ironic that in all segments of "the masses" the majority response is at least some degree of satisfaction as opposed to outright dissatisfaction. For most of the income categories, two-fifths or more indicated the

TABLE 10.3
Family Income and Satisfaction with Income: Non-South Manual Workers
(Married, Active) SRC 1964

Satisfaction with income	\	\	\	Family Income	\	\	\
	To $3999	$4000–4999	$5000–5999	$6000–7499	$7500–9999	$10,000–14,999	$15,000 or More
Pretty well	23%	44%	40%	40%	50%	70%	33%[a]
More or less	43	37	47	38	39	30	67[a]
Not satisfied	33	19	12	22	11	...	...
N =	(30)	(27)	(42)	(86)	(84)	(40)	(6)

[a] Note the small N.

higher level of satisfaction (that is, they were "pretty well" satisfied). The other point to be noted is that at the lower levels of income there must be some framework that allows what is objectively a very low and inadequate income to be interpreted by the respondents as "satisfactory."

Part of the explanation is relatively simple. Income levels vary directly with city size.[7] The high-paid jobs, for both manuals and nonmanuals, are to be found in the large communities. Costs of living, primarily the costs of food and housing, also follow the same pattern. At a given level of income, in short, it is easier to "make do" in the smaller communities. When we examine the pattern of satisfaction by income level and city size we find that with two exceptions (both involving small numbers of cases) the workers in middle-sized cities and small towns indicate fairly high levels of satisfaction and that the big-city workers indicate relatively low satisfaction.[8] (See Table 10.4.)

It is possible that one might have official statistics indicating rising real incomes and at the same time have either constant or declining satisfactions as far as the subjective appreciations are concerned. The processes of industrial-

TABLE 10.4
Family Income and Satisfaction with Income by Size of Place, Non-South Manual
Workers (Married, Active) SRC 1964

Size of Place	\	\	Family Income	\	\	\
	To $3999	$4000–4999	$5000–5999	$6000–7499	$7500–9999	$10,000–or More
	Percent "pretty well" satisfied with income					
Large city	38%	31%	29%	28%	38%	67%
N =	(13)	(13)	(17)	(46)	(40)	(27)
Middle-sized city, small town	12	57	48	53	61	63
N =	(17)	(14)	(25)	(40)	(44)	(19)

ization or of "modernization" have the consequence of moving workers out of a setting that, as seen previously, is associated with some greater degree of conservatism. It also has the consequence of moving them out of a setting in which they have significantly greater satisfaction with their incomes.[9] Calculations of income levels that fail to take into account the movement of populations from small towns to cities would overlook this peculiar source of dissatisfaction.[10]

The situation is actually somewhat more complicated. One moves to where the jobs are. The dwindling of "opportunities" in small towns pushes people out of those locations. There can be little doubt that having a job in a larger city must be more satisfying than not having one in a small town. At the same time, it does seem likely that were jobs equally available and equally rewarded in cities and towns, there would be considerably less movement to the cities and simultanously there would be considerably greater satisfaction with any given amount of income.[11]

There is little systematic connection between satisfaction with income and party identification. Among the large-city manuals, for example, 22 percent ($N = 37$) of those who were pretty well satisfied favored the Republicans and among the dissatisfied the level of Republican support was about the same— 19 percent ($N = 27$). In the combined results for the middle-sized cities and the small towns there was some systematic relationship; the Republicanism of the pretty well satisfied amounted to 32 percent ($N = 63$), of the more or less satisfied, it was 27 percent ($N = 48$), and among the dissatisfied, it was only 19 percent ($N = 16$). A closer examination of the relationship in this context showed even this confirmation of an age-old thesis to be spurious. The satisfaction-conservatism relationship appeared only among those respondents having a Republican father. And within this context the dynamics of the relationship appear to be somewhat different from those conventionally assumed. Almost all of the Republican children of Republican fathers are white Protestants and they also tend to be regular churchgoers. Those having only limited satisfaction or dissatisfaction with their incomes tend to be irregular churchgoers and it is these who defect to the Democrats. The relationship appears to be the result of differential involvement in a conservatising milieu. Those who make it economically, possibly, are able to maintain those involvements. Those who lose out become subject to new and different political influences.

A Note on Recent Trends

As already mentioned, there is a widespread acceptance of the idea that incomes are moving toward equality. This tendency is, in turn, viewed as providing the basis for a wider, more general satisfaction within the society. Since, as also indicated, there are occasions where the statistics "say" one thing and the subjects "feel" another. it is worth inquiring as to the public perception of the trends.

If there were an equalizing trend in process this would mean that those in the lower income categories should be more likely to report recent financial improvement than those in the higher brackets. Also, expectations for improvement in the future should, if not mistaken, vary inversely with current income.

The actual reports do not accord with that expectation (see Table 10.5).

TABLE 10.5
Family Income and Expectations for the Future (Married, Active, Non-South) SRC 1964

	Family Income						
	To $3999	$4000– 4999	$5000– 5999	$6000– 7499	$7500– 9999	$10,000– 14,999	$15,000 or More
In the last few years financial situation has been "getting better"							
Nonmanuals	29%	55%	47%	58%	56%	71%	74%
N =	(14)	(22)	(36)	(50)	(80)	(94)	(49)
Manuals	43	44	67	47	63	64%	
N =	(30)	(27)	(42)	(86)	(86)	(47)	
In the next few years financial situation will "get better"							
Nonmanuals	58	48	69	67	61	57	59
N =	(12)	(21)	(36)	(49)	(78)	(90)	(46)
Manuals	37	56	58	54	66	44	
N =	(30)	(25)	(40)	(84)	(80)	(45)	

Looking first at the nonmanuals, the pattern with respect to income changes over the last few years shows some tendency to vary directly rather than inversely with current income.[12] More specifically, in four of the seven income categories there is little significant difference by income level. In the upper-middle-class ranks one finds the highest level of positive reports. The working-class pattern is less regular: the lowest levels of reported improvement are also found in the lowest income categories. As far as these reports are concerned, the aggregate picture is one of the rich getting richer.

The pattern of the future expectations also does not accord with the assumed trend. On the whole, there is little clear variation by income level in the percentage anticipating improvement within the non-South middle-class ranks. Within the manual ranks the relationship also does not fit the picture necessary for the development of a "leveling" trend. Here the relationship is curvilinear, the middle-income workers tending to have the highest expectations and majorities of both the very poor and the very best-off workers tending rather to expect things to stay the same.

Of greatest importance, perhaps, is the contrast between the well-off middle class (that is, the upper-middle class as defined in this work) and the "equivalent" working-class populations.[13] A majority of the former group expect improvement whereas the majority of the latter expect things to stay as they are. These modal expectations do not accord with a picture of emerging equality. One might argue that these expectations have a tenuous or unrealistic basis; this might (or might not) be the case.[14] On the other hand, since it is the individual perception and understanding of reality that provides the basis for action rather than some distant, unknown, "objective" reality, this presentation might be the more "realistic" consideration.

Income and Careers

Earlier it was suggested that the key circumstance differentiating the lives and careers of upper- and lower-middle-class families was the kind of job held by the main earner. The major consideration is whether the main earner has a job that is intended as training for a series of subsequent advances or whether the job "leads nowhere." Jobs in the former career line are located low in the hierarchy but, as Weber pointed out, that beginning is merely a first step in a planned series of moves that would ordinarily take the individual ever higher in the hierarchy and would provide ever greater financial rewards. The second career type, the more conventional lower-middle-class job, involves performance of the same routine tasks throughout one's entire career. These jobs are, in a sense, the office equivalent of factory work.

At present, it is impossible to get a precise delineation of "uppers" and "lowers" according to this distinction. The division based on an arbitrary income line was a first and, certainly, rather crude approximation to allow exploration of some received claims about class and to indicate the need for a more precise specification. An alternative *approximation* to a definition in terms of career patterns involves the separation of the nonmanual group by background. Those persons who issue from the middle class are very much favored in terms of education, jobs, and income. We have also seen that they tend to be different in terms of their political orientations.

Families in favored circumstances are in a position to pass the favors on to their children. There was once a time when this pass-on was direct. The father, an independent businessman, simply brought his son (or son-in-law) into the firm and gave him the choice position as successor. The current situation is somewhat different given the role of a new "intervening" institution, the universities. In many accounts the change is portrayed as a shift from a "personalistic" (nepotistic) arrangement to one wherein "talent" is rewarded. This overlooks the details of the new situation.

Upper-middle-class children are raised in class-segregated housing areas and attend the school of that area. Children of that milieu, with relatively infrequent exceptions, simply "go" to college more or less irrespective of their talents. Children with talent (as determined by class-biased tests) are directed to and recruited into the "best" schools. The less talented upper-middle-class children go to somewhat less prestigeful upper-middle-class establishments. A significant number of these also, in the end, acquire a college degree.[15] The firms looking for "talent" to staff their managerial and professional ranks (what we are calling upper middle class positions) recruit from among these university graduates. There is still sufficient "personal influence" present to allow provision for those who went to the less prestigious institutions. This arrangement involves an indirect pass-on of privilege as opposed to the older, more direct procedure. This arrangement carries the additional advantage that it can be presented for public consumption under the cover of an attractive phrase, namely, the "elite of talent." This disguises the persistent class character of the process and has the aura of providing a straightforward, democratic competition.

The other part of the picture involves the working-class and lower-middle-class children who also "go to college." They do not, again with rare exceptions, go to the best schools.[16] And since the channeling from the less-than-best schools does not lead them into upper-middle-class career lines, they are eventually found in jobs that, on the whole, are very similar to those held by their parents, that is, in the working class and lower-middle class.

If this account is accurate, the income patterns associated with upper-middle-class careers, on the one hand, and with the lower-middle and manual careers, on the other, ought to be markedly divergent.

The main features of the income pattern of the manuals are a low beginning level, some rise in mid-career as the wives and children enter the labor force, and then, still later, a falloff that brings the total family income back very close to its beginning level. (See Figure 10.1.)

The typical working-class career, then, has something of a tragic fate built into it. Instead of life getting "better and better," it improves to a point (even that being largely through the efforts of second earners), and from then on the trend is downward. It seems likely that this fate would be highly visible; it could be seen in the lives and careers of parents, uncles, older brothers, and so forth, and, being widely known, it would provide the basis for much of the planning of working-class life. It seems likely, for example, that the major purchases, such as homes, household durables, and whatever luxuries, would be made during the periods of the upswing. After the peak years the career is largely a holding operation, that is, holding one's achievement as best one can.[17]

When we consider the middle-class families of working-class and farm background, a group that falls disproportionately into the lower-middle class as defined in terms of income and a group that, for the most part, did not get the benefit of higher education, we find that they, too, have an up-and-down pattern similar to that of the workers.[18] Their medians are consistently higher than those of the manuals. As for the basic pattern of income over the career,

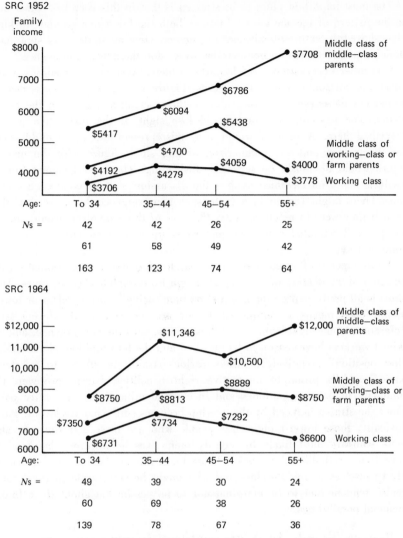

Figure 10.1. Class, age, and family income (married, non-South).

however, they also suffer the same mid-career fate as the workers, that is, from there things proceed downhill.

That segment of the middle class that comes from the middle class has a strikingly different career. Their pattern is one of steady improvement. They begin higher than either of the other two groups considered and, with one exception in the 1964 data, the gap between this middle class subgroup and the others continuously increases. The gap is greatest after age 55 because the groups are then moving in opposite directions, the one continuing to improve while the others are in the declining phase.[19]

The most important point to be stressed is that in this very key dimension, in the pattern of income over a lifetime, both the lower-middle and working-class share this feature of existence in common. Once again the most significant division proves to be that between the lower- and the upper-middle class.

One other observation is of importance here. Averages or medians would constitute horizontal lines cutting across Figure 10.1. A working-class median would cut the curve twice, once during the upswing and once on the downswing. The median, in short, would lose sight of the distinctive pattern described here. A median would also misrepresent the upper-middle-class income pattern and any comparison of that single figure with the manual figure would obviously be seriously misleading. The most frequent line of analysis based on medians involves the discussion of their convergence over time. There might (or might not) be such a convergence, but it is clear that even if they were to reach equality, the lives of those involved would still be sharply differentiated since one pattern is up and down and the other is continuous up.

A fair amount of speculative and research effort has been expended on the question of the overlap of working-class and lower-middle-class incomes. That effort is all predicated on the assumption that "being" working class or lower-middle class means something, that they are, or were in the recent past, different in some significant ways. Presumably, with the convergence, affluent skilled workers have reason to be gratified and the lower-middle class, having "lost position" (relatively), suffers various strains, is subject to a "status panic," and is prone to innovative rightist politics. Given, however, the similarity in political outlooks and in class identifications, the entire point about the strains induced by the overlap becomes somewhat irrelevant. Paradoxically, those lower-middle-class people who are most marginal are also those who are most likely to identify themselves as working class and to have Democratic-liberal outlooks. Those lower-middle-class people who identify themselves as middle class and who might be susceptible to the "status panic" tend neither to be marginal nor to be pessimistic about their future financial possibilities.[20]

Recent Trends in Working-Class Incomes

It is worth considering the incomes of working-class populations and the recent trend in working-class incomes as reported in official government publications. This is important as a sobering counter to the exuberant and inflated claims about working-class "affluence" in the contemporary United States and also to the assertions about the "dramatic" changes that are presumably in process.

A leading series bears the heading: "Average Weekly Earnings of Production or Nonsupervisory Workers on Private Nonagricultural Payrolls, by Industry Division." The average weekly earnings for all industries in 1967 was $101.99. That is a gross figure from which must be subtracted a wide range of taxes. This figure would mean, if one assumed 50 weeks of work, a 1967 gross income of approximately $5000, a figure that in most cities would be inadequate for a family of four. This figure includes women employees. In those fields where women predominate, the average is considerably lower as, for example, in retail trade where the figure was $70.95. In construction, a field where males predominate, the figure is highest: $154.19. In this field, however, it must be remembered that fewer workers are employed 50 weeks in a year.[21]

A parallel set of figures provides additional information under this heading: "Gross and Spendable Average Weekly Earnings of Production or Nonsupervisory Workers on Private Nonagricultural Payrolls." Here we have the same gross figures and a correction of that gross which translates those results into 1957–59 constant dollars. We are also given the "spendable average weekly earnings," in essence a net figure after taxes, this too being presented in current and in 1957–59 dollars.

The original 1967 figure of $101.99 translates into $87.70 when calculated in 1957–59 dollars. For a worker with three dependents, the spendable average in 1957–59 dollars turns out to be $78.23. Again that is an average that includes a wide range of experience, male and female earners, South and non-South, city and small town, and so on.[22]

Workers in cities, on the whole, tend to earn above that average, and, to the common understanding, they are the "affluent" workers one hears so much about. To indicate what big-city working-class affluence means, it is worthwhile considering an analysis of New York City wage conditions. One study, based on Bureau of Labor Statistics, indicated that in 1967 "to maintain an adequate but modest standard of living" a working-class family of four persons (husband, wife, and two children) would need a take-home pay of $167 a week or $8682 a year. No industry in the survey reached that average. Workers in New York City, on the average, do not have an "adequate but modest" living standard.[23]

The spendable average weekly earnings (for the family of four in 1957–59 dollars) figures are available for the years from 1947 through 1967. In most of those years there is an increase in the average; in some, however, in recession years 1957, 1958, and 1960 and in war years 1951, 1966, and 1967, there were slight falloffs registered. If we take the entire span and calculate the average yearly increase we find that it amounts to just over one dollar per week per year. That would mean that the average family of four earning say $70 per week in a given year would be earning approximately $71 per week in the subsequent year.[24]

One can only speculate about reactions to this rate of income improvement. It seems highly unlikely that working-class populations are going to share the waxing enthusiasm of upper-middle-class commentators. It seems unlikely that workers are major consumers, now "participating" in "the society" just like those people in the upper-middle class. From the day-to-day perspective it must appear as if they are standing still. In the longer run, however, one might sense a considerable improvement. At the end of the two decades being discussed here, one would be ahead 20 real dollars per week, a 35 percent increase over 1947. For those whose memories reach even further back, to what they were making in the 1940s or to their father's experience when they were growing up, the change may well be assessed as enormous.

This is not intended as an excuse or apology for these marginal wage levels. Such incomes are obviously only a pittance in comparison to what they could be, given adequate organization and utilization of the contemporary productive capacity. Since few people think in those terms and since few union or political activists point that out and argue in terms of that frame of reference, it seems likely that the framework that is most widely used would involve comparison of the present achievement with the past experience. In that framework the judgment for many is likely to be a positive one.

One may arrive at much the same conclusion through a somewhat different course. When we examine the distribution of income among family units ranked by decile (that is, from the poorest to the richest tenth of the population), we find that the overall pattern in recent years has been more or less constant. The poorest tenth have had a constant 1 percent of the money income received by family units and, at the other end of the distribution, the richest tenth have had a share that has fallen below 27 percent of that total. In most years their share has fluctuated between 28 and 30 percent.[25]

Income shares are one thing but, as is frequently pointed out, the "size of the pie" is increasing such that "nowadays" everyone is better off in absolute terms. We can make some assessment of that improvement for the various decile categories. If we take, for the sake of illustration, the fifth category from the bottom, we find that the lowest income there increased from $4600 per year in 1960 to $5610 in 1966. In the course of six years, there was an increase of some $1010 in the "floor" of this category or, on the average, an increase of $168 per year. That, in turn, would amount to approximately $3.20 per week per year, which is considerably more than the previous estimate. It must be remembered, however, that this is before taxes and that the dollars are current rather than constant. If those two corrections were made, it seems likely that the result would be close to that yielded on the basis of the Bureau of Labor Statistics data.

The income shares data allow still another important commentary on the received speculation. As against the six-year increase of $1010 in the fifth category, the highest tenth showed an increase of $3040 or an average of just over $500 per year. In general, during the 1960–1966 period, the amount of increase varied directly with rank. We may put these observations together with the responses to the Survey Research Center questions discussed above. When a respondent says that things have been "getting better" or that they will "get better," that response has a different meaning depending on the "context." It means an average of $52 yearly in the second decile, $168 in the fifth decile, and over $500 in the top category.

A question arises as to why such meager increases are indicated here in contrast to the enormous increases suggested in other works.[26] Much of the disparity is to be explained as the result of using gross income figures in current dollars in the one case, and of using net or spendable income figures in constant dollars in the other. In a period of going inflation, the use of gross current dollar figures is going to suggest very sizable increases. The problem is that the family unit can only use a part of that gross and obviously the remaining net income does not involve units of constant purchasing power. For a discussion of what people have to live with (that is, how much they have for groceries, for the mortgage, and to keep up a range of amenities), it is necessary to work with the net figures and with the constant dollars. To do otherwise is to engage in a rather abstract exercise having little relationship to the realities of everyday life.

Another source of misperception is the use of estimates based on hourly wage rates. The tendency is to take high and atypical hourly rates (because encomiasts chose the dazzling exceptions to make their point) and to assume a 40-hour work week and a 50- or 52-week year. Those assumptions are not entirely justified. Some of the highest hourly rates are to be found in construction work and yet year round employment is relatively rare in this field.[27] Another source of this kind of misperception is the same sort of generalization based on the hourly rates of various kinds of repairmen. The only contact with working-class people for many in the upper-middle class is with the range of skilled workers who enter their homes for purposes of repair, upkeep, and/or improvement. Here, again, one generalizes from, for example, the high hourly rate of the plumber and assumes full employment at that rate.

There is still another source of built-in perceptual distortion in a society with continuing inflation. Older and middle-aged people in the United States probably remember when the minimum wage was 25 cents an hour. Now that the minimum is $1.60 and there are some spectacular hourly rates well above this, it would seem as if there had been tremendous improvement. Again, that "seeming" does not take into account the steady extension of the income tax bite into the lower income ranges or the creeping sales and excise taxes, and it also does not make correction for the going inflation. Some upper-middle-class persons worked at manual jobs in their youth and they also, without making the necessary corrections, contrast the rates then with the rates now and draw a somewhat misleading conclusion.

Because of the lack of data, it is difficult to assess the claims about long-term trends toward convergence of incomes. Most of the information we have is based on series that begin in 1939 and continue up to the present. A leading source shows that between 1939 and 1950 there were relatively large increases achieved in the manual ranks. The percentage increase for laborers was 175, for operatives, 172, and for craftsmen, 160. In the nonmanual ranks, with the exception of those in sales (147), the increases were more modest: 114 for professionals, 111 for clericals, and 95 for managers.[28] It was on the basis of this evidence that the sweeping claim about convergence was made as well as the claim about the "blurring of class lines." The experience since 1950, however, has not supported the claim about a basic, long-term secular trend. Since 1950 the percentage increases have been approximately equal for all occupations.[29]

The discussions of that 1939–1950 convergence assumed that "something new" was occurring. Implicit in that analysis is the assumption that clericals and skilled were widely separated at some time in the past. There is, however, another possibility, namely, the possibility that a considerable "overlap" (or "blurring") existed in times prior to 1939. In the course of the depression decade, manual incomes fell disproportionately; this group, after all, suffered the massive unemployment. Although many white-collar incomes were cut during those years, nevertheless, given the more limited unemployment and the fact that price levels fell more than salaries, one consequence was that the gap between manuals and lower white-collar workers was increased as the depression deepened.[30] Later, in the upswing phase, the differences were reduced. It should be remembered that the year 1939, the beginning point in the series under discussion, was a year in which 17.2 percent of the civilian labor force was unemployed.[31] That there is a convergence of blue-collar and white-collar income levels when near full employment is reached should come as no great surprise. The convergence, however, rather than being something new may well have been no more than a return to the "normal" (that is, to the near full employment) state.[32]

The Question of Living Standards: Home Ownership

It is clear, given the data on incomes, that many of the flamboyant claims about the equalization of consumption standards must also, like the income convergence claim, be without foundation. Through the use of the Survey of Consumer Finances, also done by the Survey Research Center, it is possible to indicate something about the class differences in consumption patterns. There is little point in undertaking an examination of all the minutia associated with the purchase of durable and not-so-durable products. For the present purpose consideration will be restricted to homes and automobiles.

Taking the economically active non-South families and comparing the 1952 and 1964 surveys, we find slight increases in the level of home ownership on the part of all three groups: manuals, lower middles, and upper middles. The percentage shifts are about the same for all three groups so that the differences among the groups remain approximately the same at the later point, that is, some twelve years later (see Table 10.6).

In both 1952 and 1964, a majority of the manual families owned (or were in process of buying) their homes. That approximately three-fifths of non-South working-class families owned their homes in 1964 still does not mean equality for them, since the homes owned were, on the whole, rather modest. The median value of the non-South working-class home was $13,237 in 1964.

TABLE 10.6

Class and Home Ownership (Married, Active, Non-South) Survey of Consumer Finances

	Class		
	Working	Lower Middle	Upper Middle
Percent owning home			
1952	55%	61%	78%
N =	(724)	(395)	(181)
1964	61	67	83
N =	(354)	(182)	(122)
Value of home: 1964			
$25,000 or more	8%	4%	32%
$20,000–$24,999	10	11	20
$15,000–$19,999	19	28	21
$10,000–$14,999	36	37	24
Less than $10,000	27	20	4
Median	$13,237	$14,111	$20,375
N =	(215)	(122)	(101)

Approximately one-quarter of these homes were valued at less than $10,000. At the other extreme, 10 percent of the homes were valued at between $20,000 and $25,000 and 8 percent at above the latter figure. The typical working-class home would appear to be neither large nor elegant, at least not by the standards of the upper-middle class.

The pattern of housing in the lower-middle class is very similar to that of the workers. There is again a relatively low median ($14,111), a similar large proportion of low-value homes, and a very small proportion in the higher brackets. Only 4 percent valued their homes as being worth more than $25,000.

The median value of the upper-middle-class home is approximately $6000 dollars higher than the lower-middle-class median and $7000 higher than the equivalent working-class figure. There are practically no upper-middle-class people living in homes valued at less than $10,000. On the other hand, over half report owning units valued at more than $20,000. Thirty-two percent of the total report homes of $25,000 or more.

The lesson would appear to be that, here too, the lower-middle class and the working class share a life condition. Together they have an existence that is quite different from that of the upper-middle class. Once again, the key line of division in the United States proves to be that separating the upper- and lower-middle class.

There are some unexpected features involved in the distribution of home ownership. It was indicated previously that income levels tend to be higher in the larger communities. The level of home ownership, on the contrary, tends to be highest in the smallest communities. This involves no great surprise once pointed out; it is clear that in small towns and depopulating villages, the price of housing is very low and well within the range of people with average or even below average incomes. It is possible that for many small towners, owner-ship does not involve a purchase but rather an inheritance.[33] In this respect, then, the best paid, the urban workers, suffer a peculiar penalty. They are, with greater frequency, forced into renting and thereby obliged to forego the opportunity for saving involved in owning. On the other hand, it seems likely that in some respects the quality of the housing owned in the urban areas is superior to that in the rural areas and that there is a better market for that housing should one wish or be forced to sell.

One other point ought to be made in this connection. When one speaks of "home ownership," the tendency is to think in terms of an ordinary house. The Survey of Consumer Finances, however, also counts among the owners those having a trailer. Much of the increase in "home ownership" in recent years is actually an increase in trailer ownership, most of this being on the part of workers and lower-middle-class populations.

The Question of Living Standards: Automobile Ownership

The class pattern with respect to automobile ownership shows both some similarity to and a small difference from the home ownership pattern. Already in 1952 substantial majorities of all three groups owned automobiles (see Table 10.7). Here, again, the upper-middle class was well differentiated from the other two categories. Nearly all upper-middle-class families owned a car, and a sizable minority, approximately one-quarter, owned more than one. By comparison, one-quarter and one-fifth, respectively, of the working and lower-middle classes in 1952 did not own; also, within both categories, there were, approximately, only one in twenty with two or more such vehicles.

By 1964 an across-the-board pattern of "upgrading" could be observed. The level of ownership in the upper-middle class, obviously, could not increase much over the already high level of 1952. Ownership increased in both the working and lower-middle classes so that in 1964 only one in ten families in those categories was without an automobile. Simultaneously, the level of mul-tiple vehicle ownership increased with the upper-middle-class level jumping from 23 to 46 percent, that of the lower-middle class going from 6 to 26 per-cent, and in the working class, the level going from 4 to 29 percent. Again, the greatest division is between the upper- and lower-middle classes.

One difference from the general pattern, that is, one respect in which the lower-middle class occupies a more clearly intermediate position, is with re-spect to whether or not they bought the car new. The buying of new cars varies directly with the class level. A majority of the lower-middle-class respondents report having bought new in both the 1952 and 1964 studies, whereas in the working class, majorities at both times report having bought used cars.[34] The

TABLE 10.7
Class and Automobile Ownership (Married, Active, Non-South) Survey of Consumer Finances

Automobile Ownership	Class		
	Working	Lower Middle	Upper Middle
1952			
Does not own	26%	20%	5%
Owns one	70	74	72
Owns two or more	4	6	23
$N =$	(750)	(414)	(181)
1964			
Does not own	10	11	3
Owns one	61	63	51
Owns two or more	29	26	46
$N =$	(354)	(182)	(122)

more usual pattern appears once again, however, when we ask about the age of the car; the upper-middle class tends to have newer ones, the median age being 2.9 years as opposed to 4.9 years for the lower middles, and 5.6 years for the working class.

Looking at the type of car bought, we find that within all three groups a majority buys in the low price category and that only a very small percentage purchase in the much talked about high price range (see Table 10.8). Looking at the differences between the classes we find the expected tendency—the purchasing of new medium-priced and high-priced cars varies directly with class level. Interestingly enough, however, the opposite obtains when we are looking at the purchase of used cars. Putting that more concretely, no working-class family in the 1964 study bought a new Cadillac or Lincoln (out of a total of 354 active, non-South family units). The ten Cadillacs and Lincolns owned by workers were all bought used. These ten cases amount to a mere three percent of the non-South working-class families.[35]

It seems likely that the low-priced cars, because of planned obsolescence, are either not available or are not viewed as ideal purchases in the used-car markets. Their rapid decline means that medium-priced and high-priced cars are somewhat more likely to appear (and to be relatively more sought after) in the used-car lots. There is clearly a "trickle down" process operating, the better cars passing from the affluent to the not-too-affluent owners.

One might ordinarily expect much of what has been indicated here—for example, that ownership would vary directly with class and that ownership of expensive automobiles would vary in the same direction. There has been, nevertheless, a sustained emphasis on a very special and very exceptional minority, that is, on the workers, the poor, and the Negroes who own "big

TABLE 10.8
Class and Kind of Automobile Owned (Married, Active, Non-South) Survey of Consumer Finances: 1964

Kind of Automobile[a]	Automobile-Owning Families by Class		
	Working	Lower Middle	Upper Middle
Bought new			
High priced	2%	2%	3%
Medium priced	7	17	26
Low priced	29	32	46
Bought used			
High priced	4	4	3
Medium priced	19	13	5
Low priced	39	32	17
N =	(317)	(162)	(118)

[a] Refers to "first car" considered in the survey. For a definition, see note 35.

and expensive" automobiles, an emphasis suggesting their exceptional experience to be either a typical one or at least a very frequent occurrence.

It is worth undertaking a brief digression here to consider both the fact and the intellectual proclivity. The general tendency has been to view automobile ownership as a reward; a man who has a car is a man with a special benefit, a "good." This "conclusion" is invoked together with the fact of extensive ownership to indicate the "well-off" character of the majority of the American and, increasingly, other populations. One critic of the "income revolution" and of the correlated "massification" theses contrasted the 23 percent of the poor who owned automobiles with the 95 percent figure among the rich. A critic of the critic, using the same figure, drew another conclusion: that *even* among the "poor" a significant percentage have automobiles, suggesting in the process that this is indicative of a spurious or pseudo poverty.[36] This point is again based on the assumption that the automobile is a "good" and not a "bad."

These instances of the automobile-owning poor do present something of a problem. Is their behavior merely frivolous? Are they spending their money irrationally? Is it just a childlike attraction to glittering status symbols? A wasteful use of funds that could be better applied to other ends? A more detailed examination of the pattern of purchases suggests a quite different line of "explanation."

Taking married, active, non-South working-class families, one finds that the level of automobile ownership varies inversely with city size (see Table 10.9). This pattern obtains within each level of current income; automobile ownership is highest in the rural areas and lowest in the cities. This would suggest a simple alternative hypothesis: automobile ownership is a function

TABLE 10.9
Size of Place, Income, and Automobile Ownership (Married, Active, Non-South Working Class) Survey of Consumer Finances, 1964

	Size of Place			
Family Income	Twelve Largest Cities	Other Cities 50,000 or More	2500– 49,999	Less Than 2500
	Percent having one or more cars			
Less than $5000	56%	77%	84%	93%
N =	(18)	(13)	(19)	(27)
$5000–$6999	60	91	97	100
N =	(25)	(23)	(34)	(24)

of the adequacy or, more accurately, the inadequacy of public transportation. In areas with no public transportation or in areas with deteriorating or disappearing public transportation, people of all income levels are forced to purchase their own means of transport. In order to get from home to job and back again, even the most deprived individuals are forced into paying the costs of acquiring and maintaining their own personal transportation "system." These costs include the price of initial purchase, fueling, lubricating, licencing, repairing, and, last but not least, insuring. From this perspective, ownership of an automobile, rather than being a benefit or "good," would appear to be a formidable "bad" for poor families. It amounts to an enormous cost factor that they are forced to incur because of the unavailability of adequate bus, streetcar, or train facilities. The claim that automobile purchasing by the very poor represents frivolous status-seeking would appear to seriously misrepresent their actual situation.[37]

The benefits and the costs do not add up in any simple way. Small-town and rural workers do not receive as large money incomes as do workers elsewhere, but it is relatively easy for them to solve their housing problem given the ample supply and low costs in such setting. At the same time, however, they are forced to incur the costs of acquiring and maintaining their own transportation caused by the lack of public transportation. The problem for workers in the cities is just the opposite; it is difficult for them to find adequate housing, but, on the other hand, public transportation, in one form or another, is present.

It has been argued that as a result of presumed equalization processes, notably an equalization of incomes and of the consequent ability to acquire similar consumption standards, the "life-style" differences between the classes have been reduced. It has been indicated here, to the contrary, that there is a substantial difference in the pattern of income development over the lifetime with the upper-middle classes having a markedly different pattern than is the case with the lower middles and working class. The former career is one of continuous improvement; the latter two involve an up and down pattern. To the extent that income, and more specifically, the lifetime pattern of income, provides the basis for life-styles and determines the patterns of location and of social contacts, and, more generally, to the extent that these "income-careers" affect life plans, there would be "differences" so long as this "source" of the outlooks remained differentiated.

A limited examination of consumption patterns confirmed the expectations. In most respects, the lower-middle-class home-owning and automobile-owning habits were similar to those of the manual workers. It was indicated in this connection that the claims about similarities of appearance "away from the job" do not appear to be well-founded. The instances of "high level" consumption in the working class were shown to be very exceptional and not at all "typical" cases. Even in these cases there are likely to be special factors operating such as inheritance, multiple earners, and hard-driving salesmen.

Notes

1. See Richard Hamilton, *Affluence and the French Worker* (Princeton: Princeton University Press, 1967), Ch. VII: "Income and Politics," and Ch. VIII: "Standard of Living and Politics: Automobiles, Homes, and Luxuries." See also Hamilton, "Affluence and the Worker: The West German Case," *American Journal of Sociology*, **71** (September 1965), 144–152.

2. The medians (family incomes) in 1952 for non-South nonmanuals and manuals, respectively, were $5023 ($N = 368$) and $3890 ($N = 426$). In 1964, the equivalent figures were $9089 ($N = 349$) and $7046 ($N = 320$). In 1952 the manual median was 77.4% of the nonmanual figure. In 1964 the manual median was 77.5% of the nonmanual level.

The equivalent medians for the South in 1952 were $4692 ($N = 108$) and $3053 ($N = 158$). In 1964 the figures were $8304 ($N = 158$) and $5211 ($N = 120$). In 1952 the median income of Southern manual families was 65.1% of the nonmanual level. In 1964 the equivalent was 62.8%.

3. We are using the NORC study at this point because it has a direct question on the number of earners in the family. We can reach the same conclusion using the SRC 1964 study by contrasting the family income and the income of the main earner. The following shows the percentage of families in which the main earner's income falls in the same category as the family income:

Family Income (SRC 1964)

	$4000–4999	$5000–5999	$6000–7499	$7500–9999	$10,000–14.999	$15,000 or More
Nonmanuals	77%	81%	82%	72%	68%	81%
$N =$	(22)	(37)	(50)	(80)	(95)	(48)
Manuals	89	85	83	59	32	17
$N =$	(27)	(39)	(85)	(87)	(41)	(6)

Parallel results for West Germany appear in my article "Einkommen und Klassenstruktur: Der Fall der Bundesrepublik," *Kölner Zeitschrift für Soziologie und Sozialpsychologie,* **20**:2 (1968), 253. Also of some interest on the subject of "affluent" workers is John H. Goldthorpe, "Attitudes and Behavior of Car Assembly Workers: A Deviant Case and a Theoretical Critique," *British Journal of Sociology,* **17** (September 1966), 227–244.

4. Data from the 1964 SRC study also indicate that at any given income level the manual families are somewhat larger than the equivalent nonmanual units. Once again, the appearance of equality hides inequality since the same income in the typical working-class case must maintain a larger number of persons.

The single-earner working-class families report greater satisfaction with the income of the main earner than is the case with those families having multiple earners. For example, in the case of non-South manual families earning under $4000 (from the NORC Study No. 367, 1955), 60 percent of the single-earner units ($N = 141$) reported satisfaction with the head's earnings as opposed to 49 percent ($N = 76$) of those in units with two or more employed. This would suggest that the wife's employment in many cases is not viewed positively or with indifference. It amounts to an additional penalty.

There is a further observation of interest in this connection. At a relatively high income level for 1955, $5000–$7500, a high proportion of the working-class families report satisfaction with the head's income, the figures being 71 percent ($N = 65$) for manuals as compared to 59 percent ($N = 97$) for nonmanual single-earner families, respectively. The equivalent figures for the multiple-earner families are 66 percent ($N = 91$) and 48 percent ($N = 49$). These results would suggest that at this income level workers become satisfied, their achievements apparently approaching their expectations. The equivalent middle-class group, by comparison, shows relatively less satisfaction suggesting a greater disparity between their aspirations and attainments.

5. The question reads as follows: Q. 42. "We are also interested in how people are getting along financially these days. So far as you and your family are concerned, would you say that you are pretty well satisfied with your present financial situation, more-or-less satisfied, or not satisfied at all?" The same question was asked in the 1956 study. The marginal distributions for the two studies are presented below. One may see the very restricted impact of all the upgrading of real living standards in the intervening years.

	1956	1964
Pretty well satisfied	41%	44%
More-or-less satisfied	39	40
Not satisfied	18	15
Don't know, no answer	1	1
$N =$	(1762)	(1571)

The easiest response is to invoke the "rising expectations" cliché. As we shall see later in the text, there is another likelihood of at least equal plausibility.

6. The NORC Study No. 367 shows a similar result. Exactly 56 percent ($N = 217$) of the non-South, married respondents in economically active, manual

families with incomes below $4000 reported satisfaction with the head's earnings. In the nonmanual families the figure was 61 percent $(N = 72)$. The NORC question reads: Q. 1-A. "In general, would you say you are well satisfied, or not well satisfied, with your (main earner's) present income?"

There is a possibility of some response bias in the answers to these satisfaction questions. It might be difficult for a main earner of limited means to admit dissatisfaction with his income since he might simultaneously see that answer as an admission of personal incapacity. Suspecting that it might be easier for the wife to admit dissatisfaction to the interviewer, the separate responses of male and female non-South manuals at the different income levels were examined. Contrary to expectations the wives at each income level had the higher percentage reporting satisfaction with the head's earnings.

7. The median incomes of main earners by class and city size are as follows (SRC 1964):

	Large City	Middle-Sized City	Small Town
Nonmanual	$8466	$8229	$7124
$N =$	(170)	(100)	(78)
Manual	6590	6375	5928
$N =$	(159)	(82)	(81)

Data from the U.S. census showing the same pattern may be found in Otis Duncan and Albert T. Reiss, Jr., *Social Characteristics of Urban and Rural Communities, 1950* (New York: John Wiley, 1956), p. 104. Also, U.S. Bureau of the Census, *U.S. Census of Population: 1960 Selected Area Reports, Size of Place*, Final Report PC(3)-1B, (Washington, D.C.; U.S. Government Printing Office, 1964), pp. 22–24.

8. The unexpected reversal of this pattern among the very poorest workers presents a bit of a problem. Most of those poor workers in the middle-sized and smaller communities say they are more or less satisfied so that a total of 76 percent indicates some degree of satisfaction in those locations. In the large cities, inclusion of the more or less satisfied brings the total there to 54 percent.

9. The 1964 SRC study indicates that manual workers who were raised in middle-sized or small communities and are now living in large cities are essentially no different in their financial satisfacton from the indigenous large-city workers. Interestingly enough, those who moved in the opposite direction, that is, into the small towns, have a very high level of satisfaction as compared to the indigenous small-town workers. The percentages who are "pretty well" satisfied are: indigenous large-city workers, 41 percent $(N = 64)$; migrants to the large cities, 37 percent $(N = 92)$; indigenous small-town workers, 47 percent $(N = 62)$; and migrants to small towns 67 percent $(N = 21)$.

10. This is the case with official figures on the trends in real living standards. These are based on wages and salary data from a number of sampling points and on the price level data from the same sampling points. There is no consideration given to the fact that large numbers of people move from low-wage–low-price areas

into communities with the opposite characteristics. The figures, in other words, assume a population with no geographical mobility.

11. The same relationship between community size and satisfaction with income appears in the South. The data follow (SRC 1964):

	Family Income: Manual Workers		
	To $3999	$4000–$5999	$6000 or More
	Percent "pretty well" satisfied		
Large cities	18%	27%	42%
$N =$	(11)	(15)	(19)
Middle-sized and small towns	12	56	50
$N =$	(33)	(16)	(26)

That peculiar reversal in the poorest group appears again. Most of these counted themselves as more or less satisfied.

Another discrepancy between the statistics showing "real" improvements and the appreciation of those changes appears in the South. Although there were "real" rises in living standards throughout the South between 1956 and 1964, the level of those saying they were "pretty well" satisfied was constant in the non-manual ranks (50 percent, $N = 157$ in the former year, 51 percent, $N = 158$ in the latter). The satisfaction in the Southern manual ranks *declined* (44 percent, $N = 160$ in 1956, and 33 percent, $N = 122$ in 1964).

Despite the lower income levels in the South, both the manuals and the non-manuals in 1956 showed slightly higher levels of satisfaction than did their peers outside the South. In 1964, that was still true of the Southern nonmanuals although no longer of the Southern manual workers.

12. If one were to take the entire population, in particular including the re-tireds, the result would show an even more pronounced pattern of reported im-provement (both in the past and expected in the future) tending to vary directly with current income levels thus suggesting a strong counter-equalitarian trend. This is because the retireds fall into the low income brackets and report recent income declines and very limited prospects for the future.

13. Most of the manuals in Table 10.5 who have a family income of $10,000 or more are in the $10,000–$14,999 category. This is the case with 41 of 46 cases.

14. The tendency in such cases is to assume that the respondents are wrong; they, so it is claimed, have some malfunctioning perception processes ("they just don't see things right") preventing them from appreciating the hard, tangible realities of this world. The French sociologist, Raymond Aron, for example, states that "Public opinion polls in France reveal an astonishing, almost infinite, capacity to be uninformed about favorable events. Many workers, when questioned, say there has been no change, although their real income has gone up 5 percent a year." From *France: Steadfast and Changing* (Cambridge: Harvard University Press, 1960), p. 74. Other instances, discussion, and some French evidence are contained in Hamilton, *Affluence and the French Worker*, op. cit., pp. 73–74.

It is worthwhile, especially in view of the point about the country-to-city migration, to consider the possibility that the respondents might know what they are talking about.

15. As a case in point, a study of Wisconsin high school graduates divided the sample into four socioeconomic status categories and also, using a class-biased intelligence test, into four intelligence levels. Relatively few high-status males fell into the low intelligence quartile, but of these, 28.4 percent intended to go to college and 38.8 percent actually attended. 10.5 percent of this group graduated from college. If we take the next quartile, those high-status sons of "lower-middle" intelligence, we find that 23.3 percent graduated from college, a level that is higher than that for the sons from low-status families with high intelligence (20.1 percent graduating). In this comparison, because of the skewed distributions resulting from the class-biased intelligence test, the number of persons in the former category is approximately twice that of the latter. This data comes from William H. Sewell and Vimal P. Shah, "Socioeconomic Status, Intelligence, and the Attainment of Higher Education," *Sociology of Education,* **40** (Winter 1967), 1–23.

A followup study that picked a subsample of these graduates some seven years after high school allows some insight into the occupational retention picture. This study defined upper-middle-class families as those having a main earner in a nonmanual occupation and having an income of $10,000 or above. The study divided the respondents into three intelligence categories (because of the smaller numbers of cases) and then examined occupational attainment. Taking the low intelligence sons of upper-middle-class families, this study found that 60 percent had retained nonmanual status. About 40 percent of those who retained that status were described as "managers."

This information comes from an unpublished study by Dario Longhi and Dorothy Ellegaard, "Intergenerational Occupational Mobility and Social Class," Department of Sociology, University of Wisconsin, 1969.

16. The best simple summary picture of where high school graduates of varying backgrounds go to college appears in Burton R. Clark, *The Open Door College: A Case Study* (New York: McGraw-Hill, 1960), p. 54. Based on freshmen students from San Jose, California, his study shows the following percentages of children from manual families among the students at four nearby institutions: Stanford, 6 percent, University of California (Berkeley), 17 percent, San Jose State College, 45 percent, and San Jose Junior College, 62 percent.

Not included here are private small liberal arts colleges. These institutions are also, in all probability, very similar to Stanford in the social background of the students. Although these institutions lack the prestige of Stanford, they do serve an important "saving" function for upper-middle-class families. Very few students fail in such establishments; almost all, of those who wish to, make it through. The institutions in this part of the "educational system" cancel out the importance of ability and allow the intergenerational continuity of privilege. Low intelligence high-status children are here accredited with degrees. Those degrees in turn allow them to "enter the competition" for rewarding jobs. Those commentators who fail to see the mechanism involved in this process can then "define" the degree as indicative of talent and can argue the degree-job link as evidence in support of their "elite of talent" thesis.

17. The typical working-class man will have a very constant or stable earnings pattern since he does not, in the ordinary case, receive regular increments such as come, for example, in the career of a public school teacher. The presentation in the text simplifies what is obviously a much more complex reality. Many semi-skilled machine operatives are forced to change jobs later in life when they are no longer physically able to keep up with the demands of the machines. At that time they may be forced into unskilled jobs, or, if lucky, they may get some low-paying but secure minor white-collar job.

The 1964 SRC study shows a precipitous falloff in expectations of future improvement among the older manuals. The percentages expecting things to get better in three age categories of active, non-South manuals are: age 34 or less, 70 percent $(N = 136)$; age 35–44, 55 percent $(N = 78)$; and age 45 or over, 31 percent $(N = 96)$. The pattern of satisfaction with current incomes varies in just the opposite direction, the proportions "pretty well" satisfied being 41, 46, and 51 percent, respectively.

A useful source on the subject of life cycle and income is John B. Lansing and James N. Morgan, "Consumer Finances over the Life Cycle," pp. 36–51 of Lincoln H. Clark, ed., *Consumer Behavior*, Vol. II: "The Life Cycle and Consumer Behavior" (New York: New York University Press, 1955). This work, unfortunately for the present purpose, provides no breakdown by class. The pattern of second earners over the life cycle is shown in their Table 7, p. 41.

The study also contains some data of relevance to the income satisfaction versus rising expectation question. A 1954 Survey of Consumer Finances study (also done by the Survey Research Center) asked the following question: "How do you people feel about your present income; do you think it is about what you ought to be getting or not?" Again, unfortunately, the results were not presented by class or income level. A majority at all stages in the life cycle, however, felt they were receiving what they "ought to be getting."

18. The procedure involved here, to be sure, leaves much to be desired. Aside from the fact that background does not determine with 100 percent certainty whether one gets into an upper-middle- or a lower-middle-class career, there is the additional difficulty that a beginning on the former course is no guarantee of retention. The results shown in Figure 10.1, moreover, are based on information for husbands and wives, which would mean that in roughly half the cases we are showing the age and background of the wife and the family income. This was done so as to maximize the number of cases available for the analysis. The ages of husbands and wives are close enough so that that aspect of the procedure does little to affect the result. Separate consideration for the males only (not shown here) yielded essentially the same result. If it were possible to make a more precise separation according to the career lines, it seems likely that the differences between the two middle-class groups shown in Figure 10.1 would be somewhat enlarged.

The tendency for the educational benefits to be found within the second-generation middle-class group is indicated in the following data (SRC 1964):

Married, active, non-South nonmanual males

	To 44		45 or More	
Father middle class				
Completed college	46%	} 72%	33%	} 60%
Some college	26		27	
N =	(43)		(33)	
Father working class or farm				
Completed college	18	} 42%	12	} 22%
Some college	24		10	
N =	(68)		(41)	

19. That exception in the 1964 study among the 45–54-year olds may well be a result of the small number of cases involved and the large range in the income category ($10,000–$14,999).

Data paralleling these for West Germany are also to be found in my article "Einkommen und Klassenstruktur . . . ," op. cit.

20. This point is considered at greater length in my article "The Marginal Middle Class: A Reconsideration," *American Sociological Review*, **31** (April 1966), 192–199. More recent evidence and discussion appears in Hamilton, *Restraining Myths and Liberating Realities* (forthcoming), Ch. 3.

The question about the income overlap of skilled workers and the lower-middle class (a question which I now consider a mistaken formulation of the problem) is considered in my articles: "The Income Difference Between Skilled and White Collar Workers," *British Journal of Sociology*, **14** (December 1963), 363–373; "Income, Class and Reference Groups," *American Sociological Review*, **29** (August 1964), 576–579; and in my "The Behavior and Values of Skilled Workers," pp. 42–57 of William Gomberg and Arthur Shostak, *Blue-Collar World* (Englewood Cliffs, N.J.: Prentice-Hall, 1964). Still another contribution in the subject is that of Gavin MacKenzie, "The Economic Dimensions of Embourgeoisement," *British Journal of Sociology*, **18** (March 1967), 29–44.

21. *Handbook of Labor Statistics : 1968*, U.S. Department of Labor, Bureau of Labor Statistics, Bulletin No. 1600 (Washington: U.S. Government Printing Office, 1968), p. 166.

22. Ibid., p. 169.

23. This information comes from a study of the Teamsters Joint Council 16 and was reported in *The New York Times* of June 9, 1968.

24. It might be thought that the increases early in the period were small and that larger ones came more recently; that is, it is possible that working-class incomes have been "taking off" during this period. That is not the case. Calculating five-year averages from 1948 to 1967, we find the results for the four quinquennia, going from earliest to latest, to be $0.84, $1.31, $0.78, and $1.04.

25. Income shares data are presented for the years 1910–1959 in Gabriel Kolko, *Wealth and Power in America* (New York: Frederick A. Praeger, 1962). Data for more recent years may be found in the annual editions of the U.S. Bureau of the

Census, *Statistical Abstract*. The information in this and the following paragraphs comes from the 1968 edition, p. 323.

26. A *New York Times* account, for example, bears the headline: "Labor Day 1969: Affluence and Quiet." The article states that "The American Federation of Labor and Congress of Industrial Organizations has found that 46 percent of the nation's union members earn between $7,500 and $15,000 a year. Of the union members under 40, about 75 percent now live in the suburbs" (from p. 1, September 1, 1969).

That means, to stress what has been omitted, that just over half of the nation's trade union members earn less than $7500 per year. Left unsaid is that most of those earning more than $7500 are closer to that figure than to the $15,000 figure. Since most *unionists* are to be found in urban areas outside of the South, one must take those figures in conjunction with the high living costs in non-South cities. When it is said that three-quarters of the younger unionists live in "the suburbs," what is neglected is that they are living in working-class suburbs rather than in those communities that come immediately to the minds of *Times* readers. Another publication of Teamsters Joint Council 16 disputes this image of suburban working-class affluence; this one, paralleling the report for New York City cited in note 23, is entitled "Suburban Affluence: For Whom?"

The 1964 SRC study data indicate that the workers in the suburbs of the largest central cities are less satisfied with their financial situation than those in the cities. The data:

Married, Active, Non-South Manuals

| Residence | Financial Satisfaction | | | |
	Pretty Well	More or Less	Dissatisfied	N
Largest central cities	47%	44%	9%	= 100% (55)
Suburbs of these cities	35	43	22	= 100% (69)

27. The percentage of brickmasons, for example, who were employed 50 to 52 weeks in 1959 was 30.1 percent. The equivalent figure for carpenters was 39.1 percent, for painters, 37.7 percent, and for plasterers, 31.4 percent. Plumbers had a relatively high figure: 61.9 percent. From *U.S. Census of Population, 1960: Occupational Characteristics* Special Reports, P C (2)—7A, Table 14, pp. 206–207.

28. See, Herman P. Miller, *Income Distribution in the United States*, U.S. Bureau of the Census, A 1960 Census Monograph (Washington, D.C.: U.S. Government Printing Office, 1966), p. 82. An earlier presentation of data, also by Miller, is found in his *Income of the American People* (New York: John Wiley & Sons, 1955), p. 105. A recent popular account by the same author is his *Rich Man, Poor Man* (New York: Thomas Y. Crowell, 1964). See especially Ch. IV.

29. For the 1950–1960 data see Miller, *Income Distribution . . .* op. cit. The data also appear in "Income in 1966 of Families and Persons in the United States,"

396   Class and Politics in the United States

U.S. Bureau of the Census, *Current Population Reports*, Series P-60, No. 53, December 28, 1967.

30. This is indicated in the German experience. See J. Heinz Müller, *Nivellierung und Differenzierung der Arbeitseinkommen in Deutschland seit 1925* (Berlin: Duncker und Humblot, 1954), p. 140. The relevant figures are reproduced in my article "Einkommen und Klassenstruktur . . . ," op. cit., p. 265. Some data presented by Kolko also supports the point made here (op. cit., p. 85).

The best available study for Great Britain does not show this linkage with the economic cycle. It does, however, suggest that a considerable "blurring" of class lines was present quite early in the century. The weighted average yearly income for male clerks in 1911–1913 is given as £99. At approximately the same time, the equivalent figure for skilled men was £97. The data appear in Guy Routh, *Occupation and Pay in Great Britain: 1906–60* (Cambridge: The University Press, 1965), pp. 79, 88.

31. U.S. Bureau of the Census, *Historical Statistics of the United States: Colonial Times to 1957* (Washington, D.C.: U.S. Government Printing Office, 1960), p. 73.

32. Despite all the discussion of the collapsing of class differences, there is very little in the way of empirical support for the claim. The long-term studies (those reaching back beyond 1939) are of wages. These studies have shown a collapse in the differences between the skill levels in the first half of the century and a stability in the relationship over the last fifteen years. See, among others, the works of Harry Ober, "Occupational Wage Differentials, 1907–1947," *Monthly Labor Review*, **67** (August 1948), 127–154; Melvin Reder, "The Theory of Occupational Wage Differentials," *American Economic Review*, **45** (December 1955), 833–852; Paul G. Keat, "Long-Run Changes in Occupational Wage Structure, 1900–1956," *Journal of Political Economy*, **68** (December 1960), 584–600; Donald J. Blackmore, "Occupational Wage Relationships in Metropolitan Areas," *Monthly Labor Review*, **91** (December 1968), 29–36; and, a somewhat different picture, in Robert Ozanne, "A Century of Occupational Differentials in Manufacturing," *Review of Economics and Statistics*, **44** (August 1962), 292–299. Keat's article has a limited comparison with two nonmanual occupations—professors and public school teachers. These data support the convergence claim. He notes a number of limitations in the data. In addition to those he mentions, the original source says nothing about changes in the sex and age composition of the white-collar groups.

33. The city size classification used in the Survey of Consumer Finances differs from that used in the political studies. The categories are: (1) the central cities of the 12 largest Standard Metropolitan Areas (SMAs), (2) cities of 50,000 or more (exclusive of the 12 largest), (3) places of 2500 to 50,000 [which includes urban units within SMAs, that is, areas adjacent to the units contained in categories (1) and (2)], and (4) rural (which also may include parts of SMAs). Taking married, active, non-South, white manuals, the proportions owning their homes are 39 percent (57), 67 percent (60), 63 percent (115), and 75 percent (83), respectively. Non-South Negroes, a majority of whom fall in the first category, have a level of ownership that is very similar to that of white workers in that location, the proportion of home-owning blacks being 37 percent (30).

The levels of ownership in the South, again, despite the lower income levels there, are equal to the levels outside of that region. The 1964 result (to be compared with the data in Table 10.5 follows: percent owning: working class, 61 percent (160); lower middles, 65 percent (57); upper middles, 88 percent (75).

That 18 percent of the non-South working-class homeowners whose homes are valued at $20,000 are the very much talked about "bourgeois workers." The Survey of Consumer Finances does not allow us to give very much of a description of this group. One-third of them report some stock holding (versus 12 percent among the other working-class homeowners). Among these well-housed, stock-owning workers are two who report a capital income in excess of $5000 yearly. These are the most exceptional cases in the 1964 study. Here, again, one suspects that it is necessary to reckon with the possibility of inheritance.

34. Taking the car owners (non-South, active, married) in 1952, for example, we have the following proportions who bought new cars: working class, 39 percent (527); lower middle, 61 percent (307); and upper middle, 79 percent (130). The equivalent figures for 1964 are 37 percent (217); 53 percent (115); and 81 percent (62).

35. These results are based on inquiry about the "first car." This is defined as "the car bought in the year prior to the survey year, if any, regardless of the model year. If two cars are bought in the year prior to the survey year, the first car is the highest priced car. If no car is bought in the year prior to the survey year, the first car is the latest model year." For the most part, then, the results presented here concern the "newest and best" car. They say nothing about second and third cars. If we were to include consideration of the second and third cars, the class differences would be somewhat greater than those presented here.

36. The 23 percent figure appears in Kolko, p. 123. Specifically that reads: "In 1959, 23 percent of those earning less than $1,000 owned a car . . ." Hermann Miller has used census and survey material showing, for example, the automobile ownership of the poor as indicative of the "relative" character of that poverty. One of his efforts appears in a German newspaper under the headline: "Autos auch für die armen Leute." The matter of automobile ownership is considered under a subhead, "Reiche Arme," (Rich Poor). This is from the *Frankfurter Rundschau*, January 28, 1967.

37. The misrepresentation involves a problem characteristic of many intellectuals—the refusal to recognize the manifest uses of things. The manifest purpose of an automobile is to transport people and things over relatively long distances. Overlooking that obvious fact, in both intellectual circles and in the upper-middle class generally, attention is focused on the use of a vehicle as a "status symbol." Ferdynand Zweig's book *The Worker in an Affluent Society* (Glencoe: The Free Press, 1961) contains numerous cases of workers saying that they bought a car for shift work or so that they could do overtime. In both cases it was difficult to obtain public transportation.

There are, to be sure, some poor people who do own big and expensive cars. Using the 1964 Survey of Consumer Finances, for example, and questioning the stereotype of Negroes and Cadillacs, it was discovered, first of all, that only 54 percent ($N = 138$) of Negro family units in the nation own automobiles. Only four of the 138 units owned Cadillacs. Two of them had been bought new; the other two were used, one being five and the other seven years old. These findings parallel closely those of another study, see I. Roger Yoshino, "The Stereotype of the Negro and His High-Priced Car," *Sociology and Social Research,* **44** (November–December, 1959), 112–118.

One might easily conclude that the few cases of Cadillac ownership here were instances of status-seeking. It should be noted that there is still an alternative hypothesis that cannot be easily excluded. This ownership might be linked to the efforts of hard-driving, racketeering car salesmen. For some insight on the role of the latter, see David Caplovitz, *The Poor Pay More* (New York: Free Press of Glencoe, 1963).

Still another observation relevant to this question—the poor as beneficiaries or as victims—concerns multiple ownership. Again the question is whether this is economically frivolous behavior or whether there exists some not entirely obvious rationale. Operating on the assumption that an automobile, for most people, is a means of transport to and from work, it would seem appropriate to inquire into the relationship between the number of earners in a family and the number of automobiles. We do not have information on the number of earners but some approximation is allowed by the information on the number of adults. Taking the small-town and rural family units (where most of the multiple earning is found), there is a very striking relationship with 28 percent ($N = 63$) of the two adult households having two or more cars, 50 percent ($N = 30$) in the case of the three adult units, and 71 percent (or five of seven cases) in the case of the units with four or more adults.

11
Class and "Authoritarianism"

Introduction

In recent discussion it has been claimed, with supporting evidence, that manual workers are more "authoritarian" than the middle classes. Specifically, the claim has been made that the workers are less tolerant of racial, ethnic, and religious minorities, that they are less tolerant of political minorities, and that they are less likely to support democratic rules of procedure.[1]

Working-class persons, it is also pointed out by way of explanation, are more likely than others to have been raised in families in which the parents, particularly the father, demanded and obtained unreasoning obedience. The leading presentation of this "working-class authoritarianism" thesis contains an extended discussion of the experiences of those raised in the class, experiences that might plausibly produce individuals with "rigid and intolerant approaches to politics." Among the experiences mentioned are "low education, low participation in political or voluntary organizations of any type, little reading, isolated occupations, economic insecurity, and authoritarian family patterns. . ." The end product of such "training" is a "greater suggestibility, absence of a sense of past and future . . . , [an] inability to take a complex view . . . [they have] greater difficulty in abstracting from concrete experience, and lack imagination." Their training "predisposes them to view politics as black and white, good and evil."[2]

Discussions in earlier decades made similar claims about "the lower-middle class." This ill-defined category was viewed as a "dangerous" class, a group that, potentially at least, could provide the mass support for radical-rightist, reactionary movements. It was this group, so it is said, that gave the National Socialists their mass electoral base. The sources of their "reaction," then and now, are to be found in their strained position, their presumed loss of status relative to workers, their isolation and anomie. They are helplessly pushed by events and unable to control effectively their own life conditions. They, too, have been described along lines similar to those of the above account of manual workers. That is, they have also been portrayed as having little education and little involvement in voluntary associations. Small shop-keepers, it has been noted, work in isolated occupations; they are competing against other small shopkeepers and at the same time are being ground down by the big chain stores, and so on. They are, therefore, subject to con-siderable economic insecurity. Within the small shops one also finds the more authoritarian family patterns. Children are enlisted for roles in the family enterprise at an early age and, as such, are continuously subject to the rule of an anxious and increasingly desperate father. Unreasoning obedience is demanded; children growing up in this context are "broken," they are made into dependent submissive beings. As adults, they later become the willing followers of "tough" and "dynamic" leaders who offer the easy (and, therefore, unreal) solutions. Since they have no effective organized way of dealing with their problem, it is to be expected that they would develop hostility toward any easily identifiable groups that might plausibly be viewed as the source of their difficulty. These hostilities would also be directed toward those groups that are viewed as getting ahead at their ex-pense. Given their low level of education and of understanding, they come to be willing followers of "demagogues" who appear from time to time proffering easy solutions and defining stereotypically the "enemies."

In short, "the lower-middle class" is also thought to be "authoritarian." They, too, are felt to be intolerant of racial, religious, and ethnic minorities, to distrust political minorities, and to lack commitment to the "democratic rules of the game."

Given the plausibility of the argument and the apparent likelihood that "authoritarianism" results from those life experiences, it is not surprising that these views are widely accepted in the ranks of the upper-middle-class intelligentsia. These views have also gained widespread acceptance because of the existence of a range of supporting evidence.

The acceptance of the claim has, in turn, provided the basis for an "ap-propriate" political response—a retreat to elitism. The inverse of the two theses outlined here is the supposition of upper-middle class and elite virtue. These groups are portrayed as the tolerant ones, as the "moderates," as those who are interested in and willing to protect minority rights, as the guarantors of due process, and as the capable managers of the social and economic enterprise. It is this capable management that is going to "pay off" in the long run with increased income, education, and security for everyone, thus ushering in a universal good life for all citizens. The one contingent necessity, however, is that the political-economic mechanism not be disturbed or dis-rupted by either the lower-middle class or working-class authoritarians. For those interested in maximizing development and democracy as well as for those interested in maintaining and protecting minority rights, it is clear, given the motivational assumptions and findings, that there is a need for "containment" of the dangerous, erratic, unpredictable, and un- or even anti-democratic masses.[3]

Considering the importance of these claims and assuming that they provide the basis for a definition of appropriate political strategies that seriously undermine conventional views of democracy, it is clearly a matter of the greatest importance to explore once again the empirical support for the position.

In this chapter we shall accomplish the following: (1) We shall reassess the claim that manual workers are more likely than nonmanuals to be intolerant of racial and ethnic minorities. (2) We shall examine the claims made with respect to the lower-middle class as opposed to the upper middles. In general, as we shall see, these received claims are not supported. (3) We shall, therefore, explore some alternative explanations of the observed pattern of tolerance and intolerance. (4) Since the attitudinal evidence to be presented goes so much against the conventional viewpoint, we shall review some other kinds of evidence, involving actual behaviors. (5) We shall review evidence on attitudes toward civil liberties. (6) As a more peripheral task, we shall be concerned with foreign affairs preferences, in particular the "hard" versus the "soft" options in the conduct of military policy. (7) We shall review some of the original evidence upon which the received claims are based. (8) And finally, we shall review the evidence on Wallace voting in the 1968 election.

White Attitudes and the Rights of Blacks: Manuals and Nonmanuals

The results for the relevant questions in the two principal SRC studies (1956, 1964) and the 1965 AIPO studies are shown in Table 11.1.[4] Contrasting first the non-South manuals and nonmanuals, we find very little difference between the two groups. The greatest difference in favor of the received hypothesis amounts to only seven percentage points. There is one six-percentage-point difference. As for the remaining six questions, the best conclusion would be that there is *no difference* between the white non-South manuals and the nonmanuals.

Among the white Southerners, a somewhat more complex pattern appears. There is again no difference between manuals and nonmanuals in the responses to many of the questions, for example, to the 1956 jobs and housing question, to the 1956 school question, and to the 1964 jobs question. With respect to the 1964 school integration question, there is a fair-sized difference —17 percentage points. There is also a middling difference of ten percentage points in the response to the 1965 AIPO question on school integration. For the rest, the pattern is again one of essentially no difference in the responses to four questions and small reversals in two cases.

TABLE 11.1

White Attitudes Toward Black Rights: By Class and Region (Married, Active, Whites)

	Non-South		South	
	Manual	Nonmanual	Manual	Nonmanual

Percent "tolerant" of those with opinion

SRC 1956 Q. 12f. "If Negroes are not getting fair treatment in jobs and housing, the government should see to it that they do."

	Non-South		South	
Percent agreeing	73%	74%	63%	64%
$N =$	(348)	(315)	(90)	(123)

SRC 1956 Q. 12p. "The government in Washington should stay out of the question of whether white and colored children go to the same school."

Percent disagreeing	52	54	30	31
$N =$	(349)	(315)	(111)	(137)

SRC 1964 Qs. 22, 22A ". . . Should the government in Washington . . . see to it that Negroes get fair treatment in jobs [or] . . . leave these matters to the states and local communities?"

Percent for Washington action	47	45	32	33
$N =$	(229)	(273)	(60)	(120)

SRC 1964 Qs. 23, 23A ". . . Do you think that the government in Washington should see to it that white and Negro children go to the same schools [or] . . . stay out of this area as it is none of its business?"

Percent for Washington action	54	60	19	36
$N =$	(230)	(282)	(63)	(128)

SRC 1964 Q. 31 "Which of these statements would you agree with? White people have a right to keep Negroes out of their neighborhoods if they want to. Or, Negroes have a right to live wherever they can afford to, just like white people."

Percent for open housing	73	80	38	41
$N =$	(247)	(293)	(63)	(123)

AIPO 4/21/65—Asked of those with children in schools.

Q. 13 "Would you, yourself, have any objection to sending your children to a school where . . . half of the children are colored?"

Percent saying they would not object	72	71	25	34
$N =$	(240)	(247)	(91)	(62)

TABLE 11.1 (Continued)

	Non-South		South	
	Manual	Nonmanual	Manual	Nonmanual

Percent "tolerant" of those with opinion

AIPO 4/21/65. Q. 15 "If colored people came to live next door, would you move?"

	Manual	Nonmanual	Manual	Nonmanual
Percent saying no	64	68	46	40
N	(506)	(530)	(221)	(168)

AIPO 6/2/65 Q. 17a ". . . do you think that private organizations such as country clubs and college fraternities and the like should or should not have the right to exclude otherwise qualified Negroes from membership?"

	Manual	Nonmanual	Manual	Nonmanual
Percent saying no	54	52	22	14
N =	(654)	(573)	(214)	(183)

On the while, the evidence presented here yields only very restricted support for the "working-class authoritarianism" claim. In six of the eight comparisons of the non-South groups there is basically no support for the claim. In the remaining two comparisons, the maximum difference amounts to seven percentage points. In the South, there is again no support in six of the eight comparisons. In the Southern responses to the school integration questions in 1964 and 1965, there is some support for the received claim, the maximum difference being one of 17 percentage points.[5]

A question of definition ought to be raised at this point. If one were talking about sharp contrasts, where all or nearly all of the members of group A possess trait X and none or only a few of the members of group B possess the trait, one would be justified in referring to the X-ness of group A (as in working-class authoritarianism). If, on the other hand, the case were similar to the results here—that is, where one group is somewhat more likely (by a few percentage points) to possess a trait—then the attribution of X-ness to the entire class would not be justified. Instead of asking why one class and not the other has the characteristic, the data presented here indicate that the appropriate line of inquiry is to discover the sources of intolerance within each of the classes. Particularly outside the South, it is clear that "class" is not a significant factor and that it is necessary to look for that "something else" that may either stimulate or support intolerance in both classes.

White Attitudes and the Rights of Blacks: Lower-Middle and Upper-Middle Classes

Taking the same questions and exploring the pattern within the white-collar ranks, we find the second of the established hypotheses also to be lacking a solid basis (see Table 11.2). Looking first at the non-South middle-class populations we find the lower middles on the whole to be somewhat *more* tolerant than the upper middles. This is the case in 5 of the 8 comparisons, the differences ranging from a low of 6 percentage points to a high of 24. The latter difference occurs with respect to the school integration question, that is, whether or not there would be objection to sending one's

TABLE 11.2
Attitudes of Middle-Class Whites Toward Black Rights by Region (Married, Active)

	Non-South		South	
	Lower Middle	Upper Middle	Lower Middle	Upper Middle
Percent "tolerant" (of those with opinion)				
SRC 1956—" . . . jobs and housing"				
Percent	82%	64%	66%	63%
N =	(162)	(137)	(35)	(86)
SRC 1956—School integration				
Percent	58	50	14	37
N =	(155)	(144)	(37)	(96)
SRC 1964—". . . fair treatment in jobs . . ."				
Percent	45	44	35	33
N =	(146)	(116)	(48)	(70)
SRC 1964—School integration				
Percent	60	61	31	40
N =	(153)	(117)	(51)	(73)
SRC 1964—Housing				
Percent	79	80	31	49
N =	(159)	(118)	(48)	(72)
AIPO 4/21/65—School integration				
Percent	80	56	25	39
N =	(153)	(94)	(16)	(44)
AIPO 4/21/65—Family next door . . .				
Percent	71	60	45	38
N =	(365)	(164)	(62)	(104)
AIPO 6/2/65—Private organizations				
Percent	54	48	16	10
N =	(348)	(210)	(107)	(68)

children to a school where half the children were "colored." Only 1 in 5 of the non-South lower-middle class say they would object as opposed to 44 percent of the upper-middle category. There are three comparisons that do not show this pattern. These three, however, are cases involving essentially no difference between the lower- and upper-middle classes. The questions reviewed here, in short, provide no support for the conventional position that the lower-middle class is especially intolerant in contrast to a tolerant upper-middle class.

In the South, the pattern is again somewhat more complicated. In 4 of the 8 comparisons the Southern lower-middle class proves to be slightly more tolerant than the upper middles although all of these differences are small (ranging from 2 to 7 percentage points). There are an equal number of differences in the opposite direction, that is, in support of the conventional viewpoint. These differences are somewhat larger, ranging from 9 percentage points to 23.

To summarize: nowhere do we find any sharp differences between these classes that would justify a claim about contrasting class-specific propensities. Outside of the South, the view of a "dangerous" lower-middle class gains no support whatsoever, most of the comparisons showing just the opposite—a greater tolerance in the lower-middle class. The other comparisons show no difference. In the South, as indicated, the pattern is more complex, but it still does not show clear and consistent support for the received hypothesis.

If that received hypothesis were valid, one ought to find consistent and fair-sized differences between the lower- and the upper-middle classes. In 12 of the comparisons presented here that is not the case. In some of these the pattern is just the opposite of that expected. The best that can be said for the conventional hypothesis is that there are 4 instances of support out of a total of 16. All 4 of these, it must be noted, involve the Southern population.

Thus far, in order to address the two conventional claims, we have presented either combined or truncated results. Piecing together data from the previous two tables, we may see, simultaneously, the state of tolerance in all three class levels. For the purpose of illustration, only the 1964 SRC results will be presented. For the non-South population, we have the following:

	Manuals	Lower Middles	Upper Middles
		Percent tolerant	
Jobs	47	45	44
Schooling	54	60	61
Housing	73	79	80

It should be noted that the overall differences are, as is to be expected, very small. While there is a slight positive relationship between class and tolerance with respect to schools and housing, the opposite is the case with respect to jobs. Once again, the lesson is clear: outside the South, class is not a significant predictor of tolerance.[6]

The equivalent picture for the South is:

Jobs	32	35	33
Schooling	19	31	40
Housing	38	31	49

In the South once again, the pattern is rather erratic. With respect to the job question, there is essentially no difference. On the school integration question, there is clear support for both of the received hypotheses. On the housing question, we find the lower-middle class to be the least tolerant, the upper-middle class the most tolerant, and the working class to be in-between.

It should be noted that a presentation that did *not* make the separation by region would show an overall pattern of working-class intolerance. A similar result would appear in an overall comparison of lower- and upper-middle classes. The separation makes it clear that the little support there is for these hypotheses is to be found, not across the board, but in one region only, the region of the "peculiar institution."

There is another fact that should be considered in this discussion—the peculiar "Southern-ness" of the United States' manual ranks. The non-South white manual ranks have a somewhat higher percentage of Southern-reared members than the equivalent nonmanuals. The Southern nonmanual ranks, by comparision, have a higher proportion of persons reared outside of the region than is the case with the Southern white manuals. The likelihood (and the fact) that the characteristic regional "training" is transferred into a new location suggests that part of the above result would be caused by the inter-regional migration patterns rather than to any class-specific training or deprivations.[7]

The original formulation of the "working-class authoritarianism" claim focused on class-specific experiences in "explaining" the "fact" of worker intolerance. It was a combination of deprivations, punitive family training, and limited education, presumably, that accounted for their limited tolerance. Another line of inquiry worth considering involves the components of the classes, that is, the outlooks and relative sizes of the various class segments, in particular the socioreligious factor. This suggests, consistent with the previous analysis of the "pillars" within American society, that there are distinctive patterns of training that are independent of class and that are shared across the class lines but within the major socioreligious communities.

It should come as no surprise that Jews in the United States are overwhelmingly in favor of equal rights. A less well-known fact is that Catholics also tend to be supportive of equal rights   (see Table 11.3). The lowest levels of such support are to be found among the white Protestants. It will be noted that in response to a question of principle—the housing question—there is

TABLE 11.3
Class, Religion[a] and Tolerance: Non-South Whites (Married, Active) SRC 1964

	Manuals		Lower Middles		Upper Middles	
	Protestant	Catholic	Protestant	Catholic	Protestant	Catholic
Percent tolerant (of those with opinions)						
Jobs	46%	51%	41%	47%	37%	53%
N =	(142)	(75)	(80)	(53)	(63)	(38)
Schools	49	61	56	65	55	61
N =	(142)	(75)	(90)	(51)	(60)	(38)
Housing	72	73	78	77	75	88
N =	(154)	(79)	(92)	(53)	(64)	(34)

[a] There were too few cases to justify detailed presentation of percentages for Jewish respondents. The overall results are as follows: jobs, 72% (N = 18); schools, 85% (N = 20); and housing, 95% (N = 22).

little difference between Protestants and Catholics, at least in the manual and lower-middle categories. The consistent differences appear with respect to the job and schools questions, both of which involve consideration of federal government enforcement.

On the whole, this distribution of outlooks is to be expected. It is clearly in the *interest* of minorities, ideal considerations apart, to be supportive of equal rights. For a dominant majority the question of rights is likely to be taken for granted and would not, therefore, be high on the scale of priorities. A hands-off, laissez-faire position is, in a sense, the special luxury of the dominant majority. Moreover, the long history of nativism in the United States (which means white Protestant hostility toward immigrants, outsiders, newcomers, etc.) would undoubtedly leave some contemporary residues. For the influential and powerful groups within the majority, one might even expect an opposite commitment—an emphasis on the special rights and prerogatives of the gifted, the capable, the elect, the talented, the "fittest," and so forth.[8]

One might ordinarily assume that the white upper-middle class in the United States would be disproportionately Protestant. That, however, is not the case with the non-South population. There is a slight inverse relationship existing, the white Protestant proportion in the non-South upper-middle class being 54 percent and among the equivalent manuals, 62 percent. The Catholic proportion runs at about one-third in all three class levels. The Jewish percentage increases with the class level.

For three reasons, then, the overall picture presented above would tend to misrepresent the relative tolerance of the classes in question: (1) because of the disproportionate presence of Southerners in the white working class, (2) because of the disproportionate Protestant representation in the white working class, and (3) because of the disproportionate presence of Jews in the upper-middle class. Were we to take the non-South white Protestant majority and exclude the Southern-reared segment, it is clear that the relationship shown above would be shifted in the direction of greater relative working-class tolerance.[9]

These considerations of the composition of the various classes do not alter the basic facts about the distribution of attitudes by class shown in Table 11.1. Instead they provide some basis for interpreting the significance of that original relationship. What is indicated by this consideration of the component segments is the unimportance of, specifically, class training, low education, and economic deprivation as far as attitudes toward blacks are concerned. That traditional focus, then, is misleading; it causes one to overlook a fact of greater significance—socioreligious background and, presumably, the training associated with "growing up" in the Catholic or Jewish as opposed to the white Protestant context.

One other lesson is clear. With respect to school integration the Southern working class does prove to be less tolerant than the Southern middle class. A presentation that did not make the regional separation would suggest across-the-board support for the working-class authoritarianism thesis. The specification by region makes it clear that what is operating is not the authoritarianism of the class as a whole but instead of the Southern segment of the class.

Racism: Personal and Institutional

The main purpose of the above presentation has been to address two key hypotheses about the location of intolerance in the United States. It is worthwhile noting also the relevance of these data to some of the considerations discussed in Chapter 3, notably the potency of "race" as an issue for "cutting across" the ranks of the economic liberal majority and thus making possible a "conservative" victory.

In recent years it has been claimed with increasing frequency that the United States is a "racist" society.[10] There are two major interpretations of this "white racism" problem. The first maintains that there is widespread personal, individual hostility felt by whites toward the black population. The second position argues the existence of "institutional racism." In this latter explanation, the personal position of the whites may be tolerant, but, given the existence of a set of institutions that segregate, the personal position has little effect on the de facto realities that involve separate and very unequal conditions.[11]

The difference is an important one. If the racism were "personal," that is, if it were a case of widespread, open, aware, and committed intolerance, the problem of social change would be a formidable one. It would involve going against the will of a sizable and committed majority. If the majority attitude were tolerant, the possibilities for change would be much greater. Change, however, would have to involve the transformation of institutions. The willingness to recognize the rights of others is one thing; the willingness and capacity to make major institutional changes is another.

The available evidence offers very little support for the first of these positions, that is, the notion of widespread personal intolerance. The basic trend in recent decades has been decisively in the opposite direction, toward ever greater tolerance. This steady increase in tolerant responses has been shown in the Hyman and Sheatsley summaries and in the later Bettelheim and Janowitz account of the trends (discussed in Chapter 3).

The willingness to recognize equal rights, at least to the extent of a verbal commitment, is indicated by data in this chapter. The "purest" statement of rights is the 1964 question on housing, that is, whether Negroes "have a right to live wherever they can afford to . . . ." As shown in Table 11.1 some 80 percent of the non-South middle-class whites favor that right. Among the manuals the figure is 73 percent. The equivalent percentages for the South, expectedly, are considerably lower, being 41 and 38 percent, respectively, for the nonmanuals and manuals. The majority support for equal housing outside of the South does not guarantee social peace. The intolerant minorities, the 20 and 28 percent, respectively, who do not support the right to live where one pleases, involve tens of millions. The possibility for some kind of racist reaction from these millions, or some minorities within that minority, is obviously enormous. The possibility and actuality of such "disturbances" (which loom so large in the headlines) should not, however, lead one to overlook or to misrepresent the character of majority sentiment.

It should also be noted as an additional caution that the results presented here involve an average or "net" result covering all communities in the nation. There is a strong likelihood that the experience in these communities is not "all of one piece." In some, because of the particular stresses, population composition, or political leadership, there might well be a "reaction" occurring. In the overall pattern those developments have been submerged or hidden by the larger shift in the opposite direction. Because of the high visibility and "newsworthiness" of the instances of reaction, they tend to figure more prominently in media accounts.

The other questions in the 1964 study show lower "tolerant" percentages. These questions, however, involve two elements: the question of the rights of blacks and the question of a federal government role. It seems likely that some people who would favor the equal rights position would not favor "government intervention." This unwillingness to use the most effective political vehicle would be one of the reasons why there is a relative absence of personal racism and at the same time a persistence of racist institutions—in schools, with respect to job opportunities, and with respect to private clubs and organizations.[12]

Age and Attitudes Towards Blacks

Previous research has indicated that younger people are more tolerant and more willing to recognize the equality of other groups than are older generations. Considering the trend discussed here and in Chapter 3, that is, the long-term shift toward more equalitarian outlooks, this age relationship is not too surprising.

It would be easy to assume that increasing education, greater media attention, more "cosmopolitan" experience, and organized campaigns to build tolerance have created this result. The implication would be that there was massive intolerance within the white population at some time in the past (judging from the oldest cohorts, at the turn of the century) and that these new "educational" efforts have succeeded in "converting" the children and grandchildren to a more amicable position. One immediate alternative possibility that needs consideration, however, is the changed composition hypothesis. We have seen that white Protestants are less "liberal" than Catholics and Jews. It was also shown (in Chapter 6) that the older cohorts are disproportionately white and Protestant.

A separate consideration of the three major "pillars," the white Protestant, Catholic, and Jewish "communities" yielded a rather complicated picture. Taking first the white Protestants and using five age categories, we found, with respect to the job rights and school integration questions, that the oldest cohort (those 55 or more) was markedly less in favor of a government intervention than the younger groups (see Table 11.4). There was little systematic variation among these four younger categories. With respect to the less complex question of a right to a free choice in housing, there was a consistent increase in tolerance among the younger age groups.

A similar pattern appeared among the white Catholics. The oldest cohort was least favorably disposed to government intervention to guarantee job rights but otherwise there was no clear pattern of variation. There was no variation at all with respect to the school integration question, all age categories being more or less the same in their willingness to accept a government role. Again, with respect to the housing question, there was a fairly consistent pattern of increased tolerance among the younger age categories. There was little variation by age within the Jewish "pillar." All age groups with few exceptions were "liberal."

In summary there does appear to be a consistent tendency toward enhanced equalitarianism (as indicated by the responses to the housing question) evidenced within each of the younger age categories. Part of the overall result stems from the shift in the relative strength of the more liberal socioreligious communities, but we also found the same pattern within the two largest of such communities. The "trend," in short, results from both changes in composition and likely "conversions."

With respect to the more complicated questions (those on jobs and school-

TABLE 11.4

Age and Civil Rights Questions: Non-South White Protestants and Catholics (Married, Active, Manuals and Nonmanuals) SRC 1964

			Age		
	To 24	25–34	35–44	45–54	55 or More
White Protestants	Percent "liberal" (of those with opinion)				
Jobs	43%	48%	41%	46%	29%
N =	(37)	(66)	(78)	(68)	(42)
Schools	53	48	58	55	40
N =	(38)	(65)	(81)	(65)	(47)
Housing	87	83	73	67	67
N =	(39)	(70)	(95)	(73)	(39)
White Catholics					
Jobs	45[a]	52	52	59	32
N =	(11)	(62)	(42)	(27)	(25)
Schools	58[a]	63	58	65	67
N =	(12)	(59)	(41)	(34)	(21)
Housing	85[a]	88	76	61	74
N =	(13)	(59)	(51)	(28)	(19)

[a] Small number of cases.

ing, which involve both questions of equalitarian principles and of a government role, the picture is not as simple. The oldest cohort considered here is less willing to see that government role than the other cohorts. There is a decisive break between this older group and all the younger groups. Otherwise there is no shift indicated.

In the South, looking only at the dominant white Protestant group, we found no consistent variation at all by age with respect to the two questions on a government role. With respect to the housing question, there was, once again, a fairly consistent tendency toward increased equalitarianism in the younger generations.

In summary, both in the South and in the rest of the country there appears to be a secular trend toward increasing acceptance of the equalitarian principle. That trend exists within both the white Protestant and Catholic subgroups and is enhanced by a shift in the relative proportions of these two groups in the non-South population. Although there is an increase in the willingness to recognize equality, other than the clear break vis-à-vis the oldest cohort considered here, there does not appear to be an equivalent development of a willingness to use the federal government as an instrument to guarantee that equality.

If the interpretation given here is correct (that there is a conversion toward equality and toward acceptance of the principle), this would again suggest a diminution of the potential for radical-rightist movements based on racist appeals. These results indicate that the "center" of antiblack sentiment appears among the older Protestants. It is clear that with the passing of the years, due to declining participation and to the ultimate facts of demography, the importance of that group will be steadily reduced.[13]

Possibly the most frequently propounded claim about the source of the trend is the thesis that "education" causes tolerance. This assumes that "education" either directly involves the teaching of tolerance or, alternatively, has an indirect impact by bringing people into social and economic circumstances that then engender more "moderate" outlooks.

The assumption of a direct liberalizing influence, while perhaps applicable to the contemporary scene, is not so appropriate in times past. Much of education in the past, particularly "higher" education taught a lesson of special privilege for the "fit," for those of "good stock," for the gentry "trained for leadership." This "premodern" educational orientation is indicated by the fact that in the oldest of the cohorts considered here, the education-tolerance relationship shows a slight reversal, the least educated tending to be the somewhat more tolerant.[14]

The education-tolerance relationship, as indicated by the responses to the housing question, was positive in the three younger cohorts considered here (not shown in a table). If this result is due to education, it would again suggest a continuing erosion of the basis for any racist demogogic appeal.[15] With respect to the questions of a federal government role, on the other hand, the relationship is erratic. Particularly in regard to the government role in guaranteeing job equality, the finding is strikingly at variance with common expectations. In the youngest cohort, equal percentages of both grade school educated and college educated favored the government role. In the group age 35 to 44, there was a slight reversal. In both cohorts the high school educated, by a small margin, were most favorably disposed. Again, a lack of correspondence is indicated between the acceptance of the principle of equality and the willingness to make use of the most likely effective guaranteeing agency.

The question of a possible reaction may be approached more directly. The 1964 campaign contained an intentional effort at generating a white "backlash," that is, a reaction away from the majority Democratic party. This was supposed to occur among the economically depressed or marginal whites, or those who felt themselves threatened by the advances being made in the black revolution.[16] We have touched on the matter of "defections" among the Democratic identifiers at numerous points throughout this work. Here, however, we may explicitly link the "reaction" to both the personal financial situation and to the attitude toward the rights of blacks.

The initial point to be noted is that the Republican percentage was lowest among those who said they were not at all satisfied with their financial situation. The largest Republican percentage was to be found among those who were "more or less" satisfied although none of the differences are very large. Perhaps the best conclusion is that the individual economic condition had very little to do with Republican voting among the white workers. It is clear that sensed deprivation was *not* a factor in creating Republican voting; those who were dissatisfied were clearly *less* likely than other workers either to vote for or to favor the Republican candidate.[17]

A more fruitful line of analysis would begin with party identification. Here, as elsewhere, the key factor may be a traditional allegiance. Part of the result reported in the above paragraph, for example, is due to the fact that those who are "not at all" satisfied happen to be (21 of 24 of them) Democratic identifiers.

The overwhelming majority of the Democratic identifiers, as indicated previously, remained with their party in 1964. Those voting came out for their traditional party and those who did not vote also were loyal to that party. None of the Democratic identifiers, incidentally, who were dissatisfied with their financial situation defected. By comparison, again as indicated previously, there was a substantial counter-defection among the white working-class Republicans. The "reaction" to the attempt at generating a backlash among the white workers, then, was a net gain for the Democrats. Most of the defecting Democrats, as is to be expected, opposed a federal government role in guaranteeing job equality for Negroes. There was, however, a countering movement among the Republican workers who favor the government guaranteeing role. Even among the white Republican workers who opposed the federal role, one in three defected to the Democrats.[18]

A peculiar feature of the white Republican working class is that they are, in comparison to their Democratic peers, relatively opposed to federal government intervention in the areas of schooling and jobs. There is virtually no difference between the two groups in the responses to the housing question suggesting that the division is not on the equality principle but rather involves the question of the proper role of government.[19]

The absence of "consistency" in these attitudes points up a difference in behavior and outlooks of liberal and radical intelligentsia, on the one hand, and of the general population on the other. The liberal and radical position in respect to the three questions used here is that one should be for the equal housing option and for a government role in guaranteeing both job and school equality. At the other extreme, there is an expectation of some kind of core racism (thought to be very widespread) that would involve a preference for the three opposite positions. It is easy to sort out the white workers into the "pure liberal" and the "pure racist" categories. When that is done, it turns out that only a small minority of the non-South white workers showed this consistency. Most of those who were consistent happened to be consistent liberals, the distribution being as follows: consistent liberals, 20 percent; mixed cases, 71 percent; and consistent racists, 9 percent.[20]

Sizable majorities of all three of these working-class groups are Democratic identifiers. Both Democratic and Republican liberals came down over-whelmingly for the Democratic candidate in 1964 voting and in nonvoter preferences. Surprisingly, most of the racists who were Democratic identifiers, eleven out of twelve cases, also remained with the Democratic party. Most of the defection (both directions) is found among those with mixed positions on these issues.

There are a number of lessons of special interest to be observed here. The first is the absence of widespread "hard" or committed racism within the working class such as would be indicated by consistent intolerant responses to these three questions.[21] The most frequent case is one involving a "mix-ture" of outlooks. Within that "mix," one important cluster involves an accep-tance of the equal housing principle with, at the same time, a refusal to use the government enforcement potential in the other two areas. Another large group responded with "don't know," "it depends," and "no interest" with respect to the questions and issues raised. It is to be noted that these re-sponses do not indicate opposition to the black demands but rather suggest, if not openness, at least an "uncommittedness" that might be channeled in either a positive or a negative direction.

A second lesson involves the consistent liberals. The coherent viewpoint of the liberal intelligentsia (or of the radicals) stems from very exceptional cir-cumstances and very exceptional training. It comes from being raised in a milieu where others share that outlook. Within that milieu a continuous in-formal process of education takes place—a process of refinement, correction, and improvement in the outlooks of those located in the setting. This means that the resulting outlook is far from being a "natural" development. It means, too, that the expectation of a "pure" position on the part of those who have not had the advantages of that "training" is somewhat unrealistic.

Black-White Contacts and Attitudes

The discussion to this point has been somewhat abstract in that the com-parison has been of the attitudes present within large aggregates of the white population. These attitudes per se, do not make events (or prevent their occur-rence). Of central importance to the development of black-white relations are the attitudes of those present at the points of contact. As a consequence of migration patterns and segregation, a large percentage of manuals and an even greater percentage of nonmanuals have no significant contact with blacks either in their neighborhoods or in their workplaces (see Table 11.5). The greatest amount of contact is found among the large-city manual workers. Roughly two out of three are employed in a shop with at least some blacks, and roughly one-third live in a neighborhood with at least some blacks.[22]

In terms of the dominant convention, one would expect that those workers in the integrated settings would show the greatest hostility toward the blacks; specifically one would expect from this group the most intense competition

TABLE 11.5
Neighborhood and Workplace Integration by Size of Place and Class (Non-South Economically Active Whites) SRC 1964

	Size of Place and Class								
	Large City			Middle-Sized City			Small Town		
Class:	Working	Lower Middle	Upper Middle	Working	Lower Middle	Upper Middle	Working	Lower Middle	Upper Middle
Neighborhood									
All white	68%	77%	72%	79%	92%	92%	87%	93%	91%
Mostly white	21	17	25	21	8	8	13	7	9
Half and half, Mostly black[a]	11	6	3	...	...	...	...	...	...
N =	(133)	(81)	(75)	(82)	(61)	(39)	(82)	(54)	(23)
Workplace[b]									
All white	34	51	52	71	74	70	62	75	70
Mostly white	49	42	43	26	25	24	37	21	30
Half and half, Mostly black[a]	18	7	5	3	2	6	...	4	...
N =	(113)	(73)	(61)	(77)	(57)	(33)	(72)	(47)	(20)

[a] The overwhelming majority of these say "half and half."
[b] This mixes results for males plus those for employed females. See note 22 for details.

415

for jobs and the most formidable struggle to keep blacks out of the neighborhood.

It was possible to sort out the non-South white workers by integration settings in order to allow some testing of this expectation. The respondents were
initially divided into three categories: those who live in all white neighborhoods and work in all white shops, those who live in all white neighborhoods
and work in integrated workplaces, and those who both live in integrated
neighborhoods and work in integrated workplaces.[23]

Contrary to the popular hypothesis, those having both integrated neighborhoods and jobs also had the most favorable attitudes.[24] The least favorable
attitudes with respect to the equal job rights question are found among those
in the segregated milieu. There are no sharp differences between the segregated and the "mostly white" sections with respect to the residential segregation question, both running slightly behind the integrated group in their level
of tolerance. In short, contrary to the image of competition and struggle in
the transitional areas on the edges of the ghetto, those settings actually contain the most positive attitudes to be found in the working class.[25]

The questions discussed above indicate the attitudes with respect to rights.
Perhaps more decisive is a question on interracial friendships. Of course, it
is to be expected that there will be very few friendships mentioned by those
in the segregated or mixed settings. If competition and conflict existed in the
integrated neighborhoods, however, one would also expect to find very few
friendly contacts there. People might live side by side but they would have
little to do with each other. The reports from those living in the integrated
settings, however, indicate an opposite picture, that is, one of much friendly
contact.[26]

These findings suggest that the conventional view of ruthless struggle at
the point of contact is not accurate. This point is even more significant in
view of the fact that the whites in the integrated neighborhoods, on the whole,
are poorer, older, and are more likely to be immigrant or first-generation
American.

All of this suggests that another line of analysis might be more appropriate.
One simple, straightforward hypothesis found in the sociological literature
is the claim that continuous and sustained contact, particularly as status
equals, will lead to feelings of friendliness and solidarity. It is this kind of
contact that is present in the integrated neighborhoods and, conceivably, has
created this favorable outlook. By comparison, those whites who happened to
be born, raised, and living in small towns have never had that kind of contact and their orientations are likely to have been formed out of the remnants
of a nativist tradition together with some more recent stereotypes fashioned
out of episodes and fragments from the mass media. That would suggest that
the "competition for jobs" and the concern with housing prices in middle-
sized and small communities is of rather small importance.

Of major significance, if these findings are valid and the interpretation accurate, is the fact that, in general, the relationships at the point of contact are not hostile and competitive but are friendly and, in some instances, cooperative. This interpretation, it should be noted, is consonant not only with a less well-known alternative hypothesis but also with the findings of some famous studies, notably those involving the integration of housing projects and also the integration of U.S. Army units.[27]

This alternative to the competition-hostility hypothesis assumes that there is a change in attitude associated with integration. The data presented here, it will be noted, do not justify that conclusion. One would need a before-after study in order to show such a *change* in attitude. Another possible explanation for the observed finding might be self-selection. It might be, for example, that what we are looking at in the integrated urban setting is a kind of "residual" white community that is left over after the most intolerant whites have moved out. In other words, the positive attitudes of those living in the integrated neighborhoods might result not from attitude change but rather from a change in the location of the intolerant populations. It is also clearly a possibility that both factors are involved—that there may be both self-selection, a choice to move out, and also a conversion on the part of those remaining.[28] At minimum, however, it is clear that the points of contact are not, as has been frequently assumed, characterized by widespread hostility felt by the white population living there. Greater hostility to the equal rights of the blacks appears among those who live some distance away and who have little contact with the black population. It is worthwhile exploring the housing and job concerns separately.

The Housing Question

The major concerns that presumably lead white working-class persons to be hostile toward blacks are centered in the areas of housing and jobs. The movement of blacks into a neighborhood presumably reduces the value of housing there causing financial loss to families ill-equipped to pay such costs. The threat of such losses gives rise to hostilities or else aggravates those already present.[29]

The overall result suggests some support for this expectation. The non-South white working-class homeowners do show less support for the equal housing option than do the renters. At the same time, it ought to be noted that a majority of the owners (two-thirds of them in fact) favor the open housing option and that the difference between the owners and the nonowners amounts to only 13 percentage points.[30]

The picture is complicated by a number of related factors. Homeowners tend to be older than renters. Then, too, the proximity to blacks varies considerably by city size so that the large-city owners face the "threat" of reduced house values, but those in middle-sized cities and towns, on the whole, do not. It might be that the greater tolerance of the renters is purely a function of age, since they have been reared in a more tolerant era than that of the majority of the owners. A limited control for both age and city size, however, still shows the owners to be less approving than the renters. The most positive attitudes are found among the younger renters. The least positive attitudes are found among older owners.[31] In the case of the older owners, however, the division is still 50–50, not one of overwhelming opposition.

There are two alternative possible readings of this result. One is that the older generation is less tolerant because different attitudes were instilled in times past. The other alternative is that people change their outlooks over the years; they are tolerant early in their careers but with increasing age (as their equity increases and their earning power declines) they come around to a "defensive" intolerant outlook. There is very little evidence one can offer to resolve the matter at this point. A contrast with the older renters is difficult because there are very few cases of older working-class renters in this sample.

Another complicating factor is religion. In the large cities, older working-class homeowners are disproportionately white and Protestant. A majority of the younger white working-class homeowners, by comparison, are Catholic. A separate examination within the two religious communities still showed the homeowners to be less tolerant than the renters in all comparisons. At the same time, however, it should be noted that with one minor exception all groups of homeowners have tolerant majorities.[32]

Implicit in the above results is another complicating factor. A majority of the large-city manual workers living in mixed neighborhoods are renters. By comparison, the overwhelming majority of those living in all white neighborhoods are owners. In other words, a majority of those who have some neighborhood contact are not subject to any sense or threat of economic loss with respect to their housing. And it is this group that has the most favorable attitudes within the large-city white manual ranks, 87 percent of them $(N = 23)$ favoring the open-housing option.

It is difficult to draw any firm conclusions about the future. There are a number of contingencies still to be discussed that might affect the situation. For the moment, it may be noted that the actual distribution of attitudes with respect to equal housing is much more positive than is generally realized. Even with respect to a key source of strain—the presumed impact of integration on the value of housing—while we do find a consistent pattern of the home-owning workers being less tolerant than the renters, with equal consistency we find that only a minority of the homeowners behave as commonly predicted.[33] Among the renters and also among the owners in mixed neighborhoods, a higher level of support for equal rights is found. The absence of economic strain for the renters and the influence of personal contact in the case of owners in mixed neighborhoods appear to be the main factors yielding this result. It also appears that a reasonably friendly coexistence prevails in the mixed neighborhoods rather than, as is widely believed, a general antagonism and hostility.

The Job Question

Another area of presumed strain and tension is the job sphere. The most frequently heard assumption here is that blacks and whites, particularly those in the working class, are competing for jobs and, consequently, seek to exclude their black competition. The overview in Table 11.1 would not appear to support this assumption about the orientations of the white workers. The 1956 question, which focused on "jobs and housing," found workers in both the South and non-South regions just as favorably disposed to a government role as the middle class. The same holds for the 1964 question, which focuses exclusively on "fair treatment in jobs."[34]

Since this "competition" and struggle is likely to be most serious among the poor, a more precise test of the hypothesis would examine the attitudes by income level. Since class is not a factor, we have combined the manuals and nonmanuals for this purpose.[35] Looking first at the non-South population in the 1956 study, one finds that the pattern is just the opposite of the conventional expectation. The percentage favoring the government guarantee of equality in jobs and housing is greatest among the poor (see Table 11.6). According to the conventional hypothesis, the poor should be *less* willing

TABLE 11.6
Income and Government Guarantee of Job Equality: By Region (Married, Active Nonfarm White Population)

	Family Income						
	To $3999	$4000–4999	$5000–5999	$6000–7499	$7500–9999	$10,000–14,999	$15,000 or More
	Percent favoring government role[a] *(of those with opinion)*						
SRC 1956							
Non-South	81%	75%	76%	72%	68%	69%	
N =	(105)	(123)	(126)	(102)	(111)	(72)	
South	70	53	67	67	63	58	
N =	(50)	(38)	(49)	(30)	(24)	(19)	
SRC 1964							
Non-South	57		40	48	44	45	33
N =	(61)		(52)	(107)	(121)	(102)	(43)
South	38		30	25	24	35	48
N =	(40)		(27)	(28)	(25)	(34)	(23)

[a] See Table 11.1 for question wordings. There are significant differences in the emphasis of the two questions.

than the well-off. They should fall far short of the 81 percent indicating support for a government role as is shown in this study.

The evidence from the same study for the Southern whites shows the same pattern, the largest percentage in favor of the government guarantee of equality in these two areas again being found among the poor whites. The relationship with income, to be sure, is not a strong one, but the remarkable fact is that the tolerant response tends to be negatively related to income rather than, as is so frequently assumed, positively.[36]

This accounting focuses on the nonfarm populations. It might be that the "really" poor whites are to be found within the farm populations. An alternative stress has focused on the rednecks, the peckerwoods, and the crackers as providing the core support for the racist reaction. Separate consideration of the poor Southern white farm population, however, did not support this view. Seventy-six percent $(N = 21)$ of those farmers earning less than $4000 in 1956 gave the "tolerant" response to this question.

The results from the 1964 study, which has a less complicated question focusing exclusively on the job question, are similar to those already described. In the non-South regions, the support for government intervention is greatest among the poor and least among the rich.[37] In the South, the pattern is somewhat more complicated this time. There is a negative relationship with income up to the $10,000 cutting point. In the higher income ranges there is a sharp increase in the percentage of those favoring a government role. These higher income ranges are heavily impacted with people raised outside the South. Looking only at the Southern-reared, however, the same curvilinear pattern appeared with both the poor and the rich being most favorable to the intervention and the "middle-income groups, those between $6000 and $10,000, being the least favorable.[38]

The claims about the struggle of poor whites for jobs and their consequent hostility toward blacks are not supported by the data at hand, that is, with respect to these questions on a right to job equality. It is clear that some open and vicious struggle over jobs, housing, and so on does occur. The point suggested by these data is that it would be a mistake to generalize from the fact of street riots in working-class neighborhoods and to take that as evidence about the outlook of the entire area.

At this point and with the limited resources available, one can do little else but guess at the reasons for this unexpected development. One possibility, to be discussed at greater length below, is that the poor have a strong concern with equality and that they have a greater commitment to the equality value than any other group in the population. Another related possibility is that the very poor know what it means to be unemployed and hard up and do not wish such circumstances on anyone.

This suggestion amounts to a minor doctrinal heresy but it is worthwhile at least considering the possibility that a dominant motivation or possibly only a frequent orientation is one of common decency. A fair quantity of materials are now available that challenge the "ruthless competition" viewpoint (the "hard, realistic" outlook). These materials stress patterns of reciprocity, of helping one another out, and of behaving in ways that, through cooperation, help to ease the burden.

The correlated claim in the liberal or centrist social science tradition is that the upper-middle class is tolerant and responsible, the stress typically being on the benevolent impact of education. That focus tends to overlook some other possibilities, the most important of which is that employers of blacks (at least some of them) may find it to their advantage to maintain discriminatory conditions. This would be the case, for example, with the rich Mississippi planter who quite frankly stated that "They made me rich." Some of the "tolerance" in the middle class is likely to be "tactical" as opposed to principled. That is, it is a concession to insistent demands, an attempt to either end or avoid "trouble." In 1969, the city of Buffalo had a three-way mayoralty race between a black candidate, the Democratic mayor, and a white woman, Mrs. Slominski, who was opposed to busing of pupils, favored neighborhood schools, and so forth. A well-known businessman in town indicated his opposition to her candidacy. As he put it: "I'm not interested in the racial issues . . . I simply think that the lady would be bad for business."[39]

Some Qualitative Evidence

Since the evidence presented thus far is "statistical" and since columns of figures lack the "concreteness" of case studies, it is useful to shift to some anecdotal, illustrative materials.

A collection of biographies of poor persons, written by Ben Bagdikian, contain two instances of the kind of mutually supportive contact being discussed. The first involves one Homer Burleigh, a white from Anniston, Alabama. He had obtained a job as a punch press operator in Pontiac, Michigan at $1.80 an hour. Later, seeing a bulletin board announcement in the plant asking for buffers, he applied. This meant an increase to $2.21 an hour. He had had no previous experience as a buffer, but, a frequent experience in American industry, claimed he had. The account goes as follows:

> The foreman dubiously turned Homer over to an experienced buffer, a Negro from Meridian, Mississippi. Homer jauntily took up his first fender and burned a hole right through the metal. He looked curtly at the hole in the metal, chucked the fender back in a box, and started walking away. "Where are you going?" the Negro asked. "I'm quitting before they fire me," Homer said. . . . "That colored boy he said to me, 'You come on back here and do what I say. Now pick up another fender and hold it just like this'—he took one and made me take one and grab it the way he

did—'and you hold it just like a baby, and rock it back and forth, back and forth, gentle but fast, just like a baby.' Well, I began doing all right. I spoiled a couple after that but the colored guy fixed them up for me.

In this case the black man made it possible for the Southern white (an obvious fact, incidentally, given the accent) to earn over $100 a week. It will be noted that this is in the automobile industry, a field known both for its seasonal and cyclical layoffs, hence, job competition should have been a major concern. Both of them were laid off shortly thereafter for the annual changeover.

Another case involved a John Merrick, a Negro originally from North Carolina. At the suggestion of a friend, the Merricks moved to Providence, Rhode Island where, through the effort of the friend and his kin, Merrick got a job in a foundry. He describes his situation as follows:

My living was better but my overhead was more. I had to buy tools, brushes, socket wrenches. I was on 30-day trial, and I don't mind telling you I was nervous. I used to get headaches from the strain because I was working a $7,000 machine I could have ruined. But the other men in the foundry, white and colored, helped me learn and with their help I made it.[40]

"For instances" do not confirm or disconfirm hypotheses. The previous survey data is intended to do that. The illustrations merely pick out some individual experience for closer examination. The effort, both the statistical and the illustrative, challenges the assumption of general competition and hostility within the working-class ranks. It suggests that there are other processes operating that counter or overcome the tendencies toward disassociation. These processes are generally unknown to the distant upper-middle-class population so that the imputation of mutual distrust comes to dominate in the most prevalent analyses.

It is clear that the survey evidence considered here does not support the standard hypotheses on the subject. Outside the South there are basically no differences in the proportions of manuals and nonmanuals who affirm an equal rights position. Even within the South the differences prove to be surprisingly small. In the specific conflict areas, in housing and jobs where black versus white struggle is expected, the surveys indicate a considerable basis for harmony.[41] The attitudes of whites at the "points of contact" prove to be generally more favorable than is the case with those whites who are more distant, who live and work in all white settings.

One other point deserves some emphasis. The only point at which interracial conflict can occur is where there is some contact. The most likely setting for conflict, in other words, is in those integrated areas where the attitudes toward integration, on the whole, happen to be most favorable. Although the dominant attitude in such areas happens to be positive, there is a minority present that holds opposite orientations. It is obviously possible to draw enough "recruits" from among that intolerant minority to make a sizable "urban disturbance." This point will be considered at greater length below.

Some Behavioral Evidence

Since these findings are so much at variance with common expectations, it is important to review other kinds of evidence to see whether the surveys, which yield reports of attitudes and orientations, and the evidence of actual *behaviors* show consonant results. The first effort in this direction involves a review of some selected key elections.

The case of Senator Estes Kefauver, for many years a leading Southern liberal, sheds light on both points; that is, it yields a result that is consonant with these survey materials and also provides some explanation of the otherwise unexplainable.

In 1960 a strong attempt was made to oust Kefauver from his Tennessee Senate seat. This attempt in the Democratic primary of that year was considered to be of great significance. If the leading Southern liberal were defeated, presumably other liberal representatives would soon follow. Moreover, wavering "moderates" would "draw the lesson" both in terms of stylization of their subsequent campaigns and in terms of their legislative performances.

Kefauver was opposed by Circuit Judge Andrew T. Taylor, a man "from West Tennessee cotton country" with a "proved ability to attract votes" both there and in other parts of the state. Taylor was conservative in economic affairs and also was clearly for segregation. Moreover, in the campaign he led with every theme calculated to move an unreasoning and prejudiced mass —his opponent was soft on communism, had had a fund-raising party on a Sunday at which drinks were served, and he depended on outside, that is, Northern money; there were also some touches of anti-Semitism. Kefauver had cast the single dissenting vote against the August 1954 bill to outlaw the Communist party. He had voted in favor of civil rights measures. He was also a graduate of Yale Law School.

For his part, Kefauver "pulled no punches on civil rights." His best speeches were delivered in rural west Tennessee, an area that is "politically kin" to Alabama and Mississippi. The character of this effort is described in the following passage:

> He outlined his vote on the 1960 civil-rights bill this way: "I thought it was a fair and just bill and I could not clear it with my conscience to vote against the right to vote. I don't know how we can hold our heads up in the world if we deprive people of this right. I'll tell you something else— our friends from the North and West aren't going to help us with the TVA

if they can't reason with us and expect our support on fair bills like this. But if there's someone here who's against the right to vote, maybe he'll raise his hand and tell us why." No hands were raised.

Given the factors operating against him and given the basic assumptions about poor Southern whites, it should have been impossible for Kefauver to win. He did win, however, with 450,533 votes to Taylor's 240,609. Negroes, of course, were overwhelmingly for Kefauver. One source says that many Republicans from east Tennessee came over to the Democrats both because Kefauver himself was from that region and because "they resent segregationist campaigns." In the Deep South city of Memphis, the old Crump bastion, Kefauver led by 11,000. Even in rural west Tennessee where Taylor was expected to be strongly favored, his people anticipating a lead of 100,000 votes, he came out with an edge of only 8000.

If one assumes a monolithic Negro vote for Kefauver and eliminated that vote entirely, Kefauver would still have had a 150,000 vote lead. Unless there were some extraordinary inversion of voting patterns such that the rich and the upper-middle classes voted for Kefauver, it seems clear that both poor and middle-income whites much have voted for Kefauver despite all those things that, presumably at least, should have worked against him.[42]

The Kefauver effort involved two things that are rather unusual. First, he did not avoid the central issue in the campaign, but rather faced it squarely.[43] Second, in facing the central issue he focused on the equality theme. It seems a strong likelihood that the hidden factor in the campaign is the commitment of large segments of the population to the equality value. There is reason to believe that the middle- and lower-income groups would be most strongly committed to this value. A campaign that equivocated on the segregation issue and that did not indicate clearly that a fundamental value, equality, was involved would become both a defensive and a losing effort. Numerous commentators have pointed out this American dilemma—the competing interest in both equality and special advantage. In a diffuse struggle, where the terms of the conflict are not made clear, it seems likely that the value of special privilege would win out.

A later campaign in the same state provides similar lessons. In 1964 a special election was called to fill the position left vacant by Kefauver's death. The contenders in the Democratic primary were a liberal Congressman, Ross Bass, and a conservative Democrat, Governor Frank Clement. Bass had voted for the 1964 Civil Rights Act and Clement focused on that vote in the course of the campaign. Clement had been responsible for an expanded sales tax during his time as governor, a most unpopular accomplishment. The campaign provides another useful test case because here we have a conservative identified with a very unpopular "hard" economic issue. Clement made every effort to divert attention onto other issues, the most important of these being race. He also had the party machinery at his disposal. Again, given conventional assumptions about "mass" sentiment, particularly of the Southern white "masses," and given this advantage of having the party organization, it would seem that Clement could not lose. In his speeches he attacked foreign aid, the Medicare program, and the State Department. The speeches always ended up with the subject of the Bass vote for the Civil Rights Act and his statement that he would not have voted for it.

Bass, like Kefauver, did not avoid the key issue. He pointed out that as an elected official he had "to ask Negroes to serve in the Armed Forces, to die if necessary." He pointed out the incongruity of asking men to die and at the same time denying them service in segregated restaurants. His campaign, in contrast to Clement's, was badly organized. Many Democratic politicians were unwilling to help out fearing some later reprisal by Clement.

Bass won in the primary with a margin of 95,000 votes. That is considerably less than Kefauver's margin in the previous primary but it must be remembered that Bass was running against a well-known governor and that the governor had the party organization with him. The minimal lesson one can draw is that there were "some other factors" influencing the electorate in that Southern state sufficient to overcome the effects both of the party organization and a side-tracking campaign with a strong attempt to capitalize on racial hostilities.[44]

Bass won in the general election, defeating Howard H. Baker, and served in the Senate until 1966, the regular election for the old Kefauver seat occurring in that year. There was a repeat of the Bass-Clement struggle in the Democratic primary of that year, this time with Clement winning by approximately 8700 votes out of a 622,000 total. In the general election, Howard Baker, the son-in-law of Senate Republican leader Everett Dirkson, defeated Clement to become the first Republican elected to the Senate from Tennessee.

From a distance this turn of events might sound like a developing conservative wave. The detailed analysis, however, shows a somewhat different picture.

In 1966 Clement changed his position of the race issue. Prior to the 1964 primary he had ostentatiously refused to sign a fair employment practices code. Prior to the 1966 contest, however, he had appointed a prominent Negro leader in Memphis to be a criminal court judge. This was the first such appointment in modern Tennessee history. The result was that while Bass carried the vote in Negro areas elsewhere in the state, in Memphis he lost in 20 predominantly Negro precincts, and had only a narrow margin in 50 others.[45] Another factor contributing to the Clement victory was Republican crossover voting in the primary. One county, for example, which had 45,335 Goldwater votes in 1964, had only 3394 votes for the Republican side of the primary.

Both successful candidates, Clement and Baker, then went on to speak "enthusiastically of Negro rights" in the general election campaign. Racist appeals had disappeared from both the primary and the general election. In the general election many liberals, unionists, and Negroes who previously supported Bass found little to choose from in the Baker-Clement contest. As a result there was light voting in middle Tennessee where the Democrats usually have sizable margins.[46]

The major lessons to be gained from this limited review of electoral experience are, first, that the use of racist themes does not universally make winning campaigns and that there are strategies available that may successfully counter those appeals. Second, those people, at least so it would appear, who support the racist candidates tend to be upper-middle or upper class.[47] In the cases reviewed, poor and working-class whites appear to have provided heavy support for the liberal contenders. Another important point is that when the conservative (or neo-Bourbon) Democrat Clement eventually won, it was not through racist appeals but rather through a very limited effort in a "liberal" direction. And it was Clement's victory that, in turn, made possible the victory of the Republican Baker—a victory through indifference.

Another indication of behavior, as opposed to the attitudes indicated in surveys, is the voting in referenda. Consideration of these elections proves more useful than the analysis of campaigns of contending persons. Candidates run on a range of issues and characteristically a number of personal interest factors become involved, making assessment of the lessons difficult. In most cases, referenda involve a single issue and, hence, the significance of the outcomes are less ambiguous.

One study has reviewed the experience in segregationist referenda in fifteen Southern cities. The expectation was "the higher the socio-economic position, the more favorable [to integration] the attitudes." This study examined the vote in selected white precincts within these cities, having made some rough estimates of their class level. In only three of the cities—Atlanta, Augusta, and Winston-Salem—did the voting pattern come out as expected. In most instances there were no differences by class level. In Birmingham and Montgomery, the segregationist sentiment was directly related to class level, that is, it was just the opposite of the expectation.

It is worthwhile quoting form the conclusions of this study:

> From attitude studies and polls, it had been predicted that an inverse relationship would exist between socio-economic class and affirmative voting on segregationist referenda. The evidence, taken as a whole, was inconsistent and even contradictory. . . . this study seems to suggest that the socio-economic factor may not play as simple or as critical a role as some of us doing research in this field have been prone to assign it.[48]

In two of the cases confirming the conventional prediction, that is in Atlanta and Augusta, there was a substantial amount of organizational activity in opposition to the segregationist measure. While the opposition included the efforts of the state C.I.O. and the Georgia Federation of Labor, most of that effort had an upper-middle-class character to it. The daily newspapers were four to one against the measure, the League of Women Voters was against, there were specially formed Committees to Save Our Schools against, the directors of the United Church Women of Georgia were against, as well as the state's Superintendent of Schools and the Executive Secretary of the Georgia Educational Association. This suggests that the result in these cases may not provide an adequate indication of "natural" class sentiments since the "all other things equal" assumption appears to be less likely than usual. What is being suggested is that the organizational effort made the result. It would be a mistake to assume that this organized effort stemmed from enlightened equalitarian idealism. The author indicates that many of those opposed to the proposal objected not because it was segregationist but because it was unworkable and jeopardized education. In fact, the author tells us "many opponents in fact were segregationists. . . ." It seems likely that this pragmatic concern over the workability of a segregationist program would be felt most strongly in the upper-middle and upper classes.[49]

A more detailed study done in the city of Houston, Texas, found results that also go against the received notion. This study analyzed 20 elections from the 1960 to 1966 period, including school and municipals, state and nationals, and referenda. Rank order correlations were calculated between the socioeconomic status of 29 white precincts and the levels of "pro-Negro" voting. Nineteen of the 20 correlations were negative. That is "pro-Negro" voting was greatest in the poorer areas and least in the richest.

The image of moderate and responsible elites and of the need for and viability of a "Black-Bourbon coalition" is seriously questioned by the voting pattern in the richest of these precincts—one located in the very affluent River Oaks. With only a few exceptions this precinct had very low levels of "pro-Negro" voting. In most of the elections it had the second or third lowest level of such support out of 29 precincts. The lowest level of "pro-Negro" voting in 9 of these elections came from another precinct in this same very affluent suburb.[50]

The Use of and Excusing of Violence

In part, the image of a responsible and genteel upper-middle and upper class stems from literary presentations.[51] A favorite theme is the lynching of a black man, and the favorite villains are "poor whites." The "data" in such instances present the upper-middle-class individuals as concerned, but, because of their numbers, helpless against the ruthless masses. The available evidence, sketchy and unsystematic as it necessarily must be, shows the realities to be somewhat different.

A case of some interest in this connection is that of Ben "Pitchfork" Tillman, one-time governor and later United States Senator from South Carolina. He is frequently portrayed as a "populist" figure, his behaviors being set in contrast to the gentility of the "established" Bourbons. On the whole, however, the classification depends largely on personal style since in point of fact he came from a family that was very well established. His father bought 1864 acres of land in 1840 for $8035. The house in which Tillman grew up had twelve rooms. The family also had fifty slaves. By 1860, the family had 86 slaves and 3500 acres. In short, the family was far from being "poor white." He was not a Populist.

The family history was one long tale of violence. His older brother, a Harvard graduate, shot and killed a man in a quarrel. Two other brothers were killed in feuds; another died in the Civil War. Ben Tillman's mother raised him on tales of Tory violence during the Revolution.

As a young man Tillman and his associates were leaders in the administration of lynch justice in the post-Civil War efforts to undo Reconstruction. At one point they killed seven prisoners as an object lesson to other blacks. As his biographer put it: ". . . [that] the entire North as well as liberal Southern circles condemned the so-called Hamburg Massacre caused him no heartaches; he was contemptuous of such opinions. As he neared home that morning, he stopped at a neighbor's house and ate heartily of watermelon; he felt elated."[52]

Later, during his first term as governor, Tillman opposed lynching. In his second term, however, he returned to his earlier propensities and both argued and offered support for the institution. During his canvass in 1892 he stated that there was "only one crime that warrants lynching, and Governor as I am, I would lead a mob to lynch the negro who ravishes a white woman." The first lynching of his second administration involved a man accused of an attempted rape of a fourteen-year-old white girl. Tillman had his secretary write a local officer saying that "The villain deserves lynching and he [the governor] has been hoping to hear that you have caught and lynched him." Tillman preferred that the alleged criminal be lynched "before the officers of the law get possession of him" because the law did not provide for the death penalty in such cases. The local officer was asked "to preserve the proprieties." The man in question was captured. He asked for and obtained the governor's protection. He was then, however, returned to the local officers and was then "taken" from the local officers and lynched. Tillman refused an investigation saying it would serve no useful purpose. There had been five lynchings during his first administration. In his second and more "permissive" term there were thirteen.[53]

Largely lost from view in the literary stylizations of race relations in the South is the fact that in times past some organizations of poor whites made some, even though limited, moves in the direction of joint action with blacks. Mississippi Greenbackers made appeals for Negro votes. The later Populist movement in the state "bitterly attacked the franchise clauses of the 1890 constitution," and it was the Bourbon Democrats who answered with the "old rallying cry of white supremacy." It was the Bourbons who warned that a Populist victory would result "in Negro supremacy and the degradation of southern womanhood." The Populists also pledged free public schools to "all the children of the state without regard to race, color, or condition of life." This was the work of a party of poor whites.[54]

The links of blacks and poor whites were somewhat stronger in Georgia. The established Bourbon Democrats responded in the same ways as in Mississippi. Interestingly enough, in contrast to the contemporary claims about the "responsibility" of the established upper class, about their commitment to the "rules of the game," at this point, where their hegemony was threatened, they made extensive use of fraud. Not only did they give false counts, destroy ballot boxes, and so forth, but they also justified its use; it was a valid means to keep the Populists from "jeopardizing the social order." Another officeholder said "We had to do it! Those d—— Populists would have ruined the country!"[55]

At one point, Thomas Watson, the Georgia Populist leader addressed a crowd of four or five thousand "yeomen." He attacked the Democratic party and made a plea to "wipe out the color line, and put every man on his citizenship irrespective of color."

The Bourbons of the day also made use of violence against the insurgent Populists. At one point, H. S. Doyle, a young Negro preacher, a friend of Watson's and a very active Populist orator, was threatened with a lynching. He came to Watson for protection. Watson sent out riders on horseback and all night long poor whites, some two thousand of them, streamed in to protect a black man. Watson addressed the crowd as follows:

> . . . in this free country . . . the humblest white or black man that wants to talk our doctrine shall do it, and the man doesn't live who shall touch a hair of his head, without fighting every man in the people's party.

The reaction of the Democratic press is also instructive, This effort at coalition so alarmed them that one newspaper declared that "Watson has gone mad" and another announced that the entire South was "threatened with anarchy and communism" because of "the direful teachings of Thomas E. Watson."[56]

The accomplishment of the Georgia Populists was limited, as judged by contemporary standards, but the point remains, that in the heart of the Deep South, poor whites did, to some extent, make comon cause with blacks. When that happened, the reaction of the ruling classes and their party involved violence, fraud, and nearly the entire repertory of racist appeal.[57]

Another rather impressive instance where "high-status" persons were involved in lynching took place in New Orleans in 1891. Eleven Italians being held in the city jail were lynched. The mob in this case was led by the district attorney. The incident, understandably, caused some difficulties in Italian-American affairs. President Harrison offered apologies and satisfaction. It is of interest to note the reaction of Theodore Roosevelt to the entire episode.

Publically he approved of Harrison's actions, this being in a statement published in the *Independent*. Privately, however, writing to his sister, he indicated that he thought the lynching "rather a good thing."[58]

In a commencement address at Swarthmore College, a young man, a Quaker, referred to the New Orleans lynchers as an "aristocratic" mob. The mob acted, the speaker asserted, only after "justice" had been denied by a jury that refused to convict the Italians of murder. This was the position of Mitchell Palmer, destined to become the nation's chief law enforcement officer and leader of the "raids" that bear his name.[59]

A leading authority on lynching summarized his researches as follows:

> It would be erroneous . . . to leave the impression that all the lynchers were of shiftless, irresponsible, property-less type. At Scooba, Mississippi, where a double lynching occurred, the two men reported to have organized and engineered the mob from start to finish were leading people in the community and prominently identified with the local church, school, and other community activities. *Generally speaking, the more backward the community, the more likely were the "best people" to participate in the actual lynching.*

In addition to actual participation, this authority continued, there is also the question about those standing by, knowing about the events, but not themselves being directly involved. It is reported that:

> In every community where lynchings occurred in 1930, there were some people who openly justified what had been done. All walks of life were represented among the apologists—judges, prosecuting attorneys, lawyers, businessmen, doctors, preachers, teachers, mechanics, day laborers, and women of many types.[60]

This limited review of evidence on the subject of lynching suggests that the conventional presentations are misleading. Historically, the institution had upper-class beginnings in pre-Revolutionary days and also in the Reconstruction period in the South. In those periods, the practice was both "taught" to other participants and legitimized. In still later times, where the Populist insurgency appeared, such violence was again widely used and was again undertaken by the same "sponsors." In later periods, after the political threat disappeared, these upper classes or their children have claimed that the behavior was something done by others. The little evidence available on the subject indicates that even in the later post-Populist lynchings there was considerable involvement of the "better" people, both as participants and as apologists.

Another kind of evidence that is cited in support of the working-class authoritarianism hypothesis is the evidence of street confrontations, most of these having occurred in working-class neighborhoods. In these instances crowds of white workers have been present on the scene engaging in, advocating, or supporting violence. The pictures, in newspapers, magazines, or on television, leave little doubt as to the intensity of the bigotry involved.

Such events do not contradict the evidence and the assertions made previously. In all the tables presented, there is an intolerant group present, and, from among that group (in most instances, a small percentage of the total) it would certainly be possible to recruit large *numbers* of individuals to create a sizable street action, certainly one that would prove adequate to dominate the week's headlines.

There are a number of considerations to be noted about such experiences, considerations that would lead one to question the most frequent interpretation of such events. Ordinarily a street conflict will take place at the edge of the ghetto, that is, where there is some "integration" of blacks and whites. The next most likely context for a confrontation is in the immediately adjacent areas, which, in most cases, happen to be working-class areas. For reasons of geography, therefore, this sample of experience is almost necessarily linked to working-class contexts. The parallel experience, blacks and whites in contact in an upper-middle-class area could not occur unless one or the other of the contending parties were transported some considerable distance. This sample of experience, therefore, is biased because the possibilities for conflict are not equal.

The fact of a conflict within a working-class area does not necessarily indicate the dominant sentiment of those living there. A mob of hundreds may be only a fraction of the area's population which, in turn, might number in the tens of thousands. Still another point to be considered involves the usual tacit assumption that the active members of the mob come from the area. This is not entirely justified since there is some evidence that individual and organized bigots come from miles around to make the action.[61] It proves useful to review some cases.

In the summer of 1966, civil rights activists, under the leadership of the Reverend Martin Luther King, marched into various neighborhoods and outlying communities in the Chicago area demanding open housing agreements. On numerous occasions crowds of spectators, heckling and jeering, faced the demonstrators. The most serious confrontation of forces occurred in connection with the march into Cicero, Illinois, a working-class "suburban" community. The original march, scheduled for the last week in August, was called off when King and his group reached an agreement with "community leaders" of the Chicago area. Some blacks who were not part of this negotiating announced their plans for continuing the march and rescheduled the effort for Sunday of the Labor Day weekend.

Approximately 200 persons marched into Cicero that afternoon. Given the reputation of the community, extensive preparations had been made to "keep the peace." The police from Chicago and Cicero and from other communities accompanied the marchers. Also present were county sheriffs and units of the Illinois National Guard.

There were approximately 200 hecklers who followed the marchers, gathering strength as they proceeded. They showered stones, bottles, and cherry bombs on the protesters throughout the course of the march. As the protesters returned and crossed into Chicago, fights broke out between the demonstrators and counter-demonstrators, the latter group numbering approximately 500 at this point. The police and national guard moved in. Some persons were bayonetted and numerous arrests were made.

These events, understandably, provided what appeared to be unassailable evidence about the state of sentiment within the white working class.

It will be noted, however, that the maximum estimate of the counter-demonstrators' numbers was 500. The population of the city of Ciero is approximately 70,000. If one were to assume that all of the counter-demonstrators were from Cicero, it is still clear that the overwhelming majority of the citizens avoided the event. The other point to be noted, judging from the arrest records, is that a fair proportion, approximately one-third, of the counter-demonstrators came from outside of Cicero. It would appear that a widely advertised event of this kind draws bigots from miles around and is, therefore, not adequate testimony as to the state of sentiment within the immediate community. There were reports, for example, that both the Ku Klux Klan and the American Nazi party were involved in the events.[62]

A series of similar events occurred a year later in the city of Milwaukee. Again there was much violence with white working-class youths attacking civil rights marchers.

In late August 1967, Father James Groppi led the first of a series of marches through the city of Milwaukee in support of open housing. This march, planned for from seven to nine o'clock in the evening, took the civil rights marchers to Kosciuszko Park in the heart of the South Side, which is heavily working class and presumably Polish.[63] The police estimated that the spectators along the march route numbered 3000 and those in the park 5000. Fights broke out along the route and showers of rocks and bottles fell on the marchers at various places. Those involved in the violence appeared to be white teen-agers, their number being estimated at 500. On the following night there was a second march to the same destination. This time there was more violence, many were hospitalized, and the police used tear gas and shotgun volleys to disperse the crowd. It was estimated that between 6000 and 8000 spectators were present on the scene and that about 1000 were involved in the violent attack on the demonstrators. The evidence of working-class (and ethnic) racism seemed clear especially given the pictures and the reports of white youths shouting "We want slaves" and "get yourself a nigger."[64]

The area surrounding the park, that is, the area within a radius of fifteen or so blocks contained a population of more than 150,000 persons. If one assumes that all those present came from the area and that the very young and the very old were not present, that still suggests that fewer than one in ten of the area residents came out on these evenings as spectators and that possibly one in a hundred actively opposed the demonstrators.

A small random sample of adults from the area was interviewed by one of the local newspapers. This inquiry indicated that 80 percent of the area's residents disapproved of the white counter-protest. Some 67 percent of those questioned said that any group has the right to demonstrate legally anywhere in the city. There was strong disapproval of Father Groppi indicated, most of these persons feeling that he was doing more harm than good.[65]

Another South Side march took place on a Saturday early in September. Although this one too was viewed by "thousands of whites" there were "no major incidents." A similar march occurred on the following Saturday. This time there were again only a "few incidents." There were "no more than 500" along the march route and only an estimated 3000 in the park itself. The relative quiet, however, was deceptive. On Sunday, the police did battle with white mobs, trying to disperse them and to prevent contact with a large number of civil rights marchers on the South Side. The white mob was reported as "at times numbering several hundred persons," including many women. It was also reported that some South Side residents were "angry at the mobs, which contained many persons from other areas."[66]

On Monday, a mob of "hundreds of angry whites," after first clashing with civil rights marchers on the South Side, crossed over to the North Side intent on going into the ghetto for their counter-demonstration. The police blocked their route. This development, described as involving about 1000 whites, stemmed from some prior organizational effort. The counter-demonstrations originated in two South Side parks. The first of these efforts was organized by three men, one from the area and the other two from an outlying town. This rally was addressed by a man (a machinist) from Racine, a city to the south of Milwaukee. The other park rally appeared to be indigenous. Some local people, working together with these three, had planned the actions of this particular evening during the previous week.

Another march of the counter-demonstrators occurred on the following night. This involved approximately 650 youths and was again organized by the local forces. Some sense of the expanded base of the operation, however, may be seen in the fact that the leading speaker at the beginning rally was a field director of a national state's rights organization who had come in from Lutherville, Maryland.[67]

On Wednesday of that week there were more actions by the counter-demonstrators, they now being organized into a group called the White Power Rangers. Once again there was much violence. The police used tear gas to disperse some 2000 youths. If one took that as being exclusively South Side youth, it might appear to be a formidable demonstration of the area's views. Among those arrested, however, were members of the American Nazi Party, who were in town from Chicago. They were carrying posters of swastikas which were labeled the "Symbol of White Power." Less than half of those arrested on this evening were from the South Side. Many of the arrested persons were from the North Side of the city and some were from outlying communities. One of those arrested came from an elegant North Shore suburb.[68]

The efforts of the counter-demonstrators dwindled considerably after this conflict with the police. The marches of the open housing advocates into the South Side continued, but the reactions, measured by the numbers of spectators or of counter-demonstrators, were minimal. An effort was made to organize a more "responsible" group of South Side opposition, this having among its leaders a south side priest. They promised to have 1000 people to march on city hall to oppose open housing. On the evening of their announced march they were able to muster some fifty persons.[69]

The major lesson suggested by these two cases is that the "dramatic" instances of violence in working-class areas may be deceptive and misleading if taken as an indication of the dominant sentiment of the subcommunity. It is clear that only a small minority participates and that many of those involved are attracted from outside the immediate area.[70]

The major lesson indicated by this review of the evidence on class and attitudes toward civil rights is that the working-class authoritarianism hypothesis proves to have strikingly limited support. The review of the survey data shows that for all practical purposes, outside of the South there is no support for the hypothesis. A limited review of behavioral evidence, on voting and doing violence, also suggests that the claim has, to say the least, been somewhat exaggerated.

Civil Liberties

A second major theme emphasized by those arguing the existence of a "working-class authoritarianism" involves the area of civil liberties. One such formulation puts the matter as follows:

> There can be little doubt that in the United States the rights of dissidents and of Communists are protected primarily by the powerful classes who accept the traditional norms under which a democratic system operates. This seems to be true in other countries as well, that is, the upper and better educated strata are more likely to be tolerant of dissent, and to recognize the need for civil liberties than the workers, the farmers, and the less educated.[71]

This indicates the lay of attitudes (and also, presumably, of behavioral tendencies). There are some qualifications made about the relationship between such attitudes and political *events*, it being recognized that mass attitudes have little direct impact on the latter. In general, those attracted to this viewpoint have argued that the absence of any such direct impact is a good thing; otherwise, given the frequency distribution and the class-related tendency, civil liberties would be immediately endangered by direct mass involvement. In general, the presentations also assume that these attitudes appear as a result of training or experience *within* the working-class milieu. There is little consideration given to the obvious alternative possibility, that attitudes may have external origins.

Possibly the most striking evidence offered in support of this thesis derives from the work of Samuel A. Stouffer. In an attempt to assess the impact of McCarthyism (Joseph R.) on mass and local elite attitudes, Stouffer undertook two large national surveys of the American population and special surveys of selected community leaders. The two national surveys, both of which involved rather large samples, were conducted by different research organizations. The same questions were asked, however, and the results of the two investigations showed a striking congruence with one another. For this reason, most of the data from the study have been presented with the results from the two surveys combined.

The main presentation takes male respondents only and gives, for five major occupational groups, the percentages who are "more tolerant" with respect to civil liberties issues. The groups and the percentages follow: professional and semiprofessional, 66%; proprietors, managers, and officials, 51%; clerical and sales, 49%; manual workers, 30%; and farmers and farm workers, 20%.[72] The difference between the professionals and the manual workers is an impressive one of 36 percentage points. The former group has a "more tolerant" majority, two-thirds falling in that category as opposed to only one-third among the manuals. With such a large difference indicated in what is probably the best study of the subject ever accomplished, the case would appear to be unassailable. Should there be any doubt as to the factors operative, a second table controlling for education showed less working-class tolerance at each educational level than was to be found in the middle class.[73]

A detailed examination of the responses to the questions contained in the Stouffer "tolerance" scale indicates a rather sizable variation by occupation in the responses to some of the questions and practically none in response to others (see Table 11.7). Five of the questions asked about "an admitted Communist." In the responses to these questions, there are large differences in the levels of tolerance, the differences between professionals and manual workers averaging just under 30 percentage points. Two questions asked about "a person who favored government ownership of all the railroads and all big industries." The level of tolerance for this person is higher than for the admitted Communist. The occupational differences are still present, although in these instances they are somewhat smaller. Another range of three questions asked about "somebody who is against all churches and religion." Here, again, there are large differences by occupation, the average being just over 30 percentage points. The six remaining questions involve someone "whose loyalty has been questioned before a Congressional committee, but who swears under oath he has never been a Communist." The responses here show relatively high levels of tolerance and only very limited differences by occupation, the average difference between workers and professionals amounting to approximately 10 percentage points.

One point is immediately clear: the scale combines and therefore hides these rather diverse results. Perhaps of greatest significance is the support for "due process" on the part of manual workers in the case of the man whose

TABLE 11.7

Occupation and Civil Liberties (Males, Excluding "Don't Know" Occupation and Retirees), Stouffer Study

	Occupation				
	Professionals or Semi-professionals	Proprietors, Managers, and Officials	Clerical, Sales	Manual Workers	Farm[a]
	Percent "tolerant" (of those with opinions)				

Q. 1. "Suppose this admitted Communist wants to make a speech in your community. Should he be allowed to speak or not?"

Percent	53%	41%	40%	27%	20%
$N =$	(174)	(270)	(235)	(1001)	(265)

Q. 2. "Suppose he wrote a book which is in your public library. Somebody in your community suggests the book should be removed from the library. Would you be for removing it, or not?"

Percent	62	44	42	25	18
$N =$	(174)	(260)	(224)	(968)	(263)

Q. 3. "Suppose this admitted Communist is a radio singer. Should he be fired, or not?"

Percent	52	42	39	28	23
$N =$	(174)	(269)	(234)	(965)	(256)

Q. 4. "Should an admitted Communist be put in jail, or not?"

Percent	68	58	51	36	28
$N =$	(160)	(242)	(222)	(908)	(243)

Q. 5. "There are always some bad people whose ideas are considered bad or dangerous by other people. For instance, somebody who is against all churches and religion.

"If such a person wanted to make a speech in your city (town, community) against churches and religion, should he be allowed to speak, or not?"

Percent	72	48	50	36	23
$N =$	(174)	(267)	(234)	(993)	(259)

Q. 6. "If some people in your community suggested that a book he wrote against churches and religion should be taken out of your public library, would you favor removing this book or not?"

Percent	72	48	50	36	23
$N =$	(174)	(267)	(234)	(993)	(259)

Q. 7. "Now suppose the radio program he (an admitted Communist) is on advertises a brand of soap. Somebody in your community suggests you stop buying that soap. Would you stop, or not?"

Percent	77	68	65	58	52
$N =$	(174)	(267)	(227)	(968)	(252)

[a] Farmers, $N = 262$; farm laborers, $N = 20$.

436

TABLE 11.7 (Continued)

	Occupation				
	Professionals or Semi-professionals	Proprietors, Managers, and Officials	Clerical, Sales	Manual Workers	Farm[a]

Q. 8. "Or consider a person who favored government ownership of all the rail-roads and all big industries.

"If this person wanted to make a speech in your community favoring government ownership of all the railroads and big industries, should he be allowed to speak, or not?"

Percent	86	78	73	64	55
$N =$	(177)	(273)	(234)	(963)	(257)

Q. 9 "If some people in your community suggested that a book he wrote favoring government ownership should be taken out of your public library, would you favor removing the book or not?"

Percent	82	71	71	58	47
$N =$	(175)	(265)	(229)	(953)	(242)

Q. 10. "Now I would like you to think of another person. A man whose loyalty has been questioned before a Congressional committee, but who swears under oath he has never been a Communist.

"Suppose he is teaching in a college or university. Should he be fired or not?"

Percent	90	87	85	79	71
$N =$	(163)	(267)	(227)	(951)	(250)

Q. 11. "Should he be allowed to make a speech in your community, or not?"

Percent	91	87	86	79	71
$N =$	(170)	(267)	(233)	(961)	(250)

Q. 12. "Suppose this man is a high school teacher. Should he be fired or not?"

Percent	86	85	81	79	69
$N =$	(165)	(267)	(232)	(955)	(247)

Q. 13. "Suppose he has been working in a defense plant. Should he be fired, or not?"

Percent	89	89	84	82	74
$N =$	(164)	(265)	(226)	(940)	(242)

Q. 14. "Suppose he is a clerk in a store. Should he be fired or not?"

Percent	98	94	93	88	81
$N =$	(169)	(269)	(233)	(964)	(249)

Q. 15. "Suppose he wrote a book which is in your public library. Somebody in your community suggests the book should be removed from the library. Would you favor removing it, or not?"

Percent	92	92	88	81	73
$N =$	(163)	(258)	(225)	(930)	(245)

"loyalty" was questioned. Approximately four out of five do *not* feel he should be fired from jobs or have his free speech abridged. Even in the face of the modified conceptions of due process that characterized the 1950s, it is impressive to note that very large majorities of the manual workers still demanded proof; unsubstantiated allegations were insufficient.

Another hidden point concerns the differentiation within the working class. In most cases the tolerance of the skilled is greater than that of the semiskilled and their tolerance in turn is greater than that of the unskilled. In the case of the man accused of being a Communist, however, there is very little variation. Asked, for example, whether he should be fired from a teaching position in a college or university, 79 percent of the skilled ($N = 409$), 78 percent of the semiskilled ($N = 312$), and 85 percent of the unskilled ($N = 136$) take the tolerant position. The equivalent figure for the professionals is 90 percent ($N = 163$).

One other point that appears to be of considerable importance is the fact that in all comparisons, the farm populations are less tolerant than the workers. Since the working class is disproportionately made up of ex-farmers, it seems likely that what is being called "working-class authoritarianism" might well be "farm authoritarianism" transferred from the rural setting.

For a limited, indirect test of this possibility it is useful to consider the pattern of tolerance by region and size of place. This limited inquiry indicates the level of tolerance for Communists and atheists to be consistently lowest among the Southern populations and also, in both South and non-South, to be low in the middle-sized and smaller communities. In all comparisons, the middle classes still prove to be somewhat more tolerant than the manual ranks (see Table 11.8). It is possible that this remaining class difference might be a result of a compositional difference and also might result from the distinctive patterns of migration found in the United States.

The evidence in Table 11.8 shows the middle-sized and small-town–rural contexts to be characterized by low tolerance levels for admitted Communists and for atheists. The lowest levels of tolerance are to be found among the workers in the Southern small towns and rural areas. In general, the farm populations, particularly in the South, have even lower levels of tolerance than the small-town and rural manual workers.[74] It is clear that some features of rural life, especially in the South, have given rise to the low levels of tolerance for admitted Communists and atheists. This rural-based intolerance may then be "transferred" to other locations when one moves off the land into nonfarm occupations. Since most of that movement is into the manual ranks, it would seem likely that such transfers might either make or enhance the class differences in tolerance within their new communities. This would be the case both as a result of movement within a region or as a result of the South to North migration between regions.

It was noted earlier that there is a disproportionate migration of middle-class persons into the South. This would be likely to transfer relatively toler-

TABLE 11.8

Class and Civil Liberties by Region and City Size (Males, Excluding "Don't Know" Occupation and Retirees), Stouffer Study

City Size	Region					
	Non-South			South		
	100,000 or More	2500–99,999	2499 or Less	100,000 or More	2500–99,999	2499 or Less
	Percent tolerant					
Q. 1. *Admitted Communist's right to speak*						
Middle class	51%	46%	43%	37%	27%	27%
N =	(270)	(160)	(92)	(56)	(49)	(52)
Working class	35	28	26	26	19	13
N =	(331)	(216)	(152)	(85)	(95)	(122)
Difference	+16	+18	+17	+11	+ 8	+14
Q. 5. *Atheist's right to speak*						
Middle class	65	57	55	56	34	35
N =	(273)	(161)	(95)	(61)	(50)	(49)
Working class	42	45	36	38	29	18
N =	(336)	(221)	(153)	(86)	(96)	(123)
Difference	+23	+12	+19	+18	+5	+17
Q. 11. *Accused man's right to speak*						
Middle class	90	87	84	90	80	85
N =	(268)	(157)	(93)	(58)	(46)	(48)
Working class	83	77	81	76	70	74
N =	(318)	(210)	(150)	(83)	(87)	(113)
Difference	+ 7	+10	+ 3	+14	+10	+11

ant populations and thus would either make or enhance the class differences in tolerance there.

Briefly, the above suggests that the observed differences do not result from the experiences of working-class life (for example, child-rearing, economic deprivations, or punishments), but instead may result from training and experience occurring prior to entry in the manual ranks and from the peculiar transfers of that experience between communities and regions.[75] The focus on the "class factor," if this is the case, may be mistaken, leading one away from consideration of the real origins of the intolerance in both the South and in the small towns and rural areas. The impact of the migrations may not be investigated with the Stouffer data since a question on place of origin was not asked. For that purpose we have to return to one of the Survey Research Center studies. Before doing so, however, it is important to make one other observation about the data of Table 11.8.

The statement quoted earlier about "the rights of dissidents" being protected "primarily by the powerful classes" clearly needs some qualification. When it is a matter of the "traditional norms," as in the questions about the accused man's rights, sizable majorities of all groups affirm the tolerant position. Even among the markedly "intolerant" small-town Southern workers we find, in the response to this question, approximately three out of four supporting the traditional norm. It would appear, then, that the problem with the "state of the masses" is not one of a general, irrational, and punitive orientation. The outlooks appear to be much more precisely specified; there is little support for the idea if punishment based on unsubstantiated denunciation. The compartmentalization, indicated by the corresponding lack of support for the admitted Communist, will be taken up at a later point.

The 1956 Survey Research Center study contained a question that parallels the "accused man" series in the Stouffer study. Although one is limited to a single question, this study has the advantage of allowing exploration of the impact of farm origins.

The 1956 statement reads as follows:

Q. 12n. The government ought to fire any government worker who is accused of being a Communist even though they don't prove it.

Respondents were asked to agree or disagree, provision being made for strong or not-so-strong concurrence or dissent. Fifty-six percent of all persons interviewed *dis*agreed with the suggestion, that is, chose the tolerant, civil libertarian option. Only 21 percent agreed and the remainder were "not sure" or had "no opinion." If we take only those with opinions, that is, those agreeing or disagreeing, one finds that 73 percent, or nearly three out of four, supported the "traditional norm."

Raising once again the "working-class authoritarianism" question, one finds, taking the percentages based on those with opinions, that 72 and 80 percent of the manuals and nonmanuals, respectively, took the tolerant position, the difference amounting to only 8 percentage points. This finding is consonant with the Stouffer conclusion based on surveys done two years previously. Again, roughly three out of four manual workers respect "due process." It is clearly not possible, on the basis of responses to this kind of question, to refer to the authoritarianism of the working *class* since such a sizable majority does take the tolerant position. The best that may be offered in support of the received hypothesis is this 8 percentage point difference.

This study also shows that the contemporary farm populations are less tolerant than the nonfarm populations, this being most especially the case in the South.[76] Since some of this farm intolerance is likely to have been carried into the nonfarm sector, it is important, in order to see whether it is working-class or farmer authoritarianism we are observing, to give separate consideration to those of farm and nonfarm origins.

Outside the South there is little difference in the tolerance of those segments of the middle and working classes who have nonfarm origins. The difference here is only 4 percentage points (see Table 11.9). Those middle- and working-class people of farm origins tend to have lower levels of tolerance, and, looking at the base figures, we find approximately twice as many ex-farmers and/or children of farmers in the working class as in the middle class. If we take the non-Southern respondents of nonfarm origins shown in Table 11.9 and exclude, in addition, those of Southern origin, then

TABLE 11.9
Tolerance by Class, Region, and Farm Origins (SRC 1956, Married, Active)

	Nonfarm Origin		Farm Origin	
Class:	Middle	Working	Middle	Working
	Percent tolerant[a]			
Non-South	81%	77%	73%	64%
$N =$	(269)	(256)	(63)	(113)
South	84	73	73	67
$N =$	(80)	(55)	(48)	(57)

[a] Civil liberties question, see text.

the difference in the levels of tolerance of manuals and nonmanuals is reduced to 2 percentage points.[77]

The reduction of the class differences occurs only in the non-South regions. Once again, in a pattern similar to that indicated with respect to the rights of blacks, the Southern workers still prove to be less tolerant, both in the case of those who grew up in the farm and in the nonfarm sectors.

Upward and Downward Mobility

Thus far it has been shown that intolerant attitudes are transferred to the working class as a result of farm-to-city movement. Also, it has been shown that the non-South manual ranks receive a large contribution of intolerance as a result of South-to-non-South migrations. In short, as opposed to the Lipset formulation, which focuses on experiences *within* the working class as the source of intolerance, this analysis has shown that much of the so-called authoritarianism comes from without.

It is worthwhile considering still another possible source of "transference." A minor source of new "recruits" to the working class is the nonfarm middle class, that is, those added through downward mobility. At the same time, there is a loss of working-class persons in the case of the upwardly mobile individuals.

There has been some evidence that downwardly mobile individuals tend to be less tolerant than others in their original rank and some suggestion that upwardly mobile individuals tend to be more tolerant than those who remain in the manual ranks.[78] If this is, in fact, the case, then there is a possibility that the processes of upward and downward mobility play some role in shifting the class-tolerance pattern, through losses of tolerant people to the upper-middle class and gains of intolerant ones by the working class. The differences in attitude associated with mobility and stability are small and not always supportive of the above assumptions. If we assume that the claims are valid, the overall impact would still be small since the differences in attitude between mobiles and stables are small and the number of persons involved, particularly in the case of the downward mobiles, is also relatively small.[79] Compared to the impact of the farm transfers, for example, the nonfarm mobility factor is of rather limited importance. It is only when taken in conjunction with a range of other factors working in the same direction that this rather minor consideration gains significance.

Education and Tolerance: A Note on the Dynamics of Mobility and Attitudes

In most readings of the evidence it is claimed that education creates tolerance. On the basis of a cross-tabulation of education and tolerance, some have imputed a direction of causation and claimed that the education causes the tolerant outlook.[80] Initially, at least, it seems unlikely that tolerance would, somehow or other, "cause" education. If, however, tolerant parents looked with favor on education and, conversely, intolerant parents regarded such effort with disfavor, it could be the case that "tolerance causes education." In more detail, that means that the tolerant parents teach their children tolerant outlooks *and* see to it that their children achieve high levels of education. The intolerant parents pass along their outlooks and either prohibit or discourage achievement of higher education. If this is the case, it would mean that within the younger contemporary generations there would develop a direct relationship between years of schooling and tolerance. Whether the schooling, by itself, led to or created tolerant attitudes would be a separate and open question.[81]

If this alternative interpretation of the processes operating were correct, it would also mean that tolerant working-class parents were preparing their children for upward mobility in the course of which the children would carry along their tolerant attitudes. Intolerant middle-class parents, by comparison, would be preparing their children for downward mobility. The relative intolerance of the downward mobiles in this case would not be a result of the traumas accompanying a loss of position, but would have antedated that loss.

A very striking example of the upward mobility process occurred in the case of American Jews. The first generation was largely occupied in manual tasks, but two and three generations later, the overwhelming majority were located in nonmanual ranks. In the process, as an aid to or instrument of mobility (or in some cases, a mere by-product of mobility) very high levels of education were achieved. It was not the case, however, that the education created their tolerance. The tolerance was there long before the education.

Rather than leave this point at the level of speculation (with an illustration), an effort was made to find a study that would allow some test of this alternative reading of the causal question. For this purpose, it was necessary to find a study that had questions on both tolerance and on college aspirations (or the lack thereof) for one's children. A study undertaken by *Fortune* magazine in 1949 proved useful for this purpose.[82] It contained a number of questions about whether or not colleges should have classes in various areas or, alternatively, that there be no such discussion. The areas in question were racial and religious prejudice, sex education, religious beliefs, and communism. For the present purpose, only male respondents who had no college education were considered. They were divided into manual and nonmanual categories, and using the above questions, they were divided further into "more tolerant" and "less tolerant" categories.[83]

The less tolerant group did tend, as expected, to be less interested in having a son or daughter go to college (see Table 11.10). The differences, in short,

TABLE 11.10

Tolerance and College Aspirations for Children: Male Respondents with less than College Education (*Fortune*, Study No. 76, 1949)

	Tolerance Level[a]	
	More Tolerant	Less Tolerant

Qs. 1 & 2. "If you had a boy [girl] graduating from high school, would you personally like to have him go on to college, or would you rather have him do something else?"

	Would *not* want boy to attend college	
Manuals	9%	23%
$N =$	(532)	(122)
Nonmanuals	7	15
$N =$	(373)	(87)

	Would *not* want girl to go to college	
Manuals[b]	27	49
Nonmnuals[b]	25	31

[a] See note 83 for explanation.

[b] Same *N*s as above.

are such as would support the view that tolerance of the parents would affect the level of education achieved by the children. The tolerant manual parents, being more willing to send their children to college, are more likely to "prepare" them for upward mobility; the intolerant nonmanuals, by contrast, tend to "prepare" their children for downward mobility.

Another question in this study asked about the perceptions of the "average college student." It must be remembered that the respondents being discussed had not attended college and the date of the study was 1949. There were systematic differences in the perceptions; the tolerant respondents, both in the manual and the nonmanual comparisons, gave more positive descriptions of students than the intolerant respondents. The former group, for example, were more likely to consider college students to be intelligent, well-informed, well-mannered, hard-working, and ambitious. By comparision, the less tolerant respondents tended to portray the college students in negative terms. They were more likely to consider the students as soft, time-wasting, hard-drinking, and snobbish.[84] Given this perception, it seems likely that the intolerant parents would want to keep their children, especially their daughters, out of such an environment.

It is worth speculating on still another possibility that may yield the same effect on mobility. Only a minority of the less tolerant working-class group did not want a son to go to college; approximately three-quarters of these parents followed the dominant sentiment. It seems reasonable to assume that tolerance and intolerance, like party identification, religion, and numerous other orientations, are passed on within families from parents to children. It seems likely that the children of these intolerant parents would have a "bad experience" in college. In courses that involved what to them would be "controversial" social, political, or cultural content, it seems likely that they would be disposed to reject new information if it conflicted with their received outlooks. A likely consequence of such a rejection of information would be that they would do poorly on examinations and they would graduate with a low average. Alternatively, they might drop out. This suggests that even if they do get into college, it is probable that the children of intolerant parents will suffer a fate similar to that of their peers who never made it into college. It is also possible that the intolerent person who "drops out" (or, in his view, possibly, is "forced out") would react with increased hostility toward the universities and the people in them.[85]

Other Influences: Public Figures and the Mass Media

What has been indicated thus far is that the intolerance of the working class in the civil liberties area, in part, is caused by some peculiar contributions from outside the class milieu; the non-South manual ranks receive the "contributions" of farm intolerance and the intolerance from the Southern milieu. As indicated with the 1956 question on the rights of the accused man, there was essentially no difference in the attitudes of manuals and nonmanuals once these two factors were controlled. Within this "core" group of the working class—the non-South group of nonfarm origins—the experiences of deprivation, of child-rearing, and so on that occur "within" the class contribute nothing to the shaping of class differences in the responses to this particular question. The considerations so heavily stressed by Lipset in his original formulation of the working-class authoritarianism position, therefore, appear to be of no importance. Instead, the factors making the "working-class authoritarianism" (actually, the small percentage edge of intolerance in this case) prove to be the "flows" into the class. Whether or not one comes to the same pessimistic conclusions about the possibility of democracy would depend, then, not on the basic conditions of working-class life, but rather on the size of the flows into the working class and on the stability of the attitudes carried into the new milieu.[86]

This whole discussion depends on the admittedly inadequate base of one question from the 1956 Survey Research Center study. This question, as noted, is similar to the range of questions used by Stouffer with respect to the "accused man." With respect to "his" situation, it was noted that a majority of the population was tolerant (or "responsible") and that the class differences were very small. Were one able to follow the same line of analysis used with respect to the 1956 study, that is, were one able to exclude the impact of the two intolerant flows, it is possible that the class differences would be erased there also.

It seems unlikely, however, that this same effort would eliminate all the difference with respect to the admitted Communist and his rights. What is the source of this more sizable difference? In particular, we are once again raising the question as to whether the difference stems from factors inherent in the class situation or whether it is once again caused by an outside influence.

One immediate possibility involves the declarations of prominent public figures and the reporting of these in the mass media. In the so-called McCarthy Era, many persons made claims about the loyalty of fellow citizens, about the threat of domestic communism, about the numbers of communists in the government, and so on. In retrospect, it is easy to characterize the era with the name of one man, as if he alone were responsible for the development; it is especially convenient when that man is dead. It should be noted, however, that also participating in the wider venture were numerous surviving senators, may members of the established elites, a congressman who went on to become president, intellectuals, scholars, journalists, and many others.[87]

One characteristic of the period was that the charges made on Monday were no longer "current" by Wednesday. In their place, new charges were brought that, in turn, were displaced by Friday. It would obviously be difficult for the ordinary citizen to assess the validity of such multifarious claims. They came too fast; the events were frequently years in the past; they were distant from the lives of most citizens. The concerned citizen in Kankakee, Illinois, was not in a position to discover the "truth" about the day's accusations through his own efforts. Therefore, the average citizen was dependent on the news media both for factual material and for evaluations of that material.

One of the features of the era was a widespread acceptance of the claims on the part of local newspapers. Explicit, day-to-day approval of the specific claims was not typically the case. It would have proved difficult for even the most astute editor or publisher to assess each claim. The more frequent position was to adopt the apothegm, "where there's smoke, there's fire." In other words, while equivocating on the details of the outpouring of cases, this evaluation argued that, in essence, there must be something to it. There were very few sources present on the American scene claiming that charlatanry might be involved, although, according to one post-era source, this was recognized be some close and influential observers from the very start.[88]

The question should be raised as to whether acceptance of the claims, the sense of urgency, and the resultant sense of the priorities was a function of the "education and training" offered by the local newspapers and by some national magazine rather than caused by the character structure of workers. This is to argue (or at least to entertain the possibility) that the result indicated in the Stouffer study is better explained by "situational" factors rather than by "character." The first element of the situation was the "lesson" offered by various rightist demagogues. A second element, the crucial one in generating the mass sentiment, was that the "lesson" was assented to, vouched for, and accredited by a wide range of high-status public figures, by national political elites, and by local news media. In this connection, it would seem that the local newspapers would be the most important media since they are more widely read by manual workers (as opposed to national news magazines) and have more detail and more opinion allowed than is the case with either radio or television. Both national political figures and the various metropolitan and provincial press lords, it will be noted, are of the upper class or, at minimum, of the upper-middle class. The key agents "mediating" between the demagogues and the populace, in other words, prove to be rather powerful people of rather high status. It is suggested that these upper-class "authoritarians" made the mass sentiment of the era. Without the upper-class efforts, the *mass* hysteria of the era could never have occurred.[89]

As indicated in an earlier chapter, it is just this kind of "distant" issue that allows the most easy manipulation of public sentiment. It is possible to build up a sense of urgency in the general population, a sense of the imminent danger, and to suggest that the government is filled with persons bent on treason. For the average man living some distance from those "events" and unable to prove the validity of the claims, a likely response is the adoption of a defensive stance. As indicated earlier, working-class life, in great measure, is characterized by a wide range of fears—fear of distant and not well-known events, of war, of atomic fallout, of fluoridation, and so forth. An appropriate response is to guard against all such threats. This again means that the reaction may be "situational" rather than a result of "character." In this case, it should be noted that established upper-class figures structured the situation so as to stimulate both the fears and the reaction.

The Stouffer study indicated that the manual workers were slightly more likely than the middle classes to see a "great" or "very great" danger posed by American Communists. The differences, to be sure, were not very large. As one would expect, those perceiving a "great" or "very great" danger from the American Communists are disinclined to grant a Communist the right of free speech (see Table 11.11). Among the non-South manuals, for example, only 22 percent of those sensing a major threat would support that right, as opposed to 46 percent among those seeing "hardly any" or no danger. The perception of threat has no impact at all on the willingness to grant free speech to the "accused man." This again indicates that the original tolerance scale mixes different dimensions. It also makes clear once again that the

TABLE 11.11

Perception of Communist Threat and Tolerance by Class: Non-South Only (Stouffer: Married, Active Males)

	Communist Threat[a]		
	Very Great or Great Danger	Some Danger	Hardly Any or No Danger
	Percent tolerant		
Manuals			
Free speech for			
Communist	22%	34%	46%
N =	(250)	(242)	(89)
Accused man	80	85	79
N =	(250)	(236)	(86)
Nonmanuals			
Free speech for			
Communist	40	52	57
N =	(171)	(186)	(90)
Accused man	88	89	87
N =	(169)	(189)	(89)

[a] The question reads: "How great a danger do you feel that American Communists are to this country at the present time—a very great danger, a great danger, some danger, hardly any danger, or no danger?"

working-class response is not one of irrational hostility to all real or potential threats. The responses, in short, appear to be clearly compartmentalized.

Two things stand out in this discussion so far: manual workers are more likely to perceive a threat from the American Communists, and, also, at any given level of perceived threat, workers are more willing to abridge the free speech of the Communist. One other point deserving attention is that even among those perceiving little or no threat, there is a large proportion who are unwilling to support free speech for Communists.

In part, the pattern may be accounted for as a response to or acceptance of the new official and unofficial elite practice of the age. In both the government and in private agencies, the new practice involved denial of rights to admitted Communists. The official practice went even further and denied rights to "loyalty risks," that is, people who had been "accused" but against whom nothing had been proved. In this respect, official practice proved less tolerant than the mass sentiment of the period, the latter being, as has been shown, unwilling to accept the unproved charge. The official practice beginning in the Truman presidency and carried through into the Eisenhower period involved a major shift from traditional "rules of the game." Traditionally, the civil libertarian position was that it took *acts* in violation of law to justify abridgment of individual rights. In the extreme case, the exception to this rule, it was held that the exercise of free speech could be abridged where there was no legal violation but where there was a "clear and present danger." The practice instituted in the Truman period changed this tradition making *membership* (quite apart from any acts) in the Communist party sufficient grounds for denial of rights, the right in question being to a government job or a job in defense plants. The abridgements were extended, under the "loyalty programs" to include persons who were accused of disloyalty. Trials or proof were not required; "sufficient grounds" in the judgment of a loyalty board were all that was necessary. In communities, in colleges and universities, and in the mass media, the same new principles were used to abridge the right of free speech. The new principles were promulgated, then, by leaders in the federal and local governments and by the heads of private organizations. Also supporting the new position was an organization of liberal notables—the Americans for Democratic Action. Intellectual justification was provided in the work of an eminent liberal, Professor Sidney Hook.[90]

It seems likely that the working-class response involved little more than an acceptance of the official "sounds of alarm" and of the official position about a need for new "rules of the game." If this was the case, then the working-class responses would not indicate "authoritarianism" but instead would indicate acceptance of the leads provided by governments and private "opinion leaders." That workers prove more likely to accept the definitions of threat as valid, possibly stems from their lack of defenses. That is, they lack alternative sources of information with which to check or challenge the official claims. Because of the absent defenses, it seems likely that they react with greater alarm and concern when "threats" are dramatized for them.[91] This account would suggest a confirmation of the mass society viewpoint, the portrayal being one of a helpless, dependent, and easily swayed population. The actual situation is considerably more complicated since, as will be shown below, that alarm was *not* correlated with a simple and easy behavioral response, a vote for those sounding the alarm. As was pointed out in Chapter 3, those candidates McCarthy favored with his active support tended to lose votes rather than gain them.

The second "episode" in the history of the era involved a shift in the focus of the attacks. McCarthy, who had been sponsored and supported in his attacks on the Democrats, turned his attention to Republicans, the leading targets being members of the Eisenhower administration. When this happened, there was an understandable change in establishment sentiment. Political and economic notables now opposed McCarthy and his efforts were eventually nullified.

This belated response on the part of some "distinguished" figures contributed to the notion of the elites and upper classes as the protectors of civil liberties and as the defenders of democracy against the irresponsible demagogues with their mass (or "populist") support. An analysis of the themes stressed in the man's speeches also appeared to support the same conclusion, the themes consisting of attacks on the eastern establishment, and on the rich and well-born. Still another contribution to the image of responsible elites and irresponsible masses came from the surveys and polls of the time, most of which showed greater working-class support for McCarthy than was to be found in the middle or upper-middle class.[92]

The first of these points, however, errs in that it focuses only on the era of the "put down" and neglects the period of the build up. By considering only the put down, the analyses overlook the fact that he was both *made and broken* by "established" or, at least, very influential figures. Senator Taft's advice cannot be overlooked nor can the efforts of the newspapers that contributed to his national "success." For some, apparently, the support was merely tactical, a useful issue in the struggle against the opposition party. For others, however, the support was that of the true believer. Given the tactical and ideological support from the upper-class ranks, the notion of "responsibility" as applied to that class seems at best somewhat doubtful. The "responsibility" developed only when the thrusts began hitting their own members.[93]

Survey evidence does show the manual ranks as more approving of McCarthy and his methods than the middle classes.[94] Again, rather than taking attitudes as an "uncaused cause," it is worth while asking *why* they were that way. As was noted above, much of the urban press (Hearst and others), together with the provincial press in middle-sized cities and small towns, was arguing, in essence, that "where there's smoke, there's fire." Many newspapers also argued that given the nature of the "threat," "unusual" means were necessary and justified.

An additional problem is posed for the conventional position by consideration of behavior. The surveys show sentiments, outlooks, orientations. A more telling indicator of "responsibility" or "irresponsibility" appears in the case of actions. A rather simple but instructive action in this connection involves voting. The only population having a chance to vote directly for the man was the Wisconsin population, McCarthy having run a second time in 1952. If the upper and upper-middle classes were "responsible," that ought to be indicated in the voting pattern in that state. The same holds for the assumptions about the working class and the presumed responsiveness to "demagogic" appeals.

In the city of Milwaukee all but one of the wards turned out a majority for McCarthy's opponent. The single exception was an upper-class, North Side, lakeshore ward (see Chapter 4). In the working-class and "ethnic" South Side of Milwaukee the vote was more than two to one *in opposition to* McCarthy. In the surrounding county, McCarthy gained a majority in Wauwatosa, the large middle-class suburb to the west. He also gained heavy majorities in all the upper-middle-class suburbs on the north shore of the city. As one moves northward from the merely upper-middle class to the more exclusive settings, the size of the McCarthy majority increases. In River Hills, where the city's richest and most influential citizens reside, the vote was three to one for McCarthy.[95]

The lesson would appear to be clear. Working-class populations responded with alarm and concern over the domestic "communist threat" and felt a need for decisive action to oppose it. When, however, it came to a clear-cut choice between the leading demagogue advocating the "tough" position and a liberal Democrat, they preferred the latter. In other words, the poorly educated, ethnic, working-class population favored the "responsible" candidate. By contrast, the upper- and upper-middle-class electorates, that is, the educated, well-off, and presumably "responsible" populations, voted overwhelmingly for the "irresponsible" candidate.

The related claim, that McCarthyism had Populist, or in Wisconsin's case, Progressive, roots has been criticized recently in a detailed analysis of the voting in Wisconsin. The major conclusion of this analysis is that the areas that supported classic conservatives in the past supported McCarthy in 1952.[96] The major lesson from the evidence on voting, then, is one of continuity of orientations rather than a sweeping transformation as has been asserted. Conservatives supported conservative candidates in the past and they continued to do so now. If the "populist" themes were decisive at all in the 1952 election it would appear that they somehow appealed to the state's better-off populations. Another lesson is that the demagogic appeals seem to have had only limited impact on the behavior of the working class. The demagogic technique does not appear to be as effective as is generally believed.

Red scares, in short, are created by the upper classes. It is a simple device, long since known and recognized by the victims, the left, or, in some cases, the liberal opposition. In recent scholarship the dynamics have been obscured, it being argued that the events are made by "demagogues" who stimulate the poor and the masses while the educated and responsible elites stand to one side, appalled and helpless. In view of the Wisconsin voting pattern, however, it does not appear justified to view them as either appalled or helpless.

One other point to be considered in this connection is the persistence question. The initiators of a scare do suffer some loss of control since what they stimulate is a large movement and it is impossible for them to control all the details and directions of a sprawling, amorphous development. Senator McCarthy, for example, got out of hand. Many organizations set up to carry on the effort gain a degree of autonomy of their own. The leaders choose their own directions and reject the guidance of the initiators of the movement. When the initiators end, or at least attempt to end, the "scare," they too come to be defined as part of the conspiracy.

The point is that such movements cannot be "turned off" as easily as they are "turned on." The sentiments aroused, the militancy created, and the organizations formed will all remain after the whole effort has ceased to be of use to the initiating elites. It was noted earlier in this chapter that lynching had upper-class origins. The initial development of the Ku Klux Klan and the violence designed to undo Reconstruction had upper-class leadership and direction. After the initial purpose had been served, the practices had been legitimated and the "masses" (some of them) trained in the procedures.[97]

The Civil Liberties Question: A Summary

The following summary conclusions appear to be in order with respect to the question of class and civil liberties matters as discussed thus far.

The use of the Stouffer "scale" misrepresents the realities. Rather than there being a general working-class intolerance in all areas, there is a significant differentiation in attitude according to whether one is talking about an accused man or an admitted Communist (or a Socialist or athiest). In the case of the accused man, there is little class difference indicated and even that proves to be largely a function of extraneous contributions, notably the place of origin.

There is a consistent class difference with respect to the rights of the admitted Communist, Socialist, or athiest. The question to be considered in this connection is whether the differences are a result of factors inherent in the class situation or whether they also stem from some "outside" influence. It seems likely that the responses result from the "training" or experience gained in "red scares." As noted, the two major scares of the twentieth century as well as some of the minor ones had their beginnings in rather high places.

All that is "indigenous" to the working class is a greater general anxiety and a more extreme response when presented with the appearance or claim of a threat, claims or appearances that workers cannot easily assess. It was also shown that when it came to a vote for the rightist demagogue, in the case of Senator Joseph McCarthy, that vote varied directly with class level, rather than inversely. The surveys, thus, suggest a greater anxiety in the working-class ranks and a greater acceptance of the cues proffered by leading newspapers. The voting, however, shows another pattern; it shows workers voting for a liberal (in civil rights and in economic affairs) and the upper-middle classes supporting the "irresponsible" demagogue.

Most of the attention in this analysis has been devoted to the disparity between the attitudes toward the accused man and the admitted Communist. It seems likely that the attitude toward the Socialist may be explained along the same lines as the attitude toward the Communist, the press and various public spokesmen never having made much effort to distinguish between the two.

The attitude toward the admitted athiest, however, is another matter. It seems likely that what we have here is a cultural conservatism that has its roots in small-town and rural settings, particularly in the South. Assuming that the working class is disproportionately made up of people from such origins, the rural or small-town fundamentalist nativism finds its reflection in these data. This contribution to the Stouffer results also has "outside" origins, that is, it involves an attitude carried with one in the course of shifting from farm to city employment.

None of the above observations is intended to detract from the basic frequency distributions in the responses to this specific set of questions. Those questions involving "deviations" from conventional political and religious positions, do show a greater working-class intolerance than is found in the middle class. The question being raised in connection with this set of questions is the source of the attitudes: is it rooted in working-class family training and, hence, in working-class character, or is it rooted in some outside source such as red scares and farm transfers? If the latter is the case, then the attitudes are likely to be more mutable than if rooted in character structure. The disparity between the response to the accused man as opposed to the admitted "offender" provides strong evidence for the assumption that the response is "situational" rather than part of character.[98]

Foreign Affairs

If manual workers are more "authoritarian," that syndrome ought to be indicated in their foreign policy preferences as well.[99] In particular, it should mean that workers prefer "tough" and aggressive options when faced with choices between alternative strategies in international affairs. The educated middle class ought to prefer more restrained options such as negotiation and discussion.

The available studies allow a straightforward test of these assumptions. The 1952 study, asking about the Korean War, and the 1964 study, asking about the Vietnam war, contained questions that pose three alternatives: a pullout, negotiations to end the fighting, and a hard-hitting escalation of the struggle.[100]

The evidence indicates quite clearly that the preference for the "tough" option is greatest in the upper-middle class. Outside of the South, there is little difference between manuals and lower middles (see Table 11.12). These

TABLE 11.12
Attitudes Toward Korean and Vietnam War Policy by Region and Class (Married, Active) SRC 1952 and 1964

	Non-South			South		
	Manuals	Lower[a] Middles	Upper Middles	Manuals	Lower[a] Middles	Upper Middles
1952 preference (of those with opinions)						
Pull out	8%	7%	8%	5%	4%	4%
Negotiate	47	50	36	63	47	33
Stronger stand	45	43	56	31	49	62
N =	(411)	(272)	(73)	(150)	(49)	(45)
1964 preference (of those with opinions)						
Pull out	9	8	16	21	13	9
Negotiate	41	43	24	41	45	35
Stronger stand	50	49	60	37	42	56
N =	(200)	(134)	(99)	(65)	(40)	(71)

[a] The 1952 cutting line was $7500 (family income) outside the South and $5000 in the South. The 1964 equivalents were $10,000 and $7500.

two groups are more likely to prefer a "moderate" position, that is, negotiations to end the fighting. The results, in short, indicate just the opposite of the original expectation.

A more detailed analysis showed that the "tough" preference was strongest among younger, well-educated, white Protestants, in particular, among those who paid much attention to newspapers and magazines.[101] In part, that preference appears to result from a media influence. Since at equivalent levels of attention there are still differences both between the classes and between socioreligious groupings, it is clear that more than a media impact is operative. One possibility is that the preference is linked to nationalist sentiments of the upper-middle-class white Protestants. They appear to take a different attitude toward the "national interest" than do others at equivalent class levels. They apparently order the priorities differently, viewing it as right and proper that all necessary force be used to "successfully" complete distant military engagements. In this respect, their outlook is similar to that of the Victorian or Edwardian (or, for that matter, Bismarckian) upper class or upper-middle class with their conception of the special rights of the empire. There is a significant division within the Catholic population. Older immigrant groups in the upper-middle class share the outlooks of their white Protestant class peers. Newer immigrant groups among the Catholics are considerably more favorably disposed to either the pullout or the negotiations possibilities.[102]

The working-class response, particularly that of the poorer workers, suggests a markedly different orientation. They have little interest in the honor and prestige involved in successful completion of foreign wars. Moreover, since they tend to pay one of the most important costs, at least, in a so-called limited war, they have reason to prefer one of the other options—either negotiations or a pullout.

In summary, the evidence here does not support the image of jingoistic and warlike masses. It indicates just the opposite: that the tough, hard line is a proclivity of established, educated, upper-middle-class white Protestants.[103]

The Previous Literature

Since the findings in this chapter go against so much of the recent literature (at least so it would appear), it is necessary to undertake some discussion of the discrepancy.

Much of the literature in the area and much of the supporting data, depend on the use of "authoritarianism" scales. These scales, which are supposed to get at a character structure, may also pick up some peculiar values. Some of the questions ask about practices that are generally approved in farm areas, in small towns, and in some occupations, notably, in small independent family businesses. The responses to such questions may not provide an indication of a character structure but rather they may simply give an indication of the values that are approved in that milieu.[104]

There is a greater prevalence of ex-farmers and also small towners in the manual ranks. Since many of them are likely to have brought these "premodern" orientations with them, the scales frequently show a greater degree of "authoritarianism" in the working class.

At least, as indicated by the results presented in the first part of this chapter, that greater degree of "authoritarianism" has no evident effect on the attitudes toward the rights of blacks. The relationship with civil liberties attitudes, as has been indicated, is somewhat more complex. The illiberalism in this area is linked to small-town, rural, and Southern conditions or "training." On the surface, it would appear that the relatively greater "authoritarianism" of the working class has no payoff at all in terms of "pugnacity" as is indicated by the responses to the Korean and Vietnam war questions.

One of the major points indicated in this chapter is that much of the intolerant or illiberal working-class response to the questions explored is given by workers of farm and/or small-town background. It seems likely that intolerance and cultural conservatism is also characteristic of the small towns and rural areas in other countries. Again, assuming that the rural areas everywhere "feed" the manual ranks, it would seem likely that the "authoritarianism" reported in the manual ranks of other countries has similar roots there; that is, it is transferred "farm authoritarianism." It was shown that this process was operating in the case of the UNESCO study of West Germany used by Lipset, and the same kind of thing may well be operative with respect to the "comparable results" he reports for Austria, Japan, Brazil, Canada, Mexico, the Netherlands, Belgium, Italy, and France.[105] It has been said that "every country has its South." In this connection that means there would also be a migration from these areas of backwardness and cultural conservativism, a "feed in," which also shifts people disproportionately into the manual ranks.

To repeat an earlier cautionary statement, this explanation does not change the facts; with respect to the "civil liberties" questions and the "plural parties" questions the manual ranks do prove to be "less tolerant." The question being raised here is about the origins or sources of the differences, whether they stem from the life conditions and experience of workers and their families, or whether they stem from training and experience gained from "outside" the class, that is, experience not linked to the immediate life circumstances or milieu of the working class. The point is of obvious importance in that, depending on the source, the outlooks may be "rigid" and more or less permanent or, alternatively, they may be highly malleable. What normative conclusions one woud draw for the operations of contemporary democracy, whether participative or elitist, depend, in part, on one's reading of this empirical matter.

Another difficulty with "authoritarianism" scales, that is, in addition to their picking up culturally approved sentiments, is the problem of "response sets." Until 1955 the questions used had to be answered negatively in order to be scored as nonauthoritarian; all positive responses, that is, agreement to the statements presented, were scored as authoritarian. Some respondents, however, answer all statements positively. A smaller proportion of unselected populations tend to answer all statements negatively. This means that part of the result has nothing to do with the content of the statements. As long as the questions all had the same form, these propensities (or "response sets") injected a systematic bias into the results.[106]

A study of those who responded positively to mutually contradictory formulations, people who have been termed "Yeasayers," indicated that they tended to be persons with weak ego controls who accept impulses without reservations. The opposite group, the "Naysayers" proved to be persons who control and suppress impulses.[107] The latter would appear to be more appropriately categorized as "authoritarians" than the Yeasayers. The Yeasayers prove to be merely conformist or acquiescent. Given the scoring of the pre-1955 studies, however, Yeasayers would be classed as "authoritarian" and Naysayers as "equalitarian."

The above paragraph gives some characterization of who the Yeasayers are in personal, psychological terms. Another question to be considered is: where are they located in the social structure? In a very general way, yeasaying may be seen as an implied act of deference (or, possibly, of defense). If we ask "which populations defer or feel a need to defer?" a simple answer is those at the lower levels of formal or informal social hierarchies.[108] For some, "deference" is a trained "way of life," a set of procedures passed on over generations, a style that is intended to make life at least barely passable. For others, it is a more conscious technique for fending off threats from those with more power.

One study investigating this phenomenon found 8 percent of the respondents to be Yeasayers; that is, they responded positively to pairs of mutually contradictory statetments. They also found that "the greater the social distance between interviewer and respondent, the more often this behavior was observed."[109] Poorly educated populations—manual workers and blacks (who were responding to white interviewers)—were most likely to give this "acquiescent response set." The original results showed fair-sized differences between the manuals and the nonmanuals, 15 percent and 4 percent, respectively, giving the "authoritarian" response to one item. With the acquiescent individuals eliminated, the respective proportions were 5 and 2 percent.[110]

Because the "authoritarianism" scales pick up the approved values and orientations of small-town and rural areas and because there is a systematic response bias in the studies done prior to the mid-fifties, it seems that there is reason to either discount or reject completely the results of those studies. Much of the footnoted support for the "working-class authoritarianism" thesis involved reference to just this literatture.[111]

One of the reasons that the findings of this chapter prove to be so much at variance with the conventional wisdom of the field has to do with a "response set" on the part of social scientists. As a result of years of training, many social scientists have come to expect tolerance to vary directly with class level. As happens with the "perception" of the population generally, their understanding comes to be warped in the direction of this expectation. This was indicated in the above discussion of the *perception* of the social characteristics of lynchers as opposed to the *evidence* contained in studies of the subject. It seems likely that such perceptual distortion goes on continuously, social scientists either "not seeing" contrary evidence ("selective perception"), or if seeing it, not remembering it ("selective retention"). Another process that seems likely is the rejection of contrary (or "dissonant") information.

It is useful to consider an illustrative example. A study was concerned with the relationship between mobility and prejudice and, necessarily, had to look at the class-tolerance relationship among the stable (that is, nonmobile) populations.[112] In the review of the previous evidence, the authors report a study which found that "the higher one's class of origin or class of destination the more likely that one prefers to exclude Negroes from one's neighborhood."[113] The authors simply deny the validity of this finding. They put it as follows:

There is just too much independent evidence that prejudice toward Negroes is inversely associated with current occupational status for us to contemplates seriously the possibility that the zero order associations revealed by the Elmira data are *substantively* correct.[114]

A second study was reviewed and it, too, showed some unexpected findings. There was little overall difference in the mean prejudice scores of those currently in manual and nonmanual occupations. The children of nonmanuals, however, proved to be more prejudiced than the children of manuals. In short, the class-tolerance relationship proved to be nonexistent in the one comparison and negative in the second. Again, the findings were dismissed:

This curiosity has no obvious explanation and makes us as suspicious of these data as we were of the Elmira data studies above.[115]

The authors present their evidence showing a positive relationship between class and tolerance. In their conclusions, they once again dismiss the earlier findings:

. . . since other studies have shown that socioeconomic status tends to be inversely related to prejudice toward Negroes, this failure to support the additive model postulated in the theory built around a consideration of competition and socialization may possibly be attributable to faulty data.[116]

In this case, rather than recognizing that the evidence is contradictory, that it does not indicate clear support for the conventional notion, the reading here involves merely a dismissal of the contrary evidence. A more appropriate conclusion would be to recognize the disparate results, to note that the "established" hypothesis does not have the uniform support claimed for it, and, a useful next step, to inquire as to the conditions giving rise to the varying results.

These authors say there is "just too much independent evidence" existing to allow them to accept the findings of these two studies. In this connection they refer to three sources. The first of these is the Greenblum and Pearlin article, which contains a datum showing manual workers as more likely to agree with a stereotypic statement. In this case the evidence shows that stationary manual populations (that is, those whose fathers were also manual workers) are, by a 10 percentage point margin, more likely to agree with the following statement: "Generally speaking, Negroes are ignorant and lazy." The best conclusion would be that the differences are small and that the picture is mixed. Pending presentation of some justification, there appears to be no reason for assuming that the data are faulty.[117]

The second reference is to the original evidence and the review of previous evidence by Bettelheim and Janowitz. Their original study is of World War II veterans living in the Chicago area. The table in question shows the "anti-Negro attitude" of those earning under $3000 and those earning over $3000 (in 1946). There are smallish differences indicated. It is not entirely clear that the lower income group is the less tolerant one. The study itself is a small one, there being 102 and 28 cases in the respective income categories.[118]

Bettelheim and Janowitz preface their review of the data by noting that "a number of sociological arguments would lead one to anticipate that persons of middle and upper socioeconomic status would be less prejudiced than those of lower status."[119] "National surveys," they say, "reveal that for the population as a whole and for very broad socioeconomic groupings a limited association with very general forms of ethnic prejudice does emerge." They present no data or reference accompanying this rather restrained and cautious statement. They then say that the "realities of social stratification" may be seen "more sharply" through the use of metropolitan community samples and present data from one—a study of the Detroit metropolitan area. There are three categories of Negro prejudice indicated: tolerant, mildly intolerant, and strongly intolerant. There are essentially no differences at all in the "tolerant" percentages reported for four occupational categories. There are some differences in the percentages that are "mildly" and "strongly" intolerant, but, as Hodge and Treiman recognized in a footnote, the relationship is not "monotonic." The clerical and sales employees are *less* tolerant than the craftsmen and foremen. The latter are little different from the professionals and managers. The largest percentage of strong intolerance is found among the operatives and service workers. It seems likely that Southern origins might well be a factor here.

The third source referred to by Hodge and Treiman is a study of intergroup relations based on a number of studies of smaller communities.[120] The table in question reports findings for three communities. One of these is Elmira, New York (based on a survey in 1949), the second is Bakersfield, California, and the third is Savannah, Georgia. The number of respondents reported on for the three communities were, respectively, 314, 107, and 140. These, in turn, were then divided into three occupational categories: "professional, business, and allied," "skilled," and "semiskilled and unskilled." Inquiry was made into the "social distance toward Negroes." There were fair-sized differences indicated in Bakersfield and Savannah, a greater "distance" being desired by the white workers of those communities. In both studies, however, it must be noted that the nonmanual group consisted of less than 25 cases. In Elmira, the difference between the nonmanuals and the skilled was 15 percentage points; between the nonmanuals and the other manuals, it amounted to 22 percentage points.

It is clear that there is some evidence available that supports the received hypothesis. It is also clear that the references made by Hodge and Treiman are not appropriately summarized with the phrase "much independent evidence." There is little evidence contained in the sources cited, much of it is based on small samples, and the results do not consistently support their position. It also should be noted that many of the differences indicated that do support the received hypothesis are relatively small. There is clearly a question to be raised about the emphasis on the importance of "class" as a factor determining tolerance or intolerance.[121]

The works reviewed thus far are focused on prejudice toward Negroes. Lipset makes no distinction as to the object of the prejudice. As he states, the "evidence from various American studies is also clear and consistent—the lower strata are the least tolerant."[122] When it is a question of anti-Semitism, that conclusion is not justified. Bettelheim and Janowitz, summing up their study of veterans, report that "socioeconomic status as such is not correlated with intolerance."[123] A study by Herbert Northrup of industrial workers in five cities reported a level of anti-Semitic sentiment "similar to that found in studies of the general population at the time of the study."[124] The Greenblum and Pearlin article, as noted above, does not show "clear and consistent" evidence of "lower strata" intolerance.[125] The Robin Williams study reports "a tendency for anti-Jewish responses to go along with higher occupational position."[126] Some of the evidence presented by Herbert Stember indicates greater prejudice against Jews in the higher status groups than elsewhere.[127] Another study cited by Lipset in support of his "clear and consistent" evidence claim actually concludes as follows:

> Subjects whose parents are engaged in business or professional occupations scored significantly lower (indicating greater "prejudice") than subjects whose parents are skilled workers, clerical workers, or farmers. . . . A direct relation between income of parents and 'prejudice' was found: subjects whose parents are in the upper income groups scored significantly lower than those whose parents are in the lower income groups.[128]

Still another study cited by Lipset as supporting his position in fact reports that the "Anti-Semitism score was found to increase directly with amount of the father's income. . ."[129]

In summary, it is clear that the evidence is not "clear and consistent." Basically this review of the previous evidence indicates that the research to date does not show the manual workers to be *consistently* more prejudiced than the nonmanuals. This review has indicated that the widespread acceptance of the working-class authoritarianism claim is based on a selective appreciation of the available evidence.[130]

The evidence presented in this chapter does not justify drawing an opposite conclusion, one of "middle-class authoritarianism." The evidence with respect to attitude toward Negroes indicates that outside the South there is essentially no difference between manuals and nonmanuals. Outside the South and with the farm-reared excluded, there is essentially no difference between manuals and nonmanuals in their support for the rights of the "accused man." There is less working-class tolerance indicated for admitted Communists, Socialists, and athiests. In a third area studied, the preference for moderate or immoderate foreign policy initiatives, the upper-middle class proved to be the most "authoritarian."

Where Lipset focused on experiences within the class situation as providing the roots for the so-called authoritarianism, this study has indicated that much of the "intolerance" has its roots outside the class. It is "transferred" into the class in the course of farm-to-city migration and South to non-South moves (or possibly through downward mobility) and, in another context, has its origins in the initiatives of upper-class influentials who have sponsored "red scares" and supported rightist demagogues, and who themselves redefined the "rules of the game" in order to justify guilt by association.

A Postscript

An analysis of class and tolerance in the United States that ends with consideration of the 1964 election is a peculiarly truncated one. The result of the 1968 election, in particular, the vote for the third-party candidate, George Wallace, poses some obvious questions. His campaign is well-known for its racist themes and for its successful appeal to the white working class. This appeal would appear to outweigh in its significance any mere attitudes picked up in polls and surveys. Here, in the course of a national campaign, the alternatives were clearly formulated; there was little reason to be unfamiliar with the choices presented, and here, an action, voting, was involved (as opposed to the perhaps more frivolous expression of opinion to an interviewer). In short, it would appear that here, with the "chips down," manual workers showed their "true" character.

Once again, it is worthwhile examining the evidence. For this purpose, use has been made of the Survey Research Center's 1968 election study. For part of the following analysis, only married, active whites have been studied, continuing the practice used throughout most of this book. The results do not depend on this choice of focus since the major question has been explored using the most obvious alternative possibilities. Since region is such an important factor in the 1968 result, the findings have been presented separately for the South and the non-South.

The basic finding, taking first the non-South regions, is the *absence* of differentiation by class. Nine percent of the non-South manuals voted for Wallace as opposed to 8 percent of the nonmanuals (see Table 11.13). If we proceed somewhat differently, taking also the single persons, the widowed, the divorced, the retired, and so on, the result is still the same, a difference of one percentage point.[131]

This evidence then indicates that as far as the non-South regions are concerned, that is, combining the Northeast, the Midwest, and the West of the

TABLE 11.13
Wallace Vote in 1968 by Class and Region (SRC 1968: Married, Active Whites)

	Class	
	Manual	Nonmanual
	Percent for Wallace—1968	
Non-South	9%	8%
$N =$	(149)	(260)
South	42	23
$N =$	(45)	(85)

United States, class is no factor at all in predicting or accounting for the Wallace vote. This result corresponds very well with the data presented earlier on tolerance and intolerance in the regions, there being, it will be remembered, no clear differences in attitude toward Negroes by class outside the South.

This also means that the widespread focus on class, on the working-class support for Wallace, has seriously misrepresented the actual realities.

In the South, there is a clear and fair-sized difference between the manuals and the nonmanuals, 42 percent of the former supporting Wallace as opposed to 23 percent of the latter. This finding also shows some correspondence with findings on prejudice reported earlier in the chapter, for example, that there were class differences, at least in the area of school integration, within the South. This evidence, then, supports the view of a *Southern* white working-class authoritarianism. The evidence clearly does not support a general claim about authoritarianism of the working class. The focus of concern must be with the character and situation of the Southern white workers rather than with the working class in general.

Since this finding comes as something of a surprise, it is useful to consider some of the related evidence. The only other national study making the same division by class and region arrives at a similar result. This study indicates 9 percent of the non-South manuals voted for Wallace as opposed to 5 percent of the equivalent nonmanuals. The class difference indicated here is a small 4 percentage points as opposed to the 1 percent difference found in the Survey Research Center study.

The class differences reported in the South are, once again, fairly sizable, the Wallace figures being 53 percent for the manuals and 22 percent for the nonmanuals. This study, too, then, indicates "Southern white working-class authoritarianism" but only a miniscule difference elsewhere. When it is remembered that the non-South manual ranks are disproportionately composed of the Southern-reared, it seems likely that the 4 percent difference "overstates the case." A comparison of only non-South-reared populations would probably reduce even that 4 percentage point difference.[132]

In great measure, the prevalent misconceptions about the character of Wallace's following result from erroneous reports of his earliest "victories." One leading account, for example, states that:

Wallace astounded political observers not so much by the percentage of votes he could draw for simple bigotry . . . as by the groups from whom he drew his votes. For he demonstrated pragmatically and for the first time the fear that white working-class Americans have of Negroes. In Wisconsin he scored heavily in the predominately Italian, Polish, and Serb working-class neighborhoods of Milwaukee's south side. . . .[133]

In point of fact, the Wallace percentages were *lowest* in Milwaukee's South Side. His percentages were high in the affluent North Side districts and highest in the very affluent north shore suburbs. In Madison, the Wallace percentage was greatest in the very affluent suburb of Maple Bluff.[134]

A second problem with the above presentation is to see it as a vote for "simple bigotry." In both the Wisconsin and the Indiana primaries that year, Democratic governors had presented themselves as "favorite sons." Both of these "favorites" had recently introduced sales taxes. In both states, crossover was possible allowing Republicans to vote in the Democratic primary campaign. It seems likely that reactions to the sales tax and Republican attempts to embarrass the Democrats were factors in both cases.[135]

One small additional specification of these findings ought to be noted. It would be easy to assume that it is (or "must be") the "lower-middle class" which provided that nonmanual support for Wallace. It would be "easy to assume" because of the "training" that leads intellectuals, at least, to believe that the upper-middle class is "responsible." Much of their argument is essentially "cultural." It is difficult for the trained liberal intellectual to believe that the educated, urbane, well-to-do population would ever be attracted by the "crude" and "simplistic" claims and appeals that Wallace had to offer.[136] A breakdown by family income, however, dividing the nonmanuals at $12,000, does not support that expectation. Nine percent of the non-South "lower-middle class" voted for Wallace. In the "upper-middle class" the figure was little different—8 percent.[137]

The discussion thus far makes one rather unrealistic assumption—that a vote for Wallace is an unambiguous indication of "authoritarianism." Here, too, there are some surprises.

To give some idea as to the "dynamics" of Wallace voting, it is useful to consider first the economic liberalism area. In one key "welfare" area, medical care, the familiar question was again posed to the 1968 respondents about favoring or opposing aid from the "government in Washington" to help pay doctor and hospital costs (see Table 11.14). Working-class Wallace supporters are little different from working-class Democrats on this issue, heavy majorities of both groups favoring this option. Both groups are more "liberal" than those members of the working class who voted Republican in 1968.

Much of the same picture appears with respect to the question about a federal government guarantee of the adequate living standard. Working class Wallaceites in the North were somewhat more conservative than other workers in their responses to this question, but, like the other groups, they, too, have a fair-sized minority in both major regions favoring this option.

Middle-class Wallaceites are a different matter. They appear to be torn on the medical care question. Half of those outside the South favor this effort by the "government in Washington" as do also one-third of the Southern middle-class Wallaceites. The response to the guaranteed living standard question by the Southern middle-class Wallaceites indicates a very solid conservatism. This group is the most conservative in the entire population, manual or nonmanual, South or non-South.

These data suggest that there is a very serious division within the ranks of the Wallace followers. The working-class supporters show evidence of being for the welfare state while the middle-class supporters, particularly in the Southern stronghold, are very strongly opposed. This suggests that a strong appeal on the basis of welfare issues could divide the American Independent party and, at minimum, very seriously tempt the party's working-class supporters.

A key issue in public discussion at this time (that is, in the news media and in the speeches of political leaders) was school integration and the role of the government in this connection. The question of federal government aid to schools, for this reason, would be especially salient in 1968. Wallaceites in both classes and in both regions proved to be strongly opposed to the federal government's financial aid. Wallaceites were more strongly opposed to school aid than any of the groups in question, more so even than the generally laissez-faire-oriented Republicans. The Southern middle-class Wallaceites once again were nearly monolithic in outlook. Southern working-class Wallace voters, by comparison, were little different from other Southern white workers.

Asked whether the government in Washington was too powerful, the Wallace supporters again proved distinctive, that is, more conservative than the Republicans. There were again some interesting variations. The Southern middle-class supporters were overwhelming in their agreement on this point. In other contexts, however, there were fair-sized minorities among the Wallaceites who did not feel the government was too strong. The largest of these "deviating" minorities appeared among the Southern white working-class Wallaceites.

The pattern appearing thus far is one of strong ideological orientation on the part of the middle-class Wallaceites. Among the working-class Wallaceites something different appears to be operating. They tended to share the same basic welfare concerns as other workers and did not oppose a government role in aid of their personal situation. They did appear to be concerned about the school aid question and they did tend to react to the formal statement about

TABLE 11.14
Economic Liberalism and Civil Rights Attitudes by Region, Class, and 1968 Vote
Preference (SRC 1968: Whites; Includes Single, Divorced, Retired, etc.)

	Region					
	Non-South					
	Manual			Nonmanual		
Voter Preference[a]	Demo-cratic	Repub-lican	Wallace	Demo-cratic	Repub-lican	Wallace
Economic liberalism questions						
Medical care	81%	57%	75%	75%	47%	50%
N =	(91)	(91)	(16)	(118)	(182)	(22)
Living standard	44	42	36	43	24	29
N =	(91)	(108)	(22)	(114)	(169)	(24)
School aid	49	23	14	50	24	14
N =	(85)	(95)	(21)	(109)	(182)	(22)
Powerful gov't.	65	45	32	58	26	23
N =	(78)	(87)	(19)	(105)	(180)	(26)
Civil rights questions						
Job guarantee	55	45	41	58	39	12
N =	(83)	(106)	(22)	(119)	(182)	(26)
Equal housing	90	79	68	87	83	57
N =	(101)	(112)	(22)	(145)	(207)	(28)
Hotels, restaurants	76	65	52	75	63	35
N =	(95)	(105)	(23)	(137)	(208)	(26)
Schools	55	48	20	65	43	4
N =	(91)	(103)	(20)	(121)	(188)	(24)

[a] Includes also non-voters who indicated their preferences.

the "too powerful" government. The working-class response patterns did not show the same ideological consistency found in the middle class. There was, even that close to the campaign, much "deviation" from a "pure" Wallace position within the working-class following.

The central feature of the Wallace campaign, the core appeal, presumably, was his position on integration. It is on this basis that many commentators have taken a Wallace vote as directly equivalent to or as an expression of racist sentiment. This assumption is open to some question. The 1968 study

TABLE 11.14 (Continued)

	Region					
	South					
	Manual			Nonmanual		
Voter Preference[a]	Demo-cratic	Repub-lican	Wallace	Demo-cratic	Repub-lican	Wallace
Economic liberalism questions						
Medical care	79%	66%	73%	65%	43%	33%
$N =$	(29)	(32)	(30)	(31)	(69)	(24)
Living standard	50	27	43	34	23	4
$N =$	(32)	(33)	(30)	(29)	(64)	(23)
School aid	26	30	22	41	21	4
$N =$	(27)	(30)	(32)	(29)	(73)	(26)
Powerful gov't.	48	23	42	48	18	8
$N =$	(21)	(26)	(31)	(29)	(68)	(26)
Civil rights questions						
Job guarantee	37	32	35	45	31	27
$N =$	(30)	(37)	(31)	(29)	(72)	(30)
Equal housing	48	52	35	77	69	35
$N =$	(29)	(31)	(34)	(30)	(74)	(31)
Hotels, restaurants	53	33	20	62	53	16
$N =$	(32)	(33)	(35)	(29)	(73)	(25)
Schools	35	15	18	50	33	4
$N =$	(31)	(33)	(34)	(32)	(69)	(27)

used three of the civil rights questions used in the 1964 study. One of those questions asked about a government role in guaranteeing Negroes job equality, that is, whether one favored such intervention or whether one favored leaving those matters "to the states and local communities." Considering conventional assumptions, there should be a very simple and clear distribution of responses to this question from the Wallace supporters. As it turns out, however, a fair-sized minority of the non-South working class-Wallaceites favored a federal intervention to guarantee Negro job equality, and even in the South, one-third of the working-class Wallace supporters did the same. Non-South middle-class Wallace supporters were strongly opposed to such intervention. Curiously, their Southern equivalents did not show the same near-unanimity on this issue; a quarter of them even favored a government role.

Unexpected distributions also appear in the responses to the housing equality question. The options here, it will be remembered, were that "white people have a right to keep Negroes out" versus "Negroes have a right to live wherever they can afford to. . . ." Two-thirds of the non-South manual Wallace supporters favored the equal opportunity option and a majority of the non-South middle class did the same. Even in the South, one-third of both the manual and the nonmanual Wallace supporters favored the "open housing" alternative. The tolerant percentages in all cases are lower among the Wallace supporters than among the Republicans and Democrats, as is to be expected. The important point, however, is that the Wallace followers were divided on this issue, so one is not justified in treating the Wallace vote as a direct indication of a racist predilection.[138]

A new question in 1968 asked about the desirability of a government role to guarantee equal access to any hotel or restaurant. This possibility also gained considerable support from Wallaceites. The non-South working-class supporters divided in half on this question. Significant minority support for such an intervention appeared also in two other contexts. On this issue the Southern middle-class supporters once again showed very heavy opposition to any government role.

The most salient of the questions considered involves the government role in school integration. In this area Wallace supporters in all four contexts showed heavy opposition to the government role. The middle classes, both South and non-South, again proved to be nearly unanimous in their opposition to government action in the area. The working-class Wallace ranks, once again, were not monolithic in their outlook; a fifth of them favored the government action.

Three major points emerge from this analysis of the issue orientations of the Wallace supporters. First, the working-class supporters appear to have serious conflicts in their issue preferences. They wish the federal government to contribute to their own personal or familial welfare. At the same time, many of them have accepted the belief that the government is "too powerful" and in particular, they do not wish to see the government enforcing integration of the schools. In the long run, following the argument presented in Chapter 3, it seems likely that the persistent concerns of welfare would outweigh the concern with the somewhat more distant school question and the clearly more distant question of a "powerful" government.

The second major point has to do with the attitudes of Wallace supporters toward the rights of blacks. The evidence indicates that a large proportion of the Wallace voters have equalitarian attitudes, a point that actually should come as no surprise when one is discussing a "populist "candidate. The suggestion made by some commentators that the Wallace support represents last ditch segregationist sentiment does not hold for a large minority of Wallace's followers.

A third major point, the one most relevant for the major concern of this chapter, involves the distribution of attitudes by class. It will be noted that in all but one of the comparisons involving the civil rights questions, the working-class Wallace supporters proved to be more tolerant than the middle-class Wallaceites. It was the middle-class Wallaceites, in short, who were most antithetic to the rights of blacks. It is the middle-class segment that most adequately fits the standard portrayal of Wallace supporters as committed racists; or, put differently, it is the middle-class segment that proves to be most clearly "authoritarian." For all of the reasons indicated, it seems likely, should the movement decline, that it would lose its working-class support and persist as a movement of intransigent middle-class conservatives.

Notes

1. The leading formulation is that of Seymour Martin Lipset, "Working-class Authoritarianism," Chapter 4 of *Political Man* (Garden City: Doubleday, 1960). An earlier presentation appears as "Democracy and Working-class Authoritarianism," *American Sociological Review*, **24** (August 1959), 482–502. Some elements of the position appear still earlier in Nathan Glazer and S. M. Lipset, "The Polls on Communism and Conformity," pp. 141–165 of D. Bell, ed., *The New American Right* (New York: Criterion Books, 1955).

2. Lipset, *Political Man*, op. cit., pp. 98, 100, 109, 115. The Lipset position contains two basic elements: first, the claim of a greater "authoritarianism" among workers, and second, an explanatory claim linking the orientation to deprivation and child-rearing practices.

There are a number of criticisms of the first of these elements available. See S. M. Miller and Frank Riessman, "Working-Class Authoritarianism: A Critique of Lipset," *British Journal of Sociology*, **12** (September 1961), 263–276 (also contains a reply by Lipset); Emanuel A. Schegloff and Carole Kruytbosch, "Some Comments on 'Working-Class Authoritarianism,' " *Berkeley Journal of Sociology*, VI (Spring 1961), 99–103 (again there is a Lipset reply); Lewis Lipsitz, "Working-Class Authoritarianism: A Re-Evaluation," *American Sociological Review*, **30** (February 1965), 103–109; Richard F. Hamilton, "Working-Class Authoritarianism Reconsidered," XVIII World Congress of Psychology, Symposium 38, "Work and Personality," Moscow, September 1966; Maurice Zeitlin, "Revolutionary Workers and Individual Liberties," *American Journal of Sociology*, **72** (May 1967), 619–632 (also appears as Chapter 10 of his *Revolutionary Politics and the Cuban Working Class* (Princeton: Princeton University Press, 1967). Also of some interest in this connection is Charles Herbert Stember's *Education and Attitude Change* (New York: Institute of Human Relations Press, 1961).

For discussion and evidence on the second of the elements, the explanatory hypothesis, see Herbert Hyman and Paul Sheatsley, "A Methodological Critique," in Richard Christie and Marie Jahoda, *Studies in the Scope and Method of the Authoritarian Personality* (Glencoe: Free Press, 1954). Hyman and Sheatsley point out that the original studies of the "authoritarian personality" base their conclusions on retrospective evidence, that is, the reports about the family came from adult authoritarians. They concluded that: "In the absence of any validating data, one is compelled to qualify very seriously any conclusions which relate to the influence of *actual* childhood upon prejudice" (p. 100). Although published in 1954, Lipset does not mention the Hyman-Sheatsley critique.

A limited study that did not depend on retrospective questions, one that had direct observation of families between 1935 and 1940 and interviews with the children in 1948 asking about prejudice toward Jews and Negroes, concludes as follows: "The findings are uniformly negative. *The familial backgrounds of the openly antagonistic, the prejudiced, and the apparently tolerant men do not differ significantly on any variable.* Only the slightest of trends distinguish the bigots from the others." William McCord, Joan McCord, and Alan Howard, "Early Familial Experiences and Bigotry," *American Sociological Review*, **25** (October 1960), 717–722. Quotation from p. 721.

3. See, for example, Glazer and Lipset, op. cit., p. 150. See also the discussion in Chapter 2 of the present work.

4. It will be noted that there is a wide range of questions contained in Table 11.1. Some mix rights issues together with questions of the role of the federal government. There is a shift of focus in some cases, for example, from "jobs and housing" in 1956 to jobs only in 1964. In one of the 1956 questions, the agent in question was simply "the government" whereas in other questions it is "the government in Washington." This wide range of question wordings would suggest that the lack of sizable class differences is a genuine finding and not a result of the wording of any particular question.

One question has been omitted from this table. It reads: Q. 41. "What about you? Are you in favor of desegregation, strict segregation, or something in between?" Most white respondents chose the "in between" option, which would mean, following the percentaging procedure used in the table, that the result would not be comparable with the others, which forced choices of tolerant and intolerant alternatives, leaving no explicit middle ground. The responses to this question show a result similar to those indicated in the table, that is, one of rather limited class differences. Outside the South, for example, 28 percent of the manuals ($N = 287$) and 37 percent of the nonmanuals ($N = 340$) chose the desegregation option—a difference of 9 percentage points. For a number of reasons, which will be considered later in the text, even this exaggerates the basic "class" differences.

5. Further substantiation of these findings (with some elaboration) was found in a subsequent investigation based on the 1968 Survey Center study and on two studies of the National Opinion Research Center, one from 1963 and one from 1968. The main findings closely parallel those reported in Table 11.1. These results appear in Richard Hamilton, *Restraining Myths and Liberating Realities* Ch. 4 "Black Demands, White Reactions, and Liberal Alarms," (forthcoming). A much condensed version of this chapter appears in Sar A. Levitan, ed., *Blue-Collar Workers: A Symposium on Middle America* (New York: McGraw-Hill, 1971).

6. Again, it should be kept in mind that we have a mixture of questions. The first two, on jobs and schooling, involve a federal government role in enforcement. The housing question has a pure focus on rights.

7. The manual rank as a whole proves to be disproportionately Southern. Samuel Stouffer's study (discussed in Chapter 3) shows 31 percent ($N = 1023$) of the economically active male manuals to be located in the South as compared to 23 percent ($N = 701$) of the nonmanuals. Unfortunately, that large study does not have a question allowing one to explore the question of interregional migration. The 1964 SRC study shows that 9 percent ($N = 298$) of the non-South white manual workers were Southern-reared as compared to 7 percent ($N = 353$) among the nonmanuals. There is a much greater imbalance in the South since relatively few white workers go South in comparison to the white middle class. The respective proportion of the non-South reared in the Southern manual and nonmanual ranks are 16 percent ($N = 80$) and 27 percent ($N = 149$). In the original presentation in Table 11.1, we saw a difference of 17 percentage points with respect to the 1964 school integration question, the largest of the differences to be discovered. Taking the indigenous Southern populations still living in the South, this difference is reduced by 2 percentage points.

8. The political orientation of the Protestant minority in France is the opposite of the Protestant majority in the United States. One study shows 39 percent of them supporting the Left (Communists or Socialists) and another 34 percent backing the Radicals, an old-style liberal (and civil libertarian) party. See Lipset, *Political Man*, op. cit., pp. 244–245.

On American Protestantism and the nativist tradition, see Gustavus Myers, *History of Bigotry in the United States* (New York: Random House, 1943) and John Higham, *Strangers in the Land: Patterns of American Nativism, 1860–1925* (New Brunswick: Rutgers University Press, 1955). On the claim to special privilege, see Richard Hofstadter, *Social Darwinism in American Thought* (Boston: Beacon Press, 1955, revised edition).

Some sense of the prevalence of racist attitudes in the Civil War period and earlier may be gained from the following: Winthrop D. Jordan, *White over Black: American Attitudes Toward the Negro, 1550–1812* (Chapel Hill: University of North Carolina Press, 1968); Leon F. Litwack, *North of Slavery: The Negro in the Free States, 1790–1860* (Chicago: University of Chicago Press, 1961); Lorman Ratner, *Powder Keg: Northern Opposition to the Antislavery Movement* (New York: Basic Books, 1968); Eugene Berwanger, *The Frontier Against Slavery: Western Anti-Negro Prejudice and the Slavery Extension Controversy* (Urbana: University of Illinois Press, 1969); and V. Jacques Voegeli, *Free But Not Equal: The Midwest and the Negro During the Civil War* (Chicago: University of Chicago Press, 1967).

9. For example, among the non-South white Protestants who were reared outside the South, the proportions favoring open housing for the manuals, lower middles, and upper middles, respectively, are 75, 82, and 74 percent.

The dominant upper-middle-class white Protestants are least supportive of the equal rights options. It is the upper-middle-class Catholics and Jews who provide the "liberalism" in that setting. A presentation that fails to make the religious separation, that is, one that merely shows "class" and attitudes, is going to be seriously misleading. Some additional information on the subject comes from the Gallup studies. The data are:

Income:	White Non-South Nonmanuals			
	White Protestants		All Others	
	To $9999	$10,000 or More	To $9999	$10,000 or More
Study:	*Percent "liberal"*			
AIPO 710 4/21/65	"Would you, yourself, have any objection to sending your children to a school . . . where more than half of the children were colored?" (of those with children in school)			
Would not object				
(of totals)	43%	22%	41%	44%
N =	(91)	(59)	(68)	(41)
Same	"Would you move if colored people came to live in great numbers in your neighborhood?"			
Would not move	30	21	13	38
N =	(227)	(90)	(139)	(74)
AIPO 713 6/2/65	". . . do you think that private organizations such as country clubs and college fraternities and the like should or should not have the right to exclude otherwise qualified Negroes from membership?"			
Should not have right				
to exclude	48	40	61	55
N =	(198)	(104)	(150)	(105)

The lower-middle-class white Protestants are more "liberal" than the equivalent upper-middle-class on all three questions. The upper-middle-class white Protestant context, once again, proves to be a special center of intolerant attitudes. They are the least tolerant of the four groups shown here and their peculiarity is more pronounced than in the case of the SRC questions.

There are some differences between the SRC and Gallup results. The "others" are not uniformly more tolerant than the white Protestants, there being two instances of essentially no difference between them. There is also a reversal of the "SRC pattern" among the "others" in that the upper group proves slightly more tolerant in response to two of the three questions. The reversals are the only bits of evidence in support of the "lower-middle-class reaction" thesis although the differences are not very great, amounting to 3 percent in one instance and 7 percent in the other.

Even this modest support for the received wisdom, however, proved to be problematic. The "upper-middle-class others" have a higher percentage of Jews than does the equivalent lower-middle class, and the upper-middle-class Jews show a very high level of liberalism in response to these questions. Taking the question on "great numbers" of Negroes moving in, we find that among the Catholics the lower-middle class is somewhat more tolerant than the upper middles so that here, too, the support for the conventional hypothesis disappears. Sixty-eight percent ($N = 22$) of the upper-middle-class Jews said they would not move in those circumstances.

There was only minimal and inconsistent support for the "reactionary lower-middle class" thesis among white Protestants to be seen in the South. Taking first the SRC job rights question (1964), the proportions favoring government effort were 31 percent ($N = 42$) and 30 percent ($N = 56$) for the lower- and upper-middle classes. On the equal schooling option, the equivalent figures were 24 percent ($N = 45$) and 33 percent ($N = 58$). Some 53 percent ($N = 55$) of the lower-middle class said, in response to the Gallup question, that they "would definitely move" if a Negro family moved next door. This compares with 60 percent ($N = 94$) in the upper-middle class. The respective proportions saying clubs should not have the right to exclude qualified Negroes were 14 percent ($N = 56$) and 5 percent ($N = 84$). There were not enough lower-middle-class respondents with children in school to justify use of the school integration question. The biggest percentage difference in favor of that hypothesis is one of 9 percentage points. There are, in contrast, differences of nine and eight percentage points in the opposite direction in two other comparisons and, in the final comparison, there is essentially no difference.

10. The Kerner Commission Report described the situation as follows: "Despite these complexities, certain fundamental matters are clear. Of these, the most fundamental is the racial attitude and behavior of white Americans toward black Americans. Race prejudice has shaped our history decisively in the past; it now threatens to do so again. White racism is essentially responsible for the explosive mixture which has been accumulating in our cities . . ." *Report of the National Advisory Commission on Civil Disorders* (Washington: Government Printing Office, 1968), p. 91.

11. A useful account of the implications of institutional racism appears in Louis L. Knowles and Kenneth Prewitt, eds., *Institutional Racism in America* (Englewood Cliffs, N.J.: Prentice-Hall, 1969).

12. If, for example, we take the non-South, upper-middle-class whites favoring the open housing option, we find that 46 percent ($N = 81$) of them oppose federal government intervention to guarantee equal job opportunity. Similar results appear in the lower-middle and working classes.

13. Party identifications become stronger with increasing age, another factor that reduces the possibilities of a "defection" to racist candidates on the part of older white Protestants.

14. The number of cases is relatively small. Taking the married, active, non-South, nonfarm whites of ages 55 and over, we find 73 percent ($N = 30$) of the grade-school-educated favoring the open housing option as opposed to 68 percent ($N = 34$) of those going beyond grade school. There is no difference in the tolerance of those having high school and college educations.

15. There exists something of an obsession with the presumed impact of formal

education. It is worthwhile bearing in mind that there are a wide range of other "educational" experiences that might be more decisive than formal schooling. This is especially likely to be the case since these other experiences come *after* formal schooling. Among those deserving consideration are the following:

Mass media impacts: Many newspapers in the past were heavily laden with racist lessons, this being particularly so in the case of Hearst papers. For an initial glimpse into the subject of how newspapers once performed, one might begin with *The Chicago Tribune* treatment of the arrest for murder of a Robert Nixon. See their accounts between May 28 and June 8, 1938. A sample: "He has none of the charm of speech or manner that is characteristic of so many southern darkies. That charm is a mark of civilization and so far as manner and appearance go, civilization has left Robert Nixon practically untouched. His hunched shoulders and long, sinewy arms that dangle almost to his knees; and his outthrust head and catlike tread all suggest the animal. He is very black—almost pure Negro. His physical characteristics suggest an earlier link in the species. Mississippi river steamboat mates . . . would classify Nixon as a jungle Negro. They would hire him only if they . . . needed rousters. And they would keep close watch on him. This type is known to be ferocious and relentless in a fight. Though docile enough under ordinary circumstances they are easily aroused. And when this happens the veneer of civilization disappears." From *The Chicago Tribune*, June 5, 1938, p. 5.

Voluntary association influences: The last major resurgence of the Ku Klux Klan would have touched the generation that was of age in the 1920s. It is worthwhile speculating about the possible influence of the American Legion on the attitudes of its predominantly white membership. The impact of the Eagles and other segregated clubs should also be considered.

Special informal contacts: There are possibilities for at least some informal black and white interactions in factories and neighborhoods, possibilites that undoubtedly increase over time (this refers to the non-South population). There are also special events, such as wars and general mobilizations, that mix up the population in unusual ways and create new (although temporary) kinds of contacts.

The Hearst press probably had its greatest impact in the 1910s and 1920s. The Klan was at its peak in the twenties. It seems likely that subsequent experiences, the contacts made in World War II and to a lesser extent in Korea and Vietnam, would work in an opposite direction.

16. Prior to the election, a noted political sociologist wrote as follows:

. . . the Negro Revolution and the success of the Civil Rights movement have have increased the fears of large sections of the white population. These fears centre on what will happen if Negroes move next door—if schools are integrated —and if Negro demands for job quotas are met. All of these fears, if properly exploited, would seem to give the Republican Party a real chance to win a large percentage of the white, working-class, normally Democratic vote.

In an account written after the election, the same author said that "From the beginning it was doubtful that many normally Democratic workers, no matter how bigoted, would vote Republican." Both quotations are from Seymour Martin Lipset, the first appearing in "Beyond the Backlash," *Encounter*, **23** (November

1964), 21, and the second, as "How to Rebuild the Two-Party System," *Harper's*, **230** (January 1965), 61. The discrepant formulations were brought to my attention by Jonathan M. Wiener in his "White Workers and the Negro Revolution" (Princeton: Princeton University, unpublished B.A. thesis, 1966).

17. Taking the non-South married, active, white manual workers, we have the following results: Among those "satisfied" with their financial situation, 21 percent ($N = 100$) voted for Goldwater; among those more or less satisfied, the Republican figure was 25 percent ($N = 89$), and among the dissatisfied, it was 19 percent ($N = 26$). If we add also the nonvoters to the above figures, classifying them by their preferences, the proportions are 19 percent ($N = 124$), 25 percent ($N = 110$), and 14 percent ($N = 37$). In the South, the Republican proportion among the equivalent "satisfied" workers was 29 percent ($N = 28$) and among the more or less satisfied, it was 34 percent ($N = 35$). There were only five dissatisfied working-class respondents in the South and only one of these favored Goldwater.

For discussion of satisfaction and party identification (as opposed to voting) see Chapter 10.

18. Seventeen of the 175 white workers (South and non-South) who were Democratic identifiers and who indicated either their vote or their preference defected to the Republicans in 1964. Eleven of these 17 were opposed to a government role in guaranteeing job equality. There were 17 white workers who were Republican identifiers and who favored the government guarantee. Eight of these voted for or favored the Democrats in 1964. Fifteen of the 45 Republican workers who opposed the government role guaranteeing job equality for blacks also voted for or favored the Democrats that year.

19. Among the married, active, non-South white workers we have the following results: with respect to the federal government's guarantee of job equality for blacks, Democrats 53 percent favoring ($N = 148$) versus 29 percent among Republicans ($N = 58$); with respect to the federal guarantee of school integration, Democrats 59 percent ($N = 145$) versus Republicans, 48 percent ($N = 65$). With respect to equal housing opportunities (no government role mentioned), the Democrats had 72 percent in favor ($N = 156$) and the Republicans 76 percent ($N = 66$).

This unwillingness to use the powers of government to guarantee equality is strongly linked to party identifications in other contexts as well. Among the upper-middle-class non-South whites, for example, there is little difference between Democratic and Republican identifiers in the responses to the housing question; 84 percent ($N = 51$) and 79 percent ($N = 57$), respectively, take the tolerant position. On the question of government intervention to guarantee jobs, however, there is a sharp division, 65 percent of the Democrats favoring the option as opposed to only 31 percent of the Republicans. A similar pattern appears with respect to the school integration question (which also involved a government role). Similar results appear in the lower-middle-class ranks.

There would appear to be little question but that a strong party stand can play a significant role in determining the position of its own voters on issues. It seems likely that the role would be significantly greater when it was a case of noneconomic issues. In a series of referenda following the Civil War, moves to provide Negro suffrage were regularly defeated in Northern states. One striking exception was the state of Iowa, which in 1868 carried the proposal to change the state constitution by a two-thirds majority. This was especially instructive inasmuch as a similar proposal advanced in 1857 had been defeated by a margin of 85.4 percent. Radical reconstructionists in Iowa linked U.S. Grant's candidacy with the constitution change saying that "A vote for Grant and Colfax in Iowa, is not a *true, honest, Republican, vote,* unless it contain[s] the clause striking the word 'White' from the Constitution." The correlation between the vote for Grant and for Negro suffrage in Iowa's counties was +.92. See Robert R. Dykstra and Harlan Hahn, "Northern Voters and Negro Suffrage: The Case of Iowa, 1868," *Public Opinion Quarterly,* **32** (Summer 1968), 202–215.

Lipset does mention the role of organizational and other pressures in determining attitudes. His presentations of data, however, involve simple cross-tabulations of occupation and attitudes, or, in two cases, provide a control for education. The initial presentation in this chapter is addressed to his *practice* rather than to what is essentially an undeveloped theme in his own work.

20. The proportions of these three groups who are Southern-reared are 7, 9, and 15 percent, respectively.

The distribution of attitudes and consistency among the Southern white workers falls in an opposite direction, the intolerant group being considerably larger than the consistent tolerant one. At the same time, the overwhelming majority still showed a mixed position rather than a consistently intolerant one. The percentages are: consistent tolerant, 4 percent; mixed, 67 percent; and consistent intolerant, 29 percent ($N = 80$).

21. It should be noted that although there is no widespread racism indicated within the non-South white working class, even a "small" amount is sufficient to create enormous disturbance. The small percentage of consistent intolerance—9 percent—translates into millions of individuals. Within the mixed category there are no doubt many individuals who could fall in any direction in a racial conflict.

22. The questions used in Table 11.5 read as follows: Q. 32. "Is this neighborhood you now live in all white, mostly white, about half and half, mostly Negro, all Negro?" And, Q. 38. "Are people where you work . . . [plus the same options]?" It will be noted that there is no indication of the "closeness" of integration. If, for example, in speaking of one's workplace, one has reference to a firm employing a thousand workers, two hundred of whom are black, one might answer the question by saying "mostly white" referring to the entire unit or by saying "mostly black" if one were in a segregated shop within the enterprise. Someone in the front office might give the "mostly white" response even though his immediate work is conducted in an *all*-white setting.

The results for the job integration question are for the respondent's job. This means that the figures in Table 11.5 mix descriptions of the house head's job situation and those of the employed wives. The males are more likely to report integrated circumstances than are the women. For example, taking the non-South white working-class individuals, 69 percent ($N = 68$) of the male workers in the large cities report "integrated" jobs as compared with 62 percent ($N = 45$) of the white employed working-class women. In the middle-sized communities and small towns (combined), the equivalent figure for the males is 40 percent ($N = 75$) and for the females 26 percent ($N = 74$).

23. In what follows, the term "integrated" is used to refer to those reporting at least some Negroes in the workplace or neighborhood, that is, it includes all those categories from "mostly white" to "all Negro." There were only a few cases of respondents living in integrated neighborhoods who were employed in segregated workplaces. They have been omitted from this analysis.

24. Very few women in the integrated setting were gainfully employed, a fact that made direct comparison difficult. It was also thought, following the competition-conflict hypothesis, that a job and any resultant interracial competition would have different meaning for men and women. To increase the number of cases available, the single, divorced, and widowed males were included.

As one moves from segregated, to mixed, to integrated settings, the proportions favoring a government role in guaranteeing job equality increase from 39 percent ($N = 49$) to 47 percent ($N = 47$) to 61 percent ($N = 31$). The respective proportions favoring a right to equal housing are 70 percent ($N = 54$), 67 percent ($N = 48$), and 77 percent ($N = 35$).

I am indebted to Jonathan Wiener for this line of analysis. See his "White Workers . . . ," op. cit.

25. There are too few cases available to allow any serious analysis of the Southern setting. When these cases were dichotomized into those with both a segregated workplace and neighborhood, on the one hand, and those with some integrated setting, on the other, we find a pattern similar to that indicated in Table 11.6. There is essentially no difference in attitude indicated with respect to the job question, the tolerant proportions being 4 of 14 and 5 of 14, respectively. With respect to the open housing suggestion, the respective proportions are 7 of 20 (35 percent) and 6 of 13 (or 46 percent).

26. The percentages of non-South, white, male workers having some Negro friends increases from 11 percent ($N = 63$) for those in the segregated milieu (the first column of Table 11.6), to 15 percent ($N = 59$), to 53 percent ($N = 36$) within the integrated setting. In all settings, however, the overwhelming majority indicate that their friends are "mostly white."

27. This alternative hypothesis, in one formulation, reads as follows: "persons who interact frequently with one another tend to like one another." In another formulation it reads: "If the frequency of interaction between two or more persons increases, the degree of their liking for one another will increase, and vice versa." Both statements are from George C. Homans, *The Human Group* (New York: Harcourt, Brace, 1950), pp. 112, 113.

On the degree of integration and tolerance in housing projects see Daniel M. Wilner, Rosabelle P. Walkley, and Stuart W. Cook, "Residential Proximity and Intergroup Relations in Public Housing Projects," *Journal of Social Issues*, **8**:1 (1952), 45–69. More detailed presentations appear in Morton Deutsch and Mary Evans Collins, *Interracial Housing: A Psychological Evaluation of a Social Experiment* (Minneapolis: University of Minnesota Press, 1951), and in Wilner, et al., *Human Relations in Interracial Housing* (Minneapolis: University of Minnesota Press, 1955).

The original account of the impact of integration of army units is that of Samuel

A. Stouffer, Edward A. Suchman, Leland C. DeVinney, Shirley A. Star, and Robin M. Williams, Jr., *The American Soldier: Adjustment During Army Life*, Vol. 1 (Princeton: Princeton University Press, 1949), p. 594. More recent evidence may be found in Charles C. Moskos, Jr., "Racial Integration in the Armed Forces," *American Journal of Sociology*, 72 (September 1966), 132–148.

Also of relevance are the following works: Ira N. Brophy, "The Luxury of Anti-Negro Prejudice," *Public Opinion Quarterly*, 9 (Winter 1945–46), 456–66; John Harding and Russell Hogrefe, "Attitudes of White Department Store Employees Toward Negro Co-Workers, *Journal of Social Issues*, 8 (1952), 18–28; Ralph D. Minard, "Race Relationships in the Pocahontas Coal Field," *Journal of Social Issues*, 8 (1952), 29–44; Erdman B. Palmore, "The Introduction of Negroes into White Departments," *Human Organization*, 14 (Spring 1955), 27–28; Ralph H. Grundlach, "Effects of on-the-job Experiences with Negroes upon Racial Attitudes of White Workers in Union Shops," *Psychological Reports*, (March 1956), 67–77; Marion Yarrow, John D. Campbell, and Leon J. Yarrow, "Acquisition of New Norms: A Study of Racial Desegregation," *Journal of Social Issues*, 14 (1958), 8–28; Ernest Works, "The Prejudice-Interaction Hypothesis from the Point of View of the Negro Minority Group," *American Journal of Sociology*, 67 (July 1961), 47–52; Thomas F. Pettigrew, "Racially Separate or Together?" *Journal of Social Issues*, 25 (1969), 43–69. The latter article contains the best recent summary of the works in this alternative tradition.

28. Of those studies cited in the previous note, only the summer camp study has a before-after comparison. The study of the housing projects has a retrospective question asking about change in attitude toward Negroes. This does indicate change rather than selection operating. See Wilner, et al., "Residential Proximity . . . ," op. cit. The studies of the U.S. Army strongly suggest attitude change since "self-selection" there has such a limited role.

29. There is a sizable gap between perceptions and realities in the matter of integrated housing and property values. One of the best available studies of the subject found that "the entry of nonwhites into previously all-white neighborhoods was much more often associated with price improvement or stability than with price weakenings." (From Laurenti, see below, p. 47). There is, however, a widespread expectation to the contrary. This expectation is likely to stem from a recognition of the prices offered by "blockbusting" real estate operators. The real price, however, is what the operator, in turn, gets for the property.

See Luigi Laurenti, *Property Values and Race: Studies in Seven Cities* (Berkeley: University of California Press, 1961). A study based on 1950 and 1960 census data covering six major Ohio cities reached similar conclusions. The study was undertaken by Sherwood Ross for the National Urban League (reported in *The New York Times*, June 6, 1965, Section VIII, p. 1).

30. Taking the married, active, non-South white working class, one finds 68 percent ($N = 162$) of the homeowners favoring the open housing option and 81 percent ($N = 84$) of the renters. These results are based on those having opinions on the issue. Among the homeowners there is a larger percentage of "don't know, it depends, and can't decide" responses, which indicates, perhaps, some hidden intolerance. The respective proportions falling into this category are 20 percent ($N = 202$) and 12 percent ($N = 95$).

31. The data follow:

Married, Active, Non-South, White Manuals

Age of Head:	Large Cities		Middle-Sized Cities and Small Towns	
	To 44 Years	45 or More	To 44 Years	45 or More
	Percent favoring equal housing (of those with opinion)			
Owner	65.5	52	84	52
$N =$	(40)	(27)	(68)	(27)
Renter	83	80[a]	93	33[a]
$N =$	(35)	(10)	(30)	(9)

[a] Small number of cases.

32. In the large cities outside the South, 25 of the 36 older homeowners (64 percent) were white Protestants. In the younger group of owners only 18 of 47 (38 percent) were white Protestant, the majority, 26 of them, being white and Catholic.

White Protestants, on the whole, are less likely to have an integrated environment than are other groups. Within the non-South white working class in the large cities, for example, comparing white Protestants and white Catholics, one finds the proportions in integrated neighborhoods to be 29 percent ($N = 69$) and 41 percent ($N = 54$). The proportions (of employed men and women) in integrated workplaces are 60 percent ($N = 58$) and 73 percent ($N = 48$). The proportions having at least some black friends are 21 percent ($N = 69$) and 33 percent ($N = 54$).

33. The smallest tolerant percentage is found among the working-class homeowners in all white neighborhoods of the large cities. The figure there is 58 percent ($N = 50$).

34. Both questions, it will be remembered involve two issues, equality and a federal government role. See also the questions in my essay "Black Demands . . . ," op. cit.

35. And since the hypothesis assumes that it is poverty and desperation that stimulate the competition and conflict, this should be evidenced among poor manuals and nonmanuals alike.

Discussions of the competition for jobs, with only rare exceptions, are focused on the "threat" that blacks will take jobs from whites. One of the major job grabs in the history of the United States involved just the opposite development—whites taking the jobs of blacks. See Herbert Hill, "The Racial Practices of Organized Labor—The Age of Gompers and After," pp. 365–402 of Arthur M. Ross and Hill, *Employment, Race, and Poverty* (New York: Harcourt, Brace & World, 1967).

36. It might be argued that the data as given do not cut very low. A specification with the 1956 data, taking first the non-South whites, yields the following results: The "tolerant" proportion for those earning $1999 or less was 91 percent ($N = 11$), for those earning $2000 to $2999, 83 percent ($N = 24$), and for those

earning $3000 to $3999, 79 percent $(N = 72)$. For the South the equivalent figures are: 90 percent $(N = 10)$, 73 percent $(N = 15)$, and 60 percent $(N = 25)$.

37. One would assume, following the conventional wisdom, that the competition and resultant hostilities would be greatest among the unemployed. There are very few cases of unemployed family heads in the 1964 study (and even fewer in the 1956 study). For what it is worth, the conventional wisdom is once again not supported. The percentage of the employed favoring the government guarantee of job equality (among the married, active, white manuals) was 46 percent $(N = 209)$. Among the equivalent unemployed, the figure was 65 percent $(N = 17)$.

38. In 1964, 37.5 percent $(N = 64)$ of those Southerners earning $10,000 or more were reared outside of the South. Among those earning less than that figure, the percentage reared ouside of the region was only 19 percent $(N = 159)$. It is possible that the more tolerant in-migrants have had some effect on the attitudes of their indigenous Southern peers.

39. Some evidence and discussion of the working-class reciprocity patterns may be found in the following sources: William J. Newman, "The Culture of the 'Proles,'" *Dissent*, V (Spring 1958), 154–161; Richard Hoggart, *The Uses of Literacy* (London: Chatto and Windus, 1957); Michael Young and Peter Willmot, *Family and Kinship in East London* (London: Routledge and Kegen Paul, 1957); Andrée Michel, "Relations parentales et relations de voisinage chez les ménages ouvriers de la Seine," *Cahiers Internationaux de Sociologie*, XVII (July–December 1954), 140–153; Donald E. Muir and Eugene A. Weinstein, "The Social Debt: An Investigation of Lower-Class and Middle-Class Norms of Social Obligation," *American Sociological Review*, **27** (August 1962), 532–539; William F. Whyte, *Street Corner Society*, 2d edition (Chicago: University of Chicago Press, 1955); and Herbert J. Gans, *The Urban Villagers* (New York: The Free Press, 1962).

Some evidence on the concern with equality may be found in William Form and Joan Rytina, "Income and Ideological Beliefs on the Distribution of Power in the United States," *American Sociological Review*, **34** (February 1969), 19–31, and "Income and Stratification Ideology: Beliefs about the American Opportunity Structure," *American Journal of Sociology*, **75** (January 1970), 703–716.

The Mississippi planter's comment appears in Nicholas von Hoffman, *Mississippi Notebook* (New York: David White Company, 1964), p. 85. The "bad for business" quotation appeared in *The New York Times*, October 5, 1969. For another account of this "pragmatic" or "tactical" liberalism see Pat Watters, *The South and the Nation* (New York: Pantheon Books, 1969), p. 54.

40. Ben Bagdikian, *In the Midst of Plenty: A New Report on the Poor in America* (Boston: Beacon Press, 1964), pp. 33–34, 83. See also Reese Cleghorn, "The Mill: A Giant Step for the Southern Negro," *New York Times Magazine*, November 9, 1969, 34–35 ff, and Richard L. Rowan, "Negro Employment in Birmingham: Three Cases," pp. 308–336 of Arthur M. Ross and Herbert Hill, eds., *Employment, Race and Poverty* (New York: Harcourt, Brace, 1967).

41. The association of contact and favorable attitudes appears in still another context, with respect to school integration. These data are somewhat oblique since it is parents, or more specifically, adults, who are asked the question and this, in turn, focuses on a government role, not their approval or disapproval of the school practice. The pattern shown in the 1964 data is clear: the more integrated the

schools, the greater the percentage favoring a government role. This is the case in the South and elsewhere. Taking married, active, non-South whites (manuals and nonmanuals), we have the following results: Proportion favoring a government role among those in all white neighborhoods, 56 percent $(N = 267)$; in "mostly white" neighborhoods, 60 percent $(N = 184)$; and in "half-half" or mostly Negro neighborhoods, 67 percent $(N = 24)$. For the South, a comparison is possible only between "all white" and "other" (mostly "mostly white") neighborhoods. The respective proportions there are 23 percent $(N = 139)$ and 53 percent $(N = 47)$.

A *New York Times* story of November 10, 1969 carried the headline: "South Learning to Live with Desegregation." In the story a white teenage girl from Mississippi is quoted as saying that as a result of the experience with integrated schools she had learned "that they're not as dumb as lots of us figured." And a black girl said, "They're not as mean as lots of us thought." For an instructive view of Southern community leaders' attitudes, see Richard Cramer, "School Desegregation and New Industry: The Southern Community Leaders' Viewpoint," *Social Forces*, **41** (May 1963), 384–389.

42. This account and the quotations are from David Halberstam, "The 'Silent Ones' Speak Up in Tennessee," *The Reporter*, **23** (September 1, 1960), 28–30.

43. For example, his enemies circulated a photograph of Kefauver shaking hands with a Negro. He responded saying: "I plead guilty to shaking hands with Negroes." *Time*, **76** (August 15, 1960), 17–18.

44. See Bill Kovach, "Racism Wasn't the Issue in Tennessee," *The Reporter*, **31** (September 24, 1964), 37–38. The title points to the claim that the Clement sales tax was the issue. My point is that the attempt by Clement to divert attention with "demogogic" appeals was not sufficient. Here the combination of a "hard" economic issue and a frank defense of equal rights proved to be successful, it would seem, among the poorer white "masses."

Also a contender in the Bass-Clement primary was a third figure, one who was more conservative and more outspokenly segregationist than Clement; this man picked up only a miniscule percentage of the vote. In Nashville, again in the August 1964 Tennessee Democratic primary, liberal Congressman Richard Fulton, who provided the second Tennessee vote for the Civil Rights Act, defeated two opponents who made that vote into *the* issue. According to one account, he "overwhelmed" the two opponents. The "dean" of the Tennessee Congressional delegation, Representative Cliff Davis, a man with 24 years experience in the House, was defeated by George Grider, a liberal Memphis lawyer. Davis had voted against the Civil Rights Bill. In the Republican primary in Knoxville, a moderate defeated a Goldwaterite. It is interesting to note the conclusions reached. *The New York Times*'s headlines to their summary article stated: "Tennessee Vote Buoys Democrats: But Leaders Urge Caution After Liberal Victories" (August 9, 1964).

In Missouri, a border state, Representative Richard W. Bolling, a liberal with a "record of fighting for civil rights and medical care for the aged," fought a campaign against Judge Hunter Phillips. Phillips had the united support of the five "strong" factions of the local (Kansas City) Democratic party, the remnants of the old Pendergast machine. Phillips attacked Bolling as a "wild-eyed pink" who was "so radical that the Americans for Democratic Action always gives him its highest rating." *The New York Times*'s headline (August 2, 1964) read, "Bolling is Facing Major Challenge." The lead sentence stated that Bolling "faces a serious threat to his political life. . . ." Bolling won by a vote of 52,849 to 26,167. Although *The New York Times*'s headline to this story (August 6, 1964) reads "Negro Vote Makes Bolling a Winner," they also note that Negroes comprised only 17.7 percent of the district's population.

A *New York Times* article (September 11, 1965) reporting on the Georgia Democratic primary was also filled with gloom and fear of backlash. Halfway down in the story we learn that Representative Charles L. Weltner, who had voted for the Civil Rights Act had defeated his opponent by 36,379 to 23,287. The basis of concern was that the size of the defeated candidate's vote was greater than previously.

In another Georgia district Judge Durwood T. Pye, a staunch segregationist noted for his stiff sentences given to civil rights demonstrators, led against two other contenders. The other two, a white liberal lawyer and a Negro lawyer, together had a majority of the vote. It is also stated, a commentary on Southern Republicanism (see Chapter 7), that "Many Republicans passed up their party's primary to vote against Mr. Weltner and for Judge Pye."

There was strong segregationist sentiment indicated in a South Atlanta suburb. There, the Georgia "Grand Dragon" of the United Klans of America, Knights of the Ku Klux Klan, Inc., was running. Although gaining about 46 percent of the vote, he was defeated.

The story ends by noting that two Negroes were successful in their campaign for State Senator nominations. Weltner and James A. McKay, "both liberals by Georgia standards," defeated Goldwater Republicans in the general election in November 1964.

An analysis of Weltner's first Congressional campaign, in which he defeated conservative Representative James C. Davis, appears in M. Kent Jennings and L. Harmon Zeigler, "A Moderate's Victory in a Southern Congressional District," *Public Opinion Quarterly*, **28** (Winter 1964), 595–603. This account of Weltner's 1962 campaign does not support *The New York Times*'s claim about a decrease in his 1964 margin. In 1962 Weltner gained 47 percent in the first primary and 55 percent in a runoff primary. The *Times*'s figures for 1964 indicate a 61 percent margin.

Jennings and Zeigler also present evidence on the relationship between socioeconomic characteristics of districts and the vote for Weltner. The results are complicated by the fact of Republican crossovers in the primary. The partial correlations between median education and median income, respectively, in the primary were .54 and .42. In the general election, these results were reversed, the figures then being −.28 and −.33. They also present partials between a "ratio of managers to laborers" and the vote. These results are the reverse of the above, being −.23 in the primary and .18 in the general. It is difficult to know what to make of this. A focus on managers and laborers, by leaving out most of the employed population, possibly leads to some distortion.

In 1966 Weltner again won in the Democratic primary. At this time, however, the Democratic party had devised a "loyalty oath" that would have required him to support Lester Maddox for governor. Weltner withdrew from the campaign saying "I cannot compromise with hate." The local party committee then selected a substitute who was defeated by a Republican in the general election. The Republican vote was roughly the same as in 1964. The Democratic vote in the district was only little better than half of the 1964 level. See *The New York Times*, pp. 3–6, October 9, and October 12, 1966.

45. *The New York Times*, August 6, 1966.

46. *The New York Times*, August 7, 1966; October 3, 1966; October 30, 1966; and November 9, 1966.

An excellent account of Tennessee politics in the 1950s and early 1960s is that of Norman L. Parks, "Tennessee Politics Since Kefauver and Reece: A 'Generalist' View," *Journal of Politics*, **28** (February 1966), 144–168. It would take us too far afield were we to consider the defeat in 1970 of Tennessee's liberal Senator Gore. For some discussion of that case see my *Restraining Myths . . .* , Chapter 8.

47. Possibly the most outspoken racist in the history of the United States Senate was Theodore G. Bilbo of Mississippi. Norman Parks (op. cit., p. 146n) tells of a closed-door conference held in a Belle Meade mansion in Nashville, Tennessee suburbs. An emissary reported to a group of prominent Democratic and Republican businessmen from that city on his trip to Mississippi where he had delivered a sizable contribution for what turned out to be Bilbo's last campaign. The chairman of the group explained that though they would not receive Bilbo in their homes, "we must frankly recognize that he is our man." Bilbo, in public discussions, was viewed as the favorite of "poor whites." Since very few poor whites were voting at the time, his electoral success must have resulted from the voting of better-off whites. See Chapter 7.

48. James W. Vander Zanden, "Voting on Segregationist Referenda," *Public Opinion Quarterly*, **25** (Spring 1961), 92–105.

49. It also seems likely that the labor effort in Georgia must have been insignificant in comparison to that of the other groups active in this campaign.

Vander Zanden also indicates some organizational efforts being present in the Birmingham and Montgomery results. This involved the white Citizens Councils, the *local* units having conceived of this pro-segregationist referendum proposal as "an integrationist plot." There is some reason to believe, however, that their influence was minimal.

An open housing referendum in Flint, Michigan, carried by a very small margin. Analysis of the result indicated that Negroes, understandably, were strongly in favor of the proposal. The middle-class districts had majorities in favor while the working-class districts tended to be opposed by two-to-one margins. There would seem to be an obvious lesson here. The difficulty, however, is that the always implicit "other things equal" assumption is not justified. The organizers of the campaign concentrated their efforts in the black precincts and in the middle-class precincts. The fair housing committee refused to conduct a neutral poll of the registered voters for fear of antagonizing the opposition. The only effort, therefore, made to reach white workers was through articles in the union local newspapers, some limited leafletting, and talks at union meetings. As to the latter, one of the more active UAW locals had an average attendance at meetings of about 50 out of 4500 members.

In short, it would appear that the committee assumed white working-class authoritarianism and built their campaign on that basis. The result would seem to involve what sociologists call a "self-fulfilling prophecy." I am indebted to the work of Philip Levy for these observations on the Flint referendum.

50. From Chandler Davidson, *Biracial Politics: Conflict and Coalition in the Southern Metropolis* (Baton Rouge: Louisiana State University Press, 1972), Ch. 8. The notion of a Bourbon-black coalition is argued by James Q. Wilson, "The Negro in Politics," pp. 949–973 of *Daedelus* **94** (Fall 1965), see especially pp. 951, 953–54, 957, and 960. Wilson's claim is based, in part, on the very limited presentation of evidence in Jack Walker's "Negro Voting in Atlanta: 1953–1961," *Phylon*, **24** (Winter 1953), 379–387. Results similar to Davidson's appear in a study of the Los Angeles 1969 mayoralty campaign in which a black city council-man, Thomas Bradley, was pitted against Mayor Samuel Yorty. The latter's campaign was replete with all the themes that supposedly generate a blue-collar "backlash." This study found an inverse relationship between both education and income of the precinct (controlling for racial composition) and vote for Bradley. Put otherwise, the vote for Yorty was greatest in the high-income and high-educa-tion precincts. See Harlan Hahn and Timothy A. Almy, "Ethnic Politics and Racial Issues: Voting in Los Angeles," *Western Political Quarterly* (forthcoming). A study of a contest of black and white candidates in Massachusetts found socio-economic status had little relationship to the result; see John F. Becker and Eugene E. Heaton, Jr., "The Election of Senator Edward W. Brooke," *Public Opinion Quarterly*, **31** (Fall 1967), 346–358.

51. This is most clearly the case in the novels of William Faulkner. Black authors make a markedly different stress. They portray the violence as coming from all levels in the white community. This alternative focus appears in the work of Charles Chesnutt, James Weldon Johnson, Jean Toomer, Richard Wright, and others. I am indebted to Joel Roach who brought this to my attention.

52. The account here is based on the work of Francis Butler Simkins, *Pitchfork Ben Tillman: South Carolinian* (Baton Rouge: Louisiana State University, 1944). The quotation is from p. 63. The entire history of the "Straightout, the Shotgun, or the Edgefield policy" is recounted on pp. 57–67. An account of a similar develop-ment in pre-Revolutionary South Carolina is contained in Richard Maxwell Brown's *The South Carolina Regulators* (Cambridge: Harvard University Press, 1963).

53. Simpkins, op. cit. pp. 224–225. Tillman was a close friend of James F. Byrnes. At the time, Byrnes was a member of the House of Representatives. He later served as United States Senator from South Carolina, as U.S. Supreme Court Justice, as Secretary of State, and Governor of South Carolina. See Simpkins, p. 316n, and also James F. Byrnes, *All In One Lifetime* (New York: Harper, 1958), pp. 41–42.

At one point Tillman nominated his personal lawyer for United States district attorney, the lawyer being J. William Thurmond, the political boss of Edgefield county. Thurmond had "rashly killed a man" in a quarrel over Tillmanism. President Wilson overlooked the "alleged incompetence" of the successful ap-plicant, feeling that "the chief enforcer of Federal law in South Carolina should not be a man who had killed a fellow citizen." Through Tillman's efforts, South Carolina was divided into two Federal judicial districts, the new position this time being guaranteed successfully to Thurmond. President Wilson made the appointment. See Simpkins, pp. 531–534. J. William Thurmond was the father of J. Strom Thurmond, the presidential candidate and South Carolina Senator.

54. Albert K. Kirwan, *Revolt of the Rednecks, Mississippi Politics: 1876–1925* (New York: Harper & Row, 1965), pp. 21, 95–96. As indicated, the appeals of the Populists to the Negroes were limited. Their ticket did not include a single Negro candidate.

55. Alex Mathews Arnett, *The Populist Movement in Georgia: A View of the "Agrarian Crusade" in the Light of Solid-South Politics* (New York: Columbia University Press, 1922). The quotations are from pp. 153 and 184. See also William DeBose Sheldon, *Populism in the Old Dominion: Virginia Farm Politics, 1885–1900* (Princeton: Princeton University Press, 1935), p. 92. Also useful for its portrayal of upper-class authoritarianism and for an indication of some limited joint black-white effort is Roscoe C. Martin's *The People's Party in Texas: A Study in Third Party Politics* (Austin: University of Texas Bulletin, No. 3308, 1933). See especially pp. 95–96.

Two factors appear to have been operating in the Populist effort, one ideal and the other practical. First, the thrust of the Populist program was strongly equalitarian, against the privileges of the established wealth; and second, since Negroes did hold the balance of power in many Southern states, it was also expedient to make these appeals. It is difficult to assess the relative importance of the two considerations.

56. C. Vann Woodward, *Tom Watson: Agrarian Rebel* (New York: Oxford University Press, 1963), quotations are from pp. 231 and 240. On the force and fraud used by Democrats, see pp. 231–243.

57. Watson, according to Woodward, changed his position in subsequent years, to become a leading anti-Negro, anti-Catholic, and anti-Semitic agitator. By 1906 he was a champion of Negro disenfranchisement. He was, still later, involved in the lynching of Leo Frank (see Woodward, pp. 443–445).

The anti-Negro position in those years was still not limited to "poor whites," nor was violence the exclusive province of the "red-necks." A few days after the 1906 election in Georgia (in which the disenfranchisement issue was prominent), a race riot occurred in Atlanta with murder, destruction, looting, and acts of extreme brutality. Woodward writes that: "During the campaign the papers of Atlanta were almost daily filled with sensational stories of Negro atrocities. Lynching was openly advocated and frequently practiced. A concerted crusade of race bigotry and hatred was preached. Partly it was the result of newspaper rivalry, augmented by the recent intrusion of Hearst into Atlanta . . ." (p. 379). One account of this riot notes the involvement of members of the "best families." See Charles Crowe, "Racial Massacre in Atlanta, September 22, 1906," *Journal of Negro History*, **54** (April 1969), 150–168.

Recently a question has been raised as to whether or not Watson "changed." He and the Populists generally were led, because of the pivotal role of Negro voters, to make some concessions to Negro voters. See Charles Crowe, "Racial Violence and Social Reform—Origins of the Atlanta Riot of 1906," *Journal of Negro History*, **53** (July 1968), 234–50, and Robert Saunders, "Southern Populists and the Negro: 1893–1895," *Journal of Negro History*, **54** (July 1969), 240–257.

58. This disparity between Roosevelt's public and private position is to be found in Howard K. Beale, *Theodore Roosevelt and the Rise of America to World Power* (Baltimore: Johns Hopkins Press, 1956). The letter reports that he thought the lynching "rather a good thing, and said so," at a dinner with "various dago diplomats . . . all much wrought up by the lynching" (p. 42). John Higham reports that the mob "was led by the district attorney and other prominent citizens." See his *Strangers in the Land* (New Brunswick: Rutgers University Press, 1955). The quotation accompanies a picture following p. 210.

59. Stanley Coben, *A. Mitchell Palmer: Politician* (New York: Columbia University Press, 1963), p. 197.

Coben reports that Palmer's attitude toward southern and eastern Europeans changed little during his later career. Addressing Congress in 1912 he pointed out the large number of fatal quarry accidents, calling them a real loss to the nation since the victims were mostly Welsh immigrants, "a high class of workman —not cheap foreign labor" (p. 198). Later on, in 1919, writing about alien radicals for *The Forum*, he stated that: "Out of the sly and crafty eyes of many of them leap cupidity, cruelty, insanity, and crime; from their lopsided faces, sloping brows, and misshapen features may be recognized the unmistakable criminal type" (p. 198). It is to be noted that these are the words of the *nation's* chief law inforcement officer and that he is President Woodrow Wilson's appointee.

Some related activities of this "progessive" administration are discussed by Nancy J. Weiss, "The Negro and the New Freedom: Fighting Wilsonian Segregation," *Political Science Quarterly*, LXXXIV (March 1969), 61–79.

In 1837, an abolitionist, Elijah Lovejoy, was murdered in a mob action in Alton, Illinois. Playing a very prominent role in the events leading up to the murder was one Usher F. Linder, the attorney general of Illinois. Later, a large audience at Faneuil Hall in Boston was told that the Alton mob had acted in the hallowed tradition of Samuel Adams and the other heroes of the Boston Tea Party. The speaker in this case was James Trecothic Austin, the Massachusetts attorney general. For the details, see Leonard L. Richards, *"Gentlemen of Property and Standing" Anti-Abolition Mobs in Jacksonian America* (New York: Oxford University Press, 1970). The "gentlemen" in this case, the leading men of their communities, were also the leaders of the mobs.

60. The quotations are from Arthur F. Raper, *The Tragedy of Lynching* (Chapel Hill: University of North Carolina Press, 1933), pp. 11–12 (emphasis added). Also of some interest is James Elbert Cutler, *Lynch-Law: An Investigation into the History of Lynching in the United States* (New York: Longmans, Green & Co., 1905). This work cites a number of instances in which the "best people" originated or revived the practice, for example, in the case of Col. Lynch, the founder, who was controlling Tories in the interior of Virginia during the Revolution. In some of these instances, after the upper classes taught and legitimated the practice, the subsequent lynchings were undertaken by persons of lesser status (pp. 131–132, 147, 274–275).

One case study of a lynching stresses repeatedly the competition of Negroes and whites of the lower and lower-middle classes as being a key contributing factor. The detailed history of the event, however, tells a different story. "A prominent businessman arranged with a friend to be notified the moment the victim was removed to another jail, one which was in a building more "easily stormed." The report says: "If a 'prominent man,' who is unlikely to be punished, participates, surely lesser men may safely join the mob. . . . It was said to be well known locally that some of Longwood's prominent businessmen and citizens themselves participated in the mob. Such individuals are likely to control the machinery of punishment and be able to obstruct it if they choose. . . . A deputy sheriff stated . . . the day of the lynching that 'the mob will not be bothered, either before or after the lynching.' " A nearby radio station broadcast news of "a lynching party to which all white people are invited." It should also be said that if "prominent citizens" and "lower-class" whites are present in the same enterprise, it would seem unlikely that the prominent citizens would be *followers* in the action. The account is from Neal E. Miller and John Dollard, *Social Learning and Imitation* (New Haven: Yale University Press, 1941), pp. 243–244.

A community study reports as follows:
It is frequently said by white people that the greatest hostility toward Negroes exists among lower-class whites, and it is similarly implied that the middle- and upper-class whites love the Negroes. The middle-class Negroes, at least, do not confirm this statement. The Negro owner of a small farm said that the hostility lies mainly between the 'strainers' (the middle-class whites) and the Negroes, and not between the Negroes and the poorest whites.

See John Dollard, *Caste and Class in a Southern Town* (New Haven: Yale University Press, 1937), p. 126.

A more recent lynching also *would appear* to be the work of poor whites, this being the killing of Michael Schwerner, James Chaney, and Andrew Goodman in Mississippi in June 1964. Although those doing the actual killing have been described as fitting that picture ("a sorry lot" says one author), knowledge of the murders and complicity in the undertaking reached into some rather high places. When the murderers were finished with their task and had buried the bodies and burned the car, they returned to the courthouse square in Philadelphia where "they were met by an official of the state of Mississippi" who told them ". . . you've done a good job. . . . Mississippi can be proud of you." From William Bradford Huie, *Three Lives for Mississippi* (New York: WCC Books, 1965), p. 191.

Since one so frequently hears, in motion pictures or on television, or reads the words of poor whites advocating violence, and since, because of this training, it appears as rather implausible that upper classes would do the same, it is worth citing a case. The following is from a news report by Homer Bigart, *The New York Times*, November 30, 1964:

The banker said he was tired of hearing stories that Neshoba County Sheriff Lawrence Rainey was rough on Negroes.
"This nigger woman was trying to cash a forged check," he recalled. "I told the teller to call for the sheriff. The nigger woman snatched the check and started to run. The sheriff caught up with her at the corner. She resisted and was slamming him up against a building when I arrived."
Sheriff Rainey weighs about 220 pounds. He is under indictment on charges of depriving seven Negroes of their civil rights by unlawfully detaining and beating them.

"I don't believe in police brutality," the banker continued, "but I told the sheriff 'Take that club and knock hell out of her.' He didn't do it."

61. Dietrich C. Reitzes, "Union vs. Neighborhood in a Tension Situation," *Journal of Social Issues*, **9** (1953), 37–44. This article tells of a "Civic Club" organized to keep Negroes out of the community. The club also sent members to join in a disturbance in a nearby community (p. 38).

62. Cicero was the scene of a mob action in 1951 when a black family attempted to move into the all white community. Many of those arrested at that time were from outside the town. Earlier in 1966 a black youth had been beaten to death in the community.

The account of the march is based on the reports of the *Chicago Sun-Times* and the *Tribune* for August and September 1966.

63. Although it is customary in Milwaukee to refer to the South Side as "Polish," the *Milwaukee Journal* estimates that 100,000 to 150,000 of the 350,000 persons in the area are of Polish descent. Their issue of September 9, 1967, p. 7.

64. *Milwaukee Journal*, August 28, 1967; August 29, 1967; and August 30, 1967.

65. The survey was conducted by the market research division of the *Milwaukee Journal* and is reported in their issue of August 31, 1967. Eighty-three persons were interviewed for this purpose.

66. *Milwaukee Journal*, September 3, 1967; September 10, 1967; and September 11, 1967.

67. *Milwaukee Journal*, September 12, 1967 and September 13, 1967.

68. *Milwaukee Journal*, September 14, 1967. This evenings' activities provided the peak of counter-demonstrator activity. The struggle of the evening was between counter-demonstrators and police, not between civil rights marchers and counter-demonstrators.

69. *Milwaukee Journal*, September 21, 1967.

70. The instances cited here involve marches of protestors into working-class areas. Similar demonstrations in middle-class areas, for reason of urban geography, are relatively infrequent. One such case, however, does prove to be instructive. In August 1966, Father Groppi led marchers into middle-class Wauwatosa, a suburb of Milwaukee. The marches occurred each night for a couple of weeks, the destination being the home of a local judge and the aim being to protest his membership in the segregated Eagles club. In this setting of $40,000 homes, much of the same thing happened as occurred a year later on the South Side. Crowds of hecklers appeared and violence ensued. The police were present in great numbers and units of the Wisconsin National Guard were called out. The newspaper reports of the events are not very detailed. The observations made in the text also apply to this series of events; only a minority of the community appeared on the scene and some outside involvement was indicated. See *Milwaukee Journal*, August 20, 1966–September 2, 1966.

Discussions of "working-class authoritarianism" often make reference to the support by workers for capital punishment, that is, for "official" as well as "unofficial violence." One review of relevant evidence finds little support for this claim. Gallup has asked the following question over the years: "Are you in favor of the death penalty for persons convicted of murder?" The results from three surveys follow:

	Occupation		
	Professional and Business	White Collar	Manual Workers
Year	*Percent for capital punishment*		
1965	44	52	47
1966	43	57	40
1969	48	54	51

From Hazel Erskine, "The Polls: Capital Punishment," *Public Opinion Quarterly*, **34** (Summer 1970), especially pp. 292–293.

71. Glazer and Lipset, "The Polls on Communism and Conformity," op. cit. (note 1), p. 150.

An alternative formulation of the same point, with some different emphases, is by John W. Gardner who states: "The collision between dissenters and lower middle class opponents is exceedingly dangerous. As long as the dissenters are confronting the top layers of the power structure, they are dealing with people who are reasonably secure, often willing to compromise, able to yield ground without anxiety. But when the dissenters collide with the lower middle class, they confront an insecure opponent, quick to anger and not prepared to yield an inch." *Science*, **164** (25 April 1964), 379. See Leonard Richards for some striking evidence to the contrary.

72. See Samuel A. Stouffer, *Communism, Conformity, and Civil Liberties* (Garden City: Doubleday, 1955). The "main presentation" referred to is Lipset's, see *Political Man*, p. 104.

73. This second table (*Political Man*, p. 109) deserves more detailed attention. There are four occupational categories used, "high" and "low" white collar, and "high" and "low" manual, and five educational categories. Unlike the previously discussed table, this one contains males and females. It is not clear how the women are classified, that is, by their own or by a husband's or house head's occupation.

The table shows essentially no difference in tolerance between the high manuals and the low white-collar groups. All of the difference in tolerance levels comes in the extreme groups, the low manuals and the high white collar. Even this pattern does not appear consistently in all educational categories. The table as it stands does not justify the *"working-class* authoritarianism" formulation. What is indicated is "low manual" authoritarianism or even more specifically, low-manual-with-grade-school-education authoritarianism.

The table also indicates, a point recognized in the text, that the relationship is considerably stronger with education than with occupation. This too suggests that the phenomenon is mislabelled.

74. The proportion of non-South farmers supporting the admitted Communist's right to speak was 24 percent ($N = 151$). The equivalent figure for the South was 14 percent ($N = 114$). The right of the "accused man" to speak was supported by 80 percent ($N = 144$) of the non-South farmers and only 59 percent ($N = 106$) of the farmers in the South.

75. Still another consideration involves the religious factor. The original report indicated that little difference was found in the tolerance levels of Catholics and

Protestants. The Jews, however, were considerably more tolerant; the differences between them and the Catholics and Protestants amounted to roughly 50 percentage points. This special contribution of tolerance on the part of the Jewish population falls largely within the non-South, urban middle class. It seems likely that if one compared only the Protestants and Catholics, the class differences would be reduced, particularly in the larger communities outside the South. When only Protestants and Catholics were considered, this did prove to be the case. The tolerance of the non-South large-city middle classes for the admitted Communist fell from 52 percent to 45 percent, and the class differences were reduced from 17 percentage points to 11. In other contexts, however, this procedure had no more than a one percentage point impact on the results shown in Table 11.8.

76. The result, broken down by region, follows. Percent tolerant (SRC 1956 civil liberties question): non-South middle class, 79 percent ($N = 332$); non-South manuals, 73 percent ($N = 369$); non-South farm, 70 percent ($N = 66$); South middle class, 80 percent ($N = 128$); South manuals, 70 percent ($N = 112$); and South farm, 53 percent ($N = 30$).

77. Taking the married, active, non-South populations of nonfarm origins who were reared outside the South, we find 78 percent ($N = 231$) and 80 percent ($N = 248$), respectively, of the manuals and nonmanuals responding tolerantly to the civil liberties question.

There is much casual usage made of the *ceteris paribus* assumption. It is, of course, extremely rare that the assumption obtains. The best one can hope for in the social sciences is to hold constant as many of the other key determining factors as possible. It is rare, however, that even this attempt is made. Lipset's original presentation shows only two variables, occupation and attitude, in two of the tables which present new evidence, and in a third, education is controlled. In the present analysis an attempt has been made to go beyond that level of presentation. This discussion does nothing to change the basic, that is, the original, frequency distribution. Instead, it indicates what factors are operative in producing that original result.

It seems likely, were we able to control for farm origins and region of origin in the Stouffer data, that we would obtain a result similar to that found here. That is likely only in the case of the "accused man" series. It is doubtful that the differences would be eliminated in the case of the other questions in the scale.

In the Stouffer data, the professionals come through regularly as the most tolerant of the major occupational groups. Much of the presumed "middle-class" tolerance is, in fact, the tolerance only of this category. It is worthwhile speculating whether this result could not be specified in more detail. The Stouffer study, unfortunately, does not allow any more detailed breakdown of the professionals. The 1956 SRC study does allow some specification. Dividing the category into teachers, clergy, and engineers, on the one hand, and "all other" professionals, on the other, the respective "tolerant" proportions approving the rights of the "accused man" are 92 percent ($N = 71$) and 79 percent ($N = 53$). The latter category includes (in addition to semiprofessionals) accountants, dentists, lawyers, and doctors.

78. The best recent summary of the evidence appears in Bruno Bettelheim and Morris Janowitz, *Social Change and Prejudice* (New York: Free Press, 1964), pp. 25–36. See also Robert W. Hodge and Donald J. Treiman, "Occupational

Mobility and Attitudes Toward Negroes," *American Sociological Review*, **31** (February 1966), 93–102.

79. The Bettleheim and Janowitz study had information on 130 World War II veterans. Questions were asked about the occupation held before the war and at the time of the interview (1946). Mobility meant moving up or down one or more grades in the Edwards classification. For this reason it is difficult to assess the data for its relevance to the more conventional concern, that is, movement between the manual and nonmanual ranks. Their study does find the downward mobiles to be considerably less tolerant than the nonmobiles and the upward mobiles. There were only 18 cases of downward mobility in the sample. It must be remembered, given the definition, that this could mean a move from the "manager" category to the "clerical" category.

Reanalyzing the data from the Elmira study, this time comparing fathers' and respondents' occupations and focusing on manual-nonmanual stability or mobility, one study found the stable groups to be generally less prejudiced than the mobile groups. There was little consistency about any of the other results. Upward mobiles were more prejudiced in some comparisons, downward mobiles more prejudiced in others. The percentage differences in tolerance associated with mobility or stability were small. This is the work of Joseph Greenblum and Leonard I. Pearlin, "Vertical Mobility and Prejudice: A Socio-Psychological Analysis," pp. 480–491 of Reinhard Bendix and Seymour Martin Lipset, *Class, Status, and Power* (Glencoe: Free Press, 1953). A similar study by Fred B. Silberstein and Melvin Seeman also found small differences. See their "Social Mobility and Prejudice," *American Journal of Sociology*, **65** (November 1959), 258–264. There are a number of other studies cited in Bettelheim and Janowitz, pp. 30–31. An examination of mobility and tolerance using the Survey Research Center's 1964 study also showed small differences, varied patterns, and, hence, inclusive results.

80. It was noted above that very little difference exists in the tolerant percentages of the manuals and nonmanuals when the influence of farm origins and Southern origins are controlled. Taking only those of nonfarm and non-South origins, there is a small positive relationship between education and tolerance. Among those of grade school and high school education, the tolerance is *greater* among the manuals than among the nonmanuals. The data follow (Survey Research Center, 1956):

Married, Active, Non-South Populations of Non-Farm and Non-South Origins

	Education		
	Grade School	High School	Some College
	Percent tolerant (civil liberties question)		
Manuals	77%	79%	81%
N =	(60)	(117)	(53)
Nonmanuals	74	74	84
N =	(23)	(85)	(141)

Since it is so generally assumed that education and tolerance are positively related, it is important to note the exceptions. The relationship is negative in the case of the 1964 question on a government guarantee of job equality. The data:

Married, Active Non-South White Catholics and Protestants of Non-South Origins

	Percent tolerant (job equality question)		
Manuals	62%	46%	46%
N =	(34)	(112)	(48)
Nonmanuals	50	45	44
N =	(20)	(85)	(114)

81. Cross-sectional surveys are not the best procedure for ascertaining the direct impact of education. What is needed here, to exclude the influence of selection, is before-and-after studies. It is possible, of course, that both selection and conversion may be operating.

The use of cross-sectional surveys is also rather crude (as well as rather obscure). Merely counting years of education and relating that count to the attitudes held toward minority groups tells very little. Why each additional year of study of electrical engineering should affect one's attitude toward Negroes, for example, is not entirely clear.

82. The study in question is the Roper-Fortune Study, No. 76, dated April 1949. The sample was a large one—over 3000 interviews—based on quota procedures. I wish to express my appreciation to the Roper Public Opinion Research Center, Williamstown, Massachusetts, for making this study available.

83. The question reads as follows: Q. 17. "Should colleges have classes that take up the subject of (racial and religious prejudice, etc.), or should (racial and religious prejudice, etc.) be discussed in classes only when students ask about it, or would it be better not to discuss it at all?" The question was repeated asking about sex education, religious beliefs, and communism. For the following analysis those who favored such classes (even if with the qualification) were viewed as tolerant and those opposed as intolerant. Those failing to respond to one or more questions were excluded. Respondents giving two or more tolerant responses were classed as the "more tolerant" group. Those with only one or no tolerant responses as the "less tolerant."

These are not, to be sure, ideal "tolerance" questions. A culling of the materials at the Roper Center indicated that this was the best available study for the purpose at hand, that is, one having questions on both tolerance and on college aspirations for one's children.

84. Comparing the "more" and "less" tolerant manuals (N's = 532 and 122, respectively), we have the following results: college students seen as: hard working, 31 percent and 23 percent; intelligent, 54 percent and 44 percent; well-informed, 38 percent and 22 percent; well-mannered, 33 percent and 30 percent; and ambitious, 50 percent and 34 percent. By comparison, taking the negative descriptions, we have: soft, 5 and 10 percent; time-wasting, 11 and 23 percent; hard-drinking, 4 and 16 percent; and snobbish, 8 percent and 21 percent. It is assumed here that for most of the respondents, ambition is viewed positively and that drinking and wasting time are viewed negatively.

85. Still another possibility is that the less tolerant students choose less controversial courses of study such as, for example, engineering or business. These subject matters are less threatening, involve "mere facts," and can be treated more or less technically, that is, without any personal emotional involvement. Such a propensity, if it were the case, would have the consequence of funneling the "less tolerant" persons into different kinds of careers, into business and industry, whereas the "more tolerant" students would be likely to go into liberal arts courses and from there into the fields of education and welfare.

86. There is a tendency to treat survey research results as "fixed" or "constant" conditions, as if the population described had "hard" commitments in all areas where questioning occurred. That conclusion is not warranted, as the more methodologically sophisticated are quick to point out. Many people "merely give a response," as if to fulfill the demand of the interviewer. Many people respond with "don't know" or "no answers," and many of those who do respond are not strongly committed. The focus in this work on the "do knows" (as opposed to the "don't knows") does, regrettably, tend to feed this impression of "fixity" or "determinacy." It was shown in Chapter 6, however, particularly in the smaller communities, that there was a relatively large degree of "openness" indicated by the proportion of "don't knows" and nonresponses and by the weak identification with the parties. It seems likely that many of the small-town and rural "authoritarians" would shift position when subjected to more "moderate" or "liberal" influences. This would seem a likely eventuality for those who move out or commute out, finding jobs in larger communities.

87. Two summary works showing the wide range of involvement in what later came to be called "McCarthyism" are those of Alan D. Harper, *The Politics of Loyalty: The White House and the Communist Issue, 1946–1952* (Greenwich: Greenwood, 1971) and Athan Theoharis, *Seeds of Repression: Harry S. Truman and the Origins of McCarthyism* (Chicago: Quadrangle, 1971).

Prominent and elite figures gave McCarthy all kinds of support and in many ways made his effort both possible and credible. Some of this support was purely tactical; some did not believe his claims but saw the development as useful in the fight against "liberal" opponents. Richard Rovere says that Kenneth Wherry, the Republican floor leader, "had dutifully given McCarthy whatever parliamentary advantages it had been within his power to win, but he avoided making common cause with him" (p. 135). Although Senate leaders did not believe McCarthy's charges (his first defense of his claims before the Senate had been a fiasco), Republican leaders saw his uses. Senator Robert Taft, frequently referred to as a Republican "statesman," told him simply: "If one case doesn't work, try another" (p. 136). Rovere continues: "To Kenneth Wherry and the rest of the Republican leadership, McCarthy was, within a matter of weeks, to become pure gold—a partisan with a bipartisan following" (p. 136). Regardless of his personal reserve in the matter, Taft "gave it out that in his opinion, 'the pro-Communist policies of the State Department fully justified Joe McCarthy in his demand for an investigation'" (p. 179). The chairman of the 1952 Republican convention introduced McCarthy and set off a wild demonstration by referring to him as "Wisconsin's Fighting Marine" and as the man who was so unjustly maligned for "exposing the traitors in our government" (p. 180). Dwight David Eisenhower, the Republican presidential candidate, gave McCarthy his support when he made an appearance in Wisconsin during the 1952 campaign. The Republican National Committee Chairman, Arthur Summerfield, also a supporter, "had pleaded with Eisenhower to accept McCarthy . . ." (p. 238). While none of these personages (other than Eisenhower) were members of the "Eastern establishment," one such individual did lend some credence, although less directly, to the McCarthy enterprise. Senator Henry Cabot Lodge (together with Senator Bourke Hicken-looper) did not sign the Tydings Committee report because he did not think the investigation was broad enough to warrant a clean bill of health for the State Department. Among the upper-class supporters on the Democratic side were various members of the Kennedy family, most notably, Joseph, John F., and Robert.

The above page references are from Richard H. Rovere, *Senator Joe McCarthy* (New York: Harcourt, Brace, and World, 1959). Additional information on elite responses to McCarthy may be found on pages 10, 12–18, 98, 142, and 235. A much better source, in fact, the source for much of the information in Rovere's book, is the work of Jack Anderson and Ronald W. May, *McCarthy: The Man, the Senator, and the "Ism"* (Boston: Beacon Press, 1952), see pp. 111, 164, 191–193, 230–233, 290, 316, 352 (the Taft quotation), and elsewhere.

On John F. Kennedy, see John Hughes, *The Ordeal of Power* (New York: Atheneum, 1962). Hughes states that in 1953 "one could look in vain through the record of all deliberations of the Senate . . . for a single word or vote of criticism from the cautious young Massachusetts senator. In the year 1952, his relations with Senator McCarthy were so cordial and satisfactory as to dissuade McCarthy from entering Massachusetts, even to deliver a single speech in support of Kennedy's Republican opponent, Henry Cabot Lodge" (p. 355). For a more detailed account of Kennedy's attitude see John P. Mallen, "Massachusetts: Liberal and Corrupt," *New Republic,* **127** (October 13, 1952), pp. 10–12. Kennedy, who also supported the McCarran Act, indicated his respect for McCarthy and stated his feeling that he "may have something." He also, according to Mallen, indicated he was very happy that Richard Nixon defeated Helen Gahagan Douglas. See also pp. 426–429 of Richard J. Whalen, *The Founding Father: The Story of Joseph P. Kennedy* (New York: New American Library, 1964).

The contributions of the congressman, senator, vice-president, and later president of the United States to the "McCarthy" era are reported in William Costello, *The Facts About Nixon* (New York: Viking Press, 1960).

A little known aspect of the history of the era involves John Foster Dulles. New York Governor Thomas E. Dewey appointed Dulles (July 1949) to the United States Senate to fill a vacancy created by the retirement of liberal Senator Robert F. Wagner. Dulles later decided to run in the special election of November 1949. Governor Dewey said that New Yorkers would "thrill to the news" of their opportunity to elect "one of the greatest statesmen in the world." His opponent was Herbert Lehman. Although Dulles had originally announced that the campaign would focus on "welfare statism," it came to be heavily focused on "Communism."

Dewey declared during the campaign that ". . . the only people that don't want him [Dulles] are the Communists and their supporters" (*The New York Times,* October 4, 1949, p. 23). Dulles told an upstate crowd that if they "could see the kind of people in New York City making up this bloc that is voting for my opponent, if you could see them with your own eyes, I know that you would be out, every last man and woman of you, on election day" (*The New York Times,*

October 6, 1949, p. 26). Dulles preceded this statement with one linking his opponent to the Communists referring to "the unfailing devotion of the Communist Party to his ideals." A similar attempt was made on other occasions (*The New York Times,* October 8, p. 30; October 26, p. 1; another Dewey inuendo is reported October 27, p. 22; another Dulles one on October 28, p. 6). This last reference, reporting a speech in Syracuse, gives Dulles' words as follows: "If I am defeated . . . the greatest rejoicing will . . . be in Moscow . . . now its up to you . . . to decide whether or not you will do what the Russian Communists want."

It is difficult to reconcile these efforts with the hypotheses that attribute such behaviors to low-status or "populist" demagogues. It is also difficult to reconcile these efforts with the assumption that elites are responsible and tolerant.

Ironically, President Harry S. Truman also played a role in "setting the tone" for the subsequent period. The President's counsel, Clark Clifford, in a memorandum written in November 1947, urged that "the Communist inspiration" behind Henry Wallace's campaign should be denounced. See Irwin Ross, *The Loneliest Campaign* (New York: New American Library, 1968), p. 24.

88. Referring to a vote of appropriations for McCarthy's Permanent Subcommittee (of the Judiciary Committee), Rovere says, ". . . it is doubtful if there were more than three or four men in the Senate who had any confidence in him or felt toward him anything but distaste, distrust, and fear, [yet] eighty-five members of that great deliberative assembly voted 'Yea' on the motion to give him what he wanted in the way of money" (p. 35). That was in February 1954. A very good account of press treatment of McCarthy in his home state appears in Sharon Coady, "The Wisconsin Press and Joseph McCarthy: A Case Study" (Madison: unpublished M.A. thesis, Department of History, University of Wisconsin, 1965). This study concentrates on McCarthy's 1946 campaign rather than the key 1952 effort. For the 1952 newspaper performance, see Robert Pell, "AMPE Editorial Criteria vs. Comment on McCarthyism: A Study of Editorial Page Responsibility in the Daily Press of Wisconsin" (Madison: unpublished M.S. thesis, Journalism Department, University of Wisconsin, 1963). See also Ronald May, "Is the Press Unfair to McCarthy?" *New Republic,* **128** (April 20, 1953), 10–12.

The Milwaukee *Sentinel* (a Hearst paper) recommendation of McCarthy read as follows: ". . . there are other reasons why McCarthy must be re-elected. In spite of his dramatic and free-swinging methods—or perhaps because of them— he has become the rallying point for American patriotism in its long-delayed counter-attack on the Communist menace within our own government." (November 3, 1952, p. 18). The Janesville (Wisconsin) *Gazette* made the same recommendation justifying their preference as follows: ". . . for all the alarm about his methods, [he] has succeeded as no other individual in dramatizing the danger of Communists in government. Much of the 'threat to Americanism' which makes the headlines represents, of course, the type of political campaigning used against him. McCarthy, whatever his faults or shortcomings, is the symbol of anti-Communism not only in Wisconsin, but nationally" (editorial, November 1, 1952).

89. The same holds true for previous periods of hysteria also. For outstanding accounts of the 1919–1920 "red scare," see Coben, Ch. 11 and Higham, Ch. 9. Also of some, albeit more limited, value is Robert K. Murray, *Red Scare: A Study in National Hysteria, 1919–1920* (Minneapolis: University of Minnesota Press,

1955). During World War I the federal government created a Committee on Public Information to drum up patriotic sentiment. See the work of its head, George Creel, *How We Advertised America* (New York: Harper & Brothers, 1920). Three large voluntary associations having substantial upper-class support did the same unofficially. These were the National Security League (supported by T. Coleman du Pont, Henry C. Frick, J. P. Morgan, and John D. Rockefeller), The National Civic Federation (at this time supported by Everit Macy, August Belmont, and Elbert Gary), and The American Defense Society (which had government sponsorship and Theodore Roosevelt as honorary chairman). Murray sums the matter up as follows: "Employers . . . were brought to the realization that the issue of radicalism could be helpful in their fight against unionism. To certain politicians it became obvious that radicalism would make an excellent political issue by which free publicity as well as votes could be obtained. The general press found in the issue of radicalism an immediate substitute for waning wartime sensationalism" (p. 67). Mitchell Palmer was a "true believer" and at the same time an enthusiastic presidential aspirant; he was very much interested in the scare for its vote-getting potential. See Coben, op. cit. Murray's account contains a wealth of detail. It is marred, however, by its use of such expressions as "the public mind." He treats public concern as the key initiating factor in the event. His *evidence* makes it clear that "public sentiment" is a dependent, not an independent factor. For this reason the work should, to use his phrase, "be used with some caution."

It seems likely that the efforts of this period first instilled the basic fear of Communism, both domestic and foreign, that have been developed and reworked to the present. In this view, the events of the early fifties amount to little more than reuse of techniques that had been used on numerous previous occasions. It also involved an activation of fears, the seeds of which had been planted years earlier.

In addition to those works already cited, see John R. Mock and Cedric Larson, *Words That Won the War: The Story of the Committee on Public Information, 1917–1919* (Princeton: Princeton University Press, 1939). On the American Protection League see *The Web* (Chicago: Reilly & Lee, 1919). See also Norman Hapgood, ed., *Professional Patriots* (New York: Albert E. Charles Boni, 1928) and George Seldes, *Witch Hunt: The Techniques and Profits of Red-baiting* (New York: Modern Age Books, 1940).

On the public view of the Soviet Union (and how it got that way), see Meno Lovenstein, *American Opinion of Soviet Russia* (Washington: American Council on Public Affairs, 1941) and Walter Lippmann and Charles Merz, "A Test of the News," *New Republic*, August 4, 1920. See also the discussion of the American Legion (note 97). On the textbook purges see Bessie L. Pierce, *Public Opinion and the Teaching of History in the U.S.* (New York: Knopf, 1926).

The presence of a non-contest between the major parties in 1924 (both the Republican and Democratic candidates had rather close ties to Thomas Lamont of J. P. Morgan) and the emergence of LaFollette as a serious third-party contender led to a reemergence of the red-scare technique. See Kenneth Campbell, *The Progressive Movement of 1924* (New York: McKay, 1966), pp. 162–164.

An early, post-World War II, "scare" occurred in Oakland, California where, after many years of political quiescence, a serious opposition appeared. See Edward C. Hayes, "Power Structure and the Urban Crisis: Oakland, California" (Berkeley: unpublished Ph.D. dissertation, Department of Political Science, University of California, 1968), pp. 40–61.

90. A brief description of the new "security" procedures may be found in Herbert Hyman, "England and America: Climates of Tolerance and Intolerance—1962," pp. 226–257 of Daniel Bell, ed., *The Radical Right* (Garden City: Doubleday, 1963). See also Harper and Theoharis, op. cit.

One problem with the frequently used phrase, "the traditional rules of the game," is its lack of specificity. The 1919–1920 "red scare" made use of the same assumptions as later appeared in the early 1950s, for example, that membership in an organization was sufficient ground for denial of rights. The entire "deportation" program of Attorney General Palmer rested on that assumption. The other point to be noted is that "traditional" (or "established") elites strongly supported the attorney general's effort. Coben (p. 221) puts it quite simply. Referring to the response to the first, that is, to the November raids, he says, "Newspapers almost unanimously applauded the raids." With respect to the more extended raids in January 1920, a *New York Times*'s editorial commented as follows: "If some or any of us . . . have ever questioned the alacrity, resolute will, and fruitful intelligent vigor of the Department of Justice in hunting down those enemies of the United States, the questioners and the doubters have now cause to approve and applaud" (Coben, p. 230).

91. Given the difference in the reactions of poorly educated manual and nonmanual respondents (Table 11.11), it is clear that more than education is operating. It seems likely that "informal education" (what friends, neighbors, and associates are saying) would also play some role. In the working-class milieu, it seems likely that there would be a greater *relative* dependence on the reports and fantasies of the mass media.

92. These themes are to be found in the essays contained in the previously cited works edited by Daniel Bell, that is, his *New American Right* and, the second revised edition, *The Radical Right*. A major criticism of the positions taken by Bell, Lipset, Glazer, and others appears in Michael Rogin, *The Intellectuals and McCarthy: The Radical Specter* (Cambridge, Massachusetts: Massachusetts Institute of Technology Press, 1967).

93. For example, when McCarthy took on Robert Stevens, the Secretary of the Army.

A similar late developing "responsibility" occurred in the aftermath of the 1919 red scare. As Coben put it:

Powerful industrialists and business organizations also attacked the Justice Department in the hope that they could bring the Red Scare to an end. These businessmen, some of whom contributed earlier to the hysteria, now feared that unless nativists were curbed, immigration restrictions would soon be invoked, stopping the flow of cheap labor. As a result of business efforts, by May [1920] even those newspapers which applauded Palmer Raids were publishing articles about the value of immigrants to American industry (p. 239).

94. See Lipset, pp. 326–348 of Daniel Bell, ed., *The Radical Right*, especially p. 332. The same material appears in Lipset and Earl Raab, *The Politics of Unreason: Right-Wing Extremism in America, 1790–1970* (New York: Harper & Row, 1970), p. 227. Three of the four studies reported date from 1954, that is, after the development of the heightened sense of "responsibility." The other survey dates from 1952. It shows the smallest differences between occupations of the four studies.

95. These percentages are based on the election results as given in the *Milwaukee Journal*, November 5, 1952. A similar result appeared in Madison, the state capital. The vote in the east side working-class wards was heavily opposed to McCarthy. In the leading upper-class suburb, Maple Bluff, McCarthy drew 70 percent of the vote. From the Madison, *Capitol-Times*, November 5, 1952.

In some of the Milwaukee suburbs there are fair-sized Jewish populations. Since, in general, Jews were strongly opposed to McCarthy, it seems likely that the pro-McCarthy sentiment among the Protestants and Catholics in those communities is even greater than is indicated in the text.

An examination of the pattern by wards in Janesville, Wisconsin, also shows the highest McCarthy percentages in the upper-middle-class areas. Janesville differs from both Milwaukee and Madison in that there McCarthy did do relatively well in the working-class wards. It seems likely that the media influence is once again a factor. Janesville's only daily paper, the *Gazette*, favored McCarthy (see note 88), whereas in both Madison and Milwaukee, there were papers opposing him. There are also, to be sure, differences in the strength of unions in the three cities. The Janesville figures are from the *Gazette*, November 5, 1952.

96. Rogin, Ch. 3.

97. To some extent veterans' organizations have been created by upper-class sponsors and used as instruments for their aims. Here, too, there is some legitimation given for otherwise unseemly behaviors. For a discussion of the American Legion and other such organizations together with evidence on their impact see Hamilton, *Restraining Myths . . .* , Ch. 6.

98. Lipset has also presented data from West Germany showing that manual workers are more likely to favor a one-party regime than a democratic plural-party system (*Political Man.* p. 102). To take up his analysis of these data constitutes something of a digression from the discussion of the American scene. On the other hand, a brief analysis of these data does provide some useful lessons that have some possible relevance to this scene and certainly bear on the general claims being assessed here.

A reanalysis of the original study showed that the manual workers of farm background were the least likely to support the "several parties" option. Taking these workers of nonfarm origins, the percentage favoring the "several parties" option varied directly with size of city. Within the large cities, once those of farm and small-town origins are excluded, the class differences are minimal. The differences between the unskilled workers and the managers, for example, was two percentage points.

In great measure, the small towns and rural areas in any democratic society are de facto one-party systems; a single clique or coterie of local notables dominate the politics of the community. The "small-town" or rural response to the number of parties question may be little more than a generalization based on immediate experience.

The ex-farmers who are now manual workers and who are in trade unions differ markedly from the farmers-turned-worker who still live in small towns. This suggests the ease of "conversion" once they arrive in a "more democratic" milieu. It also suggests that their presumed "authoritarian" responses are not a matter of character structure.

The reanalysis is based on the original UNESCO study undertaken by Erich

Reigrotzki. See his *Soziale Verflechtungen in der Bundesrepublik: Elemente der sozialen Teilnehme in Kirche, Politik, Organizationen und Freizeit* [Tübingen: J. C. Mohr (Paul Siebeck) 1956] and also Juan Linz, "The Social Bases of West German Politics" (New York: unpublished Ph.D. dissertation, Sociology Department, Columbia University, 1959).

99. As is suggested by Lipset, *Political Man*, pp. 98, 99, 102, and 103.

100. The questions read as follows (1952): "Which of the following things do you think it would be best for us to do *now* in Korea? Pull out of Korea entirely? Keep on trying to get a peaceful settlement? Take a stronger stand and bomb Manchuria and China?" In 1964: "Which of the following do you think we should do now in Vietnam? Pull out of Vietnam entirely? Keep our soldiers in Vietnam but try to end the fighting? Take a stronger stand even if it means invading North Vietnam?"

101. For a more detailed presentation of these results, see Richard F. Hamilton, "El apoyo de la Masa a una política exterior de agresión," *Revista Española de la Opinión Pública*, **8** (Abril–Junio, 1967), 3–22; or, for a French publication of the same article, "Le fondement populaire des solutions militaires 'dures' " *Revue française de Sociologie*, **10** (Janvier–Mars, 1969), 37–58. Only a very brief presentation of the major findings has appeared in the English language, this in "A Research Note on the Mass Support for 'Tough' Military Initiatives," *American Sociological Review*, **33** (June 1968), 439–445. See also Hamilton, *Restraining Myths* . . . , Ch. 5.

In some subcategories, the sentiment for the strong or tough option reaches a very high level. There was a sharp cleavage in 1952 between those earning less than $3000 and those earning more. Taking those in the latter category who are white, Protestant, young, self-identified Republicans or independents, and who pay much attention to news magazines, the proportion favoring the bombing of China rose to 79 percent ($N = 33$).

102. For an additional contribution to the subject see James D. Wright, "Support for Escalation in Viet Nam, 1964–1968: A Trend Study" (Madison: University of Wisconsin, unpublished M.S. thesis, 1970). As of 1968 there was essentially no difference in the pugnacity of the well-off white Protestants and the other major population segments. A change in the position of the media on the subject of the war had brought these "upper-middle-class masses" around to a more "responsible" position.

103. This might come as a surprise to some. It is surprising simply because the bellicose propensities of "statesmen" are hidden in most of the encomiastic biographies. About Theodore Roosevelt, for example, a man frequently presented as the archetype of the responsible, pragmatic, established-rich statesman, one historian writes as follows:

He would have hesitated to proclaim openly that he liked war. Yet, there was something dull and effeminate about peace. A civilized tradition drew him back from open advocacy of war. Yet, personally he gloried in war, was thrilled by military history, and placed warlike qualities high on his scale of values. Without consciously desiring it, he thought a little war now and then stimulated admirable qualities in men. Certainly preparation for war did.

From Howard K. Beale, p. 36.

His statements, private and public, make it clear that his orientation toward war was not so "unconscious" as Beale suggests. Writing to Henry Cabot Lodge, he stated quite simply, "this country needs a war." In 1897 he wrote that "I should welcome almost any war, for I think this country needs one" (Beale, p. 37). In June 1897, Roosevelt, then Assistant Secretary of the Navy, spoke before the Naval War College telling his audience that the "great masterful races have been fighting races" and that "No triumph of peace is quite so great as the supreme triumphs of war (Beale, p. 40).

Another enthusiast from a similar background was Henry Stimson, later destined to be a secretary of war and secretary of state. He felt that a war would, in some ways, be a "wonderfully good thing for this country. . . ." He thought it would be "good to lift men out of selfish, individual work." See Elting E. Morison, *Turmoil and Tradition* (Boston: Houghton Mifflin, 1960), p. 40.

John Hay, who also later became a secretary of state, viewed the Spanish American conflict of 1898 as a "splendid little war." Richard Hofstadter, *The American Political Tradition* (New York: Alfred A. Knopf, 1948), p. 211.

William Randolph Hearst's sentiments and behavior with respect to that war are too well-known to deserve reiteration.

Tough, jingoistic orientations (and actions) do appear in other contexts as well. The actions of the construction workers in the Wall Street area in May 1970 provide an instructive case of this kind of "intervention." Many commentators have treated the action as a spontaneous "uprising" on the part of the construction workers (for example, labor columnist Victor Riesel said "The . . . confrontations were spontaneous." Madison Wisconsin, *State-Journal*, May 21, 1970). Vice-president Spiro Agnew also stated that they were spontaneous.

The original *New York Times*'s stories (May 9, 1970) indicate much advance planning and advance warning. More important, there is evidence that the event was directed by men who were not wearing hard hats or blue collars. One observer said: "I turned around and [saw] men in business suits with color patches in their lapels—the color was the same on both men, and they were shouting orders to the workers." Similar reports appeared in *The Wall Street Journal*, May 11, 1970. The most detailed account of this stimulated "reaction" is that of Fred Cook, "Hard-Hats: The Rampaging Patriots," *The Nation*, June 15, 1970, pp. 712–719. There was no mistaking the zeal of the construction workers involved. The other important lesson, however, is that it took some organizational effort from outside the blue-collar ranks to generate the action. The event, it will be noted, has some similarity to the plot of the motion picture "Z."

104. For example, the items that appear on the "Short Authoritarian-Equalitarian Scale" follow: (1) Human nature being what it is, there must always be war and conflict, (2) The most important thing a child should learn is obedience to his parents, (3) A few strong leaders could make this country better than all the laws and talk, (4) Most people who don't get ahead just don't have enough willpower, (5) Women should stay out of politics, (6) People sometimes say that an insult to your honor should not be forgotten, and (7) People can be trusted. The claims about the distribution of these sentiments by city size and region were checked out using the 1956 SRC study. Taking first all non-South respondents, the proportions agreeing to the "there must always be war" statement were 57, 51, and 66 percent in the large cities, middle-sized cities, and small towns. In the South the equivalent figures were 69, 70, and 84 percent. Southern respondents were also more likely to "strongly" agree with the statement.

The seven items listed above were developed by Fillmore H. Sanford and H. J. Older, *A Short Authoritarian-Equalitarian Scale* (Philadelphia: Institute for Research in Human Relations, 1950). These items were also used by William J. MacKinnon and Richard Centers, "Authoritarianism and Urban Stratification," *American Journal of Sociology,* **51** (May 1956), 610–620. This study was one of those cited by Lipset, p. 105. For additional discussion and analysis of the authoritarianism scale items, see the Lipsitz article (cited in note 2).

It seems likely that a number of these items, especially 1, 2, 3, and 5 would be agreed to more frequently by rural populations than by urbanites. It will be noted, a point to be discussed below, with six of the seven items, one must *disagree* in order to be scored as "equalitarian."

There are a number of complicating factors in the MacKinnon-Centers study. Sixty-nine of the 460 persons interviewed were Mexicans and another 30 were Negroes. Both Mexicans and Negroes had very high "authoritarianism" scores, the proportions being 80 and 77 percent, respectively. This is in contrast to the 42 percent figure among whites ($N = 342$) and 25 percent among Orientals ($N = 16$). The study, incidentally, was undertaken in Los Angeles.

Since most of the Mexican and Negroes are likely to be located in the semi-skilled and unskilled ranks, it seems likely that if one compared only the white populations the class differences would disappear. The working-class authoritarianism indicated in this study, if this assumption were correct, would be linked exclusively to the Mexican and Negro respondents. One must then raise the question as to whether this is "authoritarianism" in these two groups or whether it is something else, such as a "response set." For further discussion, see below in the text.

Some of the MacKinnon-Centers evidence, even without the control for ethnicity, presents a challenge to the Lipset position. Fifty-one percent of the skilled workers ($N = 81$) were "authoritarian." The "large business" group ($N = 18$) was little different from the skilled workers, 50 percent of them being authoritarian. A somewhat higher percentage of the white-collar group, 59 percent ($N = 75$), were authoritarian.

105. Lipset, *Political Man*, pp. 102–103.

106. This discussion is based on the review by Roger Brown, *Social Psychology* (New York: The Free Press, 1965), p. 511 ff. Another useful review is that of John P. Kirscht and Ronald C. Dillehay, *Dimensions of Authoritarianism: A Review of Research and Theory* (Lexington: University of Kentucky Press, 1967). The work that opened up the discussion was that of Bernard M. Bass, "Authoritarianism or Acquiescence?" *Journal of Abnormal and Social Psychology,* **51** (1955), 616–623. If item content were the sole factor measured by the received procedures, the correlation between the F Scale (authoritarianism scale) and the same scale with the items reversed should be close to -1.00. Bass showed the correlation to be only $-.20$. A later contribution to the discussion is that of S. J. Messick and D. N. Jackson, "Authoritarianism or Acquiescence in Bass's Data," *Journal of Abnormal and Social Psychology,* **54** (1954), 424–425.

107. A. Couch and K. Keniston, "Yeasayers and Naysayers: Agreeing Response Set as a Personality Variable," *Journal of Abnormal and Social Psychology,* **60** (1960), 151–174.

108. Gerhard E. Lenski and John C. Leggett, "Caste, Class, and Deference in

the Research Interview," *American Journal of Sociology*, **65** (March 1960), 463–467. They note, for example, that "Negro respondents are less likely to communicate dissatisfaction with American institutions to white interviewers than to Negro interviewers. Working-class respondents are less likely to communicate radical views on controversial issues to middle-class interviewers than to working-class interviewers" p. 463.

109. Ibid., p. 464.

110. Ibid., p. 466. See also Richard Christie, Joan Havel, and Bernard Seidenberg, "Is the F Scale Irreversible?" *Journal of Abnormal and Social Psychology*, **56** (1958), 143–159. The Survey Research Center group have also experimented with reversed items. They summarized their result as follows: "With the reversed half of the scale alone one would conclude that it is the upper educational groups who are threats to democratic institutions, for here they register as significantly more authoritarian than people at lower levels." See Angus Campbell, et al., *The American Voter* (New York: John Wiley, 1960), 512–515.

111. At least two other works cited by Lipset make use of the Short Authoritarian-Equalitarian Scale discussed above. These are Morris Janowitz and Dwaine Marvick, "Authoritarianism and Political Behavior," *Public Opinion Quarterly*, **17** (September 1953), 185–201, and F. H. Sanford, *Authoritarianism and Leadership* (Philadelphia: Stevenson Brothers, 1950).

For many readers the Lipset position is made plausible by the wealth of references to supporting literature. Much of that literature, however, depends on use of the scales being discussed here. Possibly the leading criticism of the work in the area is that of Herbert H. Hyman and Paul B. Sheatsley, " 'The Authoritarian Personality'—A Methodological Critique," pp. 50–122 of Richard Christie and Marie Jahoda, eds., *Studies in the Scope and Method of "The Authoritarian Personality"* (Glencoe: The Free Press, 1954). Hyman and Sheatsley summarize their review as follows: "Our major criticism leads us inevitably to conclude that the authors' theory has not been proved by the data they cite . . ." (p. 119). Although this criticism appeared in 1954, six years before *Political Man*, Lipset makes no reference to it. In fact, in the "Working-Class Authoritarianism" chapter he makes no reference at all to the Christie and Jahoda work. That work is referenced only in a later chapter and even then it is to refer to the essay by Edward Shils, "Authoritarianism: 'Right' and 'Left'," pp. 24–49.

Lipset devoted a paragraph to the work of H. J. Eysenck; this work, apparently at least, offered support for the working-class "authoritarianism" thesis. The work in question is *The Psychology of Politics* (London: Routledge and Kegan Paul, 1954). In a brief footnote Lipset makes reference to a study that "raises serious questions" about the procedures of this work. This is a reference to Richard Christie, "Eysenck's Treatment of the Personality of Communists, *Psychological Bulletin*, **53** (1956), 411–430. Roger Brown, reviewing the discussions of Eysenck's work refers to the criticisms as "deadly." An equally devastating critique, one based on Eysenck's own data, is that of M. Rokeach and C. Hanley, "Eysenck's Tender-Mindedness Dimension: A Critique," *Psychological Bulletin*, **53** (1956), 169–170. Lipset makes no reference to this criticism. Both the Christie and the Rokeach criticisms together with Eysenck's replies are contained in Volume 53 of the *Psychological Bulletin*. A review of the "controversy" together with the key table from the Rokeach criticism may be found in Roger Brown, pp. 526–544.

Since so much is said on the subject of "right" and "left" authoritarianism, by Lipset, Shils, and others, it is useful to note Brown's summary conclusion, which is based on a review of the relevant literature: ". . . it has not been demonstrated that fascists and communists resemble one another in authoritarianism or in any other dimension of ideology. No one thus far has shown that there is an authoritarianism of the left" (p. 542).

112. Robert W. Hodge and Donald J. Treiman, "Occupational Mobility and Attitudes Toward Negroes," see note 78.

113. This is a finding from the Greenblum and Pearlin article cited in note 79.

114. Hodge and Treiman, p. 96. Emphasis in the original.

115. Ibid., p. 98. The reference here is to the Silberstein and Seeman article cited in note 79.

116. Hodge and Treiman, p. 102.

117. Contrasting the stationary manuals and nonmanuals, Greenblum and Pearlin (p. 486) show the nonmanuals to be more desirous of keeping Jews and Negroes out of their neighborhoods; they show no difference in the percentages thinking Jews or Negroes have too much power; they show the manuals are more likely to think the "foreign born" have too much power; and, they show the manuals as more likely to think Jews are dishonest and Negroes lazy. The largest percentage difference is one of 21 points (the belief that Jews are dishonest). All of the other differences are 10 percentage points or less.

118. Bettelheim and Janowitz (see note 78), p. 328.

119. Ibid., p. 20. The following paragraph in the text summarizes their review on pp. 21–24.

120. Robin M. Williams, Jr., *Strangers Next Door: Ethnic Relations in American Communities* (Englewood Cliffs, N.J.: Prentice-Hall, 1964), p. 53.

121. This is not intended as an exhaustive discussion of the literature of class and tolerance. For additional information and references, see George E. Simpson and J. Milton Yinger, *Racial and Cultural Minorities,* third edition (New York: Harper and Row, 1965), pp. 103–108. Simpson and Yinger add only a few references to those that have already been discussed here. Another work that is frequently cited in discussions of class and tolerance is that of Melvin M. Tumin, *Desegregation: Resistance and Readiness* (Princeton: Princeton University Press, 1958), Ch. 8. This is a study of Guilford County, North Carolina (which contains the city of Greensboro). There were 287 white, male adults interviewed. The findings, as presented, are not all too useful since his "high-status" category includes craftsmen and foremen, and his "low-status" category includes farmers, farm managers, and farm laborers.

122. *Political Man,* p. 103.

123. Bettelheim and Janowitz, p. 161. Even that statement leaves something to be desired. They divided their sample by income categories (up to $2500, $2500 to $3000, and $3000 and over). The respective proportions in the categories who were "outspoken and intense" anti-Semites were 28 percent ($N = 59$), 37 percent ($N = 43$), and 39 percent ($N = 28$). This result originally appeared in these authors' book, *Dynamics of Prejudice* (New York: Harper & Brothers, 1950). This book was reprinted in its entirety in the same authors' *Social Change*

and Prejudice. See p. 160 and also p. 23 for some additional discussion. Lipset makes no reference to this work.

124. In R. M. MacIver, ed., *Discrimination and National Welfare* (New York: Institute for Religious and Social Studies, 1949), pp. 73–74. The quotation comes from the Simpson and Yinger summary of the study, p. 222. This work is also not cited by Lipset.

125. Lipset does not refer to their work in *Political Man.* It will be noted that the Greenblum and Pearlin article appears in the volume, *Class, Status, and Power,* which is edited by Bendix and Lipset (Glencoe: The Free Press, 1953).

126. *Strangers Next Door,* p. 54. This is based on evidence from Bakersfield, California (where the total number of respondents was 107) and Savannah, Georgia, (where there were 140 respondents). Williams reviews other studies of occupation and antiminority prejudice on pp. 55–56 and reports that "the findings are contradictory."

127. Stember (see reference in note 2). This work is concerned primarily with education and prejudice. In a number of tables he has controlled "socioeconomic status" (an interviewer's rating) and in some he has controlled occupation, thus allowing some indication of the class-tolerance relationship. One table, reporting on three separate studies and using occupation indicates that in most comparisons a greater prevalence of anti-Semitic talk was heard in the middle class as opposed to the working class (p. 25). There is a slight and irregular tendency for higher-status persons to believe that Jews are "not as good as other people in being fair in business" (p. 26). Higher-status persons are more likely to think Jews are "trying to get too much power" in the United States and are more likely to think Jews "stick together too much" (pp. 28 and 29).

Stember also has data showing that with education controlled, the percentages believing Negroes to have inferior intelligence increases at higher class levels (p. 48). Another study shows, again with education controlled, that the percentages willing to vote for a Jewish presidential candidate were generally greatest in the "lower class" and lowest in the "upper-middle class" (p. 65). From a 1944 study, Stember shows, with education controlled, that the percentages favoring Negro job equality tend to vary inversely with class level. A similar pattern obtains with respect to approval of integrated public facilities (p. 81).

Stember's conclusion reads as follows: "Socio-economic status has no uniform effect of its own on attitudes toward the rights of Negroes. [The same was found, earlier in this chapter, with regard to the rights of Jews.] High class status is associated with discriminatory attitudes on such issues as job or social equality" (pp. 102–103). Another relevant conclusion reads as follows:

High class status . . . stands in a direct relation to prejudice, as most of these data indicate. [A table] permits 36 comparisons of the effect of class with education controlled; in 33 instances, the lower a respondent ranks on the socio-economic scale, the less he objects to personal relations with Jews. Class, it would appear, is a much more powerful determinant of social acceptance or rejection of Jews than education; its influence extends almost uniformly through all levels of schooling, whereas education is a positive factor in only a few instances and a negative one in as many others (p. 112).

See also pp. 115, 133, 136, and 156–157.

128. Howard H. Harlan, "Some Factors Affecting Attitude Toward Jews," *American Sociological Review*, 7 (December 1942), 816–827. The quotation appears on p. 827.

129. Daniel J. Levinson and R. Nevitt Sanford, "A Scale for the Measurement of Anti-Semitism," *Journal of Psychology*, 17 (1944), 339–370. The quotation is from p. 369. Lipset refers to these studies in a note on p. 104.

130. This does not mean that there is *no* evidence in support of the thesis, merely that the results are more diverse than the "clear and consistent" assertion would suggest. Hodge and Treiman's evidence suggests support for the working-class authoritarianism hypothesis. Their result, however, does not make a separation by region. For a more detailed consideration of that study see Hamilton, "Black Demands . . . ." In addition to works cited in previous notes, the following also indicate varying degrees of support for the received hypothesis. James W. Prothro and Charles M. Grigg, "Fundamental Principles of Democracy: Bases of Agreement and Disagreement," *Journal of Politics*, 22 (May 1960), 276–294. This study is based on small samples in two university cities, Ann Arbor, Michigan ($N = 144$) and Tallahassee, Florida ($N = 100$). It focuses on the relationship between education and income (not occupation) and a set of statements on majority rule and minority rights. Another work frequently referred to in this connection is that of Herbert McClosky, "Conservatism and Personality," *American Political Science Review*, 52 (March 1958), 27–45. The key relevant table shows "liberals" to have a considerably higher educational accomplishment than "extreme conservatives." There is no data on occupation. It seems likely that age is strongly related to this conservatism scale. Education, in other words, may be as much an indicator of an age difference as a class difference. The scale in question, it will be noted, measures conservatism, not intolerance.

A review of the available studies by David O. Sears also reports support for the received claim. See his "Political Behavior," Vol. Five, Ch. 41 of Gardner Lindzey and Elliot Aronson, eds., *The Handbook of Social Psychology*, 2nd ed. (Reading, Mass.: Addison-Wesley, 1969). He states that the "proposition that status is positively associated with noneconomic liberalism is persuasively supported by available evidence." He continues that by "any of the normal indicators of status (income, occupation, or education), anti-Negro racial prejudice is substantially greater in the working class than in the middle class" (p. 401). In addition, he reports, support for civil liberties "is vastly greater at upper status levels than at lower levels" (p. 401). Some of the evidence mentioned in support of these claims has already been discussed in this chapter such as, for example, the small sample of veterans studied by Bettelheim and Janowitz and the study by Prothro and Grigg (see above). The study used by Hodge and Treiman, also discussed previously and offered by Sears as providing support for his claim, is considered in Hamilton, *Restraining Myths* . . . , Ch. 4. The findings reported there are generally consonant with those reported in the present chapter.

Most of the large differences reported in Sears' sources appear in connection with education. Since education is strongly related to age, however, and since there does appear to have been a shift in attitude among younger generations on these issues, those strong relationships probably tell more about the age-tolerance link than about class and tolerance. One of the studies which presumably showed "vastly greater" upper-status tolerance actually showed very small differences in the relationship of income level and responses incorporated in a civil rights scale. The same study showed *no* difference by income level in the responses to civil liberties scale series. There were, nevertheless, substantial differences associated with education. See K. D. Kelly and W. J. Chambliss, "Status Consistency and Political Attitudes," *American Sociological Review*, **31** (June 1966), 375–382.

131. The 1968 study also asked the preferences of the nonvoters. If we combine the indicated vote and preferences, the result is roughly the same. Taking the married, active, non-South whites, the Wallace proportion among the manuals is 10 percent ($N = 180$) and among the nonmanuals, it is 9 percent ($N = 289$). When we included the single, widowed, retired, and so on, and also included the nonvoter preferences, the class differences were somewhat greater, the respective figures for manuals and nonmanuals being 10 percent ($N = 269$) and 7 percent ($N = 361$).

The data as reported here involves a "pure" manual category, that is, following the procedure used throughout, the independent artisans and the foremen have been put into the nonmanual category. One could take the manuals and nonmanuals without this correction, that is, using the census categories without any change. Taking the married, active, non-South whites, the same one percentage point difference again appears. Taking all the non-South whites who may be classed by present or past occupation, we also find a one percentage point difference. When we include also the nonvoters who had a preference, a four percentage point difference appears—the largest to be discovered. Part of this results from the disproportionate presence of the Southern-reared in the manual ranks. Taking only the indigenous, non-Southern-reared populations, that difference is reduced from four to two percentage points.

See also Philip E. Converse, Warren E. Miller, Jerrold G. Rusk, and Arthur C. Wolfe, "Continuity and Change in American Politics," *American Political Science Review*, **63** (December 1969), 1083–1105.

132. Seymour Martin Lipset and Earl Raab, "The Wallace White-lash," *Trans-Action*, **7** (December 1969), 23–35.

One suggestion of Southern origins as a factor is the high Wallace percentage among the Baptists, 16 percent of whom reported a vote for him.

No Jews supported Wallace. Since this liberal segment of the population is overwhelmingly located in the nonmanual ranks, in particular in the non-South nonmanual ranks, their influence would also contribute to the small difference indicated in the Lipset-Raab report (p. 28). If one controlled for both religion and Southern origins, it seems likely that there would be very little remaining difference.

Lipset and Raab also present the percentages of those who "considered Wallace" at some time in the campaign but then voted for someone else. Thirteen percent of the manuals considered but did not vote for Wallace as opposed to 5 percent of the nonmanuals. Combining the two, those who voted for him and those who considered him, they have a total of 10 percent of the nonmanuals and 22 percent of the manuals who are described as "Wallace sympathizers." It should be noted that half of the middle-class "sympathizers" voted for the man as opposed to only about two-fifths of the working-class sympathizers, the remaining three-fifths finding another more adequate choice. It is an open question whether sympathy, protest, or frustration were involved in the choices made.

See also Hamilton, *Restraining Myths* . . . , Ch. 4.

133. Theodore H. White, *The Making of the President: 1964* (New York: Atheneum, 1965), p. 234. See also Lipset, "Beyond the Backlash," p. 22.

134. Michael Rogin, "Wallace and the Middle Class: The White Backlash in Wisconsin," *Public Opinion Quarterly*, **30** (Spring 1966), 98–108 and his "Politics, Emotion, and the Wallace Vote," *British Journal of Sociology*, **20** (March 1969), 27–49. See also Margaret Conway, "The White Backlash Re-examined: Wallace and the 1964 Primaries," *Social Science Quarterly*, **49** (December 1968), 710–719.

135. In the 1968 election, the pattern changes considerably. The "upper-middle-class" support for Wallace from the north shore Milwaukee suburbs and from Madison's Maple Bluff had essentially disappeared. This indicates support for the hypothesis that the voting there in the 1964 Democratic primary was "tactical," that is, an attempt to embarrass.

A comparison of the absolute number of Wallace votes in the 1964 Democratic primary and the 1968 general election indicates that he suffered a serious loss in *all* Milwaukee wards. In most cases his 1968 total was less than half of what he received in the primary in 1964. This, too, suggests that the vote in 1964 was largely punitive, that is, aimed at punishing the "favorite son" who gave the state the sales tax.

Wallace's percentage was somewhat below the city-wide average in the ward containing the University of Wisconsin's Milwaukee campus and it was, as is to be expected, nonexistent in the Negro precincts. There was no significant variation in the Wallace percentage in any of the other wards of the City; north and south side had approximately the same percentages for the man.

An interesting account of Wallace efforts in middle-class suburbs is that of Mary Kritz, "The Wallace Vote: The Organizational Factor" (Madison: unpublished M.S. thesis, Department of Sociology, University of Wisconsin, 1970).

136. Wallace, on the other hand, has declared his aims to be a "fusion" of the "working man with the large industrialists and tycoons of Mid-America." He claims: "We got part of it already . . . we got the workin' man, and now we're gonna get the other part of it—the high hoi-polloi. They gonna come around, you wait." His biographer reports as follows:

At a patio party . . . in New Orleans' French Quarter, an oil millionaire from Dallas allowed, "I'd vote for him in a minute, and give him all the money I could if I just felt I could trust him—if he wouldn't wind up getting tamed by Washington like Lester Maddox over there in Georgia. I'm a Republican, but I'd love to support him, and every one of my friends—oilmen, fellows in wheat— feel the same way."

See Marshall Frady, *Wallace* (New York: World Publishing Co., 1968), p. 10.

A report by Nan Robertson (*The New York Times*, October 31, 1968) appeared under the following headline: "The Old Georgia Names and New Money in Macon are Behind Nixon." But, after a brief mention of the Nixon candidacy, one learns something quite different:

Privately, without putting their name to it, Macon's white daughters of the Deep South of all ages will confess there is much they like in what George C. Wallace has to say about Negroes.

But he is not—well—not the kind of man you'd invite to dinner, or except in unusual cases, vote for.

One of the richest women in Macon, who has always voted Democratic, will cast her ballot for Mr. Wallace because "he's not too much for integration." She adds: "I don't believe I am in the minority around here." Her husband, a Republican, is even stronger for Mr. Wallace.

Most of the account reports rather equivocal support for Mr. Nixon. It appeared to be largely tactical, apparently for lack of a better alternative. The objection to Wallace appeared to be mainly aesthetic, a matter of tone. The report ends on the following note:

One aristocratic and imperious grandmother spoke of how integration in the schools meant her grandchildren would face intermarriage. "I could just die over it," she said. She thinks Mr. Wallace is "an ignorant man—a rabble-rouser" but goes right down the line with all of his views about "the Negro situation." She will vote, however, for Mr. Nixon.

A much younger woman said that a significant number of her friends in Macon "agree with everything that Wallace says—but they can't bring themselves to vote for him."

137. This result is for those reporting a vote for one of the three leading parties. If we added also the nonvoters who expressed a preference, the result would be essentially the same. The Jews fall disproportionately into this "upper-middle class." The Wallace proportion among the non-Jewish upper-middle-class populations is 9 percent, that is, the same as in the lower-middle class and the manual ranks.

There was no variation in the manual ranks by income. Nine percent of both high- and low-income manual categories (dividing at $8000 total family income) voted for Wallace.

138. A study of 257 white males in Gary, Indiana found a similar result. Asked about their attitude toward "Negroes living next door," Wallace supporters proved, as one would expect, to be more prejudiced than Nixon or Humphrey voters. At the same time, 31 percent of the Wallace voters said they would not mind at all. This is from an unpublished paper by Robert T. Riley and Thomas F. Pettigrew, "Relative Deprivation and Wallace's Northern Support," presented at the American Sociological Association meetings, 1969, San Francisco, California.

These findings, both in the areas of economic liberalism and civil liberties, cast considerable doubt on the claims of Kevin Philips, who feels the Wallace vote is entirely available to the Republicans. See his *The Emerging Republican Majority* (New Rochelle: Arlington House, 1969).

12
The Future of American Politics

Introduction

This chapter will consider, first, the question of stability and change in the United States. The multifarious claims about the so-called big changes will be reviewed, leading to the major conclusion that, despite the appearances, there is a remarkable lack of change. The next task will be to consider the question of why there is no change (or why the changes are so limited). Some of the theories outlined earlier will be reconsidered and, in the light of the evidence presented, it will be indicated where they prove useful and where not so useful.

Since the crux of the matter involves claims about the character of the society's majority, this discussion will be largely concerned with the theoretical accounts which make some portrayal of that majority. Rather than an image of mass satisfaction (as in liberal pluralist theory), or an image of narcoticization (as in mass-society–power-elite views), the present claim is one of helplessness, of reluctant acquiescence in the face of a situation that appears to provide no reasonable way out.

The major themes to be developed are the following. The character of majority sentiment in the United States has been misrepresented. The major division in political outlooks is between the upper class and the upper-middle class, on the one hand, and everyone else, that is, the lower-middle class and the working class on the other. A second major line of cleavage involves a religious/ethnic division between white Protestants and, again for all practical purposes, everyone else. The white Protestant upper-middle class (and also the equivalent upper class) form an "isolated mass." They are separated and cut off from the rest of the society and as a result have their own separate consciousness and understandings about what is going on elsewhere in the society. Much of the conservatism of this group would appear to be a result of their isolation and their distinctive political heritage rather than the product of some highly conscious class interest. In some respects, however, they prove to be a peculiarly moveable group. Their outlooks, in some areas, are very well explained along the lines of conventional "mass society" theorizing.

The account up to this point is intended to describe the society as it is and to give some explanation as to the sources of its relative stability. On the basis of the evidence that has been presented, an attempt will also be made to project some likely future developments. In particular, for reasons to be discussed, there are grounds for anticipating some decline in the importance of the Republican party and some transformations in the character of the Democrats. Some consideration will be given to the possibility of the development of a new party. Another possible kind of change, a revolutionary intervention, will also be discussed.

Accounts of social change tend to pay little attention to the agents of change. By reason of theoretical predisposition, most commentators avoid "voluntaristic" factors and focus rather on the "larger" structural sources of change or on the ever-imminent economic crises as providing the stimulus to change. Change is by no means the universal correlate of crisis situations. It would be difficult to argue that it is even a frequent correlate. The actual outcomes would appear to be much more closely linked to the activities, formulations, and appeals of political leaders rather than to any direct or compelling impact of the "objective" conditions themselves. If the exponents of new political directions are capable, they may generate a significant following and have an effect. If they are not capable, they may repel the potential supporters, immobilizing them, and thus provide further evidence that there is no reasonable way out. This is the concluding theme of the present chapter.

Stability and Change

In a former age, sociologists used to ask themselves and their students the following question: how is social order possible? They would present this as the most perplexing of all conceivable questions and would labor long and hard at developing an answer. They would invoke the aid of an illustrious collection of political and social theorists in this effort—Thomas Hobbes, Adam Ferguson, Herbert Spencer, Gabriel Tarde, Emile Durkheim, Ludwig Gumplowicz, Gustav Ratzenhofer, Charles Cooley, George Herbert Mead, Charles A. Ellwood, E. A. Ross, Talcott Parsons, and many others.

From one perspective, the problem is no problem at all. It is immediately clear and obvious that a social order is possible and that here, there, and everywhere "social order" has existed. It is, furthermore, immediately clear and obvious that there have been only very few, quickly passing occasions in which some kind of order did not exist. It is also clear that many kinds of "social order" are possible, or, put slightly differently, there are many ways of "ordering" a society. This means that to talk of "social order" or of "the" social order arbitrarily restricts the area of consideration. Effectively, the range of discussion becomes some present condition, which is set in contrast to some completely unrealistic opposite case, this being called anarchy. The more appropriate comparison is between Order A and Order B, or Order C, and so on.

A more useful and challenging question that has more real human importance is the following: how can this highly imperfect social order, filled with
obvious problems, difficulties, and injustices, continue with so little basic
change? Or, to return to a question posed in the first chapter, how does the
disparity between wants and performance persist?

It is worthwhile undertaking a brief review of some principal structural
features of the contemporary social order.

Unlike the conservatives of the nineteenth century, contemporary defenders
of the existing social order talk like revolutionaries, that is, they present themselves as enthusiastic supporters of a successful revolution. In this connection
it is argued that there has been an Income Revolution, an Educational Revolution, a Revolution in Leisure; a Revolution in Participation, ("previously excluded groups now integrated . . . now part of the system"), and a Revolution
of Rising Expectations. The decisive steps, it is claimed, have already been
taken; the break with previous history already made. Much of the encomium,
again unlike previous conservatism, involves a condemnation of the past, those
admitted outrages being set in contrast to the now fundamentally reformed
structures of the present.[1] Despite the talk of the completed transformations,
the realities prove to be somewhat different.

The occupational structure, it is claimed, has been drastically transformed.
A majority now work in white-collar occupations, doing less onerous, cleaner
work, carrying out jobs that provide more stability, more status, more security, and more chance for advancement. This claim is based on the experience
in the labor force as a whole and as such hides another very important point
—that most of the transformation occurred in the jobs held by women. As far
as the male side of the labor force is concerned, there has been only very limited change in the course of the twentieth century. A majority of nonfarm
males are still engaged in manual occupations and there is little reason to believe that this pattern will change dramatically in the near future. The "big
change" has come in what are essentially second jobs in the family, jobs that
supplement the earnings of the "main earner," and that are typically of less
permanence. The basic lesson, then, is a hidden one of persistence of structure
rather than change.[2]

It has been claimed that an Income Revolution has occurred. This claim too
appears to be of dubious merit. The best available evidence indicates the basic
stability of the pattern of income distribution over recent decades rather than
any "big" or "dramatic" change.[3] The so-called progressive income tax was
quickly transformed and has been continuously undermined by exemptions
that work to reduce or eliminate its "progressive" character. At the same time,
frankly regressive taxation policies—land taxes, sales and excise taxes—have
been imposed and/or increased, which makes the overall tax arrangement a
regressive one. In short, this "revolution" too provides an appearance of
change when, in fact, the basic character of the "old regime" continues.

A related claim maintains that the great fortunes have been wiped out, that
there has been an equalization of wealth as well as incomes. This, too, appears

to be a claim without foundation. Since much of that wealth is in the form of stock holdings and since there has been no significant change in the pattern of such holdings (or, as frequently phrased in the 1950s, no development of "people's capitalism"), that means the concentration in relatively few hands is still the case. In turn, it means the persistence of de jure control, the corporations remaining in the same "hands" or, more realistically, in the same families. The everyday operations of these firms may be delegated to some managers but, contrary to the claims of those arguing a "managerial revolution," the behavior of the managed firms proves to be little different from those that are still family owned.[4]

Another feature of the income picture is the persistence of poverty on the American scene, long after it is in any sense either "natural" or necessary. In part, this persistence can be said to be intended and planned. To the extent that national policy makers have chosen to create an "acceptable rate of unemployment," they have condemned about 4 percent of the population (give or take a few percentage points, depending on the phase of the cycle) to some kind of poverty. In a full employment situation, or an over-full arrangement such as exists in a number of continental European countries, that source of poverty disappears.[5] Poverty in the latter context is also reduced as many low-paying jobs disappear. With other more attractive opportunities available, no one chooses to fill them.

It is said that there has been a revolution in leisure caused by "technological advance" which has led to a continuous reduction in the work week. It is clear that the 60-hour week and the 48-hour week have given way to a 40-hour standard. But the claim about a *continuous* decline is unfounded. For all practical purposes the 40-hour standard has been a constant since the end of World War II.[6] The assumption that the remaining hours of waking time are "leisure" hours is open to some question. It seems likely that average distance from home to work has increased in these postwar years and that the time required to traverse that distance has also increased because of inadequacy of current transportation arrangements. When one subtracts this "useless time" spent in commutation, it seems likely that the postwar years have actually seen a reduction in leisure time.

Another of the "big changes" involves the educational arrangements. Here, presumably, another revolution has occurred, this one radically transforming the character of educational institutions, or, more specifically, the character of the clientele served by those institutions. This claim, too, is misleading. In great measure what has happened is an increase in the size of the ongoing units together with the addition of some new ones. As for the clientele, what has happened is that more of the same kinds of people now attend those institutions. That means, basically, that more upper-middle-class males now go to college than was formerly the case and, even more striking, considerably larger numbers of upper-middle-class girls now "go to college." This revolution, then, has amounted simply to doing more of the same. There have, to be sure, been some additions in the *numbers* of working-class children "in college." In great measure, however, they are found in the new and lower-quality institutions—the community colleges and the state colleges. Many of those who are "in" those institutions are only tenuously "of" them since for many the affiliation is one of very short duration.[7]

There are two possible developments that could legitimately be counted as revolutionary. There could be a decided shift toward equality of opportunity. Or, there could be a complete reversal of going practice, that is, working-class children could got to college and upper-middle-class children could, as one possibility, go into the factories. Neither of these appear to have occurred.

There is some redistribution of benefits associated with these institutions. The best available evidence on the subject, however, indicates that the effect is regressive, that is, it aids those who are already well endowed with the advantages of this world.[8]

Possibly the biggest of the changes of the last four decades has involved transformations in welfare institutions. The development of the welfare state, unlike those "changes" discussed previously, is real. It has involved the creation of new and rather formidable (as far as size is concerned) institutions and these do perform important services that previously were not available. Some light is shed on the quality of this accomplishment when one compares the United States' achievement with that of other advanced industrial countries. In terms of performance, that is, considering the things the American welfare state does, it proves to be rather lacking. Put simply, the accomplishment of the American system is the most limited of any of the advanced countries. Coverage is limited, services restricted, and the quality of those services leave much to be desired.[9]

Another principal feature of the arrangement was discussed earlier. The system is not redistributive, that is, it does not redistribute from rich to poor. Essentially what happens, given the tax structures, is that redistribution occurs among the less affluent populations. To the extent that the burden falls on these groups, it has the consequence of dividing them, of pitting the employed against the unemployed, the middle-aged against the young and against the old, and so forth. The solutions to the problem, when the problem is seen from this perspective, involve penalties for "welfare cheats" or, in the extreme case, a demand for elimination of or reduction of the welfare program. One peculiar irony of the New Deal liberal solution to the problem of poverty and welfare is that it provides some incentive for persons with decent orientations to support conservative, that is, laissez faire options. Many old people are simultaneously beneficiaries and victims of the arrangement; they are receiving modest payments and paying out (in property taxes and sales taxes) large portions of the benefit received. In some instances the only practical option for them on the local scene is to support rightist movements which promise to keep the municipal costs down. This is the case even though they do not personally share any of the basic values of that kind of movement.[10] Since few commentators ever study the dynamics of such "reaction," it comes to be assumed either that the development represents genuine rightist sentiment or that it is "irrational" and hence uncontrollable. The major practical conclusion is that not much can be done about it. This mistaken reading of the evidence contributes to the sense of "beleagueredness" on the part of the liberal forces. They mistakenly see their support as minority. And their responses are timid and defensive.

The urban renewal programs, which first began in the 1950s, were at one time billed as a part of the great liberal progressive revolution. Conservative community leaders had for decades fought off any "government programs" affecting urban development. In the course of the century, however, the heritage of bad initial planning and bad (or no) subsequent planning had as its consequence a major deterioration in the quality of central city living and business conditions. Perhaps most decisively for the community leaders, this "development" led to a reduction in profit margins. The retail trade shifted to outlying centers as the affluent populations moved further away from the downtown shopping areas.

Once the disaster was readily apparent to even the most obtuse of the ruling patriarchs, who themselves or whose forebears were responsible for the problem, conservative "ideals" were abandoned and a ready enthusiasm developed for the federal government subsidies. These would make possible the reconstruction of the downtown areas and they also would pay for the superhighways that would cut through the city allowing easy access, once again, to the downtown market places.

Studies now available indicate that urban renewal is by no means as "progressive" as it first appeared.[11] Both the renewal and the road programs involved a considerable amount of "urban destruction," that is, demolition of existing structures. To the extent that the demolition involved the oldest and most decrepit buildings in the city, this might have been counted a good thing. Since the people living in the oldest and most decrepit housing happened to be the poorest segments of the city's population, a program that provided no substitute, no alternative structures at equivalent rentals, proved to be a *not* very good thing. One of the first and clearest impacts of the programs was a reduction in the number of housing units available in the central city and, more specifically, a reduction in the number of low-cost units. For the poor, the programs meant a removal and higher living costs (both in terms of rent and frequently in terms of transportation, since people were generally moved out and away from the downtown area). The urban renewal programs also had indirect effects on welfare programs, therefore, by creating a need for higher payments. The removal of large numbers of properties from the tax rolls had the consequence of shifting the burden of city costs to those still on the rolls, effectively shifting it to all the other property holders in the city.

Although most of the costs of the road and renewal plans were paid by the federal government, a relatively small portion were paid by the city. This added cost came out of general revenues and would therefore be spread among the property holders and the payers of sales taxes. In great measure the programs amounted to subsidies for the downtown merchants and the owners of valuable downtown properties. Once again, what looked to some like a "progressive" innovation turned out to be regressive as far as the distribution of costs and benefits was concerned.

One area in which the continuity of development is very clear and where no revolutionary changes are evident is that of pollution. With rare exceptions, such as the Pittsburgh air pollution case, the history is one of continued destruction of pure streams, of the atmosphere, and of natural resources. As far as cities are concerned, the typical urban renewal solution, by making use of throughways and automobiles rather than electric rail transport, has only worsened the problem. In the urban context, there is again an inversion of the benefits. The well-off can afford to move out to a more attractive environment, with cleaner air and more pleasant surroundings. And they, in turn, in the course of their commutation to the city deposit huge quantities of poison gas together with sundry other impurities that are the end products of enormous quantities of gasoline being burned. If the pollution abatement programs currently being discussed are paid for out of general revenues (rather than the profits generated, in part, through careless disposal of waste products), then that, too, will involve an inversion of benefit, the standard theme being once again repeated and the poor paying disproportionately.

Amidst all the self-congratulatory talk about the big changes, one such transformation, at least until the late 1960s, went largely unmentioned, namely, the development of a massive permanent military establishment, the largest in the history of the world. In the process, large numbers of young men are impressed into service, a development which, except for some months prior to World War II, had never before been the case in peacetime America. The length of "service," moreover, is greater than that in any of the other advanced countries of Western Europe. Most of those other countries have reduced the period of service in the postwar period (thus, one might note, increasing leisure). Some advanced industrial countries, notably Japan and Canada, do not have any such forced servitude.

This big change has involved the creation of a number of giant corporations and a diversion of the effort of a number of others in order to provide manufactured products or services for the military. This manufacture of products (one would hate to beg the question by referring to them as "goods") and provision of services have some significant impacts on the character of the society. It clearly distorts the gross national effort by diverting talent and skills from the construction of decent cities, from the provision of adequate education, or from the development of quality leisure. The most important continuous short-run impact is the contribution to inflation.

Military spending is essentially no different from any other government spending in this respect. Those who are paid, directly or indirectly, by the federal government for the production of products or creation of services that do not appear in ordinary commodity markets will be making a contribution to driving up the prices of those goods and services that do appear there. If, by contrast, those persons engaged in "defense" work were producing houses, schools, hospitals, urban transportation systems, and so forth, they would be producing consumer goods and services that would reduce the inflationary pressure.

If one were to raise an old question, cui bono?—for whose good?—once again it would appear that we have a case of inversion of benefits. Those employed in the so-called defense industries benefit. That is to say, they benefit if the alternative were unemployment. If the government, however, were to invest in the schools, housing, and urban amenities package, those employees would probably benefit even more than now; they would get the same money and they would also get better cities. And, moreover, other people would also be beneficiaries. Skilled and semiskilled workers would have jobs in a genuine urban renewal effort and upon completion of such effort they would be able to live in the homes built, send their children to the schools, and get from one place to another with greater ease than is presently the case. That all has to be set in contrast to the uses of M-16 rifles, F-111's, Sherman tanks, radar machine-gun sighting devices, defoliants, and assorted other accomplishments. It goes without saying that primary and secondary military contractors are beneficiaries as are the holders of securities in those firms. That benefit too must be assessed in terms of the alternative options. It is by no means clear that this choice maximizes their returns.[12]

It would be a mistake to treat the Department of Defense and/or its related suppliers (who together form the key units of the "complex") as an independent or autonomous growth within the American enterprise. While having some degree of independence and autonomy, it is not as if they together ruled in opposition to all other segments of the population. Together they are both de jure and de facto subordinate to the president and to the persons and agencies making United States policy, in particular the foreign policy. The military, in normal circumstances, is an instrument for the execution of that larger policy.[13]

In large part it is the cold war policies, set and maintained by a civilian "establishment," that have governed the national priorities.[14] By determining that the foreign policy would be one of "containment" and that the resources of the nation would be mustered to aid in the implementation of that policy, those decision makers have diverted resources that could have contributed to the improvement of the quality of life, or could have contributed to making real changes in the areas being discussed here. The direction of United States foreign policy is undoubtedly the major area of nonchange; the priorities that follow from that determination restrict the possibilities for development in all other spheres of endeavor.

The Sources of Stability

The question remains: why does significant change not occur? Or, to consider the inverse of that question: how does this "social order" persist?

There are, currently, three dominant explanations offered in answer to these questions. All of them involve judgments about the character and orientations of the rulers and the ruled. These judgments, in turn, provide the basis for the varying policy implications that flow from each basic description.

The first of these explanations is a "power elite" formulation which is combined with a critical or leftist mass society account of the other, that is, of the non-elite segments of the population. In this reading, there exists a cohesive, knowledgeable, highly self-interested ruling class that has a near-monopoly of the means of influence and of force. The remainder of the population is said to be "bought off" and/or manipulated into "believing in" and accepting the main directions of the society.

The second explanation is a now somewhat dated liberal pluralist view. Power, it is claimed, is widely dispersed. All major groups in the society have influence with which they can have some impact on policy making. A lack of change in this view is read as consent, as indicative of satisfaction with the existing arrangements. Where that is not the case, the alternative explanation involves the assumption of a "communication problem" and/or a purely temporary failure of organization. There is thought to be some "automaticity" about the response to any functional problem; where a problem develops, awareness will be generated, some organizational response will appear (some "veto groups" or some "countervailing power"), and some adequate adjustment will be made.

The third view is presented as a more "realistic" variant on the above position. Dispensing with "populist" democratic prejudices the exponents of this position have argued that power must necessarily be concentrated in relatively restricted segments of the population. The diversity or "pluralism" of this viewpoint involves the cleavages or differences of outlook among the elites. And the "democracy" offered in this formulation consists of a role for ratification or acclamation on the part of the other groups in the society in the "periodic elections."

Elements of the revisionist Marxist theory of stratification have been introduced into this synthesis, in particular, those claims about the dangerous or threatening character of the lower-middle class. In a later period, the notion of a "working-class authoritarianism" was also added to the basic repertory of claims. The elites and the upper-middle classes, by comparison, are said to be both capable and responsible. The major lesson is that the basic direction of the society is best left as is since any sudden and fundamental democratization (enlarged, effective mass participation) would, given the character of the majority, only contribute to making things worse.

The principal effort of this work has been to assess the "realism" (or simply, the empirical adequacy, the validity) of these claims. Most of them, as we have seen, prove to be wanting. In fact, all three of these basic characterizations of the majority appear to be inadequate; that is, the views, first, that the majority is bought off and/or manipulated; second, that the majority has adequate sources of influence to effect policy; and third, that the majority constitutes a special source of danger or threat. Stated somewhat differently, those in the working-class–lower-middle-class majority have a wide range of unfulfilled wants that have not been erased by shrewd manipulative efforts; they do not, as things currently stand, have the influence to effect change in the major directions of the society; and they do not constitute the threat that some writers have claimed.

It is useful to review these positions in some greater detail so as to bring the assembled evidence to bear on the major claims.

The first of these positions, the left-critical "power elite" view (not Marxist) assumes a very self-interested set of rulers who control all significant options. They are the prime beneficiaries of the contemporary arrangements. It is to their advantage, therefore, to limit and contain any opposition that might threaten those arrangements. They are portrayed as very shrewd and knowledgeable; they are aware of their interests and they have both the will and the means to defend them. In discussions of their "consciousness" no question is raised as to whether their appreciations are "real" or "false." Their understandings are treated as "real" or, at minimum, as very accurate.

Their control of the mass media allows them to manipulate opinion, to convince large portions of the population that there are no significant social problems in the country or, alternatively, that the programs currently in operation or under consideration will quickly eliminate any remaining difficulties.

The problem of mass "consent" in this view is thought to provide no serious intellectual problem; presumably it is satisfactorily explained in terms of the manipulation efforts. The acquiescence of the majority of the American population is also, in some variants on this theme, thought to be aided and abetted by their presumed affluence. The society, basically, consists of calculating, manipulative elites and of the duped masses. The problem of order poses no special intellectual problem; it is the immobilization of the "narcotized" masses that "stabilizes" the entire enterprise.[15]

This view may be faulted on a number of grounds, some of which involve evidence presented earlier and some of which, for the moment, must remain largely speculative. Elite or upper-class political behavior has been treated only in passing in this work; hence, the judgments about that behavior must depend on outside sources or remain purely speculative. There is some reason to doubt the adequacy of the calculating and manipulative imagery. There is a question to be raised as to the realism of elite or upper-class understandings. Because of their isolation and "exclusiveness," their knowledge of the society is limited and, consequently policies based on that knowledge prove, with some frequency, to be rather strikingly mistaken. The claims of the effectiveness of the means at their disposal also might better be considered as an open question. The number of failures of the manipulative attempts are impressive. Unfortunately, given the theoretical predisposition, it is the spectacular confirmation of the manipulation claim that is written about, discussed, and remembered.[16]

The present work has presented evidence with respect to the "state of the masses." Here we have seen that the "broad masses" still remain concerned with the economic liberalism issues and that this cluster of concerns serves as a kind of anchor for orientations and outlooks. It is this anchorage that works against the manipulative efforts, particularly against the attempts to distract through the use of the distant or alarmist concerns.

There is also the problem of the restricted "reach" of the "means of manipulation." The ability of the upper or ruling class to contact the "target groups" and to achieve their desired aims is rather strikingly limited. In the case of the media, numerous studies have shown the ability of the audience to avoid the manipulative attempt—by changing the program, by not hearing (or seeing), by quickly forgetting the uncongenial message, and so forth. When it is a question of the use of organizational weapons, that is, contacting and influencing people through associations, the problems faced by the upper-class manipulators are even more severe.[17]

This is not to suggest that the viewpoint is entirely erroneous. There are some calculating and manipulative elite figures. The basic questions being raised here are, first, the question of the frequency with which such cynics are found in elite circles and, second, the question of their actual impact on the other groups in the society.[18]

The second of these views, the liberal pluralist view, does not deserve much attention here. As noted, it is already somewhat dated, having been dominant in a more ingenuous age, the decade of the 1950s. Few commentators at present would care to make the same claims about the wide distribution of power that were argued at that time. Fewer still would subscribe to the automatic corrective, to the "invisible hand" assumption, which characteristically embellished the theorizing of that period. The discussion of pluralism in Chapter 2, which focused on the limited membership in instrumental voluntary associations and the class-relatedness of those involvements, showed the basic limitation of the position.

The third view discussed here, the more "realistic" variant of the pluralist view recognizes the class differences and incorporates, as noted, elements of the revisionist Marxist social theory. This view takes account of the inequalities of existing political abilities and also recognized the unequal distributon of political means. It goes one significant step further in providing a justification for the inequalities, a justification that, presumably, has a solid empirical basis.

It is claimed that the influential upper classes and upper-middle classes are now "responsible." This means that they are not governed by any necessities of class interest, that they have, to a considerable extent, surmounted the determinants of previous eras and are now free to respond in a more generous way. And it is because of their sense of decency, their disinterested concern with others, that they perform an essentially protective function in the society, aiding the interests of the less privileged and protecting the rights of all. By comparison, the lower-middle class proves (so it is said) to have a narrow and self-interested outlook. They are quick to react to real or imagined slights to their basic interests. And in a similar vein, the blue-collar workers are also said to be intolerant of ethnic, racial, and political minorities and to have limited appreciation for the basic "rules" of the democratic "game." The "realistic" response of the disinterested and responsible citizens involves some effort at "containment" of these disruptive forces, of those who might threaten the rights or interests of other disadvantaged minorities and who might under some circumstances even threaten the entire democratic enterprise.

The answer to the question of why no change, or why only limited change occurs, in this case involves the dangers of mobilization of certain groups in the society and the need to be extremely careful in the tactics used so that the entire operation is not "destabilized"—an antiseptic term meaning "changed for the worse." The problem of limited change, in this case, is explained in terms of intention; there has been a refusal to move on some issues because of their "disruptive" potential, because the mobilization of some elements of the population might give rise to uncontrollable, noncontainable problems.

The present book has been largely concerned with a criticism of the assumptions of this position. For this reason, a brief review of the evidence on the "responsibility" question is in order.

It should surprise no one to discover that "the upper-middle class" is more conservative on economic liberalism issues than any other group in the society. This is, nevertheless, a point that is paid little attention in the writings of the "realistic" pluralists. After a "one liner" mention, the typical presentation moves off quickly to the noneconomic issues and makes the case for "responsibility" in that context. The analysis that is restricted to the noneconomic issues necessarily overlooks some significant aspects of "irresponsibility" in the economic area.

A responsible person, for example, would feel concern for those who lack adequate medical care, who are unable to pay the costs. The leading practical solution to their problem is to have the federal government pay those costs; that solution has been tried in numerous other contexts and, judging by the evidence on health, it is one that has proven very effective. And yet, approximately seven out of ten upper-middle-class white Protestants were opposed to that suggestion when it was posed in the 1964 study. Opposition to the living standard guarantee was even greater. One ought to find a different pattern with respect to federal school aid; that, after all, is not a "handout"—it does not involve direct economic aid to families. It would "provide better opportunities" for those "with talent." And that "rescued" talent should, at least according to the best-accredited technocratic assumptions, improve the condition of the entire population. Nevertheless, approximately three out of four of the upper-middle-class white Protestants disapproved even here.

The other major point to be noted in this connection is the inadequacy of the argument which speaks simply in terms of "class." As opposed to the white Protestants, the other members of the upper-middle class, principally Catholics and Jews, indicate a two-thirds majority in favor of the medical care suggestion. On school aid, the latter groups divide 50–50. It would be a mistake, therefore, to talk about upper-middle-class responsibility or irresponsibility without a specification of which segment one is discussing. Moreover, as opposed to a purely self-interested motivation, it appears that some "cultural" factor, some "training," or, if one prefers, a value difference, is present, which results in a greater sense of responsibility among the "others" than among the white Protestant group.[19]

This evidence suggests that the traditional left position has some validity, especially when one is considering the white Protestant segment of the population. These data "fit" better with a notion of a socially *irresponsible* upper-middle class than with the supposedly "realistic" pluralist stress on responsibility.

These data describe upper-middle class, not elite, attitudes. It might be that there is a sharp break between the Protestant upper-middle class and Protestant elites, although this would seem doubtful. When we took the very highest income category in the 1964 study, the white Protestant segment in that rank proved even more ópposed to the medical care proposal. One must also consider the implications of an 84 percent level of support for Goldwater in that group.[20]

In the noneconomic area, in the sphere of civil rights, it was shown that outside the South there were only very small differences in attitude associated with class. Even these small differences did not support the received claims. In short, there too, the assumption of some special repository of responsibility among the financially secure and well-educated population was simply not justified. Putting the matter somewhat differently, approximately the *same* level of "threat" exists in all classes.

Here, too, there are systematic differences between the white Protestants and the other religious groups, the latter being more tolerant, more supportive of government actions to guarantee rights, than the former category. Although the differences are not as striking as those associated with the economic liberalism questions, it is, nevertheless, still the case that Catholics and Jews prove more "responsible" than white Protestants.[21]

The key factual assumptions of the revised pluralist theory, thus, prove to be largely unsupported. The established, secure, and educated upper-middle class, in particular the more influential white Protestants, do not appear to be especially responsible, either in matters concerning immediate economic welfare or in matters at some remove such as support for more adequate education; nor are they especially supportive of civil rights initiatives, either on the level of principle or on the level of implementation. Many of the more outrageous assaults on persons and liberties, as has been shown, have stemmed from elite or upper-middle-class initiatives, the "masses" being drawn in as part of their following. Subsequents accounts, by omitting this history, have stressed the "mass" involvement and linked it instead to child-rearing practices and the deprivations of the working-class and lower-middle-class milieu.

Both the initial conclusions and the major line of "explanation," in short, prove to be erroneous. Moreover, the portrayal of the general population as ignorant of issues also proves to be misleading since much of that "ignorance" also has its roots in the behaviors of those in the "higher circles," in particular in the persistent avoidance of the issues of major concern and in the use of frivolous and distractive themes. It should be clear that the "imperatives" that flow from this line of "empirical theory" also prove to be largely unjustified. In particular, this would be the case with the assumption about the dangerous masses and the need for their containment. The findings of this work indicate that many of the dangers and threats to the democratic regime issue instead from the ranks of those who have been portrayed as the guarantors of the democratic arrangement.

Rather than proceeding further with the essentially negative task of detailing the failures of the theory of "democratic elitism" (which, as noted, is the main theoretical orientation and the central direction of contemporary sociology and political science), it proves more useful to outline a fourth alternative. The criticism of the previous three viewpoints has involved objections to the factual claims made about both the ruled and the rulers and about the relationships between them. The task here is to present a more adequate, a better grounded account, than they have done. It proves useful to begin with an account of the general population.

Within the general population there is a widespread awareness of and concern with the problems of domestic economic welfare. No amount of "manipulation" appears likely to erase that awareness. The sense of the priorities may be affected by dramatizations of distant threats and the sounding of alarms, but even those efforts, as has been indicated, have had relatively limited impact on the general population. In some instances the effects have been the opposite of those intended. These reversals were (and are), to be sure, not widely known, so that many political practitioners still think such "scare" techniques useful for purposes of distraction.[22]

There are two important differences between this viewpoint and the more optimistic or sanguine liberal pluralist viewpoint. While there is a fairly widespread concern on the part of individual respondents with the domestic economic questions, there is some evident obscurity about the extent to which that concern is shared by others in the society. Stated somewhat differently, this means that large numbers of persons may, as individuals, feel a concern without recognizing that many others, possibly even a majority, may share the same feelings. There is nothing automatic in the human condition which necessarily leads to a recognition that those sharing common concerns form a large minority or even a majority. The other point of difference involves the assumed ease of creating "aggregations." Even if there is collective awareness of the shared interests, it is still different for a large and territorially dispersed population to create an effective aggregation that can have a sustained effect on policy making.

A first prerequisite for any collective effort is an awareness of the existence of some significant (that is, non-minuscule) collectivity. An organized minority can campaign for benefits or rights and presumably gain some hearing. It helps, in a democratic society, if one can claim majority status since there is a mystique, a special privilege that accompanies those who at least appear to have 51 percent or more of the population on their side. Where, however, that majority status can be hidden or kept secret, the compelling force that comes with 51 percent status can be denied. If those who are in a de facto minority can successfully claim to be a majority, they may succeed in intimidating the real majority, the latter not feeling it to be either right or possible to "impose" their will.

In the United States, as was indicated in Chapter 3, the character of the majority has been regularly misrepresented. In brief, the majority has with some consistency been defined as a minority and the minority as a majority. This is the case with respect to economic liberal opinion in the face of rather conservative practice. And this appearance has helped to "stabilize" the domestic scene by the suggestion of a consonance of public opinion and government performance.

When, beginning in the 1950s, it was claimed that blue-collar workers no longer constituted a majority of the United States' population and, the correlate, when it was claimed that working-class demands no longer constituted the majority view, these presumed facts undercut the willingness of liberal and left forces to make demands in the name of that group. The representations of mass opinion within the white population as intolerant and opposed to black demands also has had the same impact; it has reduced the willingness to make and support those demands because of the *appearance* that it involved going against majority sentiment.[23]

The problem of misperceived public opinion has been labeled "pluralistic ignorance."[24] One might think that it would be difficult if not impossible to misrepresent the character of the majority of a population. De Tocqueville assumed that democratic arrangements would make the majority position crystal clear and, as a result, that democratic nations would have a self-legitimating charcter; elections, he felt, would provide unambiguous evidence as to which was the majority party. There are, however, three major difficulties that make elections poor indicators of majority opinion on issues. In the United States, high participation elections are a very rare event. Recent presidential elections have run at a 60 percent participation level which, in turn, means that two-fifths of the population has not "expressed" itself in these contests. The second difficulty is that parties run on a range of issues, which makes it difficult if not impossible to discern opinion on any given one of them. And finally the parties, as noted earlier, have some incentive to either submerge or obscure many issues, to refuse, in other words, to allow an expression of opinion on those matters.

Many people in public life misrepresent the character of the majority, it being clearly to one's advantage in many contexts to claim majority backing. The low electoral participation aids in such efforts inasmuch as anyone can claim the nonvoters as his own. This was a frequent claim of conservatives in the New Deal–Fair Deal–New Frontier period. Their argument was that the nonvoters were conservatives who simply refused to vote since they were faced with the limited options of Democrats or of "me too" Republicans. The 1964 election did much to destroy that fantasy. This style of misrepresentation has appeared in more recent elections as a claim about a "Silent Majority."

For some, the claiming of a majority may involve cynical misrepresentation, that is, conscious dishonesty. For others, it may simply be a function of isolated or segregated living conditions. Those who live in conservative upper-middle-class subcommunities meet nothing but conservatives in the course of their lives; the reigning fantasies in such a setting receive continuous support on all sides. It is easy, given such experience, to assume that the entire country is populated with conservatives. This is a problem of "isolated masses" no matter what their location; it is difficult for persons in isolated or segregated settings to have an accurate appreciation of the state of opinion in the society as a whole.[25]

The misrepresentation or false estimation of majority sentiment is greatly facilitated by the absence of realistic estimates. As noted earlier, there are very few attempts in American social science to provide summary portrayals of the attitudes of the American population. Newspaper polls have been very limited in their presentations and even more limited in the quality of the interpretations offered.[26] Much of contemporary social science is of little use for this purpose, one principal emphasis being heavily technical (rather than substantive) and another one being heavily deductive (called "theoretical") and thereby having only limited contact with evidence. A third difficulty is a failure to make necessary analytical distinctions (such as the differences between regions and those associated with age).

Still another factor discouraging the development of realistic estimates is the attitude of the more prominent groups of intellectuals. A persistent bias found among the literary-political intellectuals, those writing for such journals as *Commentary* and *Encounter*, is a hostility toward survey research methods and findings. Surveys, polls, or findings of mass studies are rarely mentioned in such journals without some accompanying disparagement. The same is generally true of the works appearing in the semi-intellectual journals intended for educated upper-middle-class audiences, such as *Atlantic* or *Harper's*. This same bias is also found within the most prominent circle of leftist literary-political intellectuals, those associated with the *New York Review of Books*. It seems likely that the readers of these journals would also come to share the same diligently cultivated hostilities, preferring to base their judgments on free and unhindered intuitions rather than to suffer the constraints imposed by evidence.[27] To the extent that the preference for the "informed guess" and the hostility toward systematically collected evidence have come to dominate in liberal and left circles, the consequence has been that, by default, the social sciences come into the hands of practitioners who are middle-of-the-road or conservative politically, or, more frequently, into the hands of those who are indifferent to social and economic concerns.

A second major difficulty, after the recognition of a constituency, is that those groups that are most aware of the problems and most interested in making changes simply lack adequate instruments for making those changes. Their own voluntary (or not-so-voluntary) associations are either incapable of exerting the necessary pressure, or else refuse to initiate the new programs. Or, alternatively, they may not have any voluntary association and may not have the resources to create one. It is always a formal possibility, as the more exuberant pluralists note, for the poor to mobilize their resources, such as their votes, and influence the results of elections by voting in more responsive candidates. While always a formal possibility, the actual difficulties are immense. If it were a question of an "outstate" small-town–rural congressional district, the problems of the back-roads-poor getting together, organizing, getting registered, and voting in a district covering six, eight, or more counties are clearly enormous. And even if successful, it would change only 1/435 of the composition of the House of Representatives. Under current rules it would have no effect on the naming of committee heads and, since all legislation comes out of committee, the de facto obstacles in the way of significant change would be enormous.

The long and the short of the matter is that to make a transformation in the major directions of the nation's effort it is necessary to have a widespread collective awareness of the basic problems and, based upon that constituency, it is necessary to have a formidable organization. That kind of organization is at present simply not available.

Some people, to be sure, are unaware of the problems. Some people are so much out of touch that they do not receive information available to most others in the society. Some of these people, it should be noted, are not willfully obtuse or indifferent; some of them are aged and retired and no longer follow current events. Many of these are aged widows who never had much contact with national affairs or with world events even when younger, their lives having been stylized in a conventional Victorian manner or else having been filled with household tasks that never allowed any serious attention to distant affairs.

In conventional intellectual usage, the "ignorance" or "unawareness" hypothesis is applied to the poorly educated groups in the population. They are the ones focused on in the alarmist "mass society" theories; they are the ones who are "susceptible," who are easily manipulated. It is useful to break with that convention and consider another source of "ignorance," a structural source this time, the ignorance or unawareness that stems from location in an isolated or sheltered milieu. This would be the case in some respects with the "sheltered" or "protected" upper classes and also with the upper-middle class living in communities that are separated from the larger society. One might even consider the inhabitants of such communities to be "culturally deprived" since they have a very limited range of *different* stimuli in their lives and since they are effectively denied the range of experience shared by almost all other groups in the society.

One of the peculiar ironies of modern times is that these groups, for relatively long periods, proved to be peculiarly misinformed and uniquely "out of touch." The growth and segregation of contemporary cities allowed these groups to remove themselves from contact with other population segments. From their distant communities they were dependent on the mass media of communication for their accounts of life in the "other America." Especially in the 1950s, in the radiant Eisenhower years, these accounts were singularly cheerful and filled with promise. The irony is that the group flattering itself as being "informed" and "knowledgeable" should have been so impressively misinformed. The group that pointed to the "poorly educated" as being susceptible to manipulation by the mass media was itself rather strikingly misled by the mass media.

These highly stylized optimistic presentations of domestic and world affairs appeared in all the major news and picture magazines. While one might anticipate that readership of such magazines as *Time, Newsweek,* and *U.S. News and World Report* would vary directly with class level and with occupation, it may come as a surprise to learn that the readership of *Life* and of the now defunct magazines *Look, Saturday Evening Post,* and *Collier's* also varied in the same direction. One study, for example, showed that the highest percentage of *Life* magazine readers were to be found among the bearers of Ph.D.'s.[28] Given the bland and soporific character of the content in the 1950s, there is little wonder that the "will to change" emanating from the upper-middle-class circles were very limited or, for all practical purposes, nonexistent.

For the most part there was no alternative source of information present in their life to "make up for" the failure of these media. Book reading in this rank also tended to be distractive, to be highly concentrated in the fiction selections of the leading book clubs. The few critical works of the period assumed the basic success of the larger enterprise and instead concentrated on the minor strains of life in the giant firm or on the modest problems associated with affluent life in the upper-middle-class suburbs. For those of somewhat more intellectual persuasion, the dominant focus of attention in more critical journals was the "problem" of "mass culture."[29]

The 1950s, after the years of depression and war, were also characterized by a resurgent focus on prestige, a part of the *Sturm und Drang* of upper-middle-class existence deriving from the concern with "status" and with "conspicuous consumption." This interest is largely restricted to the rich and to the very affluent upper-middle class since only they can afford to pay the costs.[30] Considerable expenditures of time were necessary in order to keep up with the approved styles, to purchase the appropriate ornamentation, and to display it properly. The "home and garden" type magazine is read almost exclusively in these ranks and the time and effort involved in "becoming informed" about appropriate display, it will be noted, is time that is not available for the gaining of basic information about more serious matters. Related to this "diversionary" effort was the ever greater attention given to lawn care, to the mowing and manicuring of the acres. That time, too, is not available for more serious "educational" effort.

Another major diversion of effort comes through the reading of another variety of "mass" circulation magazines, those directed toward upper-middle-class women, such as *Vogue, Mademoiselle, Bazaar*, and others.[31] These journals are also very much tied in with the status-seeking and conspicuous consumption effort; in this case, however, the concern is with the adornment and display of upper-middle-class wives and daughters. The time spent in managing this particular line of stagecraft is again not spent in acquiring more fundamental knowledge.

During the postwar years, there has, in all likelihood, been an increase in the amount of time spent in daily commuting. It seems probable that this increase would have been greatest in the case of the upper-middle-class segment of the population, that is, those who could afford the costs of moving out of the city, or, to put that another way, who could afford the costs of avoiding the developing problem. As public transport deteriorated in this period, more and more of this commutation was undertaken in private vehicles. The most important correlate of this development, for the purpose of this present discussion, is that when riding in public transport one can read—for example, a newspaper or a news magazine—an advantage that is not available to the driver who is "consuming" significant portions of his life in traffic jams.

One final point to be noted with respect to the character of the upper-middle-class existence involves the informal rules of social gatherings. Possibly the most important kind of gathering of this variety is the cocktail party. On such occasions, large numbers of persons, many of them only casual acquaintances, are brought into one's home. The major purpose of this activity, at least so it is claimed in the leading ethnographical study of the subject, is to allow a semipublic display of the "achievement."[32] It is the culmination of the festival of consumption. Alcoholic beverages are liberally dispensed, easing somewhat the problem of conversation among those in attendance. One of the basic informal rules governing behavior at these gatherings, however, is that serious conversation is not allowed.

The main point to be noted, therefore, is that even on these occasions there is no opportunity for a serious exchange of ideas or information or for the gaining of a more adequate understanding of the outside world. The "audience" present on such occasions must necessarily be somewhat limited as far as the range of backgrounds and experience is concerned and, more importantly, the informal rule against serious conversation prevents, or at least discourages the gaining of knowledge about either those persons present or about life and the conditions that are more distant.

The image of an intelligent, educated, and responsible upper-middle class, for a number of reasons, appears to be misleading. Although possibly intelligent and although indisputably the possessors of most of the "higher education" to be found in the society, they proved to be rather ill-informed about conditions in that society, both because of their geographical isolation and because of the peculiar workings of the upper-middle-class "life-style."

It seems unlikely that many blue-collar workers, that many blacks, or that many of the poor ever accepted the effusive claims about the arrival of general affluence and about the sweeping redistributions of benefits. They knew from their own lives that that was not the case. Moreover, unlike the upper-middle class, these groups probably never even received that message, not being readers of the celebrations, not coming in contact with, say, Frederick Lewis Allen's *The Big Change*.

Large percentages of all groups in the society were taken in by the claims of the postwar period's leading "irresponsible demagogue," Senator Joseph McCarthy. As for "susceptibility," it was the upper-middle class that gave him the disproportionate share of their votes; the manual ranks by comparison favored McCarthy's opponent, a proponent of both economic and civil libertarianism. The 1964 presidential election is instructive in that the blue-collar workers, in general, avoided the more obvious "demagogic" overtures of that campaign. On the other hand, the presumably responsible upper-middle class gave Goldwater his strongest support, which ran to seven out of ten among the white Protestants. Outside the South, it was shown that the Wallace percentages did not vary by class level, the appeal being as strong in the upper-middle class as in the blue-collar ranks. Only in the South did the middle class responsibility hypothesis gain any support.[33]

In some key foreign affairs matters, we saw that support for a tough and aggressive conduct of the Korean War was strongest in the upper-middle class, particularly in the white Protestant segment of that rank. In this respect they shared a policy preference that was advocated by some major public figures and that was conveyed by, and advocated by, most of the major news media. The same distribution of preferences appeared in the Vietnam war, as was indicated in the 1964 study. When, however, a change occurred in the policies supported by the media, it was followed by a substantial shift in attitude on the part of the same upper-middle-class groups that were previously so "hawkish."[34]

What is the character of the linkage between class position and outlooks? In one frequent reading people are said to have an "objective" class position and various features of that position supposedly force the development of appropriate attitudes. The assumption is one of a close and ineluctable linkage between position and attitudes. Some of the evidence that has been reviewed in this work raises questions about this "hard" or deterministic class analysis. The shift of attitudes toward the Vietnam war, for example, suggests that the key determinant was media attention rather than some objective features of "class position." The difference in attitudes between white Protestants and Catholics or Jews of the same class also suggests that "other factors," in this case subgroup traditions, appear to have a considerable impact on the outlooks. The *Fortune* study of top executives in the largest corporations (see note 17 of this chapter) also revealed a wide range of attitudes many of which would not be consonant with the view of class position forcing the development of a narrow and very self-interested world view.

The events of the later years of the 1960s also suggest a looser linkage between "class position" and outlooks than is suggested in some of the Marxist readings. Within the white population, the New Left insurgency was largely located within the upper-middle-class ranks, indicating that somehow or other it was possible to escape from the "determinants" of one's class.[35] The confluence of some new media impacts together with some new "personal influences" allowed the breaking up of what, in the 1950s and early 1960s, had been very well-established attitudes, behaviors, and life-styles. It is worthwhile making a brief review of some of these "dynamic" factors, that is, those which broke up the rather soporific upper-middle-class consensus of the 1950s. It was these "dynamic" factors which, in effect, generated the "big change" in the consciousness of at least some members of the upper-middle class.

A major factor in this transformation was the situation of the media themselves. The print media in particular were faced with a serious competition for the advertisers' dollars, a considerable portion of the available funds having shifted to television. This stimulated a competition among the magazines, one principal result being a shift away from the bland to the mildly "stimulating" content. New authors were "discovered" and new areas of content appeared. Norman Rockwell disappeared from the *Saturday Evening Post*, the bucolic small-town emphasis went, and in its place came the "new and exciting" content.

The civil rights movement developed at about the same time and, given the usefulness of the topic for the competitive purpose, it, too, was given considerable attention. When large numbers of upper-middle-class youth broke out of their ordinary routines and "went South," they gained an education that had been denied to previous generations and, unlike previous civil rights efforts in the South, this group was followed by television cameras and reporters, thus bringing the education about the conditions there to a considerably larger mass audience.

A competition between the television networks for the audience and for advertisers' dollars also led to the generation of "stimulating" content, this consisting of series about "fighting" lawyers, social workers, and doctors and nurses. Similar developments appeared in motion pictures, the creative forces there being freed after many decades from the sentimentality of Metro-Goldwyn-Mayer and from the pseudorealism of Warner Brothers. Commercial publishers, engaged in their own competition, were eager to join in the search for and production of "relevant" materials. And finally, the protest song replaced the sentimental ballade. *Somewhere over the Rainbow* seemed ever more bizarre in the years dominated by the Vietnam war. Nelson Eddy and Jeanette MacDonald who, curiously, were the idols of many adults in the depression decade, have come to be viewed with open disbelief.

The combination of new "educational" experiences, including both the new media content and the new orientations passed within interpersonal networks contributed to the reemergence of a "left" in the United States. The media, by itself, had a rather limited impact. Only a relatively small portion of the reading or viewing population associated themselves with the movement. The leaders of the New Left, the earliest activists, came largely among those whose initial training was such as to predispose them toward critical or leftist readings of evidence. Many of the early members of the student left were children of leftists or of "left liberals."[36] That means there is some close correspondence of the political directions of the generations rather than a "gap." In great measure the changes have been "marginal" or "stepwise" changes, children of left liberal parents become leftists, children of liberals become left liberals, and so on. And that also means that most of the children of the conservative upper-middle class are still conservative or at best "middle of the road" in their orientations.

Among students, changes in political orientations occur primarily in those locations in which conservatives or "moderates" are subject to the influence of liberals, left liberals, or leftists. In general, that occurs where persons from conservative or "moderate" families come to be located in the "liberal arts" fields within the large universities. In such cases, a considerable shift to the left takes place. In general, however, conservative students tend to locate themselves in the other contexts within the large universities, in the engineering departments, in the business school, in the sciences, in the pre-medical programs, and so forth. And in those contexts, there is relatively little change in the political outlooks. It would, therefore, be a mistake to generalize about "the students" on the basis of the new and highly visible political developments that happen to be concentrated among the liberal arts students. For the remainder of the students, while there may well be a greater general awareness than was the case with the students of the 1950s, continuity with the parental generation in basic political orientations and party preferences appears to be the rule.[37]

There are two major lessons that may be derived from this discussion of these recent changes in political outlooks. First, since the change tends to be restricted largely to people who are "upper-middle class," it means that the impact of "self-interest" as a determinant of political orientations is considerably less important than some commentators have suggested. In addition to the recent changes, it was also seen (in Chapter 5) that although the upper-middle class constitutes *the* center of conservatism in the society, there do exist some significant differences within that rank, the principal one being a division by religious communities. Here, too, there is less homogeneity than would be suggested by the notions of "self-interest" or of an "objective interest." It does seem likely that some very calculating self-interested persons are to be found in that rank. At the same time, the evidence suggests that there are traditions present that support much more decent and humane orientations. The evidence, particularly in the student case, suggests the relative ease with which the implications of the humane tradition can be made clear and significant attempts to support it can be generated.

The second lesson is that the key to attitude change and to mobilization appears to be interpersonal influences. The "objective conditions" probably provide a necessary setting for the attitude change and the mobilization. It would certainly have been much more difficult to transmit a critical reading of the evidence without the Vietnam war and without the internal ramifications of that war. But the "sufficient cause" of the attitude changes, of the new awareness, and of the mobilization appears to have been the efforts of new "opinion leaders" within that milieu.

This point is of relevance to the assessment of some of the theories discussed in Chapter 2. It suggests the major importance of the group-bases or social-influences approach. Conditions by themselves did not generate the change in the student attitudes and behavior; the "conditions" are general; the war, the deaths, the inflation and so on are known in one way or another to all groups in the society, to students in all universities and in all fields within those universities. And yet, the appearance of the New Left reaction has been partial, centered in relatively restricted locations. If this judgment is correct—that the transformation depends on the role of "opinion leaders"—then it would also mean the continuation of that direction of change would depend on the further efforts of that group, or of that group plus new adherents. In particular, further change would depend on extending that influence to hitherto untouched audiences. The distribution and character of those efforts will be discussed in more detail at a later point.

The other side of the "personal influence" coin is that if new, plausible, more appropriate, readings of the evidence are *not* provided, and if sensible alternative political directions are not made available, then the readings and choices will tend to be "fitted into" the received options.[38] The basic under-standings will be those received in the earliest political training; the political choices, for the most part, will be those instilled and supported throughout the politically active lifetime. If there is any change in political behavior in a period of "crisis" or "disturbance" it is likely to be a shift from one party to the other, as in the 1952 presidential campaign, that too being part of the "traditional" training. That does not mean that those following in the tradi-tional channels are unaware of the problems; for the most part they just do not see any other plausible way out.[39]

One may pursue further the question of stability, or, put differently, the ways in which the "objective" structural developments and the social psycho-logical or perceptual facts combine to provide that "solidity of institutions." Some of these developments have been mentioned or discussed in the previous chapters but without consideration of the likely implications.

It has been argued in this work that a class division is emerging with the upper-middle class living in a separate "quarter" of the society and possessing separate and distinctly privileged conditions. The rest of the nonfarm popula-tion, the manual workers and the lower-middle class, occupy the remainder of the inhabited territories and share many life conditions in common. There are, to be sure, differences in the level of rewards of the various subgroups within this "other" class, differences in skill level, separations into racial and ethnic communities, and so forth. Despite these differences, nevertheless, all the com-ponent subgroups of this large and diverse "other" class share much in com-mon.

There is a sharp difference between the upper middles and these "others" in the pattern of income over the respective lifetimes, the former receiving continuous improvement throughout the occupational career and the latter peaking in mid-career and suffering some relative losses thereafter. Except for the most spectacular cases on the "tail" of the distribution, the level of income in the "other" class is such as to effectively prevent the achievement of an "upper-middle-class" life-style. Those exceptional, very high income workers come into that affluence through rather unusual circumstances, largely through the employment of second and third earners. The educations of the two cate-gories differ sharply, the upper middles being the beneficiaries of most of the "best" of the higher educational offerings and the "other" class, to the extent that they receive any such education, receiving the offerings of the community or state colleges. Living in different parts of the cities (or of the metropolitan areas), these groups are subject to diverse social and political influences. It seems likely that, in the course of time, the dominant values present in these two "societies" will show an ever increasing divergence.[40]

Most commentators, irrespective of their political persuasion, assume that class divisions or cleavages more or less automatically lead to conflict. For a number of reasons, that conclusion does not appear to be justified. In some ways, barring exceptional interventions, the emergence of separate commu-nities may well have the consequence of reducing or dampening conflict.

It was noted that a slow and gradual improvement of living standards is occurring. This process is interrupted from time to time by inflation and/or limited wars, but, at least as far as the last 25 years are concerned, there have been no serious reversals of the process. The process essentially has been one of either standing still or of slow advance. The response to that objective condition is likely to vary depending on the framework used to interpret the "fact." If one took a "large view" and contrasted that limited accomplishment with "what could be" (that is, if the economy were organized more adequately and greater equity achieved) that larger view might provide the basis for some antagonism and dissent. If one were to take another "large," or in this case, a "distant" view, and contrast the United States' accomplishment with the increases in real earnings of workers in western Europe, the comparison would, once again, be unfavorable and, conceivably, that, too, might give rise to some dissent and possible "strain."[41]

Both of these responses, however, depend on the "bringing in" of a framework that is not ordinarily present in working-class neighborhoods. In the latter case, for example, it would be necessary to "find" or to develop data from European sources, from foreign language sources, and digest the lessons and then disseminate them in a working-class setting. That kind of task, when it is done at all, is usually performed by intellectuals and activists in leftist parties. The presence of such "agents" would be key to any mobilization based on such "larger" readings of the "facts." Were such activists not present, the meanings and assessments, in all likelihood, would be those generated within the immediate milieu.[42]

It was suggested that the existing frameworks for interpretation of income levels and income trends entail much less critical assessments. It seems likely that the frame of reference of most people is "how things are now" versus how they stood at some earlier point either in their own careers or, alternatively, in the careers of their parents. For most people, a comparison with how things were "when growing up" or when "just starting out" with the present allows a clear favorable judgment. If the "larger view" or the "distant" view is not present in one's assessment, then it is possible to come to an overall positive conclusion. This says nothing about the degree of enthusiasm or support for "the system." One may be dealing with the kind of ambiguities indicated by such responses as "I don't have to work as hard as my father" or "We don't have it as bad as my parents." Such responses, in translation, may be rendered as saying: "Yes, we have it better than before. We are, however, still not satisfied; there are still problems that remain." This would be consistent with the central tendencies noted earlier, in particular, with the attitudes toward the extension of the welfare state. Support for any system must, in part at least, depend on knowledge or awareness of plausible alternatives. Where no plausible alternatives are present, it seems likely that most people will remain with the present accomplishment seeing it as the best available option.

The growing separation of the classes, the differentiation that becomes more and more evident in the face of the cities, probably aids in the development

of such limited perspectives of such "accepting" frameworks. The removal of
the upper-middle classes, and, to an even greater distance, the removal of the
upper classes, serves to hide the more obvious evidences of wealth. In the
much smaller cities of the nineteenth century, those with less territorial spread,
there would be a considerably greater number of opportunities for those at
the extremes of the class structure to see one another and have at least a passing acquaintance with the conditions of one another's existence. In New York
City, to take the most obvious example, the great mansions were constructed
"far to the north" of the main population cluster, first at Washington Square
and then, even further "out" in the east thirties. Still later, the Vanderbilts
made their homes in the fifties and a later generation moved even further
north along Fifth Avenue. In the next century the moves were to Westchester,
Nassau and Suffolk Counties, to Tuxedo Park, and to Far Hills. For those
who, at this late date, happen to be born and raised in the central cities, the
very rich and the well-off are lost from view or at least they are lost to direct
and immediate contact.[43] The apparent "disappearance" of the rich and well-
off provides support for some of the elements of the new harmonist theorizing
and for the claims about the "revolutionary" changes. One points to the now
empty town houses and mansions, some of which are now transformed into
fancy shops or into the headquarters of charitable organizations, or given
over to the universities. Such changes are presented as evidence of the impact
of the new income and inheritance taxes: "they," so it is said, can no longer
afford that kind of elegance. In point of fact, what has actually happened is a
removal rather than a change in circumstances; the residences of the rich are
now further away, to some extent hidden in out-of-the-way locations. Moreover, possibly because of a change in preferences, in "style of life," the homes
are now smaller and not as flamboyant as in an earlier period.[44]

One consequence of the transformations in the geography of the city is a
hiding of the extremes. By locating the wealth of the society at some distance
from the non-affluent majority, the strains which might otherwise be generated
by daily contact have been avoided.[45]

The separation of the classes occurs in still another way. The social scientists who specialize in occupational transformations have, for some years now,
noted the decline of domestic service workers in all "modernizing" countries.
The members of the upper-middle class themselves have reacted to the same
development by noting how hard it is "to get help nowadays." The other part
of the picture involves the "help" themselves. At one time, millions of working-class women, wives and daughters, made regular appearances in upper-
middle-class households. They could then observe at first hand all of the features of the upper-middle-class way of life and, more important, they were
instructed in all of the details of its style by the mistress of the household.
With the nearly complete disappearance of domestic servitude, that kind of
inter-class contact and instruction in the details of upper-middle-class life-
styles also disappears. The working-class wives and daughters in the later era

find employment in factories, in lower-level white-collar jobs, and in service occupations. What they "see" from the vantage point of these new positions is something quite different from what was "seen" in the old ones. Even the white-collar jobs are not likely to provide much of a look into *upper*-middle-class existence since only a small percentage of them would be located in the "front offices."

It is likely that the development of geographically separate classes would eventually lead to the development of a separate working-class–lower-middle-class culture. Initially, the differences might not be substantial, but, over time, it seems likely that the routine everyday orientations of the two communities would more and more diverge. Again, that is not to say that they would conflict, merely that they would diverge, that they would be different.[46] One strong likelihood is that there would be lower levels of aspiration within the working-class–lower-middle-class setting. This is a "normal" development within any community, the aspirations coming to approximate the likely or the "realistic" levels of accomplishment. A lower level of aspiration makes "achievement" somewhat easier and that, in turn, might well provide the framework for a kind of satisfaction. What would be involved, for example, would be training in working-class schools, "opportunities" in working-class jobs or careers with working-class income levels. Success or failure would be interpreted or assessed in terms of the range of possibilities provided within that context. The upper-middle-class life would involve different communities and different schools; there would be different careers held out and a markedly different earning level and pattern. Were "common values" the case, as is so frequently asserted by the latter-day Durkheimians, there would be very serious strains posed by the increasingly awesome gap between the goals presumably shared by everyone in the society and the differing possibilities for reaching those goals. If the class differences claim is valid, those differences might be, as the Durkheimians would put it, "functional" for the "social order." What that means is that those value differences would aid in stabilizing the social arrangements as they are currently developing.

The schools in the working-class–lower-middle-class areas would appear to make a contribution to this "stabilization" process. Not as a result of any consistent plan, they nevertheless manage to teach or hold out lower levels of aspiration, thus making a contribution to the new working-class culture. Although there may be no active counseling of restricted occupational objectives, the training given in some such schools prepares its "clientele" for no other positions.[47]

A small minority of those raised in the working-class–lower-middle-class milieu do overcome the limitations of their upbringing and do manage to excel in the tests presented by the schools and in those "achievement" or "qualification" examinations used to accredit one for entrance into the various institutions of higher learning. There is, in short, "opportunity" provided for these individuals. They are rewarded and supported in their high schools and they will, many of them, be aided in securing entrance into the higher-quality educational institutions. The chances are that they will be very successful in those institutions and that they will never return to their original "home" communities. This "opportunity" enables, or in some ways forces, them from the one community and locates them in the other. While most analysts have focused on and stressed the "opportunity" posed by such mobility, the giving of "a chance" to those talented individuals, it must also be noted that this process drains off a special kind of leadership talent. The kind of leadership lost to the working-class–lower-middle-class community is that which can successfully work with the symbols and verbal constructions contained in the school tests and achievement measures, the kind of skills that are necessary, or at least very useful, in dealing with the bureaucratic requirements that govern so much of contemporary life. The school system, therefore, to the extent that it does provide such opportunity for individuals, helps to remove "bureaucratic talents" from these communities. As things currently operate, another range of bureaucratic experts do come to be placed in those communities— school experts, welfare experts, and ultimately police experts—but, given the different values, the part-time commitments, and the limited involvements, these contributions are not as helpful as those of indigenous leaders. The draining of at least some of the "natural" community leaders would also, seemingly, make a contribution to the "stability" of the existing arrangement.

The basic point is that the emerging cleavage may not lead to conflict at all; it may instead be associated with a kind of peaceful coexisting apathy or resignation.

The Transformation of the Party System

An important political correlate of these social structural developments deserves special attention. There is currently emerging what one might call a one-and-a-half-party system. Some of the evidence pointing in this direction has appeared throughout this work.

Outside the South Republican party preferences, it was noted, vary directly with age. It was also noted that there is no shift in party loyalties with advancing years, that is, people do not become Republican either in their mature or declining years. On the whole, those who currently identify with the Republican party have done so during their entire lifetimes. The key to the age distribution has to do with migrations and birth rates, the oldest cohorts being disproportionately white and Protestant, and that category, as we have seen, has been disproportionately Republican in almost all comparisons. Democratic families, moreover, have tended to be more fertile than Republican families, which also contributes to shifting the party balance. The significant point, as far as the political future is concerned, is that the removal of those older cohorts and the coming of age of the heavily Democratic younger cohorts will have the consequence of a steady increase in the likelihood of Democratic victories. In the nation, in states, and in localities, the chances of the Democrats should steadily improve over time.

The processes of demography play another curious role because upper-middle-class retirees from across the nation remove themselves to more attractive climates, notably to Florida, Arizona, and southern California. This characteristically involves the removal of the solid conservative forces (those of McKinley or Taft vintage) and their clustering in a few selected locations. There is more than just a fractional voting strength operating here since with their wealth, their influence, and their organizational involvement, a special kind of core support group is lost to the party in northern and midwestern communities. The fractional losses of retiree votes in communities throughout the country combine with the demographic losses already discussed, both working in the same direction, to reduce the chances of the Republicans and to enhance those of the Democrats. At the same time, this concentration of forces in the various retirement centers does allow them some regional victories and some "successful" candidates. The positions of these successful candidates bear some understandable resemblance to the conservatism of a previous age.

There is still another demographic contribution which works in this same direction. The processes that pull people out of rural and small-town settings are simultaneously processes that remove "traditional" Republicans from conservatising influences. When farmers, ex-farmers, and small-town workers leave the apolitical or the conservative small-town milieu and come into the somewhat more politically active middle-sized or large cities, they are for the first time freed from those inhibiting political influences; they are free to make a more appropriate political choice. While social scientific and popular attention have been focused on the relatively minor strands of movement, on the movement of workers into "the" middle class and the movement of workers to "the suburbs," the major population shift has been the small-town-to-city movement. The latter is correlated with a fair-sized net shift of political orientation—from Republican to Democratic.

It was also shown, contrary to the impressionistic speculation, that there is very little shift to the Republicans associated with upward mobility. Movement into the lower-middle class involves a movement into a context that is little different politically from the working-class ranks. The political shifting occurs with the movement from the working class into the upper-middle class, but, as was also indicated, that kind of movement involves very small numbers of cases and is certainly not of a magnitude that could reverse the impact of the trends favoring the Democrats. It was also shown that the suburban workers were little different from those found elsewhere. The suburban workers who are Republican, moreover, had Republican fathers, which suggests that their political orientations were not new; it is not something that came with the new residence.[48]

Those working-class persons who were farm-reared tend to be somewhat less active politically than are the second-generation workers or the downwardly mobile group. To the extent that the farm-to-city movement has some "politicizing" effect, that, too, should serve to increase the relative strength of the Democrats. This change would not be exactly "revolutionary" in character; it involves the shifting of large numbers of people from the apathy-inducing conditions in the small towns and their removal to locations that foster moderately higher levels of awareness and of involvement. It should mean some equally moderate improvement in the normal voting strength of the Democrats and some marginal reduction in the chances for successful diversionary or distractive appeals.[49]

In the South the revived Republicanism is heavily concentrated within the upper-middle-class segment of the population. The successes of Republicanism there appear to be dependent on upper-middle-class conversions, distractive appeals, and very low electoral participation. Given the real existential concerns of the majority of the Southern population, both black and white, it seems unlikely that the distractive appeals could have any long-term success. It also seems unlikely that the electoral participation will continue to be as low in the years to come. Should the participation increase and were the Democrats to make use of "populist" or even straightforward welfare-state issues it seems likely that the Republicans would once again be reduced to minority status.

If these developments continue unchanged, it means the emergence of the Democrats as a permanent majority party. In order for them to lose they would have to make colossal mistakes, mistakes of such a magnitude as to drive their supporters away to the opposition. They would have to, in a sense, *make* the opposition attractive. They have been relatively successful at this in the past, giving the Republicans the Bryan-induced victories of William McKinley, giving the Republicans the reaction against the promises of 1916 and the call for war in April 1917, giving away the 1952 election by the Korean involvement (in a sense making the Eisenhower "I will go" claim possible), and giving away the 1968 election, the broken promises of 1964 spawning a reaction against the party that offered "responsible" conduct of foreign policy. Given the political-demographic trends, however, they would have to make errors of considerably greater magnitude than those of the past in order to "make possible" a transfer of power. In 1968 it took a massive disaffection of routine Democrats plus a third-party exfoliation to make the Republican victory possible and that was done on the basis of only 44 percent of the vote.

It seems likely that the system which results will be a one-and-a-half-party system rather than a one-party arrangement. Parties very rarely dissolve. The party functionaries hang on with a skeletal organization and survive on the minuscule bits of patronage that they are able to glean from the few localities in which they are still able to win in the electoral "competition."

Barring the exceptional policy disaster, the arrival of the one-and-a-half-party system means the end of party competition as it is conventionally understood. The arrival of the permanent majority party has some more or less obvious consequences. Established business interests deal with governing parties, not with the permanent opposition (at least where they have any choice in the matter). That would mean that business elites, by tradition and persuasion Republican in overwhelming percentages, would be inclined to "join" in these Democratic governments either as "guests" in coalition or possibly through actual conversions as in the case of the Southern Whigs following the Civil War. The achievement of permanent majority status would entail the development of a coalition of forces, Republican and Democratic.[50] Without any kind of threat to the party's hegemony, what little incentive to responsiveness existed in the age of the flourishing two-party system would also disappear. The problem with dominant parties everywhere is one of sluggishness, of immobility.

The Parties and Their Supporters

In the past, the parties had a peculiar asymmetry about them. The Republicans, as we have seen, have a white Protestant upper-class and upper-middle-class core group. In a sense, it could be said that the initiatives within that party radiate or extend outward (or rather "downward") from that center. The remainder of the party's electoral clientele is more marginally involved, its allegiance less strong. Much of the remainder of that clientele is also white and Protestant but they happen to be lower-middle class and working class. The migrations to the cities, as noted, have the consequence of breaking the linkages of these latter groups with the party. They no longer have any ties to the small town upper-middle class, nor are they any longer subject to the more or less exclusive Republican influences present in the small towns. They make contact for the first time with trade unions and pick up some of the political orientations of their fellow workers in the cities. It was seen that, somehow or other, contact with or involvement in the Protestant churches is associated with high levels of Republican identification and voting, but that in the cities this linkage also tends to be broken. It is the defection of these peripheral groups from the Republican "coalition" and the corresponding decline of Republican chances that would provide the incentives for the upper-class and upper-middle-class Republicans to move into the dominant Democratic party. It seems likely that those doing so would be the younger, more "flexible" or "moderate" Republicans, those not irrevocably committed to the age-old Republican verities. The key to the party's loss, it will be noted, is its reduced ability to exert control "down the line" within the white Protestant pillar. Despite the wealth, the media, the organizational resources, and so on, the "power elite" and their immediate allies in the upper-middle class simply lose the lines of influence that once made a viable coalition.

The Democratic coalition is of a rather different character. Essentially it involves a collection of ethnic pillars. Each ethnic pillar has its working-class and lower-middle-class components and, in the course of time, each has developed an "upper-middle class" and, frequently, some members who might even be counted as "uppers" (although they might not be accepted into the Protestant establishment). These upper- and upper-middle-class segments contain most of the active politicians. These politicians may be said to have risen within the ethnic pillars. In the archetypical case, one began as a construction worker, later was the proprietor of a construction firm, got city contracts, then national ones, and so on. The successful man now contributes and supports the party that has made his success possible. Or he may himself hold positions within the party or possibly he may even run for office. If the latter, it is the support from "down the line" (i.e. from within the ethnic pillar) that provides the votes necessary to enable an electoral victory.

The Democratic party faces a more complex internal political problem than the Republicans. At the top levels, instead of the relative cohesion, the relatively high consensus on policy and strategy typical of the Republicans, the top levels of the Democratic party involve the ethnic chieftains, some big business interests (those whose interests were better served by the low tariff, by "interventionist" government of the New Deal, or by the "wet" propensities associated with the Democracy), plus the South. Policy decisions within the the party, decisions about candidates, programs, and appointments, have to be made with consideration of the interests of all these participants. In some instances, they also find it convenient to pay attention to the interests of the Republican elites.[51]

In the course of time some political differentiation occurs within the pillars. Those at the "top" become somewhat more conservative in their orientations, although to be sure, for strategic reasons, to protect their political base, they retain their Democratic linkages and involvements.[52] They are now in a situation in which they, too, may have some interest in repressing demands from below, since those demands may affect the personal interests of the ethnic leadership group and may also affect their relations with the other members of the Democratic coalition, that is, the leaders of the other ethnic groups, the Democratic business interests, and, on a national level, the Southern Democrats. This strain became most clear when the demands of the black population escalated. Many black leaders found themselves embarrassed by the level of the demands they were forced to make and many found themselves bypassed. Some advanced liberals in the other pillars, many of them members of "intergroup relations" organizations, also found themselves embarrassed, paying off demands not being one of their most heartfelt concerns.[53]

One of the ironies of American history involves a peculiarity of Whig and later Republican supporters. Nativist sentiments in the United States tended to be heavily concentrated in the ranks of these parties. The professionals among the party leaders knew of the danger involved in the use of nativist campaigns and yet, from time to time, some less knowledgeable talents within the party in combination with religious zealots committed the party to anti-Catholic or antiforeigner campaigns. The professionals were well aware of the impact of these efforts; any tendency toward the loosening of the ethnic attachments, toward assimilation, or toward the breakdown of the pillars would be undone. Probably nothing could have worked more effectively to shore up ethnic and religious solidarities than these direct assaults.

In the late nineteenth century, the Protestant upper class began to develop a set of separate (or "exclusive") institutions—communities, schools, universities, and cotillions, and, to clarify the sometimes obscure boundaries of the group, some guidelines were provided by the *Social Register*.[54] Anti-Semitism developed in these ranks, apparently for the first time in United States' history, and exclusion became accepted policy. The correlate of this development was the emergence of parallel institutions—for example, country clubs for the excluded populations.

The irony is that the party that needed to encourage assimilation, that had to break down the ethnic barriers in order to maintain its electoral chances repeatedly found itself engaged in campaigns that had just the opposite effect. At the elite and upper-middle-class level the white Protestants created institutions which effectively precluded assimilation there also.

It is worthwhile speculating about the likely implications of any contemporary effort at undoing the institutionalized results of the nativist effort. Were this to happen (in the new, more tolerant age), were the country clubs and city clubs to be opened to all those able to pay, regardless of race or religion, and were free and easy social intercourse to become commonplace, then it seems likely that some considerable assimilation would take place. It is generally assumed that upwardly mobile "ethnics" would assimilate the values of the white Protestants. That viewpoint, however, is peculiarly ethnocentric; it is the orientation of the dominant group itself, or perhaps of the more sycophantic aspirants, those particularly anxious to "be accepted." Many of the values of the dominant groups, however, are not especially attractive to outsiders. The more conservative tenets of Republicanism are not likely to have much appeal. Some of the lingering remnants of the Puritan tradition would also have very little appeal to any contemporaries. Some of the more nationalist orientations of the older generation of the Protestant elites are likely to be viewed as curious antique viewpoints rather than as something to be imitated and cherished.

Assuming the political party development described above, that is, the emergence of the one-and-a-half-system, it seems more likely, if anything, that a mutual accommodation would occur with some shifting in the opposite direction, the more "liberal" of the established Protestant elites joining in with the now-dominant Democrats. It seems likely that many of the viewpoints so vehemently opposed by the older generation would be espoused by the younger. The political end product would involve some acceptance of the "liberal" welfare-state arrangements and a ready acceptance of Keynesian economic policies. At the same time, it seems likely that there would be some additional sacrifice of the equality value and the acceptance of noblesse oblige conceptions, the latter taken over from the white Protestant upper class. This "conservatism" with respect to the equality value is already to be observed in the higher reaches of the "other" pillars. A merger across class ranks, a union of Protestant, Catholic, and Jewish upper- and upper-middle classes, would, in all likelihood, have the additional consequence of some attenuation of the contacts "downward" across class lines.[55]

This suggests some repetition of the white Protestant experience, this time within the Catholic and Jewish pillars. The growth of the bureaucratic hierarchies puts ever more distance between those at the top and those at the bottom. The growth and differentiation of the cities, the proliferation of areas of settlement—first-, second-, and third-generation areas which at the same time are differentiated by class levels—also serves the same function. In the area of first settlement, the ethnic group members from the richest to the poorest families attended the same schools, went to the same churches or temples, attended the same neighborhood activities, and so forth, and, as a consequence, knew each other personally. When there is differentiation by community, that same inter-class contact cannot occur. And for that reason, it becomes ever more difficult for the younger generations "at the top" to know the detailed wants of those "at the bottom" and to be able to respond to those interests in any serious way. Like the white Protestants, the upper-class and the upper-middle-class ethnic leaders must more and more "project," guess, or simply fantasize about the concerns of those elsewhere in the society. Or, they must depend on the reports and accounts of those who successfully "rise" in the ranks. Such accounts are likely to be of limited value, somewhat warped in character, and, with time, more and more out of date.[56]

The major impact of such a "merger" may be summarized as follows: there would be less difficulty in working out policy on the top level. There would be less value cleavage within the upper class and within the "supportive" upper-middle class. There would, effectively, be only one party and that one would be in relatively complete control of national and state government operations.

As was noted earlier, there is a diminution of value differences "at the bottom" also. That is, the few remaining pockets of working-class "Toryism" are disappearing. Although the *value* differences are likely to diminish, separate communities within the working-class–lower-middle-class segment appear to persist. It is unlikely, within the foreseeable future, that Italian, Polish, Serbo-Croatian, and German working-class communities will be thoroughly intermixed. It would take a considerable amount of moving within the metropolitan areas to achieve such a result, an approximation to a random distribution.[57] The separation of blacks and whites within the working-class–lower-middle-class context also seems to be a more or less permanent part of the urban landscape. There are no plans, programs, or trends in process at the present that would in any way significantly alter that pattern. For the majority of the society, then, while there is a widespread agreement on some basic political issues, the organizing of the many subcommunities for effective political action remains a formidable task. Without that organization, the direction of the society would rest largely with those in the upper echelons of the dominant party, those upper echelons being drawn almost exclusively from the removed, segregated, well-off communities.

Possibly the most important development to be anticipated were there a merger at the top would be the emergence of much sharper class differences. The relatively small differences seen at present result from the divisions in the upper-middle-class ranks, the Catholics and Jews there tending to be Democratic in party orientation and liberal on the issues. Were there a development of homogeneity of outlook in the higher circles and a corresponding attenuation of contacts with the remainder of the society, it would then seem likely that horizontal, this is, class cleavages, would come to replace the vertical ones.[58]

One very marked distinction of the development in the United States is the absence of a socialist opposition; a party based on the other part, on the majority of the society, failed to develop. It is that failure, presumably, that in large measure accounts for the limited welfare-state accomplishment and for the relatively unlimited growth of the military complex within the society.[59]

A New Third Party?

The developing social and political situation provides a setting in which the "missing" party could emerge. Some of the major impediments to the development of a left party have disappeared or their significance has been reduced. A problem that faced the old Socialist party at the time of its first appearance was the division of the working class into many foreign language subcommunities. In contrast to the experience of linguistically homogeneous countries, the educational and organizational tasks of the American party were extremely complicated. The United States' Socialist party was forced, a reasonable adaptation, to accept a federalist structure which, in essence, meant an additional layer of hierarchy staffed by "ethnic lieutenants." That structure also meant that when there were internal policy differences it was easy for the party to fragment or splinter. When the ethnic lieutenant took off his clientele, there was no way the party could maintain those members or, indeed, in many cases even communicate with them.[60]

Since the breakup of the party in the early 1920s, some 50 years have elapsed which have brought the development of linguistic homogeneity. Although there has been some continuation of geographically distinct ethnic subcommunities, the language problem is no longer there. And that means a reborn party would not be faced with the same organizational or the same educational problems. It would no longer be necessary to have the foreign language federations or the foreign language publications.

The migration patterns discussed earlier have also made things easier for the development of a left party. Any process that "pulls" blue-collar workers and/or farmers from the rural areas and the small towns and concentrates them in larger communities makes such a development easier. It is, at its simplest, easier for the organizers of such a party to reach their potential clientele when they are (relatively speaking) concentrated in the larger cities than when they are scattered in tiny communities or along the back roads in the hill country.

To the extent that the migration brings people into areas of heavy working-class concentration, it removes them from personal contact with middle-class individuals and locates them in a setting where "indigenous" blue-collar leadership may be found or may more easily develop. Unlike the small towns, where the upper-middle-class oligarchs may easily monopolize all political roles, in the urban working-class—lower-middle-class communities local leadership must come from that milieu.

That country-to-city movement, as was also noted earlier, is correlated with a fair-sized net shift to the Democratic party, a shift that contributes to the making of the "emerging Democratic majority" and that simultaneously reduces the basic Republican strength. That movement also appears to lead to some increase in the average level of political knowledge and of political ability, the product of somewhat better information received through both the formal and informal educational channels.

In 1948, when the Republicans and Democrats seemed to be approximately equal in strength, the appearance of a third party on the left, Henry Wallace's Progressives, threatened to take off enough votes so as to guarantee a Republican victory. This possibility provided a major argument used against the third-party movement; instead of making things better, they would make things worse. This assumed the accomplishments of the New Deal–Fair Deal to be threatened by a victory of the Republican candidate, Thomas E. Dewey, and assumed that the risk of losing those accomplishments was too great to justify taking any chances with a third party.

The risk is much smaller in a one-and-a-half-party system than in a flourishing two-party system. The third party can gain a fair-sized minority status before there would be any threat of putting in the more conservative Republicans. Conceivably they could have victories in a number of states (where the risks would be less) prior to any serious attempt at the presidency. Victories might also occur in the cities; the exodus of the upper-middle classes, their abandonment of the central cities would make electoral success *relatively* easy.[61] One-and-a-half-party arrangements have already existed for many years in the larger cities of the United States. Many of them have been governed by the "liberal" Democratic "organizations," which means by local parties that have worked out acceptable arrangements with the Republican elites of the city. It was, characteristically, these "liberal" Democratic organizations that brought the urban renewal programs (upgrading the properties of the downtown merchants) and the throughways into the city, sacrificing thousands of low-rent housing units and deferring the development of the working-class communities.

Some municipal elections in recent years have already shown the possibility of creating a viable political organization out of the working-class–lower-middle-class constituency. The success of Stenvig against the "liberal organization" in Minneapolis is one kind of possible development. The Atlanta experience, where Massell defeated the "liberal" organization, and the Pittsburgh experience, where Flaherty defeated both the "liberal" Democratic machine and the resurgent (and alarmed) Republicans, are more promising experiences.[62]

Whether a new party will, in fact, emerge is a separate question from that of the changed *potential* for such a development. Any new party would have to organize immense numbers of active or core supporters, it would have to bridge the remaining cleavages within its potential clientele, and it would have to capture both the metropolitan cities and many of the middle-sized cities in order to have a statewide win. It would be necessary to move in the direction of a "party of integration" as opposed to the rather loose "party of notables," the latter being the "form" adopted by both Democrats and Republicans. That does not mean that it would be necessary to imitate the "disciplined" Social Democratic or Communist parties of a previous age. It merely means that the party would have to make some limited steps in that direction; it would need more integration, more connection with its clientele than presently exists between the Democratic party and its supporters. It is that degree of integration which would allow the new party to educate, win, and hold its supporters; that "integration" would provide the counterpart to the dominant Democratic party's resource of traditional party identifications and their ability to use the media.

There is nothing "natural" about the development of a new party. It is possible that at this late point the politically underdeveloped United States can recapitulate the history of Great Britain, France, Germany, and Canada. That is, a socialist party could develop by taking supporters away from the liberal party, thus offering a more adequate political option to the majority of that population.[63] Essential to the formation of a new party is the development of a staff or cadre, one that is sufficient both in numbers and capacity to accomplish the task. The problems associated with the creation of "left" party cadres will be considered at a later point.

The task facing the creators of a new party in the United States is more complicated than in most other "advanced" countries. One talks of the organization of *a* new party, but in the United States the task actually involves the organization of 50 parties (or some number not much smaller than that). The requirements for getting on the ballot have been intentionally complicated. The George Wallace campaign, however, has shown that it can be done; he succeeded in all 50 states.

Change Through Revolution?

The political developments outlined thus far involve, first of all, what we might call the continuity-drift hypothesis, that the current trends will continue their unimpeded course. The end product of that development is the permanent

Democratic majority with upper-class and upper-middle-class domination. A second possible development involves "building in" a variation on that development, that is, building in a left opposition party.

A third possibility which one might consider is that of a revolutionary change. In one widely read formulation (that of Baran and Sweezy), the United States economy has a persistent and insoluble tendency toward stagnation. A formidable surplus is accumulated in the course of the economy's "normal" operation. There is, so it is said, a lack of adequate opportunities for reinvestment of that surplus. Numerous "make work" efforts are undertaken, essentially to salvage a difficult situation, but, in the long run, the basic problem—stagnation—recurs. The major consequence of the stagnation is unemployment, a problem that is considered fundamentally insoluble and destined to become more serious with time. And presumably, this being an unstated point, the persistent and widespread unemployment will generate a mass uprising.

This argument contains two components, one economic and one sociological. The principal emphasis has been on the first of these questions. It is possible that the economic arguments are all correct but that at the same time the assumption about the social consequences are erroneous.[64] The sociological assumptions seem questionable from two perspectives.

Some evidence of the impact of long-term and substantial unemployment is available, notably in the experience of the United States during the 1930s. Were that kind of experience "radicalizing" in its impact, it certainly ought to be indicated in the course of the Depression decade. One useful measure of radicalization, a kind of thermometer showing the political reaction to the failure of capitalism would be the support for the Socialist and Communist parties. The levels of commitment to those parties varied. One could become a highly active participant or one could merely carry on as a passive supporter. Although it is difficult to get accurate measures of organizational involvement, the best estimates, do not show any significant increases in the numbers of members. Such commitments were clearly very limited.[65]

Another indicator of the extent of depression-induced radicalism appears in the vote for these parties. To vote for the party obviously involves even less of a commitment than joining. One must simply be registered and go to the polls on election day. Although reprisals might be visited for public advocacy and militance, a vote for the party, being secret, could be cast with just as much ease as a vote for the Democrats. And yet, the history of the vote for the Communist party has been a history of a steady minuscule percentage of the total.[66] Where one might expect a steady growth of dissenting left opposition to be indicated by the vote (particularly after the formation of the Congress of Industrial Organizations), the fact of the matter is that both the percentage and the absolute numbers remained minuscule. The same is true of the vote for the Socialist party. The other part of this picture is that "the masses" continued voting for the Democratic party.

One may interpret or explain this persistence of the electoral pattern in a number of ways. No matter how it is explained, however, one lesson is clear: the long years of deprivation *by themselves* were not sufficient to generate widespread revolutionary change consciousness, let alone an uprising.

It is also significant that the same objective condition—serious depression with widespread unemployment—gave rise to markedly diverse political developments. In the United States the political correlate was essentially one of continuity with the past, there being some transformations in one of the parties that allowed some very limited welfare-state reform measures.

In Norway, the same depression saw the rise of the Social Democratic party. This development occurred through changes of the votes in rural-farm districts and has been linked to the activity of Social Democratic party members who, themselves only one generation removed from the farms, were able to form the Social Democratic party program in ways that provided a reasonable, that is, practical, appeal to farm populations. The outcome as far as policy is concerned was the development of a much more adequate welfare-state apparatus than was achieved in the United States.

In Germany at this time, in the course of the same depression and in rural areas very similar to those of Norway, a markedly different political response was occurring. These farmers were turning from the traditional parties and began voting for the National Socialists. The key to this development also appears to rest with the activists who in a sense "intervened" between the "objective events" and the population, explaining and interpreting the new developments. In the German case the traditional parties, in effect, had no solutions to offer. Being classical liberal parties, their propensities were to let things take their course, to avoid an active state intervention into the operations of the economy. The German Social Democrats, more doctrinaire than those of Norway, did not offer any solution to the farmers, in general not making any appeals to these "petty bourgeois elements." The only "new factor" present at the grass roots, the group offering "solutions" and a "dynamic appearance," that is, presenting a plausible front and suggesting that they had realistic and practical ways out of the dilemma, were the National Socialists. These grass roots efforts appear to have created the electoral strength which, in turn, made Hitler a possible choice to head the government.

The suggestion here is that an economic crisis does not have a single ineluctable outcome. Such events, in themselves, are sufficiently obscure, complex, and incomprehensible as to allow for a considerable range of alternative interpretations and to also allow a fair range of solutions, all of which, in certain circumstances, may *seem* plausible to an audience not possessing a detailed knowledge of the polity and of the economy.[67]

The expectation of success in an armed revolution seems an even more questionable assumption. If serious economic stagnation appeared with consequent high unemployment and if widespread revolutionary sentiment followed as a result, there would still remain the task of translating that sentiment into the reality of a successful takeover.

A noted expert, a man who was referred to as "the General" by his associates because of his special interest in this and related areas, summarized the matter as follows:

An unarmed people is a negligible force against the modern army of today.

The expert in this case was Frederick Engels and the date of the quotation was December 11, 1884.[68] Since then the military balance has shifted even more decisively in favor of the "modern army of today." This is true in terms of the fire power it possesses, its mobility, and the support it would have in tanks, armored troop carriers, and artillery. The United States' population, to consider the other side of the "equation," is probably the most heavily armed population in the history of the world. Most of that armament, however, is designed for hunting; the shotgun is the most frequently found weapon in the typical household armory with light, that is, small caliber, rifles following as the second most widely owned weapon. These weapons are owned, disproportionately, by the rural population and by the Southern white population.[69] The weapons tend to be concentrated among those groups in the population which, seen historically, are more likely to be involved in the counter-revolution than the revolution.[70]

Such weaponry, moreover, is clearly inferior to that possessed by "the modern army of today." For that inferior weaponry to gain its maximum degree of effectiveness, it would have to be organized, coordinated, and mobile, all of which assumes considerable prior training. None of those conditions currently obtain. Whether or not it would be possible to create the needed level of organization is an open question. Tiny cells of terrorists, clearly, can operate for relatively long periods without being stopped. A revolution, however, would demand much larger units. Any increase in size beyond that of a "cell" or an "affinity group" of a few persons would, presumably, increase the vulnerability of that organization. The moribund Communist party of the 1950s, for example, was heavily infiltrated by local and national police agencies such that, with rare exceptions, all of their moves were known to the authorities well in advance of any actions.[71] In many cases, the police agents of necessity participated in the decisions to undertake the actions.

The most likely setting for an uprising in a highly industrialized nation would be in the urban centers. Such uprisings in the past have been the most easily contained efforts. The armed forces, rushed to the scene, surround the insurgent populations and gradually close the perimeter. The surrounding forces have a relatively free choice of options; they can move in immediately if strong enough and willing to take the likely costs, or, they can cut off the supply of ammunition, food, water, electricity, and gas, and simply wait. With no internal source of supply, the issue of the struggle is never seriously in question, the only questions being how long the struggle and how serious the reprisals. With rare exceptions, the history of the urban uprisings repeats that of the Paris Commune of 1871. When an uprising is defeated—quickly, decisively, and with much bloodshed—the movement stops for decades.[72]

The Inadequacies of the Left

It would be a mistake to lay the failures of the leftist parties solely to the machinations of the established parties and their leaders. To be sure, the established parties have red-baited their left opposition, have passed punitive legislation, and in the extreme case have used fraud and force to maintain their hegemony. Those efforts, however, are more or less constants in all countries. Unless one wishes to argue that the repression was more serious in the United States than elsewhere (than in France or Germany, for example), one would be forced to look to other explanations for the failure.

A major problem with left histories is the preference for the "heroic" presentation. The contending forces are the side of· virtue and the side of villany. The former sallies forth to do battle and, where defeated, that result is attributed to the cunning, the duplicity, and the power of the opposition. The difficulty with such analysis is the failure to analyze the weaknesses of one's own forces, the failure to consider the incapacities of the defeated side. Since many of these histories are intended to serve "political" purposes, to rally the masses and to sweep them up in the enthusiasms of the movement, there is very little attention given to the errors or mistakes made by the insurgent forces. Many of the histories, moreover, are "official" party accounts and, like official records in all contexts, they hide or obscure the contribution that the leaders or the party may have made to the defeat. In this respect, left histories differ from conventional military histories, which are written in the aftermath of international struggles. Essential to the writing of a good military history is the discovery of the failures of the defeated party, not the glorification of the defeated forces—no matter how deserving they may be.

Some of the most insightful self-critical commentary (a striking exception to the above generalization) is that provided by Engels. In a discussion of the American Socialist scene, he indicated some of the problematic behavior of the German-exile Socialists, noting that they had isolated themselves in the German immigrant communities, that they had not learned the language of the country, and, most seriously, that they had not learned the local conditions but instead imposed their "imported" views of things.[73] The result, not too surprisingly, was a problem of "communication" with native American workers. This problem of the peculiar disabilities of the Socialist leadership was to plague the party for its entire history. It was even more serious in the Communist party.

The problem described by Engels was one of isolation or encapsulation of the leadership, in this case the problem being one of self-encapsulation, where the "leaders," by their own choices, separated themselves from the majority of their most likely followers. Encapsulation or isolation, that is, life within an isolated mass, results (as noted above in the discussion of the upper class) in misjudgments of the distribution of attitudes. One can very easily assume, from the vantage point of a radical subcommunity, that the ideas prevailing there are typical of the entire society. This misconception is reinforced by the character of radical literature which tends to be adulatory and euphoric in character rather than analytical.

Another difficulty associated with life in isolated subcommunities is that special meanings and understandings tend to develop in such settings. The claims made and accepted as valid within that kind of subcommunity, however, may be given no acceptance at all in the larger society. The plan that might be successful within the subcommunity—because the initiators know that community (they know how it operates and how it reacts)—may not be successful or may even have negative results when carried "outside" into relatively unknown territory. A ready belief that "the masses" have either "sold out" or have been "manipulated" aids in hiding the alternative possibility, namely, that the appeal might have involved, at minimum, a tactical error.

At another point Engels touched on an even more serious problem affecting the early development of Socialist parties. Among those who "throng to the working-class parties in all countries," he said, were:

> . . . those who have nothing to look forward to from the official world or have come to the end of their tether with it—opponents of innoculation, supporters of abstemiousness, vegetarians, antivivisectionists, nature-healers, free-community preachers whose communities have fallen to pieces, authors of new theories on the origin of the universe, unsuccessful or unfortunate inventors, victims of real or imaginary injustice who are termed "good-for-nothing pettifoggers" by the bureaucracy, honest fools and dishonest swindlers. . .[74]

The presence of such diverse types in a political organization does a considerable amount of damage. They are able to lead the party in all kinds of directions, wasting scarce organizational resources, and obscuring the main thrust of the party's effort. The presence of these elements in the party also serves to discredit it before the large public, many of whom are potential supporters. Nothing is quite so salutary in driving off potential members than the presence of large numbers of people who have a loose grasp of the realities of this world.

When these diverse types combine their efforts with others of similarly limited awareness, the likelihood of self-defeating strategies being adopted as party policy is very high. This suggests that a major reason for the lack of success of leftist parties in some American contexts has been the quality of its leaders and of its more visible followers, both of whom, in effect, discredited the party, frightened away potential supporters, and drove out the willing and able members. The presence of an incapable leadership group, which defeats the party from within, would provide yet another explanation for the stability of the current arrangements in the society. With incapables undermining the leftist effort from within, there is little need for the managers of the established social order to make serious use of repression.

As was noted earlier, the segregation of the upper-middle-class communities may have the consequence of stabilizing the existing social order. This may occur as a result of the development of separate cultures, different levels of aspiration, and different levels at which a kind of satisfaction or adjustment occurs. The division of the society may lead to "stability" in still another way. Much of the New Left thrust has been generated by people, mostly students, who come out of these upper-middle-class communities. In part because of their better education, the quality of the literature and the journals they read, and possibly because of more "demanding" moral norms, they developed quite early in the post-Eisenhower years an awareness of the persistent problems on the domestic scene and, with the worsening of the Vietnam situation, came to be informed and concerned about the direction of United States' foreign policy. A wide range of actions were undertaken by those sharing these concerns, intended to change both the domestic and foreign policy of the nation.

The efforts of the first "generations" of the New Left proved to be highly successful. That leadership was very talented, had a relatively wide range of experience, and contained many very attractive and courageous figures. They knew the interests and concerns of the immediate clientele, fellow students, and were able to build a following. It was their effort that made the movement.

Many of the later actions contemplated mobilization of other groups in the population, in particular, mobilization of "the workers." The distance separating those activists of the upper-middle class and the potential supporters made such mobilization extremely difficult. The ideas held about workers in many instances were derived from very inadequate sources. Some later New Left "generations" approached the subject armed with various "insights" gleaned from Wilhelm Reich, some from Charles Reich, and some with the contributions of Herbert Marcuse. Despite many plans and programs for "work in the factory," many of the intended activists never came near the factory gates.

Some of these activists are the children of Old Left parents. It was from their parents that they first learned of the injustices; the parents provided both the radical education and the initial lessons in strategy. The parents may have had direct contact with manual populations, many themselves issuing from the working class. After the decline of organized radical effort, many of them became "successful" and moved to the upper-middle-class suburbs. In a sense, the children with this background bear a twofold burden; they have been "sheltered" by virtue of their separated existence, and, if they have received an uncritical rendering of leftist history, they would be led to practice the same errors in strategy that led to the demise of the left when it was directed by their parents.

The second-generation radicals frequently provide the "vanguard" of the more "sophisticated" New Left development. They have, after all, both "an analysis" and "ideas" about strategy and tactics. They can, in the ordinary course of events, overcome the opposition of the less forceful (because less knowledgeable and less sure of themselves) first-generation radicals. The problem is that second-generation radicals come from very exceptional backgrounds on the American scene. And, once again, the judgments that are accepted and supported in that milieu are likely to be very different from those of the vast majority of the nation's population. In some ways, the first-generation radicals, by being more in touch with that majority, are likely to have better tactical judgment than the more forceful and seemingly knowledgeable second-generation group. The former are likely to base their judgments on immediate experience, that is, on conversations and discussions with others like them. The second-generation group are likely to base their initiatives on experience drawn from their peculiar backgrounds. Some direction is also gained through reading leftist literature—Marx, Engels, Luxemburg, Lenin, Mao, Ho, Che, Debray and others. To the extent that that "experience" is either dated or derived from other markedly different countries, it is also likely to lead to some rather eccentric initiatives.

Still another unintended "containment" effect comes with the formation of radical subcommunities. These communities develop their own "culture," the literary fare of which involves some highly intellectualized productions, much of it using a Marxian vocabulary, or, even worse from the standpoint of communication with the larger society, a rich and exotic Hegelian language. There is, on the whole, probably nothing that could more effectively limit communication between members of such a sub-community and *any* segment of the larger society than the use of a language that cannot be understood by anyone outside of that subcommunity.

Another subcommunity peculiarity is the use of very aggressive, tough formulations, a development that may again be a borrowing from the culture of the Old Left. Linked to this is the sustained use of denunciation; one's opponents, frequently even the very audience to whom one is making the "appeal," are put down in no uncertain terms as either ignorant or as dupes, as accomplices in the most heinous crimes, as the "running dogs" of capitalism, and so on. Although this may serve some useful psychological function and although some "activists" may feel better for the experience, it seems unlikely that the approach would be of much use in generating support, except in the case of the most abject masochists.

The members of the radical subcommunities have fallen into another of the practices that contributed to the demise of the Old Left. The response to the increasing frustration that comes with the recognition of ever-repeated failure is an escalation of the claims about the depravity of "the system," its leaders and supporters. Where the New Left began by "telling it like it is," that is, cutting through the cant and mythology that had come to prevail in the 1950s, in the later development the tendency is "tell it like it isn't." The regular use of obvious contrary-to-fact claims must also play a considerable role in repelling those who might otherwise support the movement.[75]

In all these respects the behaviors of the "vanguard" serve to immobilize the willing and thereby contribute to stabilizing the existing arrangements.

A standard convention in leftist dramaturgy, as already noted, is the portrayal of the left as the "helpless" victim of the oppressive forces present in the larger society. The continual recounting of the history of martyrdom presumably will generate the sense of anger, or outrage, which will then be directed against the offending "system."[76] In this connection, however, it must be noted that "the system" is in no way responsible for the exotic but self-defeating language developed within the radical subcommunities. And "the system" did not develop the aggressive and pugnacious style. "The system," in addition, probably plays only a minor role in the choice of the self-defeating initiatives. Although, from time to time there may be an agent provocateur who intentionally directs "the movement" toward some disaster, their services are scarcely necessary in a "movement" filled with enthusiastic, zealous, and hopelessly incompetent amateur field marshalls.

Of special concern in the American case is the unique support given for a highly divisive strategy. The fundamental, age-old policy of rulers everywhere has been to divide the opposition. The Roman Empire operated on the principle of *divide et impera* and the British Empire in its flourishing days followed the same guiding policy. Against this principle the leftist parties have traditionally stressed the need for working-class unity; that was an evident necessity for the majority of the population, if they were ever to counter the power of their rulers.

Although the civil rights movement began as a unitary thing, as an integrative development, it was later transformed into a movement emphasizing division, building in a very sharp line of cleavage. The adoption of the Black Power rhetoric had the added consequence of frightening large numbers of persons who were either in sympathy or, at minimum, favorably inclined to the goals of integration and improving the condition of the blacks In most times and places one would expect the left to argue the strategic advantages of unity. At this point in time, however, the divisive strategy was not only accepted by white leftists, it also gained enthusiastic support. To argue against it, one said, would involve whites tellings blacks "what to do," a direction of influence that was suggestive of plantation antecedants.[77] This refusal to employ what the ancients called "right reason" was largely inspired by guilt. Again, that may be good for one's psyche but it may not be good politics.

Much of the direction of white radical politics has been motivated by such expiational concerns. Strategies based on those concerns may work, that is, be effective, within the ranks of those who "feel guilty." The rest of the population, however, may view that behavior and the presumed "telling" thrusts (which assume guilt feelings) with some disdain. This again goes back to the problem of basing strategies on the experience of very atypical subgroups.[78]

The basing of policy on considerations of "guilt" or "identity" indicates another peculiar misdirection of effort. Both of these interests are special "luxury" concerns which, in a sense, can be "afforded" only by the relatively affluent and by relatively leisured populations. The identity concern, moreover, is likely to be much more prevalent among ethnic or religious minority groups than among the majority of a society, and, even there, it is likely to appear only among that tiny segment of the minorities who have much free time for contemplation. It is the "double vision" of the minority intelligentsia that, in part, gives rise to their distance from the dominant tendencies in the society, to their ambivalence, and to their identity problems. Having the luxury of considerable leisure, or, at minimum, having no demanding full-time occupational commitments (which, by forcing choices, would end the ambivalent relationship), these persons are "free" to think about their "identity problems," to read books about them, to write about them, to develop a language to handle those questions, and so forth.

The practical political problem involves the extension of that concern to the larger population. For people without that quantity of leisure which allows such extensive introspection and attention to esoterics, for people whose lives are dominated by jobs, by commutation, by the cost-of-living, by the persistent shortage of money, and by "crime in the streets," the problems of "guilt" and of "identity" are going to be very distant concerns.

It should come as no surprise that a political movement with such strong "personalist" or "subjectivist" bias should be indifferent or even actively hostile to empirical social scientific efforts. It is not necessary to consider the social psychology of this aversion at length; the constraints and the discipline required in such effort is antithetic to the felt demands of the "free spirit." The ideological position of the proponents of the guilt-identity-alienation syndrome is that the "subtle impulse" can never be properly studied with the "crude tools" of the contemporary social sciences.

This anti-empirical bias has a number of important consequences. It reinforces the already very serious problem of reality avoidance. The failure to make even the crudest empirical assessment of public concerns, of the distribution of attitudes, of the location of satisfied and dissatisfied groups, contributes to the already discussed problems of erratic and ill-informed policy making.

A second important consequence of the anti-empirical bias involves the impact on the social sciences themselves. When radicals more or less systematically avoid involvement with social science research, the consequence is very simple: the work undertaken in the social sciences will be done by liberals, conservatives, or by the politically indifferent. That in turn means that the principal directions in the resulting social science productions will be centrist in tone or without evident import for any political direction. Research with a radical thrust will be absent.

In the subjectivist radical circles this result is "explained," in one standard line, as due to the methods themselves. This is the "subtle impulse" argument: the "real" condition can only be apprehended by those with enlightened intuitions. In another line, it is claimed that one can only do research with the aid of large grants and that the granting agencies will give support only to the politically reliable researchers. In this case it is once again a matter of the "structure of controls." This argument, rather unrealistically, assumes close controls and policing of the research operation.[79] It also overlooks the possibilities for inexpensive research that can be done without the resources of government, private business, or the foundations.

When radicals avoid even the minimal first step in this direction, that is, learning about how to do research and how to read and interpret research reports, they make still another contribution to the distortion of the entire "social science product" in that they leave themselves unfit for the task of criticizing that resulting "centrist" or politically indifferent product. Thus, they are put in a position where they can only dismiss uncongenial findings; they cannot criticize them. Then, too, given the subjectivist first principles, dismissal comes easy.

The findings of the resultant centrist and/or indifferent social science then become the staple product offered in colleges and universities throughout the country. It is those findings and those orientations that provide the basic orientations offered to what is still essentially an upper-middle-class student population. By failing to do the radical research and by failing to make the detailed technically competent radical critique, the subjectivist radicals lose out on another opportunity to exert influence. In this case, the audience is destined to become the very influential upper-middle class. The dismissal of the basic centrist product as "irrelevant" probably carries weight only with those already convinced. After a while the repetition of that theme, with no new detail, commentary, or criticism, becomes a bit tedious, that is, it has no additional impact.

By opting out of the social research area, the subjectivist left has made another major contribution to the "stabilization" of the existing social arrangements. They have unfitted themselves as critics; they have avoided the writing of serious empirically based works; and they have allowed the more politically oriented among the centrist social scientists relatively unhindered access to the student population of the nation.[80]

It is worth noting the policy recommendations of Frederick Engels. His basic point, made in an 1895 formulation, was that in the formal democracies, just about everything was working in favor of the Socialist parties. Unlike many present-day leftists who are hostile to electoral activity, Engels recommended it and discussed in detail the advantages of that option. Continuous educational activity, he assumed, would pay off in ever larger shares of the vote. With the basic structures of the capitalist societies still unchanged, and despite some evident improvement in working-class living standards, the fundamental appeals of the Socialist parties still remained valid.[81]

The party's electoral effort allowed a number of significant developments, according to Engels. It provided an occasion for activists to carry the socialist lesson out to hitherto untouched groups. Just as important, however, was the educational impact that proceeded in the opposite direction. The electoral activity put the party militants in regular contact with many segments of the population and provided them (the militants) with an "education" as to the state of consciousness within that population. They would learn, presumably in some detail, the felt concerns of the population; they would also learn the public reactions to the Socialist party and to their leading competitors. These electoral activities would yield, therefore, a high level of "organizational intelligence," that is, they would create a large number of party activists with very realistic appreciations of the conditions in the society. That "intelligence" would, in turn, help to prevent any serious misapprehension of the state of public opinion and thus would reduce the chances of erratic policy decisions.

The elections would educate the party members in still another way; they would provide an index of their accomplishment. Election results, by providing a measure of the current achievement, helped to undercut any fantasy claims about "majority" or "mass" backing, claims that could easily develop in small and isolated conspiratorial groups. Election results, in short, constituted a guard against "premature" actions which, in turn, would have provided an excuse for the use of repressive measures.

The procedures described by Engels were, at the time of his writing, rather successful. In fact, Engels reports one conservative as saying "legality is killing us." The lesson that Engels drew was one of the necessity for the party to operate within legal limits and to avoid "provocative" attempts that would provide the excuse for the dominant powers to end the electoral contests and then rule by force. The task, in effect, was to use those electoral contests to create the understanding and support for the Socialist party and to build the Socialist majority. With majority status clearly demonstrated, it would then be much more difficult for the bourgeoisie to rule by force.

Engels puts the matter as follows:

> If [the German Socialist] party continues in this fashion, by the end of the century we shall conquer the greater part of the middle strata of society, petty bourgeois and small peasants, and grow into the decisive power in the land, before which all other powers will have to bow. . . . To keep this growth going without interruption until it of itself gets beyond the control of the prevailing governmental system, not to fritter away this daily increasing shock force in vanguard skirmishes, but to keep it intact until the decisive day, that is our main task.[82]

His comment on the violent actions which are so highly prized by some elements of the contemporary left reads as follows:

... there is only one means by which the steady rise of the socialist fighting forces in Germany could be temporarily halted, and even thrown back for some time: a clash on a big scale with the military, a bloodletting like that of 1871 in Paris.

At a later point he says that:

... if *we* are not so crazy as to let ourselves be driven to street fighting in order to please them [the parties of Order], then in the end there is nothing left for them to do but themselves break through this fatal legality.[83]

The major impacts of contemporary "street fighting" have been to increase both the weaponry and training of urban police forces, to build them into more cohesive units, to provide additional arms and training for the national guard, intended to back up the police, and the passage of much repressive legislation. At the same time as these developments were taking place, little or nothing was created in the way of ongoing political structures. Most of the available poll data indicates the impact of "street fighting" on public sentiment to have been almost wholly negative. Such are the accomplishments of those "so crazy as[to be] driven to street fighting."[84]

The major point of this extended discussion of the special pathologies of the left is to note their role in inhibiting change rather than facilitating it. This is, clearly, not to say that all activists work in that way. In the United States, however, a number of these misdirected styles have flourished and provided the central tendencies of both the Old Left and New Left movements. And these central tendencies, in turn, have been such as to discourage the growth of leftist parties; these styles of leadership repelled the willing and drove away the capable.

Stability and Change: A Summary

Of the theories discussed earlier, the social-bases–group-pressures notion appears the most appropriate for the understanding of contemporary mass political orientations. People are, in a sense, born into, or perhaps better, trained into a political tradition and from then tend to fit evidence in (or screen evidence out) so as to protect that view. There are some significant unplanned (or drift) changes in orientation that occur in the routine development of the society, these being most frequent in the case of those who have no serious party allegiance to begin with and who later find themselves subject to a different set of social and political influences. An unintended consequence of the geographical and social mobility occurring in the society is some tendency toward the development of "more appropriate" political orientations, the most important of those changes being the disappearance of the so-called Tory workers. The "drift" changes, in turn, are likely to lead to the development of a one-and-a-half party system discussed earlier. That development, by itself, promises little in the way of basic social and institutional change.

This drift to the one-and-a-half system provides a potential for a significant new electoral development and from there the possibility for significant new policy directions. Whether the first step will be taken depends on the role played by political activists—whether they take advantage of the objective situation, recognizing the potential, and, whether they do so effectively, that is, in a way that attracts, that makes sense, rather than in a manner that repels.

The effective possibilities appear to be the following. If there are no new and capable activists operating at the grass roots and offering a new and plausible political orientation, the result in normal times and in crisis times, for most people, will be to persist in their original tradition. This would appear to be what has happened in the United States. Much of the increased strength of the Democrats in 1932 appears to have come from those "returning to the fold," having (for good reason) wandered off or having not voted in 1920 and 1924. The strength of the party was already increasing in 1928. Some of the additional strength in 1932 must have been from previous nonvoters who now, largely as protest (since in terms of issues, the Democrats offered very little that was new) had some incentive to vote. The impressive fact, at that grim point in the history of the depression, is that there was no significant shift to the left.

If new and capable activists appear in sufficient numbers, a second possibility, they may make a change in the ordinary trends of electoral politics. It takes, in other words, a concerted effort, one involving a significant new influence to break the hold of the previous training and influences. Where the group-bases–social-pressures viewpoint, at least in the Lazarsfeld-Berelson formulation, was static, that is, concerned largely with the persistence of electoral traditions, the same orientation proves useful in explaining breaks with or changes in those traditions.[85]

A third option involves the appearance of incapable activists, incapable either by misuse of their own capacities (e.g., those applying inappropriate analyses and strategies) or by virtue of the highly tenuous relationship between their conceptions and the character of the external realities. Should a movement come to be dominated by such "activists," the consequence is likely to be the immobilization of those who are interested and willing to see changes made. At the same time, the latter groups might not be able to supply the leadership themselves, in which case the entire movement toward change may be stopped until the incapables remove themselves from center stage.

As already noted, there are a number of convenient "theoretical frameworks" used to "explain" or "account for" the failures. By stressing the "power and influence" of the opposition and the ramifications of that influence into all spheres of life, the incapables are able to portray themselves as the martyred victims, overwhelmed by the strength of the enemy. A variant on the theme involves the use of the "mass society" theory, one which stresses the "power" of the media in "engineering" consent, in "narcotizing" the masses. As indicated, these efforts are rarely based on data and evidence; where there is some evidence presented, it tends to be highly selective and, again, self-indulgent, stressing those cases where, for example, a "powerful boss" had won an election, thereby neglecting all the cases where, when challenged, the "powerful bosses" have gone to defeat.[86] These "explanatory" frameworks serve useful psychological functions if not intellectual ones; they allow the incapable practitioner to maintain an unimpaired self-image of virtuous character and correct analysis. In this respect the behavior is more akin to that of the Puritan divines (or some characters in Ibsen) than to that of realistic and effective political activists.

Possibly the most tragic aspect of the latter history is that it seems destined to repeat itself. Given the self-indulgent reading of the history, that is, given the externalization of blame, it seems unlikely that the detailed lessons of the organizational or movement histories will be learned. Once the movement is immobilized and destroyed it disappears from the scene. If there is any post mortem analysis it is likely to be written in the heroic vein stressing again the martyrdom, the movement as the victim of the repression. When a new movement arises, some twenty or so years later, that movement's intellectuals will review the surviving documents and, once again missing the lesson of the internal difficulties, will take no precautions and will develop no special organizational innovations to guard against a repeat of the prior history.

A Note on "General" Theories

It is worthwhile making some comment on the character of the theoretical styles that have been criticized in this work, both those of the established directions in the social sciences and those of the "critical" opposition. A common feature of both has been described by Alexis de Tocqueville in his discussion of the writing of history in democratic times.[87] What he has said of history may be seen to apply with equal force to the social sciences, in particular, to sociology and political science.

The historians in democracies, he said, "assign great general causes to all petty incidents." By way of explanation, making a contrast to the history as written in aristocratic times, he noted that the individual influences in a democracy are "infinitely more various, more concealed, more complex, less powerful, and consequently less easy to trace. . . ." The historian who tires in the face of the more complicated effort demanded in democratic times "prefers talking about the characteristics of race, the physical conformation of the country, or the genius of civilization, and thus abridges his own labors and satisfies his reader better at less cost." Quoting M. de Lafayette to the effect that the "exaggerated system of general causes affords surprising consolations to second-rate statesmen," de Tocqueville goes on to say that the same consolations are there for second-rate historians. They are thereby furnished with "a few mighty reasons to extricate them from the most difficult part of their work . . . it indulges the indolence or incapacity of their minds while it confers upon them the honors of deep thinking."

De Tocqueville carries the discussion further by noting that such historians are also given to connecting "incidents together so as to deduce a system from them." In contrast to the historians of aristocracies who see only individual actions, no plan and no interconnection, the writers of history in democracy "are ever ready to carry [the use of those general theories] to excess."

The major consequence of that kind of formulation, he asserts, is that "men are led to believe that . . . societies unconsciously obey some superior force ruling over them. "Historians who live in democratic ages," he says:

> . . . not only deny that the few have any power of acting upon the destiny of a people, but deprive the people themselves of the power of modifying their own condition, and they subject them either to an inflexible Providence or to some blind necessity. According to them, each nation is indissolubly bound by its position, its origin, its antecedents, and its character to a certain lot that no efforts can ever change. . . .
>
> To their minds it is not enough to show what events have occurred: they wish to show that events could not have occurred otherwise.

A special kind of lesson is taught with this type of formulation. Where the historians of antiquity "taught how to command," he says, "those of our time teach only how to obey; in their writings the author often appears great, but humanity is always diminutive." "If this doctrine of necessity," he continues, "which is so attractive to those who write history in democratic ages, passes from authors to their readers till it infects the whole mass of the community and gets possession of the public mind, it will soon paralyze the activity of modern society. . . ."

History, and social science, and social criticism does not have to be written in that vein. Much of the evidence presented in this work suggests that the handed down "systems" lack the solid base of supporting evidence that is claimed for them. Such systems do constitute, as de Tocqueville suggested, shortcut procedures that allow one to avoid the difficult and time-consuming task of researching one's claims. The "needlessly structural" reading of the human condition does, in fact, portray individuals as the helpless prisoners of events and discourages the beginnings of effort to change those events. The portrayal of "the masses" as manipulated dupes and as narcotized pawns when they are neither also contributes to immobilization rather than movement. It also creates unnecessary divisions between the insulter and the insulted. The definition of majorities as minorities, of the holders of decent sentiments as the holders of indecent ones, also immobilizes and thereby reduces the possibilities of transforming the human condition. These are needless obstacles that could be removed by researching the matter rather than accepting the articles of faith passed on within the interpersonal networks of academic social scientists or within the leading schools of social criticism.

The ready acceptance of such claims, in summary, stands in the way of human improvement, or worse, leads to the choice of self-defeating strategies. That kind of performance, moreover, loses sight of what de Tocqueville called "the great object in our time" (and one might hope, of any time) : "to raise the faculties of men, not to complete their prostration."

Notes

1. The archetypical work is that of Frederick Lewis Allen, *The Big Change: America Transforms Itself, 1900–1950* (New York: Harper, 1952). Another work sharing much the same perspective is that of Herman Miller, *Rich Man, Poor Man* (New York: Thomas Y. Crowell, 1964). Miller is willing to admit that there has not been much change in recent years but still insists that an "Income Revolution" did occur. He takes Kolko to task for denying that claim. See Chapter 2, note 10, for other references.

2. These points were discussed in Chapter 4.

3. See the works cited in note 38, Chapter 2.

4. An outstanding *empirical* study of the question is that of Robert J. Larner, "Separation of Ownership and Control and Its Implications for the Behavior of the Firm" (Madison, Wisconsin: unpublished Ph.D. dissertation, Department of Economics, 1968). His main conclusion is: ". . . although control is separated from ownership in most of America's largest corporations, the effects on the profit orientation of firms and on stockholders' welfare have been minor. The magnitude of the effects appears to be too small to justify the considerable attention they have received in the literature for the past thirty-six years" (p. 114). See also his "The Effect of Management-control on the Profits of Large Corporations," pp. 251–262 of Maurice Zeitlin, ed., *American Society, Inc.* (Chicago: Markham, 1970).

5. In January 1971, the unemployment in West Germany increased from 0.6 to 0.8 percent. Even that low figure misrepresents the actual condition since at the same time there were over 1.8 million "guest workers" in the country. Calculated in terms of the native population, the actual employment level would be above 100 percent. That kind of experience, the 105 percent employment level, must be set in contrast to the United States' "goal" of an "acceptable" 4 percent unemployment rate (or a 96 percent employment level). The 0.8 percent of West Germans who were unemployed constituted 175,100 persons. At the same time, the number of unfilled positions in the economy was 602,800.

The argument against genuine full employment is that it would be inflationary. In this connection it is to be noted that the United States and the Federal Republic have approximately equal rates of inflation which, in turn, indicates an obvious fact—that there are ways of controlling that threat, ways which do not entail all the penalties of the forced unemployment strategy. These figures are from the *Frankfurter Rundschau*, January 8, 1971.

6. The average weekly hours of production or nonsupervisory workers on private nonagricultural payrolls in manufacturing was 40.3 in 1946. In 1966 the figure was 41.3 hours. There are slight variations over the years, the figure being lower in recessions and higher in good times. The lowest point was 39.1 hours in 1949 and the highest was the 1966 figure. The overall figure for all employment does show some slight decline, from 40.3 in 1947 to 38.2 in 1967. Almost all of that decline appears in the field of retail trade. All other fields of endeavor show essentially no change. From the *Handbook of Labor Statistics: 1968*, United States Department of Labor, Bureau of Labor Statistics, Bulletin No. 1600 (Washington, D.C.: U.S. Government Printing Office, 1968), p. 112.

7. On the educational revolution see, for example, former University President Martin Meyerson who says that, with the exception of the very poor, "America's colleges and universities are not limited to a social, an economic, or an intellectual elite; they are educating nearly everyone. Soon most American families will have one or more members who have had some college or university education." From his "The Ethos of the American College Student: Beyond the Protests," in Robert S. Morrison, ed., *The Contemporary University: U.S.A.* (Boston: Houghton Mifflin, 1966), p. 268. Sociologist Lloyd Warner says that "we have provided the opportunity for higher education to almost all who would seek it and have the capacity to profit by it." See his and James Abegglen's *Big Business Leaders in America* (New York: Harper Brothers, 1955), p. 34. For a review of the actual condition see Dario Longhi, "Higher Education and Student Politics: The Wisconsin Experience" (Madison: unpublished M.S. thesis, Department of Sociology, University of Wisconsin, 1969).

8. For a portrait of one large public school system see Patricia Cayo Sexton, *Education and Income: Inequalities in Our Public Schools* (New York: Viking Press, 1961). For a picture of the redistribution upwards occurring in higher education see W. Lee Hansen and Burton A. Weisbrod, *Benefits, Cost, and Finance Of Public Higher Education* (Chicago: Markham, 1969) and Douglas M. Windham, *Education, Equality and Income Redistribution* (Lexington, Mass.: D.C. Heath, 1970).

9. A useful source comparing the United States performance in the welfare area with the performance of other countries is Frederic L. Pryor, *Public Expenditures in Communist and Capitalist Nations* (London: George Allen and Unwin, 1968), Ch. IV.

10. These observations are based on Robert E. Agger, Daniel Goldrich, and Bert E. Swanson, *The Rulers and the Ruled* (New York: John Wiley & Sons, 1964), Ch. 13. This work is a striking exception to the generalization in the following sentence of the text.

11. See Scott Greer, *Urban Renewal and American Cities* (Indianapolis: Bobbs-Merrill, 1965); Martin Anderson, *The Federal Bulldozer: A Critical Analysis of Urban Renewal, 1949–62* (Cambridge: MIT Press, 1964); and Jewel Bellush and Murray Hausknecht, eds., *Urban Renewal: People, Politics and Planning* (Garden City: Doubleday Anchor Book, 1967). See also Edward C. Hayes, "Power Structure and the Urban Crisis: Oakland, California" (Berkeley: unpublished Ph.D. dissertation, Department of Political Science, University of California, 1968).

12. James L. Clayton, ed., *The Economic Impact of the Cold War: Sources and Readings* (New York: Harcourt, Brace & World, 1970) ; Seymour Melman, *Our Depleted Society* (New York: Holt, Rinehart & Winston, 1965) ; and George Thayer, *The War Business: The International Trade in Armaments* (New York: Simon & Shuster, 1969).

13. Samuel P. Huntington summarizes a number of studies of postwar defense decisions. He says: "Perhaps more striking is the relatively unimportant role which [the military] played in proposing changes in policy. . . . The initiative in military policy rested with the civilian executives, the decision on military policy with the President." See his *The Common Defense* (New York: Columbia University Press, 1961), p. 115. For a more general review of the question with a wide range of supporting evidence see G. William Domhoff, *The Higher Circles: The Governing Class in America* (New York: Random House, 1970), Ch. 5. The efforts to push enhanced "defense" expenditures and to have that written into the 1960 Republican platform (carefully balanced with economic growth, medical care for the aged, and civil rights) were not initiated by the Pentagon but rather by Nelson Rockefeller; see Theodore H. White, *The Making of the President, 1960* (New York: Atheneum, 1961), p. 198.

14. See Domhoff, Ch. 5: "How the Power Elite Make Foreign Policy," and Ch. 6: "How the Power Elite Shape Social Legislation." The notion of a "power elite" that makes the major decisions of national policy is, of course, that of C. Wright Mills. The sociologist Daniel Bell has attempted to discredit the claim referring to a "detailed analysis" by Richard Rovere of the decisions Mills cited, an analysis which "broadly refuted" the notion that the power elite was "really involved." The "detailed analysis" in question turns out to be a book review in the *Progressive*. The discussions of the decisions are very casual one and two paragraph accounts. Both the Bell and Rovere works are reprinted in G. William Domhoff and Hoyt B. Ballard, eds., *C. Wright Mills and The Power Elite* (Boston: Beacon Press, 1968).

15. This reading is taken as justification for the use of armed attacks and terrorism. 'The system," so it is claimed, makes use of illegitimate means ("dope," for example) to maintain itelf and its purposes. Since the "narcotized" population cannot be reached through normal, ordinary processes of reasoning, it is justified, especially when pursuing a moral end, to also make use of what would otherwise be illegitimate means. In some formulations there exists an aware "underclass," those who have not been bought off and for whom no manipulation will work.

16. The questions of the realism of elite orientations and the adequacy of their choices of means to exert influence have been discussed briefly in Chapter 1. See also Richard Hamilton, "A Touch of Tyranny," *The Nation*, **201**:4, August 16, 1965, pp. 75–78. In contrast to the assumption of "realism" one has to consider the upper-class fantasies about "the poor" and their Cadillacs, or about the poor of the world, who, in the face of declining living standards presumably have "rising expectations." One has to consider the anti-Roosevelt passions of the rich and the intense hatreds directed against the man who, more than any other, saved their positions. An earlier Roosevelt, Theodore, also complained about the obtuseness of the rich who opposed the modest concessions of his "progressive" period, concessions that were also designed to save their prerogatives. John W. Davis,

a corporation lawyer and Wall Streeter, the Democrats' 1924 presidential candidate, told *The New York Times*'s readers that "he was still a Democrat, partly because none of his predecessors had carried the country so near to socialism as had Herbert Hoover." The latter quotation is from Norman Thomas, "The Thirties in America as a Socialist Recalls Them," pp. 104–122 of Rita James Simon, ed., *As We Saw the Thirties* (Urbana: University of Illinois Press, 1967). The quotation is from p. 109.

17. On the limits of the media influence see the discussion and works cited in Chapter 2, notes 68, 69, and 70. An illustrative account of the difficulties involved in the instrumental use of voluntary associations is contained in Hamilton, "A Note on Veterans, Veterans' Organizations, and Tolerance," Chapter 6 of *Restraining Myths and Liberating Realities* (forthcoming).

18. An archetypical case of a calculating, manipulative political leader would be that of James Forrestal, the first secretary of defense. See Arnold A. Rogow, *James Forrestal: A Study of Personality, Politics, and Policy* (New York: Macmillan, 1963). Forrestal was a strong supporter of the United States Information Service for its overseas propaganda purposes. Having in mind the effects of the pre-war Nye Committee investigations of the armament industry, he urged the formation of a domestic equivalent of the USIS. He was also concerned about the lack of coordination of domestic police efforts and urged the formation of a central internal security police (p. 129). Not satisfied with the accomplishments of others in this latter field, he organized and ran his own modest intelligence operation.

Some sense of the diversity in the elite ranks may be gained from a *Fortune* magazine study of heads of the largest corporations. Some 46 percent agreed, either strongly or partly, with the statement that "Economic well-being in this country is unjustly and unfairly distributed." Discussing the top priority problems in the nation, 62 percent stressed "supporting education," 58 percent indicated "combatting air and water pollution," and 57 percent said "ensuring equality of opportunity for minorities." These results suggest a high degree of support for decent and humane initiatives. The problem comes in what they are willing to do. Only 6 percent indicated support for a guaranteed minimum income, a figure that is consonant with the liberalism findings as presented in earlier chapters of this work.

Some 72 percent of this sample identified as Republican (the others being independents or Democrats, many of the latter apparently being Southern). And, some 80 percent of the sample voted for Nixon in 1968. Most thought he was doing a good job.

Unfortunately this study gives only the marginal distributions. It would be useful to have a discussion of the types or of the clusterings of attitudes in that rank. And also, it would be useful to have some indication of the degree of political involvement of each of the different types. It is possible that the findings are not so paradoxical as they at first seem. If the "hard-headed" conservatives were the actively involved and the more "liberal" ones were quiet and inactive, then the explanation for the direction of United States policy would not pose much of a problem. The *Fortune* report also indicates that "beyond question the nation's corporate leaders are governed by, and in their social impulses restricted by, the profit-and-loss disciplines of the marketplace."

The *Fortune* study appears in that magazine, volume **80**, September 1969, pp. 93–95, and October 1969, 139–40 ff. These results ought to be set in contrast to the claims of those who, without any evidence, *assume* widespread, near-universal viciousness in these ranks. See, for example, Paul A. Baran and Paul M. Sweezy, *Monopoly Capital* (New York: Monthly Review Press, 1966).

An as yet unpublished study of very high income groups in the state of Wisconsin undertaken by Leonard Berkowitz and Kenneth G. Lutterman comes up with a similar picture, that is, of remarkably high levels of willingness to undertake some responsible initiatives. At the same time, the political choices they made were such as to preclude any serious efforts toward accomplishment. For an indication of some of the work in this direction, see Kenneth G. Lutterman and Leonard Berkowitz, "The Traditional Socially Responsible Personality," *Public Opinion Quarterly*, **32** (Summer 1968), 169–185.

19. Chapter 5, Table 5.4.

20. See the discussion that follows Table 5.4 in Chapter 5. These findings have some obvious relevance to the claims of Edward C. Banfield and James Q. Wilson who portray the "middle class," particularly the older, more established ethnic groups, as being given to "public-regarding" orientations. See their *City Politics* (Cambridge: Harvard University Press, 1963) and their "Public-Regardingness as a Value Premise in Voting Behavior," *American Political Science Review*, **58** (December 1964), 876–887. See also the criticism of that position by Raymond E. Wolfinger and John Osgood Field, "Political Ethos and the Structure of City Government," *American Political Science Review*, **60** (June 1966), 306–326. Wilson and Banfield reply in the December 1966 issue, pp. 998–999. Wolfinger and Field reply to the reply on p. 1000.

21. See Chapter 11, Table 11.3 for the presentation of the class and religion factors. Tables 11.1 and 11.2 show the class relationship alone. For the attitudes with respect to "strong stands" in two wars, a picture which again does not accord with the notion of upper-middle-class "responsibility," see Table 11.12.

There is some support for the "working-class authoritarianism" hypothesis among the Southern whites, the blue-collar workers being less supportive of government initiatives than the middle-class groups. Even here the evidence is far from "solid." The surveys of the attitudes and the Wallace preferences show support for the claim. Chandler Davidson's review of elections and referenda show a decisive rejection of the hypothesis. See his *Biracial Politics: Conflict and Coalition in the Southern Metropolis* (Baton Rouge: Louisiana State University Press, 1972), Ch. 8.

22. See the discussions and works cited in both Chapters 3 and 11.

23. This refers to the "working-class authoritarianism" claim. Large numbers of liberals and leftists were taken in by these arguments. The strategies that evolved as a result of their being taken in have included a kind of *cordon sanitaire*. Some people on the left, assuming that the blue-collar ranks were both a minority and peculiarly corrupted, turned to the "development" of a "new" working class, one consisting largely of salaried white-collar workers—engineers, technicians, and professionals. Some sense of the outlooks of these "new" working classes may be gained from the evidence in Table 5.7. Some left reactions have involved working *against* the white manual workers rather than with them, op-

posing them as "exploiters" of blacks, as beneficiaries of imperialism, and so forth.

24. An outstanding study of this phenomenon is that of Warren Breed and Thomas Ktsanes, "Pluralistic Ignorance in the Process of Opinion Formation," *Public Opinion Quarterly*, **25** (Fall 1961), 382–392. They note that ". . . there is clear and systematic error in guessing public opinion, and the error is in the traditional direction." With respect to civil rights questions, those who favored segregation were "unable to envision even the existence of an antisegregationist public." In one survey "not a single Segregator estimated that others would take one of the three tolerant positions, while in fact 27 percent of their fellow townsmen did just this."

25. The best discussion of the "isolated mass" is that of Clark Kerr and Abraham Siegel, "The Inter-Industry Propensity to Strike: An International Comparison," pp. 189–212 of Arthur Kornhauser, Robert Dubin, and A. M. Ross, eds., *Industrial Conflict* (New York: McGraw-Hill, 1954). This kind of distortion of public opinion is a problem with all isolated communities whether it be isolated upper classes, liberal professors "lost" in giant academic enclaves, members of student radical communities, or coal miners in Wales. Most of the discussion of "isolated masses" has been focused on working-class communities while the upper-middle-class or upper-class "masses" have been neglected.

26. In the not-too-distant past the Gallup polls had a distinct anti-labor slant to them; see Arthur Kornhauser, "Are Public Opinion Polls Fair to Organized Labor," *Public Opinion Quarterly*, **10** (Winter 1946–47), 484–500. There are some responses contained in the same journal, vol. **11** (Summer 1947), 198–212.

27. The hostility toward "survey research" in left circles is especially surprising since both Marx and Lenin initiated surveys. The Marx questionnaire, the Enquête Ouvrière, is reprinted in T. B. Bottomore, ed., *Karl Marx: Selected Writings in Sociology and Social Philosophy* (New York: McGraw-Hill, 1956), pp. 203–212. Lenin's effort is discussed in Louis Fischer, *The Life of Lenin* (London: Weidenfeld and Nicolson, 1964), p. 21. Mao stated that "The CCP does not rely on terror for nourishment; it relies on the truth, on arriving at the truth by a verification of facts, and on science. . . ." This is from a speech originally published in *Chieh-fang jih pao* (Liberation Daily), June 18, 1942.

28. See, for example, a nationwide study by Sindlinger & Company conducted for Newsweek, *The Characteristics of the Reading Audiences of Newsweek, Time and U.S. News & World Report* (no date, no place). At the time of the study, 1958–1959, 6.4 percent of the population (age 12 and over) read *Time* magazine, the largest circulation of the three magazines in question. Taking employed males, one finds 25.4 percent of the professionals to be *Time* readers, 12.3 percent of the managers, 12.4 of the clerical and sales group, 7.5 percent of the craftsmen and foremen, and only 1.8 percent of the operatives and laborers. A later study by *Newsweek* adds data on *Life* and the *Saturday Evening Post*, this being their *Audiences of Five Magazines* (New York: Newsweek, 1962). It is this study which showed *Life* magazine coverage in relation to educational level. Some 55.8 percent of the households where the house head had a Ph.D. were recipients of *Life* magazine. The equivalent figure for homes in which the house head had no more than grade school education was 18.0 percent (pp. 38 and 39). A study of

executives in "million dollar corporations" done for the *Wall Street Journal* found the following readership levels: *Wall Street Journal*, 68.8 percent (of the total sample) ; *Life*, 43.0 percent; *Saturday Evening Post*, 34.5 percent; *Business Week*, 34.0 percent; and *Reader's Digest*, 26.5 percent. In answer to a further question, 5 percent of these executives reported the *Reader's Digest* to be one of the three "most important and useful" sources among the newspapers and magazines they read. See *The Reading Preferences of Corporate Officers & Executives* (New York: Ercos and Morgan, Research Service, 1962).

29. A very useful account of the book clubs and their accomplishments may be found in William Miller, *The Book Industry* (New York: Columbia University Press, 1949). The leading work on the stress and strain of executive life, both in the office and at home, was that of William H. Whyte, Jr. *The Organization Man* (Garden City: Doubleday Anchor Book, 1957). The mass culture focus was particularly dominant in the magazine *Dissent*, a Socialist Quarterly.

30. Given the extraordinary amount of attention paid the subject and given the ready and gratuitous willingness to invoke "status concerns" to explain wide ranges of behavior, it is remarkable that so little empirical work has been done to establish the actual extent of such concerns. The only work that does make such inquiry found economic interests to dominate among most of the population studied. Only among the well-off was there special concern with the other dimensions of the Weberian trinity, that is, with status and power. See Joan Huber Rytina, "The Ideology of American Stratification" (East Lansing: unpublished Ph.D. dissertation, Michigan State University, Department of Sociology, 1967).

31. The best source on the subject of these periodicals is Theodore Peterson, *Magazines in the Twentieth Century* (Urbana: University of Illinois Press, 2d edition 1964). Some sense of the audiences of one home and garden and two women's magazines may be found in a study done by Alfred Politz, *The Audiences of Nine Magazines* (New York: Politz, 1955).

32. The work referred to is that of John R. Seeley, R. Alexander Sim, and Elizabeth W. Looseley, *Crestwood Heights: A Study of the Culture of Suburban Life* (New York: Basic Books, Inc., 1956).

33. For the discussion of McCarthy and his support, see Chapters 3 and 11. The distribution of support for Goldwater may be seen in Chapter 5, Table 5.2. The Wallace case is discussed toward the end of Chapter 11. The key table is number 11.13.

34. See James D. Wright, "Support for Escalation in Viet-Nam, 1964–1968: A Trend Study" (Madison: unpublished Master of Science thesis, Department of Sociology, 1970). This study is based on the Survey Research Center's 1964 and 1968 election studies. The white Protestant upper-middle class was unusually "hawkish" in 1964, 78 percent of those with opinions favoring the "stronger stand." In 1968 only 38 percent held the same opinion, a difference of some 40 percentage points. The shift was even greater among the upper-middle-class white Protestants who were highly dependent on news magazines for their national and international political news (p. 34). See also Ch. 5 of Hamilton, *Restraining Myths* . . . .

35. The upper-middle-class character of the movement has been noted in many studies. The best account of the matter, one containing a significant specification of the received readings, is that of Henry C. Finney, "Political Libertarianism at

Berkeley: An Application of Perspectives from the New Student Left." *Journal of Social Issues*, **27** (1971), 35–61.

36. Put epigramatically, the leftist parents created the leaders of the leftist student movement. The media created the readiness that allowed those leaders a wider audience than was the case in the 1950s. It is impossible in a short space to take account of all the complexities. There is a new literature in the form of the so-called underground press. There are new motion pictures going far beyond *Rebel without a Cause*, these focusing on rebels with a cause. Most of these innovations appeared subsequent to the reemergence of the left, sustaining it perhaps, but not causing it. Within the universities there emerged a new critical scholarship that challenged the semi-official works of the cold war period. While these gained only limited acceptance within the universities, they had and still have a fair-sized outside readership. A good account of the early development of the New Left movement is that of Jack Newfield, *The Prophetic Minority* (New York: New American Library, 1966). See also James P. O'Brien, "The Development of the New Left," pp. 15–25 of the *Annals of the American Academy of Political and Social Science*, Vol. 395 (May 1971). See also Kenneth Keniston, *The Uncommitted: Alienated Youth in American Society* (New York: Harcourt, Brace, & World, 1965); Richard Flacks, "The Liberated Generation: An Exploration of the Roots of Student Protest," *Journal of Social Issues*, **23** (July 1967), 52–57; and Maurice Pinard, Jerome Kirk, and Donald Von Eschen, "Processes of Recruitment in the Sit-In Movement, *Public Opinion Quarterly*, **33** (Fall 1969), 355–369.

37. This account is based largely on the work of Dario Longhi and Henry Finney. See also, for a general review, Vern L. Bengtson, "The Generation Gap: A Review and Typology of Social-Psychological Perspectives," *Youth and Society*, **2** (September 1970), 7–32.

38. Of some interest in this connection is the work of John P. Robinson, "Public Reaction to Political Protest: Chicago, 1968" *Public Opinion Quarterly*, **34** (Spring 1970), 1–9.

39. See the discussion in Chapter 1 of the 1968 campaign in which some 43 percent of the voters indicated dissatisfaction with all of the candidates.

40. This divergence would be furthered by the differences in mass media attention. Relatively, the working-class–lower-middle-class group pay more attention to television. The upper-middle class, again relatively, are the consumers of the more well-known mass circulation magazines and the more specialized limited circulation magazines. Even within a given medium the attention tends to be focused on different programs. See also note 43 below.

41. Some discussion of these questions and some evidence bearing on them appears in Chapter 10. See also L. G. Runciman, *Relative Deprivation and Social Justice* (Berkeley: University of California Press, 1966), Ch. 9, 10, and 11.

42. The role of activists in providing alternative frameworks for interpretation of events is considered in Hamilton, *Affluence and the French Worker in the Fourth Republic* (Princeton University Press, 1967). The role of the activist-interpreters was also a key feature of the early works of Seymour Martin Lipset, notably in his *Agrarian Socialism* (Berkeley: University of California Press, 1950), and, with Martin A. Trow and James S. Coleman, *Union Democracy*

(Garden City: Doubleday Anchor Books, 1962). In the latter work we have such formulations as the following: "Few issues that arise in the union are intrinsically party issues; they are *made* political issues by the parties and their spokesmen" (p. 209). And, "These active partisans convert *potential* political arenas into *actual* ones by channeling union concerns into union politics and by injecting political issues into the networks of social relationships that flourish in the larger shops" (p. 215). Regrettably, this focus has disappeared from his later writings.

43. There do remain, to be sure, some "pictures" of these groups appearing from time to time on television. There is some question as to how they are seen by the various segments of the audience, whether as objects of envy or as members of another, distant and unreachable world. Some initial efforts in the area appear in Herbert Gans, *The Urban Villagers: Group and Class in the Life of Italian-Americans* (New York: The Free Press, 1962); Leo Bogart, "The Mass Media and the Blue-Collar Worker," pp. 416–328 of William Gomberg and Arthur Shostak, *Blue-Collar World* (Englewood Cliffs, N.J.: Prentice-Hall, 1964); Ira O. Glick and Sidney J. Levy, *Living with Television* (Chicago: Aldine Publishing, 1962), Herbert J. Gans, *The Uses of Television and their Educational Implications: Preliminary Findings from a Survey of Adult and Adolescent New York Television Viewers* (New York: Center for Urban Education, 1968); and Bradley Greenberg and Brenda Dervin, "Mass Communication among the Urban Poor," *Public Opinion Quarterly*, **34** (Summer 1970), 225–235.

Useful content analyses are those of Frank Gentile and S. M. Miller, "Television and Social Class," *Sociology and Social Research*, **45** (April 1961), 259–264 and Melvin L. DeFleur, "Occupational Roles as Portrayed on Television," *Public Opinion Quarterly*, **28** (Spring 1964), 57–74. Although content analyses have provided a considerable stimulus to speculation and inference, they are clearly only the first step in an assessment of impact. The questions "who watches?" and "with what effect?" still remain open.

44. For an interesting case study of this transformation of the housing styles of the rich, see Floyd Hunter, *The Big Rich and the Little Rich* (Garden City: Doubleday, 1965), pp. 130–33.

45. The elaborate festivities of the well-off no longer have the same high visibility they once had. A frequent image in nineteenth-century literature involved the poor watching the arrival of the guests and catching glimpses of the ball through the open terrace doors. When the neighborhoods are no longer contiguous, that kind of image must necessarily disappear from the literature. For a portrayal of turn-of-the-century flamboyance, see Charles A. and Mary R. Beard, *The Rise of American Civilization* (New York: Macmillan, 1930), Book II, Ch. XXV: "The Gilded Age."

46. Those differences would be reinforced by attention to different media, by paying attention to different programs in any given medium, and by different advertising in the different programs. They would have different stores available to them, that is, located within a convenient distance, and these stores would contain a different range of goods. There would also be differences in the accessible leisure time activities.

47. In some instances, however, there may be active counseling, as in the case reported by Burton R. Clark, *The Open Door College: A Case Study* (New York:

McGraw-Hill, 1960). Another useful source is Aaron V. Cicourel and John I. Kitsuse, *The Educational Decision-Makers* (Indianapolis: Bobbs-Merrill, 1963).

48. See the discussion in Chapter 6.

49. Similar processes appear to be operating in other economically advanced countries. There is an age-related difference in party preferences in Great Britain. One study reports a Conservative-Labour division of 45 and 36 percent in the 65 years and over category and a 34 to 45 relationship among those of ages 21 to 24. My own reanalysis (unpublished) of the Almond-Verba data indicates a very pronounced demographic edge for the Labour party, that is, the Labour families tend to be larger than those of Conservatives. My reanalysis of Eric Nordlinger's study of British workers does not indicate any pattern of shifting from Labour to Conservative such as would be necessary in order to "stabilize" the "two-party" relationship. The age relationship (based on the aggregate results of six independent samples) appears in Philip Abrams and Alan Little, "The Young Voter in British Politics," *British Journal of Sociology*, 16 (June 1965), 95–110. The Nordlinger study referred to is his *The Working Class Tories* (Berkeley: University of California Press, 1967). A slight age relationship, younger voters tending toward the Social Democrats, is also indicated in West Germany. See Juan Linz, *The Social Bases of West German Politics* (New York: unpublished Ph.D. dissertation, Columbia University, Department of Sociology, 1959) p. 856. There is also some differentiation indicated with city size (Ch. 10). It seems likely that the demise of the older generations in the small towns and the exodus from the small towns would both lead to an increase in the typical chances of the Social Democrats, that is, to the making of a permanent majority party there also. Similar findings, at least as far as the age and city size relationships are concerned, also appear in Italy. See Joseph LaPolombara, *Interest Groups in Italian Politics* (Princeton: Princeton University Press, 1964).

50. There are some foreshadowings of this development. The wartime Roosevelt government was a coalition government. Although few people think of it as such, the same can be said of the Kennedy administration, the secretaries of defense and the treasury both being Republicans, the latter in fact having served in the Eisenhower administration. Some of the candidates considered for secretary of state were also Republicans but, for reasons of party, had to be turned down. All three of the successful candidates were originally suggested by Robert A. Lovett, a Republican and the "chief agent" of the "American Establishment." See Arthur Schlesinger, Jr., *A Thousand Days* (Boston: Houghton Mifflin, 1965), Ch. V. Coalitions of a sort are already in existence in many cities where quiet support is provided for the "liberal Democratic organization," the group that has both a majority of the urban votes and which brought the urban renewal program. See note 62 below for further discussion. The Lynds account of the dominant "X" Family tells of their Republican commitments, one of them even being a member of the Republican National Committee. In the 1930s, however, after both the nation and the state had gone democratic, a second-generation "X" turned up as a Democrat and was quickly appointed to the governor's Committee on Unemployment. See Robert S. and Helen M. Lynd, *Middletown in Transition* (New York: Harcourt Brace, 1937), p. 87.

51. Richard Neustadt, who advised Kennedy on cabinet appointments, argued

that there was much to be gained by "bowing to tradition" in the appointment of a secretary of treasury from the "financial community." His daily duties, Neustadt argued, "cannot help but make him sensitive to the concerns of bankers and investors, their colleagues overseas, and their friends on the Hill. He will end as a 'spokesman' for them. He might as well begin as an effective spokesman to them." He recommended someone "of the type" of Lovett, McCloy, or Douglas Dillon, men who, it so happened, were all Republicans and closely linked to that financial community. See Schlesinger, p. 133.

52. Some indication of the relative conservatism of the higher status Democrats may be found in Tables 5.8 and 11.2.

53. For some insight on the subject see the following: E. Franklin Frazier, *Black Bourgeoisie: The Rise of A New Middle Class in the United States* (Glencoe: The Free Press, 1957); Lewis Killian and Charles Grigg, *Racial Crisis in America: Leadership in Conflict* (Englewood Cliffs, N.J.: Prentice-Hall, 1964); Daniel C. Thompson, *The Negro Leadership Class* (Englewood Cliffs, N.J.: Prentice-Hall, 1963); James Q. Wilson, *Negro Politics; The Search for Leadership* (Glencoe: The Free Press, 1960); Floyd Hunter, *Community Power Structure* (Chapel Hill: University of North Carolina Press, 1953), Ch. 5.

54. See E. Digby Baltzell, *Philadelphia Gentlemen: The Making of a National Upper Class* (Glencoe: The Free Press, 1958), and G. William Domhoff, *The Higher Circles: The Governing Class in America* (New York: Random House, 1970).

55. Some indication of the greater concern with the equality value among the poor may be seen in the work of William Form and Joan Rytina, "Ideological Beliefs on the Distribution of Power in the United States," *American Sociological Review,* **34** (February 1969), 19–31. The ideological justifications for the conception of a new and "democratic" *noblesse* are provided, in sociology, by the so-called structural-functional theory of stratification, and in political science, by the neoelitist writings, those sometimes referred to under the heading of "democratic elitism." In a sense, these orientations might be said to constitute a modern, more palatable, "functional equivalent" to the social Darwinist views which dominated in previous generations.

The discussion of a "merger" in the upper-class ranks is largely hypothetical. Although it is generally assumed that the "barriers are being broken down" and that the ineluctable processes of "democratization" continue to reduce all obstacles that stand in the way, the actual evidence provides a markedly different picture, one in which the "old" cleavages persist. See, for example, the following: Edwin Kiester, Jr., *The Case of the Missing Executive* (New York: Institute of Human Relations, 1968); Lewis B. Ward, "The Ethnics of Executive Selection," *Harvard Business Review,* **43** (March–April 1965), 6–39; Robert L. Kahn, et al., *Discrimination without Prejudice: A Study of Promotion Practices in Industry* (Ann Arbor: Institute for Social Research, 1964).

56. Some of the discussion in this paragraph, in particular the discussion of the generations and the areas of settlement, is based on the work of Marshall Sklare, *Conservative Judaism* (Glencoe: The Free Press, 1955). A very useful account of the relationship of upwardly mobile individuals to their community of origin is contained in William Foote Whyte, *Street Corner Society: The Social Structure of*

an Italian Slum, enlarged edition (Chicago: University of Chicago Press, 1955), pp. 104–108.

57. See note 52 of Chapter 2 for references on the ethnic persistence.

58. Were this kind of a merger to occur, it would mean that the religious–ethnic cleavages noted in this work would be diminished. It seems likely that there would be some change in the dominant issues. Rather than a liberalism–conservatism struggle dominating the "public" campaigning, it seems likely that the struggles would be "within" the liberal camp. To the extent that the dominant issues were mere continuations of the present themes, they would revolve around questions of the adequacy and the extent of the welfare coverage. It also seems likely, however, that populist themes would come to be much more important, with questions of income distribution, tax burdens, and de facto control of life circumstances coming to the forefront.

59. The absence of a party on the left is the key to the "malfunctioning" pluralism in the United States. A major interest is not represented. The emergence of the one-and-a-half party system entails still further depluralization and would create "a need" for some kind of repluralization. The problem is actually more serious than the above analysis would suggest. When the parties divided 50–50, it was necessary that the Democrats pay some attention to the trade unions in order to gain their support. The majority Democrats in the new party system can take the unions very much for granted and can bypass them in the conduct of legislative and executive affairs.

60. See James Weinstein, *The Decline of Socialism in America, 1912–1925* (New York: Monthly Review Press, 1967), Chs. 4 and 5.

61. The stress on the word "relatively" means in comparison to the difficulties that were present when the upper-middle class was still in the city and when the working class was ethnically, religiously, and linguistically divided. At the same time that expression—relatively easy—is not meant to overlook the fact that a victory means thousands of hours of effort, of organization, of campaigning, and so on. It should also be noted that although the win may come with relative ease, those victories do not prove to be very meaningful. When one "inherits" a city abandoned by the upper-middle class, frequently what is gained is a city with an immense debt, with no further opportunities for gaining new revenues, and one facing immense and very expensive problems.

A very useful account, one which shows the development of a third party in situations where the "second" party had been seriously weakened is that of Maurice Pinard, *The Rise of a Third Party: A Study in Crisis Politics* (Englewood Cliffs, N.J.: Prentice-Hall, 1971).

62. For an account of the Pittsburgh case, see Donald Janson, " 'Nobody's Boy' in Pittsburgh," *The Progressive* (June 1970), 32–37. For other details see *The New York Times* of 1969, issues of May 22, October 10 and 13, and November 2 and 4. For the Atlanta case, see *The New York Times* of the same year, the issues of October 5, 6, 8, 9, 17, 20, 22, and 23. The Minneapolis case is considered in the same source, the same year, in the issues of May 1 and 18 and June 10, 11, and 12. Some hidden details of this campaign (e.g., Stenvig *working* for his victory and the Democratic-Farmer Labor people coasting) are contained in the Minneapolis *Tribune,* May 1, 1969; see the editorial. A remarkable, but again largely hidden,

resurgence of populism also appeared on the state level in Virginia in 1969. See once again *The New York Times* of 1969, the issues of June 15, 16, and 17, of July 15, of August 20, 21, and 22, of October 22, 27, and 29, and November 4, 5, and 6.

63. See accounts of the European parties contained in Sigmund Neumann, ed. *Modern Political Parties* (Chicago: University of Chicago Press, 1956).

64. It is also possible that their economic arguments are erroneous. They make the point that there are, relative to the need, dwindling opportunities for investment of the rapidly growing surplus. The new "space industry," however, provides unlimited "opportunity." To address the economic questions in detail would take one too far afield. The sociological arguments, in any event, have to be considered independently.

65. The Socialist party did experience some increase in members, the figure increasing from 9560 in 1929 to 20,951 in 1934. The latter was the peak figure for the decade, there being a slight decline in 1935 and a precipitous drop in 1936. The latter was due to the defection of the New York group, the core of the "old guard." See David A. Shannon, *The Socialist Party of America: A History* (Chicago: Quadrangle Books, 1967), Chs. 9, 10, and 11. The Communist party also showed some increase in members, going from 7500 in 1930 to 23,467 in 1934. The peculiarities of this party were such as to drive away members almost as fast as it gained them. They recruited approximately 49,000 new members in this period and lost roughly 33,000. In the mid-thirties there was a change from the so-called "third period" tactics to popular front tactics. Even then the development was hindered by the difficulties imposed by the Comintern and by Soviet foreign policy. The largest growth of membership occurred during the war, in the "era of good feelings" between the U.S. and the U.S.S.R. and, at the same time, in a period of relatively high wages and full employment. See Irving Howe and Lewis Coser, *The American Communist Party: A Critical History* (New York: Frederick A. Praeger, 1962), pp. 225 and 419. See also David A. Shannon, *The Decline of American Communism* (New York: Harcourt Brace, 1959). By far the best account of the self-defeating activities of this party is that of Theodore Draper, *American Communism and Soviet Russia* (New York: Viking Press 1960). This work unfortunately does not deal with the depression years.

66. The Communist party received 48,667 votes in 1928. In November 1932, after three years of steadily increasing unemployment, they received 102,991 votes, one quarter of these being from New York. It is difficult to draw any lessons from the 1936 vote (80,160) since the party, although running candidates, was actually supporting the Democrats, this being a part of the new popular front strategy. See Howe and Coser and the contributions to the Rita Simon volume (cited in note 16) by Earl Browder and Hal Draper. Norman Thomas (same source, p. 108) comments on the impact of the depression as follows: "It is, as I look back upon it, amazing that the workers were so comparatively quiet. There were strikes of desperation, all of which were lost." The electoral accomplishments of the Socialist party in the depression were almost as limited. In the 1932 election, they took 884,781 votes (2.23 percent of the total). Four more years of the depression did not lead to an increase in their share but rather to just the opposite, 116,514 votes or 0.23 percent of the total. See Svend Petersen, *A Statistical History of the*

American Presidential Elections (New York: Frederick Ungar, 1968), pp. 209–213.

A similar result is to be found in the British experience. See either John Bonham, *The Middle Class Vote* (London: Faber and Faber, 1954), p. 150, or F. W. S. Craig, *British Parliamentary Election Statistics, 1918–1968* (Glasgow: Political Reference Publications, 1968).

67. The comparison of the German and the Norwegian experience is to be found in a brilliant contribution by Sten S. Nilson, "Wahlsoziologische Probleme des Nationalsozialismus," *Zeitschrift für die gesamte Staatswissenschaft,* **110** (1954); see especially pp. 295–311. See also Pinard's account of Quebec where the activities of the rightist Social Credit party gave them the electoral gain in the midst of depression conditions.

68. Engels, *The Role of Force in History* (New York: International Publishers, 1968). The quotation appears in the Introduction by Ernst Wangerman, p. 23. It originally appeared in a letter to Bebel, See *August Bebel: Briefwechsel mit Friedrich Engels* (The Hague: Mouton, 1965), p. 204. In another context, Engels makes the same point and elaborates on it at some length. "Let us have no illusions about it," he says, "a real victory of an insurrection over the military in street fighting, a victory as between two armies is one of the rarest exceptions." See his Introduction to Marx's *The Class Struggles in France: 1848 to 1850,* in Karl Marx and Frederick Engels, *Selected Works,* Vol. I (Foreign Languages Publishing House, 1951); see especially pp. 120–123.

69. This account of domestic household weaponry is based on my own (unpublished) analysis of a Gallup study from January 1965. I wish to thank the Roper Center, Williamstown, Massachusetts for making that study available. Approximately half of the American families owned a weapon at that time. Since then the level of armament on the homefront has increased tremendously. See *U.S. News and World Report,* October 21, 1968.

70. According to many accounts, the counter-revolutionaries are hard at work. Police raids in New York city in October 1966 resulted in the seizure of tons of weapons and ammunition ("mortars, bazookas, machine guns, semi-automatic rifles, home-made bombs and more than a million rounds of ammunition, also, machetes, crossbows and garroting nooses.") See *The New York Times,* October 31, 1966. Raids on other caches are reported in the same source on April 27, 1967, May 17, 1967, July 7, 1967, and August 24, 1967. These represent only a small sampling of the cases reported.

71. A former special agent of the Federal Bureau of Investigation wrote in 1962, when the Communist party had approximately 8500 members, that the FBI had nearly 1500 informants in the party. The Bureau, through the dues of "its" members, was "the largest single financial contributor to the coffers of the Communist Party." See Jack Levine, "Hoover and the Red Scare," *Nation* **195** (October 20, 1962), 232–235. It seems likely that state and local police forces would have provided dues and manpower above and beyond that contributed by the Federals.

72. For the fate of urban uprisings see Martin Oppenheimer, *The Urban Guerrilla* (Chicago: Quadrangle Books, 1969). Another very useful discussion is that of Barrington Moore, Jr., "Revolution in America?" *New York Review of Books,* January 30, 1969.

73. This discussion appears in a letter to Friedrich Sorge, December 2, 1893. It is reprinted in Lewis S. Feuer, ed., *Basic Writings on Politics and Philosophy: Karl Marx and Friedrich Engels* (Garden City: Doubleday Anchor Books, 1959), pp. 457–458.

74. From his "On the History of Early Christianity," in Karl Marx and Frederick Engels, *On Religion* (Moscow: Foreign Languages Publishing House, N.), pp. 322–323.

This same quotation appears in Seymour Martin Lipset, *Political Man* (Garden City: Doubleday 1960), p. 175. It is of some interest to note the treatment it is given. Engels makes very clear that the phenomenon he is describing characterizes the early stages of the party development and, to the extent that it was still possible in 1894–1895, that it could occur only in out-of-the-way districts. The sentences immediately preceding this quotation read as follows: "Everybody who has known by experience the European working-class movement in its beginnings will remember dozens of similar examples. Today such extreme cases, at least in the large centres, have become impossible; but in remote districts where the movement has won new ground a small Peregrinus of this kind can still count on a temporary limited success" (p. 322). At the end of the quotation Engels sums up, referring to his listing of diverse types, saying that *they* "all throng to the working-class parties in all countries. . . ." In Lipset's formulation this latter phrase is used to introduce the description of the "extreme cases" and in his presentation it reads as follows: "As far back as the 1890's, Engels described those who throng to the working-class parties in all countries as . . ."; he then leads into the quotation. Where Engels is speaking of minority segments whose influence has been contained in the later development of the party, Lipset's editorial emendations would suggest that the comments applied to the entire membership. He puts the following sentence immediately after the Engels quotation: "It is often men from precisely such origins who give the fanatical and extremist character to these movements and form the core of believers." Lipset also, incidentally, omits the phrase "who are termed 'good-for-nothing pettifoggers' by the bureaucracy. . . ."

75. The Gallup organization made use of the following question in 1969 and 1970: "Do you approve or disapprove of the way President Nixon is handling the situation in Vietnam?" In mid-September 1969, 45 percent of those interviewed approved of his policies. In the subsequent months the level of approval showed a continuous increase, to 52 percent in late September, to 58 percent in October, 64 percent in November, and 65 percent in January 1970 (versus 24 percent opposed and 11 percent with no opinion). See the report in *The New York Times*, January 29, 1970. At the latter date, one local leftist group circulated a statement which began as follows: "Opposition to the war has grown so that what was once the view of a tiny minority is now the desire of the overwhelming majority—get out of Vietnam now." Nixon's Vietnam policy as of that point could scarcely be characterized as getting out of Vietnam "now."

Some claims are not *obviously* contrary to fact and cannot, for that reason, be as easily disregarded. The use of the sweeping condemnation, however, frequently leads to the taking of liberties with the evidence. When that proclivity becomes a commonplace for the leftist practitioners, it is only a question of time before the "hard" evidence will be presented—justifiably discrediting those given to such practices. An instructive case of "telling it like it is not" is reported by Edward

Jay Epstein, "The Panthers and the Police: A Pattern of Genocide?" *The New Yorker*, **46** (February 13, 1971), 45 ff.

76. In some instances the tactics involve the stimulation of a clash between the followers and the forces of "law and order." That is, the effort involves leading the naive followers into a situation where there is a high probability that the police will respond with some violence. It is this response, presumably, that creates "consciousness." It also involves a deliberate "creation" of martyrs for the sake of the movement. This, too is a very difficult tactic to manage successfully since it involves manipulation and since it can, at least in some circumstances, be easily discredited. This manner of procedure is the subject of John Steinbeck's *In Dubious Battle* (New York: Random House, 1936).

77. The Black Power orientation was in part stimulated by just that kind of thing, that is, whites in the civil rights movement telling more knowledgeable blacks how to do things. For some assessment of the consequences of the development see Joel D. Aberbach and Jack L. Walker, "The Meanings of Black Power: A Comparison of White and Black Interpretations of a Political Slogan," *American Political Science Review*, **64** (June 1970), 367–388.

78. Those members of the New Left, for example, whose parents are slum landlords are likely to respond differently to a sweeping claim about "whites" as exploiters of blacks than are white workers. This is a basic difficulty of psychological or emotive politics. What "feels good" as a political strategy may not "be" a good strategy. "Doing one's thing" may well involve a refusal to think about whether or not "one's thing" is in fact a good thing.

79. An examination of the acknowledgements contained in a number of leftist critical works of scholarship showed a wide range of foundation support, from the Ford organization on down. Some listed additional support from one or more leading universities. Most of them also indicated their appreciation for intellectual aid and encouragement from rather well-established figures in the social sciences.

80. This is, to be sure, referring only of the dominant tendency. There has developed, particularly within the last decade, some very impressive work by leftist scholars, much of which has been cited previously in the present work. At the same time, however, it is to be noted that the *number* of people on the left doing that kind of serious intellectual work is very small.

81. This discussion appears in Engels' *Introduction to The Class Struggles in France* (see above), especially pp. 117–126. This is the unabridged text of the Introduction. For a commentary on the famous abridgement of this work see Hans-Josef Steinberg, "Revolution und Legalitat: Ein unveröffentlichter Brief Friedrich Engels' an Richard Fischer," *International Review of Social History*, **12** (1967), 177–189.

82. Engels, pp. 124–125.

83. Ibid., p. 125.

84. See, for example, the Robinson article cited above on the reactions to the 1968 Chicago events. With the media openly condemning the treatment of the demonstrators the public sided with the police.

85. See the discussion of the group-bases–social-pressures position in Chapter 2. For a preliminary account of the role of "personal influence" in changing a

political tradition see my "Notes on the Study of Mass Political Behavior," in Otto Stammer, ed., *Party Systems, Party Organizations and the Politics of New Masses* (Berlin: Institut für politische Wissenschaft, 1968).

86. One focuses, for example, on Mayor Richard Daley and his machine and forgets Carmine de Sapio. Before he fell, it was customary to talk about his "powerful" machine. Some people in the New York Democrats later regretted their early victory over "the Boss." Without his presence, it was no longer possible to hold together a loose coalition of forces and it was also not as easy to muster the diffuse moralistic fervor of many reformers without such a highly visible symbol.

87. Alexis de Tocqueville, *Democracy in America* (New York: Alfred A. Knopf, 1963), Vol. II, Book One, Ch. XX: "Some Characteristics of Historians in Democratic Times," pp: 85–88.

Name Index

Abegglen, James, 560
Aberbach, Joel D., 574
Abernethy, Thomas Perkins, 76, 78
Abrams, Mark, 17
Abrams, Philip, 568
Agger, Robert E., 281, 560
Aiken, Michael, 184
Alford, Robert, 64, 184, 193, 222, 226, 228, 229, 245, 279
Allen, Frederick Lewis, 64, 65, 526, 559
Allen, William Sheridan, 81
Alli, William E., 365
Allingham, John D., 331
Alliston, James R., 365
Almond, Gabriel, 36, 43, 44, 66, 68, 72, 144, 147, 149, 226, 568
Almy, Timothy A., 482
Alpert, Hollis, 80
Amster, Harriet, 17
Anderson, C. Arnold, 184, 231
Anderson, Jack, 20, 146, 492
Anderson, Martin, 560
Apter, David E., 77, 139
Arendt, Hannah, 74
Armer, J. Michael, 186
Arnett, Alex Mathews, 483
Aronson, Elliot, 503
Aronson, Sidney, 229
Austin, James Trecothic, 484
Ayres, Richard E., 279, 305

Babchuk, Nicholas, 67
Bachrach, Peter, 66
Bagdikian, Ben, 421, 478
Baker, Howard H., 425, 426
Ballard, Hoyt B., 561
Baltzell, E. Digby, 73, 223, 228, 230, 569
Banfield, Edward C., 563
Baran, Paul A., 563
Barber, Bernard, 180
Barber, James D., 20
Barth, Ernest A. T., 180
Bass, Bernard M., 499
Bass, Ross, 424, 425, 479
Bauer, Alice H., 74
Bauer, Raymond A., 17, 74, 138
Beale, Howard K., 484, 497, 498
Bean, Louis H., 145
Beard, Charles and Mary, 67, 567
Bebel, August, 572
Beccaria, Cesare, 239

Becker, John F., 482
Bell, Daniel, 64, 71, 74, 115, 145, 233, 467, 495, 561
Bell, Wendell, 65
Bellush, Jewel, 560
Belmont, August, 494
Bendix, Reinhard, 64, 76, 332, 335, 361, 362, 489
Bengston, Vern L., 566
Bensman, Joseph, 185, 275, 278
Benson, Lee, 76, 227
Berelson, Bernard R., 19, 57, 58, 59, 72, 75, 76, 77, 78, 79, 80, 81, 229, 230, 235, 277, 322, 556
Berg, Ivan, 232
Berger, Bennett, 182, 183, 276
Berkowitz, Leonard, 563
Berle, A. A. Jr., 64
Bernhard, Ludwig, 19
Bernstein, Eduard, 64
Berwanger, Eugene, 469
Bettelheim, Bruno, 150, 409, 458, 459, 488, 489, 501, 503
Bevin, Anuerin, 6
Bigart, Homer, 485
Bilbo, Theodore C., 481
Birch, A. H., 278
Blackmore, Donald J., 396
Blank, R., 226
Blau, Peter M., 236, 361, 362
Blumer, Jay G., 79
Bogart, Leo, 567
Bolling, Richard W., 479, 480
Bonham, John, 572
Booth, Alan, 67
Bottomore, T. B., 63, 564
Bowen, William G., 279, 305
Boyle, Richard P., 186
Boynton, George R., 306
Bradley, Thomas, 482
Breed, Warren, 305, 564
Bricker, John W., 8
Bright, James R., 235
Brodbeck, Arthur J., 75, 76
Brooke, Edward W., 482
Brophy, Ira N., 476
Browder, Earl, 571
Brown, Richard Maxwell, 482
Brown, Roger, 499, 500, 501
Brown, Steven R., 139
Bryan, William Jennings, 76, 77, 228, 536

Byrnes, James E., 482
Buchanan, William, 20, 101, 143
Buckley, Walter, 64
Burdick, Eugene, 75, 76
Burnham, Walter D., 76

Cain, Leila S., 149
Campbell, Angus, 19, 21, 75, 76, 77, 143,
    145, 149, 151, 275, 302, 331, 333, 500
Campbell, Arthur A., 365
Campbell, Joel T., 149, 280
Campbell, John D., 476
Campbell, Kenneth, 494
Cantril, Hadley, 20, 86, 87, 101, 139, 141,
    143
Caplovitz, David, 398
Carter, Laurier F., 17
Centers, Richard, 100, 101, 143, 499
Chaloner, W. H., 274
Chambliss, W. J., 504
Chanady, Attila, 18
Chapetz, Janet Saltzman, 331
Chase, Stuart, 20, 141
Chesnutt, Charles, 482
Christie, Richard, 468, 500
Cicourel, Aaron V., 568
Clapp, Charles L., 20
Clark, Burton R., 235, 392, 567
Clark, Joseph S., 20
Clark, Lincoln H., 393
Clausen, Aage R., 235
Clayton, James L., 561
Cleaves, Freeman, 78
Cleghorn, Reese, 478
Clelland, Donald A., 184
Clement, Frank, 424, 425, 426, 479
Cleveland, Stuart, 186
Clifford, Clark, 493
Coady, Sharon, 146, 493
Coben, Stanley, 484, 493, 494, 495
Coleman, James, 70, 138, 177, 178, 181,
    186, 566
Coleman, Richard P., 235
Collins, Mary Evans, 475
Converse, Philip E., 21, 77, 139, 235, 302,
    304, 504
Conway, Margaret, 505
Cook, Fred, 498
Cook, Stuart W., 475
Cooper, Kent, 81
Corey, Lewis, 332
Cornforth, Maurice, 63
Coser, Lewis, 571
Cosman, Bernard, 302, 306
Costello, William, 492
Couch, A., 499
Craig, F. W. S., 572
Cramer, Richard, 479
Creel, George, 494
Crittendon, John, 282
Crowe, Charles, 483
Cutler, James Elbert, 489
Cutright, Phillips, 279

Daalder, Hans, 230
Dahl, Robert A., 15, 35, 66, 71, 230

Dahlgren, Harold E., 75
Danielian, N. R., 142
Daniels, Clesbie R., 149
Dauer, Manning, 227
Davenport, Russell, 64
Davidson, Chandler, 304, 305, 482, 563
Davis, Cliff, 479
Davis, James C., 480
Davis, James W. Jr., 181
Davis, John W., 562
Davis, Kingsley, 180
Dawson, Richard E., 15
Dean, John P., 277
Dentler, Robert A., 17
Dervin, Brenda, 567
Deutsch, Karl W., 20
Deutsch, Morton, 475
DeVinney, Leland C., 476
Dewey, Thomas E., 19, 54, 60, 78, 81, 492,
    493, 542
Dexter, Lewis Anthony, 17, 138
Dickens, Charles, 362
Dillehay, Ronald C., 499
Dillon, Douglas, 569
Dirkson, Everett, 425
Dobriner, William, 182
Dolbeare, Kenneth M., 181
Dollard, John, 485
Domhoff, G. William, 66, 69, 148, 238, 561,
    569
Donifat, Emil, 80
Douglas, Helen Gahagan, 492
Downing, Willard, 183
Doyle, H. S., 429
Draper, Hal, 571
Drucker, Peter, 64
Dubin, Robert, 274, 367, 564
Dulles, John Foster, 492, 493
Duncan, Otis Dudley, 236, 274, 361, 362
Durkheim, Emile, 508, 533
Dye, Thomas R., 15, 66
Dykstra, Robert R., 474

Eberts, Paul, 232
Edinger, Lewis J., 20
Edwards, Hugh, 331
Eisenhower, Dwight D., 19, 47, 109, 112,
    128, 149, 194, 313, 322, 329, 449, 491,
    492, 536, 568
Eisenstein, Louis, 71
El-Assal, Elain, 149
Eldersveld, Samuel J., 16, 279, 333
Ellegaard, Dorothy, 392
Emery, Edwin, 80
Engels, Frederick, 63, 239, 274, 546, 547,
    548, 550, 553, 554, 572, 573, 574
Epstein, Edward J., 574
Epstein, Leon D., 150, 274, 275
Erikkson, Erik M., 227
Erikson, Erik H., 362
Erskine, Hazel Gaudet, 148, 487
Eulau, Heinz, 20, 81
Ewing, Blair, 65
Eysenck, H. J., 500

Faulkner, William, 482

Faunce, William A., 184
Fenton, John H., 18
Ferguson, Leroy C., 20
Feuer, Lewis S., 573
Field, John Osgood, 563
Finney, Henry C., 565, 566
Fischer, Louis, 564
Fischer, Richard, 574
Flacks, Richard, 566
Floro, George K., 280
Floud, Jean, 184
Form, William H., 144, 478, 569
Forrestal, James, 562
Frady, Marshall, 302, 505
Frank, Charlotte, 279
Frazier, E. Franklin, 569
Free, Lloyd, A., 20, 141
Freeman, J. Leiper, 280
Freidson, Eliot, 75
Frick, Henry C., 494
Fromm, Erich, 74
Fulton, Richard, 479
Fry, Bryan R., 15
Frye, Bruce B., 18
Fulton, Joseph F., 182

Galbraith, John Kenneth, 64
Gans, Herbert J., 182, 184, 236, 478, 567
Gardner, John W., 65, 487
Gary, Elbert, 494
Gaudet, Hazel, 75, 79
Gay, Peter, 64
Geiger, Theodor, 64
Gerschenkron, Alexander, 332
Gerth, Hans H., 15, 362
Gieber, Walter, 81
Glantz, Oscar, 231
Glass, D. V., 331
Glazer, Nathan, 71, 467, 468, 487, 495
Glick, Ira O., 567
Goldman, Eric F., 140
Goldrich, Daniel, 281, 560
Goldthorpe, John H., 389
Goldwater, Barry, 8, 80, 121, 130, 150,
    197, 198, 208, 220, 221, 267, 291, 297,
    298, 303, 304, 306, 313, 319, 325, 348,
    357, 364, 365, 367, 473, 480, 519, 526,
    565
Gölitz, Walter, 82
Gomberg, William, 232, 394, 567
Gouldner, Alvin, 70
Grabill, Wilson H., 365
Gramont, Sanche de, 70
Gray, Julius, 69
Grazia, Alfred de, 77, 262
Greeley, Andrew M., 150
Greenberg, Bradley, 567
Greenblum, Joseph, 277, 459, 489, 501,
    502
Greer, Scott, 182, 560
Gregg, James E., 80
Grider, George, 479
Grigg, Charles M., 503, 569
Groppi, James, 432, 433, 486
Gruening, Ernest, 142
Grundlach, Ralph H., 476

Grzesinski, Albert C., 274
Gurin, Gerald, 19, 21, 145, 149, 275
Gusfield, Joseph R., 74

Haber, William, 235
Hadwiger, Don F., 70
Hahn, Harlan, 474, 482
Halberstam, David, 82, 479
Halsey, A. H., 184
Hamilton, Richard F., 20, 21, 65, 74, 75,
    77, 138, 148, 181, 183, 226, 230, 232,
    233, 235, 274, 278, 280, 281, 282, 334,
    363, 364, 388, 389, 391, 394, 467, 468,
    496, 497, 503, 505, 561, 562, 565, 566,
    575
Hammond, Bray, 227
Handel, Gerald, 235
Hanley, C., 500
Hanse, W. Lee, 71, 560
Hapgood, Norman, 494
Hardin, Einar, 365
Harding, John, 476
Harlan, Howard H., 503
Harper, Alan D., 491
Harriman, E. H., 362
Harrington, Michael, 69
Harris, Louis, 149
Harrison, Paul, 70
Harsch, Joseph C., 140
Hauser, Robert M., 186
Hausknecht, Murray, 67, 560
Havel, Joan, 500
Hay, John, 498
Hayes, Edward C., 494, 560
Hays, Alden D., 275, 279, 280
Heard, Alexander, 301
Hearst, William Randolph, 498
Heaton, Eugene E. Jr., 482
Heberle, Rudolf, 275
Heller, Celia S., 277
Henderson, W. O., 274
Herberg, Will, 366
Hero, Alfred O. Jr., 147, 149
Hickenlooper, Bourke, 492
Hicks, Granville, 275
Hicks, John D., 78
Higham, John, 469, 484, 493
Hill, Herbert, 477, 478
Hodge, Robert, W., 68, 458, 488, 501, 503
Hoffman, Lois Wladis, 235
Hoffman, Nicholas von, 478
Hofstadten, Richard, 227, 469, 498
Hoggart, Richard, 478
Hogrefe, Russell, 476
Homans, George C., 475
Hook, Sidney, 63, 448
Hoos, Ida R., 365
Hoover, Herbert, 79, 562
Hoover, J. Edgar, 572
Horowitz, David, 147, 148, 150
Hoult, Thomas Ford, 181, 187
Howard, Alan, 468
Howe, Irving, 70, 571
Huckshorn, Robert J., 302
Hugenberg, Alfred, 19
Hughes, John, 492

Hugins, Walter, 228
Huie, William Bradford, 485
Humphrey, Hubert H., 506
Hunter, Floyd, 567, 569
Huntington, Samuel, 561
Hyman, Herbert H., 67, 68, 74, 145, 146,
   150, 409, 467, 468, 495, 500

Jackson, Andrew, 18, 191, 227, 228, 484
Jackson, Brian, 81
Jackson, D. N., 499
Jahoda, Marie, 69, 468, 500
Janowitz, Morris, 15, 150, 409, 458, 459,
   488, 489, 500, 501, 503
Janson, Donald, 570
Jennings, M. Kent, 480
Johnson, Benton, 230, 332
Johnson, Lyndon, 80, 109, 121, 126, 140,
   313, 362, 364, 365, 367
Johnson, James Weldon, 482
Jordan, Winthrop D., 469

Kahl, Joseph A., 184
Kahn, Robert L., 569
Kaplan, Abraham, 279
Kaplan, Sidney J., 361
Kariel, Henry S., 66
Kassalow, Everett, 180
Katz, Daniel, 20, 57, 280
Katz, Elihu, 75, 80, 235
Keat, Paul G., 396
Kefauver, Estes, 423, 424, 425, 479, 481
Kelley, Stanley Jr., 146, 279, 305, 307
Kelly, K. D., 504
Keniston, Kenneth, 499, 566
Kennedy, Edward, 17
Kennedy, John F., 17, 150, 238, 492, 568
Kennedy, Joseph, 492
Kennedy, Robert, 492
Kennedy, Ruby Jo Reeves, 366
Kerr, Clark, 274, 367, 564
Kerrick, Jean S., 80
Key, V. O. Jr., 66, 76, 77, 79, 274, 283,
   284, 301
Kheel, Theodore W., 70
Kiester, Edwin Jr., 569
Kilgo, John Wesley, 17
Killian, Lewis, 567
King, Martin Luther, 431
King, Robert, 18
Kirchheimer, Otto, 16
Kirk, Jerome, 566
Kirscht, John P., 499
Kirwan, Albert K., 483
Kisser, Clyde V., 365
Kitsuse, John I., 568
Klapper, Joseph T., 79
Knowles, Louis L., 471
Kolko, Gabriel, 71, 78, 394, 396, 398, 559
Komarovsky, Mirra, 68, 226, 235
Kornhauser, Athur, 79, 333, 367, 364
Kornhauser, William, 74, 274
Korsch, Karl, 63
Kovach, Bill, 479
Kozol, Jonathan, 186
Kraus, Sidney, 149, 151

Krauss, Irving, 185
Kritz, Mary, 505
Kruytbosch, Carole, 467
Ktsanes, Thomas, 305, 564

LaFollette, Robert, 494
Lamont, Thomas, 494
Landon, Alfred, 79
Lane, Robert E., 78, 79
Lang, Gladys and Kurt, 79
Lansing, John B., 393
LaPolombara, Joseph, 568
Larner, Robert J., 559
Larson, Cedric, 494
Lasch, Christopher, 66, 74, 146
Lasswell, Harold, 279
Laulicht, Jerome, 149
Laurenti, Luigi, 476
Lazarsfeld, Paul F., 19, 57, 58, 59, 69, 72,
   75, 76, 77, 78, 79, 80, 81, 229, 230, 235,
   277, 324, 556
Leavitt, Harold J., 365
Lebeaux, Charles N., 183
Lederer, Emil, 122, 146
Lee, Eugene C., 279
Lee, Robert, 228
Leggett, John C., 63, 144, 499
Lehman, Herbert, 492
Lenin, V. I., 63, 550, 564
Lenski, Gerhard, 64, 75, 139, 228, 230, 499
Lerche, Charles O. Jr., 302
Levin, Murray B., 17
Levine, Gene N., 149
Levine, Jack, 572
Levinson, Daniel J., 503
Levitan, Sar A., 468
Levy, Sidney J., 567
Lewis, Oscar, 69
Lichtheim, George, 63
Liebow, Elliot, 69
Lilienthal, David, 64
Linder, Usher, 484
Lindzey, Gardner, 503
Linz, Juan J., 227, 274, 278, 497, 568
Lippman, Walter, 494
Lipset, Seymour Martin, 15, 64, 65, 66, 70,
   71, 76, 81, 138, 139, 144, 145, 150, 184,
   185, 227, 228, 233, 236, 274, 280, 304,
   318, 326, 332, 335, 361, 362, 441, 455,
   459, 460, 467, 468, 469, 472, 474, 487,
   489, 495, 496, 497, 499, 500, 501, 502,
   503, 504, 505, 566, 573
Lipsitz, Lewis, 467, 499
Litt, Edgar, 72, 185
Little, Alan, 568
Litwack, Leon F., 469
Lodge, Henry Cabot, 10, 19, 73, 492
Long, Pope, 16
Longhi, Dario, 392, 560, 566
Loosley, Elizabeth W., 145, 182, 565
Lopreato, Joseph, 331
Lovenstein, Meno, 494
Lovett, Robert A., 362, 568, 569
Lubell, Samuel, 77
Lundberg, Ferdinand, 63, 71
Lupri, Eugen, 192

Lutterman, Kenneth G., 563
Luxembourg, Rosa, 550
Lynd, Helen M. and Robert S., 64, 69, 568

McCarthy, Eugene, 140, 141
McCarthy, Joseph R., 47, 113, 114, 115,
    116, 117, 145, 146, 147, 233, 435, 449,
    450, 452, 491, 492, 493, 495, 496, 526,
    565
McClosky, Herbert, 75, 503
McCloy, John J., 569
McConnell, Grant, 66
McCord, Joan and William, 468
McCormick, Richard P., 227
McCoy, Charles A., 65, 77
McCune, Wesley, 331
McGlaughlin, Doris B., 333
MacIver, R. M., 502
McKay, James A., 480
MacKenzie, Gavin, 394
McKinley, William, 19, 77, 535, 536
McKinney, John C., 302
Mackinnon, William J., 499
McPhee, William N., 19, 57, 59, 72, 75, 77,
    78, 79, 80, 81, 229, 230, 235, 277
McWhiney, Grady, 227
Macy, Everit, 494
Mallen, John P., 492
Malm, F. Theodore, 361
Mann, Michael, 144
Mannheim, Karl, 74
Marascuilo, Leonard A., 17
Marcuse, Herbert, 15, 47, 66, 549
Marmor, Theodore R., 71
Marshall, T. H., 64
Martin, Roscoe C., 483
Marty, Martin, 228
Marvick, Dwaine, 15, 500
Marx, Karl, 22, 23, 27, 30, 34, 36, 61, 62,
    63, 64, 75, 100, 203, 353, 515, 516, 528,
    550, 564, 572, 573
Massing, Paul, 18
Masters, Nicholas, 274, 333
Mather, W. G., 68
Mathews, Donald R., 297, 302, 305, 306
Matthias, Erich, 18
Maxwell, James A., 18
May, John D., 70
May, Ronald W., 146, 492, 493
Mayer, Albert J., 79, 181, 187, 333
Mayer, Kurt, 64
Mehling, Reuben, 149
Melman, Seymour, 561
Merrill, Francis E., 183
Merrill, Horace Samuel, 16
Merz, Charles, 494
Messick, S. J., 499
Metcalf, Lee, 142
Meyerson, Martin, 560
Michael, John, 186
Michel, Andrée, 478
Michels, Robert, 8, 18, 69, 70, 78, 226
Middleton, Russell, 81
Middleton, W. L., 19
Milbrath, Lester, 65
Miliband, Ralph, 226

Miller, Douglas T., 227
Miller, Herman P., 395, 559
Miller, Neal E., 489
Miller, S. M., 181, 467
Miller, Warren E., 19, 20, 21, 75, 145, 149,
    151, 235, 275, 504
Miller, William J., 19, 73, 565
Mills, C. Wright, 15, 63, 64, 65, 66, 223,
    232, 238, 332, 362, 561
Minard, Ralph D., 476
Moberg, David O., 230
Mock, John R., 494
Modell, John, 149
Montgomery, John D., 147
Moore, Barrington, Jr., 66, 572
Moore, Stanley W., 63
Morgan, James N., 393
Morgan, J. P., 494
Morgner, Ramona, 276
Morison, Elting E., 498
Morrison, Robert S., 560
Morsey, Rudolf, 18
Moscow, Warren, 16
Moskos, Charles C. Jr., 65, 476
Moskowitz, Milton, 80
Mosse, Hilde L., 149
Mott, Frank Luther, 80
Mueller, John E., 148, 149
Muir, Donald E., 478
Mukherjee, Ramkrishna, 331
Müller, J. Heinz, 396
Munger, Frank, 76
Murray, Robert K., 493, 494
Musgrove, Frank, 278
Myers, Gustavus, 228, 469

Neisser, Hans, 227
Neumann, Sigmund, 571
Neustadt, Richard, 568, 569
Newfield, Jack, 566
Newman, William J., 478
Nilson, Sten S., 332, 572
Nisbet, Robert A., 71
Nixon, Richard M., 9, 19, 112, 130, 150,
    151, 472, 492, 505, 506, 562, 573
Nordlinger, Eric, 568
Northrup, Herbert, 569
Novak, Robert N., 150
Nye, F. Ivan, 235
Nygreen, G. T., 143

Ober, Harry, 396
O'Brien, James P., 566
O'Brien, John L., 181
Older, H. J., 499
Olson, Mancur Jr., 18, 66, 82
Olson, Philip, 74
Oppenheim, Karen, 282
Oppenheimer, Martin, 572
O'Reilly, Charles T., 183
O'Toole, Thomas, 365
Ozanne, Robert, 396

Palmer, Mitchell, 430, 484, 494, 495
Palmore, Erdman B., 476
Parenti, Michael, 75

Parks, Norman L., 481
Parsons, Talcott, 64, 508
Paul, John, 149
Paul, Randolph E., 71
Pearlin, Leonard I., 459, 489, 501, 502
Pearson, Drew, 20
Pease, John, 144
Pell, Robert Harry, 146, 493
Perrow, Charles, 65, 66
Perry, James M., 17
Petersen, Svend, 571
Peterson, Theodore, 565
Pettigrew, Thomas F., 476, 506
Pflanzer, Steven I., 183
Phillips, Kevin P., 150, 506
Pierce, Bessie L., 494
Pinard, Maurice, 566, 570, 572
Pitkin, Hannah, 70
Plant, Thomas, 149
Playford, John, 65, 77
Pole, J. R., 227
Politz, Alfred, 80, 565
Polsby, Nelson W., 17, 145, 150
Pool, Ithiel de Sola, 17, 72, 138
Pope, Liston, 332
Prewitt, Kenneth, 17, 471
Pringle, Henry F., 16
Prothro, James W., 297, 302, 305, 306, 503
Pryor, F. L., 560
Puchala, Donald J., 20
Pulzer, P. G. J., 18
Putney, Snell, 81

Raab, Earl, 495, 504
Rainwater, Lee, 235
Ranney, Austin, 150
Raper, Arthur F., 484
Ratner, Lorman, 469
Reder, Melvin, 396
Rehmus, Charles M., 333
Reichley, James, 78
Reigrotzki, Erich, 497
Reinemer, Vic, 142
Reinisch, Leonhard, 80
Reiss, Albert J. Jr., 181, 274, 390
Reitzes, Deitrich C., 486
Richards, Leonard L., 484, 487
Riche, Richard W., 365
Riesman, David, 66
Riessman, Frank, 186, 467
Riley, Robert T., 506
Robertson, Nan, 505
Robinson, James A., 15
Robinson, John P., 566, 574
Rogers, David, 232
Rogin, Michael Paul, 145, 150, 495, 496, 505
Rogow, Arnold A., 562
Rokeach, M., 500
Rokkan, Stein, 227, 228, 280
Roosevelt, Franklin D., 56, 79, 561, 568
Roosevelt, Theodore, 16, 19, 77, 429, 484, 494, 497, 498, 561
Roper, Elmo, 100, 149
Rose, Peter I., 277
Rose, Richard, 17

Rosenberg, Bernard, 74
Rosenberg, Morris, 69, 185
Rosi, Eugene J., 149
Ross, Arthur M., 274, 367, 477, 478, 564
Ross, Irwin, 229, 493
Rossi, Peter H., 75
Roth, Guenther, 226
Routh, Guy, 396
Rovere, Richard H., 146, 150, 491, 492, 493, 561
Rowan, Richard L., 478
Runciman, W. G., 77, 566
Rusk, Dean, 317
Rusk, Jerold G., 504
Rytina, Joan, 144, 478, 565, 569

Sait, Edward McC., 19
Sanford, Fillmore H., 499, 500
Sanford, R. Nevitt, 503
Sartori, Giovanni, 16
Saunders, Robert, 483
Saville, John, 226
Schattschneider, E. E., 333
Schegloff, Emanuel A., 467
Schlesinger, Arthur Jr., 238, 568
Schneir, Miriam and Walter, 146
Schnitzer, Martin, 18
Schore, Leo F., 182, 184
Schorske, Carl E., 64, 226
Schreiber, E. M., 143
Schumpeter, Joseph, 15
Schwartz, Abba P., 332
Schwartz, Mildred A., 150
Scoble, Harry M., 333
Sears, David O., 503
Seeley, John R., 145, 182, 565
Seeman, Melvin, 489, 501
Seidenberg, Bernard, 500
Seldes, George, 494
Seligman, Ben B., 365
Selznick, Gertrude J., 277
Sewell, William H., 186, 392
Sexton, Patricia Gayo, 71, 185, 186, 560
Shah, Vimal P., 392
Shannon, David A., 571
Shattuck, Frances, 141
Sheatsley, Paul, 150, 409, 467, 468, 500
Sheldon, William DeBose, 483
Shepard, Marshall, 78, 79
Sheppard, Harold L., 79, 333
Sherrill, Robert, 302, 331, 362
Shils, Edward A., 74, 501
Shostak, Arthur B., 232, 394, 567
Siegel, Abraham, 274, 367, 564
Silberstein, Fred B., 489, 501
Sim, R. Alexander, 145, 182, 565
Simkins, Francis Butler, 482
Simon, Rita James, 562, 571
Simpson, George Eaton, 502
Sindler, Allen, 71, 302
Sklare, Marshall, 277, 569
Smigel, Erwin O., 362
Smith, Adam, 18
Smith, Alfred E., 16
Smith, Paul A., 17
Smithies, Arthur, 147

Spady, William G., 236
Spectorsky, A. C., 182
Stammer, Otto, 575
Star, Shirley A., 476
Stein, Maurice, 74, 182
Steinbeck, John, 574
Steinberg, Hans-Josef, 574
Steinberg, Stephen, 277
Stember, Herbert, 459, 467, 502
Stern, Philip M., 71
Stevenson, Adlai, 13, 58, 81, 140, 141, 229
Still, Bayrd, 144
Stimson, Henry, 498
Stokes, Donald E., 20, 21, 151
Stone, Edwin O., 280
Stone, I. F., 150
Storing, Herbert J., 77
Stouffer, Samuel, 85, 113, 114, 138, 145,
    146, 185, 435, 439, 440, 451, 469, 476,
    487
Street, David S., 144
Strong, Donald S., 301
Strunk, Mildred, 20, 141
Sturmthal, Adolf, 180, 181
Suchman, Edward A., 476
Sullivan, William A., 228
Summerfield, Arthur, 492
Svalastoga, Kaare, 331
Swanson, Bert E., 560
Sweezy, Paul A., 563

Taft, Robert A., 116, 449, 491, 492
Talbot, Ross B., 70
Tallman, Irving, 276
Tannenbaum, Percy, 80
Thayer, George, 561
Theoharis, Athan, 491
Thomas, Norman, 562, 571
Thompson, Charles, 141
Thompson, Daniel C., 569
Thompson, Edgar T., 302
Thompson, Kenneth, 76, 236, 331, 332
Thurmond, J. Strom, 483
Thurmond, J. William, 482, 483
Tillman, Benjamin, 427, 428, 482
Titmuss, Richard M., 71
Tocqueville, Alexis de, 40, 55, 65, 67, 78,
    135, 239, 291, 557, 558, 559, 575
Toomer, Jean, 482
Treiman, Donald J., 68, 458, 488, 501, 503
Trow, Martin, 70, 138, 233, 566
Truman, David B., 66
Truman, Harry, 19, 58, 78, 79, 208, 491,
    493
Tydings, Millard, 145, 146, 492

Underwood, Kenneth, 228, 332
Uphoff, Walter, 275

Valen, Henry, 20, 280
Vander Zanden, James W., 481
Vare, William, 79
Veblen, Thorstein, 275
Venable, Vernon, 63
Verba, Sidney, 36, 43, 44, 66, 68, 69, 72,
    149, 150, 226, 568

Vidich, Arthur, 74, 184, 275, 278
Vilas, William Freeman, 16
Voegeli, V. Jacques, 469
Von Eschen, Donald, 566

Wagner, Robert F., 492
Wahlke, John C., 20
Wakefield, Dan, 16
Walcutt, Charles, 178, 186
Walker, Jack L., 77, 482, 574
Walkley, Rosabelle P., 475
Wallace, George C., 150, 291, 302, 358,
    401, 461, 462, 463, 464, 465, 466, 467,
    504, 505, 506, 543, 563, 565
Wallace, Henry, 493, 542
Walter, E. V., 74
Wangerman, Ernst, 572
Ward, Lewis B., 569
Warner, William L., 68
Watson, Thomas, 429, 483
Watson, Walter B., 180
Watters, Pat, 478
Weber, C. Edward, 365
Weber, Max, 15, 362, 375
Weinberg, Edgar, 365
Weinstein, Eugene A., 478
Weinstein, James, 19, 226, 276, 279, 570
Weir, Stanley, 70
Weisbrod, Burton A., 71, 560
Weiss, Nancy J., 484
Whalen, Richard J., 492
Wheeler, Raymond, 75, 77, 282
Whisler, Thomas L., 365
White, David M., 74
White, Theodore H., 17, 19, 21, 150, 182,
    505, 561
Whyte, William Foote, 184, 478, 569
Whyte, William H. Jr., 145, 182, 183, 565
Widick, B. J., 70
Wiener, Jonathan, 473
Wiener, Rose, 365
Wilensky, Harold L., 183, 235, 331
Williams, Robin, 459, 476, 501, 502
Willmott, Peter, 138, 478
Wilner, Daniel M., 475, 476
Wilson, Alan B., 185
Wilson, James Q., 482, 563, 569
Wilson, Woodrow, 482, 484
Windham, Douglas M., 71, 560
Winters, Richard F., 15
Wohl, Richard, 362
Wolfe, Arthur C., 504
Wolff, Robert Paul, 66
Wolfinger, Raymond E., 75, 563
Wood, Robert C., 182
Woodward, C. Vann, 229, 483
Works, Ernest, 476
Wright, Charles R., 67, 68, 74
Wright, D. S., 274
Wright, James D., 148, 497, 565
Wright, Richard, 482

Yarmolinsky, Adam, 17
Yarrow, Leon J. and Marion, 476
Yinger, J. Milton, 502
Yoshino, I. Roger, 398

Young, Michael, 138, 478

Ziegler, L. Harmon, 66, 70, 480
Zeisel, Hans, 69
Zeitlin, Irving M., 63

Zeitlin, Maurice, 467, 559
Zetterberg, Hans, 318, 326, 335
Zimmer, Basil G., 278
Zweig, Ferdynand, 397

Subject Index

Activists, role of, 529, 531, 545, 547ff, 553-554, 556
Affluence, and workers, *see* Working class, and affluence
Age, and attitudes toward blacks, 410
  and politics, 270ff, 300ff
Anti-empirical bias, 552
Aspirations, level of, 533
Associations, *see* Voluntary associations
Authoritarianism, 115, 399ff, 515
  and class, 399ff
  in farm settings, 438, 440, 441
  literature reviewed, 454ff
  response set in scale questions, 455ff
  see also Working class
Automobile ownership, and class, 384
  by size of place, 387
Awareness, *see* Political awareness

Backlash, 130, 412-413
Blue collar occupations, *see* Manuals; Working Class
Book reading, 524
Bourgeoisification, 28, 30; *see also* Working class, and affluence
Business, influence of, 97

Centrist viewpoint, *see* Marxian revisionism
Change, attitudes toward, 104ff
  in party identification, of nonmanuals, 341ff
    of manuals, 315ff
  in United States, 507ff
Child training, as explanation of authoritarianism, 399ff, 439, 520
China, 122, 126
City size, 239ff
  and party preferences, 241ff, 286ff
Civil liberties, 434ff
Civil rights, 130; *see also* Authoritarianism
Civil rights movement, 527

Class, and authoritarianism, 399ff
  and automobile ownership, 384ff
  definition, 188-189
  geography of, 159ff
  and home ownership, 382ff
  and income, 369
  in Marxian viewpoint, 24-25
  as "objective" determinant, 527
  and politics, relationship in United States, United Kingdom, and West Germany, 190ff
  in revisionist Marxism, 29
  and schools, 174ff
  by size of place, 160ff
Classes, separation of, 168, 540
Class identifications, 100ff
Class lines, blurring of, 28
Class polarization, 193
  and city size, 245, 257
  reconsideration of Alford, 222ff
Class shift hypothesis, 30
  criticism of, 158-159
Class structure, by city size, 172
Cleavage, manual-nonmanual, discussed, 218
  within manuals, 308ff
  within nonmanuals, 349ff
Communism, attitudes toward, 112ff
Communist Party, 544
Communists, in government, 116
  rights of, 435ff
Commuting, 525
"Conditions," role of, 529ff, 545ff

Defense, Department of, civilian control, 514
Defense expenditures, 124ff
Demagogery, 47, 115
Democracy, as competition of parties, 4
  definition of, 3
Democratic Party, internal coalitions, 537ff
  gives away elections, 536

see also Party Identification; Voting
Democratic elitism, 400, 520
Democrats, low participation in small
    towns, 262
Demography, and politics, 534-535
Demonstrations, reactions to, 431
Depressions, as radicalizing experience, 544
Desegregation, 133
Disarmament, 125
Diversionary themes, use of, 9

Economic crisis, as radicalizing experience,
    544ff
Economic issues, 85ff
Economism, 210, 323ff
Education, and class, 174ff
    expanded opportunities for, 510
    lesson of special privilege, 412
    and politics of working class, 214
    role of, 32
    and tolerance, 43, 412, 442
    and working class, 212
Elites, 31
    and anti-Negro violence, 427ff
    division by religion, 519
    fantasies of, 60-61
    and intolerance, 444
    isolation of, 60, 516, 539
    merger in ranks of, 539
    responsibility, 518
    see also Upper Class
England, 190ff
Equality value, 423-424
Ethnicity, 540

False consciousness, 25, 51
Farmers, 220, 420
Father's politics, as determinant of outlook,
    51
Fears, generalized, 447
Finland, 318
Foreign affairs issues, 118, 452ff
Foreign aid, 121
Free speech, 116

General theories, 557
Germany, 190ff, 318, 545
Ghetto areas, 166ff
Goldwater, Barry, *see* entry in Name Index;
    see also Voting
Government, attitudes towards persons in,
    107

Government ownership of electric power
    firms, 96
Government power, 97, 295
Great Britain, 190ff
Group-based politics, 49-63

High schools, 177ff
Home ownership, and class, 382ff
    and whites attitudes toward blacks, 418
Housing, 512

Ignorance, *see* Political awareness
Immigrant groups, 199
Income, and careers, 375ff
    and politics, 323ff, 368ff
    satisfaction with, 371-372
    trends, 373ff
Income Revolution, the, 509
Independent businessmen, 202ff
Institutional racism, versus personal, 408
Integrated housing, and tolerance, 417
Intellectuals, 522, 531
    anti-empirical bias, 552-553
    isolation of, 547-548
    journals of, 522
    members of minorities, 552
Interests, objective, 529
Internationalism, 119ff
"Isolated mass," 507, 522
Issue avoidance, 84
Issue orientations, 83ff
    by city size, 249
    in south, 283ff

Jacksonian democracy, 191, 227
Job equality, attitudes of whites toward,
    419
Job guarantee, 89
Jobs, competition for, and attitudes of
    whites toward blacks, 419ff

Korean War, 122, 453, 526
    and 1952 election, 129
Know Nothings, 199

Labor union influence, 97
Leaders, behavior of, 84
    role of, 58
    see also Activists
Left, the, 547ff
Leftist dramaturgy, 551
Liberalism, 110

Living standard guarantee, 92
Living standards, 382
  trend in United States, 531ff
Lower middle class, 29
  issue orientations, 198
  location of, 163, 167
  politics of, 195
  structural strains, 205-206
  white attitudes toward blacks, 403
Lynching, 427ff

Majority, the, representations of, 521ff
Manuals, manual workers, affluence and
      politics, 210
  versus nonmanuals, 27-29
    cleavage discussed, 218
  occupations, defined, 152
  politics of, 206ff
    by city size, 244
  proportion in population, 154ff
  religious divisions within, 206ff
  as threatening force, 32
  white attitudes towards blacks, 401ff
  wives and politics, 211
  see also Working Class
Marxian revisionism, 27-34, 515
  optimistic and pessimistic variants, 29
Marxian viewpoint, 24-27
  determinism versus voluntarism, 26
  see also entry in Name Index
Mass media, and election campaigns, 54
  financial strains of, 527-528
  influence of, 47, 56-58, 142
  and intolerance, 444ff
  magazine readership, 524
  pattern of attention by class, 48, 524ff
Mass society viewpoint, 46-49
  criticisms of, 516-517
McCarthyism, 115ff, 445, 449ff, 526; see
      also McCarthy, Joseph R. in Name In-
      dex
Medical care, government guarantee, 89
Memberships in associations, multiple, 32
Middle class, backgrounds and political
      attitudes, 341
  class identifications of, 345
  differentiations within, 163, 349ff
  religious differentiations within, 346
  social backgrounds of, 336-338
  threat of downward mobility, 27
  transformation of, 353
  values of, 31

Migration, effect on class-tolerance relation-
      ship, 406
  and political change, 254
  between regions, 221, 535
  and size of place, 253ff, 541
Military establishment, 513ff
Mobility, 30, 52; see also Migration; Occu-
      pational mobility

National Socialists, 545
Nativism, 199, 538ff
Negroes, issue orientations, 285
  leaders, 538
  rights of, jobs, 130-131
    neighborhoods, 132
    schools, 131-132
  trend in white attitudes, 134
  voting patterns of, 424
Neighborhood integration, and interracial
      attitudes, 416ff
Netherlands, pillar system, 191
New left, origins of, 527ff, 549ff
Nonmanuals, differentiations within, 257,
      349ff
  occupations, defined, 152
  and politics, by city size, 243ff
  proportion in population, 154ff
  white attitudes toward blacks, 401ff
  see also Middle Class
Nonvoters, 291-293
Norway, Social Democratic Party of, 545

Occupational mobility, 326
  and change in party, 216, 315, 535
  effects of demography, 351
  and politics, in United States, Finland,
      and West Germany, 318
  of Protestants and Catholics, 317
  and tolerance, 441
Occupational structure, and defense indus-
      try, 514
Occupational trends, 156
Occupations, of males and females, 153
Office automation, impact of, 350ff
Opinion leaders, see Activists

Participation, dangers of, 32
Parties, Republicans and Democrats, sup-
      porters described, 537
Party competition, assumptions criticized,
      4-11
Party histories, divergences by

country, 191ff
Party identifications, 102ff
  and tolerance, 413
Party system, changing structure of, 534
Personal influence, 529ff
  interracial contacts, 421ff
  and tolerance, 414ff
Pillars, 191, 193, 197ff, 537
Plebiscitarian choice, 40
Pluralism, 34-46, 515
Pluralist ignorance, 135, 295, 521
Political awareness, 53ff
  lack thereof, 524-525
Politicization, by size of place, 259
Polls, use of, 6
Pollution, 513
Poor whites, attitudes toward job equality,
  419
Populist issues, 536
  neo-populist campaigns, 542-543
Poverty, 510
  and organizational memberships, 37
Power elite viewpoint, 516
Primary groups influences, 49-52
Proletariat, 26

Realigning elections, 530
Racial conflict, 431ff
  location of, 422-423
Racial contacts, and attitudes, 414
  by class and city size, 415
Redistribution and wealth and income,
  510ff
Referenda, as indicators of white attitudes,
  426
Reform government, impact of, 262
Religion, 507
  and attitudes toward blacks, 406
  church attendance and politics of white
    Protestants, 320
  conflict of, 538-539
  distribution by class, 407
  and exclusive institutions, 217
  and issue orientations, 197ff
  and party identifications, 195, 215
  by size of city, 252-253
  and vote, 195
Republican Party, core versus peripheral
    adherants, 360ff
  internal structure of, 537ff
  natural organization of, 263
Response set, 455

Responsibility of upper class and upper
    middle class, viewpoint criticized, 518-
    519
Revisionism, see Marxian revisionism
Revolutions, 543ff
Rich, changed appearance of, 532
Rightist candidates, 115

Salaried middle class, 202ff
Satisfaction with income, 371
School aid, federal, 93
Schools, and class, 174ff, 533-534
Secondary analysis, 12
Segregation, 133
Separation of classes, 531-532
Service workers, 155
Size of city, 239ff
  class and race in South, 289
  issue orientation in South, 286
  party preferences, 288
  and politicization, 259
Skilled workers, 167
Small towns, 256
Social Democratic Party, Germany, 190ff
  of Norway, 545
Social mobility, see Occupational mobility
Socialist Party, United States, 541, 544
South, the, 283ff
  age and politics in, 300ff
  elections and civil rights, 423
  internal divisions within, 297
  issue orientations, 284
  nonmanuals, 200, 356ff
  party competition, 298
Status, 525
Subjectivism, 552
Suburbs, 160-161
  politics of, 247-249
  working class, 166

Tax cuts, 98
Taxes, 509
Third party, 541
Tolerance, and education, 43, 442
  interrelationship of dimensions, 413-414
  by party identification, 413
  practical variety, 421

Unions, influence of, 97, 320ff
United Kingdom, 190ff
United States, international involvements,
  120

Universities, 528
Upper class, 31
  responsibility, sense of, 518
Upper middle class, 29
  avoidance of reality, 524-526
  attitudes toward blacks, 403ff
  characteristics of careers, 339
  issue orientations, 198
  politics of, 195
  white Protestants, politics of, 198
Urban renewal, 512

Viet-Nam war, 123, 453, 526
Voluntarism, 508
Voluntary associations, 35
  class and membership in, 41-42
  educational functions, 38
  extent of membership in, 36
  in group-based theory, 50
  instrumental versus expressive, 37
  internal democracy, 39
  membership trends, 44
  use of to influence policy, 36
Voting, by class and pillar, 195
  of independent businessmen, 203
  by region, 195
  of salarieds, 203
  by size of city, 196
  of working class wives, 211

Wallace, George C., support for 460-
    461
  supporters, attitutes of, 464

see also entry in Name Index
Wealth, 509-510
Welfare state, 511
  attitudes toward, 88ff
White collar occupations expansion of, 157;
    see also Nonmanual occupations
White Protestants, 194
  exclusiveness, 217, 538ff
  issue orientations, 198
  politics of, 195
Whites, attitudes toward rights of blacks,
    401ff
Working class, and affluence, 28-31, 210,
    325, 369ff, 530
  authoritarianism, 518; see also Author-
    itarianism
  change in politics of, 315
  changes, in backgrounds of, 309-310
  conservatism among, 207-208
  culture, 533
  and education, 177, 212-213
  and George Wallace, 460-461
  incomes of, 378ff
  mutual assistance pattern, 421ff
  political attitudes of, 311
  in small towns, 256
  social backgrounds of, 308ff
  suburbs, 164-165
  voting, 207-209
  white Protestants, 319
  wives, politics of, 211
  see also Manuals
Work week, 510